MURDERERS' ROW

Dedicated to the memory of
Joan and Joy

MURDERERS' ROW

An International Murderers' Who's Who

ROBIN ODELL & WILFRED GREGG

SUTTON PUBLISHING

This book was first published in 1996 by Headline Book Publishing under the title *The International Murderers' Who's Who*

This new and updated edition first published in 2006 by
Sutton Publishing Limited · Phoenix Mill
Thrupp · Stroud · Gloucestershire · GL5 2BU

British Library Cataloguing in Publication Data
A catalogue record for this book is available from the British Library.

ISBN 0 7509 4404 8

Every effort has been made to trace copyright holders. Sutton Publishing apologises for any unintentional omissions, and would be pleased, if any case should arise, to add an appropiate acknowledgement in future editions.

Typeset in 10/11.5pt Photina.
Typesetting and origination by
Sutton Publishing Limited.
Printed and bound in Great Britain by
J.H. Haynes & Co. Ltd, Sparkford.

CONTENTS

ACKNOWLEDGEMENTS

We are pleased to acknowledge a debt of gratitude to Joe Gaute, crime historian of fond memory, whose inspiration it was to compile a 'Who's Who of Murder'. The initial concept has been conveyed in various editions published over the last twenty-five years. Thanks are extended to Susan Fennell and the late Richard Floyd for providing a flow of press cuttings and crime references and to Loretta Lay and booksellers on both sides of the Atlantic for finding numerous crime titles.

The support and encouragement of Jonathan Goodman and Jeremy Beadle are gratefully acknowledged and thanks are due to the many faithful crime readers who have taken the time to write to us with information and comments.

NOTES

Subjects are listed in an A to Z format under their surname. The exceptions are those entries, such as the **Mumbai Child Killings,** which are better known by a popular reference.

An entry is referred to as a **Case** when a murder charge brought to trial has resulted in a lesser verdict or an acquittal. Unsolved murders are also listed in this way. At the conclusion of each entry are reference numbers relating to an extensive **Select Bibliography**. It is hoped that this will enable readers interested in a particular case to follow it up in greater detail in other books.

AUTHORS' INTRODUCTION

Like much else in the modern world, murder has changed and, generally speaking, not for the better. The nature and circumstances of acts of murder have evolved from the quiet domesticity of murder in the parlour for discernible motives, through an era of guns and gangsters, to lust killings and, seemingly motiveless, bizarre bloodletting. Dorothy Dunbar, the American writer, put it rather well in her book, *Blood in the Parlor*, published in 1964 when she wrote, 'On the rim of the twentieth-century loom the Titans – Seddon, Armstrong, Crippen, G J Smith and Landru, and then, in the era of booze and bullets, art descends literally to hack work. And so, crimes marches on'.

On the cusp of the twenty-first century, then, we are witness to murders committed less for recognisable motives such as gain or elimination and more for the sheer love of killing. Inflicting pain and exercising control over others to the point of death has become a kind of addiction that is almost commonplace in news reporting and has been transformed into the stuff of cinematic entertainment. The tentacles of this fascination with violence have spread to the internet where suicide and murder can be procured on demand.

In May 2004, a fourteen year old boy in Manchester recruited another teenager over the internet to murder him in what turned out to be a failed attempt. In the same year, Armin Meiwes, a German computer expert was convicted of manslaughter in a case involving a masochist he met through the internet who wanted to die. Meiwes obliged by killing Bernd Brandes, cutting up his body and resorting to cannibalism. Following an appeal against the verdict, Meiwes is to be retried. The case had echoes of **Albert Fish** in the 1930s who ate part of his victim's flesh stewed with vegetables.

Murder has captured the public imagination with renewed fervour in the first decade of the new century. A measure of this is the way that programmes about crime, both fact and fiction, dominate the television schedules. *Crime Scene Investigation* (*CSI*), a highly successful formula from the USA, has introduced a new culture depicting the relationship between crime and science with dramatic realism. It provides entertainment, lauds the wonders of forensic science and adds a touch of morality with the notion that 'crime does not pay'. CSI represents a world where murders are solved in the laboratory by forensic experts rather than in the library so beloved of Hercule Poirot.

Patterns of murder continue to change and where Bogota in Colombia was once considered to be the murder capital of the world, a fall of 20% in the murder rate was reported in 1997. Washington DC now tops the murder league with 50.82 deaths per 100,000 of population reported in 1979/99. By contrast, London reported 2.36 murders per 100,000 of population for the same period.

There was good news overall for the USA on the murder front in 2000. The FBI reported that the murder rate had dropped to a thirty-three year low. New York City in particular recorded a drop of 40% during the four years of Mayor Rudi Giuliani's administration. For the first time in thirty years there were fewer than a thousand murders a year in the city. Similar trends were noted in all of the ten largest US cities. The improvements were attributed to zero tolerance policing, better enforcement strategies, more officers on the streets and more criminals behind bars.

Baltimore was the exception to the improving trend, with the highest per capita murder rate in the USA. This was attributed to the prevailing drug culture which led to shootings in the streets, literally assassinations, as drug barons defended their territories. Nearly 90% of the killers had criminal records and were aged between sixteen and twenty-eight.

Richard Rosenfield, an American criminologist, has commented that the dramatic increase in prison numbers had taken many potential offenders off the streets. Between 1980 and the mid 1990s, the rate of imprisonment increased threefold and in 2000, there were two million inmates in the US penal system. Also in 2000, there were 3,500 prisoners on Death Row and 800 executions have taken place since 1976 when the moratorium on the death penalty was lifted by the US Supreme Court. The USA executes more prisoners than any comparable industrialised nation. The death penalty is authorised in thirty-eight states with Texas accounting for nearly half of the annual total in 2002. **Gary Heidnik**, **Aileen Wuornos** and **Karla Faye Tucker** were executed between 1998 and 2002 after spending a combined total of thirty-seven years on Death Row.

Firearms play an increasingly dominant role in murder, particularly in gangland violence, while the proliferation of guns makes all types of killing easier and has introduced new definitions to the language such as 'Drive-by shootings', 'Walk-up shootings' and 'Road rage killings'. The firearms toll in the USA is thirty times greater than in Britain. Every day, four American citizens die in gun incidents. There are 65 million gun owners in America and in 2005 advertisements appeared in British newspapers advising travellers to the USA, particularly Florida, to be alert for road rage attacks involving guns. A new law in the Sunshine State allows citizens to use a gun if they feel threatened.

The consequences of gun culture were all too evident in the **Columbine High School Killings** in 1999 when two teenagers killed themselves after shooting dead twelve students and a teacher. Rules on gun ownership in Britain are probably among the toughest in the world. Nevertheless, following the Dunblane massacre in 1997 (see **Thomas Hamilton**) and the subsequent banning of handguns, criminal firearms offences were up by 40% in 2001. Fatal homicides with guns account for about 1% of all homicides in the UK.

Serial killing, a shocking novelty in the 1960s and 1970s, has become almost commonplace. The modest total of victims whose lives were terminated by **Ted Bundy** (40 victims), **Dennis Nilsen** (15) and **Jeffrey Dahmer** (15) wilt beside the numbers killed by **Harold Shipman** (215), **Gary Ridgway** (48) and **Anatoly Onoprienko** (52). Apart from the rise in the number of victims, an associated feature is the geographical spread. Serial killers are no longer an American phenomenon; the killing syndrome has extended worldwide to include Europe, Australia and South Africa.

Offender profiling and criminal mapping have helped investigators edge closer to understanding the pattern woven by serial killers. What it is that motivates them in their remorseless hunt for victims remains a matter for speculation. Many reasons have been offered couched in terms of genetic disposition or the influence of environmental factors, the so-called nature versus nurture argument. Once caught, and they invariably go on until they are, serial killers readily become barrack-room lawyers and self-made psychologists voicing a hundred and one reasons why they are not guilty. Domineering mothers, parental sexual abuse, childhood rejection, low achievement and many other reasons spring easily enough from disaffected minds.

The ambition of criminologists is to find personality characteristics that will enable sociopaths in the making to be identified before they set out on a murderous trail. In 2004, Scotland Yard set up a Homicide Prevention Unit to study past crimes and imprisoned murderers with a view to preventing violent crime in the future. To this end, behavioural scientists are interviewing convicted serial killers to analyse offending patterns and personality profiles. Research carried out by the FBI has shown that most serial killers fall into categories according to such factors as the type of victim selected and the modus operandi employed. This kind of insight into the evolving patterns of serial killing acquired at an early stage can curtail the duration of the killing cycle and reduce the toll of victims.

Advances in neuroscience and genetics may make it possible to map changes in brain chemistry which enable a predisposition to criminality to be identified. A technique that might help in this process is so-called 'brain fingerprinting' which has been successfully used in the USA. Criminals may unwittingly signal guilt through their unconscious thoughts. The brain puts out electrical impulses when stimulated by images it matches with stored images. Unlike the lie detector, where the subject can deceive the interrogator, 'brain fingerprinting' depends on unalterable electrical patterns which betray guilt.

In the USA, a convicted murderer has pleaded that the presence of an abnormal gene in his body accounted for his violent behaviour. This was an ingenious attempt at exoneration, using a physical explanation rather than the voices in the head which murderers frequently claim as the springboard for their violence. Some forensic psychiatrists believe that the actions of many serial killers defy diagnosis. While they are sane, they operate in a world of totally self-centred evil in which they kill for pleasure. To that extent they are isolated from the world.

It has been said of **Ian Brady**, for example, that he believes himself to be 'the centre of the universe, superior to all'. He published a book in 2001 called *The Gates of Janus* in which he set out his thinking on serial killing. His tone was superior and unrepentant. Remorse is an unknown emotion for most serial killers and a number of them have used their notoriety to turn themselves into celebrity murderers. **Dennis Rader**, the BTK murderer, wrote to the media asking how many people he needed to kill to get his name in the paper and, before he shot and killed thirty-five people, **Martin Bryant** said he would think of a way in which he would be remembered.

Harold Shipman did not admit responsibility for the murders he committed, refusing to cooperate with the police to establish the number of victims' lives he took and proving to be a difficult prisoner. **Clifford Olson**, on the other hand, has expressed his willingness to provide details of dozens of murders on top of those for which he was convicted, provided the authorities consider him for parole.

The modern world seems to want to revile its murderers and then to celebrate them. Murderers on Death Row such as **John Wayne Gacy** and **Ted Bundy**, received proposals of marriage and killers convicted of the most heinous crimes are frequently deluged with fan mail. **Richard Ramirez** was reported to receive a hundred letters a week in the early 1990s and a woman who voted for the death sentence in his case claimed to have fallen in love with him. **Peter Sutcliffe** is another recipient of regular fan mail and offers of romantic attachment.

A feature of murder celebrity in the modern world is the way that some murderers capitalise either on their profession of innocence or simple exploitation of their notoriety. Ian Brady's desire to share his knowledge of serial killing has already been mentioned. There is a literary genre here going back at least a hundred years to **Florence Maybrick** and to **Nathan Leopold**, **Jack Abbott** and others who have found expression in print. A new phenomenon, though, is of relatives adding their accounts as in the case of the **Kray** brothers, **Ruth Ellis** and **Rosemary West**. And, in the exceptional case of the **Black Dahlia**, a son has accused his father of being the murderer.

In the first half of the twentieth century, crime investigation depended in large measure on the clever deduction, hunches and intuition of detectives. This picture changed as science began to play a greater role, offering analysis and corroboration instead of guesswork. Since it was first used in a murder case in 1988 (see **Colin Pitchfork**), DNA has become a major tool in crime investigation. Very often with only minute traces of material to work on, DNA has been the means of confirming guilt where previously there was doubt. Good old-fashioned determined police work still brings results in murder investigation even when there is no victim's body. **Robert Bierenbaum**, **Thomas Capano** and **Kimes**, mother and son, discovered that the absence of their victim was not proof against conviction.

Where crime evidence or body samples have been retained in laboratories or evidence stores, DNA offers the prospect of retrospective justice. This was the case in the murder of Hilda Murrell which remained unsolved for eighteen years until DNA testing in 2002 from crime scene evidence identified **Andrew George** as her murderer. DNA evidence also played a crucial role in convicting **Dennis Rader** after he had eluded investigators for thirty years. But retrospective use of DNA does not always provide the answers sought at the time. Attempts to identify **Bible John** by DNA comparison were not successful. Hopes of campaigners that **Jeremy Bamber**, **Albert DeSalvo** and **James Hanratty** would be absolved of guilt by DNA testing were dashed when there were judged to be insufficient grounds for changing the original verdict. Perhaps the most widely publicised application of DNA testing was Patricia Cornwell's attempt to identify Walter Sickert as **Jack the Ripper**, again with inconclusive results.

One of the consequences of the pre-eminence gained by forensic science is the 'CSI effect'. Popular television programmes have long drawn on crime both real and fictional as source material for dramatic entertainment. Programmes such as *Crime Scene Investigation* (*CSI*) and *Silent Witness* show science in the ascendancy, aided by computerised technology and full of certainty. This is what has been called the 'CSI effect' and some forensic specialists believe it puts pressure on expert witnesses and jurors. Max Houck, a forensic scientist at West Virginia University, told the American Association for the Advancement of Science in 2005 that defence attorneys were concerned that juries think science is infallible.

Some leading professionals in Britain share this view and believe that forensic science portrayed as an exact process devoid of doubt and ambiguity is wide of the mark and distorts the criminal justice system. In reality, crime laboratories deal less with certainties and more with probabilities. Some of these concerns came into focus in 2004 when a study in Britain commissioned by the Home Office showed that 43% of jurors failed to understand much of the terminology used in the courtroom.

Time is an important factor in the investigation of murder. Time of death, in particular, is a crucial factor to be determined in examining a murder crime scene and a new technique enables skeletal remains to be more accurately dated than previously. Radioactive dating of bones can be achieved by measuring radioisotopes, such as Lead 210, which occur naturally in them. The normal metabolism of the body ensures that the amount of radioactive lead is maintained at a constant level. This process stops with death and, because lead decays at a measurable rate, it is possible to work back to the time of death. Results are possible within an accuracy of twelve months for a subject dead for seventy years. Presentation of this type of evidence will inevitably tax the powers of experts to explain and juries to understand.

Time is also an essential component of justice. Some murder cases take years to solve and are suddenly re-activated by some new development or piece of evidence. Justice finally caught up with **Ira Einhorn** after he had eluded the system for twenty-five years and the Green River Killings, unsolved for twenty-one years, were eventually brought home to **Gary Ridgway**. Time also works in favour of exonerating some who have been unjustly convicted of murder. Thus, Leo Frank and Derek Bentley were granted posthumous pardons in 1986 and 1998 and Iain Hay Gordon had his conviction quashed in 2000, three instances of justice delayed.

Murder continues to be an activity which recognises no boundaries. When human behaviour lurches into violence, victims and murderers alike may come from any background or profession. There are no barriers. Age, gender, race, profession and status do not inhibit the dark, elemental forces of the murderous impulse. Even medical practitioners and nurses, dedicated to the preservation of life, fall prey to the addiction of murder. There is no clearer example than that provided by **Dr Harold Shipman**. Curiously, the very profession that should be best equipped by training and practice to perform murder to perfection, frequently bungle it. Dr Shipman became careless and new recruits to the ranks of medical murderers include **Dr**

Robert Bierenbaum, **Dr Michael Swango** and **Dr John Baksh**. They join the infamous ranks of **Crippen**, **Cream**, **Palmer** and many others, all of them careless to different degrees, in the pantheon of medical murderers.

Murder, both in its commission and discovery, brings together two kinds of genius. Evil intent and the guile to deceive and cover up, pitted against investigative wisdom and invention. The history of murder is the story of this conflict and *Murderers' Row* offers a glimpse of that world through the lives and crimes of some of murder's foremost exponents.

Robin Odell
Sonning Common, Oxfordshire

Wilfred Gregg
Ruislip, Middlesex

A

ABBOTT, BURTON W

Student at the University of California in Berkeley who was executed in 1957 for kidnapping and murdering a fourteen-year-old schoolgirl.

Stephanie Bryan failed to return to her home after school on 28 April 1955. After several days, searchers found her school books in a field out of town but there was no trace of the girl. On 15 July, Mrs Georgia Abbott telephoned the police from nearby Almeda to report that she had found some of Stephanie's effects in the basement. She had been looking for articles suitable for a theatrical production when she found a purse and identification card belonging to the missing girl.

Police made a thorough search of the Abbott home and found further articles belonging to Stephanie Bryan, including her spectacles and brassiere. Neither Mrs Abbott nor her husband Burton, a twenty-seven-year-old disabled veteran, was able to offer any explanation.

When the police learned that the Abbotts had a weekend cabin in the Trinity Mountains, some 300 miles from Berkeley, they decided to pay a visit. Aided by dogs, they found a shallow grave containing the decomposed body of Stephanie Bryan; she had been battered to death.

Burton Abbott was arrested and charged with kidnapping and murdering the girl. His trial began in Oakland in November 1955. The case against him was largely circumstantial although hairs and fibres in his car linked him with the victim and undermined his alibi. He simply maintained that he was out of town when the girl went missing. The prosecution described him as a constitutional psychopath and sexual deviant.

After considering its verdict for seven days, the jury found him guilty of first-degree murder and kidnapping for which he was sentenced to death. Abbott strongly protested his innocence and launched several appeals which resulted in numerous stays of execution. On 14 March 1957, he entered the gas chamber at San Quentin; at the very moment that the gas was released, a further stay of execution was telephoned to the prison, but it was too late to save him.
[*278, 948*]

ABBOTT, JACK HENRY

Convicted bank-robber and murderer whose letters to Norman Mailer, the celebrated writer, were published in 1981 in a book called *In the Belly of the Beast.*

Abbott spent over twenty years in prison, and much of his internment was in solitary confinement. In 1966, he began a fourteen-year sentence after stabbing a fellow prisoner to death. He devoted his time and energy to reading scholarly works and began writing to Norman Mailer. The author was impressed with Abbott's potential as a writer and helped him to gain parole. For a while after his release, Abbott worked as Mailer's researcher but he found adjustment to life outside prison difficult to manage.

In July 1981, Abbott was involved in an altercation with a restaurant waiter in New York and stabbed him to death. Ironically, his victim was a budding actor-playwright. Abbott went on the run for two months before being arrested in Louisiana. He was tried for murder and sentenced to fifteen years' imprisonment.

Abbott acquired celebrity status on account of his book *In the Belly of the Beast*, and the way in which he was lauded in literary circles as a major new talent. Others thought the praise was misplaced for someone who simply romanticised crime.

In 1983, the book was adapted as a stage play in Chicago by a director who said he wanted to explore the human capacity for violence. Fifty-eight year old Abbott was found dead in his prison cell in February 2002. He had apparently hanged himself.
[*1, 2*]

ADAMS CASE

John Bodkin Adams was the Eastbourne doctor who came under suspicion after several of his patients died in the 1950s leaving him valuable legacies.

In July 1956, Mrs Gertrude Hullett, widow of a stockbroker, was being treated by the doctor for a nervous breakdown. He prescribed barbiturate drugs to the extent that she became addicted to them. When she became seriously ill, Bodkin Adams spoke to the coroner to make arrangements for a private post-mortem. The coroner expressed shock at this outlandish request for a patient not yet dead.

Mrs Hullett died on 23 July and Dr Bodkin Adams certified death due to cerebral haemorrhage. The pathologist disagreed, suggesting she had died of barbiturate poisoning. Concern voiced by the dead woman's friends was heightened when they learned that she had bequeathed her Rolls-Royce to the doctor. The inquest on Mrs Hullett returned a suicide verdict and Bodkin Adams received a reprimand.

Throughout his career the doctor had been the fortunate beneficiary in over a hundred wills, receiving cars, antiques and jewellery from grateful former patients. It was common gossip in Eastbourne that the doctor always carried with him on his rounds a supply of blank will forms. This state of affairs was made known to Scotland Yard and a trail of suspicious deaths involving Bodkin Adams was traced back to 1946.

In 1950 he had treated Mrs Edith Alice Morrell, a wealthy widow who was partially paralysed and suffered from severe arthritis. He prescribed heroin and morphine to control her pain and she became increasingly dependent on his visits. The sick woman made several wills and, at one time, left her entire estate to the doctor. When she changed her will, Bodkin Adams asked her solicitor to draw up a codicil concerning her Rolls-Royce and a box of silver which he claimed she promised to leave him. When she died on 13 November 1950, the doctor acquired both the car and the silver.

On 1 October 1956, after intensive inquiries, the police confronted Bodkin Adams about the manner in which he had acquired Mrs Morrell's property. Of her death he said, 'Easing the passing of a dying person is not all that wicked. She wanted to die – that cannot be murder.' The doctor was charged with murder and in March 1957 was tried at the Old Bailey where he pleaded not guilty.

Weaknesses in the prosecution's case were brilliantly exploited by Geoffrey Lawrence QC who defended the doctor and won his acquittal. Bodkin Adams did not testify, thereby denying the prosecution the chance to present damaging evidence about other cases. For example, the nurse who told Bodkin Adams about one of his patients, 'You realise, Doctor, that you have killed her.'

After his acquittal, Bodkin Adams was convicted of forging prescriptions and was struck off the Medical Register. He remained in Eastbourne where he bore his disgrace quietly and continued to treat patients privately.

He was returned to the Medical Register in 1961 and resumed his practice. He died in Eastbourne at the age of eighty-four, leaving an estate valued at £400,000. A full account of the trial was published by Lord Devlin, the presiding judge, in 1985.

Dr Bodkin Adams was widely believed to have killed eight or nine of his patients during his thirty-five years as a medical practitioner. Some thought he murdered for greed, others believed he merely practised euthanasia.

[*52, 237, 392, 438, 900*]

ALLAWAY, THOMAS HENRY

The murder of a young woman in Bournemouth in 1921 was solved by a telegram and a set of car-tyre impressions.

Irene Wilkins, a young unmarried woman living in London, sought employment on the south coast. She inserted an advertisement in the *Morning Post* on 22 December 1921 stating her experience for a position as a school cook. She received a reply by telegram from Bournemouth on the same day. The sender asked her to 'come immediately' and offered to meet her by car, adding, 'expense no object'.

The next day, the young woman's body was found in a field outside Bournemouth. She had been bludgeoned to death and, although her clothing was in disarray, she had not been subjected to rape. Car-tyre impressions were noticed in the road close to the crime scene.

It transpired that two other telegrams similar to the one sent to Irene Wilkins, and in the same handwriting, had been sent from post offices in the area. The purpose of the telegrams appeared to be to lure women to Bournemouth.

The tyre impressions were identified as having been made by a Dunlop Magnum. A police round-up of the relatively small number of cars used at that time in the Bournemouth area resulted in an interview with Thomas Allaway. The thirty-six-year-old ex-soldier was working as chauffeur to a businessman whose car was a Mercedes fitted with three Dunlop Magnum tyres and one Michelin tyre.

To confirm their suspicions, detectives needed a specimen of Allaway's handwriting. Betting slips found on him when he was arrested in connection with forging cheques bore writing similar to that on the telegrams. Postcards and letters which he had written to his wife were also made available for comparison.

Allaway's defence when he was tried at Winchester in July 1922 was an unconvincing alibi. The jury convicted him of murder and he confessed his guilt to the Prison Governor on the eve of his execution. The lack of motive in this case has never been adequately explained. If it was sexual, why would Allaway bring a woman from 100 miles away when he could easily have picked up a girl in Bournemouth by driving his employer's Mercedes along the seafront?
[*1009*]

ALLEN AND EVANS
Two men both in their twenties, Peter Anthony Allen and Gwynne Owen Evans, were the last two persons to be hanged in Britain.

On 7 April 1964, John Alan West, a fifty-two-year-old laundry-van driver, was found dead in his house in Workington. He lived alone and was seen by a neighbour returning to his house in the evening after work. His next-door neighbour was awakened in the early hours by thudding noises in West's house. Looking out of the window, he saw a car driving away down the street.

When the police arrived to investigate, they found West dead from a stab wound and head injuries. Their search of the house produced a raincoat holding vital clues about the attackers. In the coat's pockets were a medallion inscribed to 'G.O. Evans, July 1961' and an Army Memorandum bearing the name, 'Norma O'Brien' and a Liverpool address. Miss O'Brien, a seventeen-year-old factory worker, told the police that in 1963 she had met a man known as 'Ginger' Owen Evans whom she remembered wearing a medallion similar to the one found in the raincoat.

Within forty-eight hours of finding West's body, the police had arrested and charged two men with his murder. Gwynne Owen Evans (his real name was John Robson Welby) had West's inscribed watch on him. His companion was Peter Allen with whom he lodged at Preston. Both men had been in trouble with the police before.

Evans maintained that he did not strike West and tried to shift the blame on to Allen. He admitted stealing the dead man's watch and it was fairly obvious that he had planned the crime.

Allen explained that they had stolen a car in Preston in order to drive to Workington to borrow some money from West who was a former workmate. His wife and children had apparently gone along for the ride.

Allen and Evans were tried in June 1964 at Manchester Crown Court. The judge put to the jury the question of whether one or both of the accused men had committed the murder. The jury decided they were equally guilty and they were convicted of capital murder. Their appeal was refused and both were hanged on 13 August 1964, Allen at Liverpool and Evans at Manchester.

Their act of robbery and murder, remarkable only for its callousness, nevertheless earned them a place in criminal history. [*490*]

ALLEN, ANTHONY JOHN ANGEL

Justice finally caught up with this bigamist and murderer twenty-seven years after he killed his wife and children.

Patricia Allen and her two children aged five and seven disappeared from their home in Salcombe, Devon on 26/27 May 1975. Anthony Allen did not report them missing. He said that his wife had gone to live in the USA with another man. A huge police search was mounted to find the missing trio but to no avail. Although there were suspicions about Allen, there was insufficient evidence to mount a prosecution. Within two months he had moved in to live with Eunice Yabsley, a widow.

Allen was a bigamist who was already married with two children when he wedded Patricia. He lived with his first family in Surrey where he defrauded the building company he worked for. He deserted his responsibilities by staging a fake suicide at Beachy Head, re-appearing a few years later to marry Patricia. His deception was discovered and he was given a two-year suspended sentence for bigamy, theft and false pretences. Between 1974 and 1990, he spent six years in prison for various offences.

Enquiries into the missing mother and children were re-opened in 2001 following publication of a book by Eunice Yabsley. She related that at the time of the disappearances Allen had scratches on his arm from wrist to elbow. Witnesses also came forward attesting to rows between Patricia and Anthony Allen with their children pleading with him not to her hurt their mother.

With new evidence, a prosecution was brought against Allen and he was put on trial at Plymouth to answer murder charges. His reputation as a bigamist, philanderer and fraudster was unveiled together with his bogus suicide attempt. He told the jury that he had tried to reinvent himself.

The prosecution maintained that he had disposed of his wife and two children so that he would be free to pursue his philandering ways. He was convicted of their murders and sentenced to life imprisonment.
[*173*]

ALLITT, BEVERLEY

Twenty-three-year-old nurse found guilty in 1993 of murdering four babies in her care at the Grantham and Kesteven General Hospital. Her trial drew comparisons with that of **Genene Jones** in the USA.

Beverley Allitt had always loved children and wanted to be a nurse or a midwife. She qualified as a state enrolled nurse in 1990 and, because of a shortage of qualified staff, was taken on for six months to work in the children's ward at Grantham.

Soon after her arrival, in the early months of 1991, there were twenty-four incidents of children suffering cardiac arrests and respiratory failure. Three babies and an eleven-year-old boy died. It became evident to the staff that all the emergencies occurred when Allitt was on duty. On 29 April 1991, blood tests on one of the children who came close to death revealed he had been given a massive dose of insulin.

Allitt was arrested but protested her innocence. The circumstantial evidence against her was strong and she was sent for trial. She collapsed midway through her trial at Nottingham Crown Court and received treatment for anorexia nervosa. She had a bad record for absenteeism and during her nursing training had been treated many times for either spurious ailments or self-inflicted injuries.

Her behaviour pointed to a phenomenon known as Munchausen Syndrome by Proxy, a condition in which a person seeks attention by making others ill. Allitt was found guilty of four murders, two attempted murders and seven instances of causing grevous bodily harm. She was given thirteen sentences of life imprisonment.
[*24, 223*]

ANGELO, RICHARD

Twenty-five-year-old registered nurse nicknamed the 'Angel of Death' by colleagues when he came under suspicion following a spate of hospital deaths.

Angelo was night-shift supervisor in the intensive care unit (ICU) at the Good Samaritan Hospital, West Islip, New York State. His patients were elderly people with cardiac and respiratory problems. Blue Code emergencies were fairly common and seemed to occur mostly when he was on duty.

Doctors became alarmed when the numbers of deaths in the ICU began to rise. There were twenty-five deaths in a six-week period in 1987. Crisis point was reached in October when two deaths and one near-fatal emergency occurred during a single night. The shift involved was Angelo's, and the seventy-three-year-old patient who survived death reported that the nurse had injected something into his intravenous drip before he experienced severe breathing problems. Traces of Pavulon, a muscle relaxant of the same type as succinylcholine (see **Genene Jones**), were found in his blood and also in his intravenous tube.

Angelo was suspended from duty while doctors reviewed thirty-seven cases involving death or life-threatening crisis. A search of his hospital locker turned up a hypodermic syringe bearing traces of Pavulon. He was not at his apartment when detectives arrived to arrest him but ampoules of Pavulon were found among his effects. Angelo was at Albany attending a medical technicians' conference.

He readily admitted guilt when he was arrested and made a tape-recorded confession. He said he had given unprescribed drugs to dozens of patients. He was unmarried and led a quiet life, being well-respected by his neighbours who thought he was religiously and studiously inclined. He collected rocks and was an avid reader. 'I would never in a million years think this man could do anything to harm somebody,' said an acquaintance.

Angelo described himself as an inadequate person who wanted to be seen as some kind of medical hero saving people's lives in an emergency. A criminologist endorsed this self diagnosis, saying that Angelo had decided he could play God by interfering with the medical destiny of his hospital patients.

It was thought that ten to twenty patients had died from lethal drug doses during a three-month period at the Good Samaritan Hospital. Several of the victims were exhumed and found to have

traces of Pavulon in their bodies. At his trial for murder, the 'Angel of Death' was found guilty of second-degree murder and was sentenced to over sixty years' imprisonment.
[*582*]

ARCHER-GILLIGAN, AMY

Forty-eight residents died at the Archer Home for Elderly People in Windsor, Connecticut over a five-year period in the early 1900s.

James H. Archer founded the home in 1907 and, when he died three years later, his widow took it on. She married Michael W. Gilligan in 1913 but he died after a brief illness. The following year, one of Amy's residents, Franklin R. Andrews, despite being in apparently good health, died at the home.

The citizens of Windsor voiced suspicions about the way the home was run, although the doctor who had examined the late Mr Andrews gave his cause of death as gastric ulcers. Nevertheless, the community's concerns were discussed with the editor of the newspaper and the police were prompted to launch a discreet inquiry.

It was discovered that Mrs Archer-Gilligan's conditions for accepting clients into her home for the elderly were that they paid up to $1500, for which they were promised a lifetime's care. Viewed against the high death rate, which was six times greater than the average for the area, the investigators' suspicions hardened. Two of the deaths, including that of Mr Gilligan, were re-examined. Exhumation of the bodies revealed that the real cause of death was arsenical poisoning.

Amy Archer-Gilligan was tried for murder at Hartford in June 1917. Powerful circumstantial evidence was brought against her, including her purchases of large quantities of arsenic from the local druggist. She claimed the poison was to be used for destroying rats. Amy made much of her devotion to the nursing profession and to the ideals of the church, but the poison found in the corpses of her former patients weighed heavily against her.

She was found guilty on five counts of murder in the first degree and was sentenced to death. She secured a retrial on appeal in June 1919 when her guilt was confirmed and she was sentenced to life imprisonment. She died in 1928, aged fifty-nine, in an insane asylum. As one writer observed, she must 'have been suffering from her climacteric, which deeply affects the endocrines of women and thus induces all kinds of abnormal and half-insane conduct.'
[*871*]

ARMSTRONG, HERBERT ROWSE

One of the classic English poison cases in which a solicitor and retired army officer was hanged for murdering his wife.

Major Armstrong, a small man with a mild manner, worked as a solicitor in Hay-on-Wye. He married a woman who combined a tendency towards hypochondria with the habit of nagging her husband.

Katharine Armstrong became ill in July 1920 and was certified as insane. She spent several months in an asylum before returning home where she died on 22 February 1921. The major recorded the event in his diary with the entry 'K died'. Her death, which was attributed to natural causes, had been preceded by a painful, wasting illness.

A few months later, Armstrong became involved in a dispute with a rival solicitor over a legal matter. He invited Oswald Martin to his house for tea, ostensibly to settle the argument on a friendly basis. With the apology, 'Excuse fingers', he handed Martin a buttered scone, with the result that his guest was subsequently taken ill. Suspicion was aroused when Martin's father-in-law, who was also the town's chemist, recalled that Major Armstrong had recently bought arsenic at his shop. An analysis of Martin's urine proved that he had indeed ingested arsenic.

The police made discreet inquiries about Major Armstrong who, because of his professional background, was regarded as something of a pillar of the community. Shock waves were sent around Hay-on-Wye when, on 31 December 1921, Major Armstrong was arrested at his office and charged with attempting to murder Oswald Martin. A full murder charge was brought after his wife's body was exhumed and arsenic was found.

Armstrong's trial at Hereford was dominated by medical evidence, with Sir Bernard Spilsbury testifying for the prosecution. The little major was severely questioned by the judge who wanted to know why Armstrong had a packet of arsenic in his pocket on the day he was arrested and why he had tried to conceal it. His fumbling excuse that it was for treating dandelions carried no conviction. It was far more likely that he was simply prepared to make another attempt to poison Oswald Martin.

The jury found Major Armstrong guilty of murder and he was hanged at Gloucester Prison on 31 May 1922. The Armstrong case has a number of parallels with that of **Harold Greenwood**. Both men were solicitors in Wales and both were accused of poisoning

their wives with arsenic. The difference was that Greenwood was acquitted. The Armstrong case featured in a television drama called *Dandelion Dead* in 1994. The following year, a new book, *Dead not Buried*, purported to show that Armstrong was the victim of a miscarriage of justice.
[*43*, *712*, *1022*]

ARMSTRONG, JOHN

The five-and-a-half-months-old son of John and Janet Armstrong died mysteriously at their home on 22 July 1955. Poisonous berries were first thought to be the cause of baby Terry's death but then barbiturates were found and a murder charge followed.

John Armstrong, aged twenty-five, was a Royal Navy Sick Berth Attendant serving at Haslar Hospital, near Gosport. His nineteen-year-old wife Janet had borne three children, the first having died at the age of three months, leaving Pamela, nearly three years old, as the survivor.

It was known that Pamela had eaten poisonous berries from the garden and supposed that she had given some to baby Terry. This appeared to be the case when a post-mortem showed red skins in the dead infant's stomach. The Armstrongs' son was buried but suspicions about his death lingered. Further examination was made in Scotland Yard's Forensic Laboratory of the red skins which proved to be not from naturally occurring berries but the gelatine capsules of the barbiturate drug, Seconal. Traces of the drug were found in the baby's body after it was exhumed.

The parents denied having any Seconal in their home but again suspicion lingered when it was discovered that a quantity of capsules had been stolen from the drugs cupboard at the hospital where John worked. An open verdict was recorded at the coroner's inquest and the affair appeared to be closed.

The Armstrongs drifted apart and, in July 1956, Janet's application to the Gosport magistrates for a separation order was refused. She went to the police and made a statement admitting that there had been Seconal in the house which John had been taking to help him sleep. She said that he had instructed her to dispose of it.

John and Janet Armstrong were arrested on 1 September 1956 and charged with the murder of baby Terry. At their trial in Winchester, John admitted taking drugs from the hospital but denied any involvement in his son's death. It emerged that he had returned home at lunch-time on the day the baby died and had the opportunity to be alone with him.

John Armstrong was found guilty and sentenced to death, although he was later reprieved. Janet was acquitted and, in a sensational statement a month later, admitted that she had given the baby a Seconal capsule to help him sleep. John maintained his innocence and there was pressure for him to be released from his life sentence. The Home Secretary declined to take any further action.

[*28, 314, 496*]

AXEMAN OF NEW ORLEANS

A number of violent killings committed in New Orleans between 1911 and 1919 were the work of an uncaught serial murderer.

The murderer acquired his name on account of his methods which involved smashing his way through the door of his victims' home and axing them to death. He then left the murder weapon at the scene of the crime. His motive appeared to be a desire to kill Italian grocers.

Matters came to a head on 24 May 1918 when Joseph Maggio and his wife were found murdered in the room behind their store. They had been attacked with an axe and slashed with a razor. On 28 June, Louis Besumer and his wife were attacked in their store by an axe-wielding intruder. It turned out that the axe belonged to Besumer and that his companion, who died in hospital, was not his wife. Before she succumbed to her injuries, Harriet Rowe accused Besumer of attacking her. He was promptly arrested.

On 5 August, the Axeman struck again. On this occasion, his victim, a pregnant woman, survived. The victim of an attack on 10 March was not so fortunate. Joseph Romano died of his wounds. The panic which had seized New Orleans at this violent onslaught began to subside as the months passed without further incident. But then, on 10 March 1919, the Axeman returned. The Cortimiglia family ran a grocery business in the Gretna district of the city. Neighbours rushed to their aid when they heard screams coming from their shop and found Charles and Rosie Cortimiglia bleeding from head injuries. Worst still, they found two-year-old Mary dead. A bloodstained axe was near by.

When she recovered, Rosie Cortimiglia accused her neighbours, Iorlando and Frank Jordano, of being the attackers. Both men were arrested but strongly protested their innocence. The axeman struck twice more, his last victim being Mike Pepitone, another grocer, killed on 27 October.

This extraordinary story had several sequels. The Jordanos were tried for murder and convicted, only to be released in December 1920 when Rosie Cortimiglia admitted she had falsely accused them. Louis Besumer was tried and found not guilty and, on 2 December 1920, Mike Pepitone's widow shot a man dead in a New Orleans street, claiming he was the axeman. The dead man was Joseph Mumfre, a businessman from Los Angeles.

With echoes of the infamous **Jack the Ripper** murders, a letter signed 'The Axeman' and sent from 'Hell, 13 March, 1919' was sent to the editor of the *Times-Picayune*. The writer claimed to have a 'close relationship to the Angel of Death'. The murder of Italian grocers in New Orleans ceased with the death of Joseph Mumfre but the killings remain officially unsolved.

[*901*]

B

BABES IN THE WOOD CASE

Two nine-year-old girls were founded murdered in a Brighton park in 1986. A local man was tried and acquitted and the case remains officially unsolved.

Karen Hadaway and Nicola Fellows disappeared on 9 October 1986. They returned home from school as usual and were seen playing together at 6.20 pm near Wild Park. When they did not return home, a search was mounted and their bodies were discovered the next day. They had been strangled and sexually assaulted.

A local man, twenty-year-old Russell Bishop, who had helped in the search, became a prime suspect. He knew both families and had been seen in the Wild Park shortly before the girls disappeared. He was also known to the police as a petty criminal. A blue sweat-shirt bearing a distinctive logo had been found during the search. Trace evidence on the garment established that it had been in contact with the victims' clothes. Several witnesses claimed that the sweat-shirt belonged to Bishop.

Bishop was tried for murder at Lewes Crown Court in November 1987. Forensic evidence featured strongly in the proceedings. The prosecution believed that the sweat-shirt belonged to the killer and, although it was linked forensically to the victims' clothing, there was nothing linking it to Bishop. Dog hairs which were found in abundance on all of Bishop's garments were not present on the sweat-shirt.

The prosecution evidence did not stand up and the jury returned a Not Guilty verdict. Bishop was acquitted but suffered a local hate campaign when his home was fire-bombed and leaflets calling him a 'child-killer' were distributed.

In February 1990, a seven-year-old girl was abducted near her home in Brighton when she was roller-skating in the street. She was bundled into the boot of a car and driven off to Devil's Dyke. An attempt was made to strangle her but she managed to break free. Bishop was rounded up routinely for questioning and the girl identified him as her attacker.

Bishop was tried for attempted murder in November 1990. He pleaded not guilty but paint particles on the victim's boots matched the paint on his car. He was convicted of attempted murder, kidnap and sexual assault and sentenced to life imprisonment.

After Bishop's second trial, a number of newspapers declared him to be the Babes in the Wood murderer. In their book *A Question of Evidence*, published in 1991, Christopher Berry Dee and Robin Odell argued that Bishop was correctly acquitted and that new evidence was sufficient to warrant reopening the investigation.

[71]

BAIN, DAVID

Controversial family murder in New Zealand in 1994 with echoes of the Amityville killings twenty years earlier in the USA (see **Ronald DeFeo**).

Emergency services in Dunedin were alerted on the morning of 20 June 1994 by a semi-hysterical caller saying, 'My father's dead, Mum's dead, they're all dead'. When helpers arrived on the scene, they immediately found four bodies. In separate rooms of the house, were Margaret Bain, her teenage daughters, Arawa and Laniet, and son Stephen, also a teenager. All had been shot in the head. In addition, Stephen's body showed signs of partial strangulation.

Margaret's husband, Robin Bain, was found dead in a caravan in the garden, with a rifle, which later proved to be the murder weapon, lying beside him. On the family computer police found the enigmatic message, 'Sorry, you are the only one who deserved to stay'. The only member of the family still alive was David, the Bains's twenty-two year old son, who had raised the alarm.

Initially, it was thought that Robin Bain had killed his family and then committed suicide. This assumption was to be rudely shattered when his son, David, was arrested and charged with all five murders. He protested his innocence. David Bain's trial opened on 8 May 1995. The prosecution's case was that he had killed his mother, brother and sisters before setting out on his daily newspaper round and that, on his return, he put the message on the computer and killed his father before raising the alarm. The defence argument was that it was not possible to prove beyond a reasonable doubt that David Bain was responsible for the deaths.

The whole case was perhaps encapsulated by the judge's opening remarks when he summed-up: 'Well who did it?', he asked, 'David Bain? or Robin Bain?' The jury returned their verdict on 26 May 1995, having decided that David Bain was guilty. He was sentenced to life imprisonment.

Subsequent appeals to the New Zealand Appeal Court and the Judicial Committee of the Privy Council failed and David Bain remains in prison. His conviction disturbs the conscience of many New Zealanders and former All Blacks player, Joe Karam, has been a tireless campaigner on his behalf.

[*502, 503, 630*]

BAKSH, DR JOHN

South London medical practitioner convicted of murdering his first wife and attempting to murder his second.

During a holiday at his villa in Spain in 1983, Dr Baksh killed his wife with an injection of morphine. They had been married for twenty-one years. Cause of death was given as a heart attack. Ruby was buried in Spain and Baksh returned to his medical practice in England and cashed in on her life insurance. He immediately set his sights on Madhu, a young doctor who had recently joined the practice.

Within weeks of Ruby`s death, Baksh proposed marriage to Madhu and she accepted. While they were enjoying a weekend in Paris he told her that he had killed his first wife in order to be free to marry her. Despite this shocking revelation, Madhu accepted his proposal but from then on the relationship was a fearful one.

On 4 January 1986, Baksh and his new wife shared a bottle of champagne. He gave Madhu a glass of bubbly which he had laced with sedatives and injected her with morphine. Later, he carried her drugged body to his car and drove to Keston Ponds near Bromley where he cut her throat with a kitchen knife and left her to die. Baksh returned home and called the police to report that his wife had been abducted by two men. In this way he hoped to establish a false trail.

Fortunately, Madhu had been discovered by a passer-by close to death and was rushed to hospital where her life was saved. While recovering from her ordeal, she wrote a note saying, 'My husband is a killer. Tell the judge he killed his first wife'. The body of Ruby Baksh was exhumed and traces of morphine were found.

Madhu testified at Baksh's trial at the Old Bailey in December 1986 and related his confession to murder and the attempt he had made on her life. There were also suspicions that the doctor might have been implicated in the deaths of two elderly partners in his medical practice. Dr Baksh was found guilty of murder and attempted murder and sentenced to terms of twenty and fourteen years' imprisonment to run concurrently. Inevitably, the popular press ran stories about 'Dr Death'.

[*183, 273*]

BALL, EDWARD

One of the rare cases in which a murder conviction was achieved without the victim's body being found.

A car was spotted parked at a strange angle in a road facing the sea at Shankill in County Dublin on 18 February 1936. There were no occupants in the car but the driver's door was open and bloodstains were visible on the back seat.

The car was traced to Vera Ball, wife of a well-known doctor who lived at Booterstown in Dublin. When police made inquiries at the house, they were told by the Ball's youngest son, nineteen-year-old Edward, that his parents had separated. He explained that he and his mother continued to live in the family home.

Ball said he had last seen his mother the previous evening when she left the house at about 7.45 in her car. He thought she might be staying with friends. A search of the house produced some interesting findings. Numerous items of wet, muddy and bloodstained clothing were found in Edward's room and there was a large wet stain on the carpet in Mrs Ball's room which had been locked.

Despite the failure to locate Mrs Ball's body, the police were convinced that she was dead. Edward told them that she had been depressed and had taken her own life, using a razor-blade to cut her throat. He had decided to dispose of the body at sea and, under cover of darkness, put the corpse in his car and drove to Shankill. He carried his dead mother out to the seashore and let the ebb tide carry her away.

Ball was nevertheless sent for trial and the prosecution maintained that far from committing suicide, it was more likely that Mrs Ball had been killed by her son, probably using the bloodstained axe found in the garden. The defence pleaded that Ball was suffering from dementia praecox and, after listening to the judge's direction, the jury found him guilty but insane. Edward Ball was ordered to be detained during the Governor-General's Pleasure.
[225]

BALL, GEORGE

Perpetrator of the so-called Liverpool Sack Murder in 1913.

A ship's steward waiting for his girl-friend outside Bradfield's tarpaulin works in Old Hall Street on 10 December 1913 unknowingly witnessed the removal of a murder victim from the scene of the crime. A shutter had blown down from the building, slightly injuring the waiting man. A young worker came out from the building and offered apologies. Shortly afterwards a boy left the works pushing a handcart. He was joined by the man who had come out earlier and they walked off down the street.

The next day, the gates of one of the locks on the Leeds–Liverpool canal was found to be blocked by a water-logged bundle. When the obstacle was removed it was found to be a woman's body wrapped in a tarpaulin. The corpse was identified as forty-year-old Christina Bradfield by a distinctive medallion around her neck. She managed the shop in Old Hall Street for her brother.

The police began a search for the two men seen pushing the handcart out of Bradfield's who had been identified as George Ball and Samuel Angeles Elltoft. Eighteen-year-old Elltoft was rounded up immediately but Ball evaded investigators for ten days. But when he was found, a search of his pockets produced Miss Bradfield's watch and there was blood on his clothes.

Ball's story was that an armed intruder had broken into the tarpaulin shop, striking Miss Bradfield over the head and snatching the day's takings before making good his escape. It was a story high on invention but low in credibility. Christina Bradfield had been bludgeoned to death and her body had been sewn into a sack.

Ball and Elltoft were tried for murder at Liverpool Assizes in February 1914. Ball was found guilty of murder and sentenced

to death. Elltoft was found guilty of being an accessory after the fact and was sentenced to four years' penal servitude. Twenty-two-year-old Ball confessed to his crime before being hanged on 26 February 1914.
[255]

BALL, JOE

Proprietor of a roadhouse in Texas who was thought to have fed five of his murder victims to alligators.

During America's prohibition era, Ball ran a bootlegging business at Elmdorf, a small Texan town near San Antonio. This provided him with funds at the end of the 1930s to set up a roadhouse near US Highway 181 which he called The Sociable Inn. His ideas for encouraging customers involved the employment of beautiful girls as waitresses and the novelty attraction of an alligator pool.

Some of the entertainment at the inn bordered on the sadistic. Ball amused his guests by throwing chunks of meat to his alligators and sometimes supplemented their food with a live cat or dog. The time came when regular guests noticed that none of his beautiful waitresses stayed very long. Ball's reply was, 'You know how they are; they come and go.'

Rumours began after Ball's third wife went missing and the police began to take an interest in The Sociable Inn. Until then, he had laughed off his customers' jibes about the disappearing women, but when police officers visited him in September 1938, he resorted to dramatic action. Pulling out a handgun from behind the bar, he shot himself in the head.

His missing wife proved to be living in California, having left Texas for her own protection, after Ball admitted to her that he had killed one of his waitresses. The inn's handyman told police the location of two graves containing murder victims' corpses, and a local rancher recounted catching Ball literally red-handed. Late one night, he had witnessed the proprietor of The Sociable Inn treating his alligators to a feast of human flesh. Ball threatened his life if he did not remain silent.

It was believed that as many as fourteen of Ball's waitresses met an untimely and violent end. As for the alligators, they were pensioned off to a zoo in San Diego.
[762]

BAMBER, JEREMY

Murdered five members of his family at his adoptive parents' home at Tolleshunt D'Arcy, Essex in 1985.

On 7 August 1985, Bamber reported to the police that a tragedy had occurred at White House Farm. He said his father had telephoned him from the house saying that his sister had gone berserk with a gun. Lying dead in the eighteenth-century farmhouse were Neville and June Bamber, both in their early sixties, his sister Sheila Cafell, aged twenty-seven, and her twin six-year-old boys. They had all been shot at point-blank range with a .22 rifle which lay across Sheila's body.

The immediate conclusion was that Sheila, a former model known as 'Bambi', had killed the family members and then turned the gun on herself. She had a history of psychiatric illness and, aided by Jeremy's suggestion that she had gone crazy, the popular newspapers laid the murders at her door. Jeremy appeared distraught at the funerals.

A month after the tragedy at White House Farm, Bamber's girl-friend told the police that Jeremy had confessed to the killings, boasting that he had committed the perfect murder. It became clear that he bore a certain amount of ill will towards his adoptive parents. He resented having been sent to boarding school and disliked the restriction his father had put on his inheritance. Jeremy and Sheila stood to share an estate of over £400,000, provided, in Jeremy's case, he worked on the farm. His inclinations lay less with the agricultural life than with the night life of Colchester and London. When he heard that his mother proposed to change the will in favour of her twin grand-children, he could see his ambitions of wealth disintegrating. He referred to his mother as a religious maniac and blamed her for making his sister mad.

A close look at the forensic evidence concerning the twenty-five shots fired during the killings showed that a silenced weapon had been used. The silencer bearing traces of Sheila's blood was found in the family gun cabinet. It was clear that the rifle with its silencer fitted was too long for Sheila to reach the trigger and shoot herself twice through the neck. Hence, she could not have taken her own life.

Jeremy Bamber was tried for murder at Chelmsford in October 1986. When counsel told him he was not telling the truth, he replied, 'That is what you have got to establish.' He simply denied the killings. The jury brought in a majority verdict of guilty and the judge told him the killing of his family 'was evil almost beyond belief'. Twenty-five year-old Bamber was sentenced to twenty-five years' imprisonment.

In April 1995, he lost his attempt in the High Court to challenge the Home Secretary's decision that he should remain in prison for life. A second appeal was launched in 2002 based on new DNA evidence but was judged to be insufficient grounds to alter the original verdict.

[*143, 758, 983*]

BARFIELD, MARGIE VELMA

Bible-quoting grandmother who confessed to four murders and was executed by lethal injection in North Carolina in 1984.

Velma had bad luck with her husbands. The first was burned to death in bed in 1969 and her second died of gastroenteritis in 1971. She turned to religion and became dependent on tranquillizers. She was hospitalized several times and stole in order to buy drugs.

After her mother died of gastroenteritis, Velma took a job as live-in maid to Dollie Edwards, an elderly woman who lived alone in her house in Raleigh. She impressed visiting relatives with her caring attitude and Christian beliefs to the extent that Stuart Taylor, the old lady's nephew, wanted to marry her. Old Mrs Edwards died of gastroenteritis in February 1977 and Velma grieved at her funeral.

Within two months another elderly person Velma was looking after died suddenly and then Stuart Taylor, by now her fiance, discovered that she had been forging his cheques. He said he would report her to the police but died before he could carry out the threat. An autopsy revealed that he had been poisoned with arsenic and Velma was immediately suspected.

She confessed to poisoning Taylor and admitted three other killings. Exhumation of her victims' bodies proved that their gastroenteritis had been caused by arsenic poisoning. Arsenic was also found in the body of her first husband whom she denied killing. Velma was charged with the murder of Stuart Taylor and sent for trial. She pleaded guilty by reason of insanity and her defence was that the crimes had been committed while she was in a state of drug dependency. She said, 'There wasn't a day in those ten years when my mind was free of drugs.'

Described as a wonderful mother and a loving grandmother, she expressed sorrow for all the hurt she had caused. The jury found her guilty of first-degree murder and she was sentenced to death. She spent six years on Death Row while her appeals were heard, being finally rejected by the US Supreme Court.

Under North Carolina law she was entitled to choose her form of execution – the gas chamber or lethal injection. She spent her last days reading the Bible and answering the many letters she received in prison. On 2 November 1984, Velma Barfield, a fifty-two-year-old grandmother wearing pink pyjamas, was given a lethal injection at the State Prison in Raleigh. She was the first woman to be executed in the USA since Elisabeth Duncan went to the gas chamber at San Quentin, California on 8 August 1962.
[*35, 86*]

BARLOW, KENNETH

Male nurse convicted of murdering his wife with an insulin injection in 1957.

Kenneth and Elizabeth Barlow lived in Bradford. On 3 May 1957, at about midnight, a doctor was called to their house after Barlow found his wife drowned in the bath. She had been unwell earlier in the evening and, after a bout of vomiting, had decided to take a bath. Barlow said he had drifted off to sleep and when he woke up realised that his wife was not in bed. He found her lying in the water-filled bath and, after attempting artificial respiration, called for help.

There were no apparent marks of violence on Elizabeth Barlow's body and, bearing in mind that she was unwell, she might have slipped under the water and drowned. However, her widely dilated eyes had not escaped the doctor's attention. No traces of drugs were found at the post-mortem nor were there any obvious injection marks. Two hypodermic syringes were found in the house which Barlow said he had used on himself to administer penicillin. This was not exceptional in view of his occupation. But what interested the police was the lack of water on the bathroom floor and the dry condition of his pyjamas in view of the reported attempt to revive his wife. Baffled as to the cause of the weakness which led to the drowning, doctors made a minute examination of the surface of Mrs Barlow's body. Their close scrutiny was rewarded by the discovery of two needle marks in one of her buttocks. Evidence of an injection, associated with the dilation of her pupils and the knowledge that she had vomited, indicated that insulin might have been given. Analysis of the tissue at the site of the needle marks was positive for insulin, leading to the inevitable conclusion that Mrs Barlow had been given an injection of the drug shortly before she died.

Kenneth Barlow had access to supplies of insulin at St Luke's Hospital and, most damagingly, a former nursing colleague reported that he had talked about insulin as a means of committing the perfect murder. He explained that the drug was undetectable once in the body as it dissolved in the bloodstream without trace.

His trial for murder was dominated by medical evidence. A theory put forward by the defence was that Elizabeth Barlow slipped under the bath water and, in a physiological reaction to her panic, a large amount of natural insulin was secreted into her bloodstream. Countering this, experts for the prosecution pointed out that a hitherto inconceivable secretion of 15,000 units would have been required to achieve this effect.

Thirty-eight-year-old Barlow was sentenced to life imprisonment. He was released from prison in 1984, having served twenty-six years. [*315, 794*]

BAUER, GUSTAV

Despite a murder trial jury's majority verdict in favour of conviction, Bauer was acquitted of murder in Vienna in 1928.

Lainz Zoo in the Austrian capital was the unusual setting for the death of thirty-one-year-old Katharina Kellner. Her body was found by gardeners on 17 July 1928. She had been shot several times and a man lurking in the vicinity hastily made off when he was spotted.

Mrs Kellner, who was separated from her husband, was known to have a number of followers. Her husband openly accused one of them, Gustav Bauer, a travelling salesman, of being involved with her death. Bauer, an ex-army officer with a reputation as a ladies' man, worked for a Berlin fashion house.

When he was questioned by the police, letters from Katharina Kellner were found in his possession, and he also owned a Steyr pistol for which he had recently bought ammunition. Bauer was identified by a Vienna taxi driver as the fare he had picked up on the day of the murder. He was accompanied by a woman whose description fitted that of the victim.

Gustav Bauer was tried for murder in October 1930. The proceedings were mostly taken up with conflicting identification evidence to the extent that the judge adjourned the trial in the hope that some fresh evidence would emerge.

A new trial was held in March 1931 and although the jury voted seven in favour of a Guilty verdict and five against, Bauer was acquitted. This decision resulted from a provision in Austrian law which required eight votes to carry a Guilty verdict.

The result caused considerable public disquiet but Bauer settled the matter by his own hand. On 17 July 1932, four years to the day that Katharina Kellner met her death in the zoo, he took his own life.

[*383*]

BAYLY, WILLIAM ALFRED

New Zealand farmer who murdered his neighbours over a boundary dispute.

On 16 October 1933, Christobel Lakey was found dead on her farm, located about sixty miles from Auckland. She had apparently drowned in the duck-pond. Police established that her husband, Samuel Pender Lakey, was missing from the house along with some of his clothes and two guns.

Christobel and Samuel Lakey had been seen alive on the previous day by their neighbour, William Bayly. He suggested that the couple might have had an argument, as a result of which Lakey killed his wife and then took to the hills.

Local inquiries revealed that the Lakeys and Bayly were not on the best of terms since a dispute over rights of access and siting of fences. Samuel Lakey had bought his farm from Bayly's father and difficulties arose when the younger Bayly took over the property. William Bayly took an aggressive attitude to his neighbours and they were said to be afraid of what he might do.

An initial search of Bayly's house turned up Lakey's missing guns and, with suspicions hardening, detectives discovered human remains on the farm. Traces of hair, bone and blood were found, together with broken pieces of a denture. While these were inconclusive in themselves, the discovery of Lakey's watch and cigarette lighter put the matter beyond doubt.

The police believed that after drowning Mrs Lakey, Bayly shot and killed her husband with a .22 Spandau rifle and then set about

destroying his body. He probably burned the corpse in an old oil-drum, scattered the ashes and incompletely combusted remnants in his farm garden. Bayly was sent for trial and convicted of double murder. He was hanged on 20 July 1934 at Auckland Prison.
[*996*]

BEARD, ARTHUR

A controversial murder case which raised important issues in English law.

Beard worked as a night-watchman and in October 1919, in a drunken state, raped and suffocated a thirteen-year-old girl. He was convicted of murder at Chester Assizes and sentenced to death.

When his appeal was heard, the fact that he was drunk at the time the crime was committed was taken as grounds for reducing the charge from murder to one of manslaughter. The argument was that his intoxicated state prevented him from forming the intention to commit murder and to have acted with malice aforethought.

The prosecution took the case to the House of Lords in March 1920 and a new judgement was given which reversed the previous ruling. The Lord Chancellor ruled that while Beard might have been too intoxicated to form the intention to kill, he had not been so drunk that he could not form the intention to commit rape. In committing this felony, he used violence and, according to law, was guilty of murder. His death sentence was commuted to life imprisonment.
[*715*]

BECK AND FERNANDEZ

America's so-called 'Lonely Hearts' killers of the 1940s were a pair of misfits who used newspaper advertisements to attract their victims.

Martha Beck had overactive glands which increased both her body weight (280 pounds at one stage in her life) and her sexual appetite. She had an unhappy childhood full of humiliation because of her size, and suffered as an adult by her poor choice of male companions. Eventually she sought solace by joining a Lonely Hearts club.

Through her club membership she met Raymond Fernandez, whose object in life was to prey on lonely women and charm them out of their money. He had suffered brain damage as a result of a shipboard accident and came to believe that he possessed powers to compel others to conform to his wishes.

Beck and Fernandez formed an amorous alliance in 1947 which quickly moved on to criminal exploitation. Their aim was to use Ray's ability to woo women through the Lonely Hearts clubs and then to fleece them for every penny they could get. While Ray was the bait, Martha reassured the victims by playing a role as his sister.

Using this ploy, they tricked dozens of women out of their money and possessions and murdered those who protested. But in December 1948, they threw all caution to the wind. Ray tricked a sixty-year-old widow, Janet Fay, into marriage and persuaded her to withdraw her entire savings and sell her house in Albany. Ray and Martha then killed Mrs Fay with a hammer and buried her body in the cellar of a rented house.

The Lonely Hearts killers next turned their attentions to Delphine Downing, a forty-one-year-old widow with a twenty-month-old son, living in Grand Rapids. They shot Mrs Downing and drowned the child; their bodies were buried under the cellar floor. After this success, Ray and Martha went out to the cinema. When they returned, the police were waiting for them with questions about Mrs Fay, whose body had been discovered.

Beck and Fernandez were charged with three murders although they were suspected of having committed seventeen others. Their trial in New York provided many sensational headlines, mostly on account of Martha's lurid sex life with Ray. They had confessed to killing Mrs Fay and, after a trial lasting forty-four days, were found guilty of first-degree murder.

They were electrocuted at Sing Sing Prison on 8 March 1951, but before going to the chair Martha proclaimed her love for Ray Fernandez and insisted on having her hair carefully styled.
[*121, 128*]

BECKER, CHARLES

Corrupt New York police lieutenant who was convicted of murder and sent to the electric chair in 1915. His widow proclaimed that he had been 'murdered' by the State Governor who refused to grant a reprieve.

Becker rose through the ranks of the New York Police Department to become personal assistant to the Commissioner. He used his position to control payments to the police from gangsters and politicians in return for favours and protection of their malpractices.

On 15 July 1912, Herman Rosenthal, owner of a New York betting shop, was shot dead by several gunmen outside the Metropole Hotel. Rosenthal had decided not to bow to Becker's protection racket and had begun to talk to a newspaper reporter. There were rumours that he would name a police officer in connection with corrupt practices in the city.

District Attorney Charles Whitman, determined to clean up the police department and convinced of Becker's involvement, offered immunity to anyone who could provide information leading to a conviction. In no time at all, a man known as 'Billiard Ball' Jack Rose made a statement in which he said that Becker had instructed him to hire four men to eliminate Rosenthal.

Charles Becker was tried for murder in October 1912 along with six other defendants. It was clear that he was the man who had ordered Rosenthal to be killed and he was convicted of murder and sentenced to death.

He appealed and was granted a second trial because of Whitman's zealousness in promising rewards to some of the prosecution witnesses. The trial took place in April 1914, after the four hired gunmen had been executed and the star witness, 'Billiard Ball' Jack Rose, had claimed immunity. Becker was again found guilty and sentenced to death.

Becker's wife petitioned Charles Whitman, now State Governor, for a pardon. He refused and the corrupt police lieutenant was electrocuted at Sing Sing on 7 July 1915. Mrs Becker had a plate engraved which was screwed to her husband's coffin. The inscription, written in anger and sorrow, declared that Charles Becker had been murdered by Governor Whitman. The plate was later removed.

[*525, 587, 780*]

BELL CASE

Mary Flora Bell was eleven years old when she killed two small boys in Newcastle in 1968.

Four-year-old Martin Brown was found in a derelict house. A nursery school in the Scotswood district had been broken into and police found four scribbled notes in a child's hand, one of which referred to the boy's death. Two months later, three-year-old Brian Howe was found dead on waste ground in the same district. He had been strangled and his body marked with cuts.

Twelve hundred children were interviewed by the police and those replies that were unclear or unhelpful were closely examined. Two stood out as being evasive – they had been given by thirteen-year-old Norma Joyce Bell and eleven-year-old Mary Flora Bell (the two girls were close friends but not related). Questioned further, they both changed their stories and, eventually, each accused the other of 'squeezing' Brian Howe's throat. Mary said that her friend had cut the boy's body with a razor blade.

When the girls were arrested and charged with murdering Brian Howe, Mary said, 'That's all right by me.' During their trial at Newcastle Assizes in December 1968, Norma appeared childlike in keeping with her age, while Mary was controlled and self-possessed. She seemed to have a grasp of affairs that was well beyond her tender years.

The girls admitted breaking into the nursery school and writing the notes found there. The same day, Mary had made a contribution to her school's 'Newsbook': it was a picture of a child lying outstretched on the floor beneath a window. This was how Martin Brown had been found.

The trial jury found Norma Bell not guilty and she was acquitted. Mary Bell was found guilty of manslaughter rather than murder, on account of diminished responsibility. She was sentenced to life detention and spent the first six years of her sentence in a special approved school before she was transferred to prison.

In September 1977, Mary Bell absconded from Moor Court open prison and was absent for three days. She wanted to prove that she was capable of leading a normal life outside prison. She was released in May 1980, just before her twenty-third birthday. In 2002, Mary Bell and her daughter sought a permanent order banning publication of their identities.

[*835, 836*]

BENNETT, HERBERT JOHN

Wife murderer whose execution at Norwich in 1901 was marked by the breaking of the mast flying the prison's black flag. This was interpreted by some as a token of the hanged man's innocence.

Twenty-year-old Bennett used his talents to devise dubious

money-making schemes such as selling fake-violins. When he married in 1897, his wife helped him with his business activities for a while. But he came to regard her as a burden and they separated.

Bennett went to work in London where in 1900 he met a young parlourmaid, Alice Meadows, whom he impressed with talk of his business plans and promised to marry her. In September, he invited his wife and daughter to join him for a holiday at Yarmouth.

A courting couple on Yarmouth's South Beach late on the evening of 22 September noticed another couple some ten yards away. They heard a woman's voice protesting but simply assumed that some vigorous love-making was in progress. The next morning, a woman's body was discovered on the beach – she had been strangled with a bootlace.

The police had difficulty identifying the murder victim until a Yarmouth landlady reported that one of her lady lodgers had not returned home. She recognised the corpse as 'Mrs Hood' and publicity of a laundry-mark on the dead woman's clothing produced a response from London. A laundry worker at Woolwich recognised the mark as one she issued to Mrs Bennett.

Herbert Bennett was arrested in London on 6 November and charged with murdering his wife. One of the late Mrs Bennett's favourite pieces of jewellery was a gold chain. Indeed, a beach photographer had taken a picture of her at Yarmouth wearing the chain and her landlady recalled that it was around her neck when she left her lodgings. The ornament was not found on the body but a search of Bennett's rooms in Woolwich proved fruitful.

At his trial at Norwich Assizes, witness after witness came forward to testify to Bennett's life of lies and deceit. Even the skills of the great defender Sir Edward Marshall Hall could not prevent his conviction. Bennett was hanged on 21 March 1901, having made no confession.

Eleven years later, the body of eighteen-year-old Dora Grey was found on Yarmouth beach. She had been strangled with a bootlace. Her murder was never solved.

[*156, 951*]

BENSON, STEVEN WAYNE

Son of a wealthy family who destroyed his mother in a car explosion when he thought she was about to stop funding his life of luxury.

Benson, Steven Wayne

On 9 July 1985, the quiet residential area of Quail Creek, in Naples, Florida was shattered by two explosions. Neighbours rushed to the home of the Benson family to find Margaret Benson and her twenty-one-year-old grandson Scott dead in the remains of their Chevrolet Suburban. Mrs Benson's daughter, Carole Lynn Benson Kendall, was badly injured and her son Steven was sitting nearby in a state of shock.

The explosion had been carefully contrived. Two 4- by 12-inch metal tubes packed with explosives had been secreted in the car and detonated remotely. It appeared that as the family was about to set off in the car, Steven ran back into the house to fetch something he had forgotten. Seconds later the bombs exploded. Forensic experts found fingerprint impressions on one of the bomb casings which matched his palm print. Thirty-four-year-old Steven was arrested on 22 August and charged with murder.

Margaret Benson's father had made a fortune out of tobacco which was divided between his two daughters. Margaret became a rich woman and her husband Edward became president of the family business. The Bensons enjoyed a lavish lifestyle, owning several houses in Canada and the USA and possessing ten cars. Their children shared in this wealth but it was understood that if any of them gave displeasure, luxuries would be withdrawn.

The family moved to Florida in 1980 and Edward Benson died shortly afterwards. Steven became the man of the house and engaged in grand business ventures which usually ended in failure, with his mother having to make good the finances. In addition to this burden, Margaret Benson was also coping with the backlash of her grandson's wild lifestyle.

Little by little, the family fortune was bleeding away. The final straw was Steven's misuse of a loan which his mother made him to start an electronic business. When he learned that she wanted the money back and intended dropping him from her will, he decided to kill her.

Steven Benson was convicted of murder on 7 August 1986 and sentenced to fifty year's imprisonment. Under Florida law he was not eligible to inherit any of his late mother's remaining wealth.
[*15, 368, 654*]

BENTLEY AND CRAIG CASE

Controversial case in which Police Constable Sidney Miles was murdered during an attempted break-in at a warehouse in Croydon, South London in 1952. Christopher Craig, aged sixteen, fired the fatal shot but escaped a death sentence because he was under age. Derek Bentley, his nineteen year old accomplice, who offered no violence during the incident and was under arrest at the time, was convicted of murder and hanged.

The two youths broke into a warehouse on 2 November 1952. Bentley had a knife and Craig was armed with a revolver. They were spotted by a member of the public who called the police. The would-be robbers made their way to the roof and when challenged. Craig shouted defiance but Bentley surrendered. At this point, Bentley was supposed to have incited the younger boy by shouting, 'Let him have it, Chris.' Craig fired and a detective was slightly wounded. Police reinforcements arrived and when PC Sidney Miles appeared on the roof he was fatally shot by a single bullet through the head. Still shouting defiance, and out of ammunition, Craig jumped off the roof, fracturing his spine in the process.

Craig and Bentley were tried at the Old Bailey. It was clear from the start that Craig was too young to be hanged even though he had fired the fatal shot. For Bentley, whose age would not prevent his being hanged if found guilty, much depended on the jury's interpretation of his alleged incitement to Craig.

The trial opened before Lord Chief Justice Goddard whose constant intervention was much criticised. In the witness-box Craig admitted his hatred for the police, although he denied intending to kill the policeman, Bentley, illiterate and educationally sub-normal, was ill-equipped to answer questions. The prosecution made much of his alleged words, 'Let him have it, Chris.' The jury took seventy-five minutes to find the two youths guilty of murder, Craig was sentenced to be detained at Her Majesty's Pleasure while Bentley was sentenced to death.

Various appeals from Bentley's family and massive support from both public and Parliament failed to win a reprieve and he was hanged on 28 January 1953. A storm of protest followed which was influential on the debate leading to the abolition of the death penalty in Britain.

Bentley's father died in 1974 after vigorously campaigning for a pardon for his son. The cause was taken up by Iris Bentley, and the

Home Secretary reviewed the case in 1992 but declined to recommend a posthumous pardon. Central to the campaigners' arguments were doubts about the words of incitement, 'Let him have it, Chris', and the indisputable facts concerning Bentley's mental status which were not put before the trial jury. The youth had an IQ of 66 and a mental age of eleven years. He was also an epileptic. In May 1995, press reports suggested there was new evidence that police officers had concocted the 'Let him have it' phrase.

In July 1998, Derek Bentley's conviction was quashed by the Court of Appeal. The Lord Chief Justice, in an historic judgement, ruled that Bentley had not been given a fair trial and criticised the conduct of the trial judge, Lord Goddard, for acting more in keeping with a prosecutor.

[*1035, 1036, 1038, 1053, 1062, 1066, 1069, 1076*]

BERG CASE

The killing of Alan Berg, controversial talk-show host in Denver, Colorado in 1984, led investigators to a white supremacy group called the Silent Brotherhood.

Fifty-year-old Berg, a Jewish lawyer, broadcast on Station KAO in Denver, adopting a confrontational style which earned him the title of 'The man you love to hate'. Many of the people he interviewed had reasons to hate him because of his abrasive technique.

On 18 June 1984, as he stepped out of his car on the driveway of his home, he was mown down by a hail of bullets from a MAC-10 machine pistol. Because Berg had many potential enemies, rumours circulated that he had been assassinated by Libyan agents or possibly by the Ku Klux Klan.

The murder weapon turned up in an arms haul uncovered by FBI agents in Idaho. In December 1984, FBI agents killed Robert Jay Mathews, leader of a group called the Silent Brotherhood. Other members of the group were arrested and questioned. They believed in neo-Nazism and embraced the use of violence in furtherance of their aims. Their death list included non-whites, liberals, homosexuals and Jews – Alan Berg was one of their targets.

In September 1985, eleven members of the white supremacy group were tried in Seattle on charges of conspiracy and racketeering. They were all convicted and received prison sentences ranging from forty to one hundred years. A plea-bargaining attempt was made to persuade one of the convicted men to assist in bringing murder charges in respect of Berg's death.

This failed, but in 1987, two members of the Silent Brotherhood, David Lane and Bruce Pierce, were convicted in Denver of killing Berg. Pierce said of Berg's shooting: 'He went down so fast it was like someone pulled the carpet out from under him.'

[*860*]

BERKOWITZ, DAVID

The 'Son of Sam' killed six victims and wounded seven others in New York in a reign of terror that lasted twelve months. In 1977 he was sentenced to a total of 365 years' imprisonment.

He turned New York City into a place of fear by preying on young couples and firing at them with a .44 Bulldog revolver. The first killing occurred on 29 July 1976 in the Bronx when a young woman was shot dead and her companion wounded. As the attacks extended into 1977, the NYPD mounted its largest-ever murder investigation, involving over 300 officers.

The attacks had a number of common features. They invariably occurred during the early hours of Saturdays or Sundays, the victims were all couples seated in parked cars and the same weapon was used throughout.

On 17 April 1977, two victims died in an attack in the Bronx. Investigating officers found an envelope addressed to the NYPD. Written on it was a criticism of the police for calling the killer a woman-hater and the declaration, 'I am a monster. I am the Son of Sam.'

The last murder was committed on 31 July 1977 when a girl was killed and her companion, though wounded, survived. On this occasion, the killer had parked his car next to a fire hydrant and collected a ticket. The car owner was traced to an address in Yonkers – the vehicle was parked outside and lying on one of the seats was a loaded .44 Bulldog revolver. The 'Son of Sam', in reality twenty-four-year-old postal worker David Berkowitz, was arrested when he returned home.

Berkowitz, who had at one time been an auxiliary policeman, lived alone and claimed he was tormented by voices and demons. He said that since 1974, the voices had been instructing him to kill. He also said he was kept awake by a neighbour's dogs barking into the night. The neighbour's name was Sam.

Psychiatrists who examined Berkowitz said that his mental status meant that he came under the legal definition of insanity. This was successfully challenged by the prosecution and he was declared sane. He changed his plea to one of guilty. In June 1978 he was sentenced to six consecutive life terms, twenty-five years for each of his victims.

In 1979 Berkowitz, who at the time of his arrest had drawn a picture of himself locked in a cage with the words 'I am not well, not at all', admitted that he had concocted the story about being tormented by demons.

In 2002, Berkowitz, a committed Christian, appealed to the sniper then terrorising Washington with ten fatal shootings to stop hurting innocent people. He said the killings made him relive his own nightmare past 'in all its ugliness and horror'.
[*4, 147, 163, 524*]

BERNARDO, PAUL

In a sensational murder case which shocked Canada in the early 1990s, Bernardo was convicted of the abduction, rape and murder of two teenage girls. In 1993, his wife, Karla Homolka, was convicted of manslaughter in the killing of the teenagers, following a controversial deal negotiated with prosecution lawyers before Bernardo was tried.

On 15 June 1991, fourteen year old Leslie Mahaffy disappeared from her home in Burlington, Ontario. Two weeks later parts of her body were found in a reservoir near St Catharines. On 16 April 1992, fifteen year old Kristen French was abducted while walking home from school in St Catharines. Her naked body was found two weeks later. Both girls has been sexually assaulted.

In January 1993, twenty-three year old Karla Homolka, recently married to twenty-six year old trainee accountant, Paul Bernardo, and living in Port Dalhousie, reported to the police that her husband had assaulted her. Bernardo was arrested and charged with forty-three sexual offences going back to crimes committed in 1987 in Scarborough, a town north of Toronto. After intensive questioning, Homolka was charged with the manslaughter of the teenagers Mahaffy and French, while Barnardo was charged with murdering them.

Homolka came to trial in July 1993 at St Catharines when Judge Francis Kovacs imposed a ban on reporting of the proceedings.

She was convicted on the two counts of manslaughter and sentenced to two twelve year terms of imprisonment to run concurrently. Bernardo was brought to trial in August 1995 after which the full extent of the crimes became known. The two girls, abducted in separate incidents, were raped and beaten before being strangled. The assaults were recorded on a video camera. The video was played for the benefit of the jury but court spectators heard only the sound track. The scenes in the court room were reminiscent of the trial of the Moors Murderers (see **Brady and Hindley**) when the screams of the victims provided horrific testimony. Homolka had participated in these crimes although she claimed her husband had forced her to take part.

Paul Bernardo, who changed his name to Teale, was convicted of first degree murder and sentenced to life imprisonment. Homolka secured her deal with the prosecutors before the video tape came to light. Subsequently, another tape was found recording an assault on Homolka's sister, Tammy, in 1990. The fifteen year old was drugged and raped before choking to death. In July 2005, Homolka was released from prison, having served her sentence.
[*760, 1042, 1047, 1073, 1074*]

BESSARABO, HÉRA

The controversial death of her husband in 1920 against a background of drugs and high-living led to Héra's conviction for murder.

Héra, who came from a wealthy French family, met Paul Jacques, a traveller in silks, in 1894 and they were married in Mexico. They had a daughter, Paule, and returned to live in Paris. It was there on 5 March 1914 that Jacques supposedly killed himself. He was found dead in his room with a revolver close by. The official verdict was suicide, although it was rumoured that Héra had attempted to poison him a few weeks earlier.

Héra and Paule travelled to Mexico to attend to her late husband's affairs. Her life took a dramatic new course when she met Bessarabo, a wealthy Romanian businessman. They promptly married and returned to France. Disenchantment with her elderly husband rapidly set in and Héra amused herself with drugs and young men.

On 30 July 1920, the Bessarabos had an argument, as a result of which Héra shot her husband. Aided by Paule, she put his body in a trunk which eventually ended up in Nancy. Apart from being shot, Bessarabo had also been beaten around the head.

Mme Bessarabo and Paule were arrested. In a confession that was later retracted, Héra admitted shooting her husband but claimed she did so under provocation. She was tried in Paris in February 1912 when Paule won herself an acquittal by giving a detailed statement against her mother. Héra Bessarabo was convicted of murder and sentenced to twenty years' imprisonment. [669]

BIANCHI, KENNETH ALESSIO

Bianchi and his cousin, Angelo Buono, were the 'Hillside Stranglers' who murdered five women in the Los Angeles area between 1977 and 1979.

The first murder victim was a nineteen-year-old prostitute whose nude body was found on a hillside near Hollywood's Forest Lawn Cemetery on 17 October 1977. Evidence at the crime scene indicated the victim had been dumped there, having been murdered elsewhere. Another young prostitute fell victim to the strangler two weeks later and in November there were four more victims. A characteristic of the murders was that the victims' bodies were arranged in deliberate poses with their legs spread apart. It was also evident that the women had been raped by two different men.

The police achieved a breakthrough in their investigation when one of the victims was linked to a security officer named Ken Bianchi. Two girls who had been hired as house-minders for a wealthy family on vacation, disappeared in January 1979. Their bodies were later found in a locked car. Bianchi was security supervisor for the agency which hired them.

In March 1979 Bianchi made a full confession to the police in which he implicated his forty-three-year-old cousin as the second strangler. He said he abducted the girls and took them to Buono's apartment where they were tortured, raped and strangled.

Bianchi was a handsome man with charming ways. He had at one time served on the Sheriff's Reserve and had practised as a psychiatric counsellor on the strength of forged qualifications. Bianchi agreed to be interviewed under hypnosis, with controversial results. While hypnotised he talked about an alter ego called 'Steve' who controlled Ken's personality. Doctors could not agree whether they were looking at a genuine case of multiple personality or merely an impressive faker.

Bianchi denied committing the murders himself, laying the blame on 'Steve' and Angelo Buono. Eventually, he agreed to plead guilty, thereby sparing the tax-payers the cost of his trial, in return for a sentence with the possibility of parole. He was given five life sentences. His cousin was convicted of one of the ten Hillside Stranglings in 1983 and was sentenced to life imprisonment.

Video tapes of Bianchi's interviews under hypnosis were shown on television in 1984. Some experts believed he was genuinely a borderline psychotic capable of carrying out actions which he would not recall later. Others remained sceptical, although many found his transition from Ken, the nice guy, to 'Steve', the bad guy, somewhat sinister, whether faked or not.

[*710, 827*]

BIBLE JOHN

Three women, whose common bond was a love of dancing, were murdered in Glasgow between February 1968 and October 1969. Their murderer, who was never caught, liked to quote from the Bible.

'Bible John's' first victim was found dead in a doorway near Carmichael Place on 22 February 1968. She had been strangled. The second victim, also strangled, was found in Mackeith Street on 16 August 1969. Investigators discovered that she had been seen at the Barrowlands Ballroom at around midnight in the company of a man aged about thirty-five. Witnesses' descriptions enabled a police artist to draw an impression of the man which was widely publicised.

On 30 October 1969, the mysterious murderer claimed a third victim. Helen Puttock had been dancing at Barrowlands with a girl-friend when they met two men, both of whom were called John. It was clear that the man attracted to Helen wished to be alone with her and the girls broke their prearranged pact to stay together. While they were together, their conversation covered topics such as holidays and sport, and 'John' made a number of biblical references.

After the dance hall closed for the night, 'Bible John' called a taxi to take the girls home. The other John made his separate way home by bus. Helen's friend was dropped off on the way and the taxi-driver left his remaining fares at Earl Road. Helen's body was found next day in a nearby tenement.

The murder victim's friend was able to provide the police with a detailed account of their evening with 'Bible John'. Newspapers printed his likeness and asked their readers, 'Do You Know This Man?' Every conceivable line of inquiry was pursued including an early attempt at offender-profiling and the use of a clairvoyant.

Despite one of Scotland's greatest man-hunts, 'Bible John' remained undetected. A series of murders in 1977–8 led some to suggest that he had begun killing again. There were certain similarities with the earlier murders but no definite links. When the 'Yorkshire Ripper's' crimes featured in the headlines, there were suggestions that he and 'Bible John' were the same person. In 1995, in a book called *The Power of Blood*, Donald Simpson claimed to know the identity of Bible John. John Irvine McInnes, a former furniture salesman was named as the suspect. He had been interviewed at the time of the murders but no action was taken against him and he died in 1980. As a result of new information, McInnes's body was exhumed in 1996 to take samples of DNA for comparison with stains on the clothing of the third victim and a dental comparison with bite marks on her body. After five months of forensic investigation the DNA and dental evidence proved insufficient to identify McInnes as the murderer. The Bible John murders remain unsolved.

[*216, 890*]

BIERENBAUM, Dr ROBERT

Unusual case in which a conviction for murder was obtained without a body fifteen years after the event. Dr Robert Bierenbaum was a successful surgeon and a qualified pilot, skills which he combined when he killed his wife, dismembered her body and dropped it in the ocean. (See also, **Sante and Kenneth Kimes**, **Hosein Brothers** and the **Peel Case**).

The doctor married Gail Katz in 1982 and they lived in New York City where he worked as a thoracic surgeon. The marriage proved to be unhappy and Gail suffered anxiety problems made worse by being belittled by her husband who was given to outbursts of extreme rage. Gail confided in her friends and family and told them how her husband had nearly strangled her because he disapproved of her smoking habit. She reported this incident to the police in 1983 but no further action was taken. Gail sought psychological counselling and for her own safety was advised to live apart from her husband who was regarded as dangerously psychopathic.

On 7 July 1985 Gail disappeared and the next day Bierenbaum reported her missing. He said they had quarrelled and she walked out. He described her as being depressed and thought she had probably committed suicide. The missing woman's friends suspected foul play. The dark side of Dr Bierenbaum's character emerged in reports from friends and two psychologists. While the police did not rule out homicide, without a body there was no proof.

The investigation dragged on and Gail's sister doggedly kept enquiries alive. In May 1989 a dismembered body found in the water by Staten Island police was tentatively identified as Gail and was buried as such. Nine years later, the body was exhumed and subjected to DNA testing which showed that it was not Gail. Meanwhile Dr Bierenbaum pursued his professional career, joined in community projects and re-married.

He was a qualified pilot and it was known that on the day his wife went missing he had flown a light aircraft from Caldwell Airport in New Jersey. There were no records of his aircraft's movements but it was shown that Bierenbaum had altered the entry in his log book. In 1997 the case of the missing surgeon's wife was re-opened and in 1999 Bierenbaum was indicted for second degree murder. Witnesses at his trial testified that Gail had thought her life was under threat, a fear backed up by reports from friends, family and professional advisers. The prosecution made a forceful argument that Bierenbaum had killed his wife and dumped her dismembered body in the Atlantic Ocean from his light aircraft. (See **Donald Hume**) The jury brought in a guilty verdict and the surgeon was sentenced to imprisonment for twenty years to life.
[*1044*]

BINGHAM POISONING CASE

Three deaths from arsenical poisoning at Lancaster Castle in 1911 have never been solved.

James Henry Bingham succeeded his father as caretaker and guide at the castle in January 1911 and appointed his sister Margaret to the post of housekeeper. Within days of beginning her new duties, Margaret died and Bingham asked another sister, Edith Agnes, to take on the vacant job.

Edith did not last long in the post because she neglected her duties and Bingham had to replace her. On 12 August, after eating a meal prepared by Edith, James Bingham was taken ill and died within a few days. A post-mortem examination was carried out and arsenic was found in his body. Examinations were ordered of the bodies of Bingham's father and his sister Margaret. Arsenic was found in both instances and Edith was arrested.

In October 1911, she was tried for murder and the proceedings were conducted in Lancaster Castle which was also the scene of the crimes. It appeared that she had argued with her brother over money matters and also about her relationship with a man she described as her fiance. Edith had a possible motive for poisoning her brother insofar as she might gain the property he inherited from Margaret. She certainly had access to the means of committing murder with poison because the castle had a stock of arsenical weedkiller.

Apart from some rather weak circumstantial evidence, there was no proof that Edith Bingham had at any time possessed arsenic or administered the poison to members of her family. The trial judge gave a summing-up in her favour and the jury acquitted her. The three cases of arsenical poisoning at Lancaster Castle remain unsolved.
[*286, 469*]

BLACK, EDWARD ERNEST

Insurance salesman who poisoned his wife with arsenic and failed in an attempt to take his own life.

Black's fifty-year-old wife, Annie, ran a sweetshop at Tregonissey in Cornwall. Edward Black, fourteen years younger than his wife, was an unsuccessful insurance salesman who owed money. In November 1921, while he was away from home, Annie was taken ill with gastroenteritis and died. Her doctor was suspicious about the circumstances of her death and asked for a post-mortem examination to be carried out. Traces of arsenic were found.

Ten days later, Black was traced to a hotel in Liverpool where he was found in his room bleeding from a wound in the throat which had been self-inflicted. The coroner's inquest into Annie Black's death brought in a verdict of poisoning from arsenic administered by her husband. His protestations of innocence sounded hollow in light of the local chemist's testimony that E.E. Black had bought and signed for two ounces of arsenic.

Edward Black was tried for murder at Bodmin on 1 February

1922 against a background in which he had already been publicly condemned. The proceedings took only two days and the jury took just forty minutes to find him guilty. His appeal against sentence was dismissed and he was hanged on 24 March 1922.
[113, 985]

BLACK DAHLIA MURDER

One of southern California's most intriguing homicides which produced numerous suspects and many confessions, yet remains unsolved.

On 15 January 1947, the tortured and mutilated body of a woman was found on waste ground in the Crenshaw district of Los Angeles. The corpse had been severed at the waist and the letters BD cut into her right thigh. The internal organs had been removed and the body drained of blood. Multiple minor stab wounds and cigarette burns bore mute testimony to the torture which her murderer had inflicted.

Fingerprint identification showed that the victim of this brutal killing was twenty-two-year-old Elizabeth Short, an aspiring actress. Her fondness for tight-fitting black dresses had earned her the name 'Black Dahlia'.

The 'Black Dahlia' dreamed of Hollywood stardom but only managed to obtain parts as an extra. Her love affairs ended in disaster and she began drinking heavily and developed a reputation for promiscuity.

The horrific nature of the murder inspired more than the usual number of confessions. Most were dismissed as fantasies but one at least was taken more seriously. Ten days after the murder, a mailman found a cardboard box with a note attached to the outside. Made up from letters cut from a newspaper, the note read, 'Here are Dahlia's belongings. Letter to follow.' The box contained Elizabeth Short's birth certificate, address book and social security card.

A number of pages were missing from the address book and all the articles had been soaked in gasoline and then dried to obliterate any fingerprints. As the victim was naked when discovered and her clothes and possessions were missing, it was assumed that the sender of these items must have been involved with her murder.

Over the years, there have been as many as fifty confessions to the killing of the 'Black Dahlia' but none that has stood up to the rigour of close investigation. In 1991, the *Los Angeles Times* reported that a Californian woman, recalling memories repressed for over forty years, had identified her father as the possible murderer. She believed that her father, who was killed in a car accident in 1962, had previously murdered a woman and buried some of her belongings. An LAPD detective commented, 'We have a lot of people offering up their fathers and various relatives as the Black Dahlia killer.'

In 1994, John Gilmore, in a convincing discussion of new evidence, named Black Dahlia's killer as Jack Anderson Wilson, a former soldier who died in a hotel fire in San Francisco in 1949. The case was brought to life again in 2003 when a former Los Angeles Police Department detective, Steve Hodel, published a book naming his father, Dr George Hill Hodel as the murderer. Dr Hodel had been interviewed by the police at the time of the murder but there was nothing to connect him with the crime. The doctor had led an unconventional life, working first as a crime reporter and then training as a doctor and leading a dissolute existence. Among his father's possessions when he died in 1999, Steve Hodel found a photograph album containing an image which he believed was of Elizabeth Short, the murder victim. The implication was that Dr Hodel was a respected physician by day but a sadistic killer at night. [*336, 424, 528*]

BLACK, ROBERT

Convicted in 1994 of the murders of three young girls who were abducted from their communities in a criminal career that spanned twenty years. He was sentenced to ten terms of life imprisonment.

Susan Maxwell, aged eleven, was abducted while walking to her home in Cornhill on Tweed in the Scottish Borders in 1982 and her body was found ten days later at Uttoxeter in Staffordshire. Five year old Caroline Hogg was kidnapped near Edinburgh in 1983 and her body was found twelve days later at Twycross in Leicestershire. Sarah Harper, aged ten, was abducted from Leeds in 1986 and her body was found later at Wilford in Nottinghamshire.

Forty-seven year old Black was caught by chance in 1990 when he was seen picking up a six year old girl in Stow, Scotland and putting her into his van. The police were alerted and Black was intercepted. The girl was found trussed up in the back of his vehicle. This was the breakthrough which enabled police to build up a circumstantial case against Black in what until that time was the UK's biggest murder investigation costing £12 million.

Black had a long history as a sexual offender, having been first convicted of an assault on a seven year old when he was aged sixteen. A pornographic scrapbook found at his home in London confirmed his sexual preferences and his employment as a delivery driver for a company producing billboard posters enabled him to travel the length and breadth of the country.

He was tried at Newcastle for the murders of Susan Maxwell, Caroline Hogg and Sarah Harper. He pleaded not guilty. The prosecution argued convincingly that Black's presence in the areas of the country where the victims were abducted was beyond coincidence. The evidence, though circumstantial, formed a consistent pattern. He subsequently recorded tapes for transmission on television confessing his predilection for sexually abusing young girls, taking opportunities to abduct them as he drove around in his van.

The UK's national database of child homicides was started in 1986 as a result of the enquiries into the death of Susan Maxwell. The database holds details of every child murder and suspected murder going back to 1960. Black's criminal career was believed to have extended over nearly twenty years and after conviction he was questioned about a number of unsolved child disappearances and murders.

[*179, 181, 1018*]

BOGLE-CHANDLER CASE

Unsolved Australian case in which a government scientist and a woman friend were found dead in circumstances which have never been fully explained.

On 1 January 1963, two teenagers walking along Lane Cove River in Sydney came across the body of a man. Unsure whether he was simply drunk or dead, they called the police. He was identified by papers in his pocket as Dr Gilbert Bogle, a scientist working at the Commonwealth Scientific and Industrial Research Organisation. A search of the area produced another discovery, the body of Margaret Chandler.

Bogle was naked but his clothes had been placed over his body to make it appear dressed. Mrs Chandler was wearing a dress which was bunched up around her thighs. Examination of the bodies revealed no signs of external injury and no indication of any disease. In the absence of any signs to the contrary, the deaths were ascribed to cardiac arrest.

Dr Bogle had attended a New Year's celebration at a house on Sydney's North Shore. He was on his own because his wife was looking after their child. He met Mr and Mrs Chandler, family friends, at the party and, when festivities broke up, offered to take Margaret home. Her husband returned home on his own.

Failure to establish a precise cause of death led to a great deal of speculation. A popular theory was that, under the influence of drink, the couple had sexual intercourse during which one of them lost consciousness and accidentally smothered the other. The difficulty with this was that, strangely for two people who had attended a party, no alcohol was found in their blood samples. At the inquest in March 1963, the coroner said that every technique known to science had been used in the search to establish cause of death. But he had to admit defeat.

There were stories that Dr Bogle had been working on a secret project connected with work in the USA. It was suggested that he was eliminated by enemy agents and Margaret Chandler was killed too because she was in the wrong place at the wrong time. The killing of Georgi Markov, the Bulgarian broadcaster, by a rare poison in London in 1978 was cited as an example of how such a murder might be committed.

A less conspiratorial theory was that the couple had died by overdosing on LSD at the New Year's party. Interest was renewed in 1977 following the death in London of Margaret Fowler, Bogle's former lover. Her offer to give evidence at the inquest in 1963 was denied, because it was believed she would say Bogle used LSD as an aphrodisiac. Theorists believed she might have followed the couple after the party, and when she found them dead in a compromising situation, tidied up the scene.

[*171, 854*]

BOLBER, Dr MORRIS

In partnership with his cousin, Paul Petrillo, Bolber made a small fortune by operating a murder for insurance scheme in Philadelphia during the 1930s.

The targets for their money-making plan were the doctor's patients, chiefly poor Italians. They decided that Petrillo would seduce Mrs Giscobbe who they knew suspected her husband of infidelity. After Petrillo had won her affection, he persuaded her to agree to a scheme in which her husband would be killed for his insurance.

When Anthony Giscobbe arrived home drunk one winter's evening, the plotters waylaid him, stripped him naked and put him on a bed under an open window. Mr Giscobbe died of pneumonia and his wife netted £10,000 which she shared with Dr Bolber.

The plotters decided to build on their initial success but discovered that few of the doctor's patients could afford insurance. To overcome this drawback, they used Petrillo's brother Herman, a man with pretensions to be an actor, who impersonated named Italian businessmen on Bolber's list of patients. By this means, and without the knowledge of their victims, they took out large insurance policies.

Bolber paid the first few insurance premiums, after which the hapless policy-holder met with an accident. The insurance companies paid up without question and Bolber and Petrillo were on their way to making a great deal of money.

A further development was Bolber's involvement with Carina Favato, a notorious faith healer. Known as 'The Witch', she had allegedly murdered three of her husbands and offered advice to women who wished to dispose of theirs. Favato gave Bolber the names of potential victims and she added her particular talents to those of the doctor and the Petrillo brothers.

Having decided that concocting accidents was becoming too difficult, they arranged for their victims to meet with 'natural' deaths. This involved hitting them on the head with a sand-filled canvas bag which precipitated fatal cerebral haemorrhage and left no tell-tale marks.

Bolber and his associates dispatched between thirty and fifty victims and swindled the insurance companies out of large sums of money. The scheme might have progressed further if Herman Petrillo had not spoken out of turn. In 1937, he told an ex-convict who had proposed a money-making scheme to him, that he already had one that was working satisfactorily. The police were informed and Bolber's gang was arrested.

In true form, each member of the gang proved eager to inform on the others. They were all convicted and the Petrillo brothers were sentenced to death. Dr Bolber and Carina Favato were given life imprisonment.

[*142, 202*]

BOOST, WERNER

Mass murderer from Dusseldorf who earned comparison with that city's infamous killer of the 1930s, **Peter Kurten**.

Boost made his mark with a series of double killings in the 1950s which the newspapers inevitably attributed to the

'Dusseldorf Doubles Killer'. The first occurred in November when a young couple disappeared from the city. They were later found in their car which had been ditched in a water-filled gravel pit.

In February 1956, another young couple disappeared. Their bodies were found outside the city, badly burned and shot through the head. Investigators were intrigued by the angle of entry of the fatal bullet which entered below the left jaw and exited through the right temple. This unusual injury was the same as that inflicted on a lawyer who had been killed in his parked car in 1953.

The spirited retaliation of a courting couple in woods near Dusseldorf probably prevented a third 'Doubles Murder' in June 1956 when they fought off two armed attackers. An alert forest ranger in the same area in the following week noticed a man shadowing a young couple in the woods. The ranger, who was armed, took Werner Boost into custody.

Boost came from an East German peasant family. When the Second World War ended, he made a living by escorting people across the border into the West. In 1950, he followed suit and went to live in Dusseldorf where he existed on the proceeds of theft. He took as his accomplice twenty-three-year-old Franz Lorbach and they indulged in a fantasy world, experimenting with drugs and chemicals.

Boost was obsessed with a hatred of courting couples and many of his experiments were to design methods of killing them. He was an efficient marksman and adept at firing from the hip, which accounted for the odd angle of entry of the fatal shots in some of his victims. The murder of the lawyer in 1953 was probably a trial of the method.

Lorback eventually confessed and claimed that he had been completely under Boost's domination. Boost was tried in Dusseldorf in 1959 and was found guilty of murdering the lawyer, but the other charges, the so-called 'Doubles Murders', were dropped because of insufficient evidence. Boost was sentenced to life imprisonment and Lorbach was given a three-year prison sentence. [*228*]

BORDEN CASE

Lizzie Borden, a thirty-two-year-old spinster of Fall River, Massachusetts, ranks high in the annals of American crime. She stood trial in 1893 charged with murdering her father and stepmother with an axe and was acquitted.

Andrew Borden and his family enjoyed a prosperous life. He was noted for his meanness except where his daughters Emma and Lizzie were concerned. Lizzie adored her father but hated her stepmother, who she thought was trying to exploit her father's wealth.

On 3 August 1892, an unusually hot summer's day, two drugstores refused to sell Lizzie prussic acid 'for moth-proofing her fur cape'. Murder struck the Borden household next day, but not through poison. At a time when there was no one else in the house, Lizzie found her father and stepmother dead with their heads brutally smashed in.

An axe-blade, freshly cleaned with wood ash, was found in the house. Lizzie was charged with the murders on the grounds that the killings must have been committed by someone in the house. A tidal wave of public opinion mounted against her but, by the time the trial began, it had swung in her favour. Fainting scenes in court won her sympathy and she was found not guilty.

Lizzie lived out her days in Fall River, where she died in 1927. She was buried next to her parents. The case is famous for the rhyme:

> Lizzie Borden took an axe
> And gave her mother forty whacks
> And when she saw what she had done
> She gave her father forty-one.

One explanation of the murders is that Lizzie committed them during an epileptic fit which left her with no knowledge of what she had done. Many books have been written about the case and in 1984 a new theory suggested the murders were committed by Emma Borden to protect her inheritance in the belief that her father planned to cut both daughters out of his will. The centenary of the murders in 1992 inspired more theories, and 400 academics and criminologists attended a conference to discuss them.

The search for motives has thrown up various ideas, including the allegation that Borden was sexually abusing both his daughters. Another angle was that a local physician and developer, Dr Sewell W. Bowen, eliminated Borden because he had opposed his plans for the town. Also under suspicion was the Borden's Irish servant,

Bridget Sullivan. Her testimony at the time was ruled inadmissible and remains sealed in the safe-keeping of the Massachusetts Bar Council.
[*741, 754, 764, 898*]

BOSCH, MARIETTE

When tragedy struck two families, passions were roused and murder for elimination resulted in an unusual capital case in Botswana.

In the 1990s, many South Africans, fearing the upsurge of crime in their country, moved to neighbouring Botswana. Among those setting up a new life were the Bosch and Wolmarans families. They settled in an up-market suburb of the capital, Gabarone, and became good friends. When Justin Bosch died in a car accident, the first person to come forward with help and support for his widow, Mariette, and her children, was Ria Wolmarans.

The families' lives were again visited by tragedy when on 26 June 1996, Ria Wolmarans was found shot dead in her home. The police investigation into the killing appeared to make little headway. Meanwhile, Mariette Bosch and Tienie Wolmarans became close and eventually set up house together. They told their children they intended to get married.

Their marriage plans were disrupted when Mariette Bosch was arrested and charged with the murder of her friend Ria. Nevertheless, while on bail and awaiting trial, she and Tienie were married.

During the murder trial, evidence was given to the effect that Mariette had visited South Africa to obtain a gun to take back to Botswana. Her sister-in-law, Judith Bosch, testified that the gun had been left at her house and subsequently handed over to the police. Tests on the gun proved it to have been the murder weapon.

Mariette was found guilty of murder and sentenced to death by hanging. Her appeal, led by Desmond de Silva QC, known for his international success in fighting capital cases was dismissed. When Tinie Wolmarans arrived at the prison to visit his wife on 30 March 2001, he was told it was not convenient to visit on that day and was advised to come back on the following Monday. When he returned, it was to be informed that Mariette had already been hanged.
[*491*]

BOTKIN, CORDELIA

An arsenic poisoner who eliminated her lover's wife with poisoned candy and was convicted in one of America's most celebrated murder trials.

After she was deserted by her husband, forty-four-year-old Cordelia Botkin went to live in San Francisco at the end of the nineteenth century. She was an active participant in the city's Bohemian circles where she met John Presley Dunning, a reputable journalist. Cordelia persuaded him to leave his wife and child in favour of a more sleazy existence in brothels and gambling dens.

As a result, Dunning not surprisingly lost both his job and his wife's affection. At the same time, Mrs Dunning began receiving anonymous letters warning her not to attempt a reconciliation with her husband.

When Dunning was asked to work as a correspondent covering the Spanish-American War in 1898, he readily accepted. Cordelia was not so pleased, jealously fearing that her lover would probably return to his wife. So she plotted to eliminate Mrs Dunning by sending her a box of candies laced with arsenic. The unsuspecting recipient and her sister-in-law ate some of the candy and both died as a result.

Cordelia's handwriting was matched to the anonymous letters and to the note sent with the lethal box of candy. After a trial, sensationalised by the newspapers of the day, she was found guilty of murder. On 31 December 1898 Cordelia Botkin was sentenced to life imprisonment which she served at San Quentin. She died in the prison in 1910 and left no confession.

[*101, 778, 871*]

BOUGRAT, Dr PIERRE

Doctor who practised both medicine and murder in Marseilles but who redeemed himself after a spell on Devil's Island.

The thirty-seven-year-old physician preferred the low-life of France's Mediterranean city to the higher flights of his chosen profession. He married a girl from a good family but she was unable to curb his neglect of family duties and preference for the excitement of the red-light district.

After his wife divorced him in 1924, Bougrat went downhill quickly. He took a prostitute home to live with him, an act which did not endear him to his patients who began to desert his practice. He was soon in financial difficulty and sought a desperate solution.

When one of his patients turned up at his consulting rooms carrying his firm's wages, Bougrat saw an opportunity. Jacques Rumebe was also a friend, and was sufficiently off-guard to tell the doctor that he had 20,000 francs on him.

Rumebe was being treated for syphilis and had called at the surgery that day for an injection. Bougrat gave him a lethal dose of cyanide and the man died on the spot. The doctor locked the surgery and absconded. Curious at this sudden turn of events, his housekeeper peered through the keyhole into the surgery where she could see a body lying on the examination table.

Rumebe was reported missing by his wife who told the police that he had been due to see Dr Bougrat. In the meantime, the wily doctor had returned to his house and concealed the body in a cupboard in his surgery which he had then covered with wallpaper. Rumebe's body may have been out of sight but it was not out of smell. As the spring weather arrived and temperatures climbed, so the stench arising from the doctor's house became unbearable. When neighbours complained, Bougrat simply fobbed them off with stories about dead vermin.

When, by chance, Bougrat was arrested and questioned about some fraudulent cheques, the police seized their chance to inspect his house in the hope of determining the cause of the smell. It did not take them long to find the concealed cupboard and when they opened it, to their horror, out fell the stinking body of the missing Rumebe.

The doctor explained the sensational discovery in his surgery by saying that Rumebe, in some distress, had asked for his help. The man had been set upon in the street and had his wages bag snatched. When Bougrat left him for a moment, his distracted patient took a fatal dose of cyanide. Afraid that he would be accused of committing robbery, the doctor decided to conceal the body until he could dispose of it properly.

His account was far-fetched anyway, but the discovery of two passports and his lady friend, ready for flight, suggested another explanation.

The doctor with a passion for a sleazy existence was given his wish. After being convicted of murder, he was sent to the French penal colony of Devil's Island in 1927. Like the celebrated Papillon, he escaped in due course and went to live in Venezuela where he was allowed to marry and also to practise as a doctor. He died in 1962 as a respected old man aged seventy-five years.

[*148*]

BOUVIER, LÉONE

Young woman from a poor French family whose explanation for killing her lover was that she loved him.

Twenty-three-year-old Léone was a plain-looking girl whose parents were addicted to alcohol and whose future prospects looked bleak. She had a menial job at a local factory where she was regarded as an easy conquest by the young men.

Life took on a better aspect when she began a regular friendship with a twenty-two-year-old garage mechanic, Emile Clenet. But her happiness was short-lived, for she became pregnant and then lost the child. She also suffered the anger of her parents and the displeasure of her employers who sacked her. The most bitter blow fell when Emile rejected her.

In her wretchedness, Léone resorted to prostitution. She met Emile for what she hoped would be a reconciliation but he only wanted to tell her that he was leaving the country to work abroad. Realising that she was losing the man she loved, she took out a gun and shot him dead.

Léone Bouvier was arrested at the convent where she had sought refuge after the shooting. She was tried for murder at Angers in December 1953 where her tragic circumstances and crime of passion won over few hearts. She told the court that she killed Clenet, 'Because I loved him'. She was convicted of unpremeditated killing and sentenced to life imprisonment.

[*351*]

BOWERS CASE

Much married San Francisco doctor whose loss of three wives and survival of one of California's most protracted murder trials made his case a *cause célèbre.*

Dr J. Milton Bowers married three times in the course of fifteen years. He was heartbroken at the death of his third wife, Cecilia, to whom he had been married for three years. She had been ill for several weeks and died of apparently natural causes in 1885. The only unsympathetic note to be struck came in an anonymous letter suggesting that the death of the doctor's wife might bear further investigation. Her insurance company acted on this and had the body exhumed for a second autopsy. When analysts found phosphorus in the tissues, the police called on Dr Bowers.

The doctor, who was commonly suspected of being an

abortionist, was put on trial in March 1886 and found guilty of first-degree murder. While he was in prison waiting for his appeal to be heard, Henry Benhayon, his brother-in-law, died in strange circumstances. Bowers had been heavily criticised by Benhayon who had accused him of being obstructive during his late wife's illness.

Benhayon was found dead in his lodgings on 23 October 1887 where he had committed suicide with potassium cyanide. He left a note admitting that he had poisoned Cecilia Bowers. On the face of it, this exonerated Dr Bowers, but there was some doubt whether Benhayon's death really was suicide. There were suspicions that John Dimmig, one of Bowers's visitors in prison, had procured the man's death.

Dimmig denied any complicity but he was known to have bought a quantity of potassium cyanide. He was put on trial for murder in December 1887 but the jury could not agree a verdict and a retrial was ordered. The evidence against Dimmig was entirely circumstantial and he was acquitted at his second trial in 1888.

Dr Bowers, who had remained in prison during these sensational developments, was released in August 1889 after serving four years. He resumed his medical practice and married a fourth time. He died, aged sixty-one, in 1904. The murder of the third Mrs Bowers has never been satisfactorily explained.

[*778, 871*]

BOYLE, TONY

Joseph Yablonski and his wife and daughter were shot dead in their home in 1970, following bitter arguments over the presidential election of the US Union of Mine Workers.

Yablonski, representing a mood for change in the way the union was run, stood for office against Tony Boyle, the current President. The election was fought in an acrimonious atmosphere and Boyle won. In the aftermath, there were vigorous protests about ballot-rigging and it was alleged that Boyle had misused union funds.

The arguments smouldered on but, on 5 January 1970, Yablonski and his family were found dead in their home at Clarksville, Pennsylvania. They had been dispatched in their sleep with shots fired through the head. The immediate reaction of the police was to view the killings as another incident in the mine-workers' dispute.

The murder investigation had an early and lucky breakthrough when police questioned Aubron Wayne Martin about a minor offence. His antagonistic attitude created suspicion and the questioning intensified. He had on him a list of telephone numbers which the police decided to follow up. This led them to Paul Gilly and Claude Vealey, who admitted that they had been at Yabolonski's house with Martin. They had waited outside until all the lights had been switched off and all was quiet. They then forced an entry and carried out their plan, killing all three occupants with Martin's .38 revolver.

The three conspirators were tried separately. Vealey pleaded guilty, and Martin and Gilly were convicted of first-degree murder. Tony Boyle was subsequently convicted of embezzlement and stripped of the office of union president. In 1973, he was tried for conspiracy to commit murder. He was convicted and sentenced to life imprisonment.

[*23, 119, 574*]

BRADLEY, STEPHEN LESLIE

Kidnapper whose plan to extract a ransom for the boy he snatched from a Sydney suburb in 1960 turned to murder.

In June 1960 Basil and Freda Thorne won £A100,000 in an Australian lottery, an event which was well publicised. Their initial joy quickly turned to sorrow when their eight-year-old son, Graeme, disappeared on his way to school on 7 July.

That he was in the hands of kidnapper quickly became apparent when Mrs Thorne received a telephone call demanding £A25,000 for her son's return. Kidnapping was not a crime with which the Sydney police were familiar. Instead of keeping their inquiries discreet, they allowed full news coverage of their nationwide search for the missing boy. The lesson learned from such cases elsewhere was not to do anything which would frighten the kidnapper. He made one further call to the Thornes and then contact was lost.

Graeme Thorne was found dead on 16 August. His body, wrapped in a carpet, was discovered by boys playing on waste land at Seaforth. The boy had a fractured skull and had been suffocated. Scientific examination of fungus spores on the child's clothing proved that the body had lain where it was found for five weeks. Other botanical evidence, in the form of particles from two species of cypress trees, provided important clues. Scientists told the police that these two species of trees were rarely found growing together.

Armed with this information, detectives began looking at trees. They were naturally excited when they found a house at Clontarf, about a mile from the spot where Graeme Thorne was found, which had the two cypresses growing in its garden.

It transpired that the couple living in the house had left on the day that the boy was kidnapped. They were identified as Stephen and Magda Bradley, Hungarian immigrants to Australia whose real family name was Baranyay. When the police learned that the Bradleys had boarded the liner *Himalaya*, bound for England, they arranged for Stephen Bradley to be taken off when the ship reached Colombo.

Bradley made a written confession admitting that he had kidnapped the boy, but claimed he had died accidentally after being hidden in the boot of his car. This, of course, did not explain the boy's head injuries. Bradley was tried at Sydney's Central Criminal Court in March 1961 and convicted of murder. He was sentenced to life imprisonment.

[22]

BRADY AND HINDLEY

The Moors Murderers, Ian Brady and Myra Hindley, were tried at Chester Assizes in 1966 for crimes which evoked widespread and lasting public anger.

Brady, aged twenty-eight, and Hindley, aged twenty-four, worked together in a Manchester office. They found they had much in common, including an interest in pornography and sadism. They went to live with Hindley's grandmother in September 1964 and became friendly with Hindley's seventeen-year-old brother-in-law, David Smith.

Brady showed off to his young friend, talking about his sadistic and violent interests and idly conversing about murder. He decided to stage a demonstration which would prove his credentials. On 6 October 1965, he picked up a seventeen-year-old homosexual, Edward Evans, in Manchester and took him home. He invited Smith to come on over. While Smith and Hindley looked on, Brady attacked his young victim with an axe, smashing his head in. When he had finished, he declared, 'It's done. It's the messiest yet. It normally takes only one blow.'

Smith was terrified by what he had seen and the next morning spoke to the police. Officers found Evans's body and their search of Hindley's rooms turned up two left-luggage tickets. When they were redeemed at Manchester's Central Railway Station, the police retrieved two suitcases containing wigs, coshes, photographs and tape-recordings. Some of the photographs were of ten-year-old Lesley Ann Downey, who had been reported missing in December 1964. One of the tape-recordings was of the girl pleading to be allowed to go home.

Papers belonging to Brady included notes about the murder of twelve-year-old John Kilbride, who had been missing since November 1963. Photographs featuring Brady and Hindley on the moors were sufficiently identifiable to help the police pinpoint search areas. John Kilbride's grave was found within a few hundred yards of that of Lesley Ann Downey on Saddleworth Moor.

Brady and Hindley were convicted of murder on 6 May 1966 and sentenced to life imprisonment. Their crimes continued to excite interest. Lord Longford campaigned for Hindley's release on the grounds that she was sufficiently reformed to be absorbed into society. Brady, detained in Park Lane High Security Hospital, has stated his wish never to be released.

In 1986, Hindley confessed to two further killings, those of twelve-year-old Keith Bennett and sixteen-year-old Pauline Reade. Both Brady and Hindley assisted the police at different times in their searches for further graves on the moors. Pauline Reade's body was found in August 1987, twenty-four years after she had disappeared. The Director of Public Prosecution made it known that no further charges would be brought. In 1989 Myra Hindley was awarded an Open University degree. In 1994, the Home Secretary turned down Hindley's petition for parole and ruled that she would never be released from prison.

In a signed statement sent to Channel 4 Television's *Witness* programme in 1994, Hindley pleaded that she had paid her debt to society. She expressed her remorse and said she had atoned for her crimes. There was public resistance to the idea of releasing her but failing health prompted the idea that she might be freed. In 1997 her image, based on an iconic photograph given wide coverage in 1966, was exhibited at the Royal Academy in the form of a large portrait by Marcus Harvey. The picture was attacked with eggs and ink.

Ian Brady wrote a book called *The Gates of Janus* which was published in the USA in 2001. Publication in the UK was initially banned but the High Court later lifted the injunction. The book was Brady's analysis of serial killing; the Moors Murders were not included. Myra Hindley did not regain her freedom but died, aged sixty on 15 November 2002. She had spent thirty-six years in prison. Her body was cremated because there were fears her grave might be desecrated. [*107, 352, 634, 755, 987*]

BRAVO CASE

Celebrated Victorian poisoning case which focused unproved suspicion on twenty-five-year-old Florence Bravo.

She had recently been widowed and had inherited a substantial sum. In 1875 she married a barrister, Charles Delauny Turner Bravo, and they lived in some style at The Priory in Balham, south London.

Apart from her money, Florence also brought other legacies with her. One was a supposedly terminated affair with an elderly doctor, James Gully, and another was her live-in companion, Jane Cox, a forty-three-year-old widow. It was believed that Florence drank rather immodestly.

On 18 April 1876, Charles and Florence had dinner at The Priory with Jane Cox. Florence retired early. She was recovering from a miscarriage and was sleeping in a separate room from her husband. At about 9.45 pm, Charles was heard calling from his room asking Florence to fetch hot water. The maid responded and called for Jane Cox who found Charles unconscious and obviously ill.

The doctor was sent for and Florence was awakened. The doctor believed Bravo was suffering from poisoning but was unable to identify the substance. Jane Cox confided that Bravo had told her he had taken poison. When the sick man regained consciousness, he was questioned about this. He said he might have taken some laudanum to soothe his gums.

Florence asked for the foremost physician of the day, Sir William Gull, to examine her husband. The doctor told Bravo he had been poisoned and the patient repeated his story about laudanum. Sir William knew that an irritant poison was at work and he did not hide the fact that Bravo was dying. Charles Bravo died on 21 April 1876 and a post-mortem revealed that the poison which killed him was antimony.

An open verdict was returned at the inquest which concluded that the poison had been administered in error by an unknown person.

Suicide was a possibility but there were mutterings about both Florence Brave and Jane Cox. Florence's dalliance with Dr Gully was recalled and it was known that Mrs Cox and Bravo had quarrelled.

The findings of the inquest were quashed by the Lord Chief Justice who ordered a second inquiry. This opened in July 1876 and excited a great deal of public attention. It proved to be virtually a trial of Florence Bravo and Jane Cox but they were exonerated to the extent that the coroner concluded there was insufficient evidence to establish guilt. Nevertheless, the verdict was one of wilful murder.

Twice-widowed Florence died two years later at Southsea, having drowned her sorrows in alcohol. Dr Gully made his name from his water treatment which was taken up by the rich and famous. And Sir William Gull, many years later, was accused of being **Jack the Ripper**.

A new book on the case which explored the sexual background of Victorian Britain was published in 2001 and opted for Florence as the murderer. A television programme re-examining the case in 2004 concluded that Bravo accidentally poisoned himself while trying to poison his wife.

[*798, 903, 939, 989*]

BRIGHTON TRUNK MURDERS

The popular Sussex seaside resort acquired unwelcome headlines in 1934 on account of two trunk murders, neither of which was officially solved.

On 17 June, a trunk left at Brighton railway station eleven days previously created attention on account of the smell it exuded. On close inspection, its contents proved to be the torso of a woman, minus head and legs. The following day, the legs were located in a suitcase in the left luggage office at King's Cross. Sir Bernard Spilsbury matched the parts and confirmed they belonged to one body.

The identity of the body in this first trunk murder was never established. And it was when police were making house-to-house inquiries in Brighton that they came across the second trunk murder. When detectives knocked on the door of 52 Kemp Street, they received no answer and resolved to return later. In the meantime, painters who had arrived to renovate the unoccupied house complained of the dreadful smell coming from within.

On 15 July, the house was entered and searched by the police. In one of the rooms they found a heavy trunk containing the decomposing body of a woman. Once again, Spilsbury was called to the scene. In this instance, the body was intact and it was clear that the woman, aged about forty, had been bludgeoned to death.

The victim of the second trunk murder was quickly identified as Violette Kaye, a dancer whose real name was Violet Saunders. It was known that she had been living at an address in Park Crescent with a restaurant waiter calling himself Tony Mancini whose real name was Lois England. It was also known that Kaye had gone missing after the couple had a confrontation at his workplace on 10 May 1933. She had apparently been intent on establishing that Mancini, whom she suspected of being wayward, was remaining faithful to her.

Mancini told friends who enquired about her that Kaye had gone to Paris to work. Meanwhile, he moved to fresh lodgings at Kemp Street and asked a fellow waiter to help him shift a heavy trunk. When the trunk began to cause offence to other residents, Mancini thought about fleeing to London. He had also been interviewed routinely by police investigating the first trunk murder.

Mancini was arrested at Blackheath on 17 July after he was recognised in the street by an alert policeman. He was tried for murder at Lewes Assizes in December and pleaded not guilty to the charge. His story was that he had returned to their lodgings to find Violette Kaye already dead, lying on the bed. He panicked and decided to conceal the body on the grounds that a man with a police record would not get a fair hearing.

In a defence acknowledged at the time as brilliant, Norman Birkett won an acquittal. His argument was that from the moment Mancini initially panicked, an unpreventable chain reaction of concealment and lies followed. The jury debated for two hours before bringing in a not guilty verdict.

For all his brilliance, Norman Birkett was wrong, because in a Sunday newspaper confession published in 1976, Mancini admitted he had 'got away with murder'. He said he had not meant to kill Violette Kaye but lost control in the heat of the moment.
[*233, 904, 981*]

BRINKLEY, RICHARD

Fifty-three-year-old carpenter in south London convicted in 1900 for a double murder involving prussic acid administered in a drink. A feature of the case was that the two people he poisoned were not his intended victims.

He had befriended elderly Mrs Johanna Blume who lived on her own at Fulham. Despite the fact that Mrs Blume had a daughter and granddaughter, Brinkley fancied his chances of acquiring the old lady's property. Not being very literate, he sought help from Reginald Parker, a friend who worked in the City, to draw up a will. This left all of Mrs Blume's assets to him but he disguised its contents from her by asking her to sign up for a seaside outing he was organising. Using a similar ploy, he acquired signatures from two witnesses, one of whom was Parker.

On 19 December 1899, Mrs Blume died, aged seventy-seven, of apoplexy. Brinkley produced the will and promptly moved into the house. Not surprisingly, Mrs Blume's relatives contested the will and Brinkley realised he would be questioned about its provenance. His biggest problem was that the two witnesses to the document had been duped and, if asked, would doubtless say they had not signed a will. Brinkley decided, therefore, to eliminate them.

He visited Reginald Parker on the pretext of buying a dog and took along a bottle of stout in a gesture of conviviality. This was a surprise because Brinkley was a teetotaller. But the bottle was stood on the table while the two men went out to look at the dog. Shortly afterwards, Parker's landlord, Richard Beck, appeared with his wife and daughter. Spotting the bottle of stout, they decided to pour themselves a drink. Within minutes, all three collapsed. A doctor was called and Mr and Mrs Beck died in his presence; their daughter later recovered. The cause of their deaths was the prussic acid with which the stout had been doctored.

Richard Brinkley was tried for murder at Guildford Assizes and found guilty. The question of whether he had poisoned Mrs Blume was answered by the fact that no toxic traces were found when her body was exhumed. Brinkley was hanged at Wandsworth Prison on 13 August 1900.

[*711*]

BROWN, DAVID ARNOLD

Millionaire computer expert who manipulated his fourteen-year-old daughter into killing his wife. He urged her on by saying she would do it if she really loved him.

Police were called to a rented bungalow at Santa Ana, Orange County, California on 19 March 1985 to investigate a shooting. They found Linda Marie Brown in the bedroom dying from two gunshot wounds in the chest. Also in the house were her husband David, their baby daughter Krystal, and Patti Bailey, the dead woman's seventeen-year-old sister. Cinnamon Brown, David's fourteen-year-old daughter by a previous marriage, was missing.

A search of the yard located Cinnamon, ill from a drugs overdose, lying in her own vomit in a dog kennel. Beside her was a piece of card on which she had written, 'Dear God, please forgive me, I didn't mean to do it.' There were suggestions of a rift between the teenager and her stepmother and the youngster had been exiled to a trailer in the garden.

Cinnamon Brown admitted firing the gun and was tried for murder as a juvenile. She was sentenced to twenty-seven years' imprisonment.

The case might have rested there but for the suspicions of two of the investigators who kept a watch on David Brown. In the aftermath of the killing, Patti began wearing the dead woman's clothing and jewellery and followed David about, carrying his child Krystal, as if she were hers. Brown later married Patti and had a child by her, but this news was kept from Cinnamon.

In July 1988, Cinnamon Brown had matured sufficiently after more than four years in prison to realise that she had been manipulated. She spoke to investigators about her father's concern that Linda, his fifth wife, was plotting to kill him. He discussed with Cinnamon and Patti ways of getting rid of her and it was clear he wanted them to do it.

On the evening of 19 March 1985, he made Cinnamon write out a suicide note and told her to swallow a quantity of drugs. He then left the house and, in her programmed state, Cinnamon took a revolver given to her by Patti and shot Linda dead. Out of love for her father, she was prepared to admit the killing and accept the punishment that followed. And David Brown was prepared to let her.

On 22 September 1988, David Brown and his young wife Patti were arrested and charged with Linda's murder. Patti's account of what happened confirmed Cinnamon's. While in prison, Brown plotted with an inmate to kill Patti and eliminate the two investigators working on his case.

In February 1990, David Brown was tried for murder, conspiracy to commit murder and with expectation of financial gain. The evidence against him was damning and he was found guilty on all three charges. In sentencing him, the judge made unfavourable comparisons with **Charles Manson**, and gave Brown life imprisonment without possibility of parole.

Cinnamon Brown and Patti Bailey were expected to remain in prison with the prospect of favourable parole terms.

[*801, 859*]

BROWN, ERNEST

Convicted of murdering his employer, a wealthy Yorkshire farmer, after he had seduced his wife. Brown has also been linked to the unsolved murder of **Evelyn Foster** in 1931.

Thirty-five-year-old Brown worked for Frederick Ellison Morton at Saxton Grange, a remote farm near Huddersfield. Dorothy Morton became his mistress and they maintained an affair which lasted several years. Brown had an ugly temper, though, and after a disagreement with Morton over his duties, left the farm. He was quickly back, asking for his old job to be returned. Morton agreed to take him back but in the lesser role of handyman.

Brown felt humiliated about his new position and brimmed with resentment. On 5 September 1933, he took his anger out on Dorothy at a time when Morton was away from home. Brown rampaged around the farm while Dorothy locked herself in one of the bedrooms.

There was a loud explosion in the early hours and the garage went up in flames. The fire destroyed several out-buildings and Dorothy was unable to summon help because the telephone line had been cut. Among the wreckage was all that was left of the family's two cars and in one of them were the charred remains of Frederick Morton. Far from being the victim of an uncontrollable fire, it was revealed that he had been shot.

Brown was charged with murder. He said Morton had come home the worse for drink and dropped a cigarette end which started the blaze. The prosecution believed Brown shot his employer and then started the blaze in the belief that the fire would destroy the evidence. He was found guilty at Leeds and hanged at Armley Prison on 6 February 1934. On the scaffold he is alleged to have said either 'ought to burn' or 'Otterburn', a possible reference to the scene of Evelyn Foster's death by fire.

[*190*]

BROWNE AND KENNEDY

Frederick Guy Browne and William Henry Kennedy were convicted of the brutal murder of PC Gutteridge in Essex in 1927. The case was significant because of the pioneering use in Britain of firearms evidence. It later emerged that Browne was probably innocent.

On 27 September 1927, the body of PC George Gutteridge, the village policeman at Stapleford Abbots, was found lying in a country lane about a mile from his home. He had been shot four times in the head and a particularly brutal feature of the crime was that his eyes had been shot out.

A car stolen from a local doctor on the same day as the murder was found abandoned in London. A search of the vehicle produced a cartridge case of an unusual type. High on the list of suspects was forty-seven-year-old Frederick Guy Browne, an ex-convict, who ran a garage at Clapham and took in stolen vehicles for respraying. A Webley revolver found at Browne's premises was loaded with the same type of ammunition as that which had killed PC Gutteridge.

William Henry Kennedy, aged thirty-six, another ex-convict, who assisted at Browne's garage, was arrested in Liverpool. He made a self-serving statement in which he admitted being in the car with Browne on the day of the murder and claimed that Browne fired the fatal shots. Meanwhile, another Webley revolver, identical to the first, was found in Browne's car.

The cartridge case retrieved from the stolen car was examined by Robert Churchill, the gun expert, who found on it a distinctive mark made by the gun which fired it. That weapon was the Webley found at Browne's garage of which he had, erroneously, as it turned out, acknowledged ownership. By so doing, he had virtually signed his own death warrant. That particular revolver belonged to Kennedy while the second weapon found was the one owned by Browne.

The firearms evidence, linking the murder weapon to ammunition fired from it, was an important step forward in the scientific investigation of crime. It also gave the prosecution an overwhelming advantage when Browne and Kennedy came to trial.

They appeared at the Old Bailey in April 1928 when the mix-up over the two Webley revolvers was apparent but no one bothered to pursue it. Between them, Browne and Kennedy had committed numerous crimes, but in Browne's case, the murder of the Essex policeman was probably not one of them.

Both men were found guilty and they were hanged on 31 May 1928, Browne at Pentonville Prison and Kennedy at Wandsworth Prison.
[*73, 851*]

BRYANT, CHARLOTTE

A rural *ménage à trois* resulted in murder by arsenical poisoning for which a mother of five was executed in 1936.

Charlotte and Frederick Bryant and their children lived in a farm cottage at Over Compton, Dorset. She was an illiterate, bad-tempered woman who cared little for her husband or family. Her immoral behaviour caused tongues to wag, especially when she took in a lodger.

In 1935, Leonard Parsons, a horse-dealer, came into the lives of the Bryant family. He and Charlotte became lovers and, as a result of the scandal, Frederick Bryant lost his job and his home. He did not seem to resent his lodger, for when he and his family moved to Combe, near Sherborne, Parsons went with them.

Frederick Bryant was taken violently ill in May 1935 but recovered sufficiently to return to work. The doctor thought he had gastroenteritis. He fell ill again a few months later and, following a partial recovery, died on 22 December. The doctor refused to issue a death certificate and the Home Office analyst found arsenic in the dead man's body.

Charlotte expressed the view, 'If nothing is found, they can't put a rope round your neck.' Unfortunately for her, traces of arsenic were found in the pockets of her coat and a discarded tin of arsenical weedkiller was discovered in the garden.

She was sent for trial at Dorchester Assizes and found guilty of murdering her husband. Sentence of death was carried out at Exeter Prison on 15 July 1936. Another female poisoner, **Dorothea Waddingham**, had preceded her to the scaffold in April of the same year.
[*167, 301*]

BRYANT, MARTIN

On Sunday 28 April 1996, Martin Bryant killed thirty-five people in the former Tasmanian convict settlement of Port Arthur. Mass murderers of this type frequently take their own lives (see **Thomas Hamilton** and **Michael Ryan**). Bryant survived the massacre but never offered any explanation for his actions, although, prior to the killings he was reported to have remarked, 'Nobody listens to me. I'm getting fed up. I'll think of something and everybody will remember me'.

Bryant was regarded as a loner with a difficult personality but his life improved dramatically when at the age of twenty, he found gardening work with a wealthy elderly spinster. She took a liking to him and when she was killed in a car crash her entire estate was willed to Bryant. This good fortune enabled him to buy a new car and travel widely.

On the fateful day of the shootings, he had driven ninety-three kilometers to Port Arthur, calling first at a guest house run by an elderly couple with whom he had a dispute. Sally and David Martin became his first victims, being found later stabbed and beaten to death. Bryant then drove to a popular tourist haunt, the Broad Arrow Cafe, which he entered carrying a semi-automatic rifle and opened fire on the patrons. It was estimated that he killed twelve people in as many seconds. Survivors said afterwards that he laughed as he fired.

Bryant returned to his car to collect a second rifle. He then walked the streets firing at random at anyone within his sights. One of the most horrific killings was that of a mother and her daughters aged three and six. He instructed the mother to kneel before shooting her and turning his gun on her children. The killings continued and there were thirty-two people dead and twenty wounded in central Port Arthur. Bryant took a man hostage and returned with him to the guest house where the killing had begun. This man was his final victim, despatched with a bullet to the head.

The police surrounded the house while Bryant directed his fire at them. The seige continued into the next day when the house was set on fire. Bryant emerged from the building, his clothes burning, and was arrested. Initially he pleaded not guilty to all the charges laid against him but at a special hearing changed his plea to guilty. On 22 November 1996, he was sentenced to life imprisonment on each of the thirty-five murders and twenty-one years on each of twenty counts of attempted murder. The trial judge ruled that he should never be eligible for parole. In a postscript to the case, Joe Vialls, a journalist, published a book claiming that Bryant was not guilty of the massacre.

[77, *941*]

BUCHANAN, Dr ROBERT

One of America's most celebrated medical murderers who was said to have modified the poisoning technique practised by Carlyle Harris in 1891.

Buchanan qualified in medicine at Edinburgh University and crossed the Atlantic in 1886 to start a practice in New York. Like **Dr Pierre Bougrat**, he favoured the low-life and spent a great deal of time in the city's bars and brothels. He nevertheless managed to run a successful medical practice.

He divorced his first wife in 1890 and took Anna Sutherland, a lady who had made her money running brothels, as his second. He arranged to be included in her will and life was running to his satisfaction until his patients began to desert him. They took a poor view of his choice of companion, preferring their doctor to be a man of good professional standing. As a result, Buchanan's income dropped.

Buchanan let it be known in 1892 that he planned to travel unaccompanied to Europe. But four days before he was due to sail, he cancelled the trip on account of his wife's sudden illness. He called in two other physicians to attend her but she died of cerebral haemorrhage. Buchanan became better-off to the tune of $50,000, and, in less than a month, remarried his first wife.

Injudicious references made by Buchanan about the **Carlyle Harris** poisoning case led to an inquiry by a *New York World* reporter. The give-away sign of morphine poisoning, pin-point pupils, had led to Harris's conviction for murder but Dr Buchanan had boasted that he could counteract this effect with belladonna.

The late Mrs Buchanan's body was exhumed and, although morphine was found, the pinpoint pupils were absent. The doctor was arrested and charged with murder. His boast was put to the test at his trial when, in an extraordinary court demonstration, a cat was killed with morphine. It was shown that belladonna dropped into the eyes of the animal prevented the pinpointing of the pupils.

Buchanan gave evidence but could do little to save himself from the effects of his own unguarded remarks overheard in a bar. He was convicted of first-degree murder and died in the electric chair at Sing Sing Prison on 1 July 1895.

[*320, 871*]

BUCKFIELD, REGINALD SIDNEY

The Mystery of Brompton Road, supposedly a fictional account of murder written by Buckfield, helped to convict him of the real thing.

Ellen Symes was found dead from stab wounds in Brompton Farm Road at Strood in Kent on 9 October 1942. Her four-year-old son who was with her was frightened but otherwise unhurt. He told the police that his mother had been attacked by a soldier.

Early the next morning, a man in uniform was seen in Strood and was questioned by the police. He was Gunner Buckfield, an army deserter known to his friends as 'Smiler'. He was a prime suspect but, after being held for four days, was handed over to the military authorities. At this point, he gave one of the civilian police officers a bundle of handwritten notes with the remark, 'You'll find these very interesting.'

Under the title *The Mystery of Brompton Road*, the notes purported to be a fictionalised account of a murder but with details which could only refer to the death of Mrs Symes. There were also references to 'Smiler' as the author of the ten thousand-word document and a chapter headed, 'Gunner Turns Detective'.

'Smiler' Buckfield was charged with the murder in Brompton Farm Road. Regarding his literary work, he said simply that was how he thought the murder might have been committed. He was tried at the Old Bailey in January 1943 and, characteristically, smiled throughout the whole proceedings. Although he denied killing Mrs Symes, the detailed knowledge of the incident contained in his story could only have been written by the murderer.

Buckfield was found guilty and sentenced to death. His reprieve on grounds of insanity was announced a few weeks later.

[46]

BUNDY, THEODORE ROBERT

Almost as much has been written about America's best-known serial killer as on **Jack the Ripper**. In February 1980, the man who was thought responsible for the deaths of up to forty women was convicted of three murders and sentenced to death. He spent nearly ten years on Death Row before going to the electric chair on 24 January 1989.

During 1974 and the early part of 1975, at least one young woman was reported missing in the Seattle area every month. Following an incident at Lake Sammamich in July 1974, police were on the look-out for a man called 'Ted' whose ploy was to approach girls, asking them to help him with his boat. He was a handsome fellow with a charming manner and some found him irresistible. The bodies of two girls who succumbed to his charm were discovered close to the lake.

The high rate of 'missing persons' reports continued and extended into other states. Disappearances of young women, often students, were reported in Colorado and Utah. It was in Salt Lake City, Utah that 'Ted' was arrested in August 1975. Forensic evidence in his car linked him to the death of one of the girls whose body had been discovered.

Bundy was charged with murder and held in custody in Colorado pending his trial. He spent his time in prison studying the law. On 7 June 1977, he contrived an escape but was soon recaptured. He was more successful with his second bid for freedom and on 30 December made his way to Florida.

On 15 January 1978, he committed the crimes which finally brought him to justice. Posing as a student, Bundy entered the sorority house at Florida State University at Tallahassee where he sexually assaulted and strangled two girls. He attacked two other girls in a nearby building, but they survived, and he then went to ground. Three weeks afterwards, a girl disappeared from a junior high school in Lake City; her body was found two months later.

Bundy was arrested on 12 February and his reign of terror, conducted throughout several states over four years, was at an end. He was tried at Miami and pleaded not guilty to three counts of murder, claiming that forensic evidence had been planted by the police. He also said that he was hindered by incompetent lawyers and by prejudiced media reporting. His trial was the first to be seen on national television and public interest was immense.

He was convicted and sentenced to death but maintained his innocence throughout the period he spent on Death Row. A number of books have been written about Ted Bundy and probably the most important was that by two journalists, Michaud and Aynesworth, who interviewed him before he was executed. He said that a malignant force, which he called 'the entity', took over his consciousness and induced him to commit rape and murder. Hence, the guilt was not his but that of his inner self.

By persuading their subject to talk in the third person, the authors of *Ted Bundy: Conversations with a Killer* encouraged him to

reveal a great deal about himself without needing to confess. The result was some remarkable insights into the mind of a serial killer. This handsome, charming and intelligent man had ample gifts to have succeeded in a professional career but chose a different path. Judge Edward Cowart, who sentenced him to death, commented, '. . . you went the wrong way, pardner.' Bundy told one of the police officers who arrested him, 'Sometimes I feel like a vampire.'
[*550, 656, 696, 802*]

BURKE AND HARE

Scotland's notorious pair of body-snatchers who committed murder in order to provide Edinburgh's medical schools with a supply of cadavers.

William Burke and William Hare had their origins in Ireland and moved to Scotland in pursuit of work. Burke had teamed up with a prostitute, Helen McDougal, and they were living in the West Port district of Edinburgh. There they met Hare who was living with Maggie Laird, a recently widowed lodging-house keeper. When one of the lodgers died in 1827, they hit on the idea of selling his corpse. They approached Dr Robert Knox, the famous anatomist, who bought the body, no questions asked, for the princely sum of £7 and ten shillings.

It was clear that further lucrative business was possible. But body-snatching from graves was becoming hazardous, with severe penalties for those caught in the act, and the cemeteries being increasingly well guarded. So Burke and Hare decided on another method of procuring bodies – by committing murder. At a rate of more than one a month, with each corpse earning them between £8 and £14, Burke and Hare, aided by their women, were prospering.

Ultimately, they were overcome by their greed and abandoned caution to the extent that a recently murdered victim was discovered at their lodgings. All four were arrested and in order to obtain incriminating evidence, William Hare and Maggie Laird were offered their liberty if they turned King's Evidence. Thus, Burke and McDougal were left to face the charge of murder at their trial in Edinburgh. McDougal professed her innocence and won a Not Proven verdict, while William Burke was found guilty and sentenced to death.

Burke was hanged on 28 January 1829 before an estimated crowd of 25,000 spectators.
[*39, 494, 766, 783*]

BURROWS, ALBERT EDWARD

A farm labourer whose solution to having to support a wife and a mistress was to murder the mistress.

In 1918, Burrows, who was in his early sixties, took twenty-eight-year-old Hannah Calladine as his mistress. She already had an infant daughter and then bore Burrows a child. He married the girl, only to be convicted of bigamy and sent to prison. When he failed to pay for the child's maintenance, his mistress moved into his home at Glossop. Mrs Burrows decided enough was enough, and moved out, claiming maintenance in her turn.

Hedged in by debt and besieged by both wife and mistress, Burrows decided to reduce the odds. On 11 January 1920, he took Hannah Calladine and their son out on to Symmondley Moor and threw them down a deep, disused mine-shaft. For good measure, he also disposed of Calladine's daughter in the same way. Burrows returned to his lawful wife and, for three years, maintained the fiction that Calladine was still alive.

His lies were unveiled when a search for a missing boy led to the disused mine-shaft. The body of the missing child was found and also the remains of Hannah Calladine and her two children. Burrows was suspected of having sexually assaulted Thomas Wood, the four-year-old boy who had been reported missing. No charge was brought on this count but Burrows was tried at Derby Assizes in 1923 for murdering Calladine and her children.

He called no evidence and the jury took a mere eleven minutes to find him guilty. His main concern was that, unlike Charlie Peace, he would not tremble when he went to the scaffold. The public hangman performed his duty at Nottingham on 8 August 1923.
[447]

BUSH, EDWIN.

Murderer of a shop assistant in London who was identified by the first successful use of the Identikit system in a murder inquiry in Britain.

Elsie May Batten was found stabbed to death on 3 March 1961 in the antique shop where she worked in Cecil Court, off the Charing Cross Road. She had been found by the shop owner, Louis Meier, lying on her back with antique daggers stuck in her chest and neck.

Louis Meier recalled that a Eurasian man had been in the shop on the previous day and had shown interest in buying an antique dagger. He returned later, accompanied by a girl, and asked about the price of a dress-sword. Again, he left without buying anything. It emerged later that the man stole the dress-sword and attempted to sell it to another dealer.

Using descriptions of the suspect, the police compiled an Identikit picture of him which was widely circulated. This first use of the system in a murder investigation met with spectacular success when a policeman on patrol in Soho recognised the man in the street.

Edwin Bush was put on an identity parade and picked out by two witnesses. His palm print was found on the paper wrapping of the dress-sword and his shoeprint was found in Meier's shop. He admitted killing Elsie Batten in order to steal the sword, saying he became angry after she made some reference to his colour.

Edwin Bush was tried at the Old Bailey and found guilty of capital murder. He was sentenced to death and, on 6 July 1961, was hanged at Pentonville Prison. Although the Identikit system continued to play a part in criminal investigation, it never fully lived up to its first success.

[*317*]

BUTLER, FRANK

An Australian adventurer and murderer who advertised for victims in the newspapers on the pretence of finding partners for gold-prospecting.

Emigrants recently arrived in Sydney in the 1890s eagerly perused the columns of the newspapers for opportunities. In August 1896, Butler set out for the Blue Mountains with his first applicant and returned alone, looking for repeat business.

Little suspicion was aroused until he took Captain Lee Mellington Weller on a gold-prospecting trip and, as usual, returned alone. Weller was better known than most of Butler's victims and questions were asked when he offered some of the captain's possessions for sale.

Deciding that flight was his best option, Butler took a ship to San Francisco in November 1896. While he was at sea, Captain Weller's body was found and Butler's arrest was ordered. This news was conveyed to his ship's captain by a faster ship sailing from Auckland after Butler's departure. Thus, when Butler arrived in America, he was taken into custody to await extradition. His case achieved some publicity while he was in prison in San Francisco and, always the entrepreneur, he earned money posing for artists and by selling his autograph.

In due course, he was sent back to Australia to stand trial for murder. He was found guilty at the Central Criminal Court in Sydney in June 1897, having been virtually indicted by the newspapers. He confessed to his crimes on the eve of execution.
[*187, 922*]

BYRON, EMMA (KITTY)

Sentenced to death for murdering her lover, she was reprieved, as the result of public pressure and served only six years' imprisonment.

Twenty-three-year-old Kitty and Arthur Reginald Baker, a married stockbroker, lived together in rented accommodation near Oxford Street. Baker drank heavily and frequently ill-treated his lover.

On 7 November 1902, the couple had a fierce argument as a result of which their landlady asked them to leave. Baker asked the landlady if she would let him stay provided Kitty, whom he derided as having no class, was made to leave. His request was refused and his remarks were repeated to Kitty.

On 10 November, Lord Mayor's Day, Kitty bought a knife from a shop in Oxford Street, declining the assistant's offer to wrap it for her. She then sent an express letter to Baker requesting him to meet her urgently. He responded immediately and met her outside Lombard Street Post Office. The couple argued and Kitty produced the knife. She plunged it into Baker twice and he fell dying to the pavement. Kitty threw herself on him in a final sobbing embrace.

At her trial at the Old Bailey, Kitty was defended by Henry Dickens. He pleaded for a verdict of manslaughter on the grounds that Kitty had intended to use the knife to kill herself in front of her lover. The judge, Lord Darling, told the jury that the act could only be construed as murder. They brought in a verdict of guilty but added a strong recommendation to mercy.

Sentence of death was commuted to life imprisonment and, in the face of continued public sympathy, this was reduced to ten and, finally, six years.
[*36, 361*]

C

CAILLAUX CASE

As the threat of world war came ever closer in the spring of 1914, the tension in France broke with a sensational *crime passionnel* in Paris. Henriette Caillaux, wife of the Finance Minister, shot dead the editor of *Le Figaro*, one of the nation's leading newspapers.

Henriette married Joseph Caillaux, a former Prime Minister, in 1911, after a highly publicised affair. He was not a popular minister and was heavily criticised in *Le Figaro*, first over his economic policies and then, more personally, over his pacifism. He responded by finding out some rather unflattering details about the paper's editor, Gaston Calmette.

The attacks in the newspaper increased in venom, culminating on 16 March 1914 in the publication of one of Joseph Caillaux's love letters to his former wife. This was a malicious act and completely out of context as the letter had been written eleven years previously. That same afternoon, Henriette bought an automatic pistol at a well-known Parisian gunsmith's and tested it in their underground firing range. She instructed her chauffeur to drive her to the *Le Figaro* building. Calmette was not in his office, so she waited until he returned when she shot him dead.

The trial of Henriette Caillaux was marked by an intense swing in public opinion, first against her and then in her favour. Neither she nor her husband were popular; indeed Joseph Caillaux was branded as a traitor. Like most of the European capitals, Paris was in political turmoil following the assassination of Archduke Ferdinand of Austria. When Caillaux's defence was able to show that Gaston Calmette was not the patriot he made

himself out to be, Henriette was on her way to a famous acquittal. The jury's verdict of Not Guilty was greeted with cries of 'Vive Caillaux. Vive Caillaux.'
[*68, 769, 838*]

CALVERT, LOUIE

A scheming prostitute and petty criminal hanged for murder in 1926.

Calvert lived on her wits, frequently passing herself off as a Salvation Army officer, in order to make a living. In 1925, she took a job as housekeeper to Arthur Calvert, a night-watchman who lived in Leeds. By misinforming him that she was pregnant, she persuaded him to marry her. When the expected child failed to arrive, he started asking questions.

Realising that she had to find a baby from somewhere, Calvert contrived a scheme. In March 1926, she told her husband she was going to visit her sister in Dewsbury where she would have the baby. She established her alibi by sending him a reassuring telegram from Dewsbury and promptly returned to Leeds. She took lodgings with Lily Waterhouse and advertised her willingness to take a baby for adoption. She received a quick response from a young unmarried girl who had given birth a few days before.

Calvert now returned to her husband with the baby which she passed off as their child. She also brought back a suitcase containing cutlery and other household items which she had acquired. Within days, the police were knocking on the Calverts' door inquiring about the murder of Mrs Waterhouse who had been found bludgeoned to death in her home. Detectives had been alerted by Mrs Waterhouse a few days before she died when she complained that a lodger appeared to be stealing from her.

Louie Calvert was tried at Leeds Assizes and convicted of murdering Lily Waterhouse for the sake of stealing a few household articles. Before she was executed, Calvert confessed to another murder four years previously when she had killed John William Frobisher for whom she was keeping house. The double murderess was hanged at Strangeways Prison on 26 June 1926.
[*445*]

CAMB, JAMES

Ship's steward convicted in 1948 of the murder at sea of the actress Gay Gibson. Sentence of death was not carried out because Parliament was debating capital punishment at the time. A study of the case, published in 1991, suggested that Camb was not guilty of murder.

Eileen Isabella Gibson, a twenty-one-year-old actress known as Gay, boarded the liner *Durban Castle* at Cape Town on 10 October 1947 for the voyage to England. She joined a number of mostly elderly first-class passengers bound for Southampton. On 18 October, when the ship was sailing off West Africa, Gay Gibson was reported missing. The captain reversed course and made a search of the ocean but, after a fruitless effort, resumed his original course.

The porthole was open in the cabin Gibson had occupied and the rumpled bed sheets were stained. It was brought to the captain's notice that the call-button in her cabin had been pushed in the early hours of 18 October. The galley staff member who answered saw James Camb, a deck steward, in the cabin; he shouted out, 'All right!' It was strictly forbidden for crew to fraternise with passengers and Camb denied being in Gibson's cabin. The ship's doctor examined Camb and found scratches on his forearms. The steward was relieved of his duties and handed over to the police when the liner docked at Southampton.

Camb changed his story several times but finally admitted he had been in Gibson's cabin. He claimed she had consented to sex and during intercourse suffered some kind of seizure. He tried to revive her but when this failed, believing her to be dead, he pushed her body through the porthole.

James Camb was charged with murder and stood trial at Winchester Assizes in March 1948. The prosecution argued that he had raped and strangled the girl before throwing her body out of the porthole. As there was no body, much of the evidence was circumstantial. Interpretation of the stains on the sheets in the cabin proved inconclusive. Camb gave evidence and said he panicked when the girl appeared to have died.

The jury brought in a Guilty verdict and Camb was sentenced to death. He was reprieved and given a life sentence as Parliament was then debating the abolition of capital punishment. Camb was released on parole in 1959 but was convicted of sexual offences in 1971 which resulted in further imprisonment. He gained his release in 1978 and died in the following year.

There was no doubt that Camb pushed Gay Gibson's body through the porthole. The question was whether or not he murdered her. In his book on the case, Denis Herbstein suggested that Gibson probably died of heart failure in the course of performing oral sex. This conclusion was supported by Dr Denis Hocking, the pathologist who appeared for the defence at Camb's trial, but it was not a conclusion that could be put before a jury in the 1940s. This interpretation means that Camb was not guilty of murder.
[*100, 180, 419*]

CAMDEN TOWN MURDER
Robert Wood, a young artist, won a famous acquittal at his trial in 1907 for a murder which remains unsolved.

On 12 September 1907, Emily Jane Dimmock, a twenty-three-year-old prostitute, was found dead from strangulation, at her lodgings in St Paul's Road, Camden Town. Her body was discovered by her boy-friend, Bertram Shaw, when he returned home after finishing his shift as a railway dining-car cook.

Shaw was unaware that Phyllis, as she liked to be called, belonged to the oldest profession and entertained clients while he was on night-duty. He had the perfect alibi for he was working in the galley of the Sheffield to London train at the time doctors supposed Phyllis had been killed.

The police began checking up on Phyllis's contacts and learned that one of her happy hunting grounds for clients was the Rising Sun public house. She had met a ship's cook there, Robert Percival Roberts, who had been with her on several nights prior to her death but who had a firm alibi for the night of the murder.

Roberts volunteered the information that on the morning he left Phyllis, she showed him a letter inviting her to meet someone called 'Bert' at the Eagle public house. She also showed him a postcard decorated with a picture of a rising sun, inviting her to meet 'Alice'. The burned remnants of the letter were found in the fire-grate of her room but the postcard remained missing until Bertram Shaw discovered it when he was collecting his possessions from the room they had shared.

The 'Rising Sun' postcard was widely publicised in an effort to identify the handwriting. The missive was recognised by the person who wrote it, Robert Wood, and by his girl-friend, Ruby Young. Wood explained that he had met Phyllis in a pub and they discussed some picture postcards which he had with him. In fun, she asked him to write something on one of them and post it to her. This he did, signing it 'Alice', at her request. He also asked Ruby Young to say that he always stayed with her on Monday and Wednesday nights. But she broke the confidence by telling a friend who had journalistic connections.

Robert William Thomas Cavers Wood, to give him his full name, a promising twenty-five-year-old artist engraver, was arrested on 4 October. He was identified by several witnesses who said they had seen him with Phyllis Dimmock and, when his subterfuge over the postcard was discovered, he was charged with murder.

He was tried at the Old Bailey in December 1907 and was admirably defended by Edward Marshall Hall who portrayed Wood's lies as the action of a man anxiously trying to conceal his low-grade socialising. The letter and its charred remnants were dismissed by counsel as a ploy by Roberts to deflect attention from his association with Phyllis.

For the first time since the Criminal Evidence Act of 1888 allowed a defendant to give evidence, the person in the dock won the day. Wood made a very good impression and when the jury brought in a Not Guilty verdict, crowds outside the court cheered their agreement and women wept with relief.

[*426, 691*]

CANNAN, JOHN

Convicted of murdering a young woman in Bristol in 1987 and suspected of involvement in the abduction of Suzy Lamplugh.

Shirley Banks disappeared without trace on 8 October 1987 while on a shopping trip in her home town. Three weeks later, on 27 October, John Cannan was foiled in an attempted shop robbery at Leamington Spa and was arrested. Among his belongings were the tax disc from Shirley Banks's car, and the car itself was found in the garage at his Bristol flat.

Cannan denied any knowledge of the young woman's disappearance and maintained that he had bought the car from a dealer. Shirley Banks's body was found in a wooded area of the Quantock Hills in April 1988. She had been bludgeoned to death but there were no direct forensic links to Cannan. He continued his denials but the discovery of a fingerprint left by the dead woman in his flat sealed his fate.

At Exeter Crown Court in April 1989, Cannan was found guilty on six charges which included murder, rape, buggery, kidnap and attempted abduction. He was sentenced to life imprisonment.

Cannan had a history of committing violent assaults and rape, for which he had been sentenced to eight years in prison in 1981. His involvement was strongly suspected in the disappearance of Suzy Lamplugh, a young estate agent who went missing in London on 28 July 1986. She had been on her way to fulfil an appointment with a 'Mr Kipper'.

'Kipper' was one of Cannan's nicknames and he had been released from prison only three days before. The manner of Suzy Lamplugh's disappearance bore many of Cannan's trademarks and he fitted the description of a man seen in her company. He has consistently denied any involvement.

Cannan was a handsome charmer who had the girls falling at his feet. What they did not know was that, like **Ted Bundy**, he travelled with handcuffs, rope and weapons in his car.

[72]

CAPANO, THOMAS

Attorney and member of a prominent family in Delaware, USA found guilty of first degree murder in a case where the victim's body was not found (See also **Robert Bierenbaum** and **Sante and Kenneth Kimes**).

Thirty year old Anne Marie Fahey, a secretary in the office of the Governor of Delaware, disappeared on 29 June 1996. There was no sign of a struggle or of forced entry to her apartment. Her diary contained details of appointments with 'TC', at first thought to refer to Tom Carper, the Governor. Later, 'TC' was identified as Thomas Capano, a forty-nine year old attorney with a leading Wilmington legal practice.

Capano, who was separated from his wife, admitted having an affair with the missing woman which he said had ended amicably. He described her in unflattering terms as unpredictable, depressed, anxious, anorexic and suicidal and denied any involvement in her disappearance. A search of his house revealed small traces of blood, but without a body, there was no possibility of a DNA match.

The FBI was called in to help with the investigation which lasted for more than two years. In the course of their enquiries, agents questioned Capano's youngest brother, Gerry, who admitted complying with Thomas's request for help. Capano told him that he was being blackmailed and was afraid for his life. He said he might have to kill the blackmailers and asked to borrow his brother's fishing boat. The two men loaded a cooler onto the boat and cruised some sixty miles out into the Atlantic Ocean where, after an abortive attempt to sink the cooler, Thomas pulled a body out of it which he weighted with chains and dumped into the sea.

A breakthrough came when a sample of blood was found that Anne Marie Fahey had given as a blood donor. DNA testing showed that her blood matched the traces found at Capano's home. The accused man was tried for murder in December 1998 and after two years of denial, finally made some admissions. He testified that Anne Marie had been killed accidentally when another girl friend confronted them in his home. She was wielding a gun and threatening to take her own life when a shot was discharged which accidentally killed Anne Marie. The lady in question denied being at the house. The prosecution described Capano as a skilled manipulator and the judge was obliged to curb the defendant's angry outbursts in court. Capano was found guilty and sentenced to death.

[*1030, 1065*]

CAREW, EDITH

Unusual case of poisoning among the British expatriates at the end of the nineteenth century in Japan.

Walter and Edith Carew lived in Yokohama, Japan, among a small group of foreign expatriates. When Walter Carew was taken ill in 1896, his doctor diagnosed a bilious attack but was mystified when the illness persisted. An explanation arrived by post at the doctor's surgery in a letter from a Japanese chemist called Maruya. The cryptic message said simply, 'Three bottles of arsenic in one week'. Carew died of what his doctor now knew was arsenical poisoning.

Maruya explained that Mrs Carew had sent him written instructions to supply her with arsenic. She told the inquest that the arsenic was to treat an illness from which her husband suffered. It appeared that Edith Carew, although outwardly happily married, had a liaison with a young bank employee. She spoke to him of her husband's ill-treatment and there was mention of a possible separation.

Edith Carew was charged with her husband's murder and stood

trial at Yokohama in January 1897 under the judicial authority of the British Consul. Her defence was based on stories of her husband's alleged infidelity. This contention was backed up by letters written to Walter Carew by his lover, which turned out to have been forged by Mrs Carew. She was found guilty and sentenced to death. Sentence was later commuted to penal servitude for life.

[*474, 976*]

CARIGNAN, HARVEY LOUIS

Known variously as 'Harv the Hammer' and 'The Want-ad Killer', Carignan committed various acts of rape and murder in the USA in the early 1970s.

While serving with the US Army in Alaska in July 1949, he killed and raped a young woman for which he was sentenced to life imprisonment. He avoided execution by exploiting a legal loophole. After gaining release on parole in 1960, he killed a woman in Washington State in 1972 and was suspected of being responsible for eleven other murders in northern California.

He married a divorcee with two children in 1972 and leased a Sav-Mor filling station in Seattle. In May 1973, he placed a wanted-ad in the *Seattle Times* for a pump attendant. Fifteen-year-old Kathy Miller applied on behalf of her brother. She promptly disappeared. Carignan, whose violent record was known, was questioned but the police seemed satisfied with the account that he gave of his movements. The missing girl's body was found a few weeks later – she had been bludgeoned to death.

Meanwhile, Carignan moved first to Colorado and later to Minnesota. In the latter part of 1974, there was a string of assaults in these states on hitch-hikers. Characteristics of these attacks were that they took place in remote country areas and the victims were violently assaulted by a man wielding a hammer. Many of the victims, injured and left for dead, survived their ordeal and were able to give descriptions of their attacker.

Harvey Carignan was identified in a Minneapolis parking lot by two police officers on 24 September 1974 and arrested. The alert officers had made their sighting on the basis of a physical description of their suspect. The want-ad killer had among his belongings a number of road maps bearing scores of locations marked with red circles. Numbering 181, these included known attack sites. Carignan was a stereotype for the serial killer; always on the move and driving thousands of miles, criss-crossing many state boundaries. He had successfully avoided the police for fourteen years. He was also a man given to sudden and violent rages who had been in trouble since childhood. Like other serial killers, such as **Peter Sutcliffe** and **David Berkowitz**, he claimed to have been urged on by voices.

In separate trials conducted in 1975 and 1976, Carignan was convicted of two murders and other offences and given prison sentences amounting to one hundred years plus life.

[*878*]

CASTAING, Dr EDMÉ

Landmark case involving the use of morphine for the first time in a homicidal poisoning.

Twenty-seven-year-old Castaing, recently qualified, started a medical practice in Paris in the 1820s. He had a taste for high living which he found difficult to maintain as a young doctor and he began to experience financial problems.

Among his patients was Hippolyte Ballet, a wealthy but sickly man who had property at St Cloud near Paris. The doctor believed that Ballet had cut his brother Auguste out of his will and intended to leave everything to his brother-in-law. Castaing hit on a plan to destroy the will so that Auguste would inherit and he would acquire a large sum himself.

The plan was put into effect and Hippolyte died. Despite an autopsy finding that he had died from the effects of an unknown poison, Auguste inherited his assets.

Castaing now decided to dispose of Auguste. On 29 May 1823, the two men drove to St Cloud and stopped at a roadside inn where they drank some wine. As a result of taking refreshment, Auguste fell ill and they were forced to stay at the inn overnight. Castaing called a local doctor to attend his friend while he returned to Paris. The next day Auguste died, supposedly of cholera.

The autopsy showed that Auguste had died of morphine poisoning and Castaing was arrested. He had been careful to cover his tracks even to the extent of disposing of the sick man's vomit. Many of France's leading medical men attended Castaing's trial in Paris in November 1823. It became known that the doctor's return to Paris when his friend was taken ill was to buy a further supply of morphine. Castaing was convicted of murder and sentenced to death.

[*279, 735*]

CAVANESS, Dr JOHN DALE

Medical practitioner admired by his patients in Little Egypt, Illinois who beat his wife and terrorised his sons. Mrs Cavaness left him in 1971, taking their four sons with her. She said of him, 'His patients loved him . . . but he didn't have any use for us.' His youngest son Mark was found dead beside his truck in 1977, shot through the heart by a booby-trapped shotgun. Seven years later, his twenty-two-year-old son Sean was found dead with two gunshot wounds in the head. Both sons had been heavily insured.

After the second shooting, people started to recall the mysterious circumstances of Mark's death and there were rumours about the insurance. The police reviewed the cases and Dr Cavaness quickly became the prime suspect. He was tried for Sean's murder in February 1985 but the proceedings ended in a mistrial after evidence was introduced which had not been shown to the defence.

The doctor appeared for his second trial in November 1985 when he gave evidence admitting his presence at the shooting. He claimed that Sean shot himself and then he fired the second shot to spare the feelings of the boy's mother by making the incident look like a homicide-robbery.

An expert witness for the prosecution testified that the second shot had been fired while the victim lay on the ground. The position of the wound was such that it was not possible for it to have been self-inflicted. Dr Cavaness told the judge he was dissatisfied with his attorney's questioning and asked to be allowed to put questions himself. The judge agreed and many who witnessed the outcome said that Cavaness destroyed his own cause.

The jury found the doctor guilty of first-degree murder and he was sentenced to death. While on Death Row in the State Penitentiary at Jefferson City, he took his own life on 17 November 1986 by hanging himself with electrical wire. He left a suicide note but made no reference to his dead sons.

[*709*]

CHANTRELLE, EUGÈNE MARIE

French teacher at a school in Scotland who poisoned his wife with opium and disguised her death as accidental gas poisoning.

Chantrelle crossed the English Channel in 1862 and moved to Scotland where he taught at a private academy in Edinburgh. He proved to be over-familiar with his pupils and seduced a fifteen-year-old girl, making her pregnant. Despite the great difference in their ages, he married Elizabeth Cullen Dyer in 1868 and she bore four children.

Elizabeth proved to be a dutiful wife and mother but Chantrelle treated her badly and frequently threatened her life. He boasted that he had a perfect method of poisoning which was undetectable. On 18 October 1877, contrary to her wishes, he insured Elizabeth's life against accident. On New Year's Day 1878, she was found unconscious in her gas-filled bedroom and died the next day.

Chantrelle said there had been a gas escape from a leaking pipe. An initial examination of the room failed to find any evidence of a faulty gas pipe and a post-mortem showed that Elizabeth had died from a fatal dose of a narcotic. Analysis of vomited material on the bedclothes identified the poison as opium. Inquiries also revealed that Chantrelle had bought opium extract on several occasions from a pharmacy.

Chantrelle's trial at the High Court of Justiciary in Edinburgh in 1878 was significant for the number of leading Scottish forensic experts who gave evidence on the toxicological aspects of the case. While a great deal of the evidence was circumstantial, it was clearly shown that the gas supply in Elizabeth Chantrelle's bedroom had been cleverly tampered with. Her husband was found guilty of murder and he was hanged on 31 May 1878.

[*864*]

CHAPMAN, ANN CASE

The investigation into the murder of a young journalist at a Greek seaside resort in 1971 led to allegations of political interference.

Twenty-five-year-old Ann Chapman was a freelance radio journalist travelling in Greece on an assignment for a holiday tour company. Before leaving England she mentioned the possibility of following up another story, hinting that it might be an important news item.

She left the Pine Hill Hotel at Kavouri on the evening of 15 October 1971, telling friends that she was taking the bus into Athens. She did not return and, three days later, her body was found in a field close to the hotel. Her arms and legs were tied up with wire and she had been strangled.

Many months later, in August 1972, thirty-seven-year-old Nikolaos Moundis was denounced by his relatives as the murderer of the English girl. Moundis, who had a local reputation as a 'Peeping Tom', was arrested and promptly confessed. In April 1973, he was tried and found guilty of attempted rape and manslaughter.

Moundis withdrew his earlier confession and serious questions were asked about the evidence which had convicted him. There seemed to be two crucial omissions. The man who found the dead girl was not called to give evidence and the report of the post-mortem examination was unavailable. A vital discrepancy was that the girl had been manually strangled by someone who was right-handed, whereas Moundis was left-handed. Appeals to the Greek authorities to reopen the case were twice refused by the Supreme Court.

Disquiet about the investigation rumbled on and, after his release from prison in 1983, Moundis said that he had witnessed Ann Chapman being bundled into a car outside the Pine Hill Hotel by four men who he believed were police officers. This fuelled the theories of those who thought that Ann Chapman had come across her 'big story' at a time when Greece was ruled by a military government. She had possibly caught a whiff of the resistance movement to the military regime and saw in it a major scoop. Her life became endangered when the military security service learned of her interest and decided to question her. What might have begun as a plan to rough her up ended in her death and a consequent cover-up.

In 1984, Richard Cotterell, a Member of the European Parliament, took up the case with the Greek government. Ann Chapman was believed to have been killed by government agents while Moundis was made a scapegoat. The official response was that the case had been resolved.

[*208*]

CHAPMAN, GEORGE

Thought by some to be **Jack the Ripper**, Chapman, whose real name was Severin Klosowski, was hanged in 1903 for committing murder by poisoning.

Klosowski came to England from Poland in 1888 and initially took work as a barber's assistant in Whitechapel. He also changed his name to Chapman and decided he wanted to become a publican. To achieve this, he cultivated an acquaintance with Isabella Spinks, a married woman whom he persuaded to fund him as landlord of The Prince of Wales public house in City Road.

Soon after they took over the pub, Isabella Spinks became ill and she went into rapid decline. After suffering severe gastric symptoms, she died on Christmas Day 1897.

Chapman advertised for a barmaid and among the applicants was Bessie Taylor, a former domestic servant. He not only employed her but also took her as his wife. They moved away from London and took over The Grapes at Bishop's Stortford in Essex. Sadly, like her predecessor, Bessie's health began to fail and she too died of abdominal illness.

Having moved back to London in 1901 as landlord of The Monument Tavern in The Borough, Chapman once again advertised for a barmaid. He employed Maud Marsh after the young woman's parents had first inspected his premises. She too seemed prone to abdominal illness, but, whereas her doctor was mystified by her symptoms, her mother was convinced she had been poisoned. When Maud died on 22 October 1902, Mrs Marsh voiced her suspicions and traces of antimony were found in the dead woman's body. The corpses of Isabella Spinks and Bessie Taylor were exhumed and, again, antimony was found.

Chapman was known to have bought tartar emetic (the principal salt of antimony). When he was arrested and charged with murder, Chief Inspector Frederick Abberline, the officer in charge of the Ripper investigation, remarked, 'You've got Jack the Ripper at last!'

Chapman stood trial at the Old Bailey for the murder of Maud Marsh. After hearing the evidence, the jury retired for eleven minutes before bringing in a Guilty verdict. George Chapman, a detested poisoner, was hanged on 7 April 1903.

The reasons for believing Chapman was Jack the Ripper rest chiefly on the fact that he was in the East End of London in the autumn of 1888. That an exponent of bloody murder by the knife should change to secret homicide by poison seems a little difficult to believe.

[6, *1020*]

CHAPMAN, GERALD

A man of genuine ability and intellect who turned to crime and was first made a hero by the American public and then 'Public Enemy No 1'.

While in prison, he met Dutch Anderson, an inveterate criminal who taught the younger man all he knew. On their release in 1921, they worked as con-men in Chicago and then moved to New York City. They made a great deal of money out of their daring swindles and robberies and lived a life of luxury.

Chapman was known as the 'Count of Gramercy Park' on account of his lifestyle, and his encounters with the law and escapes from prison won a kind of public admiration. He was thought of as a Robin Hood character whose crimes were excusable because he had nerve and style.

But public goodwill evaporated when robbery turned to murder. On 12 October 1924, Chapman and others held up a department store in the course of which a police officer was shot dead. Although Chapman escaped, he was named by one of his accomplices. Dutch Anderson tried to extricate Chapman from his predicament by using the gangster tactics of the past but was shot dead by the police.

'The Count of Gramercy Park' forfeited public sympathy and was tried for murder. He was sentenced to death and spent his time reading poetry by Shelley and writing his own verses. After two stays of execution, the man who the *New York Times* said possessed 'courage, persistence, ingenuity and skill' was hanged on 6 April 1926.

[*8, 475*]

CHAPMAN, MARK DAVID

Devotee of J.D. Salinger's best-selling book, *The Catcher in the Rye*, who murdered pop-star John Lennon outside his New York apartment in 1980.

The twenty-five-year-old security guard had the book with him as he waited in the street outside the Manhattan apartment building for Lennon on the evening of 8 December 1980. As Lennon and his wife approached, Chapman fired five times at close range and the singer collapsed. He died later in hospital.

The murder of the internationally known singer made headlines around the world and the music world went into mourning. Grieving fans maintained a vigil at the scene of the shooting while Chapman was sent for psychiatric examination. He apparently identified himself with the principal character of Salinger's novel, Holden Caulfield, a teenager who experienced loneliness and disillusion in the big city.

Chapman went to live in Hawaii in 1977 where he married and became a follower of The Beatles and John Lennon. But admiration turned to resentment and he bought a revolver and flew to New York. His aim was to confront Lennon, who had become the focus of his hatred, and he stalked the singer for several days before finally gunning him down.

At Chapman's trial in June 1981, his lawyer first entered a plea of insanity and then, on instructions from Chapman, changed it to guilty. Clutching a copy of *The Catcher in the Rye*, Chapman quoted from the book when he had an opportunity to address the court. The prosecution view that he killed in order to become famous secured a verdict of guilty of second-degree murder. He was sentenced to twenty years' imprisonment.

Chapman had parole hearings turned down in 2000 and 2002. In 2004 he was granted a further parole hearing against a background of opposition from John Lennon fans. An online petition was set up to make the case for denying a parole. One supporter said, 'If Mark David Chapman is let out of jail, he wouldn't last a day'. He remains in prison.

[*114, 492*]

CHASE, RICHARD TRENTON

So-called Dracula Killer who killed six times in Sacramento, California and drank the blood of his victims.

On 29 December 1977, Chase shot and killed a man in a 'drive-by' killing. Ambrose Griffin was murdered as he walked from his house to his car. On 23 January 1978, twenty-two-year-old Teresa Wallin was found dead by her husband when he returned home. She had been shot through the head and later disembowelled. A plastic yogurt pot containing traces of blood was found near the body. There was no evidence of burglary or robbery and the victim had not been raped.

Neighbours reported that a 'weird' man in his mid-twenties had been seen in the area. On 27 January, Evelyn Miroth, a single mother, and her six-year-old son were found shot dead in their home. Mrs Miroth had been savagely mutilated. Daniel Meredith, a friend of the family, was also dead from gunshot wounds and two-year-old David Ferreira, whom they had been looking after, was missing.

Police again received reports of a weird-looking man in the neighbourhood and a woman reported encountering him in a local grocery store when he demanded a lift in her car. She recognised him as Richard Chase from the days when they attended the same school.

Chase was arrested and his apartment was searched for the missing child. He denied any knowledge of the boy's disappearance but, while in custody, told a fellow inmate that he had put the body in the garbage. Extensive police searches located David Ferreira's body on 24 March in a cardboard box discarded in an alleyway.

Chase had a history of psychiatric problems and, in 1976, when he was being treated in a mental institution, fellow patients nicknamed him Dracula on account of his fascination for blood. He regularly told doctors that his heart had stopped beating or that his body was paralysed.

He was put on trial in January 1979, when he testified in his own defence, admitting to the killings but pleading insanity. He said that he had begun by drinking the blood of animals but then moved on to humans. Clear evidence of premeditation in his crimes and psychiatric testimony that although a paranoid anti-social personality, he was sane, led to his conviction. He was sentenced to death and sent to San Quentin Penitentiary.

On 26 December 1980, Chase was found dead in his cell. He had taken an overdose of anti-depressants which he had accumulated from a daily prescription.

[*78, 637*]

CHEVIS CASE

A young army officer was fatally poisoned in 1931 in an unsolved case with undertones of revenge.

Lieutenant Hubert George Chevis, a young artillery officer, lived in married quarters at Blackdown Camp near Aldershot. On 21 June 1931, he and his wife sat down to dinner and their servant dished up a brace of partridge. Chevis took one mouthful and found it so bad-tasting that he would not eat any more. He ordered the birds to be destroyed.

Fifteen minutes later, Chevis was taken violently ill. He was rushed to hospital but died an agonising death the following day. His wife was also taken ill but without such tragic consequences. The cause of death was attributed to strychnine poisoning.

An open verdict was returned at the coroner's court although few doubted that the young officer had been murdered. On the day of the funeral, his father, Sir William Chevis, received a telegram bearing the words, 'Hooray, hooray, hooray'. The message had been sent from Dublin by a J. Hartigan.

A further message from the same source came a couple of weeks later. This said, 'It is a mystery they will never solve.'

Hartigan was never traced and the suggestion was that young Chevis was poisoned by someone seeking revenge against his father who had been a judge in India.

[*345, 1068*]

CHIKATILO, ANDREI ROMANOVICH

Russian serial killer, dubbed 'The Rostov Ripper', who committed fifty-two murders between 1978 and 1990.

As a child, Chikatilo was shy and withdrawn. He dreamed of great things including gaining a place at Moscow University. He married in 1963 and had two children. He was turned down for a place at Moscow but worked for a degree at Rostov University, graduating in 1971. He took a job as a teacher at Novoshakhtinsk in the Rostov region. His pupils found him dull and uninterested in their work. What consumed Chikatilo were his sexual fantasies and, in 1973, he became a child molester.

By 1978, his urges had taken a firm grip and when he moved to another job with his family, he secretly rented accommodation and began taking girls there. On 22 December 1978, he committed his first murder, a nine-year-old girl whose body he dumped in a nearby river. In what eventually proved to be a serious miscarriage of justice, a twenty-five-year-old man was convicted and executed for this crime.

By 1981 Chikatilo was working as a supply clerk for a company in Shakhti. This gave him the chance to travel and to stay away from home. He began to kill routinely, preying on young vagrants of both sexes, enticing them to lonely areas where he subjected them to brutal violence. His victims died of strangulation or stabbing. He committed various acts of mutilation, cannibalism and necrophilia on their bodies.

The death toll mounted. Six victims in 1982, nine in 1983 and seventeen in 1984. He was arrested on suspicion in September 1984 but was released for lack of evidence. At that time he had murdered thirty-two times. What proved to be a remarkably accurate profile of the wanted man was draw up by the police in 1987 but another three years elapsed before Chikatilo was caught.

One of the factors which confused forensic investigators was that Chikatilo's blood and sperm had different typing characteristics. Until 1988, it was believed that the body fluids of every individual shared the same typing, but work in Japan showed there were rare cases when this was not so. Chikatilo was such a rare individual; his blood was Group A and his sperm was Group AB.

He was eventually arrested on 20 November 1990 and charged with thirty-six murders. He readily confessed to another nineteen. Psychiatrists pronounced him sane and responsible for his actions. He was sent for trial at Rostov and was protected from the angry relatives of his victims by being kept in a cage. The man who said 'I am a mistake of nature' was convicted of multiple murder and sentenced to death. He was executed by firing squad in February 1994.

[*197, 217, 535, 590*]

CHRISTIE, JOHN REGINALD HALLIDAY

The infamous occupant of 10 Rillington Place was one of a handful of murderers who filled the newspaper headlines in post-war Britain with stories of horror.

At the end of the Second World War, Christie, a former special constable in the War Reserve Police, lived with his wife, Ethel, in the ground floor flat of the house at Notting Hill Gate. During the war years, he had lived there alone, occasionally taking prostitutes home for his pleasure. He murdered two of them and buried their bodies in the garden. The return of his wife put a temporary stop to these activities.

Christie befriended the occupants of the top-floor flat at 10 Rillington Place, Timothy Evans, a van-driver in his mid twenties, and his wife, Beryl. They had a young daughter but Beryl's announcement that she was pregnant cast doubt on whether they could make ends meet. Beryl decided to have an abortion and Christie, who professed to have some medical knowledge, was consulted.

On 30 November 1949 Timothy Evans presented himself at Merthyr Tydfil police station in South Wales and told the amazed officers that he had found his wife dead in their London home. A search at Rillington Place revealed that both Beryl and her daughter were dead from strangulation. Evans made a number of incriminatory statements in which he confessed to the killings and later put the blame on Christie.

Christie simply denied the accusation and appeared as a prosecution witness at Evans's trial in 1950. Timothy Evans was convicted of the murder of his child and sentenced to death. He was hanged on 9 March 1950.

With this difficulty out of the way, Christie returned to his murderous pursuits. In December 1952, he strangled his wife and hid her body under the floor. During the first three months of 1953, he took prostitutes back to 10 Rillington Place where he gassed them with a special apparatus he had rigged up and then strangled them. Their bodies were concealed in an alcove in the kitchen which was papered over.

On 24 March 1953, after Christie had sub-let his rooms at Rillington Place, the new tenant discovered his secret by accident when he was trying to fix a shelf in the kitchen. Three bodies were recovered from the wall-space, one was found under the floor of another room and two sets of human remains were exhumed from the garden.

In due course, Christie admitted to killing six women, including his wife. He was a sexual misfit who could only get satisfaction by having intercourse with unconscious or dead partners. His technique was to invite women to his flat where he rendered them unconscious by stages, first with drink, then by partially gassing them and finally by strangulation.

Christie was tried at the Old Bailey in June 1953 for the murder of his wife. His defence was based on a plea of insanity. His admission that he had killed Beryl Evans created a legal furore, although he denied killing the child. John Christie, whose teenage nickname was 'Reggie no-dick', was hanged at Pentonville Prison on 15 July 1953.

An inquiry was held into a possible miscarriage of justice in the Evans case. The outcome was confirmation of his guilt but public anxieties about the verdict remained. In 1961, Ludovic Kennedy published his book *Ten Rillington Place*, in which he convincingly argued that an injustice had occurred. A further public enquiry was held in 1966 by Mr Justice Brabin, the conclusion being that in all probability Evans had killed his wife but not his daughter, the crime for which he had been convicted and executed. This was sufficient to recommend a posthumous pardon which was granted by the Queen on 18 October 1966. In a further twist to the story, John Eddowes argued in a book published in 1994 that Evans did

murder both his wife and child. This suggestion carried the implication that there were two stranglers operating at 10 Rillington Place – Christie and Evans.
[*151, 262, 480, 648, 1050*]

CHRISTOFI, STYLLOU

Middle-aged Cypriot woman of peasant culture who came to England and murdered her daughter-in-law in a fit of jealousy.

Fifty-three-year-old Mrs Christofi came to England from Cyprus in 1953 to join her son and his family in London. Stavros was a waiter in a London West End restaurant and he was married to a German girl who also worked. The couple had three children and lived in South Hill Park, Hampstead. Into their happy home came Stavros's mother, an illiterate woman plunged straight from her peasant background into a sophisticated culture which she did not comprehend.

Mrs Christofi proved to be a disruptive influence and there were furious arguments over what she saw as her son's desertion of traditional values. Late in the evening of 29 July 1954, when Stavros was out of the house, neighbours saw flames in the garden. Mrs Christofi raised the alarm, asking passers-by to help. They discovered that she was attempting to incinerate the body of her daughter-in-law. The police were called and Stavros's wife was found to have been strangled.

Mrs Christofi said she woke up because of the smell of burning and found her daughter-in-law's body lying in the yard. She had taken possession of the dead woman's wedding ring which was found in her bedroom. Styllou Christofi was tried for murder at the Old Bailey and found guilty. She achieved the distinction of being the last but one woman to be hanged in Britain when she was executed at Holloway Prison on 13 December 1954.
[*465, 1000*]

CHUNG YI MIAO

The 'Chinese Honeymoon Murder' in the Lake District in 1928 had many strange facets.

Chung Yi Miao and his bride, Wai Sheung Siu, both in their late twenties, married in New York in 1928 and travelled to Europe for their honeymoon. He was a lawyer and she was an art dealer from a wealthy family. On 18 June, they arrived at Grange in the Lake District where they stayed at the Borrowdale Gates Hotel.

During the afternoon, the couple went out for a walk but Chung Yi Miao returned on his own, explaining that his wife had gone shopping. Later that evening, Wai Sheung's body was found near a lakeside footpath. She had been strangled and the circumstances suggested robbery and sexual attack. Expensive jewellery which she had been wearing was missing.

On being told of his wife's death, Chung Yi Miao, without waiting to be told, leaped to the conclusion that she had been robbed and murdered. Two wedding rings belonging to the dead woman were found hidden among Chung Yi Miao's effects and the cord which had been used to strangle his wife was identical to the cords used to draw the hotel blinds. On the basis of little more than circumstantial evidence, Chung Yi Miao was arrested and charged with murder.

Chung Yi Miao was tried at Carlisle in November 1928 and found guilty. He was hanged at Strangeways Prison on 6 December. There was much speculation in the newspapers about the Chinese lawyer's motive for killing his wife. One theory was that his honour was at stake because his wife was unable to bear children and another was that he murdered her to raise money for one of the Chinese secret societies.

[447]

CLARK, DOUGLAS DANIEL

So-called 'Sunset Slayer' who killed six women picked up on Hollywood's Sunset Strip in 1980. He made history of a kind by sending an article about serial killing, called 'Fatal Attraction', to *The Times* in London.

Clark was an intelligent man and a handsome charmer. He was one of five children and his father was a naval officer whose family accompanied him on numerous overseas postings. Clark attended Culver Military Academy and went into the air force but his career ended with a dishonourable discharge. By 1976, he had been married and divorced, was drinking too much and had developed extreme sexual fantasies.

In 1980, he met Carol Mary Bundy (not to be confused with Carol Ann, wife of **Ted Bundy**), a woman with two children who worked as a nurse. They indulged a shared fantasy about capturing and subduing women for Clark's sexual pleasure. They bought guns and cruised the Sunset Strip looking for prostitutes.

In June 1980, patrolling on his own, Clark picked up two young girls and shot them both in his car. He took them to an empty garage where he performed necrophilia before dumping their bodies on the freeway. On 20 June, he and Carol went out together and picked up a victim. Carol sat in the back of the car while the girl performed oral sex on Clark and then handed him the gun with which he shot the girl in the head. While Clark drove on, Carol stripped the clothes from the girl's body before leaving her to die on waste ground.

Carol suggested that Clark should make each killing more gruesome than the next to make the police think they were looking for a psycho rather than a sane person. It was a proposition that presented little difficulty for him. He decapitated his next victim and kept the head for a while in the freezer.

And so the depraved violence went on, but Clark's relations with Carol were becoming strained. He told her that she did not have the guts to kill someone herself. She responded by killing one of her lovers, Jack Murray, and cutting off his head which was eventually deposited in a street garbage can.

Perhaps finally sated, Carol told a colleague that her boyfriend had murdered two girls. She then informed the police, admitting, 'It's fun to kill people . . .' Clark was arrested at his workplace and remained cool and arrogant when questioned. He denied the murders.

Clark's trial was an extraordinary affair. He fell out with his defence attorney and represented himself in court. Dressed in a pin-striped suit and looking every bit a lawyer, he impressed some with his skills at cross-examination. But his provocative style, lapsing into the obscene, did little to help his case. At one point, the judge ordered that he be physically gagged to stem the flow of abuse.

He blamed the murders on Carol while she testified for the prosecution. On 28 January 1983, the jury found Clark guilty of six charges of murder. When he was sentenced to death, he turned on the judge, demanding, 'I want the execution in ten days.' He was sent to San Quentin Prison where he writes extensively and where he married a legal researcher who believes he is innocent.

In May 1983, Carol Bundy pleaded guilty to two charges of first-degree murder and was sentenced to two terms of life imprisonment. She is in the California Institution for Women at Frontera and is not eligible for parole until the year 2012.

[277]

CLARK, Dr HENRY LOVELL WILLIAM

A lovers' conspiracy shocked the British Raj in India in 1911 and resulted in two murders.

Dr Henry Lovell William Clark worked for the Indian Subordinate Medical Service. He was married with four children but did not enjoy a state of marital bliss. He fell in love with Augusta, the wife of Edward Fullam, a government accountant, and their passion was so great that they decided to eliminate him.

Augusta suggested using a poison that would produce the effects of heat-stoke and Dr Clark decided that arsenic would do the trick. He provided a supply of the poison and Augusta administered it to her husband. Fullam was treated for heat-stroke by Dr Clark but died on 10 October 1911.

The remaining obstacle to the lovers' plan was Mrs Clark. The doctor hired four assassins with instructions to attack her and on 17 November she was assaulted in her home and killed with a sword.

When investigators interviewed Augusta Fullam, they were aware of her affair with Clark. A search of her bungalow turned up a tin box which was found underneath the bed. It contained 400 love letters, tied up in neat bundles of fifty, written by Augusta to Clark. Their conspiracy to poison Fullam was evident in one of the letters which said, 'Please send me the powder one day next week.' The exhumation of his body showed the undoubted presence of arsenic.

Dr Clark and Augusta Fullam were tried at the High Court in Allahabad. On the first occasion they were tried for the murder of Fullam and, on the second, for the contract killing of Mrs Clark. Their guilt was absolute, for Augusta Fullam, pregnant with Clark's child, turned King's Evidence against her lover, while he made a confession from the dock.

Sentence of death on Dr Clark was carried out on 26 March 1913. Augusta Fullam's condition prevented her facing the executioner but, ironically, she died of heat-stroke on 28 May 1914.

The house in which Augusta and Edward Fullam lived in Agra is said to be jinxed. Women residents are invariably taken ill and recover only when they move away.

[956, 975]

CLEMENTS, Dr ROBERT GEORGE

When he learned that his fourth wife's death in 1947 was being investigated as a murder, the fifty-seven-year-old doctor committed suicide.

He called in another doctor to attend his wife, Amy, when she became ill at their home in Southport, Lancashire in May 1947. It was recommended that she be transferred to a nursing home where she was diagnosed as suffering from leukaemia. She died on 27 May.

A post-mortem examination revealed nothing untoward and arrangements were made to bury Mrs Clement's body. At the last moment, proceedings were halted when a doctor who had worked with Robert Clements sounded a note of caution. A second post-mortem revealed evidence of morphine poisoning which had extended over several months.

By the time the police came to question Dr Clements, he was already dead by his own hand, ironically from an overdose of morphine. The coroner's inquest at Southport concluded, on the basis of exhaustive scientific testing, that Mrs Clements had been poisoned and that her husband was the murderer. He stood to gain considerably from her death as he had from the demise of his previous wives.

This case was comparable in many respects to that of **Dr Robert Buchanan** in the USA.

[*273, 320*]

COETZEE, JACOBUS HENDRIK

South African police sergeant sent to investigate the murder of a girl he had killed after she became pregnant.

The body of Gertrina Petrusina Opperman was found dead at a remote spot near the railway line to Pretoria on 1 February 1935. Her bruises and torn clothes were evidence that a grim struggle had taken place. She had been bearing a child which was born shortly before she died from the gunshot wound in her head.

Detective Sergeant Coetzee was one of the officers sent to the scene to investigate this brutal crime. The victim was not identified until the farmer she worked for reported her missing. He produced a letter received by Gertrina, signed by 'J.H. Coetzee', reassuring her, 'Everything is still arranged.'

Coetzee had been seen with the girl and it was believed he was responsible for her pregnancy and killed her to prevent her naming him as the father. The detective was arrested and sent for trial at Pretoria in May 1935.

The most Coetzee would admit was that he had a liaison with Gertrina Opperman. He did not accept responsibility for fathering her child and had disputed her allegations. He was convicted on largely circumstantial evidence – possession of ammunition of the same calibre as the fatal bullet and bloodstains on his clothing – and was sentenced to life imprisonment.
[*61*]

COFFIN, WILBERT

Convicted murderer who cleverly escaped from custody only to give himself up to be hanged.

Three American hunters journeyed to a remote area in Quebec in June 1953 intent on tracking and killing game. When they failed to maintain contact with their families in Pennsylvania, they were reported missing. On 5 July, the Canadian authorities began a search for the men and found their abandoned vehicle at an old mine close to the St John River.

As the search continued, the bodies of the missing men were found about two miles from their vehicle. They had been badly mauled by bears although it was evident that they had been shot dead first. Wilbert Coffin, a prospector, told searchers that he had seen three Americans with a broken-down vehicle on 10 June.

When it became known that one of the hunters had been carrying a large sum of money, which was now missing, it was assumed that robbery had been the motive for the killings. Coffin was arrested and, despite the lack of evidence against him, was charged with murder.

Although it was suspected that another American party had been in the area at the time, Coffin's protestations were turned aside and he was convicted and sentenced to death. When his appeal was rejected in 1955, he escaped from Quebec City Prison, by threatening guards with a revolver made from a piece of soap.

Unwisely, he took his lawyer's advice to surrender himself and he was returned to prison. After seven stays of execution, he was hanged on 10 February 1956. The feeling that Coffin was innocent of murder was strengthened by the statement of a man in Miami who said he and an accomplice had killed the three hunters.
[*58, 412, 759*]

COHEN, RONALD JOHN VIVIAN

Celebrated South African case in which the man accused of murdering his wife claimed loss of memory and, though judged guilty, escaped the death penalty.

Ronald Cohen, aged forty-one, ran a successful construction company in Cape Town and lived on 'Millionaires' Row' in Southern Cross Estate. His first marriage ended in divorce and he remarried in 1963. Susan Johnson was a beautiful woman half his age who took on her new husband's children by his first marriage and then gave him a son.

The Cohens' life, which seemed so idyllic, was shattered on 5 April 1970 when police were called to their luxury home and found Susan battered to death. Ronald Cohen, in a highly distraught state, told investigators that someone had broken into the house and he found his wife grappling with an intruder. He remembered picking up a bronze ornament with which to strike the attacker but then blacked out. He could recall nothing of what happened subsequently.

There was no evidence of a break-in and nothing was missing from the house. Suspicion fell on Cohen who was arrested and sent for trial. The case hinged on motive, or lack of it, and Cohen's state of mind. There was talk of a mysterious book salesman who had called at the house a few days before the attack, but nothing that could be substantiated. The conclusion was that something catastrophic had occurred between Cohen and his wife, as a result of which he lost control and killed her.

In September 1970, Cohen was found guilty but the judge looked for extenuating circumstances and found them in the lack of premeditation. On the grounds that he had acted at a time of diminished responsibility, Cohen was spared the death sentence and given twelve years' imprisonment.

[*61*]

COLLINS, JOHN NORMAN

The so-called 'Co-ed Murders' which occurred in Michigan between 1967 and 1969 were committed by a twenty-two-year-old student.

Seven co-eds were murdered in the Ypsilanti area of Michigan between August 1967 and July 1969. Various methods had been used to kill the victims, including shooting, bludgeoning and strangulation, and they had been subjected to sexual mutilation.

The police were frustrated by lack of any clues and brought in the Dutch 'psychic detective', Peter Hurkos, to help them. The breakthrough in their investigation came after the seventh murder when the victim, eighteen-year-old Karen Sue Beineman, was reported as having been seen with a student motor-cycle enthusiast, known as John Collins.

Inquiries revealed that Collins was regarded by his fellow students as somewhat weird, particularly in his eagerness to talk about killing. Collins was arrested but there was insufficient evidence against him to press any charges.

The picture changed when Mrs Loucks, Collins's aunt, reported a discovery in her basement. Collins had used her house while she was away on holiday. On returning, she found some strange stains in the basement which were reported to the police. They proved to be blood which matched that of Karen Sue Beineman. Clinching evidence came from hair clippings found on the victim which had originated from the heads of Mrs Loucks's two boys when she gave them haircuts in the basement.

Collins was convicted of murder on the strength of powerful forensic evidence at his trial at Ann Arbor in August 1970. He was sentenced to life imprisonment.

[*516*]

COLUMBINE HIGH SCHOOL KILLINGS

Many mass murderers are characterised by a twisted desire for revenge for perceived wrongs and the acceptance that their actions will lead to their own death, more often than not by suicide. The Columbine High School killings in 1999 were unusual in that they were committed by two teenagers acting together.

Eric Harris and Dylan Klebold, aged eighteen and seventeen respectively, were students at Columbine High School in Littleton, Colorado. They were founder members of a gang calling itself 'The Trenchcoat Mafia'. They dressed in a uniform of black trench coats and to the outsider seemed to be comparatively harmless in their devotion to the music of 'shock rocker', Marilyn Manson. They also played computer games constantly.

Harris, seemingly a very strong personality, began to preach a weird doctrine involving both Satanism and neo-nazism and talked of killing the enemy. Aided by Klebold, who appeared to be a willing follower, these doctrines took them further than the other members of the group wanted to go. Harris and Klebold set up a website which featured a poem entitled, 'The Written Works of the Trenchcoats', which called for rage and apocalypse.

On Tuesday 18 April 1999, the pair put all this talk into action. Dressed in their black coats, armed to the teeth and carrying home-made pipe bombs, they went to school and began systematically to execute their fellow students. They particularly targeted black students and athletes, moving around the school buildings laughing as they went. During the massacre, they kept shouting that they were taking revenge on those who had made fun of them. An especially horrific murder was the killing of a young girl who was on her knees praying. In addition to the shooting they planted some of their pipe bombs around the school premises with the intention of causing further destruction.

Twelve students and a teacher died as a result of the murderous attacks by the maddened teenagers. When the police arrived and began searching the buildings, they found Harris and Klebold dead in the school library. Either sated by their blood lust or realising the game was up, they had committed suicide. Another explanation was that one shot the other and then killed himself.

[723]

COOK, JONES AND NEWALL

The murderous trio of Raymond Cook, Eric Jones and Valerie (Kim) Newall were convicted in 1967 of the murder of Cook's wife.

Police were called to the scene of a car accident near Nettlebed, Oxfordshire on 2 March 1967. A red Mini had come off the road and was little damaged. The driver and passenger, Raymond and June Cook, were taken to hospital where Mrs Cook died of head injuries.

In a statement to police, Raymond Cook said they were driving home at about 10 pm after a meal at Pangbourne. Because he was feeling sick, his wife was at the wheel. He said they were dazzled by the lights of an oncoming car and veered off the road travelling at between 30 and 40 mph.

Suspicions were immediately aroused. The police believed the Mini was travelling at no more than 10 mph when it came to rest against a tree and the injuries sustained by the dead woman were entirely inconsistent with the circumstances of a minor collision.

Inquiries shed some interesting light on Raymond Cook's background. In 1966, he took a job as a student nurse at a mental hospital near Nettlebed where he met Kim Newall. He decided to leave his wife and went to live with Newall. Early in 1967, June Cook changed her will in her husband's favour in the hope of persuading him to return to her.

Cook was already in deep trouble because Newall was pregnant and he was in debt. Together with a friend, Eric Jones, he and Newall plotted to kill June Cook. Their plan was to contrive a fatal car accident. On 2 March 1967, Jones waited on the winding Nettlebed road to flag down the Cooks' car on the pretence that his vehicle had broken down. Raymond Cook offered him a lift and the two men proceeded to attack June. She was eventually bludgeoned with a car-jack and the car pushed off the road in an unconvincing attempt to fake a road accident.

The three conspirators to murder were convicted at Oxford in June 1967 and sentenced to life imprisonment.

[*16, 593*]

COOKE, ERIC EDGAR

A former Australian serviceman who graduated from burglary to murder and terrorised the city of Perth with his night-time killings in 1963.

A married man with a large family, Cooke hit on the ideal plan to make money by working as a truck-driver by day and as a burglar by night. But stealing was not enough and he developed a taste for violence. In January 1963, he shot and wounded a couple in their car at Cottesloe before moving into the suburbs of Perth where he killed three people in separate incidents.

Perth became a city of fear while the police hunted for the killer. After several months of uneasy calm, he struck again, shooting dead a girl baby-sitting for a family in Crawley on 10 August. The police identified the murder weapon as a .22 rifle and test-fired 60,000 firearms in their hunt for the gun.

The breakthrough in the investigation came by chance when a passer-by found a .22 rifle hidden in bushes in the Mount Pleasant district. This proved to be the murder weapon and officers lay in wait for the owner to retrieve it. Thirty-two-year-old Eric Cooke was arrested on 1 September 1963. He admitted the killings and also confessed to an unsolved murder in 1959.

His trial defence was that he suffered from schizophrenia as a result of which he could not distinguish right from wrong. The prosecution argued that he was simply a sociopath bent on violence. The jury found him guilty and he was sentenced to death.

What appeared to be a straightforward case became complicated when Cooke confessed to a murder committed in December 1949 for which another man had been convicted. He thereby created a major controversy because Darryl Beamish, a twenty-year-old deaf-mute, although he had at first admitted the murder, later claimed that he had done so under duress.

In light of Cooke's confession, Beamish appealed against his conviction in March 1964. Amid mounting public concern, his appeal was rejected on the grounds that Cooke's confession was false. Cooke was executed on 26 October 1964 and the arguments over his confession continued to rage until March 1971 when Beamish was released from prison on parole. In April 2005, on his sixth appeal, Beamish's conviction was quashed when the judges accepted that Cooke's confession was genuine.

[*83*]

COPPOLINO, Dr CARL

The states of Florida and New Jersey argued over who should first try Dr Coppolino for first-degree murder.

Coppolino came from an undistinguished immigrant background to qualify as a doctor. His wife, Carmela, was also a doctor and they appeared to be enjoying successful careers.

In 1962, while they were living in New Jersey, Coppolino became friendly with a patient's wife. Marjorie Farber was the wife of a retired army officer who was receiving treatment from Dr Coppolino. After Colonel Farber died of coronary thrombosis in 1963, the Coppolinos moved to Florida.

The doctor next turned his attentions to a divorcee, thirty-eight-year-old Mary Gibson, whom he married within weeks of his wife dying suddenly of a heart attack. But he had reckoned without the intervention of Marjorie Farber who had come to live in Florida as a near neighbour. She now accused Coppolino of murdering his wife and, as if that were not enough, claimed that acting under his instructions, she had given her husband an injection which had hastened his death.

The lethal agent used was named as succinylcholine chloride, a muscle relaxant used in surgical procedures. Carmela's body was exhumed and needle marks were found. Colonel Farber's body was also exhumed and the internal structures of his throat were found to be damaged.

In December 1966 Dr Coppolino was tried in New Jersey for murdering Colonel Farber and acquitted. Next he was tried in Florida for murdering his wife. In April 1967, the jury found him guilty of second-degree murder. He was given a life sentence and was paroled in 1979 after serving twelve years. The highly circumstantial nature of the evidence in the Coppolino case came in for some heavy criticism.
[*205, 431, 617*]

CORLL, DEAN

This homosexual murderer of twenty-seven boys in Houston, Texas during the early 1970s was America's greatest mass murderer until **John Wayne Gacy**'s conviction in 1980.

Corll's murderous career came to light on 7 August 1973 when one of his accomplices, eighteen-year-old Elmer Wayne Henley, shot him dead. Henley feared that Corll, for whom he and another teenager procured victims at between $5 and $10 a time, planned to kill him as well.

Thirty-three-year-old Corll, who worked in Houston as an electrician, was well thought of by acquaintances. But they knew nothing of his secret life as a sexual sadist. He had a torture room in his house containing a plywood board on which he spread-eagled his victims and secured them with handcuffs prior to shooting them. After he had finished with his captives he strangled or shot them and hid many of the bodies in a boat-shed.

Houston police recovered the remains of seventeen bodies from the boat-shed and ten more from coastal and woodland areas in East Texas. After moving his murder factory to Pasadena, Corll lost his power over his accomplices as they saw him becoming a threat to them. Henley killed him with six shots.

The steady disappearance of youngsters in the area had been notified by parents to the police in the form of Missing Persons reports. The explanation that they had probably absconded to join the hippies seemed to be largely accepted.

Wayne Henley, who had implicated himself in some of Corll's killings, was tried for murder in July 1974. He was convicted on nine counts and given sentences totalling 594 years. His teenage

accomplice was sentenced to life imprisonment. Henley won a new trial in 1979 but it did not change his sentence.
[*382, 1061*]

CORONA, JUAN VALLEJO

Migrant Mexican fruit-picker turned contractor who murdered twenty-five middle-aged migrant labourers in 1970–1 in California.

From menial beginnings, thirty-eight-year-old Corona had built up his own contracting business in Yuba County by 1960. When the mutilated bodies of migrant workers were found in local fruit orchards, the trail led to Corona. In the pockets of some of the murder victims were found bank deposit slips and receipts bearing his name.

When the police arrived at his ranch with a search warrant in May 1971, they found a wealth of incriminating evidence. Apart from knives and weapons, they discovered twenty-five bodies which had been buried in shallow graves. Most damning of all was Corona's so-called 'Death Ledger' which contained the names of many of his victims.

At his trial in January 1973, Corona pleaded not guilty, but he was convicted and sentenced to twenty-five consecutive life terms. While in prison he was attacked by a fellow inmate and stabbed repeatedly, losing the sight of one eye.

In 1978, he was granted a retrial on the grounds that his defence had not been adequately presented because an insanity plea had not been entered. His conviction was confirmed but he was sent to a medical unit for observation. His trial and retrial cost the Californian tax-payers over $4.5 million.
[*211, 518, 942*]

COTTINGHAM, RICHARD FRANCIS

Thirty-four-year-old computer expert who killed fifteen prostitutes in New York City between 1977 and 1980.

On 22 May 1980, police were called by the manager of the Quality Inn Motel at Hasbrouck Heights, New Jersey to deal with a violent situation. Residents had been disturbed by screams from one of the rooms. Officers found a terrified eighteen-year-old prostitute who had been subjected to several hours of torture and sexual assault. Her tormentor was arrested as he tried to escape.

Richard Cottingham, married with two children, was a computer operator who worked a late shift in Manhattan, finishing at 11 pm. He had picked up his victim in the street and drove her to the motel. He restrained her with handcuffs and said, 'You have to take it. The other girls did.'

Cottingham had led a double life for several years and a room in his home, which he normally kept locked, was full of women's clothing. This evidence linked him to a number of rape attacks and to numerous unsolved murders of prostitutes going back to 1977. Survivors of some of the attacks identified him and one of them recalled that he had said that 'prostitutes needed to be punished'.

Following trials in New Jersey and New York to face nineteen charges of rape, kidnapping and murder, Cottingham was convicted on fifteen counts of murder. He could hardly deny his assault on the young woman in the New Jersey motel but refuted survivors's accounts of previous assaults. He promised Judge Paul Huot that if he was ever released from prison he would never do anything wrong again. His prison sentences totalled 250 years.

[563]

COTTON, MARY ANN

For over a century Cotton was regarded as Britain's worst mass murderer. Her total of fifteen victims looked meagre against the more than two hundred attributed to **Dr Harold Shipman** in the 1990s. Cotton, a former Sunday school teacher, was hanged at Durham Prison in 1873.

When she left the Durham pit village where she was born, Cotton worked as a nurse on the fever ward at Sunderland Infirmary. She had a succession of husbands and children and her life seemed to be dogged by death and disease. She was promiscuous, taking bigamous husbands and lovers at will and being surrounded by both her own children and various stepchildren.

Suspicions were roused in 1871 when her husband, Frederick Cotton, died of a gastric disorder and Joseph Natrass moved in as her lodger. Within months, Natrass also died under her roof, along with her baby and one of her stepchildren.

Mary Cotton did not intend to be denied a male companion for she quickly took in a lodger. She became pregnant and named a local excise officer, Quick-Manning, as the father. After another of her stepchildren died in July 1872, wary neighbours drew the spate of deaths to the attention of the authorities. A post-mortem examination on the body of her stepson showed that he had been poisoned with arsenic. The same poison was found following exhumation of two other bodies.

Mary Cotton gave birth while in custody at Durham awaiting trial for murder. She pleaded not guilty to the charge of poisoning her stepson but her purchase of arsenic for killing bedbugs proved she had access to poison. She was found guilty and sentenced to death. More than twenty persons related to or associated with Mary Cotton had died suddenly.

She was hanged at Durham Prison on 24 March 1873 after the Home Secretary refused to recommend a reprieve.

[*20, 972*]

COURVOISIER, FRANÇOIS BENJAMIN

Twenty-three-year-old Swiss valet who robbed and murdered Lord William Russell in 1840.

On the morning of 6 May 1840, a housemaid at 14 Norfolk Street, London found her employer, Lord William Russell, dead in bed with his throat cut. The house had been broken into and money and jewellery were missing. The elderly peer lived alone and was looked after by three servants, including Courvoisier.

Suspicion fell on the valet when a five-pound note and six sovereigns were found in his possession. He claimed that Lord William had given the money to him but he was later found to have given some of his lordship's silver to a French woman acquaintance for safe-keeping. Bloodstained clothing found in his room also proved difficult to explain.

Courvoisier was tried for murder at the Old Bailey six weeks after the tragedy occurred. He pleaded Not Guilty, claiming that an intruder had killed Lord William Russell. His defence counsel tried to show that there was prejudice against his client because he was a foreigner. 'Murder is a rare crime in Switzerland,' the jury were told. They nevertheless found the evidence sufficiently damning to bring in a Guilty verdict and Courvoisier was sentenced to death.

He made several confessions, giving conflicting accounts of what happened, but finally admitted that he killed in the course of robbery. It seems he was motivated by envy and a desire for money. Courvoisier was hanged at Newgate on 6 July 1840.

[*652*]

CREAM, Dr THOMAS NEILL

Compulsive poisoner who murdered on both sides of the Atlantic and who, some believed, was **Jack the Ripper**.

Cream was born in Glasgow and emigrated with his family to

Canada in the 1850s. He attended McGill University and graduated as a doctor of medicine in 1876. He practised for a while in Chicago but preferred crime to medicine. In 1881 he was found guilty of murdering his mistress's husband with strychnine and entered Joliet Prison to serve a life sentence.

Following his release in July 1891, Cream crossed the Atlantic to take up residence in south London. From his rooms in Lambeth Palace Road, he made excursions into the night to pick up prostitutes whom he tried to interest in his potions for improving complexion. His pills were laced with strychnine and his satisfaction came from fantasies about the agonising deaths which resulted.

He murdered two women in October 1891 and, as he had in America, did his best to draw attention to himself. Cream was a classic example of the 'murder must advertise' principle. He complained to Scotland Yard that he was being followed and, for £300,000, offered to name the 'Lambeth Poisoner'. After a brief visit to America, he returned to London and, in April 1892, poisoned two more unsuspecting victims. Before expiring, the two women described their tormentor down to his moustache and squint.

Once again, Cream drew attention to himself and he was finally brought to account by a young woman who he believed had taken his pills but who had only feigned to swallow them and lived to tell the tale. She gave evidence at his trial as did the chemist who had sold him nux vomica and capsule-making equipment. Seven bottles of strychnine were found at his lodgings and his guilt was judged to be sufficiently obvious for the jury to take a mere twelve minutes to decide that he had committed murder.

Cream was hanged at Newgate Prison on 15 November 1892 and his alleged utterance, seconds before he went through the drop, 'I am Jack the . . .', led to subsequent speculation. He made no confession of his murders by poison and his moral degeneracy was speculatively attributed by his optician to the squint which was a birth defect.

[*623, 852*]

CREIGHTON AND APPELGATE

Mary Frances Creighton and Everett Appelgate formed a bizarre alliance which resulted in the death of Applegate's wife.

Mary and John Creighton had a remarkable record. In the early 1900s, they had been jointly tried and acquitted of the charge of murdering Mary's brother. Later, Mary alone was tried and acquitted of the charge of murdering her mother-in-law. In both instances, arsenic poisoning was the cause of death.

Having twice escaped conviction for murder, Mary and her husband moved to Long Island, New York with their two children. They befriended another couple, Everett and Ada Appelgate, and in view of the hard times caused by the Depression, the two couples decided in 1935 to share one house.

Four adults and two children lived cheek-by-jowl in the Creightons' small house. To ease the accommodation problem, Appelgate slept with the Creightons' fifteen-year-old daughter. Ada, his overweight wife, knew that he was having regular sexual intercourse with the teenager and complained. To silence her, Appelgate, aided and abetted by Mary Creighton, poisoned her food.

When a post-mortem on Ada Appelgate showed that she had died of arsenic poisoning, her husband and Mary Creighton were charged with murder. It appeared that Appelgate used his knowledge of the Creightons' past to secure Mary's acquiescence over the rape of her daughter and complicity in the murder of his wife. Mary Creighton admitted feeding the obese Ada with milk laced with arsenic.

The couple were convicted of murder – at the third attempt in Mary Creighton's case – and they were executed on 16 July 1936. [*425*]

CRIMMINS, ALICE

Attractive New York housewife who made headlines by being tried twice for murder in connection with the deaths of her two children in 1965.

Twenty-eight-year-old Alice Crimmins was separated from her husband and lived in the Queens district of New York with her five-year-old son and four-and-a-half-year-old daughter. On 14 July 1965, the children's father reported them missing. The girl's still-warm body was found later the same day on waste ground; she had been strangled. Her brother's body was found a week later in a badly decomposed condition.

The mother told police that she had given both children a meal of manicotti and beans at 7.30 pm and that they were both soundly asleep at 4.00 in the morning. Her explanation that the children were taken from the house after that time was not supported by the post-mortem. An examination of the stomach contents of the dead girl confirmed the composition of her last meal but the process of digestion showed that she had died within two hours of eating it.

Alice Crimmins was charged with the murder of her daughter nearly two years later. There were suggestions that the children were victims of a custody dispute. Detectives noticed a hook-and-eye fastener on the door leading into their bedroom. Crimmins said this was to stop them raiding the refrigerator but another explanation was that she did not want to be disturbed when she was entertaining. At her trial in May 1968, Alice Crimmins was convicted of manslaughter and sentenced to twenty years.

Following an appeal, a second trial took place in March 1971. This time, she was charged with the murder of her son. A possible explanation of her actions was that she killed the children rather than let her husband win custody. Crimmins was found guilty of murder and sentenced to life imprisonment. She was released on parole in 1977.

[*162, 379*]

CRIMMINS, CRAIG

Twenty-one-year-old stage-hand who murdered a violinist at New York's Metropolitan Opera House in 1980.

During a concert interval at the Opera House on 23 July 1980, thirty-year-old Helen Mintiks, an attractive blonde violinist with a promising career, disappeared. She had been seen with a man in the back regions of the vast building but failed to return to her position in the orchestra pit.

Detectives searched the labyrinthine interior of the Opera House the next day and found the woman's naked body at the bottom of a ventilator shaft. She was bound and gagged and it appeared that she had fallen down three floors of the building.

Evidence of attempted rape threw suspicion on the backstage personnel. A palmprint at the spot where Helen Mintiks fell to her death was identified as belonging to Craig Crimmins. He proved evasive under questioning, but when his alibi collapsed, he admitted the murder.

He told detectives that he propositioned the violinist and when she resisted, he pinioned her and took her up to the roof where he attempted rape. When she struggled to free herself from her bonds, he kicked her off the roof to her death below.

At his trial for murder in April 1982, a sordid picture emerged of back-stage life at New York's prestigious Opera House. Drugs and crime were rife and there was overt resentment against performers. Despite allegations that detectives had brought undue pressure on Crimmins to confess, the jury found him guilty of felony murder.

Crimmins encountered **Mark Chapman**, while in custody at Riker's Island. His opinion of John Lennon's killer was that he was 'a nut case'. Crimmins was sentenced to twenty years to life.
[*82*]

CRIPPEN, Dr HAWLEY HARVEY

One of Britain's most celebrated murder cases in which a mild-mannered little man poisoned his overpowering wife. Since his execution in 1910, Dr Crippen has attracted a certain amount of sympathy.

Crippen was an American citizen who came to England in 1900 to represent a Philadelphia-based patent medicine company. He was accompanied by his wife, Belle Elmore, whose real name was Kunigunde Mackamotzki, and they lived at 39 Hilldrop Crescent in north London. To help finance her extravagant ambition to be an opera singer, Belle took in paying guests and her husband was expected to do the housework.

Life in the Crippen home was stifling, with Belle compensating for her lack of talent by browbeating her husband. They argued frequently, and he took refuge in his relationship with Ethel Le Neve, a young secretary whom he had met in 1907.

Early in 1910, it was evident to their friends that Belle was no longer about. Crippen explained that she had returned to America to visit a sick relative. It was observed that Ethel Le Neve had moved into the Crippen home and she was seen wearing jewellery and furs belonging to Belle. Crippen now told friends that Belle had died. These strange circumstances were reported to the police and Scotland Yard sent Chief Inspector Walter Dew to 39 Hilldrop

Crescent. Nothing untoward was found but Crippen had been alerted.

The little doctor took flight with Ethel to Antwerp where they took a ship for Canada. As the SS *Montrose* began its voyage and Crippen's disappearance from London was noted, a detailed search was made at Hilldrop Crescent. Human remains were discovered buried in the cellar. While much of the body was missing, Dr Bernard Spilsbury examined an operation scar on some of the flesh which identified the remains as those of Belle Elmore. Traces of hyoscine were also found after analysis.

On board the SS *Montrose*, Crippen and Ethel Le Neve, disguised as a boy, were spotted by an observant Captain Kendall. He radioed his suspicions to London, thereby using wireless for the first time to help a murder inquiry. Walter Dew took passage on a faster ship and overhauled the *Montrose* before it reached its destination. He arrested Crippen and Le Neve on 31 July 1910 and escorted them back to England.

Crippen was tried for murder at the Old Bailey and Spilsbury's evidence proved unassailable. The doctor was found guilty and sentenced to death. Ethel Le Neve was subsequently acquitted of being an accessory. Crippen was hanged at Pentonville Prison on 23 November 1910 and Le Neve went to live in Australia.

It was reported in the press in 1981 that when Sir Hugh Rhys Rankin met Le Neve in Australia in 1930 she told him that Crippen murdered his wife because she had syphilis. Papers released by the Home Office in 1993 indicated that Crippen attempted to commit suicide while waiting execution.

In May 1997 some of Crippen's memorabilia were auctioned in London. His pocket watch was sold to an unnamed bidder for £9000.

[*198, 218, 335, 353, 564, 1024*]

CROSS, Dr PHILIP

Retired army doctor convicted at Cork in Ireland for murdering his wife in 1887.

Dr Cross lived with his wife and six children at Shandy Hall in County Cork. He was not popular locally on account of his bad temper, so the doctor and his family led a somewhat isolated life.

In 1886, Mrs Cross appointed Miss Effie Skinner as governess to her children. The twenty-one-year-old girl had an attractiveness that completely seduced Dr Cross. He became so besotted with Effie that Mrs Cross could not fail to observe what was happening and dismissed the girl.

Effie went to Dublin where she was pursued by Dr Cross and they became lovers. The couple maintained a clandestine relationship for several months until Mrs Cross became seriously ill. She was treated by her husband for a gastric disorder but died on 2 June 1887. Dr Cross prepared her death certificate and gave typhoid fever as the cause. Laura Cross was buried and, two weeks later, her grieving husband married Effie Skinner by special licence in London.

Tongues began to wag and talk of foul play led to the exhumation of Mrs Cross's body. Traces of arsenic were found and the trail soon led to the arrest of Dr Cross. There was evidence enough of motive and proof that he had bought a large quantity of arsenical sheep-dip.

Dr Cross was tried at Munster Assizes at Cork in December 1887. He claimed that his wife used arsenic in a hairwash formula and said he remarried quickly because he was lonely. He was found guilty and sentenced to death. Rejected by the world and also by his new wife, it was said that his hair turned white overnight. Dr Cross was hanged in January 1888.

[252, 546]

CROYDON POISONINGS

The fatal poisoning of three members of a Croydon family in the late 1920s remained unsolved for over forty years.

Fifty-nine-year-old Edmund Creighton Duff had been retired from the Colonial Service for eight years. He lived with his wife, Grace, and three children in South Park Hill Road, South Croydon. Close by, in Birdhurst Rise, lived Grace's widowed mother, Violet Sidney, and her unmarried sister Vera.

On 26 April 1928, Edmund Duff returned home after a fishing trip to Hampshire. He went to bed feeling feverish and sick, and never recovered, dying the next day, supposedly of a weak heart. Hardly had the family coped with the tragedy of his death, when Vera Sidney died on 15 February 1929, after a short illness. Again, death was attributed to natural causes but, when sixty-eight-year-old Violet died on 5 March 1928, the doctor declined to issue a death certificate.

After arsenic was found in Violet's medicine, all three bodies were exhumed and traces of arsenic detected. The Coroner decided to hold separate inquests, which led to considerable confusion over the evidence. The discovery that organs taken from Duff's body at the original inquest had become mixed up with samples from a different body did not help matters.

It seemed fairly conclusive that arsenic had been administered to the three deceased members of the family either in food or in prescribed medicine. Although there were suspicions that a member of the family was responsible for the poisonings, nothing could be proved. The outcome of the inquests was that poison had been wilfully administered by some person or persons unknown.

There the mystery rested until 1975, when Richard Whittington Egan made a case for Grace Duff as the poisoner. It was suggested that she wanted her husband out of the way so that she could be free to pursue a love affair and that she murdered her mother and sister for gain. [*389, 980*]

CUMMINS, GORDON FREDERICK

Murderer of four women in wartime London who earned comparison with **Jack the Ripper**.

His first victim was found in an air-raid shelter in Marylebone on 9 February 1942. She had been strangled and there were indications that the assailant was left-handed. The following night, a former Windmill Girl was found strangled in her flat in Soho. She had been savagely mutilated by a left-handed individual.

On 13 February, a third victim was discovered, strangled and mutilated in her flat near Tottenham Court Road. Within a few hours, a fourth woman was found dead in similar circumstances, this time in the Paddington area. The close proximity of the murders brought eerie reminders of Jack the Ripper's activities in Whitechapel.

But the wartime Ripper gave himself away. On the same evening as the last two murders, he picked up a woman in Piccadilly and took her into a darkened doorway where he started to attack her. Passers-by were attracted and her assailant ran off. In his hasty escape, he left behind a service respirator bearing his name, rank and service number.

525987 Cummins, Gordon Frederick, was arrested at his billet in North London. His fingerprints matched those left at two of the crime scenes and he proved to be left-handed. Articles belonging to some of the murdered women were also found in his possession.

Cummins, a married man, known to his fellow servicemen as 'The Count' because of his educated ways, was tried at the Old Bailey in April 1942. A wartime jury found him guilty and sentence of death was carried out on 25 June 1942.
[*176, 813*]

CURRAN CASE

Patricia Curran was the nineteen-year-old daughter of a Northern Ireland judge. She was reported missing by her parents on 13 November 1952. She was a student at Queen's University, Belfast and had failed to return home after attending her lectures. Her brother made a search of the grounds at the family home and found her lying injured in the driveway. Her face and chest were peppered with wounds suggesting shotgun injuries. She did not recover.

The forensic pathologist established that she had been stabbed thirty-seven times and found indications of attempted sexual assault. A curious feature of the murder was that the victim had been killed so close to home. Following a report that the dead girl had been seen with a man, police directed their attention to Edenmore Royal Air Force base.

Every man working at the base was questioned and suspicion fell on twenty-one-year-old Leading Aircraftsman Iain Hay Gordon. He was judged to have given an unsatisfactory account of his movements on the day of the murder. He confessed to killing the young woman after he met her walking home from the bus-stop and she resisted his advances. The prosecution case was that he lost control and attacked the girl with a thin-bladed knife.

Gordon was tried at Belfast Assizes in March 1953 when the jury found him guilty but insane. He was sentenced to be detained during Her Majesty's Pleasure and spent the next seven years in a mental hospital. He was released in 1960 with a new identity and an undertaking that he would not discuss his case. He went to live in Glasgow and maintained his silence until 1995 when he finally protested his innocence. His cause was supported by a number of prominent figures and in July 2000 he was granted an appeal on the basis that the confession he made in 1952 had been coerced. New evidence led to his conviction being quashed by the Court of Appeal in Belfast in December 2000.
[*158, 291*]

D

DAHMER, JEFFREY LIONEL

American serial killer who murdered fifteen times between 1978 and 1991.

Dahmer's secret world was discovered by chance on 22 July 1991. Two police officers knocked on the door of his apartment at 924 N. 25th Street, Milwaukee, following a complaint from a man who said he had been threatened by the occupant.

Thirty-one-year-old Dahmer was unhelpful and belligerent. An all-pervading sickly smell assaulted the officers and when one of them opened the refrigerator he recoiled in horror with the exclamation, 'There's a goddamn head in here!' Remnants of eleven male bodies were found in the one-bedroom apartment. The gruesome tally included four heads and seven skulls, trophies which Dahmer said he kept for company.

He proved cooperative when taken into custody and admitted killing seventeen individuals, all males and all strangers. He picked up hitch-hikers and others, luring them to his apartment with promises of money. He put sleeping draughts in their drinks and then strangled them. He cut them up and took photographs of their broken bodies. Sometimes he had sex with his victims before and sometimes after killing them.

Neighbours recalled hearing weird noises coming from Dahmer's apartment at night including the sound of an electric saw. For several weeks during the summer there had been complaints about the smell.

Dahmer had been a failure throughout his life. He dropped out of university and was discharged from the army because of his heavy drinking. He had worked for over six years as a labourer at a

Milwaukee chocolate factory. The week before he was arrested, he had been dismissed for chronic absenteeism.

His teachers described him as always on the edge and a relative said he shunned any kind of physical contact. She described him as 'a walking zombie'. He had been convicted of a sexual assault in 1989 for which he received a non-custodial sentence. He later admitted that he killed five times during this period.

Dahmer went on trial in January 1992. He pleaded guilty but insane. The jury found him guilty of fifteen murders and he was sentenced to life imprisonment. The State of Wisconsin has no provision for the death penalty. Dahmer was clubbed to death by fellow inmates in the Columbia Correctional Facility at Portage on 28 November 1994.
[*40, 472, 646*]

DAVIES, MICHAEL JOHN

Controversial case in which a man was convicted of murder on uncorroborated evidence of identification.

On 2 July 1953, on a warm summer's evening, members of a gang called 'The Plough Boys' attacked four youths on Clapham Common. In the ensuing fight, a knife was produced and seventeen-year-old John Beckley was fatally wounded. He had attempted to escape by boarding a London bus, but his pursuers dragged him off the vehicle and he was left dying in the street. The incident was witnessed by a number of members of the public.

The gang members were mostly known to the police and house calls followed. Six were charged with murder but, when the trial opened on 14 September 1953, four were released and a fifth was acquitted on Mr Justice Pearson's directions.

That left Michael Davies alone to face the charge. He had been identified on the sole testimony of a passenger on the London bus who saw the final moments of the incident. None of the other witnesses, participants or passers-by identified Davies. On the strength of this uncorroborated testimony Davies was found guilty and the twenty-one-year-old labourer was sentenced to death.

He spent three months as a condemned person while appeals were heard and, finally, his sentence was commuted to life imprisonment. He had protested his innocence throughout and

there were widespread feelings that he had been wrongfully convicted. He was released from prison after serving seven years of his sentence.
[*319, 732*]

DEAN, MINNIE

Baby-farming was the Victorian forerunner of child-minding. It was defined as the nursing and maintenance of an infant under the age of nine years apart from its parents. Minnie Dean took up baby-farming when she emigrated from Scotland to New Zealand in 1868. Like **Amelia Dyer**, she ended up committing murder.

Minnie and her husband lived in a small house at East Winton on South Island. One of her passions was gardening and visitors commented on her well-kept flower beds. To earn extra money, she took in babies but her services ceased to be used when two infants in her charge died.

To overcome her bad reputation, Minnie advertised under different names and, by this means, was successful in attracting new enquiries in April 1895. She undertook to look after a one-month-old child but there was a problem when the mother came to reclaim her baby, which apparently had disappeared.

Despite Minnie's denials that she had been minding the baby, police searched her house and found some of the infant's clothing. One of the detectives, while admiring the luxuriant blooms in Minnie's garden, noticed a wet patch in an otherwise bone-dry flower bed. He pulled some of the flowers out by their roots and exposed a shallow grave containing two tiny human corpses. A third set of infant remains was discovered in another part of the garden which was identified as the missing baby.

Traces of morphine were found in one of the corpses and there were drug containers in the house. Minnie's husband was released from custody when the police were satisfied he had no knowledge of the babies' deaths. Minnie was found guilty of murder at Invercargill and, on 12 August 1895, became the only woman to be hanged in New Zealand.
[*435, 770, 950*]

DEEMING, FREDERICK BAYLEY

A Victorian villain whose crimes included bigamy, fraud and murder and whom some believed to be **Jack the Ripper**.

Deeming fled to Australia after murdering his wife and four

children at their rented house in Liverpool in October 1891. The remains of his family were discovered when police were told of the disagreeable smell associated with the house. The bodies of his wife and children were found under a freshly cemented hearthstone in the kitchen fireplace. Maria Deeming had been bludgeoned to death.

Deeming had married bigamously before leaving England and he and his new wife, calling themselves Mr and Mrs Williams, rented a house in Melbourne. History repeated itself when a new tenant in March 1892 complained of the smell in one of the bedrooms. When the police broke up the hearthstone, they found the remains of Mrs Williams. The hunt was now on for Deeming alias Williams and he was located in Southern Cross where he was arrested on 11 March 1892 and charged with murder.

The Australian public had been kept well informed of Deeming's criminal background through widespread newspaper coverage. He was tried at Melbourne for the murder of his bigamous wife and pleaded a defence of insanity. The jury found him guilty and he was sentenced to death. A crowd of over ten thousand people stood outside the prison when he was hanged on 23 May 1892.

Deeming was supposed to have told police officers when he was arrested that he was the 'Whitechapel Murderer'. This was later repudiated but there were other reports alleging that he was Jack the Ripper. After his execution, Deeming's skull was delivered into the hands of a noted anatomist for examination. The unflattering conclusion was that the executed murderer was more ape than man.

[*186, 642, 725*]

DE FEO, RONALD

High Hopes was the name of the house in Amityville, Long Island in which twenty-three-year-old De Feo shot and killed his family in 1974.

Police were called to the house on 13 November 1974 after De Feo told a friend that his parents had been shot dead. The destruction of life at High Hopes later inspired a film called The Amityville Horror, and there were suggestions that the house had been tainted with evil. Ronald De Feo Sr and his wife had been shot dead as they lay sleeping, and thirteen-year-old Alison was shot in the head as she stirred in bed. John and Mark, aged nineteen and eleven, died in their beds and eighteen-year-old Dawn was gunned down as she left her room.

The gunman had carefully collected the expended cartridge cases and disposed of the murder weapon. The sole survivor of this carnage was Ronald De Feo Jr. He told detectives that his father had been killed by Mafia assassins but then changed his story so many times that he became the chief suspect. Under skilful questioning De Feo admitted that he had killed his family with his .35 Marlin rifle.

De Feo had an unhappy history of teenage psychiatric problems and drug-taking. He expressed bitter hatred for his family and said they were trying to kill him. He was charged with murder and pleaded an insanity defence at his trial. The argument was that he had been driven by paranoid delusions that his life was in danger from his family, so he took pre-emptive action. Evidence of premeditation and concealment supported the counter-argument that he was a sociopath.

In December 1975 Ronald De Feo Jr was found guilty and sentenced to twenty-five years to life on each of six counts of second-degree murder, the sentences to run concurrently.
[433, 896]

DE KAPLANY, Dr GEZA

Hungarian-born doctor who killed his wife with acid in a crime which shocked California in 1962.

Thirty-six-year-old de Kaplany was a refugee from central Europe whose medical qualifications secured him a position as a hospital anaesthetist at San Jose. He married a beautiful, twenty-year-old model called Hajna and the couple moved into a new apartment in August 1962.

On 28 August, neighbours were disturbed by the sound of loud music coming from the de Kaplany apartment. Some of those who complained thought that they could detect the anguished tones of a human being in distress and called the police.

Officers found an appalling scene in the bedroom where Hajna was found naked and suffering third-degree corrosive burns from acid which had been poured over her body. The whole apartment reeked with acid fumes and Dr de Kaplany, dressed only in his underclothes, presided over a scene of torture.

After thirty-six agonising days in hospital, Hajna de Kaplany died and her husband was charged with murdering her. A note on a medical prescription form was found in the bedroom. It read, 'If you want to live – do not shout; do what I tell you; or else you will die.' De Kaplany explained that he had suffered impotency because he believed his wife was unfaithful. He decided to destroy her beauty so that no man would ever be attracted to her. He had bought bottles of hydrochloric, nitric and sulphuric acid to carry out his purpose. At his trial in January 1963, the acid doctor pleaded not guilty by reason of insanity. The jury found him guilty and he was sentenced to life imprisonment. De Kaplany was released on parole in 1975 and was deported to Taiwan to work in a missionary hospital.

[*18*]

DE LA POMMERAIS, Dr EDMOND

Parisian doctor with social pretensions beyond his means who committed double murder in the 1860s solely for gain.

Count de la Pommerais, as he liked to be called, was already deeply in debt when he met his future wife in 1861. Mlle Dubisy brought with her a substantial dowry which allowed the profligate young doctor to continue to live in the manner to which he was accustomed. This included maintaining his mistress, Seraphine de Pawr.

Having acquired his wife's money, De la Pommerais cast his eyes in the direction of his mother-in-law who was a wealthy woman. When she died unexpectedly, he became rich overnight. His spending was so great that within two years he had used all his money and resorted to other means to acquire more funds.

He contrived a ploy with Seraphine de Pawr whereby, after her life was insured for half a million francs, she would feign illness and persuade the insurance company to pay her an annuity as the price for annulling the policy. Seraphine duly became ill but died unexpectedly of cholera despite the administrations of Dr de la Pommerais. The insurance company refused to pay out on the life assurance policy, choosing instead to initiate an investigation into the affair.

Seraphine de Pawr's body was exhumed and traces of digitalis were detected. De la Pommerais was promptly arrested and charged with murdering both his mother-in-law and his mistress. The first charge was rejected when he went to trial but he was found guilty

of poisoning Seraphine. The tide of public opinion ran strongly in his favour and it was expected that the Emperor would intercede on his behalf. In the event, Napoleon III declined to influence the judgement of the court and De la Pommerais went to the guillotine in 1864.
[*103, 220*]

DE LEEUW, HUIBRECHT JACOB

Town clerk at Dewetsdorp in South Africa who killed three people in 1927 in an explosion designed to destroy evidence of financial malpractice.

De Leeuw found that he could not manage on his town clerk's salary and his initial solution was to borrow money from his friends. When this source ran dry, he began taking money from official funds for which he was responsible. He hid the deficit in the town's revenues by keeping the ledgers in arrears.

He maintained this deceit until the town mayor asked to look at the accounts and discovered that the books were in poor shape. Mayor P. J. von Maltitz gave the clerk a piece of his mind and told him to sort out the mess. De Leeuw tried desperately to find sufficient funds to make good the deficit but his failure was evident when the books were next examined. Mayor Maltitz gave him a week to rectify the situation or face dismissal.

The day of reckoning came on 8 April 1927 when Mayor Maltitz and two colleagues arrived at the town hall to meet De Leeuw. At about 3.00 pm, there was a tremendous explosion which destroyed part of the building, instantly killing the mayor and leading to the subsequent deaths of his colleagues.

In a dying declaration, one of the men accused De Leeuw of malpractice and the town clerk was arrested. He was tried for murder at Bloemfontein. He tried to persuade the court that the evidence against him was purely circumstantial. A witness for the prosecution testified that minutes before the explosion, De Leeuw had rushed into his shop to buy a box of matches. The bomb which caused the loss of three lives had been a petrol/dynamite device which needed a flame to ignite it.

De Leeuw was convicted of murder and went to the scaffold on 30 September 1927.
[*66*]

DE MELKER, DAISY LOUISA

A nurse who made use of her medical training with lethal consequences, by poisoning two of her husbands and one of her children.

Like **Mary Ann Cotton**, she left a trail of death behind her. She married William Cowle in 1909 and four of their five children died young. In 1923, William Cowle died after a sudden illness from what doctors believed was a cerebral haemorrhage. As a result, Daisy benefited from his substantial life insurance.

By a strange coincidence, in 1927, Daisy's second husband, Robert Sproat, also died of cerebral haemorrhage. She inherited a larger sum of money this time and, although there were suspicions, no accusations were made. In 1931, Daisy married Sydney Clarence de Melker, a noted South African sportsman, and they moved to Johannesburg. The surviving child from Daisy's first marriage, Rhodes Cecil Cowle, went to live with them.

Her teenage son gave Daisy a hard time. He proved to be unreliable in his behaviour and could not get work. One of his irritating habits was to tell his friends that he would acquire a large inheritance when he was twenty-one. Young Rhodes suddenly became ill in March 1923 and died within days of what was thought to be malaria.

Suspicions were voiced to the police and it was learned that Daisy had been buying arsenic. Traces of arsenic were found in Rhodes's body and, following exhumation of their corpses, strychnine was found in both William Cowle and Robert Sproat. A review of the circumstances in which her two husbands had died revealed that they had both demonstrated the classic arched-back sign of strychnine poisoning which was not recognised as such by the doctors. Daisy was convicted of murder and sentenced to death. She was hanged on 30 December 1932 without making any confession.

[66]

DEMETER, PETER

Hungarian-born immigrant to Canada convicted in 1974 of the non-capital murder of his wife after a sensational trial.

Demeter arrived in Canada in 1956 with a few dollars to his name. By 1962, he had formed his own property company and within ten years he was a wealthy businessman. He married

Christine, an Austrian model, in 1967 and the couple lived in a luxury home near Toronto with all the trappings of success.

Friends noticed tensions between the couple and Christine intimated that all was not well. She said she feared for her life because of her knowledge of her husband's business methods. On 18 July 1973, Peter and Christine Demeter entertained friends at their home. Peter took them to Toronto on a shopping trip, leaving Christine behind to look after their three-year-old daughter.

When he returned later in the evening, he found a bizarre scene – Christine lay dead in the garage while his daughter was in the house watching television. Christine had been bludgeoned to death for no apparent motive. Sexual assault and robbery were ruled out.

Demeter had a cast-iron alibi but he came under suspicion when detectives learned of the fears which Christine had expressed. He was arrested after one of his business associates claimed he had asked him about various ways of getting rid of Christine.

The trial in October 1974, the longest in Canada's criminal history, produced some sensational evidence. A number of shady characters from the Hungarian underworld gave confusing testimony. Among the numerous revelations was that reported by a convicted arsonist who claimed that Christine Demeter had approached him to kill her husband. He rejected the offer of $10,000 but mentioned a Hungarian fixer called Laszlo Eper who had allegedly argued with Christine over money. The police were unable to follow up this allegation because Eper was shot dead in a police-car pursuit in Toronto in August 1973 following a prison escape.

Peter Demeter was convicted of non-capital murder and sentenced to life imprisonment. He continued to feature in the headlines following his release on parole in 1982. His luxury home was destroyed by fire and he appeared in court in 1983 on a charge of arson. Following a separate police investigation, he was charged with plotting to murder his cousin, Stuart Demeter, whose father had been appointed legal guardian of his daughter.

He hired two contract killers to kill his nineteen-year-old cousin out of revenge. Sentencing Demeter, District Court Judge G. Bourke Smith described him as 'a very dangerous man, intelligent but diabolical'. Demeter harangued the court with a speech lasting an hour and a half protesting his innocence. He returned to prison to serve two concurrent life sentences.

[*489*]

DESALVO, ALBERT HENRY

The 'Boston Strangler' raped and murdered thirteen women in Boston in a two-year reign of terror in the early 1960s.

The strangler's technique was to talk his way into the homes of women living on their own, frequently on the flattering pretence that he was scouting for a model agency. Once inside the front door, he raped and throttled his victim, tying a ligature around her neck in a characteristic bow. He also left his victim's body with the legs spread apart.

A fifty-five-year-old divorcee was the first victim, found dead in her apartment on 14 June 1962. In the months that followed, a dozen women fell victim to the strangler. Boston became a city of fear with women afraid to walk the streets and the police under pressure to find the killer. As usual in cases where the motive is essentially sexual, the police had to deal with a string of false confessions.

In January 1964, there was a lull in the series of murders and Bostonians began to think the worst might be over. But, on 27 October 1964, the strangler attacked a young woman in her home and, uncharacteristically, left without killing her. He threatened his victim with a knife and tied her hand and foot but then, muttering apologies, left her apartment. The woman called the police and provided them with a full description of the assailant.

He was quickly identified as Albert DeSalvo, a man with a police record, who had been released from prison in April 1962. When he was arrested and questioned it soon became apparent that he needed psychiatric treatment. He was taken to the Bridgewater Mental Institute at Cambridge, Massachusetts where he eventually confessed to thirteen murders. Corroboration of his modus operandi came from numerous women who reported assaults to the police after DeSalvo's photograph was published.

DeSalvo came from a violent family background and was soon in trouble for breaking and entering. During service with the US Army in Germany he met and married a local girl. They returned to Boston in the mid 1950s but the marriage was soon under stress because of DeSalvo's insatiable sexual desires. He was driven by lusts which his wife could not satisfy and he began to seek release through molestation and rape. It was later estimated that he may have raped as many as 300 women before he resorted to murder.

While in hospital, he described his assault on a young student: 'Once I stabbed her . . . I couldn't stop,' he said. 'I hit her and hit and hit her . . .' The key question was DeSalvo's mental status and doctors agreed that he was schizophrenic and not fit to stand trial. Consequently, he was charged only with sex offences which occurred before the murders and not with the murders themselves.

In June 1966, he was sentenced to life imprisonment and admitted to Walpole State Prison, Massachusetts. On 26 November 1973, he was found dead in his cell, stabbed through the heart by a fellow prisoner.

The family of one of The Boston Strangler's victims believe her real killer is still at large. DeSalvo's body was exhumed in October 2001 to allow DNA samples to be taken and compared with the victim's DNA. Forensic findings announced in December 2001 concluded that the DNA found on the last victim belonged neither to her nor DeSalvo. This left a legacy of unanswered questions, with some believing that DeSalvo, an admitted sex offender and robber, only confessed to the murders out of a need to achieve notoriety.

[*33, 299, 507, 765, 849*]

DESCHAMPS, Dr ETIENNE

Fifty-five-year-old dentist of French origin who shocked New Orleans in 1889 by sexually assaulting and killing a twelve-year-old girl.

Deschamps, who claimed to be a faith healer and an exponent of magnetic physiology, set up a dental practice in New Orleans, in 1884. He talked one of his patients, Jules Deitsch, into helping him with a scheme to retrieve lost pirate treasure through his exercise of hypnotic powers. To achieve this feat, he needed the services of a pure young girl to act as a medium. The gullible Deitsch offered his twelve-year-old daughter, Juliette, to the dentist.

During the next six months, Deschamps regularly had sex with the girl, first rendering her insensible with chloroform. On 30 January 1889, his plan went horribly wrong when he was found suffering from knife wounds in his lodgings with the naked body of Juliette Deitsch lying on the bed. He had accidentally killed the girl by overdosing her with chloroform and had then attempted to take his own life.

At his trial, Deschamps maintained that the twelve-year-old was a willing partner but the jury believed he killed the girl to ensure

her silence. An attempt to establish his insanity was successfully opposed and, after two reprieves, he was hanged on 12 May 1892, loudly protesting his innocence.
[*901*]

DEVEREUX, ARTHUR

Chemist's assistant who poisoned his wife and two children because he could not support them and concealed their bodies in a trunk.

Twenty-four-year-old Devereux was regarded as an odd personality by those who knew him and he proved emotionally incapable of dealing with family life. He kept a bottle containing a chloroform-morphine mixture to hand in case he might be forced to commit suicide. He married in 1896 and the birth of a son was followed by twins. Three youngsters proved a great financial burden and he was reduced to a state of impoverishment.

At the beginning of 1905, his wife and twins disappeared from their lodgings in Harlesden, north-west London, and his mother-in-law reported the matter to the police. Three months later, a trunk belonging to Devereux was located in a warehouse at Kensal Rise. It had been carefully sealed to make it airtight. On 13 April 1905, the police opened it and found the body of Beatrice Devereux and the twins. Their eldest son survived this tragedy, having been enrolled in a private school.

Devereux claimed that he came home one day and found his wife and twins lying dead on the bed. He believed their poor prospects had led Beatrice to commit suicide by taking morphine after she had killed the children. In the classic explanation given by murderers to explain their attempts at concealment, he panicked and hid the bodies in a trunk.

While mental derangement was suggested as a cause of Devereux's actions, an insanity defence was not mounted. Evidence that before his wife's death he had described himself as a widower did not enhance his chances of winning an acquittal. He was found guilty of murder at the Old Bailey and sentenced to death. He was hanged at Pentonville Prison on 15 August 1905.
[*393, 814*]

DICK CASE

Evelyn Dick was tried twice in Canada for the murder of her husband, successfully appealing against the death sentence and eventually being acquitted.

A man's body, minus head and limbs, was discovered by walkers in the mountains near Hamilton, Ontario on 16 March 1946. The corpse was identified by relatives as thirty-nine-year-old John Dick, a Hamilton bus conductor, who had been missing for ten days. His wife, Evelyn, aged twenty-four, to whom he had been married for five months, said they lived apart.

The couple's domestic arrangements were strange indeed. It seemed that Evelyn, who lived with her mother and daughter from her previous marriage, continued to see other men. One of her lovers was Bill Bohozuk, a steelworker. Her parents lived separate lives and her father, Donald MacLean, worked for the same bus company as John Dick.

Evelyn told the police she had been telephoned by a man who said he had been hired to kill her husband. She was instructed to borrow a car and rendezvous with the caller. This she did and picked up a man carrying a sack which he said contained part of John Dick's body. She drove out to the mountains where the man disposed of the contents of the sack.

Evelyn was arrested and detectives set about unravelling her complicated life. Bloodstained clothing was found at Bohozuk's home and MacLean owned a collection of weapons. But in the furnace at Evelyn's home, debris sifted from the ashes contained fragments of human bone and teeth.

On 22 March, further searches at the house turned up a suitcase which contained a cement-filled box. When the cement was broken up, the strangled body of a newborn infant was discovered. Evelyn admitted the child was hers and had been fathered by Bohozuk who killed it days after she was discharged from hospital. She claimed that her husband had found out about her affair with Bohozuk who killed him to silence his accusations. She also implicated her father.

In September 1946, Evelyn Dick, Donald MacLean and Bill Bohozuk were charged with murdering John Dick. Evelyn was found guilty and sentenced to death. The case against the two men was referred to a second trial, because the chief witness, Evelyn Dick, declined to give evidence.

Evelyn won her appeal for a new trial which began in February 1947. There was doubt that she had killed her husband and the jury returned a Not Guilty verdict. A few days later, she was tried for the murder of her child and was found guilty of manslaughter for which she was sentenced to life imprisonment. In separate proceedings, Bill Bohozuk was acquitted and Donald MacLean was found guilty of being an accessory after the fact of murder for which he was sentenced to five years' imprisonment.

Thus, the murder of John Dick remains unsolved. Evelyn was paroled in 1958 and went to live in obscurity.

[*150, 938*]

DICKMAN, JOHN

Convicted and hanged for the murder of a man on a railway train in 1910 on the strength of questionable circumstantial evidence.

The body of John Innes Nisbet, a forty-four-year-old colliery wages clerk, was found dead in a compartment of the 10.27 am train from Newcastle when it arrived at Alnmouth on 18 March 1910. He had been killed with five shots to the head and robbed of £370 which he had been carrying in a leather satchel.

A number of passengers had seen Nisbet on the train at Newcastle in the company of another man who was identified as forty-three-year-old John Dickman. He was a bookmaker who readily admitted being on the train which he left when it stopped at Morpeth. Dickman was known to be in debt and, when a search of his home turned up £17 in sovereigns, suspicions hardened. He was picked out at an identity parade as the man seen travelling with Nisbet. The missing wages satchel, minus its contents, was found in a mine-shaft some two miles from Morpeth.

Dickman was tried for murder at Newcastle Assizes in July 1910. All the evidence against him was circumstantial and the defence suggested that as the dead man had been shot with weapons of two different calibres, the police should be looking for two murderers. Despite discrepancies of identification and the lack of a murder weapon, Dickman was found guilty and sentenced to death, dramatically proclaiming, 'I declare to all men that I am innocent.'

His appeal was rejected and John Dickman was hanged at Newcastle Prison on 10 August 1910. The case continued to arouse controversy and in 1939 his name was linked to the murder in 1908 of Mrs Caroline Luard (see **Luard Case**).

[*791*]

DIPENDRA, CROWN PRINCE

Although the Royal Family of Nepal are regarded by their people as descendants of Vishnu, the antics of Crown Prince Dipendra were far from godly. The Eton-educated heir to the throne was addicted to alcohol and drugs and obsessed with guns. It was his practice to walk around the palace grounds shooting at any animal that came within his sights. The makings of disaster were in the air.

On 1 June 2001, Dipendra attended a reception at the Narayanhiti Palace in Kathmandu hosted by his parents, King Birendra and Queen Aishwaraya. During the event he became drunk and was carried back to his quarters with the expectation that he would sleep off the effects of the alcohol.

He re-appeared at the reception some time later armed with a semi-automatic rifle. He opened fire as soon as he entered the reception hall claiming his father as his first target who collapsed dying under the impact of three bullet wounds. Dipendra continued to spray the room with semi-automatic fire and shot dead his younger brother, Prince Nirajan and his sister, Princess Shrutti. His mother, Queen Aishwaraya stood her ground but was quickly despatched with a bullet to the head. Surrounded by his dead, dying and wounded relations, Dipendra finally shot himself in the head.

When rescuers arrived at the scene, they found ten members of the Royal Family dead, but Crown Prince Dipendra was still alive. He was taken to hospital where, according to Nepalese protocol, mass murderer or not, he was bizarrely proclaimed King. A constitutional crisis was avoided when he died soon afterwards.

It was reported later that Dipendra had been told by his parents that his position as Crown Prince would be revoked if he went ahead with his intention to marry a girl they regarded as unsuitable. An ancient prophecy proclaimed that the ruling Shah dynasty would be in danger on the death of the tenth King – Birendra was the tenth King.

[*369, 986*]

DOBKIN, HARRY

Convicted of murdering his wife in wartime Britain as the result of outstanding forensic work by Professor Keith Simpson.

Workmen clearing a bomb-site in the London borough of South Lambeth in July 1942 discovered the mummified remains of a female corpse in a damaged Baptist church. The body had been dismembered, partially burned and buried in soil which had been treated with lime.

Professor Keith Simpson determined that the head and limbs had been deliberately severed from the body and he suspected foul-play. Cartilaginous tissue on the body indicated that death had occurred within the previous eighteen months.

The victim's identity was established by means of dental information. It was known that forty-seven-year-old Rachel Dobkin, wife of the fire-watcher whose territory included the bomb-damaged church, had been missing for over a year. Her dental records were available and Simpson was able to compare them with the teeth left in the corpse. They matched and he confirmed identification by superimposing a portrait photograph of Rachel Dobson over the skull, using the technique pioneered in the **Ruxton** case in 1935.

When told that his missing wife had been discovered, Harry Dobkin made the mistake of mentioning details about the manner of her death known only to the police. He adopted a high-handed attitude when he was tried for murder at the Old Bailey in November 1942, complaining that the police had lied. It was brought out that he had failed to make maintenance payments to his wife and that she had repeatedly asked him to comply. The jury took a mere twenty minutes to find Harry Dobkin guilty. He was hanged at Wandsworth Prison on 27 January 1943 and Professor Simpson carried out the post-mortem on his body.

[*48*]

DODD, WESTLEY ALLAN

Twenty-nine-year-old killer of three children in Washington State who asked the judicial system to execute him.

On 4 September 1989, Dodd went hunting for victims in David Douglas Park. He found two brothers riding their BMX bikes in the park; Cole Neer, aged eleven, and William Neer, aged ten. He enticed them away from the main cycle path and into a secluded area where he tied them up and performed oral sex before killing them with a knife.

On 29 October, Dodd abducted four-year-old Lee Iseli from a school playground near Portland, Oregon. He took the boy to his apartment where he spent the night molesting the child. Finally, he strangled him and suspended his body from a rope in the closet. He later attempted sex on the body before disposing of his victim in a garbage sack. The dead boy was found in Washington State Game Reserve on 1 November.

Dodd, who worked as a shipping clerk for a packaging firm, fantasised about his murders and his future plans. He recorded his thoughts in a diary: 'I now ask Satan to guide me', was one of his entries. He was arrested on 13 November after attempting to abduct a child from a cinema and being cornered by members of the public.

When questioned by the police, Dodd spoke of his sexual experiences with young children before finally admitting the three murders. He said his fantasies had reached the point where sex was no longer enough and he needed violence to satisfy his urges.

On 11 June, he formally pleaded guilty to his crimes before a judge, thereby making a trial unnecessary. A specially convened jury decided he should be sentenced to death. Dodd opted for hanging rather than lethal injection. Washington was one of only three states that used hanging.

He rejected all suggestions that he should appeal, saying he wanted death because if he was ever to regain his freedom, he would kill again. The authorities granted his wish and he was hanged at Washington State Penitentiary on 5 January 1993, the first man to be hanged there for thirty years.

[*520, 883*]

DOMINICI, GASTON

Sir Jack and Lady Drummond, together with their eleven-year-old daughter, were killed by an elderly French farmer while on holiday in France in 1952.

Drummond, an internationally known biochemist, with his wife and daughter, were touring southern France in their car. On 4 August 1952 they camped in a field near the village of Lurs in Provence. Near by was a farmhouse called Grand-'Terre owned by seventy-five-year-old Gaston Dominici.

The next morning Dominici's son, Gustave, reported finding a girl's body in the field. The police were called and Sir Jack and Lady Drummond were also found dead from gunshot wounds.

Detectives suspected that Dominici and his family knew more about the deaths than they were saying. Gustave had let it be known that the little girl was still alive when he found her but that he was too afraid to fetch help. He was arrested for failing to help a dying person and sent to prison. It was Gustave who finally broke the impasse by telling investigators that his father had committed the murders.

Old Gaston Dominici eventually admitted the killings. He said he watched Lady Drummond undress and when Sir Jack realised there was a 'Peeping Tom' in the field, remonstrated with him. There was a struggle during which Drummond was shot and his wife and daughter were also killed.

The elderly farmer changed his story several times, made numerous confessions and generally prolonged the investigation. But he was tried for murder at Digne Assizes in November 1954 where he was found guilty by a majority verdict. He was sentenced to death but this was commuted to life imprisonment of which he served six years. He died in 1965.

In July 2002, a French historian opened up a fresh line of enquiry by suggesting that Sir Jack Drummond had been in France in the 1950s on an espionage mission related to chemical weapons in the aftermath of World War Two. Questions were raised about an allegation that a German operative had confessed to being one of four hit men who killed the Drummonds. According to this account, the Dominici family were pawns in a political game.

[*342, 540, 1026*]

DONALD, JEANNIE

Convicted of murdering a neighbour's child in Aberdeen in 1934 – the result of a ploy to frighten the child which went wrong.

Eight-year-old Helen Priestly went missing on 21 April 1934 and her body was later found in a sack under the stairs in the tenement block where she lived in Aberdeen. Her mother had sent her on an errand in the middle of the day to buy bread. The alarm was raised when she failed to return and an extensive search was made for her. She was found early the next morning. The sack containing her body was dry despite heavy overnight rain.

The girl had been asphyxiated and it appeared that she had been raped. Inquiries began to focus on the Priestly's neighbour, Jeannie Donald. There was a history of friction between the two families after Mrs Donald had punished Helen for some misbehaviour by striking her. In retaliation, Helen referred to thirty-eighty-year-old Mrs Donald as 'Coconut'.

The case against Jeannie Donald rested on a sequence of trace evidence, the examination of which pushed contemporary forensic capabilities to the limit. Human hairs found in the sack containing the dead girl's body matched Jeannie Donald's hair and other trace material in the sack was believed to have originated in her home.

Jeannie Donald was tried for murder at Edinburgh in 1934 when the complex forensic evidence was presented to the court. The most telling piece of evidence was the discovery in her kitchen of a part of a Cooperative bakery loaf, bread which she did not ordinarily use, but which Helen Priestly had been sent to buy. Mrs Donald did not give evidence but her defence argued that if the child had been raped, she must be innocent.

In fact, there was no rape, only a simulated attempt. This suggested an explanation of the crime. Jeannie Donald might have decided to teach the girl a lesson for ringing her doorbell and then running away. She lay in wait and jumped out on Helen when she returned from her errand, but with catastrophic results. The girl was sick with fright and choked on her own vomit. Donald dragged her into her house, realised she was dead and simulated rape on the body before putting it outside in the sack when the coast was clear.

Jeannie Donald was found guilty and sentenced to death. She was reprieved a week before the planned execution date and spent the next ten years in prison. She was released in 1944.

[997]

DOUGAL, SAMUEL HERBERT

A former soldier with a reputation as a womaniser who seduced and murdered Camille Holland at Moat Farm.

Dougal served for over twenty years in the Royal Engineers and fathered children at every posting. His first wife died in 1885, supposedly of food poisoning, and his second died of the same cause a year later. He married a third time in 1892 but he abandoned his spouse. Always short of money, Dougal resorted to forging cheques and served a prison sentence in consequence.

While working as a clerk in London in 1898, he met Camille Cecile Holland, a spinster in her fifties whose chief attraction was her bank balance. Dougal turned on the charm and they went to live at a remote farmhouse in Essex, near Saffron Waldon, for which Miss Holland provided the purchase money. Dougal named it Moat Farm.

In no time at all, the philanderer was up to his old tricks and when Camille caught him trying to proposition the maid, she gave him his marching orders. After all, they were not married and the house belonged to her. Camille's absence was noted in May 1899 and Dougal explained that she had gone on a yachting holiday. He drew attention to himself by openly entertaining a string of women at Moat Farm, some of whom presented him with offspring.

He was kept under police surveillance and, in March 1903, was arrested for forgery. Four years after she had disappeared, a thorough search was made for Camille at Moat Farm. Her remains were found in a drainage ditch and it was apparent that she had been shot in the head. Dougal was tried for murder at Chelmsford Assizes but argued that Camille had been shot accidentally. He was convicted and sentenced to death. He confessed his guilt prior to being hanged on 14 July 1903.

[*479*]

DREW CASE

Philip Yale Drew, an American actor performing in Reading, was 'tried' by a coroner's court in 1929 for the murder of a tobacconist in the town. Although never charged with the crime, the ordeal ruined Drew's career.

Sixty-year-old Alfred Oliver was attacked and robbed in his shop in Cross Street, Reading on 22 June 1929. He subsequently died of the severe head injuries he had received. Several witnesses claimed to have seen a man near the tobacconist shop at the time of the murder. He was identified as Philip Yale Drew, an actor employed by a touring company performing at the nearby county theatre.

Drew was not charged with any crime but was questioned at the coroner's inquiry as if he were an accused person. Sixty witnesses were heard in what was virtually a full trial with the result that the jury recorded a verdict of wilful murder against some person or persons unknown. Drew's plight had won the admiration of the people of Reading who gave him a rapturous welcome when he left the inquiry.

The ordeal proved disastrous for Drew who lost his confidence, with the result that his career waned. He died in 1940, aged sixty. The incident resulted in changes in the law to reduce the powers of coroners to conduct trial by inquest.

[*978*]

DUFFY AND MULCAHY

Described at his trial in 1988 as a 'predatory animal', John Duffy, otherwise known as 'The Railway Murderer', was convicted of five rapes and two murders. Eleven years later, justice finally caught up with his accomplice, David Mulcahy.

A 'Railway Rapist' had been at work in London and the Home Counties since 1982. His crimes were all committed close to railway stations. During the winter and spring of 1985–6, three murders occurred in similar locations, leading the police to think the rapist had become a killer.

The body of Alison Day, a nineteen-year-old secretary, was found in a canal near Hackney Wick station on 15 January 1986. She appeared to have been garrotted. On 17 April, Maartje Tamboezer, the fifteen-year-old daughter of a Dutch family living in England, went missing. The next day her body was found near the railway line at East Horsley. She had been beaten, raped and her corpse partly burned. She too had been garrotted. On 18 May, Anne Lock, an employee at London Weekend Television, went missing on her homeward-bound journey to Brookman's Park. Her body was found nine weeks later in thick undergrowth beside the railway line. She had been beaten and raped.

The police believed the three murders and the previous rapes had all been committed by the same individual. Files of 5000 known sex offenders were examined. One of the names on the list was that of John Duffy, aged thirty, on account of a reported rape attack. When he responded to the police request to report for questioning on 17 July, he turned up with his solicitor and refused to give a blood sample. He then put himself out of reach by being admitted to a mental hospital for a month claiming he was suffering from amnesia.

Meanwhile, the police asked Professor David Canter at Surrey University if he could devise an offender profile based on the known facts of the crimes. The results of his analysis were fed into the police database of sex offenders and the name that came out was that of John Francis Duffy.

He was placed under surveillance for a while and then arrested on 23 November 1986. A former railway employee, Duffy was well acquainted with the rail network and the opportunities it offered the careful planner for abduction of young female passengers at unmanned suburban stations. He was an insignificant man obsessed with violence who went to karate classes and watched kung-fu videos at home.

At his trial at the Old Bailey in February 1988, Duffy was found guilty on two charges of murder and five charges of rape. The judge instructed the jury to discount the Anne Lock murder due to lack of evidence. Duffy was sentenced to life imprisonment.

After his arrest, Duffy remained silent about any mention of an accomplice. But, eventually, in an interview with a prison psychologist, he implicated David Mulcahy. As schoolboys in north London they indulged in petty crime and graduated to burglary, car theft and, ultimately, sex crimes. They worked together for four years in the early 1980s committing multiple rapes and three murders. They tossed a coin to decide who would be the first to rape their victim. Mulcahy was arrested in 1999 and in 2001 was tried at the Old Bailey on three murder charges. He was convicted and sentenced to life imprisonment.

[*154, 640*]

DUMOLLARD, MARTIN

Aided by his wife, Dumollard murdered at least ten girls over a twelve-year period, ostensibly to steal their clothes but primarily as victims of sexual assault.

The forty-five-year-old farm labourer from Montleul, near Lyons in France, lured young women to his cottage on the pretext of engaging them as servants at a nearby chateau. He murdered them and stripped the bodies, before burying them. Madame Dumollard sold the clothes, keeping some items for herself.

The murderous pair were caught in May 1861 when Dumollard approached Marie Pichon, a young widow looking for work in Lyons. He gave her his usual line about seeking servants to work at the château and persuaded her to accompany him. They made the short journey from Lyons to Montluel by train and then on foot to Dumollard's cottage. At some point on this last stage, Marie Pichon became suspicious and baulked at going further. Dumollard's response was to try to strangle her but the high-spirited girl struggled free and made a run for it. A chase ensued but the overweight farm labourer was no match for the young woman.

The Dumollards were arrested the next day and the full extent of their activities began to emerge. Clothes belonging to ten different women were found in the cottage. Madame Dumollard gave a full account of the murders and firmly placed the blame on her husband. He confessed to the crimes and admitted disposing of his victims either by burying them or throwing their corpses into the River Rhône.

At least nine young women were thought to have escaped the clutches of the evil pair and lived to identify them. The Dumollards were tried at Bourg in January 1862. They were convicted of murder and he went to the guillotine while she was condemned to the galleys for life.
[*1050*]

DU PONT, JOHN ELEUTHÈRE

Eccentric American millionaire and heir to the Du Pont family's riches descended into a world of fantasy and instability that ended in the murder of his closest friend.

On 26 January 1996, he drove to the home of David L Schultz and shot him three times with a .38 pistol witnessed by the victim's wife. Schultz, a gold medal winner in wrestling at the 1984 Olympics collapsed on the snow-covered driveway and died. Du Pont returned to his home on his 800 acre estate called Foxcatcher Farm, at Newton Square near Philadelphia.

Du Pont was fascinated with firearms and owned a helicopter and armoured personnel vehicle. After the shooting, he remained holed up in the house refusing to communicate with the police who had laid seige to his property. Reports of his increasingly bizarre behaviour made the authorities wary. Du Pont had started to call himself the Dalai Lama and Golden Eagle and claimed that Nazi spirits haunted his estate. After forty-eight hours the police were able to arrest him without a struggle when he came outside to attend to the heating boiler. They found an arsenal of weapons inside the house.

John Du Pont was a sportsman and biologist whose collections are housed in the Delaware Museum of Modern Art. He was also a philanthropist and made generous donations to sport, particularly to the pentathlon and wrestling. In the 1980s he built a training camp on his estate to encourage US Olympic hopefuls and installed David Schultz as coach.

By the early 1990s, his relationships came under strain as he resorted to drugs and heavy drinking and he rarely left his estate. Schultz was close to him and tried to wean his friend away from drink. This led to arguments and Du Pont threatened to kill one of the wrestlers. He also mutilated himself and a visitor witnessed him cutting his legs with a penknife to extract bugs which he said were eating into his flesh.

After his arrest Du Pont was subjected to psychiatric examination and found to be schizophrenic. Concerns about his sanity delayed his trial for murder. The judge was presented with an unusual contradiction. On the one hand Du Pont`s lawyers claimed he was mentally unbalanced and unfit to stand trial while legal advisers in another court claimed he was sane and fully competent to run his financial affairs.

John Du Pont was tried for first degree murder and, despite his lawyers' defence pleas of insanity, was found guilty. He was sentenced to twenty to forty years' imprisonment, the early part of which was expected to be spent in a mental facility.

[865]

DURRANT, WILLIAM HENRY THEODORE

Sunday School superintendent who murdered two young women in the Emanuel Baptist Church in San Francisco in 1895.

Twenty-four-year-old Theo Durrant was a student at Cooper Medical School and an active member of the Emanuel Baptist Church. He fulfilled numerous duties at the church and was also secretary to the Christian Endeavour Society.

On 3 April 1895, he took eighteen-year-old Blanche Lamont into the church where he strangled her and then dragged her body up to the belfry where it lay undiscovered for over a week.

On 12 April, he took twenty-year-old Minnie Williams into the church and left her mutilated body in the library where it was found the next day. Theo denied any knowledge of Minnie's brutal murder but the discovery of her purse among his effects prompted a search of the church and Blanche's body was found.

Theo was arrested and charged with murder, giving the newspapers a field day. One paper published a sketch of his hands so that readers could identify the hands of a murderer. Durrant's trial was a major event in San Francisco, not least because news emerged of his secret fantasies. The regular churchgoer was, apparently, also a regular customer at the city's brothels.

He was found guilty and sentenced to death but numerous appeals delayed his execution until 7 January 1898. He protested his innocence and asked the executioner to hold on while he made a statement. The sheriff in charge of proceedings overruled him and told the hangman to get on with it. Theo's parents seemed to

enjoy the glare of publicity and, in a macabre footnote to his execution, ate a full roast dinner in the room where their hanged son's body lay in a coffin awaiting the mortician.
[*463, 612, 744*]

DUTROUX, MARC

Serial child rapist and murderer sentenced to life imprisonment in Belgium in 2004 after nine years of investigation and bitter public recriminations. In 1996, following his arrest, over 300,000 people marched in the streets of Brussels to condemn the police and the justice system.

Against a background of missing children during the early 1990s and suspicions about an international paedophile ring, police raided a house at Marcinelle near Charleroi in 1996. The house was one of several owned by forty-seven year old Marc Dutroux, an unemployed electrician. In the basement, police found two twelve year old girls who had been drugged and sexually abused but were still alive. The bodies of two eight year old girls who had starved to death as captives in one of Dutroux's houses were found buried in the garden.

Outrage followed when it was learned that Dutroux, a convicted child kidnapper and rapist, had been released from prison for good behaviour and went on to commit further crimes including murder. Worse still was the revelation that, acting on a tip-off, police had twice visited his house in 1993 while two kidnapped children were held there. They accepted Dutroux's denials of any involvement with the missing children.

Dutroux worked with accomplices, one of whom he murdered, and his former wife was also implicated. He was tried at Arlon in 2004 for kidnap, rape and four murders. The remains of seven dead children had been recovered at different sites and six other missing children were unaccounted for. Dutroux claimed that he did not act alone but was part of an international paedophile network for which he was the procurer. It was known that he had visited The Netherlands and the Czech Republic but there was no substantiation for his claims about a network involving public figures.

He admitted his crimes without a trace of emotion and boasted about the dungeon he had built to hold his victims. Referring to the two girls who had starved to death, he said, 'I put them both in the freezer for more than a month. I had other things to do'. Dutroux was sentenced to life imprisonment and his ex-wife was a given a prison sentence of thirty years. Another accomplice, Michel Lelievre, was jailed for twenty-five years for his part in a conspiracy to kidnap.

Dutroux became a hate figure in Belgium and there were calls to put convicted child rapists to death.

[*1046*]

DYER, AMELIA ELIZABETH

Former member of the Salvation Army thought to be responsible for the deaths of seven children in her care.

In 1895, fifty-seven-year-old Amelia set up in the Berkshire town of Reading as a child-minder or what the Victorians preferred to call a baby-farmer. She advertised her services and, for a fee, trusting mothers would leave their babies in her care.

In March 1895, a child's body was found floating in the River Thames. The ligature used to strangle the baby was still tied around its neck. An important clue was a Reading address on the paper which had been used to wrap up the body. This led to Mrs Dyer, but the baby-farmer, adept at the use of aliases, had moved on to another house in the town.

The police caught up with her in April 1896 when she was arrested but by then the bodies of six more dead babies had been found. They had all been strangled and wrapped-up in paper parcels. Amelia accepted that strangulation with a ligature was her hallmark. 'You'll know all mine by the tape around their necks,' she told the police. She exonerated her son-in-law who had been arrested with her and took the full blame for the child deaths herself.

Her motive, like that of her contemporary in New Zealand, **Minnie Dean**, was one of greed. She killed the babies soon after they came into her care and then charged the mothers minding fees. A defence plea of insanity at her trial was rejected and she was convicted of murder.

Amelia Dyer had been in the baby-farming business for fifteen years and it was unlikely that the deaths at Reading were the first. She was executed at Newgate Prison on 10 June 1896.

[*328, 1007*]

DYER, ERNEST

Remarkable case in which chance played a vital role by revealing the whereabouts of the victim after the death of his murderer.

Eric Gordon Tombe and Ernest Dyer, ex-army officers in their twenties, joined forces after the First World War to start a motor business. Their first venture failed and they did little better with their second. Tombe had the money and Dyer the ideas.

In 1920, they set up a racing stables at Kenley in Surrey called The Welcomes. Once again, they were dogged by ill-fortune, or so it seemed when The Welcomes was destroyed by fire in April 1921. Dyer had insured the property for four times the purchase price and his insurance company refused to pay out.

Friendship turned to acrimony when Dyer began to borrow from Tombe to finance his gambling and then forged cheques in his friend's name. There were bitter arguments and, suddenly, Tombe disappeared. The missing man's father, a clergyman, began to make inquiries and started with his son's bank. He was told that Eric Tombe had given power of attorney to Ernest Dyer and was horrified to find that the bank account was virtually empty. Worse, he declared that the letter of instruction to the bank was a forgery.

The next step was to find Dyer. Fate intervened in November 1922 when the police in Yorkshire decided to interview a man called Fitzsimmons whom they suspected of initiating a fraud. When Fitzsimmons was confronted, he attempted to pull a gun and was shot dead during a struggle. The dead man proved to be Ernest Dyer and among his effects were found Eric Tombe's passport and cheque book.

Ten months later, fate intervened a second time when Reverend Tombe reported to the police. He told detectives that his wife had been experiencing recurrent nightmares in which she saw her son's body lying at the bottom of a well. There was a well at The Welcomes and in it detectives found the body of Eric Tombe. He had been killed with a shot to the head.

[*160, 375*]

E

EDMUNDS, CHRISTIANA

Frustrated spinster who developed a passion for her doctor and laid a poison trail to deflect suspicion from her main purpose which was to kill his wife.

Forty-two-year-old Christiana had a reputation as a sharp-tongued, ill-tempered person. She lived in Brighton with her widowed mother and suffered from a number of minor ailments. Dr Beard treated her sympathetically, realising that his patient's problems were more emotional than physical.

The result was that Christiana became infatuated with him, sending him love letters in the expectation that he would leave his wife. When this did not happen, Christiana decided to eliminate Mrs Beard by means of a gift of chocolates laced with strychnine. On 10 August 1871, the doctor's wife was taken sick but did not die, and Christiana, fortunate not to be prosecuted, was told that Dr Beard would no longer see her.

Devastated by the turn of events, she realised that she was now regarded as a poisoner. In order to deflect this accusation, she hit on the idea of contriving other poisonings by means of doctored chocolates. In an elaborate plan, she tampered with a local confectioner's stock with the result that a four-year-old child was fatally poisoned and others made seriously ill.

The fatal poisoning was traced to Christiana. She had bought strychnine, her handwriting matched that on anonymous letters which she had sent, and several children implicated her in the scheme to tamper with the confectioner's chocolates.

Christiana announced that her intimacy with Dr Beard had inspired her action. Her claim that she was pregnant was disproved.

At her trial in 1872, her plea of insanity was rejected and she was found guilty of murder. Sentence of death was commuted and she was sent to Broadmoor.
[*953, 990*]

EDWARDS, EDGAR
A quiet man characterised by his good manners who turned to murder for profit and, despite every indication of insanity, was hanged in 1903.

On 1 December 1902, Edwards responded to an advertisement offering a greengrocery business for sale. He went to the shop in Camberwell, south London, armed with a lead sash-weight which he used to kill John William Darby and his wife Beatrice. For good measure, he strangled their ten-week-old daughter.

Edwards took possession of the shop's cash and then proceeded to strip the premises of its contents which he moved to a house he had rented in Church Road, Leyton, some six miles away. He also dismembered the bodies of his victims and packed them into sacks. These too were transported to Church Road, where under cover of darkness, but not unnoticed by his neighbours, he buried them.

Several weeks later, Edwards attempted to repeat his murder for gain ploy, by attacking another grocer who was offering his business for sale. He completely bungled his task and had some explaining to do when the police were called. A search of his house turned up some business stationery bearing the name of John Darby who had been reported missing. A search of the garden at Church Road soon highlighted a patch of disturbed soil under which was the grave of the Darby family.

Edwards was tried at the Old Bailey and pleaded a defence of insanity. There was a strong streak of mental instability in his family; his mother and a great aunt had died insane, one of his cousins was in an asylum and two others were mental defectives. He was nevertheless found guilty and burst into laughter when he was sentenced to death. As he stood on the scaffold on 3 March 1903, he gleefully told the prison chaplain, 'I've been looking forward to this lot!'
[*226, 588*]

EINHORN, IRA

A fugitive from justice who jumped bail in Philadelphia in January 1981 before his trial for murder.

Forty-year-old Einhorn was a 'hippie' during the 1960s and subsequently made a name for himself as an intellectual luminary. He was well known in political, journalistic and cultural circles and the academic world was willing to listen to his ideas for saving the planet. He impressed with his encyclopaedic knowledge of various subjects and lectured widely both in the USA and abroad. He held a fellowship at Harvard's Kennedy School of Government.

He had a high opinion of his abilities, calling himself 'The Unicorn', and was a powerful debater with a strong following. In 1972, Einhorn met a beautiful young Texas girl, Holly Maddux, and within weeks they were living together in his apartment in Philadelphia. According to friends, they had a passionate affair but one that was prone to stormy disagreements. Einhorn had a domineering personality but Holly, despite being attracted to his charisma, also wanted to be independent. They separated at various times but usually made it up again and in 1977 went on holiday together in Europe.

The couple returned separately from their holiday and in September 1977 Holly disappeared. Holly's parents had not heard from their daughter since August and called Einhorn for news. He told them she had left the apartment on 11 September to go shopping but did not return. He expressed concern. When October came and there was still no news, Holly was reported missing.

Police inquiries revealed that Einhorn had a reputation for violence, having assaulted two previous girl-friends, although no charges were brought. It also transpired that he had asked two friends to help him move a trunk from the apartment and dump it in the Schuylkill River. The task proved too great because the trunk was too large to get in the car.

On 28 March 1979, detectives arrived at Einhorn's apartment with a search warrant. In a closet, they found a trunk containing the mummified remains of Holly Maddux. Einhorn, denying any knowledge of Holly's death, was arrested and charged with murder. He implied that his work had national security implications and said he had been set up by intelligence agents.

He was granted bail but fled from the USA before he could be brought to trial. After several years in Ireland where he was protected by the lack of an extradition treaty with the USA,

Einhorn went to France in the early 1990s. In 1993 a Philadephia court sentenced him in absentia to life imprisonment. In 2000, France agreed to his extradition on the understanding that he would not face the death penalty.

In July 2001, after losing his appeal against extradition from France, he failed in an attempt to commit suicide. He appeared on trial for murder in Philadelphia in October 2002. He claimed he had been framed by the intelligence agencies. After twenty five years on the run, Einhorn was convicted of first degree murder and sentenced to life imprisonment.
[572]

ELLIS, RUTH

The young night-club manageress shot her lover in an act which had all the ingredients of a *crime passionnel*, except that was not a defence recognised in English law. She was executed for her crime in 1955, the last woman to be hanged in Britain.

Twenty-eight-year-old Ruth who, at various times, had worked in a factory, as a waitress and a model, was a club manageress and call-girl when she met David Blakely, a twenty-four-year-old racing driver, in 1953. They had a tempestuous relationship, marked by their emotional dependence on one another. There were frequent jealous quarrels and, at different times, each tried to withdraw from the relationship.

In 1955, Blakely made a determined effort to break with Ruth and she became obsessively jealous. When he tried to obscure his whereabouts, she sank into a bitter mood heightened by a recent miscarriage. On 10 April 1955, Ruth tracked him to a public house in north London and shot him dead as he walked to his car. She then calmly waited for the police to arrive.

She made no excuses. When asked at her trial what her intention was when she fired the revolver, she answered, 'I intended to kill him.' At the scene of the shooting, after Blakely had collapsed on to the pavement, she had emptied the gun into his body. The jury's deliberation took fourteen minutes. They found Ruth Ellis guilty of murder and she was sentenced to death.

While under sentence of death at Holloway Prison, public petitions were raised clamouring for a reprieve which did not come. She was hanged on 13 July 1955. When her executioner, Albert Pierrepoint, returned home via Euston Station, someone asked him,

'How did it feel to hang a woman?' He did not reply, although he was soon to resign from the post of official hangman.

In December 2003, the Court of Appeal heard arguments brought by Ellis's family that the murder conviction should be quashed and replaced with a verdict of manslaughter. The grounds were that Ruth Ellis suffered from battered woman syndrome. The judges rejected the appeal, noting that Ellis herself had not lodged an appeal after the original sentencing.
[*270, 357, 395, 473, 638*]

ELLSOME CASE

Unique case in which a man convicted of murder had his conviction quashed on appeal on the grounds that the trial judge had misdirected the jury.

On 21 August 1911, the body of a nineteen-year-old prostitute, Rose Render, was found in the street stabbed through the heart. Later, a man on his way to work in the South London borough of Camberwell earlier that morning reported that he had heard a woman cry out, 'Don't Charles, don't!'

The dead woman's immoral earnings had gone into the pocket of Charles Ellsome, a twenty-two-year-old labourer, with whom it was reliably stated she had quarrelled. Ellsome was charged with murder and sent for trial. The witnesses mustered by the prosecution were of doubtful character. A convicted thief, Jack Fletcher, testified that Ellsome had told him, 'I have killed Rosie dead.'

Mr Justice Avory's advice to the jury that Fletcher's statement had been corroborated by Ellsome himself was a major factor in determining a Guilty verdict. Ellsome was sentenced to death but appealed to the Court of Criminal Appeal which had been set up in 1907.

The Appeal Court ruled that the trial judge had been in error in advising the acceptance of Ellsome's statement because it had not been introduced as evidence during the trial. As a result of this omission, Ellsome's conviction was quashed and a guilty man went free because of a judge's mistake.
[*49, 717*]

EMMETT-DUNNE, FREDERICK

Murder made to look like suicide followed a barrack-room quarrel at a British army camp in Germany in 1953.

On 30 November 1953, Sergeant Reginald Watters was found

hanging in a stairwell at Glamorgan Barracks at Duisberg. The popular NCO was thought to have committed suicide and that was the verdict of an army inquiry.

A strong undercurrent of opinion in the sergeant's mess suggested that the death was not what it seemed and that foul-play might be involved. Suspicion was focused on thirty-three-year-old Sergeant Emmett-Dunne, an NCO disliked as much as the dead man was respected. Since the tragedy, Emmett-Dunne had returned to England where, in June 1954, he married Mrs Watters.

The inquiry was reopened by the army's Special Investigation Branch and Emmett-Dunne was questioned. He admitted that he and Watters had quarrelled about his liaisons with his wife. He claimed that Watters drew a gun and, in order to defend himself, struck out and killed him. He and another soldier then rigged what he claimed was an accident to look like suicide.

When the dead man's body was exhumed, pathologist Dr Francis Camps established that he had been killed by a karate blow to the throat. Emmett-Dunne was tried for murder at a court martial in Dusseldorf in June 1955 and found guilty. The sentence was death by hanging and, although this was confirmed by the military authorities, it was not carried out.

Britain had signed an agreement with the German government prohibiting capital punishment for crimes committed by members of the armed forces in its territory. Frederick Emmett-Dunne was accordingly sentenced to life imprisonment, of which he served ten years before being released.

[*313, 467*]

ENGLEMAN, Dr GLENNON

'I like to kill. Not everyone has the strength, the guts to kill. It sets a man apart from his fellow men if he can kill.' Thus did Dr Engleman set out his credo in his confession to murder.

Over a period of twenty years, Engleman, whose dental practice was in St Louis, Missouri, murdered seven times in a highly premeditated fashion for gain. He operated his dental surgery on a strictly no frills basis. There were no appointments and he expected cash payment for treatment. His clients were mostly working-class from the south side of the city and if they were in financial difficulties he sometimes waived his fees.

While 'Doc' Engleman was well respected in the local

community, he was frequently in arrears with his payments to the Inland Revenue Service. He needed money to pay his taxes and hit on the time-honoured idea of murder for profit. His technique was to use his considerable sexual charisma to influence young women to marry men who could be set up as insurance targets.

His first victim was twenty-seven-year-old James Bullock whom he shot dead in the street in December 1958 to gain a share of his life insurance. In 1963, he killed another man by blowing him up with dynamite, again with a view to benefiting from the insurance. Other murders followed in well-spaced incidents, including three members of the Gusewelle family in 1977 and 1979 in the expectation of gaining half a million dollars.

The game was up for Engleman when one of the conspirators talked about his involvement. On 19 June 1985, he pleaded guilty to committing three murders in exchange for not facing a death sentence. He was given three consecutive life sentences without parole.

Those who had been his patients could not believe that the mild-mannered figure in a blue suit, who looked every inch a professional man, was a self-confessed murderer.

[29]

ERROLL CASE

Controversial unsolved murder with overtones of jealousy and blackmail involving members of the British aristocracy in wartime Kenya.

Fifty-nine-year-old millionaire racehorse owner, Sir Henry John Delves Broughton, married Diana Caldwell, thirty years his junior, in 1940. Their plan was to live in Kenya where they would sit out the war. While on honeymoon, they met Lord Erroll, aged thirty-nine, a farmer and a man with a reputation as a playboy.

Within months, Erroll had fallen in love with Diana and they had a clandestine relationship. They realised that Broughton would have to be told and Diana broke the news to him in January 1941. His reaction was unexpectedly rational. He suggested that time was needed for calm deliberation and proposed that he and Diana should go away for three months.

Erroll disagreed with this plan and Broughton gave in. The older man was prepared to honour a promise he had made to his wife that if either of them fell in love with someone else, the other partner would stand aside.

Life continued with an appearance of outward calm and, on 23 January, Diana and Erroll and the cuckolded Broughton had dinner together at the Muthaiga Country Club. After they had dined, Erroll proposed to take Diana to a dance. Broughton did not object but stipulated that his wife should be home not later than 3.00 am. Broughton was driven home in a drunken state around 1.30 and nearly an hour later, Diana was returned home by Erroll.

Lord Erroll was found dead behind the wheel of his car the next morning. The vehicle had gone off the road about three miles from Broughton's home. Erroll had been shot dead with a bullet in his head, later proved to have been fired from a gun owned by Broughton. He told the police that three days previously two revolvers had been stolen from his house.

Broughton was arrested and put on trial for murder. The event created headlines around the world and not least in wartime Britain which was scandalised by the antics of a few wealthy aristocrats in Kenya. Undoubtedly, Broughton had a motive for murder, but the prosecution failed to show beyond a reasonable doubt how a man who suffered from night blindness could have committed the murder.

The jury acquitted Broughton and he returned to England where he took an overdose of barbiturates in a Liverpool hotel on 2 December 1942. Diana, who remarried, died in 1987.

In 1982, James Fox, in a book called *White Mischief*, later made into a film, exposed the wayward lifestyle and questionable standards of British expatriates in Kenya during the early war years. The author revealed that Broughton had confessed to a friend that he was responsible for Erroll's death.

In 1993, a letter written to Diana by Broughton three months after his acquittal was made public. Riven with vindictiveness, Broughton accused his wife of ruining him financially and said he was determined to punish her. Diana gave the letter to the Attorney-General of Kenya because of the blackmail threats contained in it. James Fox believed the letter confirmed Broughton as the murderer.
[*297, 321, 930*]

ERSKINE, KENNETH

Twenty-four-year-old West Indian who murdered seven elderly people in south London in 1986.

'The Stockwell Strangler' terrorised the community with his

stealthy killings of old people of both sexes. The first murder occurred on 10 April 1986, followed by three in June and three more in July. The victims, whose ages ranged from sixty-seven to ninety-four, all lived on their own or in old people's accommodation.

The victims were strangled as they lay in bed; five of them were sodomised. The killer pulled the sheets up tidily over the corpses so that, to all intents and purposes, they looked as if they were peacefully asleep. One of his quirks was to turn to the wall any framed photographs that might have been in the victim's room.

Over a hundred detectives were deployed in the hunt for 'The Stockwell Strangler' and their best clues lay in the recollections of an elderly man, Fred Prentice, who survived an attack on 27 June, and a palmprint found at one of the later murder scenes. The police laboriously checked through many thousands of fingerprint records looking for a match with the palmprint. Their efforts were rewarded when they came up with the name of Kenneth Erskine.

Erskine had no fixed address but it was known that he collected his social security payment from a Southwark DHSS Office. When he called in on 28 July, he was arrested. Mr Prentice picked him out of an identity parade.

The police obtained little of value from Erskine during questioning. He had a low mental age and seemed incapable of answering simple questions. In an unprecedented move, his photograph was published in the newspapers on 12 August asking for information about him.

He had been disowned by his parents at the age of sixteen and had lived on his wits. A loner, with no family or friends, he slipped into robbery as a way of life. He had served time in prison and in 1982 had attracted attention because of the gruesome drawings he used to decorate his cell. They depicted old people being tortured and fellow inmates said he talked about murder. He claimed that a woman's voice tried to control him; 'It blanks things from my mind,' he said.

He was tried at the Old Bailey on 12 January 1988 and pleaded not guilty to seven counts of murder. The jury convicted him and he was sentenced to forty years' imprisonment – the longest sentence ever passed at a British murder trial.

[*738*]

EYLER, LARRY

Suspected serial killer of more than twenty young men in Indiana and Illinois over a period of ten months who was arrested in 1983 but released to kill again.

In August 1993, the mutilated body of twenty-eight-year-old Ralph Calise was found in woodland close to a main highway in Lake County, Illinois. He was the twelfth victim in the series. An ABC news journalist reporting the murder suggested that the serial killer who had been operating in Indiana since October 1982 might have found the police getting too close for comfort and decided to dump his victims in neighbouring Illinois. The two police forces compared notes and Larry Eyler came up as a suspect. He was a known homosexual who worked in a Chicago liquor store and frequented gay bars in the city. He had been in trouble with the police in 1978 over a stabbing incident.

Eyler was taken in for questioning in connection with the Calise murder. His boots had human blood on them and the tyres on his pick-up truck matched impressions at the crime scene. He was released in February 1984 after a judge ruled that he had been illegally detained. An exasperated police officer said, 'He's freed to kill . . . it's only a matter of time.'

Six months later, on 21 August 1984, refuse collection workers emptying a dumpster outside a Chicago apartment block found human remains in a garbage sack. In all, eight garbage sacks were found containing the dismembered body of Danny Bridges, a sixteen-year-old homosexual prostitute. The apartment block janitor recalled seeing Larry Eyler making trips to the dumpster carrying garbage sacks.

Eyler's apartment smelled of new paint from freshly decorated walls and ceilings. Forensic examiners found traces of human blood on the floor of the carefully cleaned apartment and vestiges of human tissue in the drains. It was believed that the young victim had been killed in the apartment and dismembered in the bath.

At his trial in July 1986, Larry Eyler was found guilty of murder, kidnapping and concealment. Sentencing him to die by lethal injection, the judge said, 'You are an evil person. You truly deserve to die for your acts.' His appeal against sentence was rejected by the Illinois Supreme Court in June 1988. In 1990, he was sentenced to sixty years' imprisonment for the murder of Steven Agan in December 1982.

Reports that Eyler would provide information on more than twenty murders if his death sentence were lifted came to nothing. He is strongly suspected of being responsible for at least twenty-three deaths.
[*531*]

EYRAUD AND BOMPARD
Celebrated French trunk murder of the 1890s in which the victim was identified by inspired forensic work.

On 27 July 1889, forty-nine-year-old Toussaint-Augssent Gouffé, a Parisian court bailiff, was reported missing. His description was circulated to police stations throughout France.

On 13 August, police in Lyons found the decomposing body of a man in a sack on the bank of the River Rhône at La Tour de Millery. Close by there were the disintegrated remnants of a wooden trunk which had contained the corpse. A still-intact label indicated that the trunk had been dispatched by express train from Paris to Lyons on 27 July 1889.

The great forensic pioneer, Professor Alexandre Lacassagne, identified the remains as those of Gouffé by the teeth and a tubercular lesion on the foot which had given the bailiff a characteristic limp.

When detectives learned the identity of the people seen with Gouffé shortly before he disappeared, they began a search for Michel Eyraud and Gabrielle Bompard, a couple of well-known swindlers. The nationwide manhunt soon became an international operation. In January 1890, Eyraud sent a letter to the head of the Sûreté from New York demanding to know why he was being branded as a murderer. On 20 January, Bompard turned up at police headquarters to report that Eyraud had used her to lure Gouffé into a trap in order that he could be robbed and murdered.

Bompard was arrested and Eyraud was eventually tracked down in Cuba and returned to France. They were tried for murder in December 1890 and found guilty. Eyraud was guillotined on 2 February 1891 and Bompard began her sentence of twenty years' forced labour.
[*674, 936*]

F

FAHMY CASE

One of the great murder trials of the twentieth century in which Marguerite Laurent Fahmy was acquitted of killing her husband in their suite at London's Savoy Hotel in 1923.

In July 1923 Prince Ali Kamel Fahmy Bey, a wealthy Egyptian with a minor diplomatic post, arrived in London with his beautiful French wife, Marguerite, to whom he had been married for six months. During the evening of 10 July, they had a public quarrel in the hotel dining-room. In the early hours of the following morning, while a dramatic storm raged outside, there were shots and Prince Fahmy was found dying in his suite. His distressed wife simply asked, 'What have I done?'

The shooting created considerable public interest and there were feelings of excitement when Marguerite Fahmy appeared at the Old Bailey on trial for murder. She was defended by the combined talents of Sir Edward Marshall Hall and Sir Henry Curtis Bennett. It came out in evidence that Prince Fahmy's sexual desires bordered on sadism and he subjected his wife to abuse and humiliation.

Marguerite Fahmy gave evidence, discreetly referring to her husband's perverted practices and describing their final, fatal argument. He threatened to kill her if she did not submit to his wishes and put his hands around her throat. In desperation, she seized the pistol which her husband kept in the bedroom and shot him three times.

There was no doubt that Prince Fahmy had been shot by his wife; the question was, did she intend to kill him? Using all the skills of oratory for which he became famous, Marshall Hall won an acquittal on the grounds that Marguerite Fahmy did not realise

the automatic pistol was primed to fire. It was a popular verdict and one which has a secure place in the criminal hall of fame.
[*781*]

FIELD AND GRAY

Two ex-servicemen brutally murdered a seventeen-year-old girl on the beach near Eastbourne in August 1920 after she apparently refused their sexual advances.

Twenty-eight-year-old William Thomas Gray lived with his wife in Eastbourne and provided lodgings for his friend, nineteen-year-old Jack Alfred Field. Neither man had a job and they spent their time in the public houses or on the beach at the Crumbles trying to make female conquests while Mrs Gray worked as a domestic servant.

On the afternoon of 19 August 1920, Irene Munro, who worked as a typist in London and was spending a holiday at the seaside, went for a walk on the beach where she was seen in the company of two men. Later that afternoon, a boy picnicking on the beach saw a foot protruding from the shingle. He rushed home at once and blurted out his discovery.

A young woman's body was removed from its shallow grave on the beach. She had been bludgeoned to death and was quickly identified as Irene Munro. Witnesses' descriptions of the two men seen with the young woman led to Field and Gray who were taken in for questioning. Their attempt to establish an alibi foundered at the first test and they were charged with murder.

Sir Edward Marshall Hall, defending Gray at his trial, argued that a refined girl like Irene Munro would hardly have fallen in with two undesirable characters like Field and Gray. Against this was the suggestion that the young woman was not so pure as might be imagined and had led the two men on. When she spurned their sexual advances, they became violent and bludgeoned her to death with a brick. Field and Gray were found guilty. At their appeal, each accused the other of the murder but their pleas were rejected and sentence of death confirmed. They were executed at Wandsworth Prison on 4 February 1921.
[*253, 487*]

FINCH AND TREGOFF

Dr Raymond Finch and his mistress, Carole Tregoff, conspired to murder Mrs Finch. Their case was put to three trial juries in California before a verdict was reached.

Finch and Tregoff

Forty-two-year-old Dr Raymond Bernard Finch was part-owner of the West Covina Medical Center. He married his second wife, Barbara, in 1951 and the couple were popular members of the local social scene. By 1957, Dr Finch was complaining to friends that his wife lacked affection for him and, for her part, Barbara was aware of her husband's indiscretions. They agreed to separate but Barbara ruled out divorce.

Using a false name, Dr Finch rented an apartment where he entertained twenty-three-year-old Carole Tregoff, a former model who was undergoing divorce. Her divorce became legal in 1959 and the only stumbling block to their plans was Barbara.

Because of her husband's adultery, Barbara was entitled, under Californian law, to claim their entire estate in any divorce settlement. This would be the whole of Dr Finch's interest in the medical centre together with high alimony payments. In short, Finch would be financially ruined.

The doctor and his mistress hatched a plan which involved obtaining compromising evidence against Barbara. As the plan evolved, it took on a more violent aspect when they hired John Cody, a former serviceman with a criminal record, to kill her. His fee was to be $1400 but when he failed to act, Finch and Tregoff carried out the deed themselves.

On 18 July 1959, they drove to see Barbara at her home to discuss the divorce situation. Shots were heard and Mrs Finch was found on the driveway with a bullet in her back. Her Swedish maid saw Dr Finch standing over the body with a gun in his hand.

Finch and Tregoff were arrested and sent for trial at Los Angeles. The doctor admitted confronting his wife, alleging that she produced the gun. During the ensuing struggle, he disarmed her and threw the weapon to the ground where it discharged the shot which killed her. The jury was unable to reach a verdict and a second trial jury also failed. In January 1961, at the third attempt, Dr Finch was convicted of first-degree murder and Carole Tregoff of second-degree murder. They received life sentences.

During their years of imprisonment Finch regularly wrote to his lover but she did not reply. Tregoff was paroled in 1969 and worked under another name. Dr Finch returned to medical practice after he was released in 1971.

[493]

FISH, ALBERT HOWARD

Harmless-looking man who murdered children and practised every known perversion including cannibalism.

The sixty-six-year-old former house painter was arrested in New York City in 1934. Six years previously, he had abducted twelve-year-old Grace Budd from her family on the pretext of taking the child to a party. He precipitated his own arrest by writing anonymously to her mother, years after the event, to explain what he had done. He admitted killing the girl and cutting up her body. Over several days, he made pieces of her flesh into a stew with carrots and onions.

Fish was traced through this letter and readily confessed to murders in at least twenty-three states. He was thought to have killed and eaten as many as fifteen children and, although questioned several times, slipped through the police nets. As an itinerant painter, he had access to empty houses and his kindly demeanour was his greatest asset as an abductor.

Although married with six children, Fish engaged in numerous masochistic acts. When medically examined after his arrest, doctors found over twenty needles which had been inserted around his genitals. He was also subjected to intense psychological examination. His own assessment was that he was not mad but he was interested in purging and suffering.

He nevertheless pleaded a defence of insanity at his trial in March 1934. A procession of experts on human behaviour gave their testimony, at the end of which the jury pronounced him sane and guilty. He relished the idea of death in the electric chair because of the unique sensation it would afford him. He was electrocuted on 16 January 1934 at Sing Sing, although the needles in his body allegedly short-circuited the first electrical charge.

[*17, 413, 820*]

FOLBIGG, KATHLEEN

A violent childhood may have been a factor affecting the personality of a mother who murdered four of her children. When she was eighteen months old, Kathleen's father stabbed her mother to death in a street in Melbourne, Australia. Thomas Britton, was convicted of the killing and was jailed for life. He was a British immigrant and after serving fourteen years imprisonment was deported from Australia.

Kathleen was placed in an orphanage and later found a home with a family who fostered her. At some stage, she discovered the truth about her background and her parents. At the age of twenty, she married Craig Folbigg, a twenty-five year old steel worker. Their first child, Caleb, was born in February 1989 and three weeks later he died. Cause of death was given as sudden infant death syndrome.

A second child, Patrick, arrived in June 1990. Four months later, he was rushed into hospital, barely breathing. He recovered but was diagnosed with epilepsy and blindness. On 13 January 1991, Patrick was again rushed into hospital but was found to be dead on arrival. Death was certified as due to asphyxiation caused by an epileptic fit. A daughter, Sarah, was born in October 1992 but, eleven months later, she too was dead and, like Caleb, death was certified as due to sudden infant death syndrome.

A second daughter, Laura, was born in August 1997. She died on 1 February 1999, apparently having stopped breathing. Her death was recorded as undetermined. A police investigation followed into the deaths of all four children. After Laura's death, Kathleen left her husband. Meanwhile Craig had discovered her diary which included disturbing references to the deaths of their children. There were outbursts of rage and hate against the children and the comment, 'I am my father's daughter'. The diary was given to the police.

Kathleen Folbigg was arrested on 19 April 2001 and charged with three counts of murder and with inflicting grievous harm on Patrick. After a strongly contested trial lasting two months, she was found guilty of the murders of Sarah and Laura, the manslaughter of Caleb and inflicting grievous harm on Patrick. On 24 October 2003, she was sentenced to forty years imprisonment. On appeal, her sentence was reduced to thirty years and the non-parole period to twenty-five years.

[*1034*]

FORSYTH, FRANCIS

Eighteen-year-old member of a four-man gang who waylaid and killed a pedestrian in the course of theft.

Late on a June evening in 1960, the four attackers – Francis Forsyth, Norman James Harris and Christopher Louis Darby, both aged twenty-three, and Terence Lutt, aged seventeen – sprang out on Alan Jee as he was walking home in Hounslow, west London. Their victim collapsed to the ground under a flurry of blows and Forsyth, as he put it later, 'kicked him in the head to shut him up'.

Alan Jee died of his injuries two days later and his attackers were quickly rounded up. When arrested, Forsyth had his victim's blood still clinging to the toe of the shoes he was wearing. Darby denied taking part in the attack and was eventually convicted of non-capital murder and sentenced to life imprisonment. The remaining three were convicted of murder committed in the furtherance of theft. Lutt was sentenced to be detained during Her Majesty's Pleasure while Forsyth and Harris were sentenced to death.

The carrying out of the death sentences on 10 November 1960 resulted in considerable criticism. Harris had not delivered the fatal blow but he was equally responsible as the law stood because he had used force on the victim. In the case of Forsyth, it was his youth which some believed was a factor that should have saved him from capital punishment.

[326, 327]

FOSTER CASE

Evelyn Foster died from burns sustained when her car was destroyed by fire in an unsolved act of murder on the evening of 6 January 1931.

Twenty-seven-year-old Evelyn Foster was found lying near her blazing car on the moor alongside the Newcastle to Otterburn road. She operated the car as a taxi and explained that she had picked up a fare who asked her to drive to Ponteland. Before reaching their destination, the man instructed her to turn back and then threatened her. She was made to stop the car on the moor and she thought the man intended to rape her. He threw some fluid over her face and set her and the car ablaze.

Evelyn gave a detailed description of the man but did not survive her injuries. In her dying words to her mother, she said, 'I have been murdered.' Doubts were cast on her story when doctors were unable to find any evidence that she had been raped. Stories began to circulate that she had set fire to the car herself to claim the insurance and had been burned accidentally.

The coroner's inquest returned a verdict of wilful murder against some person or persons unknown. This was well received by the public who believed Evelyn Foster's character had been impugned. Disquiet over the case was provoked by the attitude of the police who expressed dissatisfaction with the inquest's verdict and said they did not believe the man described by Evelyn Foster existed.

The conviction of **Ernest Brown** in 1934 for a murder involving a blazing car was linked to the Foster Case.

[*354*]

FOX, SIDNEY HARRY

Unprincipled rogue who murdered his mother for gain in a hotel at Margate on 23 October 1929.

Thirty-one-year-old Fox and his sixty-three-year-old mother turned up in Margate on 19 October and took rooms at the Hotel Metropole. Mother and son led an itinerant life marked by a trail of unpaid bills. He created a plausible aura by posing as a former public school boy or a Royal Air Force officer looking after his elderly mother, Rosaline.

Earlier in the year, Fox had insured his mother against accidental death and he increased the premium substantially when they arrived in Margate. Late on the evening of 23 October, the fire alarm was raised at the Hotel Metropole by Sidney Fox. While he stood around, apparently distraught and helpless, his mother was dragged from her smoke-filled room and found to be dead.

Rosaline Fox's death was put down to misadventure and her son lost no time in claiming the insurance. As a result of the insurance company's suspicions, Sir Bernard Spilsbury was asked to examine Mrs Fox's exhumed body. His verdict was that she had not died as a result of the fire but had been strangled.

Sidney Fox's trial for murder at Lewes Assizes was marked by a disagreement between the experts about the medical evidence. Spilsbury won the argument and the prosecution claimed that Fox had strangled his mother and used petrol to start a fire under her chair. In giving his evidence to the court, Fox made it clear that he was more concerned about preventing smoke spreading in the hotel than he was in saving his mother.

Fox was convicted of the unusual crime of matricide. Also unusually, he declined to appeal against sentence of death and was duly hanged on 8 April 1930 at Maidstone Prison.

[*481, 619*]

FRANK CASE

Leo Frank, Superintendent of the National Pencil Company at Atlanta, Georgia, was lynched in 1915 by an anti-Semitic mob after he was convicted of murdering fourteen year old Mary Phagan. He was granted a pardon by the State of Georgia seventy-one years later.

Twenty-nine-year-old Frank, a graduate of Cornell University, was working in the factory on 26 April 1913 which was a public holiday. At midday, fourteen-year-old Mary Phagan called at the factory to collect her wages. Some time later, her body was found in the basement of the building by Newt Lee, the black nightwatchman. She had been strangled and beaten, although not sexually assaulted. Beside her body were pencilled notes in semi-literate form accusing 'that negro hire doun here' as her attacker.

Lee was arrested and Leo Frank was questioned by the police. The two men were charged with murder. The case against Frank rested on the testimony of James Conley, a black worker at the factory, who alleged that Frank had shown him the body and instructed him to write the pencilled note. He also accused Frank of sexually abusing the girls who worked at the factory.

Frank's Jewish background led to infamous anti-Semitic publicity before his trial. The allegations against him were repeated but Georgia law did not permit him to give evidence on oath. He was allowed to make a statement and completely rejected the accusations. While the jury deliberated, crowds outside the court bayed their hatred of the 'Jewish Monster'. No white man had hitherto been convicted on a black man's testimony, but Frank was to be the exception. He was found guilty and sentenced to death.

There was a massive public response in Frank's favour from other US states and petitions raised demanding commutation of the death sentence. In June 1915, despite threats against him, Governor John M. Slaton commuted the death sentence to one of life imprisonment. On 17 August, a group of vigilantes, calling themselves The Knights of Mary Phagan, took Frank from Milledgeville Prison to Marietta, the murdered girl's home town, where they lynched him. Photographs showing the lynch mob surrounding Frank's suspended corpse were widely displayed.

Despite many appeals and the emergence of new evidence, the Georgia Board of Pardons resolutely refused to clear Leo Frank's

name. One witness said Jim Conley, who she knew was a sexual fantasist, told her he had killed Mary Phagan. In 1982, a former worker at the pencil factory came forward, implicating Conley and confirming that Frank was not the murderer. Finally, in 1986, Frank was pardoned but the case continued to excite passions. A controversial list of prominent townspeople alleged to have organised the lynching of Leo Frank was posted on the internet in 2000.
[*241, 306, 358, 724, 750*]

FRANKLIN CASE

Highly publicised case in the USA in which a man was convicted of first-degree murder as a result of his daughter recalling a repressed memory of the crime.

Eight-year-old Susan Nason was murdered in Foster City, California on 22 September 1969. Her killer remained publicly unidentified for twenty years. In 1989, Eileen Franklin was at home playing with her young daughter when she suddenly recalled the face of her childhood friend. Under therapy, she remembered witnessing her father sexually assault and then kill Susan Nason.

A statement was made to the police and fifty-one-year-old George Franklin was traced to Sacramento. He denied the allegations made against him but a preliminary hearing decided he should be brought to trial.

Franklin was tried for murder at Redwood City, California in October 1990. Eileen Franklin gave evidence, describing the incident which had occurred over twenty years previously. An additional allegation was that she too had been sexually abused by her father when she was a child. Her mother and sister spoke of the climate of constant verbal and physical abuse which prevailed in the family home. It was later made known that when Franklin was arrested, police found a large quantity of child pornography in his possession.

The defence argued that there was neither physical nor circumstantial evidence to link Franklin to the crime. Doubt was shed on the validity of repressed memory but Dr Lenore Terr, a specialist in traumatisation of children, testified that recovered memories were not less reliable because they had been repressed. George Franklin was found guilty of first-degree murder and sentenced to life imprisonment.

The degree of reliance which can be placed on recalled memories without benefit of factual verification is a matter of continuing debate. In 1995 a federal court overturned Franklin's conviction on the grounds that his civil rights had been violated.
[*303*]

FREEDMAN MAURICE

Married man with few prospects who murdered the girl he was courting when she attempted to break off their relationship.

Thirty-six-year-old Freedman, a former policeman, told Annette Friedson who worked in the City of London as a typist, that he wanted to marry her. Annette's family realised that Freedman was no catch, especially as he was already married, and advised her to break off the relationship.

On 26 January 1932, Freedman waylaid the girl while she was on her way to work in Fore Street. Her body was found later on the stairs leading to the office of the firm she worked for. Her throat had been cut, severing the arteries.

Freedman took refuge at a friend's house but he was arrested the following day and, a few days later, a blood-stained razor, which proved to be the murder weapon, was found on a London bus. The blood was of a rare type and the same as Annette Friedson's.

Freedman was tried for murder at the Old Bailey in March 1932. His story was that he had approached Annette Friedson with a cut-throat razor intending to take his own life if she truly rejected him. There was a struggle in which she grabbed the razor and slashed her own throat. None of this conformed with the finding of the safety razor in a patent handle which bore the victim's blood. Freedman's fate was sealed by the conductor of the bus who identified him as a passenger on the vehicle in which the razor was found.

He was convicted of murder and sentenced to death. Freedman was hanged on 4 May 1932 at Pentonville Prison.
[*703*]

FRIEDGOOD, Dr CHARLES

New York doctor who signed his wife's death certificate after murdering her and who was dramatically arrested at Kennedy Airport before he could escape.

Charles and Sophie Friedgood, married for twenty-eight years and with grown-up children, lived on Long Island. He practised as a surgeon and, outwardly, their lives seemed to be happy and fulfilled. In reality, the couple were at each other's throats most of the time. Friedgood compensated by having extra-marital affairs and, in 1972, had a child by his girl-friend. When a second child arrived, he found himself having to support a new young family.

Friedgood managed to keep these developments from his wife for a while but eventually she learned what was happening. More rows followed and, on 18 June 1975, Sophie Friedgood died suddenly, apparently of a stroke. Her husband certified the cause of death and burial was about to take place when the police intervened. Suspicion had been aroused because of the unusual circumstances which would ordinarily have called for a second doctor to confirm cause of death.

Examination of Mrs Friedgood's body indicated injection marks, and traces of the pain-killing drug, Demerol, were found. By this time, Dr Friedgood was preparing for flight. He had fraudulently obtained access to his wife's jewellery and money and headed for Kennedy Airport. His London-bound plane was turned back from the runway and the doctor was taken off by police officers.

Charles Friedgood was convicted of wife murder by a New York court in 1977 and sentenced to imprisonment for twenty-five years to life. The following year a state law was passed making it illegal for a medical practitioner to sign a death certificate when the deceased was a relative.

[*570*]

FRISBEE, ROBERT WILLIAM DION

Fifty-nine-year-old homosexual found guilty of murdering an elderly widow at sea on a cruise ship.

Seventy-nine-year-old Muriel Barnett was found dead in the suite she shared with Frisbee on board the *Royal Viking Star* on 19 August 1985. She had been battered to death with a champagne bottle. When the ship docked at San Francisco, Frisbee was charged with murder. He had on him cheques worth over $300,000 drawn on Mrs Barnett's account.

Frisbee told the police, 'I won't deny it or I won't say I did. I don't know what happened.' Psychiatrists thought he was genuinely suffering from amnesia. Following an argument about whose territorial waters the ship was in when the murder occurred, proceedings were moved to Canada.

Frisbee cut a pathetic figure. He had been a lifelong homosexual and took his name from Dwight Frisbee, a wealthy lawyer for whom he worked as secretary and chauffeur. They were also lovers. After Dwight died in 1958, Frisbee met Philip Barnett, another lawyer, and became secretary/companion to his wife, Muriel.

Frisbee lived in the Barnett's apartment and the three led a life of luxury, travelling widely and eating at expensive restaurants. Philip Barnett died in 1984, leaving $250,000 to Frisbee if Muriel predeceased him. In a codicil to her own will, two-thirds of her estimated $4 million estate would go to him. Frisbee continued in his role of faithful companion to Muriel.

Frisbee was extradited from the USA in December 1986 to stand trial in Victoria, British Columbia. While in prison at San Francisco, he had written an autobiography, *A Demented Paradise*, in which there was an account of Muriel's death. He claimed it was a fictionalised story with an invented ending.

The prosecutor argued that Frisbee had committed murder in order to benefit from his victim's wealth. The defence, headed by William Deverell, a Canadian writer and lawyer, believed Frisbee had acted while under the influence of alcohol and tranquillizers. He had committed an act of violence while in a state of altered consciousness.

In January 1987, Frisbee was found guilty of first-degree murder and sentenced to life imprisonment. He died in prison on 21 July 1991, claiming to the end that he did not remember what had happened on the fateful night that Muriel Bennett died.

[*236*]

FURNACE, SAMUEL JAMES

Builder who struck hard times and tried to escape his debtors by destroying a murder victim in a fire with the intention of faking his own death.

On 3 January 1933, residents in Hawley Crescent, Camden Town, north London observed a blaze in the garden of No 30. The shed, which was rented to Samuel Furnace, a jobbing builder, was on fire and access was impeded by a locked door. The blazing shed was broken into and the badly burned corpse of a man was found inside. A note at the scene, signed by Samuel Furnace, seemed to bear out the notion of suicide.

Closer inspection of the corpse produced another conclusion. The man had died before the fire started from a bullet wound in the shoulder. Papers on the body identified him as Walter Spatchett, who acquaintances said had lent money to Furnace.

The missing builder was arrested in Southend after a nationwide manhunt and charged with murder. He admitted meeting Spatchett in his shed and they were looking at his Webley revolver when the weapon discharged accidentally and shot his friend. He then hit on the idea of burning the body and letting it be thought he was the fire victim.

It was not an explanation that was ever likely to stand up in court but Furnace succeeded in short-circuiting justice by taking his own life. While in custody at Kentish Town Police Station, he swallowed some hydrochloric acid and died from corrosive poisoning. The coroner's inquest on Spatchett's death returned a verdict of murder against Furnace.
[*206, 289*]

G

GACY, JOHN WAYNE

Sentenced to death for killing thirty-three boys between 1972 and 1978, Gacy holds the record in America for the greatest number of murder convictions. After fourteen years on Death Row, he was executed on 10 May 1994.

Gacy served a prison sentence in 1968 for committing sodomy but could not curb his sexual perversions. He worked at various times for the Kentucky Fried Chicken organisation, as a shoe salesman and then as a building contractor. In 1971, he moved into a house in Norwood Park, a suburb of Chicago, which provided a base for his contracting business.

In 1972, he married a second time and, during that summer, his wife complained of the smell coming from the crawl space beneath the house. He put lime down to neutralise the smell which he attributed to a broken sewer pipe. His wife left him in 1976 at a time when he found a role in the community, performing as Pogo the Clown at charity functions.

In January 1978, a serious charge was made against Gacy. A nineteen-year-old boy told the police that he had been abducted from the street at gunpoint by Gacy and raped by him. Charges were not pursued because Gacy said he had made a deal with the boy who only reported him because he had not been paid. But the net was drawing closer and, in December 1978, police with a search warrant arrived at Gacy's home. The parents of a missing boy reported that their son said he had a job with a contractor called Gacy.

While in the house, one of the officers, who had worked in a mortuary, detected a familiar smell coming up through the forced air-heating system. In the crawl space underneath the house, searches found the remains of seven boys and eight more bodies were disinterred from the garden. Of the thirty-three boys that Gacy killed, only twenty-four were identified.

He trawled the streets for boys to satisfy his sexual needs. He handcuffed and tortured them before committing deviate sexual acts and finally strangling them. He sometimes passed himself off as a police officer even to the extent of putting a flashing light on his car roof.

According to the police, he confessed to his crimes, but Gacy later refuted this. He refused to give evidence at his trial in 1980 where a plea of insanity was pleaded on his behalf. The jury convicted him and demanded the death sentence and he remained on Death Row. He spent his time painting and drawing and wrote an account of his trial called *A Question of Doubt*. He maintained that he had not confessed to the murders.

On 10 May 1994, John Wayne Gacy was executed by lethal injection at Stateville Correctional Center, Illinois. He was fifty-two years of age. Demonstrators outside the prison, some dressed as clowns, mocked him at his moment of death, chanting 'Justice, Justice, Not Too Late – John Wayne Gacy Meet Your Fate.' Two businessmen were reported to have spent $7000 buying up Gacy's paintings so that they could be consigned to a bonfire for the satisfaction of his victims' relatives.

[*144, 532, 580, 776, 899*]

GARCES, MANUEL

A teenage male prostitute who murdered and robbed his elderly lover out of disillusionment.

Enrique Mercier was a respected lawyer who practised in the Chilean city of Valparaiso. On 7 May 1962, he was found dying from head wounds in his office on the fourth floor of the Consorcio Italiano building. He had been battered about the head with a heavy stone which lay on the floor and died before he could be transferred to hospital.

The office safe had been ransacked and the dead man's wallet had been stolen. While this suggested robbery was the motive, the victim's state of undress indicated another possibility. Mercier was known to invite male prostitutes up to his office after business hours and the lift attendant recalled that a youth went up to the fourth floor at about 6.45 pm on the evening in question.

A description of the youth was circulated but he played into the hands of the police by cashing a cheque stolen from Mercier. Manuel Garces, aged seventeen, came from a poor background and had drifted into delinquency and prostitution. He told the police that he hated the whole idea but it was a way of making a living out of wealthy clients.

Initially Garces claimed he was a scapegoat for a homosexual gang who were carrying out revenge killings. Later, he explained how he selected a stone from the beach which he intended to use as a weapon to kill Mercier. Using both hands, he struck the lawyer twice on the head in an act of fatal vengeance.

Garces was convicted of murder for which he was sentenced to ten years' imprisonment and robbery for which the sentence was five years.

[*461*]

GARDINER CASE

William Gardiner was tried twice for murder in the famous Peasenhall Case which remains unsolved.

Married with six children, Gardiner worked as foreman carpenter at a small factory in the village of Peasenhall in Suffolk. He was an elder of the Methodist Church and regarded locally as a rather pious man whose nickname was 'Holy Willie'.

In 1902, Gardiner who was in his mid-thirties, was linked by local gossip with twenty-three-year-old Rose Harsent. She was a member of the church choir and was employed as a housemaid by Deacon Crisp, an elder of the Baptist Church. Gardiner appeared before the elders of his church to answer questions about his morals. He admitted nothing more than a minor indiscretion and undertook to put himself beyond reproach.

Following a violent storm on 1 June 1902, Rose Harsent was found dead in the kitchen of her employer's house. Her throat was cut and her body had been partly burned. Paraffin from a broken lamp had been used to fuel the fire. Lying near the body was a broken medicine bottle and in Rose's room were two letters and an unsigned note of assignation addressed to D.R. which read, 'I will try to see you tonight at 12 o'clock at your place . . . I will come round to the back.'

As the dead girl was six months pregnant, there was an apparent motive for her death. Gardiner was arrested and charged with her murder. He was tried at Ipswich Assizes in November 1902. His wife testified that he had been with her the whole night apart for half an hour at about 11.30 pm. Gardiner proclaimed his innocence and denied writing the note. The medicine bottle had contained camphorated oil prescribed for Gardiner's children which his wife had lent to Rose who had a cold. The jury failed to agree and the judge ordered a retrial.

Gardiner was tried a second time at Ipswich in January 1903 when the previous evidence was repeated. Again, the jury failed to agree and the prosecution decided not to pursue a third trial. Gardiner was released to vanish into obscurity. He died in 1941.

A book published in 1990 thoroughly reviewed all the evidence and concluded that Gardiner was indeed innocent.

[*284, 417, 728, 795*]

GARTSIDE, JOHN EDWARD

A furniture dealer whose inventive claims to self-defence in a double killing were rejected by a trial jury.

Percy and Alice Baker lived at Standedge Tunnel, in a lonely part of the Pennines. On 22 May 1947, a friend made her way to their house and was surprised to see men loading a van with their furniture. She questioned the driver who told her the couple had quarrelled and decided to sell up their house.

Dissatisfied with this explanation, she contacted the removal firm and was told that they had a receipt signed by Mr Baker. It was plain that Baker's signature had been forged and the police were called. The removal firm said they had instructions to deliver some of the effects to a general dealer in Saddleworth. A watch was kept at the address and, in due course, a man calling himself Percy Baker drew up in a car.

He was twenty-four-year-old John Gartside, a general dealer, who claimed he had bought Baker's furniture and car. He said it was Baker's idea that he should use his name because he did not want the neighbours to know he and his wife had parted.

A search of the Bakers' house revealed forensic traces indicating foul play. Gartside admitted he had buried the two bodies on the moors. 'What am I supposed to say now?' he asked. His explanation was that he had driven to the house to find a full-scale row in progress. He had brought two loaded guns with him as he and Baker planned 'to try them out'. After Alice Baker was shot by her husband, Gartside struggled with him for possession of the gun which discharged and killed him.

Gartside's explanation did not convince the jury at Leeds Assizes who found him guilty of murder. He was hanged in August 1947.
[*398*]

GARVIE AND TEVENDALE

Maxwell Garvie was murdered by his wife's lover because of the perverted demands he made on her.

Sheila and Max Garvie, a couple in their mid-thirties, appeared to be happily married. They had three children and lived in a remote farmhouse at West Cairnbeg in Aberdeenshire. Strains began to show in their relationship when Garvie took up nudism and began to develop an interest in pornography. Perverted sexual demands followed, but in 1967 Sheila found an escape from her increasingly distasteful life.

She met twenty-two-year-old Brian Tevendale and they became lovers. When Tevendale introduced his sister, Trudy Birse, to Max Garvie, everyone seemed happy. The two couples were frequently seen out together but drama ensued when, in March 1968, Sheila Garvie and Brian Tevendale went off together. Max Garvie reacted angrily and threatened his wife in one breath while promising to curb his sexual demands in another.

On 14 May 1968, Garvie disappeared. He left home on that day bound for Stonehaven and was reported missing by Sheila one week later. Sheila and Tevendale were regularly seen together and the local community openly discussed Max Garvie's fate. Within days of her husband's disappearance, Sheila confessed to her mother that he was dead. On 16 August 1968, Sheila Garvie and Brian Tevendale were arrested.

Max Garvie's body was found in a culvert at Lauriston Castle at St Cyrus. He had been beaten and shot in the head. Garvie and Tevendale were tried for murder at Aberdeen and while Sheila denied direct involvement in the killing, she admitted moral responsibility. Tevendale shot Garvie while he lay asleep in bed at the farmhouse. The jury brought in a Guilty verdict and Sheila Garvie and Brian Tevendale were sentenced to life imprisonment.
[*325, 397*]

GEIN, EDWARD

America's most bizarre murderer whose acts of cannibalism and necrophilia at his Wisconsin farm in the 1950s made him a model for the films *Psycho* and *Silence of the Lambs.*

Gein and his brother worked on the family farm at Plainfield under the strict domination of their mother. She strongly believed in the work ethic and sexual abstinence. When his brother died in 1944 and his mother in the following year, Gein was left to his own devices. He kept his mother's room as she had left it and gradually withdrew into his own inner world, neglecting the farm and all other activities.

He fed his curiosity and fantasy by studying books on human anatomy and, as his mind deteriorated, he resorted to digging up corpses from graveyards in order to examine them. Among the bizarre practices in which he engaged was that of adorning himself in the skin stripped from a dead body. By 1954, Gein's perverted needs had reached the point where he committed murder in order to obtain fresh material to satisfy his crazy lusts.

On 16 November 1957, a fifty-eight-year-old widow disappeared from the store where she worked in Plainfield. Suspicion focused on Gein, the middle-aged farmer, because he had made inquiries about the victim being on her own. When police went to Gein's farmhouse their searches produced nightmare discoveries. His refrigerator was filled with body parts from at least fifteen human corpses. There were skulls decorating the bedposts in his room, a heart in a saucepan in the kitchen and lamp-shades made from human skin.

Ed Gein made a confession in which he admitted robbing up to eleven graves and he was subjected to extensive psychiatric examination. In 1957, he was committed for life to an institution for the criminally insane. His farm at Plainfield was mysteriously destroyed by fire in March 1958 before the house and its contents could be auctioned.

In 1974, Gein's attempt to win a sanity hearing as a prerequisite to gaining his freedom was turned down. Judge Robert H. Gollmar, who presided over Gein's trial in 1968, wrote a book in 1981 which established the full facts of the case. The bachelor recluse who became a stereotype for ghoulish murder died in 1984.
[*19, 359, 821*]

GEORGE, ANDREW

The controversial murder of an elderly rose grower led to allegations of a high level-conspiracy to cover up the actions of British Intelligence. The case remained unsolved for eighteen years before DNA evidence uncovered the murderer.

Seventy-eight-year-old Hilda Murrell was a spinster who lived on her own near Shrewsbury. On 21 March 1984 she was abducted from her home. Her body was found three days later in Moat Copse about seven miles away. She had been kicked in the head and stabbed several times, although death resulted from exposure. There were semen traces on her underclothing.

Her white Renault car was found near by and witnesses later recalled having seen it in the centre of Shrewsbury driven by another person. There was evidence of a struggle having taken place in her house and of the building being systematically searched. The telephone connection had also been torn out of its socket.

The police view was that the elderly woman had been the victim of a vicious burglar. But when news emerged of Miss Murrell's involvement with the anti-nuclear lobby, there were stories that she had been silenced. Comparisons were made with the Karen Silkwood case in the USA. In December 1984, another story alleged that she had been killed by British Intelligence agents in connection with a search for information about the sinking of the Argentine battleship *General Belgrano* during the Falklands War. Miss Murrell's nephew had served with naval intelligence during the war in the South Atlantic.

The police reopened the inquiry in 1993 following a report that the identities of three men hired by the security services to carry out a contract killing were known. The result was that the police confirmed their belief that Miss Murrell had been killed by a burglar. This view was vindicated in 2002 when West Mercia Police initiated a review of the case and reassessed all the evidence. As a result Andrew George was accused of committing the murder. He had been sixteen years old at the time and had entered Miss Murrell's house intent on burglary. Semen traces left on her clothing matched George's DNA and confirmed his guilt. He was tried at Stafford Crown Court in May 2005, convicted and sentenced to life imprisonment.

[*200, 872*]

GEORGE, BARRY

Convicted of the murder in 1999 of Jill Dando, a popular television presenter, in a high profile and controversial case.

Thirty-seven year old Jill Dando was shot dead at the front door of her house in Fulham, London on the morning of 26 April 1999. She was killed with a single shot fired at close range to the head. The manner of killing muffled the noise of the discharge but eye witnesses saw a man running down the street after the incident.

The silent nature of the shooting, the custom-made bullet fired from a smooth-bore weapon and the execution style of the killing led to speculation about motive. The weapon, which was not recovered, was judged from the spent cartridge case found at the scene, to have been a 9 mm semi-automatic handgun using a 'signature' bullet.

Jill Dando presented BBC television's *Crimewatch* programme which was regularly seen by eight million viewers. There were suggestions that she had been murdered in an underworld revenge attack related to the content of one of the criminal probes pursued by the programme. Other theories were that she was killed by a lone, obsessive stalker or by a politically motivated assassin.

Thirteen months after the killing, forty-seven year old Barry George, an unemployed man who lived less than half a mile from the murder scene, was arrested and charged. Several large rewards had been offered for information and the arrest was made as the result of information given to the police. George was a fantasist with a history of personality disorder. He had learned to use firearms at a gun club. The forensic evidence linking him to Dando's death was a minute particle of explosive material adhering to his coat which was similar to residues found on the victim. Eye witnesses who had seen a man running in the street after the murder failed to pick out George on an identity parade.

George was tried at the Old Bailey, pleading his innocence, but the jury reached a majority guilty verdict on 2 July 2001. He was sentenced to life imprisonment. Doubts were expressed at his ability to carry out such an execution style killing using a customised weapon. The nature of the shooting led to speculation that it was carried out by a hitman acting for East European interests because of Britain's involvement in the war in Serbia.

When George's appeal was dismissed in August 2002, one newspaper referred to the case as one which had produced no murder weapon, no witness to the killing, no confession and no motive.
[*1056, 1059*]

GIFFARD, MILES

Convicted of murdering his parents after his tolerance of a bullying father erupted into violence.

The Cornwall police were contacted on 8 November 1952 by the Giffard family's maid who reported that her employers were missing. Detectives made a search of the house at St Austell and immediately found signs of foul-play. There were bloodstains in the garage and also in Charles Giffard's car. A trail in the grounds of the house indicated that a wheelbarrow had been pushed from the house towards the clifftop.

Some of Giffard's possessions were strewn along the trail and, when detectives peered over the edge of the cliff, they saw the sixty-two-year-old solicitor on the rocks below. His head had been smashed in the fall. Further along the beach lay the lifeless body of his wife. The third member of the family, the dead couple's son, Miles, aged twenty-seven, was missing.

Miles was known to have been at odds with his father over his future career and had taken refuge in his relationship with a girl in London. His father disapproved and demanded that he give up the girl. Police kept watch at the girl's London home and arrested Giffard when he returned with her. The young man readily confessed to battering his parents to death and throwing their bodies over the cliff. He had written to his girlfriend in a mood of deep frustration over his father's attitude towards him saying, 'Short of doing him in, I see no future in the world at all.'

Miles Giffard was tried for murder at Bodmin Assizes. He pleaded insanity and his medical records showed that he had been sent for psychiatric examination at the age of fourteen. It was clear that he had been subjected to a lifetime of bullying by an arrogant father. He was convicted of double murder and was hanged on 24 February 1953.
[*698, 992*]

GILLETTE, CHESTER

Factory worker with dreams of marrying a rich girl whose ambition ended in the electric chair.

Twenty-two-year-old Gillette worked in his uncle's shirt factory at Cortland, New York State. While he aspired to high society, he did not spurn the opportunity to seduce a young woman secretary at the factory. When eighteen-year-old Billie Brown sent him a letter explaining that she was pregnant, he could see his plans start to disintegrate.

After he turned down Billie's pleas that he should marry her, the distraught girl threatened to tell his uncle. To reassure her, Gillette took her on a holiday to Big Moose Lake in the Adirondacks. They booked into separate rooms in the Glenmore Hotel. On 11 July 1906, the couple rented a boat and, carrying a picnic lunch, rowed out on to the lake.

Gillette returned alone from their boating trip and his companion's body was washed ashore three days later. Billie Brown had not drowned but had died from blows to the head and face. Gillette, who had moved to another hotel at Eagle Bay, was arrested and charged with murder. He gave conflicting accounts of what had happened, claiming first that Billie had committed suicide and then that the boat had capsized. Neither story accorded with the injuries which the dead girl had sustained.

Gillette's trial attracted a great deal of public attention, much of it from female admirers. He enjoyed specially prepared meals in his custody cell by selling signed photographs of himself. After a trial lasting twenty-two days, he was found guilty of murder and sentenced to die in the electric chair. After numerous appeals and refusing to confess, he was electrocuted at Auburn Prison on 30 March 1908. Theodore Dreiser's novel, *An American Tragedy*, published in 1925, was based on Gillette's life.

[*109, 125, 811*]

GILMORE, MARK GARY

Committed two brutal murders in Utah in 1976 for which he was convicted and sentenced to death. His insistence that sentence be carried out caused a sensation at the time and his execution by firing squad was headline news.

In July 1976, Gilmore held up a filling station in Oren and ordered the vacation student on duty to lie face down on the floor.

He shot him twice through the head. The following day, he held up a motel in Provo and, again, killed the manager with two shots to the head as he lay on the floor.

He made no attempt at either concealment or escape, with the result that he was quickly arrested. Gilmore was a heavy drinker who found it difficult to cope with life. He spurned offers of help from his family and resorted to crime which led to several terms of imprisonment. By the time he was released on parole three months before the fatal shootings, he had spent half of his adult life in prison. His attitude was one of hostility to all forms of authority.

Gilmore was tried at Provo in October 1976 and found guilty of first-degree murder. The jury decided his punishment should be death. Gilmore was allowed to decide the means – hanging or firing squad. He chose the firing squad and demanded that the state carry out its duty.

After two suicide attempts and two stays of execution, Gilmore finally got his wish on 17 January 1977. He was strapped into an office chair at Utah State Prison with a mattress and sandbags piled behind it to absorb the firing squad's bullets. When the prison governor asked him if he had anything he wished to say, he retorted, 'Let's do it'.

Gilmore's lawyer had bought the rights to his story and negotiated with Norman Mailer, the distinguished author, to write it. The result was *The Executioner's Song*, a best-seller which won Mailer a Pulitzer Prize.

In 1994, Gilmore's youngest brother, Mikal, wrote a sensitive account of the family's background. He referred to the constant beatings handed out to his sons by their father and of his mother's gloomy refuge in the supernatural. Gary had potential as an artist but seemed bent on self-destruction. One brother left home, another turned to religion and the third was murdered. In his own rationalisation of his actions on the night of the first murder, Gary had said, 'I knew I had to open a valve and let something out.'

[*339, 631*]

GIRARD, HENRI

Financial entrepreneur who used his knowledge of toxicology and bacteriology to procure murder for gain.

Forty-six-year-old Girard had a chequered background as a

womaniser and an insurance swindler. He kept ahead by weaving a complex pattern of deals and, although he enjoyed an apparently lavish lifestyle, was always short of money.

One of his followers was Louis Pernotte, a rather dull man who worked in Paris as an insurance broker. He was mesmerised by Girard and was easily drawn into a scheme whereby he allowed the financier to take control of his assets. Having acquired power of attorney, Girard next insured Pernotte's life for 300,000 francs.

The Pernotte family took a short holiday in August 1912 at Royan and both parents and their two children were taken ill. The doctor diagnosed possible typhoid. After he returned to Paris to recuperate, Louis Pernotte received regular visits from Girard who persuaded him to accept medical treatment which he administered. This consisted of injections of camphorated camomile, with the result that the patient became paralysed and died of cardiac embolism on 1 December 1912.

Girard next came to the attention of the insurance companies in April 1918 following the death of a war widow soon after he had insured her life. She collapsed in the Metro after visiting Girard in his apartment. Following inquiries, Girard was arrested four months later. It was discovered that he had a laboratory where he experimented with drugs and cultures. One of his experiments involved the use of *Amanita phalloides*, a poisonous mushroom, to procure the deaths of two people whom he had insured. This attempt failed but he eluded the authorities by taking his own life with one of his concoctions in May 1921.

[515]

GLATMAN, HARVEY MURRAY

Sadistic murderer who passed himself off as a magazine photographer in order to entice young women to pose for him.

Glatman served a term of imprisonment in 1945 for robbery and was convicted of a series of assaults on women in California during the early 1950s. His mother paid for him to receive psychiatric treatment and in 1957 her money enabled him to set up as a TV repairman in Los Angeles. He also took up photography as a hobby.

In August 1957, he persuaded nineteen-year-old Judy Dull, an aspiring model, that he could help her career by taking photographs of her. Once he had her confidence, he raped her and took pictures of her while she was bound and gagged. Then he drove her out to the desert and, after committing various perverse acts, strangled her with a sash-cord. The girl's body was left in a desert grave.

Glatman committed two similar murders on would-be models but after that his technique began to slip. One of his intended victims became sufficiently suspicious to escape when she had the chance and another managed to turn the tables on him. Twenty-eight-year-old Lorraine Vigil was shot in the leg by Glatman as he attempted to tie her up and, in a desperate struggle, the victim wrested the gun from her tormentor. She held him at gunpoint until police arrived.

Found guilty of murder, Glatman, like **Gary Gilmore**, told the state that he wanted to die. 'I knew this is the way it would be,' he said. He died in the gas chamber at San Quentin Prison on 18 August 1959.

[*701*]

GLOVER, JOHN WAYNE

Australia's so-called 'Granny Killer' who murdered six elderly women in 1989–90.

The murder of eighty-two-year-old Gwendoline Mitchelhill on 1 March 1989 began a reign of terror in Sydney's north shore area. The elderly victim was found badly injured near her home and died later. She had been bludgeoned and strangled in broad daylight on returning home from a shopping trip.

Four victims followed in 1989 in murders of unmistakable similarity. The victims were elderly women living on their own, murdered close to their homes with robbery as the apparent motive. The police seemed powerless and there was little they could do beyond advising elderly residents about security measures.

On 19 March 1990, sixty-year-old Joan Violet Sinclair was found battered and strangled in her home at Beauty Point, a Sydney suburb. To their surprise, police officers discovered an unconscious man in her water-filled bathtub. He was John Wayne Glover, a fifty-seven-year-old sales representative, who had been visiting Joan Sinclair for several months. He was also the elusive 'Granny Killer'.

Glover recovered in hospital from his attempt to commit suicide by taking anti-depressant drugs and was charged with murder. Tried at Darlinghurst in November 1991, he pleaded Not Guilty by reason of insanity. He admitted that he had bludgeoned his victims with a claw hammer and confessed to six killings although he denied they were premeditated.

He was a happily married man with a decent job and was well respected in the community. Apart from the evidence of his sexual fantasies, which came out after the trial, Glover did not fit the stereotype for a serial killer. He made a tearful statement in court, expressing sorrow over the deaths, and explaining how he had begun to develop a compulsion to molest elderly women. A medical expert said that he was suffering from a severe psychosexual disorder.

Glover was found guilty on 30 November 1991 and given six life sentences. Australian police continued their interest in him regarding numerous unsolved murders dating back to 1980. He was found hanged in his cell at Lithgow Prison on 9 September 2005.

[*512, 856, 1002*]

GOLDENBERG, JACK

A case of 'Murder Must Advertise' in which a young soldier who committed murder and robbery could not resist trying to help the police.

In April 1924, the bank which served the army camp at Bordon in Hampshire was raided. The manager was shot dead and over £1000 was stolen. Police were convinced that the attacker had been known to the manager and began their inquiries at Bordon Camp.

The Commanding Officer organised a roll-call and no absentees were reported among the several thousand men stationed there. But a young lance-corporal volunteered the information that he had seen a car outside the bank when he went in to cash a cheque. Eighteen-year-old Jack Goldenberg described the occupants of the car to the police and offered his opinion about the incident to local newspaper reporters. He boasted that it would be through his evidence that the criminals would be caught.

Two days after the raid, notes stolen from the bank appeared in local circulation. Goldenberg had already drawn attention to himself, and a warrant officer decided to investigate when he saw the young soldier emerge furtively from one of the huts at the camp. Inside the hut, he noticed footmarks on a window-sill and by pulling himself up to this vantage point, spotted a parcel in the roof space. It contained £500 in stolen notes.

Confronted with this evidence, Goldenberg confessed to the robbery and murder. He was convicted and sentenced to death, which was carried out following the rejection of his appeal.

[*402, 437*]

GOLDSBOROUGH, FITZHUGH COYLE

Neurotic son of a wealthy family who shot and killed a popular novelist in the erroneous belief that the writer had slighted his sister.

Twenty-one-year-old Goldsborough was an idle, over-indulged young man obsessed with his sister. He saw himself as her protector and mentor and even argued with members of the family when he believed they thought ill of her. He spent much of his time reading, including the novels of David Graham Phillips, whose themes often dealt with political and social problems.

He took exception to one of the novelist's books published in 1909 under the title, *The Fashionable Adventures of Joshua Craig*. The central character was a young social climber who Goldsborough equated with his sister. Believing the novelist had maligned her, he lay in wait outside his new York apartment.

On 23 January 1911, forty-four-year-old Phillips was confronted by Goldsborough as he left his Manhattan apartment. Shouting, 'Here you go', Goldsborough fired five shots at the writer before putting the gun to his own head and exclaiming, 'Here I go'.

The reason for Goldsborough's action was not immediately obvious and was only solved when his parents explained their son's jealous protection of his sister's reputation and his belief that David Phillips had cast a slur on her.

[*692*]

GOOLD, MARIA VERE

Self-appointed member of the aristocracy who resorted to murder after losing heavily at the gambling tables in Monte Carlo.

Thirty-year-old Maria Goold, who liked to use the title 'Lady', had twice been widowed and was married to a dissolute Irishman. After running through his money and that provided by his family, this ill-assorted couple found themselves in Monaco without a penny.

When, by chance, they met a wealthy widow in 1907, they persuaded her to lend them some money. This went the same way as their previous funds and Mme Levin demanded that her loan be repaid. Maria Goold's reaction was to stab their one-time benefactor and dismember her body.

The pieces of their victim's corpse were put into a trunk which the Goolds took with them from Monte Carlo to Marseilles. There, they made arrangements for the trunk to be forwarded to London.

If the smell emanating from the trunk was not enough to arouse the suspicion of the railway staff, the blood oozing from it was. Despite Maria's protestations that the trunk contained poultry, she and her husband were held until the police arrived.

'Lady' Goold's explanation was that she was present when a man she thought was Mme Levin's lover burst into her house, stabbed her and then fled. In their panic and to avoid trouble, she and her husband decided to cut up the body and take it to London. It was not an explanation likely to carry much conviction and so it proved when the Goolds appeared on trial in Monaco. Maria was sentenced to death and her husband to life imprisonment.

Maria Goold's sentence was commuted to life imprisonment and she died of typhoid in the French penal colony at Cayenne. Her husband took his own life a year later.
[575, *804*]

GORSE HALL MURDER

Unsolved murder case of 1909 which resulted in two trials but no solution.

On 1 November 1909, George Harry Storrs, a wealthy builder who lived at Gorse Hall, near Stalybridge in Lancashire, was fatally attacked by an intruder brandishing a revolver. In front of witnesses, he struggled with the man who produced a knife and stabbed Storrs several times before running off. The wounded man died from loss of blood within an hour and, asked if he knew who his assailant was, answered, 'I don't know.'

A description of the murderer was published and attention was directed at Cornelius Howard, aged thirty-one, a pork butcher with a dubious background who was the dead man's cousin. Four people who had witnessed the fatal encounter identified Howard as the assailant. Howard was tried at Chester on 1 March 1910. He claimed an alibi which was supported by witnesses and he was acquitted.

On 10 June 1910 a courting couple were attacked by a man with a knife close to Gorse Hall. The spirited young man fought back and disarmed the man, twenty-eight-year-old Mark Wilde, who was charged with attempted murder. After questioning Wilde, the police were convinced that he was also the murderer of George Harry Storrs.

Following his conviction for attempted murder, Wilde was tried for Storrs's murder. He appeared at Chester Assizes in October

1910 and the witnesses who had identified Howard as the murderer now identified Wilde. The accused man protested his innocence and, like Howard, claimed an alibi. Amid confusing evidence, Wilde was also found not guilty. He joined Cornelius Howard as two men who made history by being tried and acquitted for the same crime.
[356]

GRAHAM, BARBARA
Thirty-two-year-old call-girl who became involved in organised crime and murder and was the subject of the film *I Want to Live*, in which she was portrayed by Susan Hayward.

Barbara Graham came from an unhappy family background and ran away when she was nine years old. She spent her earlier years in reformatories and slid into crime. By 1947, she was a call-girl in San Francisco and had joined one of the city's robbery gangs whose methods included torture and murder.

On 9 March 1953, the gang, led by Jack Santos, attempted to extract money from an elderly widow who lived in Burbank. They believed Mabel Monahan owned a large amount of jewellery and Graham's job was to use a pretence to gain access to the house and let in the other gang members. She succeeded in this ploy and the widow was tied up and beaten prior to the house being ransacked. In her pain Mabel Monahan cried out and Barbara Graham silenced her by bringing her gun butt down on her head and killing her.

The gang went away empty-handed because there was neither money nor jewellery in the house. Santos, Emmett Perkins and Barbara Graham were rounded up and charged with murder. Graham was tricked by the police into bribing an officer to furnish her with an alibi. This was used to good effect by the prosecution and Graham responded by asking the court if they knew what it was like to be desperate. This was presumably a reference to her early life. All three were convicted and sentenced to death.

Barbara Graham went to the electric chair at San Quentin on 3 June 1955 leaving behind her nineteen-month-old child. Three years later, Hollywood produced *I Want to Live*, which sentimentalised the life of a callous criminal.
[567, 947]

GRAHAM, ERIC STANLEY GEORGE

New Zealand mass murderer who became the subject of that country's greatest manhunt in 1941.

Graham had a reputation as a quarrelsome neighbour in Koiterangi where he ran a dairy farm. His attempts to breed pedigree cattle failed, and with failure came a change in personality. He was withdrawn and bad-tempered and given to violent exhibitions of anger.

On 7 October 1941, he had a disagreement with a neighbour and threatened him with a gun. Graham was acknowledged as an excellent marksman. The incident was reported to the police who sent an officer up to the farm to warn Graham about this intimidating behaviour. The policeman was treated with abuse and called for back-up. Three other officers arrived at the farm and Graham confronted them holding a rifle. They tried to persuade him to surrender the weapon but his reply was to begin shooting.

In the space of minutes, three police officers lay dead, another was fatally injured and a neighbour who had tried to help was also shot. Graham made off into the bush where his experience as a hunter would be an asset. He returned at night to his farm only to find it occupied by soldiers, two of whom he shot dead while being injured himself.

On 12 October, Graham was spotted and wounded again in an exchange of fire. By this time, a manhunt of massive proportions had been mounted and Graham was finally cornered on 15 October when he was fatally wounded by a policeman and died in hospital. [*991*]

GRAHAM, JOHN GILBERT

Like his namesake, **Barbara Graham**, the man who planted a bomb on an aircraft which destroyed forty-four lives was intent on proclaiming that he had a deprived childhood.

On 1 November 1955, a United Airlines flight took off from Denver bound for Alaska. Ten minutes into its journey, the aircraft exploded, killing everyone on board. Aviation inspectors examining the wreckage determined that the bomb had been planted in a piece of luggage taken on board when it stopped at Denver.

One of the passengers who had boarded at Denver was Daisy King, who had been visiting her son and daughter-in-law before flying north. Her son, John Gilbert Graham, had insured his mother for $37,000. Graham confessed to the crime which had involved placing a bomb wrapped as a Christmas gift in his mother's luggage.

Graham showed no remorse, bearing in mind the enormity of his crime, and was concerned only that the world should realise the resentment he felt over his disadvantaged childhood. He had been placed in an orphanage by his mother after she had been widowed an although she remarried and tried to make it up to her son, her efforts were never good enough. In any case, Graham had resorted to crime, mostly theft and forgery, and nurtured an abiding hatred of his mother.

At his trial, he tried to withdraw his confession but the damage had already been done. He was found guilty of the crime which had created public outrage and was sentenced to death. Before going to the gas chamber on 11 January 1957, he rejoiced in his mother's death.

[*84, 616*]

GRAVES, Dr THOMAS THATCHER

New Hampshire doctor convicted of poisoning one of his patients for gain who took his own life by poison while awaiting a retrial.

Josephine Burnaby was the widow of a successful businessman in Providence, Rhode Island. The couple lived apart and, when Mr Burnaby died, he left only a small allowance for his wife. With the help of Dr Graves, the widow contested the will and secured the greater part of her late husband's wealth. Out of gratitude, Josephine Burnaby granted the doctor power of attorney.

Having dispatched Mrs Burnaby to California for her health, Dr Graves began systematically to plunder her assets. When she grew suspicious, he threatened to have her declared *non compos mentis.* Nevertheless, at the end of 1892, she announced that she was returning home and proposed to take charge of her affairs. She broke her return journey in Denver, Colorado to visit a friend. It was there that she received through the mail a mysterious package containing a bottle of whisky. With it was a note saying, 'Wish you a Happy New Year's. Please accept this fine old whisky from your friend in the woods.'

Mrs Burnaby and her friend drank some of the whisky and, within six days, both were dead. The two women had been poisoned and the whisky was suspected. Because of the ill-feeling created by his attempts to fleece Mrs Burnaby, Dr Graves was suspected of having procured the deaths. He was charged with murder but there was little evidence against him. Nevertheless, a witness came forward at his trial who claimed that Dr Graves had asked him to write the note which had been sent with the whisky.

Graves was virtually tried and condemned by the press before he was found guilty by a trial jury. He successfully appealed against the death sentence and in April 1893 was awaiting a retrial when he took a fatal dose of poison.

[*196*]

GREEN RIVER MURDERS: (see under **Ridgway, Gary)**

GREENWOOD CASE

Harold Greenwood's wife died of arsenic poisoning in 1919 and he was acquitted of the charge of murdering her.

Greenwood, aged forty-five, practised as a solicitor in the Welsh town of Llanelly. His wife came from a wealthy family and the couple lived in style at Kidwelly. Despite indifferent health, Mabel Greenwood was active in the community and was well respected. Her husband, on the other hand, had a reputation as a ladies' man and was not well liked.

After eating Sunday lunch on 15 June 1919, Mabel became unwell. She had heart pains and later suffered vomiting and diarrhoea. She was attended by her general practitioner who suspected food poisoning. Mrs Greenwood died early the following morning.

After the funeral, rumours of foul-play began to circulate and Harold Greenwood lived up to his reputation as a ladies' man by remarrying a few months later. As a result of mounting concern, it was decided in April 1920 to exhume Mabel Greenwood's body. Arsenic was found in her corpse and a coroner's inquest concluded that she had died of acute arsenical poisoning administered by her husband.

Harold Greenwood was tried at Carmarthen Assizes in November 1920 where he was defended by Sir Edward Marshall Hall. It was contended that Mrs Greenwood had drunk a glass of wine from a bottle that had been doctored with arsenic by her husband. This allegation was undermined by the testimony of Greenwood's daughter who had drunk a glass of wine from the same bottle.

Greenwood was acquitted but died in reduced circumstances nine years later. His case is invariably compared with that of Major **Armstrong**, another solicitor charged with murdering his wife with arsenic.

[*1048*]

GREENWOOD, DAVID

A military badge and a button were the evidence which convicted an ex-soldier of murder on Eltham Common, London in 1918.

On 9 February 1918, sixteen-year-old Nellie Trew was reported missing by her father. The following morning, the young girl's body was found not far from her home on Eltham Common in the London borough of Greenwich. She had been raped and strangled. Near the body police officers found a military badge depicting the motif of the Leicestershire Regiment and a button with a piece of wire attached.

Illustrations of the button and badge were widely reproduced in the newspapers and, as a result, a man who worked at a factory in Oxford Street spoke to one of his work-mates. Twenty-one-year-old David Greenwood was in the habit of wearing a Leicestershire Regiment badge and his colleague noticed that he no longer had it. Greenwood explained that he had sold it and was advised to report the incident to the police.

Shown the badge found at the murder scene, Greenwood admitted it was his but said he had sold it to a man he met on a tram. Police officers noted that Greenwood's overcoat was bereft of buttons and that, in the bottom position, there was a tear as if the button had been pulled off. Suspicion against Greenwood was confirmed when the wire still attached to the button found on Eltham Common was shown to be the same kind of wire used in his place of employment.

Greenwood was tried for murder and the jury found his explanations for losing the button and badge unconvincing. The former soldier who had suffered in the First World War trenches was found guilty and sentenced to death. He was subsequently reprieved and his sentence commuted to life imprisonment.

[*434, 448*]

GRIFFITHS, PETER

A case of child murder made notable on account of the successful use of mass fingerprinting as the means of capturing the murderer.

Staff on the children's ward of the Queen's Park Hospital in Blackburn were disturbed to see an empty cot early on the morning of 14 May 1948. Four-year-old June Anne Devaney was missing and a frantic search of the hospital and grounds resulted in the discovery of her body in a nearby field. She had been sexually assaulted and her head smashed by swinging her against a stone wall.

The polished floor around the empty cot bore the imprints of stockinged feet. More significantly, a Winchester quart bottle had been moved on a trolley, probably by the murderer, leaving behind a set of fingerprints. Once impressions belonging to hospital staff had been eliminated, the police were left with those of the murderer.

In order to identify the murderer, senior police officers decided to fingerprint the entire male population of Blackburn. This massive undertaking involved taking over 46,000 sets of fingerprints and comparing them with the crime prints. On 12 August 1948, this gamble paid dividends, when prints number 46253 matched those found at the hospital. The owner of the matching fingerprints was Peter Griffiths, a twenty-two-year-old former Irish Guardsman, then working at a local flour mill.

After consuming eleven pints of beer, Griffiths had broken into the hospital and silently abducted June Anne Devaney. He admitted hitting her head against the wall in order to make her quiet. At his trial at Lancaster Assizes, he pleaded insanity as the result of schizophrenia. The jury found him guilty and he was hanged at Walton Prison on 19 November 1948. He had told police officers, 'I hope I get what I deserve.'

[*158, 349*]

GRIGGS CASE

Unsolved Australian murder in which, after two trials, a clergyman was acquitted of poisoning his wife with arsenic after he took a lover.

Ronald Geeves Griggs married in 1926 after he had graduated from theological college and moved to Omeo in Victoria, where he practised as a Methodist minister. He was an active clergyman, travelling the length and breadth of his parish to administer the gospel. As a result, his wife was left on her own a great deal and there was talk among the parishioners that their minister's marriage was in trouble.

This appeared to be confirmed when Griggs was regularly seen in the company of the nineteen-year-old daughter of a local farmer. Even though his wife, Ethel, was pregnant, Griggs continued to see Lottie Condon and occasionally slept overnight at the farm. Not surprisingly, Ethel Griggs complained about her husband's behaviour but to no avail. In July 1927, she decided to go home to Tasmania for a while.

Soon after Ethel returned to Omeo, she became ill and died suddenly. Her demise was attributed to the excitement of returning home combined with the effects of the intensely hot weather. After the funeral, tongues wagged and the authorities ordered that her body be exhumed. Traces of arsenic were found and Ronald Griggs was charged with murder.

The prosecution case relied heavily on circumstantial evidence and it was pointed out that Griggs had ready access to poisons through the farming community. He admitted his extra-marital liaison and it was suggested that his wife took her own life in an act of desperation. The judge was obliged to order a retrial when the jury failed to agree a verdict. A Not Guilty verdict was reached at Griggs's second trial at Melbourne in April 1928.

[*127*]

GROESBEEK, MARIA

An attempt by a wife who used poison to intimidate her husband into granting a divorce ended in murder.

Maria and Christiaan Buys married in 1953 and, for the next seventeen years, led an itinerant life. Their marriage suffered because of the constant upheaval of moving home and arguments ensued about Maria's alleged waywardness.

When twenty-year-old Gerhard Groesbeek came into Maria's life, she was immediately smitten. The young railwayman had been a friend to her husband from whom she now demanded a divorce. Buys refused and there were allegations that he beat his wife.

This *ménage à trois* culminated in the unexpected death of Buys on 14 February 1969. He was taken ill with severe gastric symptoms and admitted to hospital where he died several weeks later. Tests carried out by hospital doctors confirmed that he had died of arsenical poisoning.

Maria lost no time in marrying Groesbeek, but their wedded bliss was interrupted by the police who arrested them both on charges of murder. Maria had bought a proprietary arsenical antkiller in February 1969 and admitted dosing her husband with it. She claimed that she just wanted to make him sick so that he would consent to give her a divorce.

She and her new husband were tried separately. At Bloemfontein in November 1969, Maria was found guilty of murder and sentenced to death. Gerhard Groesbeek was acquitted. Almost exactly a year later, on 13 November 1970, Maria Groesbeek was hanged.

[65]

GRUPEN, PETER

The shooting of two young girls in a remote Silesian castle led to accusations of sexual perversion and murder against the stepfather of one of the victims.

Peter Grupen had fought with the German army at the battle of Verdun and, after the war, made a living as a speculator. In 1921, he visited Silesia where his twelve-year-old step-daughter, Ursula, was staying with her cousin. At the age of fourteen, cousin Dorothea lost both her parents and inherited Kleppelsdorf Castle. The young girl was guided by her grandmother and looked after by a governess. Grupen stepped into this strange environment where he exerted a powerful influence over the two girls.

Drama ensued on 21 February 1921 when both girls were found dead. They had been shot, Ursula supposedly killing Dorothea and then shooting herself. A note had been left which read, 'I shot Dörte first and then myself . . . Your unhappy Ursel'. There were a number of doubts about the shooting because the wounds did not appear to have been inflicted at close range. Also, the revolver used in the incident had the safety catch in the on position.

Suspicion fell on Grupen who, it was rumoured, had been involved in sexual activities with the girls. He was tried for murder at Hirschberg in December 1921 and a story of a Svengali-like personality emerged. He was in the habit of having sex with servants and members of his family. It was suggested that he used hypnosis to persuade his victims to become his slaves. Dorothea resisted his advances and paid with her life while Ursula took the blame for her death.

The evidence, although riveting for a 1920s reading public, was highly circumstantial. Nevertheless, Grupen was found guilty and, protesting his innocence to the end, was executed in January 1922.
[*383*]

GUAY, ALBERT

Twenty-three passengers on a Quebec Airways flight perished when a bomb placed on board by Albert Guay and his confederates exploded in mid-air.

The DC-3 aircraft was en route from Montreal north to Seven Islands in the mouth of the St Lawrence River on 9 September 1949 when disaster struck. The plane crashed on the slopes of Cap Tourmente, killing everyone on board. Crash investigators viewing the wreckage concluded that an explosion had occurred in the left-side forward baggage hold.

The aircraft had made a stop at Quebec when this hold was emptied of luggage on arrival and then reloaded. Among the items loaded was a parcel addressed to Alfred Plouffe at St Baie Comeau. A baggage handler reported that the parcel was checked in by a middle-aged woman who he remembered because of her size and raven-black hair. Inquiries showed that Alfred Plouffe did not exist.

The police carefully reviewed the passenger list and also checked their insurance cover. They hesitated over the name Rita Guay when they learned that her husband, a jeweller in Quebec, had been fined for illegal possession of a firearm. Local police reports mentioned that Albert Guay had a mistress, whose description matched that of the woman who had checked in the parcel. She was Marguerite Pitre who had at one time worked in an armaments factory. Her brother, Genereux Ruest, a crippled watchmaker, worked for Guay.

All these elements confirmed suspicion against thirty-two-year-old Albert Guay who was brought to trial. He was found guilty of murder and sentenced to death. Before being executed on 12 January 1951, he made a full confession of the plot to kill his wife for her insurance. Ruest and Pitre were tried separately and found guilty. They were executed in 1952 and 1953.
[*386, 763*]

H

HAARMANN, FRITZ

Serial killer who preyed on young vagrants in Hanover during the years of Germany's economic collapse after the First World War.

Haarmann had been dismissed from the army before the war ended in 1918 and lived on his wits. He suffered from epilepsy and existed by a combination of theft and informing. He was useful to the police who were on the look-out for deserters.

Acting as an informer provided Haarmann with an opportunity to pick up young refugees arriving at Hanover railway station. Pretending to be a police officer, and assisted by Hans Grans, a young criminal, he gained the confidence of potential victims with promises of food and shelter. Once in the seclusion of his lodgings at Neuestrasse, the victims were sodomised before being murdered and cut up for meat to be sold at the market. Their clothes were also sold.

It was estimated that between 1918 and 1924 the 'Hanover Butcher' killed fifty young men; towards the end of his murder spree, Haarmann was killing twice a week. He attracted the attention of the police in July 1922 when he was accused of indecent behaviour. A search of his lodgings revealed clothing belonging to missing persons. At the same time, boys playing by the river found a discarded sack of human bones. These proved to have come from twenty-three different individuals.

Haarmann had no hesitation in naming Grans as his accomplice and readily made a confession. At his trial in Hanover in 1924, Haarmann was found guilty of murder and was sentenced to death. Grans was given a twelve-year prison sentence. Before his execution by decapitation, Haarmann made a further detailed

confession in which he admitted killing for the pleasure it gave him. Although convicted of twenty-seven murders, he claimed at least forty.
[*244, 569*]

HAIGH, JOHN GEORGE

Britain's notorious 'Acid Bath Murderer' who killed for profit.

Haigh came from a restrictive family background in which religion played a major part. As an adult he threw off the restraints and adopted a work-shy attitude. He became a petty criminal and a smooth entrepreneur preying on the unsuspecting.

His murderous career came to light in 1949 following the disappearance of a wealthy widow, Mrs Durand Deacon, from the Kensington Hotel in London. It was known that he had invited her to visit his factory in Crawley, Sussex on 18 February. When detectives visited the premises, they found large quantities of sulphuric acid and a recently fired revolver.

Forty-year-old Haigh told the police he had destroyed Mrs Durand Deacon with acid and taunted them by saying, 'You can't prove murder without a body.' He had reckoned without the skill of the pathologist who found gall-stones and bone fragments from the victim in the sludge from the 40-gallon oil drum used as an acid bath, together with her acrylic denture.

In a statement to the police Haigh admitted other murders. In 1944 he killed Donald McSwann and, after extorting money from his victim's parents, murdered them too. In 1948, he murdered Dr Archie Henderson and his wife at his Crawley factory. In every case, he claimed to have destroyed his victims' bodies in acid.

Haigh was tried at Lewes Assizes in July 1949 and pleaded an insanity defence. Newspapers of the day made much of his claims to have drunk his victims' blood but his careful planning indicated a calculating mind at work. The jury had little difficulty in deciding their verdict, taking a mere seventeen minutes to find Haigh guilty. He was hanged at Wandsworth Prison on 10 August 1949.
[*116, 141, 257, 468, 538, 874*]

HALL, ARCHIBALD THOMPSON

So-called 'Monster Butler' who murdered a former Member of Parliament and his wife in order to pilfer their valuable antiques.

Hall had worked professionally as a butler and had all the

credentials of that calling, including natural charm which he could switch on and off as required. He also had a prison record for theft. In November 1977, using impeccable references, he obtained a position as butler in the home of Walter Scott-Elliot, an elderly former MP.

Scott-Elliot was a wealthy man who lived in a flat at Knightsbridge surrounded by antiques and works of art. Mrs Scott-Elliot was arthritic and not very mobile. The new butler quickly enlisted two assistants, Mary Coggle, his mistress, and Michael Kitto, a thief, to help him carry out a robbery.

On 8 December 1977, Kitto was smuggled into the flat but his appearance disturbed Mrs Scott-Elliot who was callously suffocated with a pillow. Her husband, sleeping in another room, was unaware of what had happened. On the following day, Mr Scott-Elliot was drugged and put into a car with Mary Coggle who pretended to be his wife. Mrs Scott-Elliot's body was stuffed into the car-boot and the gang drove north with their victims.

Mrs Scott-Elliot's body was disposed of en route to Scotland and her husband was later beaten to death with a garden spade and buried. Between these incidents, Hall and Kitto returned to London and ransacked the Knightsbridge flat. When Mary Coggle failed to comply with Hall's wishes over the disposal of a mink coat, she too was murdered.

The two murderers sold some of the proceeds of their robbery and, with money to spend, stayed with Hall's brother in Cumbria over Christmas. Donald Hall's curiosity cost him his life, when he was killed for asking too many questions. With his body in the boot of their car, the pair headed north again. They broke their journey at a hotel in North Berwick whose manager was suspicious of them. He called the police to run a check on their car which proved to have false registration plates.

The body in the boot was discovered when police arrived to question Hall and Kitto. The two men were tried for murder at Edinburgh, and Hall survived a suicide attempt while in custody. He made a full confession and, with Michael Kitto, was found guilty and sentenced to life imprisonment. Hall died in Kingston Prison, Portsmouth in 2002.

[*204, 391, 595*]

HALLS-MILLS CASE

Celebrated American unsolved double murder in which a church minister and a choir singer were the victims.

A couple out walking in New Brunswick, New Jersey on 16 September 1922 stumbled across the bodies of a man and a woman under an apple tree in a lovers' lane. They were lying on their backs and had been shot in the head. There were letters strewn about the scene.

The man was forty-one-year-old Edward Charles Wheeler Hall, rector of St John's Episcopal Church, who had been shot once. His fellow victim was thirty-four-year-old Mrs Eleanor Mills, wife of the church sexton, who had been shot three times and had her throat cut. The letters had been written by Mrs Mills to the minister who was known to hold her in high affection.

The investigation of the double murder made little progress despite the colourful intervention of a widow, known as the 'Pig Woman'. Mrs Gibson kept pigs at her place near the murder scene and claimed that she saw four people on the night of 14 September arguing in the lovers' lane. Shots and screams followed.

There was a sensational development in 1926 when a witness came forward who claimed that the minister planned to elope with Mrs Mills. It was alleged that his wife, Frances Hall, became aware of his intentions and, with her two brothers and a cousin, conspired to kill the couple. Mrs Hall and her supposed co-conspirators were arraigned for murder in a high-profile trial at Somerville, New Jersey in November 1926. The 'Pig Woman' was the star prosecution witness who created a scene in court and was removed, shouting, 'I've told the truth, so help me God, and you know it . . .' Mrs Hall made a calm denial of the charges and, with the other three accused, was acquitted. After the sensations of the trial, she disappeared from public view, leaving the murders unsolved.

[*98, 536, 918*]

HAMILTON, THOMAS

The shooting dead of sixteen children and their teacher in the Scottish town of Dunblane in 1996 is considered to be one of the worst instances of mass murder. While many other cases have involved higher numbers of victims, it was the deliberate targeting of children which put this incident into a different category. (see also **Columbine High School Killings**).

Thomas Hamilton, the perpetrator of the killings and a resident of Dunblane, had long been regarded locally as a strange individual, earning the nickname of 'Mr Creepy'. He was a loner who failed in his efforts to establish himself as a youth worker both in the scouts and boys club movement. His pursuit of this ambition had led to complaints from parents of boys placed in his care. He was a closet paedophile whose actions were at times brutal and demonstrated a great desire to dominate his charges. He insisted that they changed their clothes in his presence and took photographs of the boys in their swimming trunks. Police enquiries followed complaints about his behaviour from parents. While no action was taken, this brought his youth work to an end.

Hamilton nursed feelings of resentment, believing he was the victim of prejudice. He contacted the local council, badgered his Member of Parliament and even wrote to the Queen about his perceived grievances. When he joined the local shooting club he was seen to practise his marksmanship on every possible occasion. His application for a firearms certificate resulted in an interview with the police but he was not prevented from acquiring guns and ammunition.

On 13 March 1996, Hamilton drove to Dunblane Primary School. He stopped to cut telephone lines which he mistakenly thought served the school but were actually those of nearby houses. He then entered the gymnasium armed with two semi-automatic pistols, two revolvers and 700 rounds of ammunition. He interrupted a class of five and six year olds and began shooting at them from the doorway. As the children lay dying and injured, he cold-bloodedly walked among them firing further shots into their bodies. Leaving the gymnasium, he fired randomly at anyone within range before returning to the scene of carnage and killing himself with a bullet to the head. He had killed sixteen children and one teacher and wounded another seventeen.
[*1045*]

HAMMERSMITH NUDES MURDERS

The victims of an unsolved series of murders in London in the mid 1960s were stripped naked and left for dead in locations close to the River Thames. The victims were also prostitutes which led to newspaper references to 'Jack the Stripper'.

The first murder victim was thirty-year-old Hannah Tailford whose body was found near Hammersmith Bridge on 2 February 1964. Between then and January 1965, the murderer claimed another five victims. The last was twenty-eight-year-old Bridie O'Hara whose body was found on 11 February on a factory site. The victims had either been strangled or suffocated and the bodies of the last four had tiny particles of paint on them.

The evidence of the paint spots suggested that the naked bodies of the victims had been kept in locations where paint spraying was carried out. Analysis of the paint traces indicated that the paint was of a type used for car-spraying.

The detectives began to build up a pattern of timings which they hoped would point to the identity of the murderer. It was known that the victims had disappeared from their usual haunts at night between 11.00 pm and 1.00 am the following morning. It was judged that their bodies were dumped in the early hours of the morning between 5.00 and 6.00 am.

This pattern indicated that the murderer was most likely a man who worked regular night-shift hours and inquiries proceeded along those lines. When the police learned of the suicide of a forty-five-year-old security worker in south London who had a paint shop on his patrol, they made the connection to the murders. The man had left a note saying he could not take the strain any longer. He was never named but John du Rose who led the murder hunt said, 'I know the identity of Jack the Stripper – but he cheated me of an arrest by committing suicide.'

[*609*]

HANRATTY, JAMES

His conviction and execution in 1962 for the A6 murder is widely regarded as a miscarriage of justice.

Michael Gregston was shot dead and his lover Valerie Storie was raped and left for dead on a lay-by on the A6 road in Bedfordshire on 22 August 1961. The couple had been in their parked car near Slough in Buckinghamshire when they were menaced by a man with a gun. He sat in the back seat and ordered them to drive away. After travelling north for about thirty miles, he told Gregston to pull into a lay-by on the A6 at a spot known as Deadman's Hill. There, he shot Greston dead and, after raping his companion, fired at her several times before driving away.

Although badly injured, Valerie Storie was able to describe the gunman sufficiently for the police to issue an Identikit picture. A second Identikit picture was published, based on the description of a man seen driving Greston's car which was found abandoned at Ilford in Essex. The murder weapon was discovered on a London bus, and two .38 cartridge cases linked to it were found in a London hotel room. The room had been occupied on the night before the murder by James Hanratty using an alias. On the night of the murder, the room had been used by Peter Alphon.

Hanratty was arrested in Blackpool on 9 October. Despite his lack of resemblance to the Identikit pictures, he was identified as the A6 attacker. Peter Alphon, who did resemble the Identikit description, was not picked out on an identity parade.

Hanratty claimed an alibi which placed him in Liverpool at a time that made it impossible for him to be the murderer. First he refused to name witnesses who could corroborate his alibi and then he changed his story, saying he had been in Rhyl. After lengthy deliberation, the jury found him guilty and he was hanged at Bedford on 4 April 1962.

Public disquiet over Hanratty grew and a number of voices suggested that an innocent man had been hanged. The Home Office was disinclined to reopen the case but in 1967, after hinting that he was the murderer, Peter Alphon made a confession. He said he had been offered money to end the relationship between Gregston and Valerie Storie. The plan was to frighten them but the gun was fired accidentally, killing Gregston. Alphon said that Hanratty, a known petty criminal, was framed for the murder.

Despite various books and television documentary programmes setting out the case against Alphon, who has continued to utter confessions, no official action has been taken.

In April 2002, the Court of Appeal heard submissions that Hanratty's conviction was fatally flawed. The appeal was based on alleged non-disclosure of evidence by the police and insufficient weight given to Hanratty's alibi. Also, traces of DNA had been discovered on garments that were mislaid until 1991. These were compared with samples of DNA taken from Hanratty's body which was exhumed in 2001. The results of the tests on the DNA ruled out Alphon as a suspect and the appeal judges concluded that the new evidence provided certain proof of Hanratty's guilt.

[*88, 294, 409, 659, 806, 1003*]

HANSEN, ROBERT

Respected businessman in Alaska who became a serial killer with a lust for hunting humans. He admitted to murdering seventeen women after raping and torturing them. His ten-year reign of terror from 1973 to 1983 was brought to an end by a girl who managed to escape his clutches.

Hansen picked up a seventeen-year-old prostitute in the red light district of Anchorage and invited her to his home in a quiet suburb. He took her down to the basement where she was handcuffed before being tortured and sexually assaulted. He told her he was going to fly her out to his cabin in a remote woodland, explaining that he often took girls there before killing them. As they were about to board his private aircraft, his captive broke loose and ran away to safety.

The girl reported her ordeal to the police and led them to the house where she had been held. Knowing the owner to be a respected businessman, the police were disbelieving at first although they knew Hansen was a keen hunter who flew his own plane. When he was questioned, Hansen's denials were accepted as he had an alibi for the time in question which was corroborated by friends.

A few months later, against a background in which several women employed in local bars and clubs had disappeared, hunters reported the discovery of two shallow graves about twenty-eight miles from Anchorage. When the bodies were identified and proved to be two of the missing women, the police reviewed the statement made by the girl thought to have been abducted by Hansen. Further questioning of his friends resulted in their withdrawal of support for his alibi. A search of Hansen's house turned up a map of the area with various locations marked, two of which corresponded with shallow grave sites.

Hansen was arrested on charges of kidnapping and rape. He offered to plead guilty to four murders if he could be saved from further prosecutions. He made a taped confession in which he admitted killing seventeen women, although the true number may well have been greater. His technique was to submit his victims to rape and torture in his remote cabin and then turn them loose so that he could hunt and kill them.

In February 1984, he was sentenced to a total of 461 years' imprisonment.

[*250, 340*]

HARRIS, CARLYLE

An aspiring doctor who was found guilty of murdering his girl-friend with morphine in New York in 1891.

Twenty-three-year-old Harris, still only a medical student, prescribed drugs for his teenage girl-friend, Helen Potts, to treat her insomnia. As a result of taking his specially made capsules, she died at her boarding school in New York.

It emerged later that Harris had married nineteen-year-old Helen Potts in secrecy, after she had an abortion. According to the girl's outraged mother, Helen had a weak heart and Mrs Potts proclaimed that Harris had no right administering medicine to her. She accused him outright of murder.

In a show of confidence, Harris offered his capsules containing quinine to the authorities for analysis. He was nevertheless indicted for murder and stood trial in New York in January 1892. His reputation as a gambler and ladies' man had been exposed by the newspapers and the prosecution argued that he simply wanted to dispose of his wife. It was alleged that he had put morphine in one of the capsules he had made up for Helen.

Most of the trial was taken up with medical evidence. Morphine had been found in the dead girl's body and the doctor who examined her reported that she had pin-pointed pupils. This was the widely recognised sign of morphine poisoning. Harris did not give evidence and an acquittal was widely expected as it was not thought possible to convict him on the evidence.

He was nevertheless found guilty of first-degree murder and sentenced to death. Harris went to the electric chair at Sing Sing on 8 May 1893. His mother had a plate attached to his coffin declaring that he had been murdered. The Harris case was said to have influenced **Dr Robert Buchanan**, who believed he knew how to commit the perfect murder with morphine.

[97]

HARRIS, JEAN

Schoolteacher who shot and killed her lover, Dr Herman Tarnower, the internationally known author of *The Scarsdale Diet*, in 1980.

Fifty-seven-year-old Jean Harris was head teacher of a private school for girls in Virginia. She had a relationship with Dr Tarnower which lasted fourteen years but appeared to be coming to an end when the sixty-nine-year-old doctor devoted his attention to a younger woman.

Jean Harris had reached a crossroads where she felt her career was in decline and then had been rejected by her long-time lover. In a state of deep depression, she made the long drive from Virginia to Tarnower's home in Westchester, New York State on 10 March 1980. She had made her will and, with a .32 revolver in her purse, was ready for an emotional showdown.

Late that evening, she confronted Tarnower and fatally shot him. She was found cradling him in her arms on the floor of the bedroom. She told police officers, 'I did it.' Her explanation was that in a mood of depression she produced the gun and asked Tarnower to kill her. He struggled to dispossess her of the weapon which discharged accidentally. Four shots were fired.

When she was tried for murder, Jean Harris persisted with her defence of an accidental killing. It came to light that she had written a letter to Tarnower in which she poured out her bitter grievances and lavished jealous scorn on his new woman friend. It also emerged that Tarnower had prescribed drugs to help her cope with the stresses of her job and, for ten years, had been taking the stimulant, methamphetamine.

It took the jury eight days to reach a verdict of guilty of second-degree murder. Jean Harris was sentenced to fifteen years' imprisonment. She was granted a pardon in 1992.

[*10, 222, 396, 927*]

HAUPTFLEISCH, PETRUS STEPHANUS FRANÇOIS

A butcher who killed his mother because she tried to curb his drinking habits.

Forty-year-old Hauptfleisch, an aptly named slaughterer, worked in Richmond in Cape Province, South Africa. He had been married but his wife and daughter left him on account of his heavy drinking and the violence which followed. He went to live with his widowed mother but continued in his former violent ways.

In a drunken rage he threatened to stone his mother to death and a few days later, on 13 January 1924, he told neighbours that she had been burned while cleaning the fire. The sixty-seven-year-old woman was found precariously perched across the top of the kitchen stove. She was dead and had sustained severe burns to the face and chest.

Hauptfleisch explained that she had been in the process of cleaning the flue with petrol which ignited with fatal results. It was plain to the doctor called to the scene that the victim was dead, probably from asphyxiation, before being burned.

Hauptfleisch protested his innocence but his use of his mother's money to pay for his legal defence did nothing to endear him to the public. At his trial in Cape Town the prosecution reconstructed events at the Hauptfleisch home when the slaughterer suffocated his mother in bed and, in a bungled attempt to feign death by fire, placed her body on the kitchen stove and ignited it with petrol.

Found guilty of the unusual crime of matricide, Hauptfleisch was sentenced to death. He was executed on 23 December 1926. [*61, 675*]

HAUPTMANN, BRUNO RICHARD

His conviction for the kidnapping and murder of the Lindbergh baby in 1932 and subsequent execution was probably a miscarriage of justice.

The twenty-month-old son of Charles A. Lindbergh, the pioneering US aviator, was kidnapped from his parents' home in New Jersey on 1 March 1932. A broken wooden ladder used to gain access to the child's room was found outside the house along with a ransom note for $50,000. Spelling errors in the note suggested a foreign origin and the signature was given in the form of two overlapping circles.

The kidnapping created headline news and a nationwide search began to find the missing child. In a letter published in the *Bronx Home News*, Dr John F. Condon offered to act as go-between in any negotiations regarding the return of the child. Two days later he received a reply, crudely written and full of spelling errors. The ransom demand had also been raised to $70,000.

A meeting was arranged and the kidnapper identified himself as 'John'. In order to prove he had the Lindberghs' child, he sent them the baby's night clothes. The kidnapper promised to reveal the child's whereabouts after he received the money. The ransom was handed over and the distraught father was sent on a wild-goose chase to the coast. On 12 May, the baby's body was found in a shallow grave in woods at Mont Rose not far from the Lindbergh home.

Several months later, on 15 September, an alert filling-station attendant in upper Manhattan examined a ten dollar bill he was tendered by a motorist to pay for 98 cents' worth of fuel. He noted the registration number of the car. The bill was from the ransom payment and the motorist was Bruno Hauptmann. He was a thirty-six-year-old German who had illegally entered the USA in 1923. Four days later Hauptmann was arrested at his home in the Bronx and over $11,000 of the ransom money was found in his garage.

Hauptmann was tried for kidnapping and murder in January 1935 at Flemington, New Jersey. Public interest in the trial was immense and crowds waited all night for seats in the public gallery. Hauptmann protested his innocence but was identified as 'John', who had negotiated the ransom, and his handwriting was linked to that of the demand notes. He was found guilty and went to the electric chair at Trenton State Prison, New Jersey on 3 April 1936, still proclaiming his innocence.

The Lindbergh case continued to be in the news and Anna Hauptmann tried several times to clear her husband's name, claiming that he had been wrongfully convicted. There was little sympathy for this view and the US Court of Appeal rejected it.

In 1985, Ludovic Kennedy, the campaigner for justice, in a new book on the case, maintained that Hauptmann had been the victim of faked evidence and false testimony. In a book published in 1994, Noel Behn re-examined the affair and concluded that Hauptmann was not the murderer. He suggested that the Lindbergh baby was killed by his aunt, Elisabeth Morrow, in an act of revenge against his mother. Elisabeth had wanted to marry Lindbergh herself but was passed over in favour of her sister. When Lindbergh realised what had happened, he concocted the kidnap plot to protect his family from scandal and was prepared to allow an innocent man to forfeit his life.

[*195, 292, 513, 818, 954, 969, 970*]

HAY, GORDON

Teenaged youth who raped and strangled a fifteen-year-old girl and was identified by his teeth marks on the victim's body.

Linda Peacock was reported missing from her home in Biggar, Scotland on 6 August 1967. Her body was found the next day in a nearby cemetery. She was partly clothed and a bite mark was clearly visible on her right breast. The police took photographs of the injury which proved to be vital evidence.

A dental specialist who examined the photograph was of the opinion that the attacker could be identified by means of his teeth impressions. Police inquiries concentrated on a local reformatory school for boys and on one youth in particular who had apparently asked his mates to provide an alibi for him.

When he was interviewed, seventeen-year-old Gordon Hay denied any knowledge of the attack on the girl but he agreed to have an impression taken of his teeth. To ensure their procedures were objectively based, the police asked twenty-eight other boys to give dental impressions. Specialists at Glasgow Dental Hospital compared the impressions with the photographed bite marks. The characteristics of Hay's teeth exactly matched the bite marks.

Gordon Hay was tried in January 1968 at Glasgow and pleaded a special alibi defence. His lawyers attempted to have the dental evidence ruled inadmissable. It was argued by the prosecution that Hay had an unusual dental structure which clearly identified him as the person who had attacked Linda Peacock. This pioneering use of forensic dental evidence was accepted.

The jury returned a Guilty verdict and Hay was ordered to be detained during Her Majesty's Pleasure. His appeal was rejected by the High Court of Appeal at Edinburgh.
[*685*]

HEARN CASE

Sarah Ann Hearn was successfully defended by Sir Norman Birkett on a charge of murder by arsenical poisoning.

Mrs Hearn, a middle-aged widow, lived in Lewannick, Cornwall with her ailing sister. After her sister's death, she was befriended by her neighbours, William and Annie Thomas.

On 18 October 1930, Mr and Mrs Thomas invited their lonely neighbour to go out with them for a drive in the country. In preparation for the trip, Mrs Hearn made some sandwiches from a tin of salmon. During the afternoon, they stopped for a picnic on the way home and, shortly afterwards, Mrs Thomas became ill. She was taken to hospital in Plymouth where she died eighteen days later. Hospital pathologists found arsenic in the dead woman's body which led to ugly rumours about Sarah Hearn.

Mrs Hearn's reaction was to leave the locality and she tried to give the impression that she had committed suicide by throwing herself into the sea. In reality she went to Devon where she took up work as a housekeeper. In the meantime her sister's body was exhumed and traces of arsenic were found. Mrs Hearn was traced to Torquay where she was arrested and charged with murder.

At her trial in Bodmin in June 1931, she was defended by Sir Norman Birkett. He proved to the satisfaction of the jury that Mrs Thomas did not die from arsenic-laced salmon sandwiches. With the help of foremost pathologist Sir Sydney Smith, he showed that when arsenic was mixed with tinned salmon it produced a blue effect. He did not believe that anyone would eat a blue sandwich.

Sarah Ann Hearn was acquitted and left the court a free woman whose main ambition was to return to obscurity. The murder of Annie Thomas remained unsolved.

[*258, 982*]

HEARN, JOHN WAYNE

Former Vietnam veteran who placed an advertisement in *Soldier of Fortune* magazine offering his services for high-risk assignments. He received hundreds of replies, many of which asked him to carry out contract killings. In 1985, he committed three murders.

One of the callers was Debbie Banister who lived in Florida. She wanted her husband and brother-in-law killed. Hearn fell in love with Debbie and accepted $10,000 to kill her brother-in-law, Cecil Batie. On 6 January 1985, Hearn shot Batie dead in his Gainsville home. A month later, on 2 February, he shot and killed Joe Banister as he was driving on the highway.

Hearn had spoken several times to Bob Black, a former US Marines officer, who wanted someone to kill his wife. A deal was struck for $10,000 and on 21 February 1985, Hearn laid in wait for Sandra Black at her home in Bryan, Texas. When she entered the house, he shot her dead.

By turning his wife's funeral into a spectacle, Bob Black succeeded in drawing attention to himself. Before he hired Hearn, he had asked four local men if they would kill his wife for him and it was well known that he was pursuing an affair with a woman in Houston. The police were already on Hearn's trail and knew that he had received money from Black.

Arrest warrants were issued for both men. Hearn turned himself in on 15 March 1985 and admitted the two killings in Florida. In June, he pleaded guilty to murder in the first degree and was sentenced to life imprisonment. In April, Debbie Banister was tried for the murder of her husband and sentenced to seventeen years' imprisonment.

In February 1986, Bob Black was convicted of the capital murder of his wife. Hearn was given a second life sentence in return for his trial testimony. Black was executed by lethal injection at Huntsville, Texas on 22 May 1992. He had confessed to hiring Hearn to kill his wife.

Both Hearn and Black were former Marines who wanted to pursue military careers but were thwarted for various reasons. Neither man settled to civilian life. Hearn drifted from job to job and married four times. He also suffered from post-traumatic stress disorder as a result of his three tours of duty in Vietnam. Black, known as 'Crazy Bob', had a reputation for being quick-tempered and in 1976 had been diagnosed as a paranoid schizophrenic.

In January 1987, a lawsuit was brought against *Soldier of Fortune* magazine alleging that its advertisements included 'guns for hire'. In February 1988, a jury found against the magazine, awarding damages totalling $9.4 million to Bob Black's mother and son. This judgement was overturned by appeal in August 1989.

[*365*]

HEATH, NEVILLE GEORGE CLEVELY

The former Royal Air Force officer committed two sadistic murders which created a sensation in Britain at the end of the Second World War.

Since 1936, Heath's career had entailed being made an officer and then disgracing himself. He was cashiered from both the RAF and the Royal South African Air Force for theft and unlawful use of rank. He ended up in London after the war where he frequented the bars and clubs wearing insignia and decorations to which he was not entitled. He was a plausible rogue.

On 21 June 1946, thirty-two-year-old Margery Gardner was found dead in a hotel room in Kensington. She had been beaten and mutilated. Heath wrote to the police saying that he had met Margery Gardner and had agreed to let her use his room while he was out of the hotel. When he returned, he found her dead.

While the police were looking for Heath, the former officer, posing as Group Captain Rupert Brooke, was in Bournemouth luring another woman to her death. He had dinner with twenty-one-year-old Doreen Marshall on 3 July 1946. Her body was found several days later at Branksome Chine. The young woman had been mutilated and beaten.

Still posing as Group Captain Brooke, Heath went to the Bournemouth police to help them with their inquiries. He was instantly recognised and held, pending the arrival of Scotland Yard detectives. Among his effects was a metal-tipped woven leather whip which had been used on both victims.

Heath was tried at the Old Bailey for the murder of Margery Gardner. His defence was that he was insane at the time the murders were committed. This contention was at odds with the planning that went into his crimes. The jury found Heath sane and guilty. He was hanged at Pentonville Prison on 16 October 1946.
[*118, 140, 214, 421, 834*]

HEIDNIK, GARY MICHAEL

Proprietor of Philadelphia's 'House of Horrors' where he kept women captive so that he could torture and rape them daily.

On 24 March 1987, twenty-six-year-old Josefina Rivera escaped from a dilapidated house on North Marshall Street and turned up in an appalling state at her boy-friend's home.

She had been missing for four months and told an horrific story of being held captive in a basement with other women who were systematically tortured and abused.

She told police she had been kidnapped on 26 November 1986 by a bearded, respectably dressed man who drove a Cadillac. She directed them to his house which was guarded by two dogs. Officers forced an entry and arrested Heidnik after two naked women were found chained by their ankles in the filthy basement. A third woman was found shackled in a hole in the floor. All the captives were weak and bruised. They spoke of daily torture and rape committed by Heidnik.

A search of the house revealed human remains in the refrigerator and elsewhere, and a stock of pornographic literature. The starving captives reported that they had been fed minced human flesh blended with dog-food. From their stories, it appeared that at least two girls had been murdered in the house.

Heidnik had the classic serial killer's biography. He came from a broken home. His father was a racist and a heavy drinker who beat his son. The boy did poorly at school and was a loner who dreamed of becoming a millionaire. He joined the army but was discharged in 1963 and given a 100 per cent disability pension because he was diagnosed as schizophrenic.

Heidnik had been in and out of mental hospitals and had attempted suicide on numerous occasions. In 1978, he served a term of imprisonment for sexually abusing a mentally retarded woman. When he was paroled in 1983 he successfully played the stock market and was worth over £300,000 by the time he was arrested.

He also founded the United Church of the Ministries of God and proclaimed himself a bishop. Services were held at his house with a congregation of mentally retarded individuals. Neighbours complained because he played noisy rock music and the sound of an electric saw disturbed their sleep.

Heidnik was tried at Philadelphia and found guilty of two counts of murder and four of rape. His father was reported as saying that he would serve as his executioner and 'hold the rope'. He was sentenced to death and joined the other ninety prisoners on Death Row in Pennsylvania. He was executed by lethal injection on 7 July 1999. [*271*]

HEIRENS, WILLIAM

A teenage offender with disturbing behaviour traits who progressed to murder and was found insane.

Heirens began house-breaking and stealing women's clothing at a young age and was in the habit of carrying a gun. When police went to his home in Chicago, they found a hoard of hidden weapons. After a spell in reform school where he impressed the authorities with his above-average intelligence, he enrolled at Chicago University.

He continued to commit crimes while at university and probably realised that he was losing his mind. In March 1945, he entered an apartment where Josephine Ross lay alseep. He cut her throat and stabbed frenziedly at her body. In October, he attacked another woman in her home, shooting her twice and sticking a bread-knife into her neck. He left a message scrawled in lipstick on the wall: 'For heaven's sake catch me before I kill more I cannot control myself'.

In January 1946, six-year-old Suzanne Degnan was abducted from her home. A ransom note was left demanding $20,000 for her return. Her body was dismembered in a nearby basement and pieces were dropped into the sewers through gratings in the street.

Heirens was caught a few months later when an alert apartment block caretaker spotted an intruder and raised the alarm. At first he denied the killings, insisting they were committed by George Murman, his alter ego. Still only a teenager, Heirens was judged insane and given three consecutive life sentences with the recommendation that he never be paroled.

In 2002 a new investigation into the case of the 'Lipstick Killer' dscribed Heirens's conviction as 'one of the grossest miscarriages of justice in the history of the United States'. His lawyers argued that neither the ransom note nor the lipstick confession were written by him. It also appeared that his confession was published in *The Chicago Tribune* before he had made it.

[*247, 305, 500, 506*]

HEPPER, WILLIAM SANCHEZ DE PINA

Man with an unorthodox background as an artist, BBC translator and agent for the intelligence services who raped and murdered an eleven-year-old girl.

Sixty-two-year-old Hepper was an eccentric character prone to bouts of amnesia as a result of head injuries sustained in a car accident. He had a flat in Brighton with a studio where he painted portraits.

Hepper and his wife were friendly with the Spevick family who lived in London and whose eleven-year-old daughter Margaret had broken her arm. In order to give the child a change of scenery, Mrs Hepper offered to have her stay at Brighton for a few days. The young girl went to Brighton on 2 February 1954 and all was well until the time came for her mother to pick her up. Mrs Spevick called at Hepper's flat which appeared to be deserted. A helpful caretaker let her in and she discovered the dead body of her daughter. The child had been raped and strangled.

Hepper was found three days later at Irun in Spain where he was arrested. Following extradition to England, he appeared on trial for murder at Lewes Assizes in July 1954. He gave evidence on his own behalf, pleading loss of memory and hallucinations and claiming to be sexually impotent. The defence plea of insanity was not easily reconcilable with Hepper's hasty disappearance after the killing.

The portrait painter was found guilty of murder and received sentence of death. He was executed at Wandsworth Prison on 11 August 1954.

[*372, 527*]

HEYS, ARTHUR

Leading Aircraftsman based at a wartime RAF base who raped and murdered a radio operator, knowing that he could be identified as a suspect.

During the night of 8 November 1944, twenty-seven-year-old Winifred Mary Evans was sexually assaulted and suffocated at the RAF base near Beccles in Suffolk. Her body was left lying in a ditch.

Earlier that same evening, a bunch of revellers who had attended a dance returned to their billets but noticed that one of their number, Arthur Heys, was missing. He appeared later in the women's quarters and was chased off by an NCO.

In the manhunt that followed. Heys's indiscretion was reported by the NCO and his alibi broke down completely. He claimed to have been back in his quarters by 12.30 but his fellow airmen said it was later. It was also noted that he had spent an inordinate amount of time cleaning his uniform.

Trace evidence linked Heys to the crime scene and he was charged with murder. While he was in Norwich Prison awaiting trial, his commanding officer received an anonymous letter naming another airman as the murderer. The letter was written in crayon, of a type issued to inmates at Norwich, and contained details of the murder known only to the police and the person who committed it.

Heys was tried for murder at Bury St Edmunds and Superintendent Fred Cherrill proved that the writing in the blue crayon letter was his. The letter, with its intimate details, was the airman's undoing. A married man with young children, Heys was convicted and sentenced to death. His appeal was rejected and Mr Justice Humphreys observed that the letter was as good as a confession.

[*366*]

HICKMAN, EDWARD

College student whose attempt to raise money by kidnap and ransom ended in the murder of a child and one of California's greatest manhunts.

Twelve-year-old Marion Parker was abducted near her home in Los Angeles on 15 December 1927. Shortly afterwards, her father received a ransom demand for $7500 signed by 'The Fox' who warned, 'Very sly you know. Set no traps.'

Other notes followed, headed with the word 'DEATH', and there were letters from Marion. In one she wrote, 'Daddy please do what the man tells you or he'll kill me if you don't' and in another, 'If you don't meet us this morning, you'll never see me again.'

On 17 December, Perry Parker drove to a spot outside the city to exchange the ransom money for the safe return of his daughter. The kidnapper, gesturing to a blanket-wrapped figure in his car, told Parker to give him the money and he would leave the girl further down the road. When Parker reached the bundle left by the roadside, he found the mutilated body of his daughter. She had been strangled and attacked with a knife.

Twenty-three-year-old Edward Hickman was arrested in Seattle when police identified him from a description. He was taken under guard by train to Los Angeles and twice tried to commit suicide on the journey. At his trial for abduction and murder, his plea of insanity was discounted by the jury who found him guilty. The reason he gave for demanding a ransom was to raise $1500 to pay for his college fees. He was hanged on 19 October 1928 at San Quentin Prison.

[155]

HICKOCK AND SMITH

The murders of Herbert Clutter, a Kansas wheat-grower, his wife and two children in 1959 were the basis of Truman Capote's best-selling book *In Cold Blood.*

The Clutters lived at River Valley Farm, Holcomb, Kansas where they were found dead on 15 November 1959. The family had been shot dead at close range with a shotgun after having been bound and gagged. The motive appeared to be robbery and the killers had been sufficiently astute to retrieve the expended cartridge cases before leaving the scene.

The cold-blooded background to the killings emerged from an account given by an inmate of Kansas State Penitentiary. Floyd Wells, who had worked on the Clutter farm, reminisced with fellow inmate Richard Hickock about his background. Hickock showed inordinate interest in the Clutter family and their farm and talked about committing robbery.

After hearing about the murders, Wells feared that Hickock might have carried out his plan. He reported his concerns to the authorities who traced thirty-three-year-old Hickock to Las Vegas. He admitted being present when the murders were committed but blamed the killings on his accomplice, Perry Smith. They believed Clutter kept $10,000 in cash but were disappointed when their robbery produced only $50. Yet they stuck to their plan to eliminate all the witnesses.

At their trial in Kansas City in March 1960, Hickock and Smith disagreed over who did the killing. Hickock blamed Smith for the shootings but admitted that he cut Herbert Clutter's throat. Smith said he killed only Mrs Clutter and her daughter. Anxious that they should not shirk their duty, the prosecutor warned the jury against being 'chicken-hearted'. Both men were found guilty of all four murders. They were hanged at Lansing Prison, Kansas in April 1965.

[*157*]

HILLEY, MARIE AUDREY

Fifty-four-year-old secretary who murdered her husband with arsenic and attempted to murder her daughter before successfully feigning her own death for four years.

After her husband died in 1975 at the age of forty-five from hepatitis, Marie Hilley claimed the $31,140 insurance and bought a few things for herself. She continued to work as a secretary at a foundry in Anniston, Alabama.

Colleagues and friends began to think that she was spending beyond her means and noticed a change in her personality. She developed a persecution complex, complaining to the police about harassing telephone calls and reporting numerous burglaries.

In 1979, her eighteen-year-old daughter, Carol, became ill with a curious wasting disease. She underwent numerous medical tests but the cause remained a mystery. In discussing her problem with a friend, Carol mentioned that her mother had been giving her injections. When a urine sample showed traces of arsenic, the source of the young woman's illness was apparent.

The bodies of Marie Hilley's husband and mother were exhumed and, in both cases, traces of arsenic were found. Marie was charged with the attempted murder of her daughter but she jumped bail and promptly disappeared.

The authorities caught up with her four years later in New Hampshire where she had remarried and perpetrated an amazing fraud. At the height of the police search for Marie Hilley, she told her new husband that she had to go to Houston because a relative had died. There she feigned her death, even to the extent of publishing an obituary, and returned to New Hampshire in the guise of her twin sister, Teri Martin.

She pleaded her innocence of the charges at her trial and an attempt was made to discredit her daughter. She was found guilty of the first-degree murder of her husband and of the attempted murder of her daughter. Marie Hilley was sentenced to life imprisonment, a punishment which she declined to serve. She disappeared in February 1987 while on weekend release and died from exposure.

[*341, 615*]

HINKS, REGINALD IVOR

A vacuum-cleaner salesman who resorted to murder after various other methods of procuring the death of his elderly father-in-law had failed.

Thirty-two-year-old Hinks was working as a salesman in Bath when he met Constance Anne Pullen. She was a divorcee with one child and he courted her assiduously in the knowledge that she would inherit from her eighty-five-year-old father.

Hinks married Anne Pullen in March 1933 and moved into the house where she lived with her child and her aged father. Hinks' first action was to make life difficult for the old man's nurse who soon left. He then began to wheedle money out of Mr Pullen and secured £900 with which he bought a property. Further plans to milk his father-in-law's assets were thwarted by Mr Pullen's solicitor who could see what was going on.

Hinks began taking the frail, senile old man on long walks in Bath, often abandoning him in busy streets full of traffic. Despite his weak condition, James Pullen did not succumb to this callous treatment.

On 1 December 1933, Bath Fire Brigade received a telephone call from Hinks reporting that he had found Mr Pullen in the kitchen with his head in the gas oven. When the police called at the house, he advised them that, should a bruise be found on the back of the old man's head, it probably happened when he pulled him out of the oven.

James Pullen undoubtedly died of gas poisoning but he was already unconscious from a blow to the head administered beforehand. Hinks was arrested and charged with murder. Owing to

strong local feeling, his trial was moved to the Old Bailey in London. The jury found him guilty and he was sentenced to death. He was hanged on 4 May 1934 at Bristol.
[*477, 792*]

HIRASAWA, SADAMICHI

Japan's most celebrated criminal who was convicted of the mass murder by cyanide of twelve bank employees in Tokyo in 1948.

On 26 January 1948, Dr Jiro Yamaguchi presented himself at the Shiinamachi branch of the Imperial Bank. He identified himself as an official of the Tokyo Metropolitan Disinfection Corps and explained that he had orders to treat the staff as part of a campaign to eradicate dysentery.

The bank employees readily fell in with this plan and lined up to swallow pills administered by Dr Yamaguchi. The effect was dramatic for, within seconds, ten of the staff were dead and six others were taken ill, two of whom died later. Dr Yamaguchi grabbed money and cheques worth 180,000 yen and disappeared.

The victims had been poisoned with cyanide and it became known that a Dr Shigeru Matsui had 'immunised' staff at a neighbouring bank a few months previously but with no ill effects. The practice of exchanging business cards gave the police their first clue. Dr Shigeru Matsui had read newspaper reports of the Tokyo bank killings and believed he recognised Dr Yamaguchi as someone he had met. He thought it likely that he had exchanged business cards with him. By a process of elimination, Yamaguchi was identified as the artist, Sadamichi Hirasawa.

Survivors of the bank killings identified Hirasawa as Dr Yamaguchi. After finding medical equipment at Hirasawa's apartment, the artist was arrested and made a confession. He was tried for murder and pleaded partial insanity; he also withdrew his confession on the grounds that he was put under pressure to give it. The court found him guilty and he was sentenced to death.

Hirasawa's lawyer saved him from hanging by arguing that the penalty was contrary to Japanese law which protected individuals from participating in their destruction. The principal was that, to be effective, hanging required the victim's weight to break the spinal cord. Hirasawa thus spent the remainder of his life in prison.

During his long imprisonment of nearly forty years, Hirasawa became a celebrity. He painted and wrote an autobiography while supporters campaigned on his behalf. There were allegations that he was the victim of a plot by the Japanese and American governments to cover up war crimes. The real perpetrator of the bank killings was said to have been a former Japanese army officer who had served in a secret biological warfare unit which carried out assassinations behind the lines using various toxins. Fears that these activities would come to light led to a plot to protect the former officer by finding a scapegoat.

Hirasawa died in 1987 and, despite threats of revenge for his alleged wrongful imprisonment and the unmasking of various treacheries, the Tokyo bank killings remain one of Japan's most intriguing crimes.

[*928*]

HOCH, JOHANN

Multiple bigamist who married for money and either deserted or poisoned his wives, earning himself the title of America's greatest mass murderer in 1906.

Hoch worked in one of Chicago's packing-houses and, between 1892 and 1905, made an industry out of marrying and burying his wives. It was estimated that he went through fifty-five marriages, using advertisements placed in the city's German-language newspapers to contact aspiring brides.

This extraordinary practice might have continued but for the advertisement which he placed in December 1904. Portraying himself as a quiet and home-loving widower, Hoch sought the acquaintance of a 'congenial widow without children'. Julia Walcker, the forty-six-year-old owner of a candy-store, replied and, within days, she became the umpteenth Mrs Hoch.

Marriage to Hoch was always short-lived and Julia Walcker proved no exception; she died four days after taking her wedding vows. A few days later, he married the dead woman's sister, Amelia, and absconded with her savings. Amelia reported him missing and his photograph appeared in the newspapers.

As a result of this publicity, a number of women who had been deserted by Hoch came forward to tell their stories. Little by little, Hoch's amazing career was exposed. When he was arrested, he was carrying a fountain pen filled with arsenic. Exhumation of several of his late wives' bodies showed they had died of arsenical poisoning.

Hoch boldly confessed his bigamous strategy for making money.

Of his many wives, he said, 'When I found they had money, I went after that.' He was tried for the murder of Julia Walcker and found guilty. 'The Stockyard Bluebeard' was hanged on 23 February 1906 at Cook County Jail before a hundred witnesses.
[*871*]

HOFMANN, MARK

Dealer in historic documents who committed the 'Morman Murders' in Salt Lake City in 1985 in order to resolve his financial problems.

On 15 October 1985, Steve Christensen, a thirty-two-year-old businessman and member of the Mormon Church, died in a bomb explosion at his office in Salt Lake City. Ninety minutes after he was killed, there was a second explosion in a suburban district in which Kathy Sheets, wife of millionaire Gary Sheets, lost her life. In both incidents, a parcel bomb had been the instrument of destruction. There was also a link between the victims; Gary Sheets was head of Coordinated Financial Services (CFS), a company in which Steve Christensen had been a vice-president.

The police thought the explosions might be an act of revenge against CFS. On the following day, there was another explosion in Main Street, which seriously wounded thirty-one-year-old Mark Hofmann. He was a dealer in antiquities, with no connections with CFS, but he was linked to Steve Christensen who had bought an historic Mormon document from him in 1984 for $40,000.

Hofmann had a reputation for making spectacular discoveries of rare documents relating to the early history of the Mormon Church, including an item which, if authenticated, was reputedly worth $1.5 million. Hofmann was nevertheless in financial difficulties because he had borrowed money from the church but had defaulted on the repayments.

Try as they might, the police were unable to link Hofmann with the bomb explosions. In 1986, however, they achieved a breakthrough when it was established that many of Hofmann's great discoveries were clever forgeries. Painstaking investigation showed that he had used a false name to commission various engravers' shops to do work for him.

It was shown that Hofmann had procured large sums of money for his forgeries but that his elaborate lifestyle had led him into debt. He borrowed $185,000 from the Mormons to buy an important document but faced bankruptcy because he could neither repay the loan nor produce the document. Christensen had been told to put pressure on the young dealer.

Hofmann's answer was to plant a bomb to kill Christensen and arrange a second explosion, aimed at killing Gary Sheets, in order to make it look like a vendetta against CFS. The third bomb was intended to be his own death by suicide.

Mark Hofmann confessed to the murders in January 1987. He was eventually found guilty and sentenced to life imprisonment. He told the Utah Board of Pardons that his survival and that of his family was more important than the lives of his victims.
[*1055, 1060, 1075*]

HOFRICHTER, ADOLPH

Infantry lieutenant in the Austrian army who reacted vengefully to being passed over for promotion by poisoning a staff officer.

Several General Staff officers stationed in Vienna in December 1909 received postal deliveries containing capsules which promised 'increased potency'. The unsolicited gifts were thrown away by most recipients but Captain Robert Mader decided to try the remedy which promised 'startling results'. The officer was found dead in his quarters by his batman. He had been poisoned with potassium cyanide.

It was found that twelve officers had received boxes of poison-laden capsules. The news reached the ears of Emperor Franz Josef who suspected treason and demanded action. The explanation of the poisoning, while it was dramatic enough, did not have the political connotations that the emperor feared.

Because of the status of the intended victims, army investigators suspected that the poisoner was an officer who had failed to gain promotion. A simple process of elimination led them to twenty-eight-year-old Lieutenant Hofrichter, a married officer, based at Linz. His home was searched and a number of capsule boxes were found.

Pressure was put on Hofrichter to confess which he did after his wife was arrested and charged with being an accessory. Despite withdrawing his confession, the lieutenant appeared at a secret court martial in June 1910. News that his trial would not be held in the civil courts created public concern which was only dispelled by stories that Hofrichter led a debauched life which included drugging young women to make them comply with his desires. Hofrichter was sentenced to death but this was commuted to imprisonment on the grounds that he was 'morally abnormal'. [*383, 1016*]

HOLMES, H.H

Holmes, properly known as Herman Webster Mudgett, killed at least twenty-seven people and ran a virtual murder factory at his hotel in Chicago.

Holmes had a keen interest in human anatomy which led him to become a medical student before he embarked on an amazing career combining hotel-keeping with robbery and murder. In 1888 he worked as a drug-store chemist and took over the business when the proprietor mysteriously disappeared. He lived above the store and shared the accommodation with a jeweller and his wife, Icilius and Julia Conner. Mrs Conner worked as Holmes's secretary.

Using the proceeds from numerous funds, Holmes built a Gothic-style hotel in Chicago at 63rd Street which was completed in 1891. The hundred-room building, known locally as 'Holmes's Castle', welcomed many guests but they did not all survive the experience. Among the visitors who disappeared was Julia Conner.

Holmes next became involved in an insurance fraud with a swindler named Benjamin F. Pitzel. When their plans started to go wrong, the thieves fell out and, like many of Holmes's acquaintances, Pitzel disappeared. The hotelier fled and Pitzel's murdered body was found.

When Holmes was arrested in Philadelphia, the full extent of his activities became known. His hotel was a death factory where some of the rooms had chutes down which murder victims were propelled to the basement. Some rooms were fitted out as gas chambers and others were sound-proofed and equipped with surgical instruments. The basement contained the skeletal remains of several bodies.

Holmes was tried for the murder of Pitzel, and one of the staff at his hotel described helping his employer strip the flesh from human bodies. The hotelier conducted his own defence and changed his confession several times. He admitted twenty-seven murders but the real number was thought to be nearer forty. He was inevitably found guilty and sentenced to death, being hanged at Philadelphia on 7 May 1896.
[*99, 300, 332, 551, 819*]

HOLT, FREDERICK ROTHWELL

Army officer of questioned sanity convicted of murdering his girlfriend on a Lancashire beach in 1919.

After being invalided out of the army, Rothwell worked for a while in Malaya. He returned to his native Lancashire in 1918 where he met Kitty Breaks, a young woman separated from her husband. They fell in love and lived together in an apparent state of romantic bliss. But, on Christmas Eve 1919, Kitty was found dead at St Anne's near Blackpool. Her body lay half buried in the sand dunes; she had been shot three times in the head. Close by was a revolver belonging to Holt, and footprints in the sand matched his shoes.

Holt was charged with murder and sent for trial at Manchester Assizes where he was defended by Sir Edward Marshall Hall. The prosecution argued that Holt murdered the girl for her life insurance which was worth £5000 and because he had tired of her. Marshall Hall countered forcibly with a plea that Holt was insane. There was a history of insanity in his family and his experiences under bombardment in the First World War trenches had left him subject to amnesia and bouts of depression.

Marshall Hall read from letters which had passed between Holt and Kitty Breaks showing a tender relationship. Holt sat emotionless throughout the proceedings as his defence counsel said that he had killed the woman he loved in a moment of irresistible impulse. It was not an argument which found favour with the jury and they brought in a Guilty verdict. When he was sentenced to death, Holt remarked, 'Well, that's over. I hope my tea won't be late.'

The case went to appeal but the verdict was upheld despite the introduction of further evidence regarding Holt's mental state. He was hanged at Strangeways Prison on 13 April 1920.

[*466, 636*]

HOSEIN BROTHERS

Arthur and Nizamodeen Hosein were convicted of murder without a body following the kidnapping of Muriel McKay in 1969.

On 29 December 1969, Mrs McKay, the wife of the deputy chairman of the *News of the World*, was kidnapped from her home at Wimbledon. This was followed by a ransom call to Alick McKay demanding £1 million and threatening to kill his wife if the money was not paid within two days.

In the ensuing weeks the kidnappers made numerous telephone demands and sent Mr McKay letters written by his wife asking him to comply with her abductors' wishes and not to inform the police. In February 1970, Mr McKay received instructions by means of a trail of telephone messages to leave the ransom money in a suitcase at a spot in Bishop's Stortford, Essex. The police laid a careful trap but were thwarted by the unknowing intervention of members of the public who spotted the unguarded suitcase.

The kidnappers failed to pick up the ransom money but were spotted circling in their blue Volvo. The car was traced to thirty-four-year-old Arthur Hosein at Rooks Farm, Stocking Pelham where he lived with his younger brother Nizamodeen. There were no signs of the kidnap victim but a search of the property turned up an exercise book from which one of the ransom notes had been taken. Fingerprints on the ransom notes matched those of the brothers who were charged with kidnapping and murder.

Arthur denied any knowledge of the crime but his younger brother admitted shadowing the Rolls-Royce which Mr McKay used to travel from his office to Wimbledon. The brothers, who were in financial difficulty with their farm, had targeted the Rolls-Royce which was regularly used by the *News of the World*'s chairman, Rupert Murdoch. It was the misfortune of the McKay family that the deputy chairman had the use of the car while Mr Murdoch was abroad.

The Hosein brothers were tried at the Old Bailey in September 1970 and found guilty of murder, kidnapping and blackmail. They received sentences of life imprisonment. Muriel McKay's body was never found, despite the most extensive searches at Rooks Farm. It was widely believed that her remains were fed to the pigs at the farm.

[*203, 229, 596, 720*]

HUME, BRIAN DONALD

Tried twice and acquitted of a murder to which he subsequently made a confession in a national newspaper and went on to kill again.

A headless torso was found on the Essex mud flats at Tillingham on 21 October 1949 by a farm labourer hunting wild fowl. The human remains were dressed in a silk shirt and underpants and wrapped in a grey felt parcel tied with rope. There were stab wounds in the chest and the legs had been severed with a sharp knife and saw.

The torso victim was identified as forty-six-year-old Stanley Setty, a car dealer whose fingerprints were on file at Scotland Yard as the result of a conviction for fraud. Setty was known as a black marketeer and, when last seen on 4 October, had completed car deals worth over £1000. One of his associates was Donald Hume, a former serviceman in the Royal Air Force who had a civilian pilot's licence.

When the police checked up on Hume, they learned that he had hired an Auster aircraft at the United Services Flying Club at Elstree on 5 October. He had apparently taken off, carrying two parcels as freight. Hume was finally tracked down and questioned on 26 October. His story was that he had undertaken for a fee of £50 to ditch at sea two parcels containing parts of a printing press used for counterfeiting petrol coupons. When he returned, the two men who paid him asked him to make another trip to dump a single parcel for £100. He described the parcel as bulky and, when he moved it, there was a gurgling noise. He wondered if it might be a body.

None of Hume's story could be corroborated and he was arrested and charged with murder. He was tried at the Old Bailey in January 1950. The prosecution believed that Setty was killed in the living room of Hume's London flat, the carpet from which was taken for cleaning on 5 October. Despite a meticulous search, not a single fingerprint belonging to Stanley Setty was found in the flat. The jury were unable to agree a verdict and were discharged. A new jury was sworn in but the prosecution declined to present any evidence. In consequence, the judge ordered that Hume be found not guilty on the murder charge. He pleaded guilty to being an accessory after the fact and was sentenced to twelve years' imprisonment.

When he was released in 1958, knowing that he could not be charged again with the same offence, Hume confessed to murder. His account was published in the *Sunday Pictorial* under the headline, I KILLED SETTY . . . AND GOT AWAY WITH MURDER. Hume went to live in Switzerland where, on 30 January 1959, he shot and killed a taxi driver in Zurich while escaping from a bank robbery. Subject to Swiss trial proceedings, he was found guilty of murder and sentenced to life imprisonment.

On 20 August 1976, Hume, at the age of fifty-seven, was returned to Britain and, following psychiatric examination, was sent to Broadmoor. Hume died in Broadmoor at the age of sixty-seven, on 19 April 1988.
[*138, 988*]

HUNTLEY, IAN

School caretaker convicted of murdering two ten-year old girls, Jessica Chapman and Holly Wells, at Soham, Cambridgeshire in 2002. His former fiancé, twenty-six year old Maxine Carr, was found guilty of conspiring to pervert the course of justice.

Twenty-nine year old Huntley, a man with a background of sexual offending, took a job as caretaker at Soham Village College in November 2001. Separated from his wife, he lived in Soham with Maxine Carr who was a teaching assistant at the local junior school.

During the evening of 4 August 2002, Jessica and Holly, who were best friends, disappeared from their homes. Huntley said he saw them when they walked past his house. The police mounted a huge search for the missing girls and Huntley helped at police briefings and public meetings. He also gave interviews to the media saying, 'I just pray that they are alive and well'. The *Sun* newspaper offered a reward of £150,000 for information about the disappearances.

Two weeks later, two bodies found in Thetford Forest in Norfolk were identified as Jessica and Holly. By this time, Huntley and Carr were already under arrest following searches made at their house. Huntley's house and car had evidently been 'sanitised' but the key discovery was the missing girls' clothing and related forensic traces in a rubbish bin in the grounds of the school. The caretaker was charged with abduction and murder. He was initially held at Rampton psychiatric hospital but was later transferred to a maximum security prison after being found competent to stand trial.

The Soham murders prompted public anger and crowds gathered to shout abuse at Huntley when he was driven to and from hearings. There were demands for the return of hanging as a punishment for murder. The police also came in for a great deal of criticism for their failure to pass on intelligence between forces about Huntley's history of sex offences going back to 1995.

At his trial at the Old Bailey in December 2003, Huntley was described as a 'latent predatory paedophile'. He was accused of luring the two girls into his home with the intention of assaulting them. There was no forensic evidence of sexual assault on the victims' bodies due to their advanced state of decomposition. The jury brought in a guilty verdict and Huntley was given two sentences of life imprisonment. Carr was jailed for three and a half years for providing a false alibi to protect Huntley.
[*1021, 1051*]

HYDE, Dr BENNETT CLARKE

Physician who presided over the demise of three members of a wealthy family and was tried for murder four times.

Dr Hyde married a niece of Colonel Thomas H. Swope, the American railway millionaire. Hyde was much older than his bride and her parents were not in favour of the marriage. Nevertheless, the wedding went ahead and Hyde joined the Swope family, becoming in due time physician to the eighty-two-year-old Colonel.

The old man entrusted his financial affairs to James Moss Hunton, who became ill in September 1909, and Dr Hyde was asked to attend him. Apoplexy was diagnosed and he died within weeks. Colonel Swope, deeply grieved at the loss of his friend, became ill himself and was given treatment by Dr Hyde. In a very short time, the doctor lost a second patient.

Colonel Swope left about $2 million to various members of his family, including Hyde's wife. One of his wishes was that, if any of the heirs died, that share of his legacy could be divided up among the rest. In the weeks following the deaths of Hunton and Swope, a typhoid epidemic hit the family and six of its members were treated by Dr Hyde. All but one survived.

The remaining members of the family suspected Hyde of murder and called in another doctor. Authority was given to exhume the bodies of Hunton and Swope and traces of strychnine were found in their organs. Gossip led to outright allegations and, following a coroner's inquest on 9 February 1910, Dr Hyde was formally accused of murder.

Medical evidence showed that Hunton and Swope had been poisoned with both cyanide and strychnine, and that one of the nephews had been deliberately infected with typhoid bacteria cultured by Hyde. The doctor was found guilty of first-degree

murder and sentenced to life imprisonment. He immediately appealed and was granted a second trial on the grounds that some of the evidence against him was unreliable. A mistrial occurred and a third trial resulted in the jury's failure to agree a verdict. On a fourth court appearance in January 1917, the charges against Hyde were dropped.
[*21, 320*]

I

INGENITO, ERNEST

Unruly soldier from a poor background whose life was one long brawl which culminated in seven murders in 1950.

Ingenito was dishonourably discharged from the US Army after attacking two officers and served two years in a federal prison. On his release in 1946, he married Theresa Mazzoli whose parents ran a trucking business in Gloucester, Pennsylvania.

The young couple lived with the Mazzoli family but tensions began to mount as Ingenito first argued with his wife and then quarrelled with his in-laws. In particular, he suffered at the hands of his mother-in-law who nagged him about his indolence. His answer was to seek refuge in drink which invariably led to bar-room violence. When Mike Mazzoli found out that Ingenito had been unfaithful to his daughter, he kicked him out of the house.

Following an argument over access to his two children, Ingenito appeared at the Mazzoli home on 17 November 1950 armed with a machine pistol and a carbine. He demanded to see his children but his wife refused. In a whirlwind of shooting, he wounded his wife and killed his father-in-law. He then went in search of his mother-in-law. She had fled the house and sought sanctuary in her parents' home near by. Ingenito followed her there and killed her. He also shot and killed four members of the Pioppi family.

Determined to revenge himself fully on his wife's family, Ingenito drove to the home of Frank Mazzoli in Mintola, New Jersey where he shot and killed Mazzoli and his wife. Theresa Mazzoli survived her husband's attack and called the police. Ingenito was arrested and tried for murder in 1951. He was judged to be insane and was sent to the New Jersey State Hospital for the Insane at Trenton.

[*882*]

IQBAL, JAVED

When he complained to the police in Lahore, Pakistan that he had been mugged and robbed by two boys, Iqbal was incensed when officers dismissed his claim and threatened to investigate him for sodomy. This occurred in June 1998 and he decided to exact his revenge by killing 100 boys. To that end, he recruited three accomplices; a twenty year old man called Sajid and two juveniles.

This quartet systematically lured young boys to Iqbal's home with promises of food and money. Once under his roof, the boys were drugged, raped and strangled with a chain. The bodies were dismembered and the parts dissolved in a vat of acid with the resultant sludge being poured into the sewer. The victims' clothes and shoes were kept as trophies.

In December 1999, when Iqbal reached his target of 100 victims, he sent a detailed account of the killings to a magazine and also to the police. The enquiries which followed led to a search of his home and the discovery of his murder factory. Police found the acid vat, body parts, bloodstains and the clothes which had been kept as souvenirs. In addition, there were photographs of each young victim.

Iqbal and his accomplices appeared on trial for murder in February 2000. There were many witness statements and Iqbal claimed that his confession was false and an attempt to discredit the police. On 16 March 2000, all four were found guilty. Iqbal was convicted of 100 murders and Sajid of ninety-eight. Their young accomplices were convicted of lesser numbers of murders.

Judge Allah Baksh passed the most bizarre capital sentence on Iqbal and Sajid. He directed that they should be publicly executed in the presence of the victims' relatives. The method was to be strangulation with the chain the murderers had used, after which their bodies were to be dismembered and destroyed with acid. This was reported to be in line with an Islamic law whereby the punishment was made to fit the crime. The two juveniles were spared this judgement and received long prison sentences.

In the event, Iqbal and Sajid did not suffer the prescribed punishment as they were both found dead in their prison cells on 8 October 2001. The authorities claimed the pair had committed suicide.

[442, 822]

IRELAND, COLIN

Self-proclaimed serial killer convicted of murdering five homosexual men in London in the course of three months in 1993.

A common feature of the murders was that the victims were all known to frequent a public house in the Old Brompton Road used by gay men. They also had a predilection for sado-masochism which made them vulnerable to a marauding killer who picked them up and then murdered them in their own homes.

Most of the murder locations had been wiped clean of evidence but the murderer carelessly left a fingerprint at the fourth crime scene. He also began telephoning the police, taunting them that he was going to kill once a week. After his fifth murder on 15 June, he called again to say he now regarded himself as a qualified serial killer.

Detectives had traced the movements of the last victim and discovered that he had been recorded on the security cameras at Charing Cross Railway Station. The tapes showed the victim in the company of a tall man with close-cropped hair. The pictures were widely publicised and the man decided to reveal himself.

He was Colin Ireland, aged thirty-nine, who admitted being in the company of the last victim but denied murdering him. Comparison of Ireland's fingerprints with the one found at the fourth murder scene quickly proved he was lying. Faced with the inevitable, he admitted the killings.

Ireland professed admiration for the character of Hannibal Lecter in the film Silence of the Lambs, and said he had made a New Year's resolution to become a serial killer, for which he had the stereotype background, being an illegitimate child, bullied at school and a failure at work. He was convicted at the Old Bailey in December 1993 and given five sentences of life imprisonment.

[*330, 714*]

ISHAAK, MUHAMMAD ADAM OMAR

The reputation of Yemen's first medical school at the University of Sana was thrown into disrepute in 2000 by the revelation that one of its employees, a mortuary attendant, had been using the dissecting room to commit rape and murder and disposal of his victims' bodies.

Muhammad Adam Omar Ishaak was evidently a compulsive confessor, firstly claiming that he had killed fifty-one women, then reducing this number to sixteen and finally to just three.

At his trial, the prosecution presented all of his murder confessions but when one of the final three victims turned up in court, alive and well, lawyers were obliged to reduce the indictment to two cases. The two victims were Zeineb Saud Aziz, a twenty-four year old Iraqi and Hosn Ahmed Atteya, a twenty-three year old Yemeni. They had been identified from remains recovered from the mortuary drains.

The Judge, Yahya al-Islami, convicted Ishaak and ordered that he be taken to the mortuary where, before the assembled faculty members and students, he should receive eighty lashes for his admitted use of alcohol and then be executed by beheading or shooting. Punishment was postponed until the end of Ramadan in December. The following year, after receiving the prescribed eighty lashes, Ishaak was executed by shooting outside the medical school. [*822*]

J

JACK THE RIPPER

Probably the best-known, yet anonymous, murderer of the last two centuries. The East End of London was terrorised in the autumn of 1888 by the murders of five prostitutes. The killings were characterised by throat-cutting and mutilation. The police of the day were unable to capture the killer although he has since been 'identified' by the authors of countless theories.

The victims were dispatched without a struggle in dark corners of the mean streets of Whitechapel and Spitalfields. The murderer melted into the darkness and, although there were many descriptions of suspects, no one for certain saw him. The circumstances of the killings suggested someone who was not a stranger to the area and who was familiar with the local geography.

The murders created a sensation in Victorian England and the Metropolitan Police came under fierce criticism for their inability to capture the killer. Contemporary theories were that the murders had been committed by a madman or a doctor. The selection of prostitutes as victims suggested a religious fanatic and hints of medical knowledge in the manner of the killings indicated a doctor.

In the century that has elapsed since the murders, probably more has been written about them than about any other crime attributed to a single individual. Jack the Ripper has acquired an aura of drama and mystique without parallel in criminal history. The desire to solve the mystery by identifying the killer has reached the point where objectivity has been swamped by fantasy. The plethora of books, plays, articles, films, stage-shows, television programmes, video programmes and other revelations is unprecedented for a series of murders.

A number of solutions have been proposed by naming Jack the Ripper from the ranks of known murderers. **Neill Cream**, **Frederick Deeming** and **George Chapman** have been suggested, along with countless others from the realms of fact and fantasy such as the Duke of Clarence, J.K. Stephen, M.J. Druitt, Sir William Gull, Dr Alexander Pedachenko, Dr Stanley, Dr Roslyn D'Onston and James Maybrick. Added to these is a galaxy of butchers, black magicians, midwives, policemen and sundry lunatics.

A plausible and well-argued case accusing the Freemasons of a plot to protect the Duke of Clarence was aired in 1976, only to be condemned as a hoax. And in 1993, *The Diary of Jack the Ripper* was published, purporting to be the scribblings of the murderer himself who was revealed as James Maybrick. He is better known as the victim of a famous Victorian poisoning in 1889 for which his wife was convicted. The original publisher of the diary dropped it because it could not be authenticated, and the *Sunday Times* subsequently condemned it as a hoax.

In 1995, a hitherto unknown candidate was proposed in a new book. Dr Francis Tumblety, an American doctor who died in 1903, was named as Jack the Ripper.

In 2002, Patricia Cornwell, the best-selling US crime novelist, published *Portrait of a Killer*. Her thesis was that Walter Sickert, the English impressionist painter, was the Ripper. Her claim was based on an analysis of some of the so-called Jack the Ripper letters held in the public archives and on DNA evidence. Seasoned Ripperologists found her arguments unconvincing. In 2005, an entirely new candidate was put forward in a theory carrying little substance, naming Sir John Williams, a distinguished Victorian doctor, as the murderer.
[*53, 54, 713, 803, 895, 977*]

JACOBSON, HOWARD 'BUDDY'

Millionaire New York businessman whose obsessive attachment to Melanie Cain, a young model, led to him to murder.

Jacobson was a successful property dealer and horse trainer who owned a luxury apartment block on 82nd Street in New York City's Upper East Side. One of his tenants was nineteen-year-old Melanie Cain, a rising star in the fashion world. She fell for his charm and moved into his penthouse suite.

While Jacobson was rich and charming, he was also eccentric and obsessive. He fixed the electricity meters in his apartment building to give low readings and kept outlawed electric guns in his home in order to deal with any intruders. As his bizarre behaviour increased, Melanie decided she had to escape. She did so by starting a relationship with Jack Tupper who lived in a neighbouring apartment.

Tupper and Jacobson thus became rivals for the young model's affections and the latter waged a war of attrition. He constantly harassed Melanie and offered money to Tupper if he would leave her. This state of affairs lasted for several months and then ended sensationally.

On 6 August 1978, Melanie returned to her apartment to find Tupper missing, with signs that he had been taken away by force. Later that day, Tupper's body was found on wasteland in the Bronx. He had been shot and stabbed and a crude attempt made to burn his body. A passer-by had seen a Cadillac at the location and noted the registration number. The vehicle was traced to Jacobson who was arrested.

Jacobson claimed that Tupper had been killed in his apartment building by drug dealers. He decided to dispose of the body with help from a man called Sal Prainito. Jacobson was charged with second-degree murder but created a sensation by escaping from custody during the trial proceedings. On being recaptured, he was convicted in 1980 and sentenced to a minimum of twenty-five years' imprisonment. He escaped a second time and, having six weeks of freedom, regularly telephoned his story to the *New York Times.*

At the age of fifty-eight, in 1989, the man who held the record for training horse-race winners in the early 1960s at Buffalo died in prison of natural causes.

[*384, 614*]

JACOBY, HENRY JULIUS

Eighteen-year-old pantry-boy whose execution for the murder of Lady White in a London hotel raised questions about the fairness of the system of justice.

On 14 March 1922, a chambermaid found Lady Alice White unconscious in her room at Spencer's Hotel. The sixty-five-year-old widow lay on the bed unconscious from severe head injuries. She died the following day. The police concentrated their inquiries on hotel staff because the lack of a struggle or of forced entry to the room seemed to rule out an intruder.

Among those questioned was Henry Jacoby whose replies created suspicion. When bloodstains were found in his quarters, he admitted that he had been in Lady White's room. He said he had heard noises which he thought were caused by burglars. Arming himself with a hammer, he went to investigate. He found the door to room 14 open and, seeing someone inside, struck out with the hammer before realising that he was attacking Lady White.

Jacoby was tried for murder at the Old Bailey. The prosecution argued that he had set out to steal from one of the hotel guests and found Lady White's open door a tempting opportunity. When his intrusion woke her up, he struck out to silence her. The jury agreed that Jacoby had been intent on theft but were unsure that he had intended to commit murder. Mr Justice McCardie told them that in law Jacoby was guilty of murder if he intended to cause grievous bodily harm and his victim died as a result. The pantry-boy was found guilty and sentenced to death. He was hanged at Pentonville Prison on 5 June 1922.

Three days later, **Ronald True** was found guilty of murder but escaped execution when he was declared insane. The two cases were compared on the basis that a working-class youth who killed a titled lady was hanged, whereas the officer who killed a prostitute was saved from a similar fate.

[*695, 726, 753*]

JEGADO, HÉLÈNE

Suspected mass poisoner convicted in a French court on purely circumstantial evidence.

Jegado, a Breton woman in her thirties, had an undesirable reputation as a thief and a poor cook whose employers frequently fell ill and died. She diverted suspicion by affecting deep grief and lavishing unstinted care on the victims. She also occasionally disappeared into a convent until the fuss subsided and then moved to another position.

In 1850, she went to work for Théophile Bidard, a professor at the University of Rennes. In no time at all, a young servant in his household fell ill and died. Jegado exhibited her usual grief-stricken response and disarmed any suspicion. When Rosalie Sarrazin joined the professor's household, she became a firm friend of Jegado's although her employer warned her about being too influenced by the older woman. The friendship between the two women held fast until Rosalie was promoted to take charge of the accounts. The illiterate Jegado immediately grew jealous of her younger colleague's success.

Rosalie Sarrazin was taken ill with stomach pains in July 1851 and died soon afterwards. When the examining magistrate called at the house, he was received by Jegado who declared that she was innocent. As she had not been accused of any offence, it was a remark designed to create suspicion.

An investigation of Jegado's background revealed a trail of deaths in the various households where she had worked. She was charged with murdering Rosalie Sarrazin with arsenic. The evidence against her was circumstantial, no poison was found in her possession and no clear motive for the possible murders of twenty-three persons was established. Nevertheless, her record proved her guilt to the satisfaction of the court and she was found guilty. Hélène Jegado went to the guillotine in 1852.

[*418*, *990*, 1011]

JENKINS AND GERAGHTY

Alec de Antiquis, a family man with six children, was shot dead in a London street in 1947 while attempting to prevent the escape of armed shop-raiders. His death and the subsequent execution of two of the robbers caused a great public outcry.

On 29 April 1947, in broad daylight, masked raiders entered Jay's jewellery shop in Charlotte Street. Brandishing revolvers, they threatened the director of the firm and demanded the keys to the safe. The situation quickly got out of control as one of the staff was attacked and another attempted retaliation. The raiders fired a shot and ran out into the street towards their car. Passers-by scattered, but Alec de Antiquis, on his motor-cycle, tried to thwart the fleeing criminals by driving into their path. He was shot through the head and lay dying in the street while the robbers escaped.

Police were quickly on the scene, including Superintendent Robert Fabian ('Fabian of the Yard'). Witnesses provided descriptions of the raiders and a taxi-driver said he had seen two masked men in Tottenham Court Road. A discarded raincoat was found in the vicinity which was traced to twenty-three-year-old Charles Henry Jenkins, a man with a criminal record.

A schoolboy found the murder weapon on the muddy foreshore of the River Thames at Wapping. It was fully loaded, except for one chamber, the gun expert Robert Churchill proved that it had fired the fatal shot.

Jenkins was arrested and two of his friends were also rounded up; twenty-one-year-old Christopher James Geraghty and seventeen-year-old Terence Peter Rolt. Geraghty and Rolt both confessed and implicated Jenkins. They were all charged with murder and appeared on trial at the Old Bailey in July. Geraghty and Rolt admitted involvement but denied their intention amounted to anything more than robbery. Jenkins claimed to have an alibi.

The jury returned a verdict of Guilty against all three. Geraghty and Jenkins were sentenced to death while Rolt, being under age, was ordered to be detained during Her Majesty's Pleasure. On 19 September 1947, the death sentences on the two men were carried out at Pentonville Prison. The executions provoked public protests and high-lighted arguments about capital punishment. Less fuss was made about the death of a family man who lost his life four months previously performing his duty as a citizen. Terence Rolt was released in 1956.

[*275, 964*]

JONES, ARTHUR ALBERT

While serving a prison sentence for a sexual offence, he was convicted of murdering a young girl after confessing the crime to a fellow inmate.

Brenda Nash disappeared on her way home from a Girl Guides meeting on the evening of 28 October 1960. She and a friend went their separate ways about a quarter of a mile from Brenda's home at Heston in Middlesex. A massive search was mounted involving police and service personnel.

Earlier, in September, there had been an attempted abduction of a young girl in the same area. The man released the girl after assaulting her. The victim gave a description of both the man and his car. The police believed this individual was also involved with the disappearance of Brenda Nash.

There followed a painstaking search for a black Vauxhall car which, on 24 November, led to Arthur Jones. Although he matched the description of the earlier attacker, he appeared to have an alibi for 28 October. On 11 December, Brenda Nash's body was found on common land near Yately in Hampshire. She had been strangled. The next day, detectives were given a piece of information which led them back to Arthur Jones. A member of the public reported that a relative had been asked to provide an alibi for Jones on the night Brenda Nash was abducted.

Jones admitted no more than that he was in the habit of consorting with prostitutes. He was tried in March 1961 for the assault committed in September 1960 and sentenced to fourteen years' imprisonment. While in Wandsworth Prison, Jones confided to a fellow prisoner that he had murdered Brenda Nash. Once again, he found himself at the Old Bailey when he was identified by two witnesses who had seen him in his Vauxhall car not far from Brenda Nash's home. He was convicted of murder and sentenced to life imprisonment.

[*496, 592*]

JONES AND HULTEN

Elizabeth Marina Jones, and Gustav Hulten, playing the gangster and his moll, killed a taxi-driver in London in 1944.

George Edward Heath, a thirty-four-year-old cab-driver, was found dead by the roadside near Staines in Middlesex on 7 October 1944. His car was missing. The vehicle was spotted by detectives two days later parked in Fulham Palace Road. Officers maintained surveillance and arrested the man who tried to drive the car away. He identified himself as US Army Lieutenant Ricky Allen.

Allen's bluff failed and he was identified as an American GI who was absent without leave from his unit. His real name was Karl Gustav Hulten. He claimed that on the night Mr Heath was abducted in his taxi, he was with his girl-friend, Georgina Grayson, a strip-tease dancer.

This was a stage name used by eighteen-year-old Elizabeth Jones who lived in rented accommodation at Hammersmith. She said she had known Ricky for a few days. She believed he was a paratrooper and he told her he had been a gunman in Chicago. Hulten claimed later that the girl said she wanted to be his moll and was looking for something exciting to do. They decided to rob a cab-driver and it was George Heath's misfortune to pick them up. Jones claimed that Hulten shot the driver and made her go through his pockets; Hulten counter-claimed that the girl incited him to commit robbery with violence.

Jones and Hulten were jointly tried for murder at the Old Bailey in January 1945. The couple were found guilty and sentenced to death. A recommendation to mercy was made in the case of Jones and she was eventually reprieved. Hulten was hanged on 8 March 1945.

[*50, 771, 831*]

JONES, GENENE

A licensed nurse who worked in the Paediatric Intensive Care Unit (PICU) at the Bexar County Hospital, San Antonio, Texas. In 1981, the unit experienced a rise in the number of infant deaths. Out of thirty-one deaths, sixteen came to be regarded as questionable and, of those, eleven occurred during the 3.00 to 11.00 pm shift worked by Nurse Jones.

Genene Jones had a reputation for being domineering and a know-all, sometimes arguing with doctors over treatment matters. Nevertheless, she was regarded as a skilled nurse, always willing to work an extra shift and, coincidentally, usually on duty where there was a Blue Code emergency alert.

After five deaths had occurred in the PICU in September 1981, there were mutterings against Jones and it was noted that when she was away on leave there were no Blue Code alerts. A whispering campaign was mounted and one nurse told an inquiry quite bluntly that Nurse Jones was killing babies.

No official action was taken and in 1982 Jones left the hospital to work for a paediatrician who had set up a practice in Kerrville, Texas. After several emergencies involving Nurse Jones, disaster struck when a fifteen-month-old child died following routine inoculations. The child had a seizure and died of cardiac arrest after Jones had inserted an intravenous needle.

Irregularities in the records concerning the use of the muscle-relaxing drug succinylcholine (see **Richard Angelo** and **Beverly Allitt**) were attributed to Genene Jones and she was dismissed from her job.

Two years later, following the exhumation of the child who had died unexpectedly at Kerrville, she was indicted for first-degree murder. Traces of succinylcholine had been found in the infant's body by means of pioneering forensic techniques. The media responded by calling her the 'Death Nurse' and the prosecution claimed she had created the hospital emergencies in order to draw attention to herself. She was found guilty and given a ninety-nine-year prison sentence.

Despite extensive inquiries at Bexar County Hospital over the spate of deaths which had occurred there, Jones was charged with involvement in only one infant death. She was convicted and received a sentence of sixty years to run concurrently with her previous term.

[*268, 667*]

JONES, HAROLD

Teenager acquitted of murder who went on to kill again and made a full confession to both crimes.

Eight-year-old Freda Burnell was sent on an errand to a seed-merchant near her home in Abertillery, Monmouthshire on 5 February 1921. When she failed to return, a search was made of the local area and her body was found near the shop. An attempt had been made at rape and the girl had died of shock as a result of partial strangulation.

It was established that she had been served at the shop by the fifteen-year-old assistant, Harold Jones, who came under suspicion. The discovery of the girl's handkerchief in the shed at the back of the shop suggested that she had been assaulted there. Jones was arrested and tried for murder at Monmouth. The jury's Not Guilty verdict was greeted with public acclaim but the joy was short-lived.

Two weeks after being acquitted, Jones was under arrest for another murder. Eleven-year-old Florence Little went missing and a search of Jones's home revealed bloody marks around the door to the attic. In the roof-space, detectives found the young victim with her throat cut. Jones admitted killing the girl and also confessed to the earlier crime.

Once again he appeared at Monmouth Assizes where he was found guilty. He was spared the death penalty, being under the age of sixteen, and was sentenced to be detained during His Majesty's Pleasure.

[*606, 999*]

JUDD, WINNIE RUTH

Twenty-six-year-old doctor's wife, known as 'The Tiger Woman', convicted of the sensational 'Phoenix Trunk Murders' in 1931.

Winnie worked in her husband's medical clinic in Phoenix, Arizona where she befriended twenty-seven-year-old Agnes LeRoi and another young woman, Hedvig Samuelson. LeRoi and Samuelson shared an apartment which was the scene of a shooting incident on 16 October 1931. LeRoi failed to appear for work the following morning and Winnie was late arriving.

A local delivery company was asked by Winnie to call at the apartment later that night to ship a heavy trunk. Two days later, Winnie left Phoenix by train bound for Los Angeles – her baggage consisted of two trunks. When she reached her destination, station staff noticed dark fluid dripping from one of them. Winnie was asked to open her trunks but made a quick exit instead. The trunks were found to contain the bodies of LeRoi and Samuelson, the latter having been dismembered.

Following a plea from her husband, Dr William Judd, Winnie gave herself up to Los Angeles police on 23 October. Her personal effects included a letter, amounting to a confession, which she had written to her husband.

Her account of what had happened was that she and the other two women had an argument during which Samuelson produced a gun. In the struggle to disarm her, she shot them both. In reality, she had killed them in a fit of jealousy and shot herself in the hand to substantiate her story of self-defence.

She was extradited to Arizona where she stood trial for murder and was convicted. She was sentenced to death but, while in prison, psychiatrists decided she was insane. There was a history of insanity in her family and during the hearing Winnie bore this out by acting hysterically. Her death sentence was commuted to life imprisonment.

Winnie Ruth Judd was regularly in the news due to her seven escapes from prison. Her last escape was in 1962 when she found her way to California and worked for several years as housekeeper to a family in Concord. She was sent back to prison in 1969 and eventually gained parole in 1971 when she returned to work in California. Judd died in October at the age of ninety-three. Commenting on her crimes, she was on record as saying, 'I've asked God many times to forgive me'.

[95, 242]

K

KALLINGER, JOSEPH

Borderline personality whose feelings of persecution edged him towards insanity and murder.

Kallinger was an adopted child who was sexually abused by his parents. They told him he had been emasculated in order to ensure that he could not indulge in the wickedness of sex. The child grew into a confused adult who found refuge in eccentric behaviour.

With the help of his children, he fortified his house to prevent people spying on him. This included excavating a huge cavity in the basement to serve as a kind of fall-out shelter. He also collected junk and wore wedges in his shoes to adjust his balance. Behaviour that was merely weird degenerated into mental disorder and anti-social feelings. He had hallucinations in which he claimed to converse with both God and the Devil. Joseph Kallinger, a shoemaker from Philadelphia, believed he had been chosen to destroy mankind.

He began his assault on society in the early 1970s by enrolling his twelve-year-old son to help him commit robbery. Kallinger's actions took on a sinister tone on 7 July 1974 when he abducted and murdered a child and followed this by killing one of his sons. On 8 January 1975, he took several people hostage and killed one of them before fleeing.

Kallinger made no attempt to cover his tracks and was easily apprehended. With his young son, who had been present during all his violent acts, he was charged with kidnapping, robbery and murder. The courts dealt with the boy under juvenile law while Kallinger himself was convicted of the kidnapping and robbery charges in 1975. The following year, he was convicted of murder and sentenced to a minimum of forty-two years' imprisonment.

[*248, 826*]

KAPPEN, JOSEPH

Killings in Swansea in the early 1970s that became known locally as the 'Saturday Night Strangler Murders' remained unsolved for almost thirty years. The breakthrough investigators had hoped for came in 2001, but by then, the murderer had been dead for eleven years.

In November 1973, two sixteen year old girls, Geraldine Hughes and Pauline Flood, left a Swansea night club after an evening's dancing. They did not return to their homes. Their bodies were found in a copse at nearby Llandarcy where they had been raped and strangled. Three months earlier, a similar killing had occurred when another sixteen year old girl, Sandra Newton, had been raped and strangled in the same area.

A witness came forward who had seen a man driving a white Austin car pick up two girls around the time the night club closed. The man was described as having bushy hair and a large moustache. Police enquiries concentrated on men known to have been present at the club and also male employees. Among the men who had worked at the club was Joseph Kappen. His appearance broadly matched the description given by the witness and he drove a white car. There was no firm evidence against him and he furnished an alibi that satisfied detectives. In mid 1974, the murder investigation was closed.

The case was re-opened in January 2001 when scientists managed to extract DNA from the clothing of the dead girls. Samples taken from Sandra Newton matched those from the Llandarcy victims, indicating that all three victims had been killed by the same person. When attention turned to likely suspects, it was found that Joseph Kappen had died of cancer in 1990. His son, a child at the time of the murders, agreed to provide a sample of DNA which indicated a possible match. On 15 May 2002, Kappen's body was exhumed and DNA was taken from tooth and bone samples. The following month, police announced that the DNA taken from Kappen's remains matched that left on all three victims. If he had lived, he would have been charged with their murders.
[727]

KAPPLER, Dr JOHN FREDERICK

Retired physician convicted of second degree murder in a hit-and-run case which hinged on issues of sanity.

Dr Kappler had a history of paranoia since 1966 and while

working as an anaesthetist in California there were allegations that he had attempted to kill patients. (See **Michael Swango**). He was admitted to hospital and treated for schizophrenia but continued to practise medicine. By 1975, he spoke of hearing voices which directed his behaviour and colleagues noted his often bizarre actions. In 1980 he injected a patient with a potentially lethal dose of a drug which caused a non-fatal cardiac arrest.

Matters finally came to a head after Kappler had retired. On 14 April 1990 he was in Boston visiting his daughter. While driving his car he jumped a red light, mounted the kerb and mowed down and killed a thirty-two year old doctor training for a marathon. Kappler then accelerated and drove his car at Deborah Brunet-Tuttle, a thirty-two year old mother, causing her severe injuries. He did not stop but drove away from the scene and hid his car. Using public transport, he made his way to New York City where he checked into a cheap hotel.

The hit and run doctor was located by his family and taken to hospital where he was kept in a secure unit. He was charged with murder and appeared on trial at Cambridge Superior Court in December 1990. Much of the testimony concerned his background and record of mental instability. His defence team admitted that he drove his car on the day in question and argued that his act was the result of a diseased mind and that he was completely insane. Experts discussed the nature of psychotic disorders and the voices or command hallucinations which might have prompted Kappler's actions.

The prosecution's case was that he had murderous intent and was sufficiently aware of what he had done to flee from the scene and hide his car. On 21 December 1990, the jury returned a verdict of second degree murder and Dr Kappler was sentenced to life imprisonment.

[*1029*]

KASSO, RICKY

Suspect in a killing inspired by Satanism who took his own life before facing an indictment for murder.

Ricky Kasso led a troubled life at Northport, Long Island. He began using drugs when he was barely a teenager and dropped out of school. Increasingly alienated from his family, he became obsessed with ideas about Satanism. In April 1984, accompanied by a group of friends, he went to Amityville to look at the house called

High Hopes made famous by the murders committed there by **Ronald De Feo**.

In June 1984, Kasso accused one of his friends, teenager Gary Lauwers, of stealing some 'angel dust' from him while he was asleep. This became something of a running feud and he again accused Lauwers, in front of two other friends, on 16 June when they met in Aztakea Woods to play heavy metal music and get high on mescaline.

An argument ensued in the early hours of the morning and Kasso stabbed Lauwers, demanding that he declare his love for Satan. Although local residents heard noises in the night, no action was taken. It was several days before Lauwers's body was found and the full extent of the circumstances of his death became apparent. He had been subjected to a frenzied attack in which his eyes had been gouged out. Newspaper headlines called it a ritual killing.

Kasso was arrested on 4 July 1984 as a murder suspect. He told several friends that he had killed Gary as a sacrifice to Satan but warned that he would take his own life rather than go to prison. Two days later he was found hanged in his police cell. Two of his teenaged friends admitted being present during the killing of Gary Lauwers. One of them stood trial but was acquitted on the defence argument that he had not participated in the actual killing.
[*881*]

KEMPER, EDMUND EMIL

Physically imposing man with a high IQ who murdered his mother and seven other women in acts accompanied by decapitation and gross sexual perversions.

Kemper was judged insane in 1964, when at the age of sixteen he shot and killed his grandmother and grandfather. As a child, he developed a liking for torturing animals and was regarded as a sadistic individual. In 1969, he was released from the Atacadero State Hospital into the care of his mother, supposedly having been cured.

He worked as a labourer and spent his time travelling the state highways looking for student hitch-hikers. Kemper became a serial killer before the term came into fashionable use. In the early 1970s he assaulted dozens of girls before turning to murder. In 1972 there was mounting panic at the Santa Cruz campus as female students were reported missing. He usually decapitated his victims after carrying out acts of cannibalism and necrophilia. In order to protect the interior of his car, he carried a supply of plastic bags in which to put dismembered pieces of their bodies.

On 20 April 1973, Kemper killed his mother by battering her to death with a hammer and mutilated her body. On the same day, he also strangled and killed a neighbour. Three days after the double killing he gave himself up to the police and admitted his catalogue of death. He asked for death by torture but he had to be satisfied with life imprisonment. The jury at his trial in Santa Cruz found him guilty of eight murders.

[*175, 221*]

KIMES, SANTE AND KENNETH

Mother and son found guilty of murder in a case where the victim's body was not found. (See also **Robert Bierenbaum** and **James Camb**).

Irene Zambelli Silverman, an eighty-two year old widow of a multi-millionaire, disappeared from her Manhattan apartment on 4 July 1998. She was last seen by her maid whom she had sent on an errand and was missing when the maid returned. Detectives found no sign of a struggle but suspicion focused on Kenneth Kimes who, using a false name, had recently become a tenant in the apartment house.

Kimes was arrested on 5 July along with his mother and they were charged with stealing a car from a dealer. It soon became apparent that the Kimes, mother and son, were among America's most wanted. The FBI had tracked them for months to answer charges of fraud and arson in several states and enquiries about a murder in Los Angeles and a missing person in the Bahamas.

Sante Kimes was the sixty-five year old widow of a wealthy Californian property developer. They owned several houses and lived an opulent life. Young Kenneth had a privileged up-bringing and was looked after by nannies and schooled by private tutors. He had a close relationship with his mother and the pair had a record of suspect dealings going back to the 1970s which included arson and false insurance claims. In 1985, Sante was tried for theft and the illegal treatment of Mexican immigrants for which she served a three year prison sentence.

When Sante and Kenneth were arrested, some of Irene Silverman's belongings were found in their possession including keys, passport, bank books and asset transfer documents with forged signatures. They were also carrying a quantity of sedatives and a 9 mm handgun. But with no body, no witnesses and no forensic evidence, the NYPD faced problems.

After two years of investigation, Sante and Kenneth Kimes finally faced trial for murder in New York in 2000. During the pre-trial hearings, mother and son appeared on the *60 Minutes* television news programme. Their close relationship was evident in their whispers and hand-holding. Detectives had pieced together details of an elaborate plan to take possession of Irene Silverman's Manhattan mansion. They had moved into an apartment above hers and plotted to obtain her signature and social security number.

The prosecution presented a case based on circumstantial evidence in which the Kimes were described as a prolific and pitiless con artist team. In sentencing each to a term of imprisonment exceeding a hundred years, the judge described Sante as a sociopath of unremitting malevolence.

[*949*]

KING, Dr WILLIAM HENRY

Wayward physician who fell for one of his patients and disposed of his inconvenient wife with poison.

William King was born in Brighton, Ontario and married a rather plain girl from a wealthy family. They parted company after their first child died and King went to Philadelphia to study medicine. He qualified in 1858 and returned to practise in Brighton. He was also reconciled with his wife Sarah.

Dr King was a successful physician and made a particular hit with the ladies. He was smitten by a twenty-year-old patient, Melinda Vandervoort, who possessed all the physical charms lacking in his wife. Completely infatuated with his new conquest, he neglected Sarah who soon became ill. She suffered from stomach pains for several weeks and did not respond to the treatment prescribed by her husband. She died on 4 November 1858.

The dead woman's parents were suspicious of their son-in-law and their fears grew when they chanced upon letters written by Melinda which suggested it would be convenient if Sarah were out of the way. Further inquiries resulted in the exhumation of Mrs King's body and arsenic was found in her organs. While this was going on, King had fled to Cleveland where he joined Melinda.

The amorous doctor was arrested and returned to Canada to face trial at Cobourg. His parents-in-law testified that they had seen him administering a white powder, presumed to be arsenic, to their daughter. Dr King was found guilty and while in the condemned cell, confessed to killing his wife; but he claimed that the agent he used was chloroform, not arsenic. He was publicly hanged before a crowd of several thousand onlookers on 9 June 1859.
[*149*]

KISSEL, NANCY

What became popularly known in Hong Kong as the 'Milkshake Murder made headlines in November 2003 when wealthy American banker, Robert Kissel, was found murdered.

His body was discovered bundled up in an expensive carpet in the store room of the luxury apartment block where he had lived with his wife and three children. A post mortem examination showed that he had died from severe head injuries, including a fractured skull. Traces of the date rape drug, rohypnol, and other sedatives were found in his stomach.

Investigators established that the rolled-up carpet and other objects had been moved to the store room on the instructions of his wife, Nancy Kissel. She was arrested and charged with murder. Her trial, which lasted for sixty-five days, provided some sensational headlines. The prosecution claimed that the couple's marriage had been failing for some time and in 2003 Nancy and the children returned to the USA because of the SARS epidemic in Hong Kong. During this visit home, she began an affair with a TV repair man.

When Robert Kissel became suspicious about his wife's activities, he hired a private detective to obtain evidence of her infidelity. Meanwhile, Nancy, who was the beneficiary of his will, devised a plan to gain control of his estate, worth several million dollars, and free herself to link up with her lover. She used their computer to search for details of sedative drugs and the prosecution maintained that she gave her husband a milkshake laced with sedatives to render him unconscious. When he was incapable of offering any resistance, she beat him to death with a heavy ornament.

Giving evidence in her own defence, Nancy Kissel denied the milkshake allegation and insisted that she still loved her husband in spite of his being a cocaine addict and subjecting her to violent sexual abuse throughout their marriage. She said that on

3 November 2003 he had attacked her with a baseball bat and, in fear of her life, she fought back and killed him in self defence.

On 1 September 2005, the seven members of the trial jury returned a unanimous guilty verdict and Judge Michael Lunn sentenced Nancy Kissel to life imprisonment, the mandatory penalty for murder in Hong Kong.

KLENNER, FRED (FRITZ)

A family feud in North Caroline ended with five murders by shooting and four by explosion.

Dr Fred Klenner, a man of eccentric habits but acknowledged as a leader in vitamin therapy, practised in Reidsville. His son Fritz helped in his clinic but his ambition to become a doctor seemed dashed when he failed to qualify. He told his father that he had, and the myth was perpetuated by the old man's patients who referred to 'Young Dr Klenner'.

Fritz said he was going on to take further studies at Duke Medical School but, in reality, he spent his time at a local gun shop where he was known as 'Dr Crazy'. He still helped his father at weekends and in the early 1980s made the acquaintance of Susie Newsom Lynch. Separated from her husband and in poor health, she had been advised to spend some time with her uncle, Dr Klenner.

Susie came from a background of growing bitterness between her parents and her parents-in-law. Although she had custody of the two children, there were legal problems about her husband's rights of access.

In May 1984, old Dr Klenner died and his clinic was closed. His son used a modest inheritance to buy guns and to fit out his Blazer station-wagon with survival equipment and a bomb which was wired-up under the passenger seat. Fritz also drew closer to Susie Lynch and empathised with her over her family problems. Her family were concerned over her association with Klenner whom everyone regarded as unbalanced. He fed Susie with stories that her husband was involved in illegal dealings.

On 24 July 1984, Susie's mother-in-law and her daughter were found dead at their home in Prospect, Kentucky. They had been shot with an assault rifle. There was talk of a 'gangland killing' but the police had few ideas who was responsible.

In March 1985, Fritz moved in with Susie and they fuelled each other's neurotic fantasies. He referred to her as his wife and she became completely estranged from her family. Fritz continued to buy military equipment and Susie's two boys were made to wear combat uniforms.

In May 1985, there was a triple murder in North Carolina at the home of Susie's grandmother. Her father, mother and grandmother were all shot dead in another mysterious killing episode. Both Susie and Fritz were questioned and suspicion that Fritz was involved in the shootings intensified when it was learned that he had been in the vicinity of the latest murders and was known to be armed. He told a friend that he had been engaged on a CIA mission.

On 3 June 1985, Fritz and Susie put the two boys into their Blazer and drove into Greensboro. The police gave chase with several patrol cars and Fritz began firing at them with an Uzi machine gun. Three officers were wounded. Suddenly, the Blazer came to a halt and exploded, killing everyone in it.

Searches of the Klenner properties showed that Fritz was preparing for war. In addition to 8000 rounds of ammunition, he had access to fifteen handguns, eight shotguns, two machine guns, two assault rifles and five semi-automatic rifles.

[*85, 700*]

KIRWAN, WILLIAM BURKE

Controversial case in which wife-murder was dressed up to look like an accident.

Kirwan made his living as an artist in Dublin and in June 1852 went to Howth in County Dublin with his wife intending to do some sketching. Maria Louisa Kirwan was a keen swimmer, so the visit to a picturesque part of the coast suited both of them. They made several trips to Ireland's Eye, a small uninhabited island with pleasant beaches about a mile from Howth.

On 6 September, the couple hired a local boatman to row them out to Ireland's Eye. He had instructions to pick them up at 8.00 pm that evening. When the boatman returned, he found Kirwan alone. The artist explained that he had not seen his wife for over an hour. The boatman began a search and found Maria Kirwan lying on rocks at the bottom of an inlet called Long Hole. Her body was still warm but she was dead, apparently from drowning. Her face and upper body were bloody and bruised.

A coroner's inquest returned a verdict of accidental death and

Maria Kirwan was buried. It emerged that Kirwan was a known philanderer and he was openly talked about as a murderer. His wife's body was exhumed and it was decided that she had died of asphyxia before drowning. William Kirwan was arrested and charged with murder.

He was tried in Dublin in December 1852. The Kirwans' landlady at Howth testified that the couple quarrelled constantly and William was heard to threaten his wife: 'I'll finish you,' he said. Arguments were put forward claiming Mrs Kirwan was epileptic and that she died accidentally. The prosecution believed that she was suffocated by her husband who then tried to make murder look like an accident. Kirwan was found guilty and sentenced to death. He was reprieved and served twenty-seven years of a life sentence.

[*115, 552, 790*]

KISS, BELA

Mass murderer who successfully disposed of his lovers and other victims and disappeared into obscurity.

Bela Kiss was a tinsmith with a business in the Hungarian village of Czinkota. When his wife Marie left him for her artist lover, Kiss appeared distraught. But he soon had tongues wagging with his own philanderings as a succession of buxom widows came and went from his house.

All this came to an end in 1914 when Kiss was drafted into the army. He secured his house with locks and chains and left Czinkota for the war. In May 1916 word was received that Kiss had been killed in action. Shortly afterwards, the security of his house was breached by police searching for hoarded petrol.

When officers found seven metal casks in the attic of Kiss's house, they assumed they had found a black market supply of fuel. They were astonished when they prised the lid off one of the casks and revealed a woman's body. Six of the other casks contained similar gruesome remains and seventeen more corpses were found buried in the ground around the house.

Among Kiss's possessions were found numerous letters from women who had replied to his advertisements. By this means he had lured well-off widows to his home where he strangled them and pawned their clothes and jewellery. The victims included Marie Kiss and her artist lover.

After the war, people who knew Kiss claimed to have seen him in Budapest despite reports that he had died in Serbia. Inquiries into the circumstances of his supposed death showed that he might have swapped civilian life with a new identity. Other rumours had it that he fled to the USA or joined the French Foreign Legion.
[*302, 885*]

KNIGHT, KATHERINE

When the former abattoir worker killed her partner, John Price, in Aberdeen, New South Wales in 2000, it proved to be one of the most brutal and bizarre murders in Australia's criminal history.

The couple had been together for about six years but Price indicated that he wanted to leave her. He had shown his work mates a stab wound which he said Knight had inflicted on him with the threat that she would kill him if he left her. When Price failed to turn up for work on 1 March 2000, police went to his home and found a scene of utter horror. Hanging by a steel hook near the kitchen was a shapeless mass barely recognisable as the skin flayed from a human body. Nearby were the skinned remains of the body which had been decapitated. The head was found boiling in a pot on the stove and there was a lump of congealing flesh in the oven. There were also vegetables on the stove.

Katherine Knight, who was asleep in one of the bedrooms, was arrested and charged with murder. Examination of the corpse showed that Price had been stabbed thirty-seven times. Under police questioning and psychiatric examination, Knight insisted she remembered nothing of what had happened other than that they had sex and recalled seeing Price in the bathroom.

She pleaded guilty to murder at her trial in October 2001 and Justice Barry O'Keefe sentenced her to life imprisonment with the recommendation that she should never be considered for parole.
[*541, 560*]

KNOWLES CASE

Doctor in Ashanti convicted of killing his wife despite her dying declaration that she had been wounded by accident.

Benjamin Knowles and his wife Harriet served in the colonial administration of the Gold Coast territory of Ashanti in the 1920s. He was Medical Officer for the Bekwai District and attracted the sympathy of his friends on account of the overbearing behaviour of his wife. Harriet, a former stage personality, was a domineering woman who constantly nagged her husband.

Dr and Mrs Knowles gave a lunch party at their home on 20 October 1928 and the guests included the District Commissioner, Thorlief Mangin. Some two hours after the guests had departed, Knowles's houseboy appeared at Mangin's quarters to tell him that a gun had been fired in his master's home. Mangin went to enquire and was assured by Knowles that there was nothing wrong.

Mangin was uneasy and returned the next day. Knowles now said that he and his wife had quarrelled and that she had been shot. Harriet was found with a gunshot wound in her abdomen and was taken to hospital. She died from her injury but made a dying declaration in which she said she put her husband's loaded revolver on a chair and then inadvertently sat on it. The weapon discharged accidentally as she attempted to pull it out from beneath her.

Knowles was believed to have pressed his wife into making her dying declaration. He was charged with murder and put on trial at the Chief Commissioner's Court in Kumasi in November 1928. There was no provision in law for counsel to act for either defence or prosecution. Knowles defended himself and was prosecuted by the Police Commissioner. The Acting Circuit Judge of Ashanti, sitting without a jury, decided that Knowles was guilty and sentenced him to death.

Sentence was commuted to life imprisonment by the Governor of the Gold Coast. In November 1929, the sentence was quashed by the Judicial Committee of the Privy Council in London which heard appeals from the colonies. They decided that the trial judge erred by not considering manslaughter. Dr Knowles died in 1933.

[5, *576*]

KNOWLES, JOHN PAUL

Serial killer who took eighteen lives in several US states before being shot dead by an FBI agent.

Knowles was shot and killed on 18 November 1974 while attempting to escape from custody. He had been arrested on the previous day following a trail of rape and murder lasting four months. He had spent nearly half his twenty-eight years in prison for committing theft and burglary. He was released on parole in May 1974 and quickly returned to a life of crime, only now he added murder to his repertoire. On 26 July, he broke into a house in

Jacksonville, Florida and robbed a retired teacher, killing her in the process. He followed this by killing two schoolgirls and dumping their bodies in a swamp.

Fully in the grip of a murderous impulse, Knowles travelled the freeways in a stolen car looking for opportunities to rape and kill. He selected his victims at random by picking up hitch-hikers or by entering people's homes on false pretences. He killed three times in August and five times in September.

In between killings, he had spells of dangerous normality. One such was his encounter in Atlanta with London journalist Sandy Fawkes who was on a visit to the USA. Calling himself Daryl Golden, Knowles disarmed the young woman with sinister charm. They spent several days and nights together before she suspected his motives. They parted company after he threatened her with a gun and she had a lucky escape.

Within days, Knowles claimed two more murder victims in Florida but, with the police hard on his heels, tried to drive through a road-block in Georgia. He fled from his crashed car and was hunted down by officers using tracker dogs. The man with the unhappy childhood who dreamed of fame and fortune was shot dead the next day.

[*280*]

KORDIYEH, ALI REZA KURAN

A serial killer dubbed the 'The Tehran Vampire' terrorised the citizens of the Iranian capital in 1997. The victims' bodies were found dumped in various parts of the city.

The dead women bore similar marks of violence. They had been raped and repeatedly stabbed, their bodies were then doused in petrol and set on fire, presumably to destroy any forensic evidence. Nine women, including a mother and her ten-year old child were despatched in this fashion.

The police were unable to make any progress in their investigation because of the killer's destructive modus operandi. But he became careless and when two intended victims escaped his clutches, detectives were able to create a photofit impression from their descriptions. When a man behaving suspiciously in a shopping mall was detained, his appearance matched the photofit. Ali Reza Kuran Kordiyeh had been charged with rape and theft in 1993 but had been on the run since escaping from custody.

A search of Kordiyeh's car revealed traces of blood and under interrogation he confessed to the murders and described how he cruised the city posing as a taxi driver and looking for victims. His trial proved to be a media event and was shown on Iranian television. The outcome was a death sentence – a public execution preceded by lashes inflicted by the victims' relatives.

The execution took place at dawn on 12 August 1997 in one of Tehran's main squares before a crowd of thousands. Kordiyeh was brought to the square and thrown onto a bench where he was lashed with a leather belt. Guards intervened to prevent members of the public from joining in and beating him to death before the executioner could do his work. When the flogging was completed, he was hanged from the lifting arm of a large crane.

Before the grisly business of the execution was started, the assembled crowd was harangued by a Muslim cleric declaring that 'this is punishment for criminals but for us witnesses it is a lesson to be learned'. From later reports of similar crimes committed in Iran, it seems that, despite its brutality, the deterrent is not working.
[*370*]

KRAFT, RANDY STEPHEN

Gifted computer analyst who led a double life as California's 'Freeway Killer'. He was convicted of murdering sixteen young men between 1972 and 1983 and was thought to be responsible for as many as sixty-seven killings.

Kraft was an exception to the stereotype serial killer. He was an only child from a stable family background and did well at school. Although he was reserved, he was not a loner. His main problem was his sexuality and in 1967 he declared that he was a homosexual.

He had a male lover with whom he lived in Long Beach for several years before his arrest. He held a well-salaried job as a computer specialist, played bridge regularly with a group of friends and was well liked. His friends had no inkling of the appalling double life which he chose to lead.

His job kept him mobile and he roamed California's freeways at night looking for murder victims. He picked up lone male hitch-hikers, frequently young servicemen. Kraft plied them with beer and overdoses of tranquilisers before subjecting them to torture, mutilation, sodomy and murder. When he had finished with them, he tossed their ravaged bodies on to the roadside.

Kraft's reign of terror in southern California was complicated by the activities of another freeway killer, William George Bonin. Working with an accomplice, Bonin murdered ten hitch-hikers between 1974 and 1980. But the killings went on after he was taken into custody.

The police finally caught up with Kraft on 14 May 1983 on the San Diego Freeway when a patrol pulled him over because they thought he was drunk. His passenger, a young Marine, appeared to be either asleep or drunk. He proved to be dead from strangulation. The likelihood is that Kraft was in the process of disposing of his victim's body when he was arrested.

When Kraft's home at Long Beach was searched, detectives found clothing and possessions belonging to some of his victims. There was also a coded list which included references to his victims' names. There were sixty-seven entries in all. He also had a well-used guide to prescription drugs and nine different types of tranquillizers were found in his car.

Kraft was held for five years in custody in Orange County before finally coming to trial. On 12 May 1989, he was found guilty of sixteen murders and sentenced to death. He was taken to Death Row at San Quentin to join close on 300 inmates under sentence of death in a state that had not executed a murderer for over twenty years. At the time he was convicted, Randy Kraft was forty-four years of age. He plays bridge with a select group of Death Row prisoners, Lawrence Bittaker, William Bonin and **Doug Clark**.
[*1057*]

KRAY TWINS

The Kray Twins, Reginald and Ronald, were born on 24 October 1933. During the 1960s they dominated London's criminal underworld in a manner reminiscent of Al Capone. 'The Firm', as it was known, engaged in rackets, protection, violence and, ultimately, in murder.

The twins were professional boxers at the age of seventeen before they were called up for National Service. Much of their time was spent in military prisons and in 1954 they were dishonourably discharged. They established themselves in an East End billiards hall which became the hub of their criminal empire.

Ronnie, a self-confessed homosexual, was the more dominant twin and was called 'The Colonel'. He studied the life of Al Capone and the Chicago gangsters and fantasised about violence and power.

Reggie provided the business acumen so that, by 1956, 'The Firm' reigned supreme in London's East End crime world.

Reggie's marriage in 1965 ended in tragedy when his wife committed suicide two years later. From then on, in an atmosphere of mounting violence, the twins were involved in freeing Frank Mitchell (the 'Mad Axe Man') from Dartmoor. His subsequent disappearance is still a mystery, but the Krays appeared at the Old Bailey when a man claiming to know they had ordered Mitchell's killing turned Queen's Evidence. Nevertheless the twins escaped conviction.

The Krays next turned to gun-law, and in their feud with the rival Richardson Gang, Ronnie killed George Cornell in the Blind Beggar public house. Then Reggie, consumed with bitterness after his wife's death, fatally stabbed Jack McVitie ('Jack The Hat') because he had threatened Ronnie.

A full-blooded but discreet police investigation was mounted against the Krays. The twins were arrested while in bed, following a tip-off about a proposed gangland killing. They were tried at the Old Bailey in 1969 for the murders of Cornell and McVitie. They were found guilty and, at the age of thirty-five sentenced to life imprisonment of not less than thirty years.

In 1987, Charles Kray started a parole campaign for the twins as they came up to serving twenty years of their sentences. At that time Ronnie was detained in Broadmoor Hospital and Reggie at Gartree Prison. In 1988, they published a book called *Our Story* which was criticised for its unrepenting glorification of violence. A film called *The Profession of Violence* was also made about their exploits. Ronnie Kray died in hospital on 17 March 1995, aged sixty-one, from a heart attack.

Reggie Kray was married in 1997 in Maidstone Prison. After thirty-two years in prison, he was released on account of terminal illness and spent his last days in hospital. He died, aged sixty-six on 1 October 2000 and his funeral procession was attended by an estimated two thousand people.

[*243, 533, 534, 544, 739, 742*]

KÜRTEN, PETER

The 'Monster of Dusseldorf' began a reign of terror in 1929 and, by the time he was caught in the following year, had committed nine murders. He admitted to a lifetime of crime involving practically every offence and perversion.

On 9 February 1929, the body of a nine-year-old girl was found on a building site in the Flingen district of Dusseldorf. She had been sexually abused and killed with multiple stab wounds. An attempt had also been made to burn the body. Three days later, a middle-aged man was found dead in a neighbouring district, again with multiple stab wounds.

The killings continued, the victims being mainly women and girls who were dispatched by a variety of methods, including stabbing, strangulation and hammer blows to the head. In some cases, murder was accompanied by rape and several assault victims survived their injuries and gave descriptions of the attacker.

The shock-waves of panic which rocked the public and the criticism of the authorities which followed were reminiscent of the **Jack the Ripper** murders in London. The hysteria spread to countries neighbouring Germany and there were reports of similar attacks in Belgium, Poland and Czechoslovakia.

The 'Dusseldorf Monster' was caught by chance. On 14 May 1930, a young woman set out by train from Cologne bound for Dusseldorf where she had taken a position as a housemaid. At the city's railway station she was approached by a man who offered to take her to the home of her new employer but first persuaded her to visit his home in Mettmannerstrasse. His attempt at rape was strenuously resisted and he let her go.

Instead of reporting the incident to the police, the girl wrote about it to a friend but incorrectly addressed the envelope. The letter was opened at the post office so that it could be returned to the sender and an alert official notified the police of its contents.

Detectives descended on 71 Mettmannerstrasse and arrested forty-seven-year-old Peter Kürten, a married factory worker. He told the police that he was the person they were seeking and his identification was confirmed by two of the surviving victims. This inoffensive-looking man admitted to all the murders known to the police and to many more, including his first killing when he was aged sixteen. His catalogue of crime included theft, arson, fraud, murder by strangulation, stabbing and bludgeoning, rape and a whole repertoire of sexual perversion. His wife was unaware of his double life, seeing him as a hard-working man and a regular churchgoer.

Kürten's incredible secret life was exposed by Professor Karl Berg who plotted his early sexual activity from 1899, through acts of arson interspersed with attacks on women and children, until his arrest in 1930. He was stimulated by the sight of blood and expressed the hope that he might hear the sound made by his own blood when he was executed. He professed to be an admirer of Jack the Ripper.

His plea of insanity was discounted by the jury at his trial in Dusseldorf in April 1931. He was found guilty of nine murders and sentenced to death. He was guillotined at Cologne on 2 July 1931. [*69, 348, 944, 1070*]

L

LABBÉ, DENISE

Young mother who killed her child to prove her commitment to her lover, who demanded total submission.

Denise Labbé came from a one-parent family and took low-paid jobs in order to make ends meet while educating herself at night-school. In due course she obtained a job as a secretary at the National Institute of Statistics at Rennes.

She enjoyed an active social life but soon became an unmarried mother. In May 1954, twenty-eight-year-old Denise, mother of a two-and-a-half-year-old daughter, met Jacques Algarron. He was a high-flying officer cadet at the Saint-Cyr military school noted for his promiscuity and with two children by previous relationships.

Denise and Algarron lived together in circumstances where he was the master and she the slave. He demanded complete obedience from her to the extent that she should sleep with other men and then seek his forgiveness. This was his warped idea of testing her faithfulness but the ultimate trial came in August 1954 when he suggested she killed her daughter as a mark of her love for him. She realised he was serious when he began to threaten her. In September and October, Denise sought to comply with his wishes and made three failed attempts to kill her child. She finally succeeded on 9 November by drowning her while staying with her sister at Vendôme.

Having killed her daughter, Denise now suffered Algarron's indifference. When she was questioned by the police she implicated him in what she termed a 'ritual murder' and the pair were charged with murder. The 'Demon Lovers', as they were

called by the press, were tried at Blois in May 1955. They were found guilty, Denise with extenuating circumstances, and sentenced to imprisonment, she for life and he to twenty years' hard labour.
[*351*]

LACROIX, GEORGE

Escaped convict from the French penal settlement on Devil's Island who murdered 'Red Max Kassell' in London in 1936.

Kassell's body wrapped in a blanket was found in a hedge by the roadside near St Albans in Hertfordshire on 24 January 1936. He had been beaten and shot. Of Latvian origin, he was known to deal in drugs and prostitution in Soho, where detectives began their inquiries.

One of his partners was George Lacroix, a French criminal whose real name was Marcel Vernon. He had offered to collect a loan made by his mistress, Suzanne Bertron, to 'Red Max'. There had been a shooting incident at Bertron's flat in Soho the night before Kassell's body was discovered. Neither Lacroix nor Bertron could be questioned as they had fled to France.

Attempts to extradite the pair to Britain were blocked by the French authorities. Both wanted persons were French citizens and Lacroix was an escaped prisoner. They were tried in Paris in 1937, Lacroix for murder and Bertron for being an accessory. British detectives gave evidence and the two accused were found guilty. He was sentenced to ten years' hard labour, followed by expulsion from France, and she was acquitted.

Kassell had been lured by Bertron to her flat in Soho where Lacroix confronted him over the loan. There was an argument and Lacroix killed 'Red Max' by shooting him six times. With the help of another man he dumped the body near St Albans. 'Red Max', a denizen of London's underworld, lost his life over a £25 debt.
[*842, 933*]

LAFARGE, MARIE

Young Frenchwoman who poisoned her husband with arsenic and paved the way for the new science of toxicology.

Most of Marie's friends married into the aristocracy while she had to settle for a more humble future. She married Charles Lafarge, a businessman close to bankruptcy and living in reduced circumstances. While he worked in Paris, she stayed home at Le Glandier in a vermin-infested house.

Age ♂ ? Unknown Fire in Motor Car, I
[illegible].30. Rex v A A Rouse
Northampton Body severely burned. Top of head
ē vault of skull completely destroyed. Brain
exposed, shrunken + burned on top. Skin of face
destroyed + ears. Fairly deep burning of front
of neck + of chest. Whole chest wall destroyed in
part + front of heart + lungs exposed + partly burned
Skin of abdom. wall destroyed in part but
abdomen not opened. Ext genitals destroyed
+ skin of limbs. . Forearms + hands completely
destroyed + part of each upper arm quite half [illegible]

Sir Bernard Spilsbury kept his post mortem notes on file cards.

atrick Mahon: ladies' man
/ho resorted to murder
nd dismemberment.

Jean-Pierre Vaquier: committed murder at the Blue Anchor Hotel.

harlotte Bryant: hanged for
oisoning her husband.

14514/10 County Gaol. Durham
7th March 1873

Sir,

I beg to inform you that at the Assizes holden in Durham on Friday the 7th day of March 1873. Mary Ann Cotton was convicted of Wilful Murder and sentenced to be hanged, Consequently in accordance with the Rules laid down in your Order dated 13th August 1868. Mary Ann Cotton will be executed on Monday the 24th Inst. at 8 o'clock Am.

I have the honor, to be,
Sir,
Your most Obedt Servant
[illegible]
2d Colonel
Governor

The Right Hon H. A. Bruce
Secretary of State
Home Department
Whitehall
London

Mary Ann Cotton: Sunday school
teacher and mass murderer.

Ronald True: his mental instability saved him from the hangman.

John Norman Thorne: murdered his pregnant girl friend.

Alfred Arthur Rouse: confessed to the 'Blazing Car Murder'.

Edith Thompson and Frederick Bywaters: Edith between her lover and husband.

Sidney Harry Fox: killed his mother for gain.

Herbert Rowse Armstrong: the solicitor who turned to arsenic.

POLICE · BUDGET · EDITION

EDITED BY HAROLD FURNISS

FAMOUS CRIMES

PAST AND PRESENT

ONE · PENNY.

MRS DYER

THE · BABY · FARMER

FROM · HER EFFIGY IN Madame Tussaud's

CONTENTS OF THIS NUMBER

Baby Farming Exposed: The Detestable Dyer.

Burglars Three Thousand Years Ago.

ELIZABETH CANNING,
She Nearly Swore Away a Life.

LIPSKI'S CRUEL CRIME

Catherine Churchill.
How She Slew Her Husband.

Inhuman Tortures.
The Close of a Clever Series.

Killed by a Clergyman.
The Sin of Curate Hackman.

HOW to PREVENT CRIME.

Amelia Dyer: child minder with murderous intent.

George Joseph Smith: the Brides in the Bath murderer.

Frederick Seddon: murdered his lodger for her money.

Hawley Harvey Crippen: poisoned his wife and buried her in the cellar.

Hawley Harvey Crippen: the 'doctor' returns to England under arrest.

Gordon Frederick Cummins: the so-called wartime Ripper.

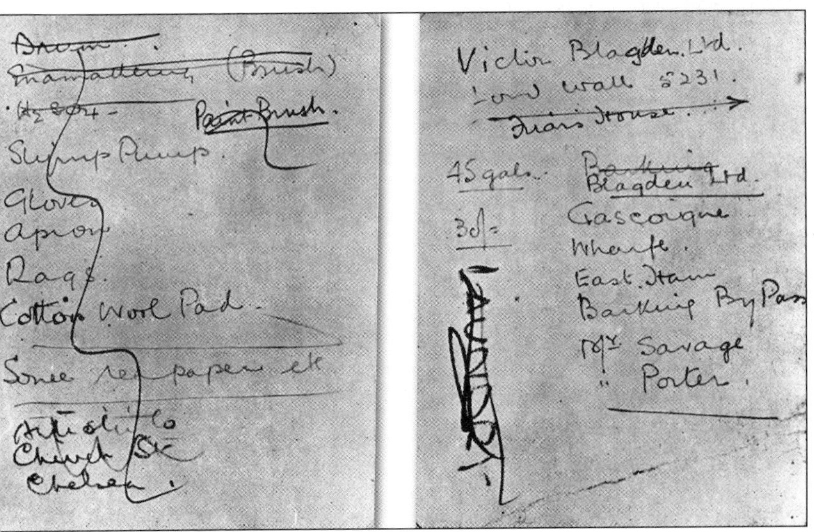

Paint Brush.
Stirrup Pump.
Gloves
apron
Rags.
Cotton Wool Pad.
Some ... paper etc
Church St
Chelsea.

Victor Blagden Ltd.
Lon wall 8231.
45 gals.
Blagden Ltd.
30/-
Gascoigne
Wharfe.
East Ham
Barking By Pass
Mr Savage
" Porter.

John George Haigh: the murderer's order for sulphuric acid.

Daniel Raven: executed for murdering his wife's parents.

Walter Graham Rowland: twice convicted of murder.

Donald George Thomas: mortally wounded police officer named his killer.

Ernest Ingenito: wiped out his wife's family.

Christopher James Geraghty: executed, along with Charles Henry Jenkins, for killing a man in the street following an armed raid.

Marie decided to eliminate the rats and bought some arsenic for the purpose. In January 1840, during a visit home, Charles Lafarge was taken ill and died within a few days. He had been ill a few weeks previously in Paris after receiving some cakes from his wife.

Suspicion focusing on Marie was confirmed when traces of arsenic were found in her husband's body. Feelings against her were compounded when an aristocratic friend accused her of stealing a necklace during a visit in 1839. The necklace was found at Le Glandier and Marie was charged with its theft. She was given a two-year suspended sentence for the offence.

Meanwhile, she faced the more serious charge of murder for which she was tried in September 1840 at Tulle. Her lawyers consulted Professor Mathieu Orfila, a chemist of high reputation who would subsequently be regarded as the father of toxicology. Much of the evidence concerned the scientific and medical aspects of arsenic poisoning. To the dismay of Marie's supporters, the professor testified that Charles Lafarge had died of unlawfully administered arsenic.

Marie was found guilty and sentenced to hard labour for life. This was commuted by King Louis-Philippe to life imprisonment which she spent at Montpellier. She wrote her memoirs in prison and died of tuberculosis in 1851.

[*400, 816, 843, 935*]

LAMSON, Dr GEORGE HENRY

Medical practitioner whose financial difficulties led him to murder a relative by means of aconitine poisoning.

Lamson served with distinction as a surgeon with the Serbian forces in the Russo-Turkish war. He was wounded in the fighting and the treatment he was given induced drug addiction. He returned to England after the war and married in 1878. His wife, together with her four brothers, was a beneficiary of her dead parents' estate.

With the aid of his wife's legacy, Lamson bought a medical practice in Bournemouth in 1880 and made two trips to America in the following year, supposedly to escape his debtors. He was in such desperate financial straits that he had been obliged to borrow from his friends.

On 1 December 1881, he wrote to his brother-in-law, Percy Malcolm John, saying he would like to visit him before going on a trip to Paris and Florence. Percy was an eighteen-year-old cripple confined to a wheelchair as the result of paralysis. He lived at Blenheim House School in Wimbledon, where Dr Lamson arrived on 3 December. Like Lamson's wife, Percy was a beneficiary under his parents' will.

The visitor took tea with Percy and the school principal. Thoughtfully, he had come prepared with a Dundee cake, already conveniently sliced. He also had some capsules containing medicine which he had prescribed for Percy and invited Percy to show them how easy it was to take. Lamson left to catch his train; within ten minutes Percy was ill with convulsions and died later that evening.

The police were eager to interview Dr Lamson who returned voluntarily from Paris. He was charged with murder and sent for trial at the Old Bailey in March 1882. Traces of aconite, a relatively rare poison, had been found in Percy John's body. It was proved beyond doubt that Lamson had bought two grains of aconite in London on 24 November 1881. The poison was administered in the cake and not in the capsule which was a diversion.

Lamson was found guilty and sentenced to death. He admitted his crime to the chaplain at Wandsworth Prison before being hanged on 28 April 1882.

[*7, 124, 261, 880*]

LANDRU, HENRI-DÉSIRÉ

Unlikely French sex symbol in the early part of the century who murdered elderly widows for gain.

When Landru proved less than successful as a businessman, he exploited his talent for attracting women. During the early years of the First World War, he sought out elderly widows and tempted them with prospects of marriage. As soon as he had access to their bank accounts, he withdrew their assets and disappeared.

He deceived hundreds of lonely, gullible women in his fraudulent career and, in due course, turned his hand to murder. He placed advertisements in the newspapers, offering himself as a matrimonial catch with entries such as 'a widower with a comfortable income and an affectionate nature'. He received dozens of replies which he recorded in a notebook, together with details of the respondents' financial position.

Landru spirited his new wives off to his rented villa at Gambais and they promptly disappeared. Over a four-year period between 1915 and 1919, he murdered ten women. His activities came to light when relatives of some of the missing women began making inquiries at Gambais. The trail led to Landru, despite his generous use of aliases. Distinguishing features of the French 'Bluebeard' were his red beard and bald head.

When the authorities caught up with Landru, his notebook gave him away because, among the 283 names listed, were those of the missing women. One of the changes he had made at Gambais was to install an oven, the ashes of which included fragments of human bones and teeth. He was tried for murder in 1921 and found guilty on eleven counts. He protested his innocence but was guillotined at Versailles on 25 February 1922. Many years later, it was reported that he had scribbled a confession on the back of a picture given to his lawyer.

[*34, 55, 566, 946*]

LAURIE, JOHN WATSON

Opportunistic murderer who killed a holiday-maker in what came to be called 'The Goatfell Case'.

Edwin Rose was a thirty-two-year-old clerk from London enjoying a holiday in Scotland in the summer of 1889. On the steamer from Rothesay to the Isle of Arran, he met John Laurie, a pattern-maker from Glasgow, and the two became travelling companions.

When they reached Arran, Laurie, using a false name, invited Rose to share his lodgings at Mrs Walker's boarding house. The pair teamed up with two other young men and the quartet enjoyed the beauty of the island, going off on walks and hiring a boat. When Laurie proposed to climb Goatfell, the island's 2866-feet-high peak, one of the other men warned Rose against it. They would not be making the climb as they intended to return to the mainland.

Rose ignored the warning and, on 15 July, set out with Laurie. They did not return and it was reported later that Laurie had been seen leaving the island on his own. After several days had elapsed and no sign of Rose, a search was made on Goatfell and his body was found hidden under a pile of rocks. He had been clubbed to death and robbed. Several witnesses had seen Laurie returning from the peak unaccompanied and he was now wanted by the police. He had left Glasgow and played cat-and-mouse with the police by writing to the newspapers with taunts. He was run to ground on 3 September and attempted to take his own life when arrested.

Laurie was tried at Edinburgh and, while he admitted robbing

Rose, denied killing him. He was convicted on a majority verdict and sentenced to death. This was commuted to life imprisonment when he was judged insane. He escaped from Peterhead Prison in 1893 but was recaptured and spent the rest of his years at Perth Criminal Asylum where he died in 1930.
[*439, 784*]

LEE, JEAN

Prostitute whose practice of blackmailing her clients ultimately led to murder.

Jean Lee worked as a prostitute in Australia during the Second World War, drawing her clients from visiting servicemen. Her good looks and engaging manner guaranteed her success and her interests were protected by Robert David Clayton.

In the changing social scene following the war years, she began to look for a different clientele. With Clayton's help she developed a money-making racket whereby men were lured into a relationship and then found *in flagrante*. Clayton, posing as her irate husband, demanded money with menaces.

Their blackmailing scheme took on a more sinister aspect when they enrolled Norman Andrews as an enforcer. On 7 November 1949, in the bar of a hotel in Carlton, New South Wales, Lee targeted seventy-three-year-old William George Kent as a likely client. They succeeded in enticing the elderly bookmaker to his room in the hotel where he was plied with drink.

He resisted attempts to rob him and, in her frustration, Lee hit him with a bottle. This was the cue for Clayton and Andrews to get rough. They took his money and tied him up. While he was defenceless, they attacked him with a broken bottle. They left their victim to die while they celebrated at a night-club.

The police had no difficulty in establishing the identity of the attackers. They were rounded up in Sydney and eventually stood trial for murder. All three were convicted and sentenced to death. A retrial was granted on appeal because a statement from one of the accused was used to incriminate the others. It made no difference to the outcome; the death sentences were confirmed and the three were executed at Pentridge Prison on 19 February 1951.
[*508, 1001*]

LEE, JOHN HENRY

Teenage servant convicted of murder in 1885 who made criminal history by surviving three attempts to hang him.

John Lee went to work as footman for Emma Keyse, a wealthy spinster who lived at Babbacombe in Devon. On 15 November 1884, there was a great commotion at the house when a fire-alarm was raised. The blaze was bought under control and the body of Emma Keyse was found in the dining-room. Her throat was cut and she had been beaten about the head. It was clear that the fire had been set deliberately with the aid of paraffin.

Suspicion fell on Lee who was suspected of having murdered his employer because she had penalised him for some misdemeanour by reducing his wages. In an atmosphere of considerable local hostility, the Torquay magistrates named John Lee as the wilful murderer of Miss Keyse. He was tried in February 1885 and found guilty. After he had been sentenced to death, Lee spoke for the first time, declaring that God knew he was innocent.

Hangman James Berry was entrusted with Lee's execution at Exeter. On 23 February 1885, he went through his routine but the trap beneath Lee's feet refused to open. It resisted his frantic attempts to make it work and the condemned man was removed from the scaffold. The apparatus was successfully tested and Lee was brought back. Again the trap refused to open. A further delay ensued while carpenters worked to ease the wooden doors. Lee was placed on the drop a third time but the trap still refused to budge. Lee was returned to prison and was reprieved within hours.

'The Man They Could Not Hang' served twenty-two years in prison. He was released in 1907 and emigrated to America where he died, aged sixty-seven, in 1933.

[*428, 429, 559*]

LEFROY, PERCY

Failed writer in delicate health and poor financial condition who set out to rob and murder a railway passenger.

On 27 June 1881, Isaac Frederick Gold, a retired businessman who lived in Brighton, took a train from London Bridge station to return home. Before the train reached Croydon, a passenger heard four explosions which he took to be fog signals. When the train pulled into Preston Park, just outside Brighton, attention was drawn to one of the passengers whose clothing was heavily stained with blood.

Percy Lefroy, a journalist who lived near Croydon, was questioned by the police. He explained that he had occupied a compartment on the train with two other men. When the train entered Balcombe tunnel, he was attacked and knocked unconscious. When he regained his senses he found himself alone.

A railway worker had found Mr Gold's body on the line near Balcombe tunnel. The elderly businessman had been shot and stabbed. His gold watch was found in Lefroy's possession together with a number of Hanoverian medals. Police officers accompanied Lefroy to his lodgings but he gave them the slip and went into hiding in the East End of London. He was recaptured a week later.

Lefroy was tried at Maidstone Assizes in November 1881 before the Lord Chief Justice. He pleaded Not Guilty and confided to the prison officer, 'When I am acquitted, I hope I shan't be mobbed.' His confidence was shattered when the jury convicted him of murder and he was sentenced to death.

Before his execution on 29 November 1881, he admitted that he had been penniless and the purpose of his train journey had been to find a likely passenger to rob and, if necessary, murder.

[*324, 833, 971*]

LEHNBERG, MARLENE

Young woman infatuated with an older man who contrived to eliminate his wife to clear the way for marriage.

Marlene came from a religious family background and had a restricted upbringing. She left home when she was sixteen years old to live in Rondebosch near Cape Town and worked as a hospital receptionist. She also modelled, posing nude for amateur photographers.

In 1971, she met Christiaan van der Linde, a hospital technician, and fell in love with him. He was a married man with children who was flattered by Marlene's attentions but did not intend to destroy his marriage. Marlene set about prising him away from his wife. First she telephoned Susanna van der Linde, telling her about her husband's affair. This failed to have the desired effect, as did her claim that she was pregnant. With increasing frustration, she plotted murder.

Marlene befriended Marthinus Choegoe and manipulated him with promises of gifts and sex. He was a poor coloured man, handicapped by the loss of a leg in an accident, and putty in her hands. After two failed attempts, Choegoe, accompanied by

Marlene, drove to Belville on 4 November 1974. Susanna was stabbed to death with a pair of scissors.

Christiaan van der Linde was a suspect but inquiries soon led to the limping Choegoe who had been seen in the neighbourhood. He made a long statement admitting his part in the crime and naming Marlene as a participant. At the so-called 'Scissors Murder Trial' in March 1975, Marlene testified that she had not taken part in the killing and did her best to dissociate herself from Choegoe. The jury were more inclined to believe the coloured man who had clearly been her pawn. Marlene Lehnberg and Marthinus Choegoe were sentenced to death which, in both cases, was commuted to life imprisonment.

[67]

LEONSKI, EDWARD JOSEPH

American serviceman based in wartime Australia who terrorised the city of Melbourne with three murders in 1942. He explained that he killed in order to capture the soft voices of his victims.

In February 1942, a young woman survived a strangulation attempt after a man broke into her apartment. The next month, a woman was accosted by a man who told her, 'I was going to kill a girl tonight. You might as well be the one.' Her screams frightened off the attacker. These attacks went unreported.

On 2 May 1942, the body of Ivy McLeod was found in a shop doorway near Albert Park. She had been strangled. A week later, Pauline Thompson, a policeman's wife, was strangled and her body left in the street. The publicity resulting from these two murders inspired the survivor of the February attack to report to the police. She described her attacker as a serviceman, aged about twenty-eight years, with an American accent.

There were two other attempted strangulations during May and, on the 28th, Gladys Hosking, a young secretary, was found dead near Camp Pell. The whole of Melbourne, blacked-out for fear of a Japanese invasion, was in a state of terror as a result of the crimes committed by the anonymous 'Mad Yank'.

On 28 May, an alert sentry at the Royal Park military base, apprehended a returning GI on account of his muddy, unkempt appearance. Edward Joseph Leonski was arrested and the Melbourne police were contacted. He denied involvement in the spate of crimes but forensic evidence linked him to the last murder victim. He was tried by a US Army court martial and found guilty.

His insanity defence failed and the baby-faced Texan, who had boasted to room-mates about his killings, was hanged at Pentridge Gaol on 9 November 1942.
[*172, 401, 633*]

LEOPOLD AND LOEB

The 1924 trial for murder of two teenagers, Nathan Leopold and Richard Loeb, sons of prominent Chicago families, is one of America's outstanding criminal cases.

On 22 May 1924, workmen found the naked body of fourteen-year-old Bobby Franks in a culvert on waste ground in Chicago's northern suburbs. Franks was the son of millionaire businessman, Jacob Franks. Next to the body lay a pair of spectacles.

Jacob Franks had received a typewritten note from 'George Johnson' demanding a ransom of $10,000 before his son's body was found. Every individual with the name of Johnson was checked and the sons of several wealthy Chicago families were interviewed. Among those who readily offered help was eighteen-year-old Richard Loeb, son of the vice-president of Sears Roebuck.

The police had few clues apart from the spectacles found at the crime scene. The eyeglasses were traced to an oculist who said the prescription had been made up for Nathan Leopold. Nineteen-year-old Leopold was the son of another wealthy family who had a brilliant future ahead of him. Shown the spectacles, he told the police, 'If I were not positive that my glasses were at home, I would say these are mine.' Asked to produce his spectacles, he admitted that he was unable to find them.

The police were also determined to find the Underwood typewriter on which the ransom note had been produced. When questioned about this, Leopold denied that the machine he used regularly was an Underwood. Yet the notes of fellow students who had borrowed his typewriter obviously matched the ransom note. Meanwhile, Loeb had broken down under questioning and made a full confession implicating Leopold and himself in the murder of Bobby Franks. He spoke of a perfect murder committed for excitement that would be incapable of detection.

The youths were tried for murder in Chicago in July 1924 with Clarence Darrow, the renowned lawyer, presenting their defence. He faced strong public demands for the deaths of the killers. But Darrow pleaded mitigation on the grounds of reduced responsibility and mental illness. The social mores of the time did not permit him to say that the accused were homosexuals. His appeal, though, was only against capital punishment, and he argued passionately to save the two youths. They were convicted of the murder charge and sent to prison for life. An extra sentence of ninety-nine years' imprisonment was imposed for kidnapping.

Richard Loeb was killed in a prison brawl in 1936, while Nathan Leopold served thirty-three years and won his freedom in 1958. He married in 1961 and worked as an X-ray technician in Puerto Rico. He died in 1971. Film versions of the celebrated case were *Rope*, directed in 1948 by Alfred Hitchcock, and *Swoon*, in 1992, which explored the links between crime and homosexuality.

[*420, 565, 627, 832*]

LEY, THOMAS JOHN

It is unusual for a judge at a murder trial to find himself sentencing to death a former Minister of Justice. Such was the irony when Thomas John Ley, accused of the 'Chalkpit Murder', came before Lord Goddard in 1947.

On 30 November 1946, a man returning to his home in Woldingham, Surrey found the body of a man with a rope around his neck lying at the top of a chalkpit. The dead man was identified as thirty-five-year-old John McMain Mudie, a barman who worked in a hotel at Reigate. Mudie had been strangled with the rope and had also been beaten about the head. It was apparent that he had been killed elsewhere and dumped at the chalkpit.

Two weeks after Mudie was found dead, John William Buckingham, who ran a car-hire business, reported an interesting story to the police. He said that a porter he knew at a London hotel had alerted him to a driving job which required discretion. He was told to contact a Mr Ley who lived in Kensington, London.

Thomas John Ley, aged sixty-six, was a former Minister of Justice in New South Wales who had returned to London in 1929. He had been emotionally involved with a widow, Maggie Brook, for twelve years, to the point of insane jealousy. He was convinced that John Mudie, who had lodgings in the same house as Mrs Brook, was having an affair with her.

Ley's plan, for which he needed assistance, was to abduct Mudie and force him to sign some kind of confession. He recruited Lawrence John Smith, a building foreman, and John Buckingham, the driver. He spun them a tale about dealing with Mudie who he said was a blackmailer. Buckingham told the police that the plan went wrong and Mudie was killed.

Ley and Smith were questioned by the police. The former Minister of Justice denied everything while Smith's account broadly coincided with Buckingham's. All three men were arrested and charged with murder although Buckingham was later released.

Ley and Smith were tried at the Old Bailey before Lord Goddard in May 1947. It turned out that Smith and his car had been seen at the chalkpit on the day before the murder, suggesting that he had carried out a reconnaissance. Both men were convicted and sentenced to death. Ley, who had some harsh things to say to the judge, was considered to be insane and was reprieved by the Home Secretary and sent to Broadmoor. The death sentence on Smith was also lifted and he was given life imprisonment. Ley died at Broadmoor on 25 July 1947 following a stroke.
[*51, 482, 600, 671*]

LIGHTBOURNE, WENDELL WILLIS

Sex killer who vented his rage on the wealthy inhabitants living in Bermuda.

Scotland Yard detectives were called to the British colony in the West Atlantic in 1959 to help investigate a series of murders. An elderly widow was found dead on 7 March 1959 near her home. She had been raped and bludgeoned to death. A second rape murder was discovered on 11 May. Again the victim was an elderly woman living on her own.

The 40,000 population of the normally peaceful islands were shocked and frightened by what had happened. It was at this point that help was sought from Scotland Yard but, after a six-weeks' investigation that produced no results, the detectives returned to London. On 28 September, a twenty-nine-year-old woman recently arrived from England was reported missing after cycling to the beach. The body of Dorothy Rawlinson was found in a coral cove. It was apparent that she had been badly beaten before being cast into the sea.

Scotland Yard detectives were again called to help the island police force. Their inquiries led to the identification of a young coloured man who had been seen on the beach where Dorothy Rawlinson had been swimming. Wendell Willis Lightbourne worked as a caddie at the nearby golf-club. At first he denied seeing the girl on the beach but, under persistent questioning, admitted killing her: 'I bashed her,' he said, 'I know I can't go to heaven now.' He was charged with murdering Dorothy Rawlinson.

He was found guilty but the trial jury added a recommendation to mercy. In January 1960 sentence of death was commuted to life imprisonment to be served in Britain as there were no adequate prison facilities in Bermuda.

[*350, 629*]

LIPSKI, ISRAEL

Convicted of committing murder in 1887 by the unusual means of corrosive poisoning in a case that remains controversial.

A doctor was called to 16 Batty Street, Spitalfields, London on 28 June 1887 to attend Miriam Angel who had been found dead by a visitor. Angel, who was pregnant, lived in a second-floor room in the East End lodging house. After examining the yellow stains around her mouth, the doctor suspected corrosive poisoning.

The room was searched in the hope of finding the poison container. A look under the bed resulted in the discovery of a semi-conscious young man with the same discoloration around his mouth. Israel Lipski was revived and explained that he and Miriam Angel had been attacked by two workmen who forced them to drink nitric acid. Lipski occupied a room in the attic and a more likely explanation was that he had spied on the girl while going to and from his room and felt emboldened to make sexual advances. When he bungled his attempted sexual assault, he poisoned her and then tried to take his own life.

Lipski was tried in July 1887 and evidence that he had bought a quantity of nitric acid seemed to prove his guilt. Mr Justice James Fitzjames Stephen introduced the notion that Lipski had killed out of lust. This proved prejudicial for, whereas this had been speculated, it had not been mentioned during the trial. Lipski was convicted and sentenced to death.

There was considerable public disquiet about the verdict but the Home Secretary declined to recommend a reprieve. Lipski was hanged at Newgate after making a full confession. Controversy continued to surround the case and many believed that the confession was made out of fright rather than remorse.

[*308*]

LIST, JOHN EMIL

Accountant and churchgoer who murdered his wife, daughter, two sons and eighty-four-year-old mother at their home in Westfield, New Jersey in November 1971. The bullet-ridden bodies of the victims were found just over three weeks later. List had disappeared but he left behind a letter of confession in which he wrote, 'I know that what has been done is wrong . . .' In a postscript he pointed out, 'Mother is in the hall way in the attic – 3rd floor. She was too heavy to move. John'.

John List was a mild-mannered person whose career history was that of a man who secured jobs with impressive-sounding titles but which did not last. In 1965, he took up an appointment with the First National Bank of Jersey City and over-reached himself buying an expensive mansion in Westfield. His commitments pushed him beyond the limits of his salary, added to which he had a sick wife to look after.

Within a year he had lost his job but kept the news from his family. For six months he went through the daily charade of pretending to go to the office. He only told his wife after he had found a new job, but with a salary half that of his previous earnings, his financial troubles deepened.

List's neighbours regarded him as an old-fashioned figure. He kept himself to himself and was never seen without a coat and tie whether it was summer or winter. He mowed his own grass in a neighbourhood where such tasks were carried out by hired help. He taught at the local Sunday School and was co-leader of the cub-scouts pack. He was regarded as too strong on discipline and was described as a martinet and tinhorn tyrant.

Having taken additional mortgages and acquired heavy debts, List decided to lighten his burden by killing his family and starting a new life on his own. He went to Colorado where he changed his name to Robert Clark and worked as a kitchen night-shift cook. He remarried in 1985 and lived in Brandermill, Virginia. Perhaps he thought he was safe after eighteen years of anonymity but he had reckoned without the persistence of public curiosity. Fox Television's *America's Most Wanted* programme featured the List killings and a viewer called the hotline number to report that a man living in Brandermill answered John List's description.

In April 1989, List was found guilty on five counts of first-degree

murder. He was given five consecutive life sentences and the trial judge said, 'The name of John Emil List will be eternally synonymous with concepts of selfishness, horror and evil.'
[*60, 810, 840*]

LITTLE GREGORY

The case of four-year-old Gregory Villemin, who was murdered by drowning in the river near his home in eastern France in 1984, has rarely been out of the newspaper headlines.

On 16 October 1984, the boy's body, with its hands and feet tied, was found in the Vologne River near his home at Lepanges. For two years, his parents had been harrassed with anonymous telephone calls and poison-pen letters. On the day after the murder, Little Gregory's father, Jean-Marie Villemin, received a letter posted in Lepanges the day before the boy was drowned. It contained the hate-filled message, 'Look where you are now with all your money. Your son is dead and I have my revenge.'

Suspicion fell on Gregory's uncle, Bernard Laroche, who was supposed to be jealous of Villemin's success and whose own four-year-old child was mentally handicapped. The investigating authorities believed Laroche's handwriting was similar to that in the poison-pen letters. He was charged with the murder but then cleared. On 29 March 1985, Jean-Marie Villemin sought out Laroche and shot him dead in front of witnesses.

Three months later, in July 1985, Christine Villemin, Little Gregory's twenty-five-year-old mother, was charged with murdering her son. She and her husband had been receiving poison-pen letters since 1981, some 800 in all, containing threats, insults and abuse. Graphologists now said that Christine Villemin's handwriting resembled that of the letter writer.

She was eventually cleared in 1992 after an inquiry lasting seven years during which she had given birth to another child, attempted suicide and written an autobiography proclaiming her innocence.

In November 1993, Jean-Marie Villemin was tried at Dijon for the murder of Laroche. He was found guilty and sentenced to five years' imprisonment. In December, he was freed, as he had already spent three years in prison.

The mystery of Little Gregory's murder remains unsolved despite the close attention of the police, amateur detectives, examining

magistrates, graphologists, psychologists and novelists. The only thing that is certain is that an innocent boy was made victim of the dark, narrow prejudice that characterises the remote regions of France. Gregory's tombstone in the cemetery at Lepanges bears the inscription, 'In memory of an angel'.
[*747*]

LOCK AH TAM

Prominent member of the Chinese community in Britain who shot his wife and daughters in a fit of anger.

He was the representative in Europe of the organisation of Chinese dock-workers and was well respected for his welfare work on behalf of Chinese seamen. He lived in Liverpool with his Welsh wife and their two daughters. Lock Ah Tam was often called on to separate the protagonists in fights between seamen. In one such altercation in 1918, he suffered a severe head injury, an effect of which was that he became prone to fits of sudden rage.

In 1924 he lost heavily in a shipping investment and was made bankrupt. His behaviour became more mercurial with bouts of geniality interspersed with drinking and violence. On 1 December 1925, Lock Ah Tam gave a party at his home in Birkenhead to celebrate his son's coming-of-age. The occasion was a great success but, after the guests departed, the host flew into a rage. Armed with a revolver and a shotgun, he killed his wife and two daughters. His son fled to summon help.

When the police arrived, Lock Ah Tam told them simply, 'I have killed my wife and children.' He was sent for trial at Chester Assizes and members of the Chinese community throughout Britain contributed to his defence fund. Sir Edward Marshall Hall pleaded a defence of 'unconscious automatism' resulting from an epileptic fit. Counsel argued that this condition was initiated by the head injury sustained in 1918. He killed his beloved wife and daughters like a man walking in his sleep and unaware of what he was doing.

After retiring for twelve minutes and convinced that Lock Ah Tam was aware of his actions, the jury found him guilty of murder. He was hanged on 23 March 1926 at Liverpool's Walton Prison.
[*106, 632*]

LONERGAN, WAYNE

High-profile murder case in which pre-trial newspaper publicity was a prejudicial factor.

After returning to her apartment in New York City after a party on 23 October 1943, Patricia Burton was found dead. The twenty-two-year-old heiress to a brewery fortune had been strangled and beaten with a candlestick. She was separated from her husband, Wayne Lonergan, a serviceman in the Royal Canadian Air Force.

When detectives learned that Lonergan had been on leave in New York during the weekend of the murder, an alert was put out to the Canadian authorities and he was arrested in Toronto. He was subjected to many hours of police questioning which resulted in bureaucratic recriminations. He supposedly confessed to killing his wife after a quarrel, and details of his alleged violent sexual activity were leaked to the press. Lonergan was thus branded a murderer before coming to trial.

Worse was to follow when his arraignment in February 1944 ended in a mistrial and, in the course of his trial the following month, doubt was thrown on his confession. His statement had not been signed and was thus invalid as evidence. Although he had been in New York at the time the murder was committed, it was not proved that he had been at the murder scene.

Despite the irregularities of the prosecution case, Lonergan was convicted of second-degree murder and sentenced to thirty years to life imprisonment. He was released in 1965 after serving twenty-two years in Sing Sing prison and was deported to Canada.
[*414, 748*]

LORD LUCAN

The murder of the Lucan family's nanny and the disappearance of the earl remain one of the greatest mysteries of the twentieth century.

Richard John Bingham went to Eton and was an officer in the Coldstream Guards. He married in 1963 and the following year succeeded to the title of Seventh Earl of Lucan. He moved in elite social circles and developed a reputation as a gambler, winning or losing as much as £5000 in a day.

His marriage faltered and in 1974 he and his wife Veronica separated. He lost custody of his children following a legal battle which, together with gambling losses, put him in a bitter mood.

Lady Lucan and their three children continued to live in their home in Lower Belgrave Street, London.

On 7 November 1974, an assault occurred at the Lucan home which resulted in Lady Lucan running into a nearby pubic house exclaiming that she had been attacked. Police found bloodstains on the stairs leading to the basement, at the foot of which was a canvas mail-bag containing the body of Sandra Rivett. The twenty-nine-year-old nanny had been beaten to death.

Lady Lucan explained that they had all been watching television upstairs and Sandra left the room to make tea. Because she was gone a long while, Lady Lucan went downstairs to find her, only to be attacked by her husband. She struggled with him and he said he had killed Sandra in mistake for his wife. When he calmed down, she seized her moment to flee from the house and summon help. At that point, Lucan disappeared.

In the immediate aftermath, Lucan telephoned his mother and told her he had found an intruder attacking his wife. Late on the night of the murder, he visited a friend in East Sussex to whom he explained that his wife had accused him of hiring someone to kill her. Two days after the murder Lucan wrote to another friend, saying that in view of what had happened he proposed to lie low. His car was found the next day at Newhaven on the Sussex coast. The interior was bloodstained and a length of lead piping was found in it.

Despite nationwide searches, there was no trace of Lucan's whereabouts. The inquest into Sandra Rivett's death held in June 1975 concluded that she had been murdered by Lord Lucan. Changes were later made in the law depriving coroners of the power to charge an individual with murder but, in Lucan's case, the charge remained.

Immense speculation ensued regarding Lucan and supposed sightings came in from all around the world. In 1987, two separate accounts of the case were published. Both excluded Lucan as the murderer. It was argued in one that Lucan hired a contract killer to dispose of his wife so that he could regain custody of his children. In the other, the murder was supposedly committed by a thief who was disturbed by Sandra Rivett. If either of these explanations is correct, the murderer remains at liberty.

The twentieth anniversary of Lucan's disappearance in 1994 brought a flurry of books and television programmes. Claims that he was dead were counter-balanced by renewed assertions that he had been seen in South Africa, South America and Australia. In 1995, there was fresh evidence about his movements after the murder when it was alleged he had been seen with friends after the last previously reported sighting. Scotland Yard said the file remains open.

In September 2003, *The Sunday Telegraph* carried a feature headed, 'Is this Lord Lucan?' A photograph showed a bearded individual, said to resemble Lucan, who, according to former Scotland Yard detective, John MacLaughlin, had been living as a hippy in Goa. The man turned out to be Barry Halpin, also known as 'Jungle Barry', a well known pub character in the UK in the 1960s.

[*331, 594, 639, 668, 768, 775*]

LOUGHANS, HAROLD

Judged to have been incapable of strangling a murder victim because of a physical disability but subsequently driven to confess after losing a libel action.

Rose Ada Robinson, the licensee of the John Barleycorn public house in Portsmouth, was found dead in her room over the pub on 29 November 1943. The sixty-three-year-old widow had been strangled and robbed. It was rumoured that she kept the cash from the pub takings in her room. The police maintained surveillance on a number of known criminals. One of these was Harold Loughans, a thief with a long record, who was arrested in London. He admitted breaking into the John Barleycorn and assaulting Mrs Robinson to stop her screaming, but he did not intend to kill her.

At the magistrates' court, Loughans withdrew his statement, claiming the police had talked him into making admissions. He was tried at Winchester in March 1944 and witnesses were produced who provided him with an alibi. The jury failed to agree a verdict and the judge ordered a retrial. At the Old Bailey two weeks later, the alibi evidence was repeated and Sir Bernard Spilsbury testified that because of his mutilated right hand, Loughan would have been incapable of exerting enough pressure to cause strangulation. He was found not guilty.

Subsequently, Loughans was imprisoned for attempted murder in the course of burglary at St Albans. While in prison in 1960, he issued libel proceedings against *The People* newspaper which published extracts from the autobiography of J.D. Casswell, prosecuting counsel at his Winchester trial. Loughans claimed that

he was portrayed as lucky to escape conviction. In 1963 he lost his case when the jury found in favour of the newspaper and effectively ruled that he had been guilty of murder. *The People* subsequently published his confession to the murder and Loughans died in 1965 soon after being released from prison.
[*28, 955*]

LUARD CASE

Unsolved murder linked thirty years later with a man who was hanged for another crime.

Shots were heard during the afternoon of 24 August 1908 at the home of Major General Charles Edward Luard at Ightham in Kent. When the general returned from a walk on the nearby golf course, he found his wife in the summerhouse in Fish Pond Woods. Caroline Luard had been shot in the head and both her purse and rings were missing.

Sixty-nine-year-old General Luard was distraught and was not helped by anonymous letters accusing him of killing his wife. The fact that the shots could be precisely timed at 3.15 pm ruled out the general as a suspect for he was seen half a mile away at that time. It was widely supposed that Mrs Luard was killed by an opportunistic thief.

Despite his exoneration by the murder investigators and the coroner, General Luard continued to receive hate-filled letters. In a state of despair, he took his own life on 18 September 1908 by throwing himself in the path of a train. He left a note saying he could not bear the horrible imputations made against him and that he cared for nothing but to join his wife.

A suggestion was made in 1939 that **John Dickman**, hanged at Newcastle in 1910 for the murder of John Innes Nisbet, had been implicated in the murder of Mrs Luard. He was supposed to have made an appeal in the newspapers seeking support as a 'distressed gentleman', to which Mrs Luard responded by sending a cheque. When he altered the cheque for a larger amount, Mrs Luard threatened to inform the police, with the result that Dickman felt obliged to murder her. It was alleged that highly placed officials who were friends of the Luards determined that Dickman was her murderer and would not benefit from a reprieve after the verdict went against him at the Nisbet trial.
[*733, 943, 1015*]

LUCAS, HENRY LEE

America's most infamous serial killer who confessed to over 300 murders. In 1986, he was sentenced to death for killing an unidentified hitch-hiker whose body was found near the Interstate Highway in Texas seven years earlier.

Lucas experienced a brutal childhood. He was the last of eleven children whose mother was a prostitute and his father a cripple. As a child aged eight years, Lucas was beaten senseless by his mother and suffered permanent brain damage as a result. He also lost an eye in a childhood fight.

He claimed to have committed his first murder when he was fifteen years old. In January 1960, he killed his mother after an argument and was sentenced to twenty years' imprisonment. While in prison, he suffered hallucinations and several times attempted to commit suicide. He was recommended for parole in 1970 because the Michigan prison system was overcrowded. He was paroled against his wishes and killed again within an hour of leaving the prison.

Lucas killed several times during the early 1970s and in 1977 met Ottis Toole with whom he had a homosexual relationship. Toole introduced him to his nephew and niece and the four made a kind of criminal family, robbing banks and filling stations. Lucas took Toole's niece, Becky Powell, not yet in her teens, as his common-law wife.

In 1982, Lucas and Becky stayed in Ringgold, Texas with elderly Kate Rich for whom he worked as a handyman. On 24 August, he killed Becky after an argument and, the following month, killed Kate Rich because she asked too many questions.

Lucas was arrested in Montague County, Texas on 11 June 1983. He immediately attempted to commit suicide. While in custody, he astounded detectives by confessing to hundreds of murders in every state except Hawaii and Alaska. In October 1983, he was sentenced to seventy-five years' imprisonment for the murder of Kate Rich and, in November, was given a life sentence for murdering Becky Powell. In 1986, he was convicted of the murder of a hitch-hiker in Texas and was sentenced to death.

At this point, Lucas went back on his earlier confessions, although the police had substantiated his accounts to the extent that they were able to close the files on over 200 cases. He now said, 'I never killed nobody but Mom.'

He claimed to have committed incest, necrophilia, rape, bestiality and murder. He was diagnosed as schizophrenic and clinical tests confirmed that he had extensive neurological damage. He was also a chronic alcoholic and drug abuser over many years. Dr Joel Norris, the forensic psychologist, described Lucas as belonging to the walking dead. His death sentence was commuted to life imprisonment in 1998. He died in prison from a heart attack on 13 March 2001, aged sixty-four. Over five hundred people attended his funeral.

[*146, 210, 707*]

LUETGERT, ADOLPH LOUIS

A lady-killer from Chicago who murdered his wife to clear the way for his extra-marital affairs.

Luetgert was the owner of a sausage-making business in Chicago whose products were widely acknowledged by lovers of German sausage. He was a man of considerable appetite. He kept several mistresses at a time and had a bed installed at his factory to facilitate his liaisons.

Luetgert was married but his wife Louisa was probably as tired of his excesses as he was of her. On 1 May 1897, Louisa disappeared and Luetgert told her relatives that to avoid a scandal he had hired private detectives to find her. Suspicious of his motives, Louisa's family eventually went to the police.

A search of his factory led to the emptying of one of the steam vats used for sausage-making. Among the debris in the tank were pieces of bone, some teeth and two engraved rings belonging to Louisa. Luetgert insisted that the bone fragments were of animal origin but tests proved they were human.

Luetgert was tried for murder and his former mistresses told their stories of his sexual activities which made sensational headlines in Chicago's newspapers. He continued to deny murdering his wife but one of his mistresses related how he had spoken of crushing Louisa. It was assumed, but never proved, that he killed her with a knife and consigned her body for destruction in one of his factory's steam vats.

He was convicted and sentenced to life imprisonment. He never confessed and died in 1911 in Joliet Prison.

[*415, 586, 960*]

M

MACDONALD, Dr JEFFREY

The murder of an army doctor's family in their home at Fort Bragg was blamed first on intruders and then on Dr MacDonald who was brought to trial and convicted nine years after the event.

Captain Jeffrey MacDonald was a 'Green Beret' medical officer based at Fort Bragg in North Carolina where he lived with his wife and family in married quarters. He raised the alarm early on the morning of 17 February 1970, telling base military police that there had been a stabbing.

Officers found Colette MacDonald in the master bedroom: she had been clubbed to death with such force that both her arms were broken in her attempts to defend herself. She had also been stabbed. The two children lay dead in their separate bedrooms – they too had been bludgeoned. Dr MacDonald was slightly wounded. He spoke of three hippie intruders whom he called 'acid heads' who had attacked his family.

News of the murders, possibly committed by drug-affected hippies, stimulated comparisons with the **Manson** murders which had occurred in the previous year. The absence of signs that might be associated with an attack by intruders led to suspicions that MacDonald himself was the murderer. His father-in-law held this view and pursued a relentless investigation.

In 1975, after he had left the army and was working as a private physician, Dr MacDonald was called before a Grand Jury. His indictment on three counts of murder was overturned on appeal because his rights had been violated. But in 1979, he was tried for murder at Raleigh. He denied the charges but various contradictions emerged regarding the forensic evidence and his version of what had happened.

It was believed that MacDonald, portrayed as a perfectionist, had flown into a rage and murdered his family in a fit of uncontrollable violence. He was convicted of second-degree murder in respect of his wife and eldest child but of first-degree murder regarding the death of his youngest child whom it was believed was killed in a deliberate act designed to bolster the story of an attack by intruders. He was sentenced to three terms of life imprisonment.

The story of the murders was told in 1983 by Joe McGinniss in the book *Fatal Vision* which was also the title of a television programme on the case. Dr MacDonald maintained his innocence in an interview with *Playboy* magazine in 1985 and resolved to continue his appeals against conviction.
[*626, 756, 884*]

MACKAY, PATRICK

Serial murderer recognised as a psychopath at the age of fifteen who killed eleven times before being captured.

Mackay was brought up in a family dominated by a drunken father who beat up his mother and sisters. His father died when Patrick was ten years old but the habit of violence was already ingrained in the boy. He bullied his fellow pupils at school, threatened his mother and sisters and tortured the family pets.

He was educationally backward and devoted his waking hours to violent pursuits including an unhealthy interest in Nazism. He was referred for psychiatric examination and at the age of fifteen was classified as a psychopath. Mackay committed numerous thefts, burglaries and assaults and was twice discharged from mental hospitals.

On 21 March 1975, he attacked and killed sixty-three-year-old Father Anthony Crean at Shorne in Kent. The priest had tried to help Mackay lead a more constructive life but was killed for his trouble. He was felled with an axe and stabbed several times. Mackay was known to have visited Father Crean and was easily rounded up by the police at his flat in London. He admitted murdering the priest and told detectives, 'I thoroughly enjoyed killing him – the blood made me more excited, it just made me worse.'

Under questioning, Mackay claimed that he had committed his first murder in June 1973 and killed nine other victims, mostly elderly people, before murdering Father Crean. He was charged

with three murders and sent for trial at the Old Bailey in November 1975. Despite his undoubted history of mental disturbance, Mackay was not found insane. He was convicted and sentenced to life imprisonment.
[*182*]

McDONALD, WILLIAM

A series of murders committed as revenge by an ex-soldier whose mind was unbalanced by a homosexual attack made on him seventeen years earlier.

The deaths of four male vagrants found in the environs of Sydney over a two-year period between June 1961 and November 1962 were attributed to a serial killer. They had died of multiple stab wounds and mutilation of the genitals indicated a possible homosexual motive. The newspapers lost no time in referring to the killer as 'The Sydney Mutilator'.

The killer was discovered by chance when one of his victims was mistakenly identified as Allen Brennan, a postal worker. After workmates had expressed their sympathy by contributing to a wreath sent to his funeral, Brennan was seen in downtown Sydney. The postal worker, whose real name was William McDonald, had some explaining to do. When he was arrested in Melbourne, he admitted he had an urge to kill.

Medical evidence regarding McDonald's state of mind took up most of the court's time at his trial for murder in September 1963. An important trauma in his life was a homosexual attack made on him by a fellow serviceman in 1944 when he was in the British Army. As a young man he harboured fears of becoming mad and this attack altered his personality. He was discharged from military service after being diagnosed a schizophrenic and was subsequently in and out of various mental institutions.

McDonald emigrated to Australia where his mental health deteriorated and he began to seek revenge for the homosexual attack which he believed had so damaged him. He heard voices which inspired him to commit murder and mutilation. The jury declined to accept evidence of insanity and convicted him of murder. He was sentenced to life imprisonment and sent to Long Bay Penitentiary where he was in due course found to be insane.
[*517, 823*]

McELROY CASE

An extraordinary murder case in which the inhabitants of a small American town meted out fatal rough justice to the local bully.

Forty-seven-year-old Kenneth Rex McElroy was a successful farmer in the town of Skidmore, Missouri which had a population of fewer than 500 souls. A heavily built man who usually carried a rifle with him, McElroy had a reputation as a bully. He terrorised the local people and committed violent acts, including rape and robbery. On one occasion he shot and wounded a man but, as always, people were too frightened to take action.

In July 1981, McElroy got into an argument with an elderly store-keeper, Ernest Bowencamp, and shot him in the face leaving him severely injured. McElroy was arrested but was quickly released on bail and swaggered about the town carrying his rifle.

For the citizens of Skidmore he had gone one bridge too far. They held a public meeting to decide what to do. Afterwards, the men made their way to the town's bar and ordered drinks. McElroy was present with his wife Trena. The unusual presence of so many of the town's men carried with it an air of menace even for the bully.

When McElroy left the bar and made his way to his pick-up truck in the street outside, he was followed by about forty-five men. They crowded around the vehicle. Suddenly a man appeared with a rifle and, firing repeatedly at McElroy, shot him dead at the steering wheel. A typical newspaper headline was, 'Farmer Shot to Death in Apparent Vigilante Attack'.

No one could be found to verify the course of events described by Mrs McElroy. A Grand Jury was called but no indictment was made. Trena McElroy testified at the coroner's court and the sheriff and postmaster also gave evidence. The jury returned a verdict of a felony committed by a person or persons unknown. The state authority in Kansas City convened a Grand Jury but again no indictment was issued.

In 1982, McElroy's farmhouse was burned down. Local inhabitants said it had been struck by lightning. The killing of Ken McElroy remains unsolved.

[*387, 608*]

MAHON, PATRICK HERBERT

Ladies' man who resorted to murder and demonstrated the difficulty of destroying his victim by dismemberment.

Marriage seemed to turn Mahon from a law-abiding citizen into a felon. In 1910, when he was twenty, he married an eighteen-year-old girl and they had two children. She stuck by him despite his numerous philanderings and prison sentences for fraud and robbery.

Mrs Mahon was also responsible in 1922 for securing a job for her husband as a salesman which ultimately led to disaster. While working for a company making aerators at Sunbury, Mahon exercised his charm on a thirty-seven-year-old secretary, Emily Beilby Kaye. She became besotted with the handsome charmer and they talked about living together as an experiment.

In fulfilment of this plan, Mahon rented a cottage located on a lonely part of the Sussex coast known as the Crumbles. The couple carefully prepared the way for their rendezvous at the cottage on 12 April 1924. Mahon told his employer he would be in Eastbourne on company business and Emily told her friends she was visiting South Africa with her fiancé.

Fed up with her husband's wayward behaviour around Easter time, Mrs Mahon did a trawl through the pockets of one of his suits. She found a cloakroom ticket issued at Waterloo station. A friend retrieved a Gladstone bag containing bloodstained female clothing from the left luggage office. The bag was replaced and detectives had no difficulty apprehending Mahon when he arrived to collect it. The bag, which Mahon explained had been used to carry dog meat, also contained a knife and a tennis racquet with the initials EBK.

Police descended on the cottage at the Crumbles and found the grisly remains of Emily Beilby Kaye. Pieces of her dismembered body were contained in a saucepan, hatbox, trunk and biscuit tin. An attempt had been made to destroy parts of the body, and bone fragments were found in the fire-grate. Sir Bernard Spilsbury pieced together the remains of Emily who was found to be pregnant; her head was never recovered.

Mahon explained that he and Emily had argued and she had fallen, accidentally striking her head on the coal-bucket. In view of the fact that he was known to have bought a knife and a tenon saw on the day he went down to Eastbourne, his real intentions seemed obvious. Moreover, he had been busily extracting money from Emily's savings account.

Mahon was tried at Lewes Assizes when his contrived explanations were exposed to the jury. There seemed to be a moment of divine intervention when he denied wishing to see Emily dead and the court was shaken by a violent burst of thunder and lightning. He was found guilty of murder and sentenced to death. Mahon was hanged on 2 September 1924 at Wandsworth Prison.
[*227, 767, 952, 966*]

MAIN LINE MURDER

On 25 June 1979, Susan Reinhart, a teacher at Upper Merion High School in Pennsylvania, went missing. Her nude body was later found in her car at Harrisburg. She had apparently died of asphyxiation and marks on her body suggested that she had been restrained with chains. Her two children were missing.

The Main Line Murder Case, named after the area west of Philadelphia that was home to a cluster of academic institutions, proved to be highly controversial. Newspaper reports of Reinert's death referred to alleged occult and bizarre sexual practices at Upper Merion. It became known that the murder victim had taken out a large life insurance policy naming fellow teacher Bill Bradfield as beneficiary.

In 1983, Bradfield was charged with the murder of Reinert and her two children whose whereabouts were unknown. The prosecution maintained that Reinert was killed for the insurance money but her killer had probably been assisted. Bradfield was convicted of first degree murder and given three consecutive life sentences. In June 1983, Dr Jay Smith, a former colonel in the US Army Reserve and Principle of Upper Merion, was also charged with murder. Largely on the strength of circumstantial evidence, he was convicted in April 1986 of three counts of murder. Smith was sentenced to death by unanimous recommendation of the jury. In December 1989, the Pennsylvania Supreme Court overturned his conviction on the grounds of misconduct by the prosecution. A new trial was ordered but this decision was reversed and Smith was discharged.
[*207, 828, 957*]

MAJOR, ETHEL LILLIE

Poisoner who drew suspicion to herself by the careless disposal of tainted food given to her husband.

Ethel and Arthur Major married in 1918 and lived with the bride's parents until they could afford a place of their own. They moved to Kirkby-on-Bain, Lincolnshire in 1929 and appeared to lead a settled family life. Their contentment was disrupted when rumours reached Arthur Major about an alleged illegitimate child born to his wife in 1915. From his inquiries he learned that Auriel, his wife's 'sister', was in fact her daughter. To avoid a scandal at the time, Ethel's parents had treated the infant as their own.

Major was resentful that his wife had not told him about the child and demanded to know the identity of the father. Her refusal to tell him led to bitter arguments and their marriage disintegrated. In 1934, Ethel learned that her husband was receiving letters from another woman. She reacted jealously and complained to everyone, including the local Chief Constable.

This emotional episode ended with Arthur's death. On 22 May 1934, he fell ill with violent stomach pains which were blamed on a meal of corned beef. He died two days later. Foul-play was suspected when the police received an anonymous letter claiming that a neighbour's dog had died after eating food scraps put out by Ethel. The dog was exhumed and traces of strychnine found in its organs. Arthur Major's funeral was stopped and a post-mortem carried out which showed that he had died of strychnine poisoning.

Ethel gave herself away by volunteering a reference to strychnine poisoning which had not previously been mentioned. She was tried for murder at Lincoln Assizes and convicted. The jury made a recommendation to mercy but she was nevertheless hanged at Hull Prison on 19 December 1934.

[*372, 1027*]

MALENO AND SOLI

Steven Maleno and Salvatore Soli murdered John S. Knight III, the wealthy newspaper owner, in his Philadelphia penthouse.

On the evening of 7 December 1975, Knight entertained an old school-friend and his wife in his apartment. The couple stayed overnight and were disturbed in the small hours by intruders. They found three armed men ransacking the apartment and in the midst of his possessions strewn about the floor was the body of John S. Knight. He was bound and gagged. 'We came to settle a grudge,' said one of the intruders. The intruders escaped and Knight died of knife wounds in his chest.

Although a wealthy man, Knight kept very little money in his apartment. It emerged that he was in the habit of picking up young homosexuals and inviting them back to his home. A diary listing prostitutes of both sexes was found which provided police with a basis for questioning suspects. Within days, police had narrowed their search to three individuals. One of these, Steven Maleno, turned himself in and Salvatore Soli was arrested in Miami. The third man, Isaias Felix Melendez, had been shot and killed after the murder by Maleno.

The men belonged to Philadelphia's underworld where gangs of youths preyed on rich homosexuals like Knight who prowled the bars looking for prostitutes.

Both attempted to put the blame for the penthouse killing on the now-dead Melendez but eventually Maleno confessed. He was sentenced to two consecutive terms of life imprisonment. Soli made no admissions but was convicted of murder and sentenced to life imprisonment.

[56]

MALIK, ABDUL

A devotee of Malcolm X, the American Black Power leader, Malik preached extreme racialism which ended in the murder of two of his followers in Trinidad.

Michael de Freitas, a Trinidadian, changed his name to Abdul Malik when he converted to the Muslim faith in 1963. He founded a movement for racial advancement in London in the 1960s but was soon in trouble with the police. He attracted media attention and talked openly of killing white people. He left Britain in 1970 after being convicted of robbery and returned to Trinidad. He made his base at a house in Port of Spain called La Chance where he surrounded himself with a few close associates. His hopes of becoming a political focus on the island did not materialise – he was a man with no influence.

There was a fire at La Chance on 19 February 1972 and the house was completely destroyed. Three of Malik's followers talked to the police but he had disappeared. An alert detective looking around the garden noticed unusually lush growth in a bed planted with lettuce. Probing of the soft soil located the remains of a human corpse and further digging at the site turned up a second body.

The bodies were identified as Gail Benson and Joe Skerrit, who had been members of Malik's clan. Malik was arrested in Guyana and returned to Trinidad where he stood trial for murder. He exerted a powerful influence over his band of followers and had ordered Gail Benson's killing because she was disruptive. Two of her erstwhile companions hacked her to death and buried her alive. Skerrit was bludgeoned to death because he objected to plans to carry out a robbery.

Malik was convicted of Skerrit's murder and sentenced to death. Two of his followers were convicted of Benson's murder. Abdul Malik, a failed leader, was hanged on 16 May 1975.

[*449, 841, 1031, 1032*]

MALTBY, CECIL

An act of murder was concealed for several months by the perpetrator confining himself in the house with the steadily decomposing corpse.

Cecil Maltby was a tailor with a shop near Regent's Park in London. He had taken to drink and neglected his business but nevertheless proved attractive to Alice Middleton, the lonely wife of a Merchant Navy seaman. During the summer of 1922, while her husband was at sea, she went to live with Maltby.

It was known that the couple went to race meetings but Alice was not seen after August. When Mr Middleton returned from his travels and found his wife missing, he reported this to the police. They attempted to question Maltby but, beyond confirming he had not seen the missing lady since 15 August, he admitted nothing. Nor would he allow officers into his house.

A watch was kept on the premises and Maltby was seen occasionally at one of the windows but did not emerge from the building. Finally, an entry was forced on 10 January 1923 after a health order had been issued because the premises were regarded as a hazard.

As the police broke in, a single shot rang out and Maltby was found in a locked bedroom where he had shot himself.

In a bath in the kitchen were the decomposing remains of Alice Middleton where she had lain for several months. She had been shot three times in the back. Notes near the body purported to show that she had committed suicide on 24 August 1922. Letters

written by Maltby were found in other parts of the house which gave details of how he allegedly struggled with her when she attempted to take her life and the gun went off accidentally. The coroner's jury had no difficulty in reaching a verdict of murder and suicide against Maltby.
[*206, 695*]

MANNING, MARIA AND FREDERICK

Celebrated Victorian murder case in which husband and wife murdered for gain.

Maria was born in Switzerland and her maiden name was De Roux. She came to England in the 1840s and worked as a ladies maid in Devon. She met Frederick Manning, a former publican and railwayman, and they were married in London in May 1847. The couple went to live at Minver Place in Bermondsey and existed on the proceeds of Manning's previous robberies.

One of Maria's admirers was Patrick O'Connor, an Irishman working in the London docks, whom she had known before her marriage to Manning. They continued their liaison and O'Connor was a frequent visitor at Minver Place. Apart from his work as a gauger at London docks, he ran a profitable sideline as a money-lender and made a considerable fortune. By contrast, the Mannings were always in financial difficulty.

On 8 August 1847, O'Connor received a note from Maria inviting him to dinner at Minver Place. When the Irishman failed to report for work, the police began to make inquiries. The Mannings were questioned but could offer no explanation. When the police returned on 17 August, they found the house devoid of occupants and stripped of furniture. Signs of disturbance to the kitchen floor prompted officers to lift some of the flagstones. They discovered O'Connor's body lying in a quicklimed grave. He had been shot and bludgeoned to death.

Maria was traced to Edinburgh and Frederick Manning to Jersey. They were returned to London to face murder charges. At their trial at the Old Bailey, he blamed Maria while she maintained she was not even at Minver Place at the time the murder took place. They were both found guilty and sentenced to death, Maria exclaiming, 'There is neither law nor justice here.'

On 13 November 1847, the Mannings were executed before a large crowd in front of Horsemongers' Lane Gaol. Maria wore

a black satin dress which was said to have made that material unpopular. Before he was hanged, Frederick Manning made a confession to the murder in which he implicated Maria.
[*12, 96, 446, 651*]

MANSON, CHARLES MILLER

Leader of a cult commune in California who ordered the execution of Sharon Tate and others in a plan code-named 'Helter Skelter'.

Manson was born in Kentucky, the son of a prostitute. While he was still a child his mother was imprisoned for robbery and he spent his formative years in different institutions. He committed his first crime, an armed robbery, when he was thirteen years old and progressively became alienated from society. He married and divorced and in 1960 began a ten-year prison sentence for fraud and theft.

On his release in 1967, Manson joined the hippie community in San Francisco and established his own community called the 'Family'. He had a personal magnetism that attracted people and was regarded as a Christ-like figure to be followed and obeyed. The 'Family' experimented with drugs and indulged in free-love. In the autumn of 1967, he moved with the 'Family' to Spahn Ranch near Hollywood and attempted to establish himself as a popular musician. This failed and it served to strengthen his deep-seated hatred of society. He drew up a death-list of 'pigs'.

On 9 August 1969, three of Manson's followers broke into the home of Hollywood film-director Roman Polanski. The film-maker was away but his pregnant wife Sharon Tate was at home with friends. She and her three companions were shot, stabbed and clubbed to death, and the words 'Pig' and 'War' were daubed in blood on the walls of the house. Two days later, Leno and Rosemary La Bianca were similarly murdered in a neighbouring house. The words 'Death to pigs' were smeared on the walls.

One of the women who had participated in the Sharon Tate killing boasted about it to a fellow prisoner while in custody. This resulted in Manson and the women being tried on six counts of murder in 1970. The trial proved to be sensational. Manson was accused of ordering the executions and, while his followers admitted their guilt, they claimed he was innocent. Lawyers refused to question them and they declined to testify after the judge ruled they could only do so without the jury being present. Manson told the court that he cared nothing for society and described his 'Family' as people who had been discarded.

Manson was found guilty and sentenced to death although this was commuted to life imprisonment when California gave up the death penalty. Members of the 'Family' received life sentences for their part in the killings. He became eligible for parole in 1978 but his applications have been consistently rejected. He has become a symbol of the drop-out, drug-oriented culture prevalent in California in the 1960s and his music made a comeback in the 1990s.

[*25, 129, 338, 556, 805, 815, 825, 963*]

MANTON, HORACE WILLIAM ('BERTIE')

Chance intervened to allow a woman murder victim to be identified after she had been deliberately disfigured.

The body of an unidentified woman was found in the River Lea near Luton by two men on their way to work on 19 November 1943. She had been strangled and an attempt made to render her features unrecognisable. Despite the circulation in the Luton area of descriptions of the dead woman and photographs of her reconstructed face, no one came forward to identify her. The breakthrough came by chance when a woman's coat was found on a refuse dump. A dry-cleaning tag sewn into the garment enabled it to be traced to a shop in Luton where it had been handed in by Mrs Caroline Manton.

Police visited her home and Manton, a driver for the National Fire Service, told them that his wife had left him to stay with her brother and produced letters which he claimed she had written to him. He denied that the woman depicted in the police photograph was his wife.

Manton proved to be the author of the letters allegedly written by his wife, and a fingerprint left by Mrs Manton on a pickle jar in her pantry confirmed the identity of the dead woman. Faced with this evidence, Manton made a full confession describing how he and his wife had quarrelled. He battered her with a wooden stool and wheeled her body, wrapped in a sack, on his bicycle to the river's edge where he tipped it into the water. His assault on his wife was not quite the spontaneous attack he made it out to be, for he had first strangled her.

He was tried at Bedford Assizes in 1944 when he was found guilty and sentenced to death. This was commuted to life imprisonment and the 'Luton Sack Murderer' died in Parkhurst Prison in November 1947.
[*471, 855*]

MANUEL, PETER THOMAS ANTHONY

Cast in the true mould of the cold-blooded killer, he murdered at least seven people.

Manuel lived with his parents in Glasgow and, by the time he reached the age of sixteen, already had a long criminal record for theft. He was an habitual offender and his record grew to include convictions for rape and assault. On 16 September 1956 the home of William Watt in Glasgow was broken into and Mrs Marion Watt, her daughter and sister were all shot dead. The killings seemed motiveless, for nothing had been stolen. Manuel was questioned and released, although he was put under surveillance.

In January 1958, there was another triple murder in Glasgow. Peter Smart, his wife and eleven-year-old son were shot dead in their home. Manuel was questioned after he had passed some recently issued £1 notes of a new design. Notes of this type had been stolen from the Smart's bungalow. House-breaking tools were found in Manuel's home and he and his father were arrested. Manuel agreed to talk provided his father was released. He admitted the two triple murders and also confessed to killing two seventeen-year-old girls in separate incidents. Anne Kneilands was murdered in East Kilbride in September 1956 and Isabelle Cooke in January 1958. The police found Manuel to be a hardened killer, completely lacking in any feelings for his victims and unable to say why he had taken their lives.

Manuel was tried in Glasgow in May 1958 for eight murders. After dismissing his counsel, he conducted his own defence. He was found guilty on seven counts of murder. There was insufficient evidence regarding the charge that he had murdered Anne Kneilands. The judge, Lord Cameron, remarked, 'A man may be very bad without being mad.' Manuel was hanged at Barlinnie Prison on 11 July 1958.
[*76, 245, 529, 599, 998*]

MAREK, MARTHA

Compulsive spender who resorted to fraud and then murder by poisoning as a means of acquiring fresh funds.

Martha Lowenstein was only fifteen when her beauty attracted a customer at the Viennesse dress shop where she worked. She was an orphan who had been adopted by a poor family. Elderly Moritz Fritsch was a wealthy man who in 1919 asked her to become his ward and paid for her to be educated at finishing school. When he died five years later, he left his property to her.

In 1924 Martha married an engineer, Emil Marek, and life appeared to be rosy indeed. Unfortunately, she had become accustomed to living beyond her means and discovered that her legacy was running out. In order to acquire more funds, the couple devised a plan to defraud Emil's insurance company. He was insured against accident for £10,000 and soon fell victim to one. While cutting down a tree, the axe slipped and so severely damaged his leg that the limb had to be amputated below the knee.

Suspicions were aroused when the leg wound was seen to be self-inflicted. The Mareks were charged with fraud but avoided conviction although they were imprisoned as a result of bribing medical staff to give false evidence. Following a failed business venture, they sank deeper into poverty and first Emil and then one of their children died of tuberculosis.

Martha moved in with an elderly relative, Susanne Lowenstein, and inherited her property when she died. She took in lodgers and again attempted an insurance fraud after one of them died. Suspicious relatives accused Martha of being a poisoner. Exhumations were ordered which showed that Emil and Ingeborg Marek, Susanne Lowenstein and an elderly lodger had all died of thallium poisoning. Martha was tried and found guilty on four counts of murder. Sentence of death by beheading was carried out on 6 December 1938.

[*857*]

MARWOOD, RONALD HENRY

One of a group of youths involved in a brawl whose admission that he had stabbed a police officer led to his conviction for murder.

Police Constable Raymond Henry Summers intervened in a vicious gang fight in Seven Sisters Road, Holloway on 14 December

1958. Knives, bottles and razors were used by the North London gangs to sort out their differences in a long-running feud. As he was leading one of the gang members away, the twenty-three-year-old policeman was stabbed to death with a ten-inch knife.

As the stricken man fell, the brawling mob dispersed. Eleven youths were questioned about the incident, including Ronald Marwood. He was released on the strength of an alibi and promptly went to ground. Convinced of his involvement, the police began a manhunt to find Marwood and, on 27 January 1959, he gave himself up.

He told detectives that he stabbed the police constable but later said he had merely pushed him, not realising that he had a knife in his hand. He accused the police of 'putting things down' which told against him.

At his trial, Marwood's defence was that there was nothing to show that he had delivered the fatal knife wound. If he had struck the policeman in the course of the general brawl and while he was under the influence of the ten pints of brown ale he had drunk the outcome was manslaughter not murder. The jury disagreed and brought in a Guilty verdict. Marwood was the first person to be sentenced to death under the new Homicide Act of 1957. He was hanged on 8 May 1959 at Pentonville Prison.

[*316, 465*]

MARYMONT, MARCUS

American serviceman based in Britain after the Second World War who disposed of his wife by arsenic poisoning.

Master Sergeant Marymont was posted to the US forces serving in Britain in 1956 and based at Sculthorpe in Norfolk. His wife Mary Helen was a little older than Marymont but they appeared to enjoy the social life of the air force base.

On 9 June 1958, Mary Helen collapsed after eating lunch at a friend's home in King's Lynn. She was taken to the base hospital where she died. Marymont gave unsatisfactory answers to questions and seemed more intent on discussing his sexual problems with doctors. It was decided that a post-mortem examination was required to determine cause of death. Marymont at first gave, then withdrew his permission. He was overruled and analysts found traces of arsenic in his wife's body.

Marymont was involved with a twenty-two-year-old married

woman living apart from her husband whom he met in Maidenhead. He found warmth in his relationship with her which he said was lacking in his wife. He had tried to buy arsenic from a chemist shop in Maidenhead but found the rules too strict. He stole arsenic from the laboratory at the air force base and even spoke to the cleaners about it. He had been poisoning his wife slowly over a period of several months before she finally died.

Marymont was tried at Denham by a US General Court Martial in December 1958. He was accused of having poisoned his wife to eliminate her in favour of another woman. There was no doubt that Mary Helen had died of arsenical poisoning but the evidence of administration was circumstantial and Marymont denied the charge. The court found him guilty of murder and of misconduct and sentenced him to life imprisonment. He was returned to the USA to serve his sentence at Fort Leavenworth in Kansas.
[*178, 916*]

MASON, ALEXANDER CAMPBELL

An army deserter and criminal convicted of murdering a cab-driver who escaped execution because of doubts about the evidence.

A passer-by in Bay Tree Lane in the London borough of Brixton on the evening of 9 May 1923 saw two people struggling near a taxi-cab. One of them cried out, 'Save me! He is killing me!' The other man flung him to the ground and fired two shots at him before running off. Jacob Dickey, the cab-driver, died in the street.

At the scene of the shooting, police found a revolver, a jemmy wrapped in paper, a bloodstained right-hand glove and a gold-mounted walking-stick of distinctive design. Newspaper photographs of the walking-stick produced immediate results. It was recognised as the property of 'Eddie' Vivian, a convicted thief who frequented the night-spots of Soho. In a statement to the police, Vivian admitted ownership of the walking-stick but implicated 'Scottie' Mason who had borrowed it from him to 'look a bit posh'. Vivian said later that he was ill at home when Mason turned up looking very dishevelled and saying that he had shot a taxi-driver.

Mason was tried for murder at the Old Bailey where Vivian was the main witness. He recounted a plan to carry out a house robbery but said Mason had bought a revolver with the intention of

robbing a cab-driver and went out on his own. Mason's defence was a simple denial. He claimed that he and Vivian were out together and that Vivian did the shooting. Mason was not believed and he was convicted of murdering the cab-driver. He was sentenced to death but reprieved because of doubts about some of the evidence. He served fourteen years of a life sentence, being released in 1937. He joined the Merchant Navy during the Second World War and was drowned when his ship was torpedoed.
[*70, 113, 681*]

MAYBRICK, FLORENCE ELIZABETH

Convicted of poisoning her husband with arsenic in one of the celebrated trials of Victorian England.

Florence was a young girl still in her teens when she met James Maybrick who was more than twice her age. She was described as a southern belle from Alabama and he was an English cotton merchant. They married in 1881 and lived for three years in the USA before moving to England to settle in Liverpool.

Maybrick's family did not approve of the marriage and, in addition, Florence had to contend with her husband's hypochondria. Despite continually dosing himself with medicine, he had sufficient vigour to keep a mistress and sire a number of children out of wedlock.

Florence found consolation in the company of Alfred Brierley, a friend of her husband's, and they became lovers. After spending a weekend in London with Brierley in March 1889, she returned to Liverpool to face her angry husband. Words and blows were exchanged. He made a new will which excluded provision for Florence.

James Maybrick was taken ill on 28 April 1889. Florence told the doctor that he had been taking a white powder. He died at their home, Battlecrease House, on 11 May. A letter which Florence had written to Brierley was opened by one of her servants and given to the dead man's brother. The family was hostile to the widow and she was kept a virtual prisoner.

Traces of arsenic were found in Maybrick's body and Florence was arrested. A packet of arsenic was found in her room, labelled as a poison for cats, and it became known that she had bought three dozen arsenical fly papers from local chemist shops. She was committed for trial, charged with poisoning her husband.

The trial opened in Liverpool in July 1889. Medical experts could not agree on the cause of death. Maybrick's self-administration of many different drugs was a complicating factor. There was no doubt that Florence had bought large quantities of arsenic which she claimed she used in a cosmetic preparation.

Mr Justice Stephen's controversial summing-up criticised Florence's adultery and weighed heavily against her. She was found guilty and sentenced to death. The result of the trial produced an outcry on both sides of the Atlantic and the Home Secretary commuted the sentence to life imprisonment. Florence was released in 1904 after serving fifteen years and returned to her native America where she died in 1941. Mr Justice Stephen was subsequently admitted to a mental asylum.

In a bizarre footnote to the case, a claim was made in 1992 that James Maybrick had committed the **Jack the Ripper** murders in London in 1888. This was based on the discovery in Liverpool of a diary signed by Jack the Ripper and allegedly written by Maybrick. It was later pronounced a hoax.

[*177, 459, 571, 618, 650, 677, 809*]

MERRETT, JOHN DONALD

He walked free from a murder charge in 1926 with a Not Proven verdict and committed double murder twenty-eight years later.

In 1924 Merrett and his mother came to Britain from New Zealand. The Merretts went to live in Scotland where Donald became a student at Edinburgh University. Although he was an intelligent youth, his interests lay more in sampling the social life. He soon outstripped his allowance and remedied the deficit by forging cheques on his mother's account.

On 17 March 1926, a gun was fired in the Merrett household and Donald told the maid, 'My mother has shot herself.' Mrs Merrett was bleeding from a head wound and gave an incoherent account of what had happened before dying on 1 April. Her death was treated as a suicide. Discovery of Merrett's forgery led to suspicion about the cause of his mother's death. He was charged with forgery and murder and tried at Edinburgh in February 1927. In a clash of experts over the nature of the fatal gunshot wound, the outcome was a stalemate insofar as the jury brought in a Not Proven verdict. Merrett was sentenced to a year in prison for forgery.

On release, he inherited a substantial legacy, married a girl whom he met in Hastings and changed his name to Chesney. When the money ran out, he resorted to fraud and blackmail. He served in the Royal Navy Volunteer Reserve during the Second World War and afterwards went to live in Germany to exploit the black market. In February 1954, he returned to England to visit his wife and mother-in-law who were running an old people's home in Ealing. He drowned his wife in the bath and strangled her mother because she knew too much. He fled to Germany where he was found dead in a wood near Cologne on 16 February. He had shot himself. An inquest in London determined that he was responsible for the deaths of his wife and mother-in-law.

[*404, 628, 786, 932*]

MERRIFIELD, LOUISA MAY

She poisoned an elderly widow for gain and, while carefully covering her tracks, gave herself away with loose talk.

Louisa was a woman who liked variety. She had as many as twenty different jobs in the space of three years and, by the time she was forty-six, had been married three times. In March 1953, she and her seventy-year-old husband, Alfred, went to work as live-in housekeepers for Sarah Ricketts, an elderly widow who lived in Blackpool. Within two weeks Louisa had instructed a solicitor, on Mrs Rickett's behalf, to draw up a new will leaving the old woman's property to her. Her next act was to boast to friends that she had inherited a bungalow.

Mrs Ricketts died on 14 April and a post-mortem showed that cause of death was phosphorus poisoning. When detectives searched the house, Louisa requested a Salvation Army band playing in the street outside to strike up 'Abide With Me'.

Louisa and Alfred Merrifield were charged with murder and stood trial in Manchester in July 1953. Evidence of Louisa's ill-judged remarks about her inheritance told against her and while the cause of Mrs Rickett's death was clear, no traces of poison were found in the bungalow. Rat poison was the most likely vehicle for phosphorus. Louisa Merrifield's contribution to the proceedings was to explain the charges against her as due to jealousy and gossip.

The jury found Louisa guilty of murder but were uncertain

about the guilt of her husband. She was sentenced to death and Alfred was released. Louisa was executed at Strangeways Prison on 18 September 1953 without making a confession. Alfred continued to live in Mrs Rickett's bungalow and, after a legal battle with her relatives, inherited a sixth of the property's value. He died, aged eighty, in 1962.
[*291, 445, 794*]

MESRINE, JACQUES

Bank robber, prison escapist and master of disguise who terrorised Paris with his daring crimes in the 1970s and earned the title of 'Public Enemy Number One'.

Mesrine spent his childhood in German-occupied France during the Second World War. He was conscripted into the army in 1956 and served in Algeria where he was decorated with the Military Cross for Valour. After demobilisation, he found civilian life boring and gradually slipped into a life of crime.

Starting as a petty criminal in 1962, he became France's most wanted criminal by 1973. His speciality was bank robbery and he eluded capture by moving from country to country. He went to Canada in 1968 and hatched a plot to kidnap a millionaire in Montreal. His planning let him down on this occasion and he was sentenced to ten years' imprisonment for kidnapping. He served a year of his sentence before staging a sensational break-out from jail. He fled first to the USA and then to South America, financing his travels by means of robbery.

Mesrine returned to France in 1973 and continued his pattern of daring robberies. After a nationwide manhunt, he was picked up in Paris and put in La Santé prison to await trial. He kept himself busy by writing his autobiography, *The Death Instinct*, in which he reported details of murders he had committed. In May 1977, he was sentenced to twenty years' imprisonment. But prison could not contain him and, within a year, he had managed to escape. He resumed his career as a bank robber and impudently planned to kidnap the judge who had sentenced him. Mesrine pushed his luck and the police force he had taunted and goaded finally had their revenge. On 2 November 1979, he was ambushed in a Paris street as he walked to his car. Marksmen from the anti-gang squad, using high-velocity ammunition, gunned him down. The President of France sent his congratulations to the head of police.

In September 2002 film evidence came to light suggesting that the police did not call on Mesrine to surrender before riddling his car with bullets and killing him. The film made by detectives rehearsing the ambush seemed to confirm that Mesrine had been effectively assassinated.
[*824*]

MILAT, IVAN ROBERT MAKO

What became known as the 'Backpacker Murders' first came to light in September 1992 with the discovery of two bodies in a remote part of New South Wales, Australia.

The remains of two British girls, Caroline Clarke and Joanne Walters, were found buried at a place with the sinister name of Executioner's Drop in Belanglo State Forest. In October 1993, the bodies of two Australians, James Gibson and Deborah Everist, were found in the same area and on 1 November, a fifth body was found, that of Simone Schmindl, a German national. The total rose to seven the following day with the discovery of two skeletons, later identified as Gabor Neugebauer and Anja Habschied, also from Germany. All the victims had been stabbed and their bodies had been placed face down alongside a fallen tree with their hands positioned behind their backs.

The first break in the investigation of the crimes came in February 1994. Following accounts of the murders in the press, Paul Onions, a British backpacker, came forward with information. He told the police that while visiting the area where the bodies had been found in 1990, he had accepted a lift from a driver who had attempted to shoot him. Fortunately, the shot missed and Onions escaped. He identified the man from police mugshots and also identified his car.

In May 1994, forty-nine year old Ivan Milat was arrested and officers took possession of a rifle which he kept in his home. The weapon bore his fingerprints and firearms evidence linked it to cartridge cases found at the scenes of the murders. Milat was charged with seven murders and with the attack on Paul Onions. He pleaded not guilty to all the charges when his trial opened on 26 March 1996. Proceedings lasted for four months and on 27 July 1996, the jury found him guilty on all counts. Justice David Hurst sentenced him to life imprisonment for each of the murder charges and six years for the attack on Paul Onions. Milat's appeal against

conviction was dismissed and he remains under investigation for other unsolved murders.
[*844, 974*]

MILLER, JAMES WILLIAM

Australian serial killer brought to justice by the death of his partner in a car crash after they had killed six young women.

Miller, an habitual thief who had spent much of his life behind bars, had a homosexual relationship with twenty-three-year-old Chris Worrell. The two men picked up a girl in Adelaide on 24 December 1976 and other disappearances followed in 1977. When the bodies of some of the missing women were found in the hills around Truro, the police offered a reward of A$30,000 for information.

On 19 February 1977, Worrell and a girl-friend were killed in a car crash of which Miller was the sole survivor. Miller, already under suspicion in connection with the disappearances, volunteered information about the location of some of the bodies. He claimed that Worrell killed the girls, while his part in the crimes was to help bury the corpses.

Worrell had received psychiatric treatment while serving in the Australian armed forces and Miller claimed his partner was subject to moods of extreme violence. At his trial on six charges of murder, Miller was described as acting in concert with Worrell in committing the crimes and consequently shared the guilt. He was convicted and sentenced to life imprisonment.

Miller maintained he was innocent of murder and wrote a detailed account of what took place in his relationship with Worrell. This was designed to help his appeal against sentence in 1984 but his application failed.
[*658, 689*]

MILLS, HERBERT LEONARD

Teenage misfit who carried out what he believed was a perfect murder in order to profit by telling the newspapers about it.

On the evening of 2 August 1951, Mabel Tattershaw, a Nottingham housewife who took in lodgers while her husband was in prison, went to the cinema. There, she met a pasty-faced young man who engaged her in conversation. She was not seen alive again.

On 9 August, the chief crime reporter for the *News of the World* received a telephone call from a man asking him about the price for a murder story. The caller explained that he had discovered a murder in Sherwood Vale near Nottingham. He was kept talking while the call was traced. Nottingham police officers apprehended Herbert Mills in a street-call box. He led detectives to the woodland area where they found the body of Mabel Tattershaw who had been strangled. Mills had no regular job but existed on the proceeds of gambling. His real interests lay in reading poetry. He gloried in the interest his discovery had generated in the press and said he thought it would earn him a lot of money.

He had written an account of the murder which amounted to a confession. He took his victim to a secluded spot where he went to read poetry and killed her. He said, 'The strangling itself was quite easily accomplished . . . I applied most pressure to the right-hand side of her neck.' His admission was corroborated by debris under the victim's fingernails clawed from Mills's suit during her struggle.

Mills was tried at Nottingham Assizes. He claimed that he found the dead body and concocted a false confession in order to make money from the newspapers. The jury did not believe him and he was found guilty. Mills was sentenced to death and hanged at Lincoln on 11 December 1951.
[*398, 792*]

MILSOM AND FOWLER

Albert Milsom and Henry Fowler were a couple of bungling thieves who murdered their victim and left behind a vital clue.

Henry Smith was a retired engineer in his late seventies who lived alone at Muswell Lodge, a large house standing in its own grounds in Muswell Hill, north London. He was concerned about being burgled and had arranged various alarm devices to protect his property. On 14 February 1896, Mr Smith was found dead in his kitchen. He had been tied up and beaten about the head. There were signs of forcible entry in the kitchen and the safe in his bedroom had been ransacked. A child's lantern was found near the body.

Two prowlers had been seen near Muswell Lodge a few days before the murder. They were identified as Albert Milsom and Henry Fowler, criminals known to the police, who lived in Kentish Town. The two men were missing from their homes but detectives were delighted when Milsom's brother-in-law, a fifteen-year-old lad, identified the lantern found at the crime scene as his.

The wanted men kept on the move, but were finally apprehended in Bath on 12 April 1896. Milsom went quietly but Fowler offered violent resistance. Milsom quickly confessed but claimed that Fowler had committed the murder. In the best tradition of thieves falling out, Fowler alleged the opposite.

The two villains continued their disagreement in the dock at the Old Bailey when they appeared on trial. It took warders several minutes to subdue Fowler who was intent on strangling his partner. They were found guilty and sentenced to death. They were hanged on 9 June 1896 with double murderer, William Seaman, between them. His last words were reported to be, 'This is the first time I've ever been a bloody peacemaker.'

[*239, 545, 876*]

M'LACHLAN, JESSIE

Notable Scottish murder trial in which public pressure led to an unsatisfactory verdict being challenged. It was believed that the convicted murderess may only have been a witness to the crime.

Twenty-five-year-old Jessie McPherson worked as a domestic servant in the home of John Fleming, an accountant who lived at Sandyford Place, Glasgow. He was in the habit at weekends of going straight to his house at Dunoon, leaving his elderly father, James Fleming, to be looked after by McPherson.

When he returned to Glasgow on 7 July 1862, John Fleming was told by his father that McPherson had gone missing. The door leading to the servant's room was locked but on gaining entry Fleming found the semi-naked body of the young woman lying on the bed. She had apparently been hacked to death with a cleaver and there was blood everywhere, including footprints on the bedroom floor. Some silverware had also been stolen and old Mr Fleming was arrested. Two days later, it was learned that the silverware had been pawned by Jessie M'Lachlan, a former servant in Fleming's employ. She claimed to have been acting under old Mr Fleming's instructions. But when her foot impression was found to match exactly with the bloody footprint at the murder scene, she was arrested and Mr Fleming was released.

Jessie M'Lachlan was tried for murder in September 1862.

Witnesses testified that McPherson was frightened of old Mr Fleming and called him 'that auld deevil', a reference to his unwanted advances. Jessie M'Lachlan admitted being in the house, saying she had attended McPherson who told her that Mr Fleming had assaulted her. The judge was not disposed to accept these allegations and summed up against M'Lachlan who was duly found guilty.

Following public concern about the outcome of the trial, sentence of death was lifted and M'Lachlan was condemned to penal servitude for life. She was released from prison in 1877 and went to live in America where she died on 1 January 1899.

[*13, 108, 785*]

MOLINEUX, ROLAND BURNHAM

High-flying socialite who resorted to murder to achieve his ambitions.

Molineux was manager of a pharmaceutical factory in New York in the late 1890s. He belonged to the fashionable Knickerbocker Athletic Club where his arrogant behaviour failed to amuse the club regulars and they did not support him when he sought to have fellow member Harry Cornish disbarred.

Cornish had beaten Molineux in a weight-lifting competition which the latter thought he should have won. When the club failed to agree to his demands to have Cornish thrown out, he resigned. Following this incident, on 23 December 1898, Cornish received a bottle of Bromo-Seltzer sent through the post. When his landlady complained of a headache, she took some of the Bromo salts and dropped dead. The bottle was found to have been poisoned with mercury cyanide. The address written on the postal package was found to match Roland Molineux's handwriting.

A previous incident was recalled involving the death of another club member. Henry C. Barnet had died mysteriously in October 1898 after receiving a bottle of laxative salts sent anonymously through the post. Barnet and Molineux had been rivals for the attention of the same girl whom Molineux married less than three weeks after his friend's death.

At his trial, fourteen document experts testified that the writing on the Bromo salts package was that of Molineux. It was also shown that he had ordered a quantity of mercury cyanide. He was found guilty of murder and sentenced to death. He appealed and

won a second trial in 1902 at which he successfully contested the previous verdict. Molineux worked for several newspapers but his wife divorced him and he ended his days in an asylum where he died in 1917.
[*523, 558, 740, 745*]

MONSON, ALFRED JOHN

Wheeler-dealer who was charged with staging the faked suicide of a youth under his charge in order to benefit from the insurance.

Monson worked for Dudley Hambrough, a retired army officer who farmed at Ardlamont in Argyllshire. Monson was hired in 1890 as tutor to the major's seventeen-year-old son Cecil, who went to live with him in Yorkshire.

Hambrough was in financial difficulty and Monson offered to help him resolve his problems. Hambrough's life interest in some of his estates had been mortgaged to an insurance company for £37,000. He borrowed from a moneylender, Beresford Loftus Tottenham, with the aim of buying back the life interest. In January 1893, Monson, who had been declared bankrupt the previous year, attempted to buy the major's interests.

The two men fell out and Monson's next move was to take a house in Argyllshire in which he installed his family and Cecil Hambrough. He then insured Cecil's life for £20,000 and persuaded the youth to agree that in the event of his death, the insurance payment would be made to Mrs Monson.

On 10 August 1893, Monson took Cecil and a man named Scott on a rabbit shoot. They entered the woods near Ardlamont House and, later in the day, Monson returned to the house reporting that Cecil 'has shot himself'. The youth was found lying on his back, with a gunshot wound in the head. The local doctor certified death which he defined as accidental. Monson arranged for the body to be buried on the Isle of Wight.

The insurance company was suspicious of the circumstances of the shooting but could not question Scott who seemed to have disappeared completely. Cecil's body was exhumed so that his injury could be re-examined and as a result Monson was charged with murder.

Monson was tried at Edinburgh and won a famous Not Proven verdict. The prosecution revealed the extent of Monson's lies and chicanery but sufficient doubt remained to win his freedom. The

mysterious Scott turned up in Edinburgh in 1894 but he was not questioned by the police.
[*670, 789*]

MOORE, ALFRED

Convicted of killing two police officers on the strength of an identification made by one of them before he died.

Moore made a subsistence living by farming a few pigs and poultry on the Yorkshire moors near Huddersfield. To make ends meet, he boosted his earnings by burgling local farms and office premises. The West Yorkshire police had been on his trail for several months and on 14 July 1951 had laid a trap for him late at night at his apparently empty farmhouse. They intended to catch him red-handed when he returned with his latest spoils.

The early hours of the following morning were shattered by the noise of gunfire and the police were dismayed to find two of their colleagues injured. Detective Inspector Duncan Fraser was dead and Police Constable Gordon Jagger died later in hospital. Moore had apparently regained the safety of his farmhouse where he protested he had been since midnight. He was arrested and taken to Huddersfield Infirmary where he was identified by the dying police constable.

Moore admitted to ownership of a shotgun but a search of his farm failed to produce a revolver which had been the murder weapon. He consistently denied being involved in the shooting, maintaining that he had been inside his farmhouse during the incident.

He was nevertheless tried for murder at Leeds Assizes in December 1951. Moore repeated his denials but the dying policeman's identification carried more weight. He was found guilty of murder and sentenced to death. A reprieve was denied and he was hanged at Armley Jail, Leeds on 6 February 1952.
[*113, 287*]

MOREAU, PIERRE-DÉSIRÉ

Pharmacist who poisoned two wives for gain in an unsubtle demonstration of the poisoner's art.

The son of a peasant family, Moreau was befriended by a priest who paid for his education. After a spell in the army he studied pharmacy and ran a herbalist shop in the Saint-Denis district of

Paris. In 1869, he married the woman who had waited for him while he served in the military. She was not well off and her family were not keen about her marriage plans. On 16 August 1873, Mme Moreau made a will in which she left the little she possessed to her husband. Two days later she was dead.

Mme Moreau died on 18 August 1873 after a brief illness characterised by constant vomiting. She was thirty-three years old. Moreau appeared distraught and bemoaned his loss to the dead woman's parents.

Shortly afterwards, Moreau remarried. This time his wife came with a considerable dowry and a property. Within a few months, she too was taken ill with symptoms of vomiting and gastric pain. She was cared for by her husband but grew steadily worse. Just before she died, she confided to her cousin, 'Moreau had poisoned me.'

Traces of copper were found in the body of the second Mme Moreau and a similar discovery was made when the first wife was exhumed. There was a treatise on pharmacy in Moreau's shop in which the entry for copper sulphate had been marked. It was learned that under the terms of his second marriage, Moreau only acquired the first half of his wife's dowry. The second half became available only on her death.

He was found guilty of murder at his trial and sentenced to death. Twenty thousand people gathered in the Place de La Rouquette to see him guillotined on 14 October 1874.

[749]

MOREY, EDWARD HENRY

An extraordinary inquiry known as 'The Hand in Glove Case' involving the unorthodox identification of the murder victim and a woman's attempt to protect the murderer.

Fishermen on the Murrumbidgee River near Wagga Wagga in New South Wales, Australia pulled a body out of the water on Christmas Day 1933. The corpse, of a man aged about fifty, was so badly decomposed that identification by the facial features or by fingerprinting was impossible.

A search of the river bank revealed another grisly relic in the form of the glove-like skin from one of the corpse's hands. It proved possible to retrieve a fingerprint enabling the dead man to be identified as Percy Smith.

Smith led a nomadic life and had last been seen in the company of Edward Morey, a trapper. Morey was questioned and incriminating bloodstains on his clothes led to his arrest. While he was on trial at Wagga Wagga, one of the prosecution witnesses was shot dead. Lillian Anderson claimed that her husband had been shot by intruders and also declared that he, and not Morey, had murdered Percy Smith.

Confusion reigned when Lillian Anderson, who evidently had a low mental age, had been writing love letters to Morey under the name of Thelma Smith. For his part, Morey, who had been found guilty of murder and sentenced to death, said he did not know Mrs Anderson. She was eventually convicted of manslaughter and sentenced to twenty years' imprisonment. Morey, whom she had sought to protect, was reprieved.

[*406, 858*]

MORGAN, SAMUEL

Soldier who committed rape and murder in wartime Liverpool and was incriminated by a finger bandage left at the scene of the crime.

Fifteen-year-old Mary Hagan was reported missing from her home in Liverpool on the evening of 2 November 1940. She had gone out to buy a newspaper and not returned. An immediate search was organised, hampered by the wartime blackout restrictions, but the girl was quickly found. She lay dead on the muddy floor of a concrete blockhouse where she had been raped and strangled.

Close to the body was a disused finger bandage which had been made from a military dressing impregnated with acriflavine disinfectant. After intensive local inquiries, the Lancashire police detained a soldier based at nearby Seaforth Barracks. He had a cut on his thumb which he said was caused by handling barbed wire. His sister had used part of one of his standard issue military dressings to bandage the small wound.

Samuel Morgan had been seen in a local hotel on the night of the murder. He was out of breath and agitated and was bleeding from a cut on his right thumb. The remains of the field dressing were retrieved from Morgan's sister and comparisons made with the bandage found in the blockhouse. Forensic tests showed that the materials matched, and further corroboration came from comparisons with a batch of dressings issued to the stores at Seaforth

Barracks. All the dressings came from the same factory and bore the same stitching characteristics. Tests also showed that mud on Morgan's uniform matched that on the floor of the blockhouse.

Morgan was found guilty of murder and sentenced to death. He was executed at Walton Gaol on 4 April 1941.

[*291*]

MORRIS, RAYMOND LESLIE

Sex murderer who preyed on young girls, daringly abducting them in broad daylight.

Seven-year-old Christine Darby was abducted while playing in the street in Walsall, Staffordshire on the afternoon of 19 August 1967. Her friends said that she went off with a man driving a grey car. They recognised him as a local person from his accent. The child's body was found in the woods at Cannock Chase three days later. She had been suffocated and sexually assaulted. There were car-tyre tracks close by. Witnesses who had been at Cannock Chase recalled seeing a man driving a grey car, possibly an A55 or A60 Austin model. The owners of over 23,000 such cars were questioned by the police throughout Britain and an Identikit picture of the driver was published.

Just when the trail was going cold, a man attempted to abduct a ten-year-old girl in Walsall on 4 November 1968. Heeding the warnings she had been given, the child resisted and an alert passer-by took a note of the car number as the man drove away. The registration was traced to a man who lived in Walsall.

Raymond Morris, an engineer who worked for a company at Oldbury, was identified by witnesses as the man they had seen at Cannock Chase. His wife provided an alibi for him on the day that Christine Darby was abducted, but later admitted that she had been mistaken. Morris had previously owned a grey A55 car. He was a well-respected man and his wife had no inkling of the double life he had been leading since 1964. Morris was suspected of abducting six girls, four of whom were killed.

He was tried at Staffordshire Assizes for the murder of Christine Darby and other offences and found guilty on all charges. He was sentenced to life imprisonment.

[*296, 407, 664*]

MORRISON, STINIE

A Russian Jew and former convict living in the East End of London who sold jewellery. In January 1911, he was implicated in the murder of Leon Beron whose mutilated body was found on Clapham Common.

Forty-eight-year-old Beron, also a Russian Jew and a property dealer, frequented the Warsaw Restaurant in Whitechapel. He was seen there on New Year's Eve 1910 in the company of Morrison. The following day, his body was discovered on Clapham Common. He had been stabbed and beaten about the head; the letter 'S' had been crudely cut in two places on his face. Beron's death came two weeks after the Houndsditch murders in which three police officers were killed by anarchists. It was thought that the 'S' might signify the Russian word for spy.

The main evidence against Morrison came from three cab-drivers who said they had picked him up as a fare on different journeys on the night of the murder. Morrison was arrested on 8 January and charged with Beron's murder which he denied. He was tried at the Old Bailey in March when discrepancies emerged in the cab-drivers' evidence. But, in a controversial move, his defence counsel sought to discredit the prosecution's witnesses. This left the way open for the prosecution to blacken Morrison's character by citing his criminal record. The judge's summing-up was less damning but the jury returned a Guilty verdict. When sentence of death was passed, Morrison burst out that he declined the court's mercy.

The Home Secretary granted a reprieve and Morrison was sent to Parkhurst Prison for life. He protested his innocence and asked for sentence of death to be carried out. In the face of refusals from officialdom, he starved himself to death. He died in prison on 24 January 1921. It has been suggested that Morrison was framed by the anarchists who killed Beron in the belief that he had betrayed them.

[*3, 41, 80, 583, 682, 782*]

MÜLLER, FRANZ

The man who made history by committing Britain's first train murder in 1864.

Thomas Briggs, aged seventy years, was chief clerk at Robarts Bank in Lombard Street, London. On 9 July 1864 Briggs travelled on a

North London Railway train from Fenchurch Street bound for Hackney Wick. Two passengers entering a first-class compartment at Hackney Wick found blood on the seat and raised the alarm. The body of Mr Briggs was found on the line between Hackney Wick and Bow. He had evidently been beaten up and robbed and then thrown out of the train. Briggs died later from his injuries.

In the train compartment, police officers found a walking-stick and bag which belonged to the dead man and a hat which did not. A check of jewellers' shops revealed that the gold chain from the murdered man's watch had been exchanged for a new one by a man who spoke with a foreign accent. The hat found at the crime scene was identified as belonging to Franz Müller, a German tailor who had lodgings in Bow.

But Müller had already taken flight, bound for America on board the SS *Victoria*, a slow-travelling sailing-ship. Detectives followed him on the *City of Manchester*, a faster-moving steamship. They were waiting at New York for Müller when he disembarked. The tailor was wearing Thomas Briggs's hat which he had adapted for size and he was in possession of the murdered man's gold watch.

Müller was returned to England for trial at the Old Bailey in October 1864. The evidence against him was powerful enough to detain the jury for a mere fifteen minutes before finding him guilty. He was sentenced to death and, despite a request for clemency from the King of Prussia, he was hanged before a large crowd outside Newgate Prison on 14 November 1864.

[*458, 589, 833*]

MÜLLER, Dr RICHARD

A blazing car murder in Germany in 1954 with echoes of the **Rouse** Case in England in 1930.

Dr Müller arrived home late on 18 February 1954 in a distressed state. Tearfully he explained to his son that there had been an accident and that his mother had been burned to death. According to Müller, he stopped the car on the journey home to Otterbach because they had seen a hedgehog in the road and his wife asked him to retrieve it. He left her in the car while he walked back along the road. Suddenly there was a roaring noise and, looking round, he saw that his car was ablaze with his wife still inside. He rushed back and fought the flames in an effort to pull her free but was beaten by the ferocity of the fire. By the time help arrived, Frau Gertrude Müller was dead.

Examination at the scene of the fire raised suspicions which were confirmed when Dr Müller was questioned. It seemed he was in the habit of travelling with several full cans of petrol in the boot of his car. On the night of the fire, he had parked the car so close to the edge of the road that kerbside trees obstructed the door on the passenger's side. In the burned-out car, there was an empty petrol can in both front and back seats. Inquiries revealed that Müller had been unfaithful to his wife, most recently with the young receptionist at his dental practice. When Gertrude learned of this liaison, she confronted her rival and begged her not to destroy their marriage. As a result, the young woman left her job and moved away.

Müller was tried for murder at Kaiserlautern in November 1955. He denied that he had killed his wife in order to marry his mistress. It was alleged that he had rendered her unconscious before splashing petrol around the interior of the car and setting it ablaze. The jury found him guilty and he was sentenced to six years in prison – a very light sentence for the crime of murder.

[454]

MULLIN, HERBERT WILLIAM

A mentally disturbed individual whose multiple murders raised several issues about American attitudes to treating psychiatric illness.

Mullin was a promising Californian student who decided in his late teens that he would drop out of college. He adopted an anti-war stance and studied mystic religions. He became increasingly disturbed and by the late 1960s. was receiving psychiatric treatment for paranoid schizophrenia. During the next few years he was in and out of hospital and began hearing voices giving him instructions.

In October 1972, Mullin's voices commanded him to kill, to take human sacrifices, as a means of averting imminent natural disasters such as earthquakes. He first killed a vagrant and then a college student in opportunistic murders in the Santa Cruz area but, after buying a gun, killed indiscriminately. In the course of twelve months, he murdered thirteen times.

After he was arrested on 13 February 1973, he said that he was a scapegoat 'made to carry the guilt feelings of others'. He confessed to thirteen murders and pleaded insanity at his trial in Santa Cruz in July 1973. Despite ample evidence to the contrary, he was judged sane and convicted of two murders in the first degree and nine in the second. He was sentenced to life imprisonment.

Mullin told the court that if his early criminal offences had been adequately punished he would have been prevented from committing more serious crimes. His case was used to highlight the policy in California of closing down mental hospitals for cost-cutting reasons. Had Mullin received the treatment his condition required, a dozen killings might have been prevented. In the following year, legislation was passed which prohibited further hospital closures.

[*221, 598*]

MUMBAI CHILD KILLINGS

Police in Mumbai (formerly Bombay) in India investigating the kidnap and murder of a nine-year old girl in October 1996 uncovered a systematic plot to exploit young children for gain.

Anjanabai Gavit, the former wife of the dead girl's father, her daughters, Renuka Kiran Shinde and Seema Mohan Gavit, and Renuka's husband, Kiran Shinde, were arrested. Searches at their homes in Maharashta uncovered the remains of several small children.

Under interrogation, Kiran Shinde confessed that the family had been kidnapping and killing children for some time. The children, usually aged between one and five years, were used as diversions or decoys while the family members engaged in an organised campaign of street robberies. Shinde claimed that Anjanabai, a known prostitute and thief, was the leader of this monstrous band. No doubt, in order to save his own neck, he agreed to give evidence against his family and the women were charged with thirteen counts of abduction and the murders of nine of the children.

Prior to their trial, Anjanabai avoided justice when she died of a brain haemorrhage in December 1997. The trial took place at Kolhapur local court and over a hundred and fifty witnesses gave evidence. The mainstay of the prosecution was the testimony of Kiran Shinde who described an occasion when Seema was held by a would be victim and Anjanabai had thrown a baby onto the road to create a distraction and allow her daughter to escape.

This same infant was eventually so traumatised that Anjanabai smashed its head with an iron bar to prevent its continual crying. The policy was to kill or dump the children when they had served their purpose.

On 22 June 2001, Renuka and Seema were found guilty of abduction and murder. The judge accepted that there was insufficient evidence against them on three of the murder charges but he believed the testimony of Kiran Shinde. On 28 June, Renuka and Seema were sentenced to death by hanging while Shinde was formally released in view of the evidence he had given.
[*1037*]

MURDOCH, BRADLEY

Former mechanic and drug runner convicted of murdering a British tourist and attacking his girl-friend in 2001 after one of Australia's biggest manhunts.

Peter Falconio and his girl-friend, Joanne Lees, were touring central Australia in their camper van. On the night of 14 July 2001, they were flagged down by a truck driver on a remote stretch of road north of Alice Springs and threatened at gun point. Falconio was shot and his companion was assaulted and abducted. She managed to escape her attacker and hid in the bush until rescued.

Every means available was used to locate Falconio, including aborigine trackers, but without success. Police learned the possible identity of his killer when James Hepi was caught with drugs hidden in his vehicle. He gave them the name of his former business partner, Bradley Murdoch, in return for a lighter sentence. The hunt was on for forty-seven year old Murdoch and he was arrested in August 2002. He was known to the police on account of a firearms offence and acquittal on a rape charge. On the night of the attack, he was high on amphetamines and was carrying 10kg of marijuana on a drug run across Australia. When he returned home, witnesses noticed that he had cut his hair and shaved off his distinctive moustache.

Murdoch was tried at Darwin in October 2005 for murder, abduction and assault. He pleaded not guilty. Key evidence was given by Joanne Lees who identified him as her attacker. Linking forensic evidence was provided by a blood stain on Lees's T-shirt which matched the attacker's DNA. The jury reached a unanimous

guilty verdict and on 13 December 2005 Murdoch was sentenced to life imprisonment. The investigation and trial attracted wide publicity and a number of books have been written about the case. The body of Peter Falconio has not been found.
[*1078, 1079*]

N

NASH AND MARGOLIES

('The CBS Murders'). Three CBS employees were shot dead in a New York City car park on 12 April 1982 when they accidentally interrupted a contract killing.

Margaret Barbera, a thirty-seven-year-old accountant, was the victim of a contract killing when she was shot dead next to her BMW in the parking lot at Pier 92. The killer was moving her body when three men appeared to collect their cars. Realising he had been seen, the gunman killed them all with a silenced weapon. A fourth CBS employee escaped and saw the gunman making his getaway in a van.

The nature of the dead men's employment guaranteed the murders maximum news coverage. The police realised they were looking for a hired gunman and knew that the key to their inquiries lay in Margaret Barbera's background. She worked for Irvin Margolies, a jewellery manufacturer, whose business had suddenly taken off in 1981, making him a millionaire.

Suspicions arose that Margolies's new-found wealth had not been earned honestly and it was later shown that he had perpetrated a massive fraud. Margaret Barbera kept a set of doctored books for him but she had an intuition that if things went wrong she had been set up to take the blame. To protect herself, she kept some of the incriminating documentation at home. In due course, when the bubble burst, Margolies fled to Israel for six months. When he returned, he said he was unaware of any fraud, which must have been perpetrated by Barbera.

For her part, Barbera claimed she was the wronged party and could prove it. In order to silence her, Margolies hired Donald Nash, a burglar and forger, to kill her for $8000. He started by killing a woman called Jenny Soo Chin, Barbera's friend and confidante, and followed this several months later by shooting Barbera herself. The luckless men from CBS were in the wrong place at the wrong time.

Police traced Donald Nash through his van when they learned that drivers of vehicles using the Pier 92 parking lot had to have a monthly pass.

In May 1983, Nash was convicted on four charges of murder and sentenced to 108 years' imprisonment. The following year, Margolies, who was already serving a prison sentence for fraud, was also found guilty of murder and sentenced to fifty years.
[*394*]

NEILSON, DONALD

His quest for military-style action led to the post-office murders in the early 1970s and culminated in the abduction and murder of a teenage girl.

The high spot in Donald Neilson's life was the time he spent in Kenya during his National Service in the 1950s. He enjoyed military discipline and the excitement of guerilla warfare. He found civilian life rather dull as a jobbing builder in Yorkshire, although he married and had a daughter. They joined him on the military manoeuvres he carried out on the moors but were unaware of his secret life as an armed robber. Between 1971 and 1975, he committed numerous armed raids on post offices and killed three sub-postmasters. The police were searching for a killer whose practice of wearing a black hood earned him the name 'The Black Panther'. On 13 January 1975, seventeen-year-old Lesley Whittle was abducted from her home near Kidderminster. A ransom demand of £50,000 was made by the kidnapper who the police knew from their inquiries was 'The Black Panther'.

The investigation centred on the underground drainage shafts at Bathpool Park near Kidsgrove. On 7 March 1975, the missing girl's naked body was found in one of the shafts suspended from the neck by a wire. Neilson eluded capture for several months but was finally arrested near Mansfield on 11 December 1975. A search of his house at Bradford turned up a treasure trove of hidden military equipment and weapons.

Neilson was tried for murder at Oxford in June 1975. He based his defence on the claim that his kidnap victim had fallen to her

death accidentally and that the sub-postmasters died because his gun discharged accidentally. It was an explanation which defied belief and Neilson was found guilty on four counts of murder. He was sentenced to three terms of life imprisonment for the post-office murders and twenty-one years for murdering Lesley Whittle.
[*408, 937*]

NELSON, DALE MERLE

In a night of drunken and possibly drug-enhanced violence, he killed three adults and five children.

Nelson worked as a logger in British Columbia and lived with his wife and three children at West Creston. He was regarded as a sociable individual although prone to surliness. His work was physically demanding and he escaped occasionally by going on drinking sprees. He went on such a spree on 4 September 1970, drinking steadily from midday until late in the evening. Finally, he got into his car as if to drive home. But he stopped on the way at the home of Shirley Wasyk, a relative whose husband was away, leaving her alone with her three daughters who were his cousins. Nelson battered Shirley to death and choked her seven-year-old daughter, ripping open her body and later dismembering it. He sexually assaulted the eight-year-old while the third daughter ran screaming into the night for help.

Nelson drove two miles to the Phipps household where he shot dead Ray Phipps, his common-law wife and three of their four children. He abducted the eight-year-old whose abused body was subsequently found in the countryside. An intensive police hunt was mounted and thirty-six hours after going on the rampage Nelson gave himself up without resistance. He told the police, 'Must have been the LSD.'

There was no doubt that Nelson had consumed considerable amounts of alcohol but it was not proved that he had taken LSD or acid. He was tried for two of the eight murders at Cranbrook in March 1971. The defence pleaded insanity and Nelson was reported to have experienced hallucinations and said of his acts, 'It seemed like it wasn't me.' The court heard graphic accounts of their night of terror from the two girls who survived his attack. The jury convicted Nelson of murder and he was sentenced to life imprisonment.
[*601, 889*]

NELSON, EARLE LEONARD

Terrorised the USA and Canada with a series of rape murders in 1926 and 1927 in which he killed at least twenty women.

Nelson was orphaned soon after birth and was brought up by an aunt. As the result of a childhood accident, he suffered occasional intense head pains throughout his life. He became a Bible fanatic and was given to moralising about the lives of others. He was imprisoned in 1918 after he raped a young girl but regularly escaped from detention.

He married in 1919 but, as a result of being constantly harangued and sexually ill-treated, his wife had a nervous breakdown. In February 1926, he raped and strangled the landlady in his lodgings in San Francisco. Thus began his reign of terror in which he moved from state to state, leaving a trail of dead landladies behind him. Between February 1926 and November 1927, he murdered at least twenty times.

With the police of several states desperately seeking to capture the rape killer, Nelson crossed the border into Canada where in June 1927 he took a room in Winnipeg. He spared his landlady on this occasion, who remembered him as a devoutly religious man, but killed two other women in the city. Before fleeing, he stole a fountain pen and some clothing from his last victim's home which he then sold to a dealer. The police were hard on his heels and, aided by the dealer's description, arrested Nelson four miles from the border.

Nelson was tried for murder in Winnipeg in November 1927 when he pleaded insanity. His careful planning, moving from place to place and changing his name, suggested the workings of a logical mind. He was found guilty and sentenced to death. Protesting his innocence, he said he forgave those who had wronged him. Nelson was hanged on 13 January 1928.

[244, 692]

NESSET, ARNFINN

Scandinavia's greatest mass murder occurred over a period of three years at an old people's nursing home in Norway where twenty-five elderly people died.

The unusually high number of deaths at the Orkdal old people's home between 1977 and 1980 was a cause of concern to the staff. But suspicion was aroused when the manager, Arnfinn Nesset, asked a nurse to obtain large amounts of the drug, curacit, used as a muscle-relaxant during surgical operations. He said he wanted it to put down a dog. When discreet inquiries established that Nesset did not own a dog, he was arrested and admitted killing twenty-seven people.

Sufficient curacit to kill 200 persons was found in Nesset's office. Many witnesses had seen him giving injections to inmates of the nursing home but no one knew what he was giving them. One theory was that he was administering euthanasia. If so, he chose an unsuitable drug, for curacit in toxic doses is slow-acting and painful in its effects. The fact that the drug breaks down when it enters the body ruled out the possibility of finding any traces in the victims.

Nesset was tried for murder at Trondheim in 1982. He withdrew his previous confession and pleaded not guilty. The evidence against him was entirely circumstantial and the jury was asked to believe that he was practising euthanasia. A more sordid motive was that he was embezzling sums of money from his patients. He claimed this was to fund charity work. Despite any clear evidence of motive, Nesset was found guilty on twenty-one counts of murder and sentenced to twenty-one years' imprisonment. Nesset was an illegitimate child who had been brought up in a rural community. He was known to suffer feelings of inferiority and rejection and he offered schizophrenia as a possible cause of his behaviour.

[582, 994]

NEU, KENNETH

Singer turned murderer who told his executioner, 'I'm fit as a fiddle and ready to hang.'

Kenneth Neu's ambition was to be a night-club entertainer. He had good looks and the right personality, although his singing talent was not exceptional. He was one of many young men seeking an outlet for their talents in New York during the 1930s, but secured only a few poorly paid engagements.

On 2 September 1933, while walking aimlessly in the streets near Times Square, he met Lawrence Shead, a theatre owner who said he might be able to help him. Shead took him back to his apartment where they spent several hours drinking. When Shead made homosexual advances, there was a struggle and the aspiring singer strangled his would-be benefactor. When he left Shead's apartment, Neu was wearing one of the dead man's suits.

Two weeks later in New Orleans, Neu met Eunice Hotte, a waitress whom he promised to give a good time in New York. To finance his promise, Neu went to the Yung Hotel and struck up conversation with Sheffield Clark, a visitor from Nashville. Once in Clark's room, he demanded money and when he was refused, killed a second time. Taking Clark's car and substituting its registration plate with a crudely painted sign, declaring 'New Car in Transit', Neu drove to New York with his girl-friend.

When he was stopped by the New Jersey police, Neu laughingly admitted to killing Lawrence Shead. He was extradited to Louisiana to stand trial at New Orleans for the murder of Sheffield Clark. He pleaded insanity, which failed when the jury found him guilty, but he continued his charade by breaking into a song-and-dance routine. He continued his hilarious antics until his execution on 1 February 1935, reportedly dancing his way to the scaffold.

[*191, 901*]

NEWALL, RODERICK

Ex-army officer convicted in 1994 of murdering his parents seven years previously following a quarrel in their home on the island of Jersey.

Nicholas and Elizabeth Newall disappeared in October 1987. Friends contacted their sons, Roderick and Mark, who worked on the mainland but neither could explain why their parents were missing. There had been a family party in a Jersey restaurant on 10 October to celebrate Mrs Newall's birthday and it was reported that an argument had marred what should have been a happy occasion.

Despite intensive searches throughout Jersey, no trace of the Newalls could be found. To all intents and purposes, they had vanished. They were declared dead in January 1991 and their sons inherited nearly £1 million.

Nicholas and Elizabeth Newall were wealthy enough not to need to work and spent their time travelling and sailing. While they seemed devoted to each other, they had little time for their boys who, early in their lives, had been sent to boarding schools. Nicholas had been a teacher and his colleagues regarded him as arrogant and domineering. He bullied his sons to such an extent that an acquaintance said, 'You would be kinder to your cat or dog.'

At school, Roderick had a reputation for violent behaviour while Mark seemed withdrawn. Roderick went into the army and Mark became a financier. One thing they shared, however, was a hatred of their parents who were so consumed by their own lives that they afforded scant love or concern for their sons. After their parents were declared dead, Roderick pursued his interest in sailing and Mark used his financial acumen to good advantage.

The Jersey police suspected that the brothers were involved in their parents' disappearance and, in July 1992, Roderick admitted as much to his uncle. He was picked up from his yacht by the Royal Navy off the coast of Morocco on 5 August 1992.

The former army officer admitted killing his mother and father after an argument which had stirred bitter childhood memories. The apparent spontaneity of this act was undermined by the knowledge that he had bought a pickaxe, spades and plastic sheeting which were used to dispose of the bodies. His brother helped him bury the bodies in a shallow grave at Greve de Lecq near their childhood home.

The brothers were tried at the Royal Court of Jersey in August 1994. Roderick, aged twenty-nine, was convicted of murder and sentenced to life imprisonment. Mark Newall, aged twenty-eight, was convicted for helping his brother and was sentenced to six years' imprisonment.

[*120, 497, 643, 1006*]

NEWELL, SUSAN

Murder of a young boy by a woman in a seemingly motiveless crime for which she paid with her life.

On a June morning in 1923, a lorry driver in Glasgow stopped to offer a lift to a woman and child pushing a loaded cart along Duke Street. He drove her into the centre of the city and set her down as she instructed. As the driver helped her with the cart, the bundle fell into the road and was hastily scrambled up by the woman.

This minor incident was witnessed by a woman looking out of an upstairs window who noticed a head and a foot protruding from the bundle. She followed the woman and then called the police. When the suspicious bundle was opened, the body of a thirteen-year-old boy was discovered. He had been strangled and trussed up. The woman was Susan Newell and the dead boy was John Johnston, one of a family of five from Coatbridge. Mrs Newell explained that her husband had killed the boy and she was protecting him by disposing of the body.

John and Susan Newell were charged with murder and sent for trial. The case against Newell collapsed and his wife was left to answer the charge on her own. The Newells' eight-year-old daughter testified and innocently explained how the 'wee laddie' had come to the house selling newspapers and described helping her mother 'put him in a bag'.

Susan Newell pleaded insanity but the jury found her guilty with a recommendation to mercy. The Secretary of State for Scotland could find no grounds to grant a reprieve and Newell was hanged at Duke Street Prison in Glasgow on 10 October 1923.

[*445, 1000*]

NICHOLSON, WILLIAM LAWRENCE WARREN

Former South African police officer who killed his wife and admitted to concealing the murder weapon.

Late on the evening of 1 September 1956, the peace was disturbed in a residential area of Fish Hoek, a South African resort town. Residents heard screams rising above the loud music coming from the Nicholson home. Suddenly, William Nicholson rushed into the street, shouting, 'My wife! I think she's been murdered!'

Sylvia Nicholson lay severely injured inside the house, her head smashed in with a hammer. She died later in hospital. Her husband told the police that when they returned home, he disturbed a coloured intruder who attacked his wife and ran off.

Dissatisfied with his explanation, police took Nicholson in for further questioning. He claimed that it was his hammer which the intruder had wielded with such deadly effect and dropped as he fled. Foolishly, he picked it up and, realising that the hammer now bore his fingerprints, he wiped it clean and hid it. Detectives found it unbelievable that a former police officer, used to preserving crime evidence, would have behaved in such a way.

Nicholson was tried for murder at Cape Town in 1957. He portrayed himself as a dutiful husband devoted to caring for his wife whose health was poor. His story of the intruder could not be substantiated and his replies under cross examination were ineffectual. He was found guilty and, protesting his innocence, was hanged on 12 August 1957.

[65]

RACHEL NICKELL CASE

The murder on Wimbledon Common of a young mother out walking with her two-year-old son in 1992 created immediate outrage and later sensation.

Twenty-three-year-old Rachel Nickell was discovered on 15 July 1992 at a spot some 200 yards from the Windmill on Wimbledon Common. Her small son was clinging to her dead body. She had been stabbed repeatedly and her throat was cut. She had also been sexually assaulted.

News of the murder in a public park used by many people for recreation created a sense of outrage in London and throughout Britain. A massive murder inquiry was mounted and the police used psychological profiling as a means of determining the likely character of the murderer. He was seen as a man fascinated by sadistic sex and notions of dominance over women. He was probably a low achiever who lived alone and in the vicinity of the murder location.

In September 1992, this profile was made public by the BBC on its *Crimewatch* programme, together with photofit pictures of two men seen on Wimbledon Common on the day of the murder. As a result, four viewers called the police to say they recognised one of the photofits as thirty-one-year-old Colin Stagg who lived at Roehampton.

Colin Stagg admitted to the police that he had been out on the Common with his dog on the day in question. Many of his personal characteristics matched those of the psychological profile and this influenced the police in setting up an unprecedented undercover operation. In an exchange of letters with Stagg extending over seven months, a policewoman drew out his sexual fantasies which included violence, pain and domination, but he made none of the hoped-for admissions about Rachel Nickell's murder.

Nevertheless, after consultation with the Crown Prosecution Service, Colin Stagg was charged with murder in August 1993. His trial at the Old Bailey in September 1994 collapsed when Mr Justice Ognall ruled that the prosecution evidence was inadmissible. He criticised the police for manipulating a suspect and trying to trap him into self-incrimination.

Colin Stagg was declared innocent and discharged. Recriminations followed with the police, prosecution lawyers and psychological profiling coming in for severe criticism. Colin Stagg threatened to sue the police and Scotland Yard announced that they had reopened the inquiry into Rachel Nickell's murder.

[*285, 743, 879*]

NILSEN, DENNIS

Thirty-seven-year-old civil servant who murdered fifteen young men in London between 1978 and 1983. He picked up his victims in wine bars and lured them to his home with the promise of giving them accommodation. There he strangled them and cut up their bodies.

Nilsen served in the army as a cook and for a short time was an officer in the Metropolitan Police. After working for a security firm, he became a civil servant in 1974 and worked in a London Job Centre. This gave him an ideal opportunity to contact lonely young men who had dropped out of society and were looking for shelter and accommodation. He also spent a great deal of time in bars where he communed with other lost souls during heavy drinking sessions.

In February 1983, a firm of drain-cleaning specialists was called to Cranley Gardens in north London to unblock the street drains. Workmen found the source of the blockage in the pipe outside No 23. Their immediate reaction was that the pieces of rotting flesh which they pulled out must be dog-meat. Laboratory examination proved otherwise – the foul-smelling material was human flesh.

Dennis Nilsen appeared anxious to tell his story when police officers knocked on his door. Talking in a nonchalant way, he admitted killing and dismembering fifteen people, adding 'I didn't keep a body count.' Three severed heads were found in plastic bags in the wardrobe, and a tea-chest contained other parts of human bodies. He mentioned that as well as the three bodies at Cranley Gardens, there were thirteen others buried in the back garden of the house he had previously lived in at Cricklewood.

Nilsen had slid into violence after his flat-mate left him. Often insensible with drink, he took his victims home, not even knowing who they were. After he had killed them and dismembered their corpses, he was faced with the problem of disposal. As many as five sets of remains were stored under the floorboards of his flat and their organs reposed in suitcases in his garden shed. Periodically he had bonfires to destroy the remains but his mistake was to start flushing them down the WC.

He was tried at the Old Bailey in October 1983 and defended on the grounds of diminished responsibility. He was portrayed by the prosecution as a cold, remote personality lacking any sense of remorse. The man who had described himself as a 'creative psychopath' was judged to be responsible for his actions and found guilty of murder. He was sentenced to life imprisonment.

Killing for Company was the title of a book about Nilsen by Brian Masters published in 1985. The author had access to his subject in prison and described an unloved child who grew into an estranged adult obsessed with the sexuality of death. In this context, Nilsen's victims were not real people but props in his fantasy world.

Nilsen was not welcomed by his fellow inmates and suffered a razor attack in Wormwood Scrubs. His house in Cranley Gardens was put up for sale in November 1983. It did not sell quickly despite attracting a number of morbid sightseers. Some of Nilsen's furniture ended up in Scotland Yard's Black Museum. His 'House of Horror', as it was dubbed, was sold in 1984.

In 1993, Nilsen was in the news again due to a controversial TV programme called *Murder in Mind* which featured an interview with him. The TV company needed a judge's ruling to overcome the objections of the Home Office to the programme in which Nilsen gave a graphic account of how he had disposed of his victims' bodies.
[*584, 610, 644*]

NODDER, FREDERICK

Child abductor whose crime was fully revealed when his victim's body turned up ten months after he killed her.

Ten-year-old Mona Lilian Tinsley, one of a family of seven children, failed to return to her home in Newark, Nottinghamshire after school on 5 January 1937. She was last seen in the company of a man at the local bus station.

She was reported missing by her parents and police began to receive information from the public. A passenger on a bus travelling from Newark to Retford saw a man accompanied by a young girl. The man was identified as Frederick Nodder, a lorry driver who lodged with the Tinsley family under a false name and was known to the children as 'Uncle Fred'.

Nodder at first denied seeing Mona but later admitted taking the girl at her request to Sheffield because she wanted to see her aunt. He said they travelled together to Worksop where he left her with instructions and money for her onward journey. He returned to Retford.

House-to-house inquiries and the widest possible searches failed to reveal any traces of the missing girl. While the hunt continued,

Nodder was charged with abduction and, in March 1937, was convicted and sentenced to seven years' imprisonment.

Three months later, Mona Tinsley's body was found in the River Idle. The child had been strangled but it was not possible to determine any other injuries. In November 1937, Nodder was tried for murder at Nottinghamshire Assizes. Sentencing him to death, Mr Justice Macnaghten told him, 'Justice has slowly but surely overtaken you.' Nodder was executed at Lincoln Prison on 30 December 1937.

[*57, 134, 254*]

O

OAKES CASE

Controversial unsolved murder in the Bahamas in 1943 during the governorship of the islands by the Duke of Windsor.

Sir Harry Oakes, a Canadian citizen and millionaire businessman, was found dead in his bed at Westbourne, his house at Nassau, on 8 July 1943. He had been battered to death and an attempt made to burn his body. Ignoring the local police, the Duke of Windsor called for help from Captains Barker and Melchen of the Miami Police Department. Their investigations prompted the arrest of Oakes's son-in-law, Alfred de Marigny, who was subsequently put on trial.

De Marigny was acquitted as the result of defective evidence-handling and deported from the island. Oakes's daughter Nancy called in Ray Schindler, an American private detective, to help with her husband's defence. He exposed many inconsistencies about Sir Harry's death and tried to have the case reopened.

Rumours persisted about the involvement of the criminal underworld, in Oakes's murder. It was alleged that Meyer Lansky, a Mafia syndicate leader, was intent on introducing gambling to the Bahamas. Oakes opposed him and Lansky sent emissaries to convince the businessman to accept his plans. What began as verbal persuasion ended in violence and Sir Harry's body was taken back to his house.

Various attempts were made to cast blame in de Marigny's direction, including a planted fingerprint in the bedroom. It was Captain Barker's failure to substantiate the provenance of the print which led to de Marigny's acquittal. Barker was shot dead by a member of his family in 1952 and Lansky died in 1983, aged eighty-one.

[*92, 231, 232, 441, 555, 693*]

OLSON, CLIFFORD ROBERT

Canadian serial killer who negotiated payments from the authorities to reveal the location of his victims' graves.

Between winter 1980 and summer 1981, forty-year-old Olson abducted and murdered at least eleven youngsters of both sexes. His first victim was twelve-year-old Christine Weller who went missing from her home in Vancouver in November 1980. Her stabbed and mutilated body was found on Christmas Day.

Children disappeared from their homes in the Vancouver area at regular intervals during the early months of 1981. The last sighting of a nine-year-old boy who went missing was talking to a man in a shopping mall. Publicity resulted in numerous witnesses' descriptions which enabled the police to build up an artist's impression of the man. Calls flooded in from the public after the picture was published.

Suspicion began to focus on Clifford Olson, a Vancouver man, married with a child, who had a string of convictions for robbery and sexual assault. He was put under surveillance and trailed for many hours while he relentlessly patrolled the highways, frequently picking up girls on the way.

When he was finally arrested, Olson's address book was found to contain the name of one of the murder victims whose mutilated body had been found near Agassiz in the Frazer Valley. He was charged with her murder but the evidence against him remained largely circumstantial.

Realising that he faced the possibility of imprisonment as a sex offender, Olson attempted to negotiate a deal with the police whereby he would trade the locations of other victims' bodies in return for a guarantee that if convicted he would be sent to a psychiatric unit rather than the penitentiary.

In an extraordinary development, Olson changed his mind and asked for money in return for information. The authorities agreed to pay $10,000 for each missing child recovered, the money going to his wife. Olson led search teams to a number of graves and enthusiastically recalled the details of each murder.

He was tried on ten counts of murder at Vancouver in January 1982. To everyone's surprise, he did not use insanity as a defence but pleaded guilty to murder. Revelation of the deal he had struck caused a police uproar. It was labelled morally and legally wrong, and politically inept.

Clifford Olson was convicted and sentenced to life imprisonment, which meant that he would be eligible for parole after serving twenty-five years.

In 1997, at a judicial hearing in Vancouver, Olson said he was prepared to reveal the truth about sixty unsolved murders in Canada and dozens of killings in the USA. This was part of his strategy to gain approval for parole in under twenty-five years. He also offered to donate the profits from his proposed memoirs to the families of his murder victims in Canada. His willingness to make amends was denounced as 'blood money'.

[*283, 432, 684*]

ONOPRIENKO, ANATOLY

Ukrainian serial killer nicknamed 'The Terminator'. With a tally of fifty-two victims, he matched his Russian counterpart, **Andrei Chikatilo**, the 'Rostov Ripper'.

On Christmas Eve 1995, Onoprienko broke into a forester's home at Garmarnia wielding a shotgun and killed a family of four. He then set fire to the house. A week later another family suffered the same fate at Bratkovychi. His next attack was at Enerhodar where he killed seven people before returning to Bratkovychi and murdering a family of five. In the space of less than a month he had killed twenty times using brutal methods including shooting with a double-barrelled shotgun, stabbing and mutilation with an axe.

By the time the police caught up with him, Onoprienko had claimed fifty-two victims including ten children. During the early 1990s, he travelled throughout Europe while a huge manhunt for 'The Terminator' was in full swing in the Ukraine. He was finally arrested at his girl friend's house near Lviv where the couple were apparently living a normal life.

Onoprienko, a former forestry student, had been treated for schizophrenia but psychiatrists pronounced him sane and fit to stand trial. His claims to hear voices and that his actions were influenced by higher authorities were regarded as false. He pleaded guilty to killing twelve people in 1989 and a further forty in 1995/96.

Spectators at his trial held in Zhytomyr, near Kiev, demanded that he be tortured before execution. The trial lasted for three months and five judges sitting without a jury heard the evidence. Thirty-nine year old Onoprienko said the killings were 'all a kind of experiment', adding, 'There is no better killer in the world than me'.

He expressed no remorse and on 1 April 1999 was convicted and sentenced to death. Sergei Rogozin, his accomplice for some of the crimes, was sentenced to thirteen years' imprisonment. Onoprienko remains in prison while the Ukraine upholds its moratorium on carrying out death sentences.
[*442*]

ONUFREJCZYK, MICHAEL

Farmer convicted of murdering his partner on their Welsh farm in an unusual case in which no body was ever found.

Routine police checks on aliens living in Britain in 1953 led officers to a remote farm at Llandilo in Carmarthenshire. Cefn Hendre was supposedly run by two Poles, Stanislaw Sykut and Michael Onufrejczyk. The officers were told that Sykut had returned to Poland leaving his interest in the farm to his partner.

Further inquiries ensued but no record could be found of Sykut having left Britain. Various parts of Onufrejczyk's statement were contradicted by people who knew him. The ex-Polish army man who had a distinguished service record talked himself deeper into trouble. Finally, on 19 August 1954, despite the absence of a body, Onufrejczyk was charged with murdering Sykut.

Against a background in which no conviction for murder had been made in England for 300 years without identification of the body, the Pole was sent for trial. He appeared at Swansea in November 1954 to answer the charge that he had murdered his partner to gain sole control of the farm. The two men were known to have quarrelled but the evidence was entirely circumstantial. Onufrejczyk maintained that Sykut was still alive but his lies to the police helped to incriminate him.

Onufrejczyk was found guilty and sentenced to death. His appeal was dismissed, but in January 1955 his sentence was commuted to life imprisonment. He was released on parole in 1966 and went to live in Yorkshire. He was killed in a traffic accident a month later. A popular local theory was that, like the **Hosein** brothers, Onufrejczyk had disposed of his victim to the pigs on his farm.
[*312, 374, 906*]

ORROCK, THOMAS HENRY

Young man intent on being a villain who killed a police officer and escaped detection for eighteen months.

Apparently influenced by the boastful talk of local villains, Orrock decided to try his hand at crime. He bought a revolver which he test-fired in the Tottenham Marshes to impress his friends. On 1 December 1882, armed with house-breaking implements and his revolver, Orrock set out to commit a robbery at the Baptist Chapel in Dalston, north London.

Although a pea-soup fog shrouded his criminal act, he was spotted by an alert policeman, PC George Cole, and arrested on the spot. While he was being escorted to the police station, he pulled out the revolver and threatened the police officer with it. There was a struggle, four shots were fired and PC Cole was hit in the head. Orrock escaped into the gloom. Two women had witnessed the shooting but were unable to give a description of the assailant beyond saying he wore a wide-brimmed hat. This proved an important clue, for another policeman, Sergeant Cobb, had seen Orrock earlier that evening wearing such a hat. Orrock was put on an identity parade but released when the witnesses failed to identify him.

Several months later, Sergeant Cobb was told about the shooting practice in the Tottenham Marshes. He was taken to the spot and shown the tree which had been used as a target. Using his penknife, he eased out a number of bullets from the bark of the tree. These proved to be of the same calibre as those which had killed his colleague.

By this time, Orrock was serving a prison sentence at Coldbath Fields for burglary. He was now charged with murder and, in September 1884, nearly two years after the crime, was found guilty and sentenced to death. He was hanged in October 1884.
[*189, 886*]

P

PACCIANI, PIETRO

The 'Monster of Florence' was the name given by the media to a mysterious killer who carried out a series of murders between 1968 and 1985 in the Italian city of Florence.

The victims, with one exception, were couples making love in cars. The first killing occurred on 21 August 1968 and resulted in the deaths of Barbara Locci and Antonio Lo Bianco. Locci's husband, Stefano Mele, was convicted of the murder and imprisoned as a result of a verdict that was widely held to be unsafe.

There was another double killing on 14 September 1974 when the murder weapon was found to match the gun used in the 1968 killings. Further double killings occurred on 6 June and 22 October 1981 and two double killings on 19 June 1982. Two homosexuals were shot dead while sleeping in their van on 9 September 1983 and two more couples were murdered on 29 July 1984 and 8 September 1985. A characteristic of the killings was that in many cases the women's breasts and sexual organs were attacked. These mutilations became more pronounced as the killings progressed.

In November 1993, a sixty-eight year old farmer was arrested and charged with sixteen murders attributed to the 'Monster of Florence'. Pietro Pacciani had already served time in prison for murder and repeatedly raping his daughters. He was sent for trial in November 1994 and after a six-month hearing was acquitted of the 1968 murders but found guilty of all the other killings. He was sentenced to life imprisonment.

On 13 February 1996, an appeal court overturned Pacciani's conviction and set him free. His release came hours after police had arrested two of his associates, Mario Vanni and Giancarlo Lotti, and charged them with five murders. Then, in another dramatic twist, Italy's Supreme Court reviewed Pacciani's appeal in December 1996 and decided that he should be retried and new evidence heard.

Meanwhile, Vanni and Lotti went on trial in May 1997 and were found guilty. Vanni was jailed for life and Lotti was sentenced to twenty-six years' imprisonment. Pacciani did not live to face retrial. He died, apparently of a heart attack, in his home on 23 February 1998. Post mortem examination revealed the presence of drugs in his body which led to suggestions that he had been silenced to prevent him naming well-connected people involved in a supposed Satanic cult.

[*822*]

PALLIKO, ALAN

Ex-police officer whose ambition of becoming a rich man turned to murder for elimination.

When his marriage faltered, Palliko turned his attentions to Sandra Stockton whose husband was mysteriously shot dead in their Los Angeles home in December 1966 while watching television. Sandra Stockton benefited from a $75,000 insurance policy on her husband's life.

Palliko's wife, Katherine Drummond, filed divorce papers and experienced two attempts on her life. The first was a hit-and-run incident and the second involved an attack in the street in which she identified Palliko as her assailant. He was arrested but she declined to press charges.

In March 1968, Palliko remarried after moving to Burbank where he managed a bar. His new wife, Judy, was a swimming-pool instructor and, with business going well, they enjoyed a luxury lifestyle. But as passion died, tension mounted and soon the new marriage was in difficulties. On 18 April 1968, Judy Palliko was found dying from gunshot wounds to the head in her car, a yellow Jaguar parked near their apartment. The distinctive car was a gift from her husband. She died in hospital. Palliko confided to a friend that he had killed his wife and he also admitted the Stockton shooting two years earlier. He was known to be a gun freak and a veritable arsenal was found in his house. Palliko and Sandra Stockton were charged with conspiracy to murder.

It was believed that Palliko gave his wife the brightly painted Jaguar in order to make her a more visible target. Vincent Bugliosi,

the famed prosecutor in the Manson trial, put forward an overwhelming case. Palliko and Stockton were convicted. While she was sentenced to life imprisonment, he was given the death sentence, although this was later commuted to life.
[*130*]

PALMER, Dr WILLIAM

One of England's most infamous murderers who poisoned as many as fourteen people to acquire money to fund his gambling debts.

Palmer was a recalcitrant child whose mother paid for his early misdemeanours. He fathered a number of illegitimate children but stuck to his studies sufficiently to qualify as a doctor in 1846 and set up in practice at Rugeley in Staffordshire. He was moderately successful as a physician but could not curb his appetite for gambling.

Constantly in poor financial straits, Palmer built up huge debts and resorted to murder and insurance swindles in order to pay his way. His mother-in-law died within days of coming to live in his house in 1848 and her assets went to his wife. Four of his five children died, along with an uncle and, in 1854, after heavily insuring her life, his wife died, leaving him £13,000. The following year, his brother died after a heavy drinking session with the doctor, but the insurance company refused to pay out on this occasion.

On 13 November 1855, with the moneylenders pressing him for payment, Palmer had a day at Shrewsbury Races with a friend, John Parsons Cook. As usual, Palmer lost, but his friend's horse came in a winner. To celebrate his win, Cook invited his friends to supper at the Talbot Arms Hotel in Rugeley. During the celebrations, Cook was taken ill and was treated by Dr Palmer. Cook died on 20 November and his relatives demanded a post-mortem examination. Traces of antimony were found in the organs of the dead man and the inquest returned a verdict of wilful murder against Palmer.

Such was the local hostility against Palmer, that his trial for murder was transferred to London. A new Act of Parliament was passed to make this possible in cases where public opinion might inhibit a fair trial. Palmer was therefore tried at the Old Bailey in May 1956. The circumstantial evidence against him was strong although the toxicological evidence was conflicting. Palmer was nevertheless found guilty and sentenced to death. He was publicly hanged outside Stafford Gaol on 14 June 1856 to a chorus of verbal abuse.

Mock funeral cards were circulated, one of which was dedicated to 'The infamous memory of Dr William Palmer of Rugeley who so doctored his friends' food and drink that they never required medical assistance again.'
[*37, 124, 293, 362, 495, 526, 880*]

PANCOAST, MARVIN

On 7 July 1983, thirty-three-year-old Pancoast, who worked for a talent agency, walked into a Hollywood police station and told officers, 'I killed Vicki. I did it with a baseball bat.' He was referring to the death of thirty-one-year-old Vicki Morgan whose battered body was found in her Los Angeles apartment. A bloodstained baseball bat lay beside her corpse.

Vicki was a model and small-part actress whose twelve-year affair with Alfred Bloomingdale, founder of Diners' Club, made the headlines in 1982 when she filed a palimony suit against him a week before he died. She claimed that Bloomingdale, a man in his mid-sixties, had promised to support her for life in return for her services as confidante and adviser. Media interest was guaranteed when she alleged that Bloomingdale had an appetite for sadistic sex practices.

Her eleven-million-dollar claim was thrown out of court and the judge described her relationship with the late Alfred Bloomingdale as one based on 'meretricious sexual services'. This amounted to sex for hire which he said was illegal in California. From this point on, her monthly support cheques of $18,000 ceased.

She then developed a relationship with Pancoast who moved into her apartment, but they argued over money. He had a history of psychiatric treatment and it was later argued that he was an unstable personality. Despite Pancoast's confession to the killing, no fingerprints were found on the murder weapon and none of his prints were found in the apartment.

The case was thrown into disarray when it was announced that three pornographic video tapes depicting Vicki Morgan and Alfred Bloomingdale had come to light. More importantly, the tapes were said to feature a number of senior political figures. As the participants would certainly have been known to Vicki, it was now suggested that she might have attempted blackmail and been murdered as a result.

At his trial, Pancoast pleaded not guilty by reason of insanity.

Defence lawyers argued that his confession was an illusion induced by his desire to take the blame for a crime committed by someone else. The jury held that he was sane and, following his conviction for first-degree murder, he was sentenced to twenty-five years to life.
[*215, 661, 1005*]

PANZRAM, CARL

One of the USA's worst mass murderers responsible for twenty-one killings and countless other crimes.

He spent most of his life in prisons and correction establishments. When he emerged from Fort Leavenworth Prison at the age of nineteen, he said that all the good that was in him had been beaten out of him. He embarked on a career of robbery and violence aimed at exacting revenge on society. His brutal instincts were honed by further spells in prison and frequent escapes.

While at liberty in 1920, he carried out numerous robberies and killed several times. He also resorted to sodomy as an expression of his hatred for his fellow men. The man who had been chained up and beaten in prison said, 'I hate the whole damned human race including myself.'

In 1928, Panzram once again ended up in Leavenworth Prison and warned his custodians, 'I'll kill the first man who bothers me.' True to his word, on 20 June 1929, he killed the foreman of the prison laundry. He was convicted of murder and sentenced to death. When the Society for the Abolition of Capital Punishment campaigned for a reprieve, he wrote to President Herbert Hoover demanding his constitutional rights, including his wish to be hanged.

He finally got his way on 5 September 1930 when he was hanged at Fort Leavenworth. His last words were addressed to the executioner whom he urged to 'hurry it up'. While in prison, Panzram wrote his autobiography and passed the pages to one of his warders. His portrait of violence was so frank that forty years passed before his *Journal of Murder* was published.
[*323*]

PARKER AND BARROW

America's legendary crime duo of the 1930s whose small-scale robberies were overshadowed by their brutal murders. Bonnie Parker, aged twenty-three, and Clyde Barrow, aged twenty-five, killed at least thirteen people during a three-year reign of violence.

Barrow, who came from a poverty-stricken background in Texas, had already embarked on a life of crime when he met Bonnie Parker, a waitress from Dallas, in 1930. He made a shortlived attempt to earn a living as a saxophone player, but resorted to robbery when that failed.

Bonnie and Clyde decided their future lay in crime and they began robbing banks and filling stations. While the proceeds of their robberies were small, they were able to work off their frustration in violence. Bonnie was an easily bored young woman with a sexual appetite bordering on nymphomania, while Clyde was a homosexual. Killing was the means by which they achieved satisfaction.

The two became four when they were joined by Clyde's brother Buck and his wife Blanche. They equipped themselves with an arsenal of guns and liked to pose for photographs with them. They tantalised the police of several states with their daring raids, trail of killings and getaways in stolen cars. The newspapers covered their crimes with bold headlines and turned them into heroes of a kind with names such as 'Suicide Sal' and 'The Texas Rattlesnake'.

But the police were closing in and, in July 1933, Blanche was captured and Buck was shot dead. Bonnie and Clyde continued robbing and killing for several months but their time was also running out. On 23 May 1934, they were shot dead in a police ambush when their car was riddled with bullets.

With a degree of prescience, Bonnie had sent to a newspaper her five-verse 'Ballad of Bonnie and Clyde' which concluded with the lines:

> Some day they will go down together,
> And they will bury them side by side.
> To a few it means grief,
> To the law it's relief,
> But it's death to Bonnie and Clyde.

Yet the law had the last word by burying the desperadoes in separate cemeteries in Dallas, Texas.
[*230, 423, 731, 924, 945*]

PARKER AND HULME

Two teenage girls, Pauline Parker and Juliet Hulme, committed a murder in 1954 which shook New Zealand society to its foundations.

Pauline Parker found life dull in Christchurch until she formed a friendship with Juliet Hulme, recently arrived from England. But it was more than a friendship. The two girls engaged in fantasies which Pauline's mother regarded as unhealthy and there were overtones of lesbianism as well. Mrs Parker did her best to break up the relationship but matters came to a head when it became known that Juliet's father intended taking her away to South Africa.

Determined not to be separated, the girls decided they would both go to South Africa but knew that Pauline's mother would oppose them. They decided to kill her. Mrs Honora Parker was found dead on 22 June 1954, her head smashed in and the murder weapon, a half-brick in a stocking, lay near by. The two girls reported finding the body and said Mrs Parker had injured herself in a fall.

Under questioning, Pauline admitted killing her mother and Juliet said they had intended to frighten her into allowing them to go to South Africa. During their trial for murder at Christchurch, the girls were portrayed as precocious and capable of careful planning. Pauline's diary was all-revealing in its references to 'moidering' mother and their decision about the weapon to be used. The defence argued that the pair were paranoid and delusional and should be considered insane.

The jury brought in a Guilty verdict and, being under age, they were sentenced to be detained during Her Majesty's Pleasure. They were released less than six years later and took new identities. The case of the schoolgirl killers was made into a successful film in 1995 called *Heavenly Creatures*.

[*347, 381, 607*]

PATRICK, ALBERT T.

Crooked Texas lawyer who resorted to fraud and murder out of greed.

Patrick was an attorney with an eye for contentious litigation. First in Houston and then in New York City he built up a lucrative practice in the 1890s by means that were not always applauded by other members of the bar. In 1899, he became involved in a legal action against William Marsh Rice, an eighty-four-year-old Texan millionaire. Rice, twice married but with no children, lived with his second wife in a stylish mansion at Dunellen, New Jersey. When his wife died in July 1896, Rice moved to more austere accommodation in New York.

The old man had a shock when he realised that his late wife had made a will whereby, under Texan law, she bequeathed half of his estate to her relatives. The community law of Texas held that a husband and wife were joint owners of all property. Rice resisted legal manoeuvres to execute Mrs Rice's will on the grounds that he lived in New York, not Texas. To help him, he took on Charles F. Jones as his secretary and adviser.

Patrick's assistance was enlisted on behalf of Mrs Rice's executors. He persuaded Jones to help him refute Rice's claim to New York citizenship. The idea was that Jones would prepare a letter on Rice's stationery making clear his Texas allegiance, and Patrick would get the old man to sign it. Then Patrick went a stage further. He had Jones prepare a will leaving half of Rice's estate to Patrick and naming him as executor.

Overcome with greed, Patrick made out a cheque for $25,000 payable to himself and forged Rice's signature on it. Jones had inadvertently made the cheque out to 'Abert T. Patrick' whereas the lawyer had correctly endorsed it. An astute bank clerk spotted the discrepancy and telephoned Jones about it. He was assured that the cheque was in order but, still concerned about it, he decided to speak directly to Mr Rice only to be told that the old man was dead.

Understandably, the doctor certified Rice's death as due to old age. Patrick demanded that the body be quickly cremated which he said was the millionaire's wish. But Patrick's forged cheque caught up with him and suspicions hardened about possible foul-play. He and Jones were arrested on 4 October 1900.

Jones turned State's Evidence and exposed Patrick's plan to fleece William Rice of his millions. The old man's life had been snuffed out by making him inhale chloroform in his sleep. Patrick was tried for murder in March 1902 and found guilty. He was sentenced to death but registered appeal after appeal. Finally, in 1906, his sentence was commuted to life imprisonment. In 1912, he was granted a full pardon and returned to the south to practise law. He died in 1940.

[*136, 159, 307, 888*]

PAYNE, ARTHUR D.

Crooked Texan lawyer who killed his wife in a car explosion in order to make way for another woman.

Payne had a successful practice in Amarillo, Texas where he was widely respected as an attorney and a family man. On 27 June

1930, he uncharacteristically decided to walk from his home to his office. With the car at her disposal, Mrs Payne decided to use it to do some shopping, taking her nine-year-old son with her.

About half a mile from the house, the car began to emit clouds of smoke and suddenly disintegrated in a violent explosion. Mrs Payne was killed outright and her small son suffered severe injuries. Townspeople were shocked by the incident and the editor of the *Amarillo News* vowed that he would get to the bottom of it. When it became known that the car had been blown apart with high explosive triggered with a time fuse, fingers were pointed at Arthur D. Payne.

The newspaper hired crime reporter A.B. MacDonald to probe into Payne's life and discovered that he was having an affair with his secretary. His promise to marry her, allied with insurance cover recently obtained on his wife, led to the newspaper making an outright accusation of murder. When she was interviewed, the secretary said Payne had told her he would get rid of his wife.

Aware that his denials were wearing thin, Payne eventually confessed, making a statement running to tens of thousands of words. He was tried for murder and the jury had little difficulty in finding him guilty. He had the last word, though, for he escaped the executioner by taking his own life. He killed himself by detonating an explosive charge strapped to his chest. A.B. MacDonald went on to win a Pulitzer Prize for his investigative reporting.

[*360*]

PEARCEY, MARY ELEANOR

She killed her lover's wife and child in a fit of jealous rage and entertained Scotland Yard's Head of CID to a recital on the piano.

On 24 October 1890, a policeman on patrol in Hampstead, north London found a woman's body lying in Crossfield Street. Her throat had been cut and her head battered. An hour later, another patrolling policeman in a street about a mile away came across an abandoned bloodstained perambulator. And, on the following morning, the body of an eighteen-month-old child was found on waste ground near Finchley Road.

The dead woman was Phoebe Hogg who had left her home in Kentish Town for an outing with her baby daughter. She was identified by her sister Clara, who was accompanied at the mortuary by her friend, Mrs Mary Pearcey. It transpired that Mary Pearcey had been having an affair with Frank Hogg, the dead woman's husband. A search of her home in Priory Street showed signs of a struggle having taken place and there were bloodstains in the kitchen. During the police search of her house, graphically recounted in Sir Melville Macnaghten's memoirs, Mary Pearcey played the piano and attributed the bloodstains to killing mice. Blood on her clothing told a different story and she was arrested.

During her trial at the Old Bailey in December 1890, some of her letters to Frank Hogg were read out in court. Her expressions of undying love for him gave her a strong motive for wanting to eliminate his wife. She lured Phoebe to her house where she killed her and the baby and wheeled both bodies in the perambulator to the places where she dumped them.

Mary Pearcey, whose father had been hanged for murder at St Albans in 1880, kept her appointment with the hangman on 23 December 1890.

[*478, 552, 716*]

PEEL CASE

A Florida judge hired contract killers to eliminate another judge in a case that remained unsolved for five years.

Curtis Eugene Chillingworth had been a judge on the Florida bench for thirty-two years but he failed to turn up for a scheduled court appearance on 15 June 1955. There were ominous signs of foul-play at his house on the beach at Manalapan, near Palm Beach. The judge's car was parked in the garage and there were bloodstains and signs of a struggle on the steps leading down to the beach. Both Judge Chillingworth and his wife had completely disappeared. Among the judge's likely enemies was a fellow member of the bar, Judge Joseph Alexander Peel, a young lawyer recently elected to the bench. Peel had been criticised for professional negligence and had been reprimanded by Chillingworth concerning his future conduct.

After they had been missing for two years, the Chillingworths were declared dead and substantial rewards were offered for information. Rumours abounded and when a local businessman saw Judge Peel and his companion, Floyd Holzapfel, he told them that the Chillingworth's bodies had been found. This proved to be false but Holzapfel, already disillusioned with Peel, let it be known that he knew something about the Chillingworth case.

In 1960, Holzapfel was questioned by the police and made a confession. He and a convicted criminal, Bobby Lincoln, had been

hired by Judge Peel to kidnap and murder the Chillingworths. The couple were taken out to sea and drowned. Lincoln turned State's Evidence and was freed and Holzapfel was tried for murder. He was convicted in 1962 and sentenced to death, subsequently being reprieved. Peel, who protested that it was all a plot to discredit him, was found guilty of being an accessory before the fact. He was sentenced to life imprisonment.
[*81, 101, 453, 1014*]

PELTZER BROTHERS

Two Belgian businessmen conspired to eliminate the husband of the woman one of them admired.

Guillaume Bernays, a well-known solicitor with a practice in Antwerp, disappeared on 14 January 1882. He had taken the train from Antwerp to Brussels, alighting at Schaerbeek where he was seen walking out of the station. The missing man had prominent friends and there were demands for results from the police. During their inquiries, detectives learned that among the solicitor's clients was Armand Peltzer who, it seemed, was sweet on Madame Bernays. Angered by this behaviour, Bernays had angrily confronted Peltzer and warned him off. When he was questioned, Peltzer provided a satisfactory alibi but the police remained suspicious.

Further inquiries revealed that Peltzer's brother Léon had travelled to Belgium from Germany and, using the name Henry Vaughan, had consulted Bernays on a legal matter. It was arranged that the two men would meet in Brussels on 14 January, the day Bernays disappeared. Two days later, the missing man's body was discovered at 159 rue de la Loi in Brussels as a result of a letter sent to the city coroner by Henry Vaughan. The letter explained that while Bernays was examining a pistol which Vaughan had on his desk, the weapon went off and killed him. Vaughan was so unnerved that he fled.

Armand Peltzer denied knowing anyone called Henry Vaughan but after circulating a description throughout the European capitals, Belgian police finally identified Léon Peltzer. He was arrested in Brussels and put on trial with his brother Armand in November 1882. Léon admitted the murder but exonerated his brother. Both were convicted and sentenced to death. The sentences were commuted to imprisonment and Léon served thirty years. He drowned in 1922. Armand Peltzer died in prison three years after being convicted.
[*220, 399*]

PERRY, ARTHUR

A clever ruse to incriminate another man for murder was uncovered by forensic evidence.

The body of twenty-year-old Phennie Perry was found on waste ground in Queens County, New York on 2 July 1937. She had been battered to death but her two-year-old child who was with her was unharmed. Near the body detectives found a man's black left shoe with a hole in its sole. There were also bloodstained papers scattered about including letters addressed to Ulysses Palm. The police believed that Mrs Perry had been robbed and in the struggle had caused her assailant to leave behind some of his possessions.

Ulysses Palm, who was deacon at the Amity Baptist Church in Jamaica, New York was well regarded in the local community. He emphatically denied killing Mrs Perry despite the discovery in his room of a black shoe which matched the one found at the murder scene.

When told about his wife's murder, Arthur Perry immediately exclaimed that Palm had threatened to kill her if she was not more friendly to him. He said that he had confronted Palm but suspicions grew when detectives found that on the given date Palm was working several miles away.

It was the shoe with the hole in it which clinched Perry's guilt. One of his socks bore a muddy patch that matched the hole in the shoe, and analysis of the stain on it corresponded with blood and mud at the crime scene. Perry was tried in November 1937 and convicted of first-degree murder. His plan to throw guilt on Ulysses Palm was undone by forensic evidence which clearly incriminated him. He succeeded in winning a second trial on a technicality, but this reached the same verdict as the first. Arthur Perry was executed in August 1939.

[*194*]

PETERSON, SCOTT LEE

Convicted in 2004 of murdering his wife in a landmark California case that allowed the death penalty to be imposed when the victim's unborn child is killed.

On 23/24 December 2002, Laci Peterson disappeared. She was eight months pregnant and the expected child was to be called Conner. Four months later, the decomposed corpse of a woman and a separate male foetus were found on the shore of San Francisco

Bay. Thirty-two year old Scott Peterson, a fertilizer salesman, seemed to be unmoved by the concern shown by family and friends over the tragedy.

The Petersons seemed to be a happy couple and there appeared to be no motive for murder. There were no witnesses and no forensic evidence linking Peterson to the disappearance. Later, though, it emerged that he had a mistress to whom he confided that he would be spending Christmas alone. This was before his wife went missing.

Detectives carried out surveillance on Peterson and picked him up in San Diego close to the Mexican border. He had disguised his appearance, was carrying a considerable sum of money, together with a credit card and driving licence not registered in his name. In his car were items of survival equipment.

President Bush had signed a law in April 2004 designed to protect unborn victims of violence. This law already existed in California and it meant that, if convicted, Peterson would be liable for the death penalty. Despite the circumstantial nature of the evidence, Peterson was indicted for murder and in 2004 stood trial at Redwood City.

The prosecution argued that he had killed his wife, put her body in his car and driven to the marina where he kept his fishing boat. He weighted the corpse with concrete blocks and dumped it in San Francisco Bay. Peterson said he had been fishing on the day in question for which he had a valid licence. His defence attorneys contended that Laci had been kidnapped while out walking, held captive and murdered some time later which explained why her body when found was separate from her child's.

The jury favoured the prosecution case and found Peterson guilty of first degree murder in respect of his wife and second degree murder in the case of Conner. He was sentenced to death and is held at San Quentin pending the outcome of the appeal process.

[*1039, 1049*]

PETIOT, Dr MARCEL

French doctor who ran a murder for profit scheme in German-occupied Paris in the 1940s, killing dozens of people and acquiring their possessions.

After suffering for several days from the stench of the black smoke emitted from the chimneys of 21 rue Lesueur, neighbours complained to the police. On 11 March 1944, gendarmes went to the house and found a note pinned to the door informing callers that the occupant would be away for a month. The fire brigade was called and they found a basement furnace roaring away and using human corpses as fuel.

The owner of the house, Dr Petiot, had disappeared and the German occupying authorities in Paris issued a warrant for his arrest. The dismembered remains of twenty-seven bodies were found at the house which had been adapted as a death factory. Petiot sought to profit from the desire of wealthy French Jews to escape the German occupation. They came to his house with high expectations of freedom but met death and destruction instead. At his brother's house in Auxerre, Petiot had lodged forty-nine suitcases containing the clothing and possessions of his victims. The contents included 66 pairs of shoes, 115 men's shirts, 79 dresses and over 300 handkerchiefs. The doctor had disappeared and, in the turmoil following the D-Day landings, managed to keep clear of the police until 31 October 1944.

He readily admitted killing over sixty people whom he claimed were Nazi collaborators. The forty-nine suitcases and their contents told a different story of murder for gain. It was believed that Petiot had made the equivalent of a million pounds out of his so-called escape route. The once successful doctor and former town mayor was found guilty of committing twenty-seven murders. He was sentenced to death and, when he walked to the guillotine on 26 March 1946, advised those present that it would not be a pretty sight.

[*238, 273, 378, 625, 837*]

PIKUL, JOE

New York stockbroker who died of AIDS before his appeal against conviction for wife murder could be heard.

Diane Pikul's body, covered with a tarpaulin tied with string, was found blocking a highway drain in Orange County, New York State on 28 October 1987. She had been strangled and battered about the head.

Diane had been reported missing. Joe Pikul said she had walked out after an argument but he had since disappeared himself, leaving their two children in the care of a baby-sitter. The couple had met in 1977 at Alcoholics Anonymous after experiencing broken marriages. Diane worked for *Harpers Magazine* in New York and Joe was a successful stockbroker.

Joe Pikul accidentally encountered police officers during a visit to his lawyer and was prompty arrested. He admitted being responsible for Diane's death but gave a rambling account of what happened. He believed she had taken a lover and described her as a malicious person. When Pikul was searched, officers were astonished to find that he was wearing women's underwear.

After their marriage in 1978, Diane discovered that Joe indulged some unusual sexual inclinations. He bought a complete wardrobe of women's lingerie and took photographs of himself in drag. He also made a video. In addition, Joe was eating and drinking heavily, experimenting with drugs and frequently resorting to violent behaviour.

In January 1978, Diane sent the photographs and video to her lawyer for safe-keeping. Her instructions were that in the event of her death they were to be returned unopened to her husband, unless her death was suspicious.

Joe Pikul was tried for his wife's murder in January 1989. Much of the evidence, including the photographs, was deemed inadmissible. Asked if he caused Diane's death, Joe answered yes; asked if he had murdered her, he answered no. He claimed that there had been a confrontation about her alleged infidelity and an argument ensued. During a struggle in which he said she attacked him with a knife, he choked her in self-defence.

His explanation did not explain Diane's multiple head injuries. The jury convicted him of second-degree murder but legal complications delayed sentencing. Joe Pikul died on 2 June 1989 aged fifty-four. In December, it was announced that his conviction had been erased because he had died before the appeal was heard. *[751]*

PIERRE, DALE SELBY

US airman who, aided by fellow serviceman William Andrews, committed the 'Hi-Fi Shop Murders' in Ogden, Utah in 1974.

On 22 April, intruders entered the hi-fi shop intent on committing robbery. They held the proprietors captive and also three friends who called by. The victims were herded into the basement where they were tied up and forced to lie on the floor. Their wallets, purses and jewellery were taken from them and then they were subjected to brutal violence.

A bottle of Drano, a caustic compound used to unblock drains, was produced and the victims were told to drink the liquid. 'We're going to have a cocktail party,' they were told. Next, each victim was shot in the back of the head while they lay on the floor; the teenage shop assistant was raped first. With three of their victims dead and one badly wounded, the intruders devoted their attention to the remaining victim who was assaulted and had a ballpoint pen forced into his ear.

Doctors saved the lives of the two who were injured, and one of them was able to give the police descriptions of the murderers. Suspicion quickly focused on Dale Pierre, an airman at nearby Hill Field, a US air base. He was known to have discussed a prospective crime in which the witnesses would be eliminated. He had talked of his intention to rob the hi-fi shop and had been overheard to say, 'If anybody gets in my way, I'll kill 'em.'

Police found some of the personal possessions of the murder victims in a garbage dump close to Pierre's quarters. A search of the airman's quarters turned up a rental agreement for a garage store which contained $24,000-worth of stolen hi-fi equipment. Detectives also found a half-used bottle of Drano in the store. Pierre was arrested along with William Andrews and a third man who was eventually convicted of aggravated robbery.

Pierre and Andrews were tried for murder at Farmington, Utah and found guilty. They were both sentenced to death but destined to remain on Death Row for many years. Pierre was reprieved five times but was executed by lethal injection on 28 August 1987. Newspapers reported that advocates of capital punishment celebrated Pierre's execution by holding parties in restaurants near the state prison.

William Andrews was on Death Row for eighteen years, longer than any of the other 2500 inmates awaiting execution in US prisons at the time. He was executed by lethal injection in Utah State Prison on 30 July 1992.

[521]

PITCHFORK, COLIN

The murders of two fifteen-year-old girls in the Narborough area of Leicestershire in the 1980s signalled a scientific breakthrough in the use of DNA.

Lynda Mann disappeared after making a visit to a schoolfriend on the evening of 21 November 1983. Her body was found a few hours later. She had been raped and strangled. Semen traces found on the body showed that the murderer belonged to a fairly rare blood group.

Initial investigations centred on nearby Carlton Hayes Hospital which accommodated a number of sex offenders. Despite intensive police activity, no progress was made in finding the murderer.

Then, on 31 July 1986, he struck again when Dawn Ashford failed to return home. She too had been raped and strangled. Once again attention focused on the nearby hospital and a teenage porter there confessed to the murder. Inconsistencies in his account meant that corroboration was necessary. By comparing his DNA with that of the murderer's, it was shown conclusively that he was not the killer.

Dr Alec Jeffery of Leicester University had discovered that every individual could be identified by means of the unique genetic material present in their tissues, blood, saliva and semen. This revolutionary discovery which had eliminated one suspect was put to use to trap another.

In a decision reminiscent of the mass fingerprints carried out in Blackburn in 1948 which led to the identification of **Peter Griffiths**, Leicestershire police officers proposed to carry out a mass blood-sampling exercise. All males aged between seventeen and thirty-four who lacked alibis for the murder dates were requested to give samples of blood and saliva.

Over 4000 men gave samples without a positive result and the exercise was beginning to founder when chance intervened. A group of bakery workers became aware that one of their number had been asked to give a blood sample for someone else. The facts were reported to the police and within twenty-four hours Colin Pitchfork was under arrest. His blood sample matched the DNA characteristics of the murderer of the two girls and he readily confessed.

Twenty-seven-year-old Pitchfork was a baker with a history of sexual offending. He said that he had intended only to expose himself to the girls but that led first to rape and then to murder when he realised they could identify him.

Pitchfork was tried in January 1988 and found guilty. He was sentenced to life imprisonment and the judge, Mr Justice Otton, acknowledged the important part played by DNA profiling in bringing him to justice.

[958]

PODMORE, WILLIAM HENRY

He committed murder to cover up a fraud and was incriminated by forensic evidence.

Police were called to a locked garage in Southampton on 10 January 1929. Inside, they found the body of fifty-eight-year-old Vivian Messiter, an oil-company agent, who had been bludgeoned to death with a hammer. The murder weapon, with one of the victim's eyebrow hairs adhering to it, was found at the scene.

Detectives searching Messiter's rooms for clues that might lead to his murder found a reply to an advertisement he had placed in the newspapers to recruit local agents. The response was from William F. Thomas, who was known to the police and wanted in connection with robbery. Thomas had long departed from his lodgings but left behind sufficient evidence to establish that his real name was William Podmore. When the missing man was located in London, he admitted knowing Messiter. Unable to tie him in with the murder, police had to settle for charging Podmore with fraud. He received a six months' prison sentence.

The murder investigation continued and an oils sales receipt book provided a breakthrough. This contained records of sales made by William Thomas on which he earned commission. The problem was that the sales were made to non-existent customers. The top copies of the receipts had been removed but the impression of the writing on them remained on the pages beneath. Using special photographic techniques, scientists were able to reveal the details of the fraud perpetrated by Thomas.

Podmore was suspected of murdering Messiter to silence him after his boss confronted him with evidence of fraud. The one-time sales agent was tried for murder at Winchester in December 1929. The jury found him guilty and he was sentenced to death. He was hanged on 22 April 1930.

[*309, 466, 850, 1010*]

PODOLA, GUENTHER FRITZ ERWIN

The murder of a police officer in the streets of London in 1959 led to the arrest of Podola who subsequently claimed to be suffering from amnesia.

On 3 July 1959 the South Kensington flat of Mrs Verne Schiffman was burgled. A thief stole jewellery and furs and then attempted blackmail. He telephoned Mrs Schiffman, claiming to be in possession of compromising photographs. She went straight to the police and the next time the blackmailer called, she kept him talking while the call was traced.

Detective Sergeant Raymond Purdey and a colleague raced to a call-box in South Kensington tube station where the caller was still talking to Mrs Schiffman. The man was arrested but while being taken to the officers' patrol car, broke free and ran off. They gave chase and he was cornered in a block of flats at Onslow Square. The man pulled a gun and fired at Purdey, killing him instantly and escaping into the London traffic.

The gunman was identified from palmprints which he had left in the entry to the flats. He was Guenther Podola, a German criminal who had been deported from the USA. A manhunt ensued and Podola was found holed up in a London hotel. On 16 July, police burst into his room, knocking him to the floor and rendering him partially unconscious.

Podola claimed to remember nothing of what had happened. He was examined by numerous doctors who were divided on whether he was genuinely suffering amnesia or merely trying to avoid responsibility for his acts. He was tried for murder at the Old Bailey and faced overwhelming evidence from the prosecution. After all, a police officer had witnessed him kill his colleague. The real issue was the question of amnesia but in a trial lasting under two days the jury found him guilty. He was hanged at Wandsworth Prison on 5 November 1959.

[*318, 464*]

POMMERENCKE, HEINRICH

Sexual offender who became a serial killer, claiming that his lusts were triggered by watching films in which there was a sexual component.

Pommerencke was an only child with a shy and introverted character. He experienced powerful sexual urges but lacked the confidence to establish normal relationships. He lived a solitary existence, indulging in fantasy and petty crime. While living in northern Germany in the mid 1970s, he committed several rapes and then, on 27 February 1959, turned to murder. He attacked a girl after leaving a cinema in Karlsruhe but was scared off by a passer-by. But his lust was so strong that he went on the prowl for another victim. He found eighteen-year-old Hilda Knothe, whom he raped and murdered.

On 3 June 1959, he killed again, this time targeting a young woman with a group of students travelling by train from Heidelberg to Italy. He made advances to twenty-one-year-old Dagmar Klimek and when she resisted, pushed her off the train. He pulled the communications cord and went back up the line to find his victim whom he raped and stabbed to death. Pommerencke killed twice more before being arrested in Hornberg in June 1960. A description of 'The Beast of the Black Forest', as the killer had been dubbed, was circulated and an astute tailor told the police of his suspicions about one of his customers. A waiter had ordered some new clothes which he took away, leaving behind a suitcase which he asked the tailor to keep for him. While moving the heavy case, the lock gave way and an assortment of knives and guns fell out.

Pommerencke was initially charged with robbery but eventually made a full confession to murder. He was tried at Freiberg in October 1960 and convicted of four murders, twelve attempted murders, twenty-one sexual assaults and several robberies. He was given eight life sentences.

[*597, 640*]

POULIN, ROBERT

Eighteen-year-old who became obsessed with deviant sexual behaviour and killed twice before taking his own life.

The son of professional parents in Ottawa, Canada, Poulin began to withdraw from family life when he was seventeen. Increasingly he spent his time in his basement bedroom where, unknown to his parents, he indulged in a world of sexual fantasy. He bought pornographic books, fantasised about bondage, rape and murder and also acquired weapons.

Poulin's parents led an active life in the community and respected their son's wish for privacy by not intruding. On the evening of 27 October 1975, Mrs Poulin returned home to find the house on fire. When firemen dowsed the blaze, they found the body of Kimberley Rabot, one of Robert's school-friends, in the basement bedroom. She was handcuffed to the bed and had been raped and stabbed to death.

Robert Poulin turned up the next day at St Pius X Catholic High School where he was a student. He was carrying a pump action Winchester shotgun with a sawn-off barrel. He went into Father Robert Bedard's classroom and opened fire. He killed one of his fellow students and wounded six others before turning the gun on himself.

He left behind a diary which recorded the actions he proposed to take, including arson and suicide. He suffered acutely from loneliness and depression even to the point of advertising for a friend just two weeks before he died. He was a devotee of pornographic literature and rented a post-office box so that he could receive it discreetly through the mail.
[*188, 387*]

PRITCHARD, Dr EDWARD WILLIAM

Physician who poisoned his wife and mother-in-law and became the last person to be publicly hanged in Scotland.

After service in the navy as a surgeon, Dr Pritchard married and took up private practice in Glasgow in 1860. He was not respected in the city's medical circles on account of his loud and boastful behaviour. He was also subject to controversy, particularly when a young servant lost her life in a fire at his home in 1863.

In 1864, the doctor seduced a fifteen-year-old servant and made her pregnant. He aborted her child and promised that he would marry her. Mrs Jane Pritchard conveniently fell ill on 1 February 1865 and her mother, Mrs Taylor, came to look after her. She too fell ill and although Dr James Patterson was called in to give a second opinion, and suspected poisoning, he took no action.

Mrs Taylor died on 25 February and her daughter followed on 18 March. Pritchard did not endear himself to his late wife's relatives by ordering the undertaker to remove the lid from her coffin so that he could kiss her corpse. As the result of an anonymous letter sent to the Procurator-Fiscal, an investigation was started. The bodies of both victims were exhumed and traces of antimony were found in their tissues.

Pritchard was tried for murder at Edinburgh in July 1865 and faced the weight of circumstantial evidence which was customary in poisoning cases. He also faced an embittered barrage from Dr Patterson which earned a rebuke from the bench. The doctor was found guilty and made several confessions of his crimes. He was the last person to be publicly hanged in Scotland. An estimated crowd of 100,000 people saw the hangman carry out his duty on 28 July 1865.
[*26, 261, 440, 787, 909*]

PUTT, GEORGE HOWARD

A wave of killings in Memphis, Tennessee in 1969 created a panic until the perpetrator was caught in the street with a bloody knife in his hand.

The killing began on 14 August 1969 when Roy and Bernalyn Dumas were strangled in their apartment. The middle-aged woman had been sexually assaulted and her body mutilated. Two more murders were committed before the end of August including the frenzied stabbing of a twenty-one-year-old woman in a public park. Citizens of Memphis took extreme measures with people locking themselves in their houses and being afraid to walk the streets.

On 11 September, neighbours were attracted by the sound of screams coming from an apartment block but were too late to save Mary Pickens, a widow living alone, who had been stabbed to death. But alert citizens spotted an intruder and pursued him through the streets. After a considerable chase, the man, bloodstained and with a knife in his hand, was arrested by the police. George Putt's explanation that he had cut himself while climbing over a fence did not carry much weight.

Putt said that he began by planning robbery but once he had entered the apartment occupied by Roy and Bernalyn Dumas, he was overcome by feelings of violence. In between his killings – five in the space of a month – he returned home to his wife and a normal background.

He was tried for the murder of Mary Pickens and pleaded insanity. In October 1970, he was found guilty and sentenced to death. Execution was put off while various appeals were heard and finally put aside when the US Supreme Court suspended the death penalty. At a second trial in April 1973, Putt was found guilty of murdering Roy and Bernalyn Dumas and given prison sentences amounting to 497 years.

[655]

PYJAMA GIRL CASE

An unusual Australian case, involving the death of a young woman, which took ten years to solve.

The partly burned body of a woman clad in pyjamas was found in a roadside culvert at Albury, New South Wales on 1 September 1934. She had been severely beaten, causing fractures to the skull, and also shot in the head. Identification was not immediately apparent and a description of the dead girl, including photographs and fingerprints, was circulated to police forces to initiate their missing persons routines. The 'Pyjama Girl', as she had been called, was put in a tank of preservative at Sydney University pending identification. The one distinctive facial feature, the lack of ear-lobes, led to a provisional identification. It was thought that she might be Linda Agostini, the wife of an Italian waiter working in Sydney.

Antonio Agostini was questioned by detectives and confirmed that he had been married to an English girl by the name of Linda Platt but that they had since separated. He was shown photographs of the 'Pyjama Girl' but denied that she was his wife. With the Second World War looming, the matter rested there. Agostini, as an Italian immigrant, was interned while the 'Pyjama Girl' remained preserved in formaldehyde.

A further attempt at identification was made in 1944. New photographs were prepared and seven witnesses said they would testify that the dead girl was Linda Agostini. Now Agostini explained that his wife had been drinking heavily and during an argument threatened him with a revolver. The weapon discharged accidentally and killed her. This failed to account for the blows to the head which she had received but he said he took her body to the place where it was found and attempted to burn it with petrol. Agostini was tried for murder in June 1944 and was convicted on the lesser charge of manslaughter. He was deported to Italy after serving six years' imprisonment.

[*185, 193, 274, 508*]

Q

QUEEN, PETER

Medical opinion was divided on whether an unusual death by strangulation was murder or suicide.

Queen appeared at a Glasgow police station on 21 November 1931 and put his house keys on the duty sergeant's desk. He told the officer, 'Go to 539 Dumbarton Road. I think you will find my wife dead.' Twenty-eight-year-old Chrissie Gall, with whom Queen had been living, lay on the bed in her pyjamas. She had been strangled and a cord was tied tightly around her neck. There were no signs of a struggle. Queen said he had found her on the bed and believed she was asleep until he saw the cord around her neck.

It was widely acknowledged that Chrissie was an alcoholic and her friends had tried to reform her. She had threatened suicide and told them that one day they would find her strung up. Neighbours testified that Chrissie had been drunk on the day before she was found dead and was depressed. Queen, who was reported to have said that he thought he had killed her, was charged with murder.

Two top-ranking forensic pathologists, Sir Bernard Spilsbury and Sir Sydney Smith, believed Chrissie Gall had strangled herself. Experts for the prosecution argued the opposite case, pointing out the neat position of the body and the orderly arrangement of the bedclothes. Queen was tried at the High Court of Justiciary in Glasgow in January 1932. He maintained that his alleged admission of guilt was misinterpreted – he had told the police, 'Don't think I have killed her.'

The jury convicted Queen on a majority verdict with a recommendation to mercy. He was sentenced to death but later reprieved. He died in 1958, following his release from prison.

[*123, 529, 873*]

QUERIPEL, MICHAEL

Murder on a golf course using a tee-marker as the murder weapon led to a successful local investigation to identify the perpetrator's palmprint.

Elizabeth Rosina Currell was reported missing from her home in Potters Bar on 29 April 1955. Her husband told the police that she had left home in the evening to walk their dog on the golf course. When the dog returned without its mistress, the alarm was raised.

A search was organised and Mrs Currell was found the next day lying by the seventeenth tee on the golf course. An attempt had been made at rape and she had been partially strangled although the injuries which killed her had been inflicted by a metal tee-marker. The bloodstained murder weapon lay near by and detectives found the clear impression of a partial bloody handprint on it.

The print was not filed in the criminal records so police made house-to-house inquiries in Potters Bar requesting householders to allow their palmprints to be taken. In an exercise with echoes of the massive fingerprinting carried out in Blackburn several years earlier (see **Griffiths**), officers hoped to find a matching print. Nine thousand impressions were taken and a match was found with number 4604. It belonged to Michael Queripel. At first he told police that he had found the body on the golf course but then admitted killing the woman out with her dog while he was suffering a migraine. He attempted to conceal his crime by slashing his arm with a razor to explain the presence of blood on his clothes.

Queripel was tried for murder at the Old Bailey on 12 October 1955. He pleaded guilty and was ordered by Mr Justice Hallet to be detained during Her Majesty's Pleasure.

[*373, 543, 647*]

R

RABLEN, EVA

Extrovert young wife whose war-disabled husband proved an encumbrance to her.

Carroll Rablen was a lonely figure as he sat in his car outside the dance hall at Tuttletown, California on the evening of 26 April 1929. He had been injured by an exploding shell in the trenches during the First World War and was deaf as a result. He was also rather withdrawn and hated dancing as much as his vivacious wife loved it. As he did most weekends, he sat and watched while his wife danced with other men. Around midnight Eva left the dance floor and bought some coffee and sandwiches which she took out to her husband. They had a brief conversation and she returned to the dance-hall. Moments later, Carroll Rablen's screams brought people rushing to his side. He was convulsing in agony and complained about the bitter taste of the coffee. He died and his wife collapsed sobbing beside him.

The popular explanation for Rablen's sudden death was that he was depressed and had committed suicide. When the autopsy failed to establish cause of death, an analysis was made of the dead man's stomach contents. This, too, proved negative. Rablen's father told the police that he thought his son had been poisoned by his wife. When a second search was made of the dance-hall, a bottle labelled 'Strychnine' was found. It had been sold by a local pharmacist to a woman whom he identified as Eva Rablen. Traces of strychnine were found in the dead man's stomach after a second analysis.

Eva was charged with murder and her trial took place in an open-air pavilion in order to accommodate the great public interest. She altered her plea to Guilty in face of overwhelming forensic

evidence and proof that she had signed the pharmacist's poison register in a false name. She was sentenced to life imprisonment and taken to San Quentin.
[*87*]

RADER, DENNIS

A serial killer terrorised the population of Wichita, Kansas in the 1970s, creating a climate of fear similar to that inflicted on San Francisco by the **Zodiac Killer**. It took thirty years before the BTK murderer (Bind, Torture and Kill) was identified and brought to justice.

The first victims were three members of the Otero family who were found gagged, bound and strangled in their home in January 1974. During the next three years, other victims were killed in their homes and a feature of the murders was that the perpetrator sent cryptic messages taunting the police and media. The messages stopped in April 1980 and the BTK murders seemed to have ended. But in 2004, the messages began again and the *Wichita Eagle* newspaper received a letter enclosing photographs of the body of Vicki Wegerle who had been murdered in 1986 but whose death had not been linked to the previous killings.

The rate of messages increased but then came the breakthrough the police had been hoping for. One of the messages was sent on a computer disk which was traced to a Lutheran Church in Wichita. Suspicion fell on sixty-year old Dennis Rader, the local dog-catcher, who was also president of the church. A search of his home turned up files and photographs relating to the BTK victims and Rader's DNA matched semen traces found at some of the crime scenes. He was arrested in February 2004 and confessed to ten murders.

In June 2005, Rader appeared on trial and told the court how he had trawled for victims and carried a 'hit kit' which included ropes and other equipment. He acknowledged sending messages to the media including one which asked, 'How many do I have to kill before I get my name in the paper. . . ?' He pleaded guilty to the ten murders and in August 2005 was given ten consecutive life sentences with a minimum of a hundred and seventy-five years, thus ensuring that he would never be freed. The man who had terrorised a community for thirty years avoided the death penalty as capital punishment was not in force in Kansas at the time the BTK murders were committed.
[*1033*]

RAMIREZ, RICHARD

Serial killer, known as the 'Night Stalker', who terrorised the Los Angeles area with a spate of violence in 1985.

The killings reached a peak in early August after six months in which thirteen people had been murdered and eleven others raped or injured. The killer favoured suburban locations close to main highways and struck at night when his victims were sleeping, a mode of operation which earned him the name of 'Night Stalker'. His technique was to enter houses by means of unlocked windows or insecure doors. He usually shot dead any male occupant before sexually assaulting the female.

A number of victims survived his assaults and a picture emerged of a man dressed in black whose distinctive features were his gaunt face and rotten teeth. He frequently made reference to the devil and told one victim, 'Swear upon Satan that you won't scream for help.' The inhabitants of houses in the Los Angeles area began equipping themselves with electronic security, guard-dogs, guns and knives. The increased vigilance deterred the 'Night Stalker' for he switched his venue to San Francisco where he attacked a couple on 17 August.

A week later he attacked again, this time leaving the scene of murder and rape in an orange-coloured car, the registration number of which was recorded. Police found the car abandoned and succeeded in obtaining fingerprints from it. Within hours detectives had identified the serial killer from police records as twenty-five-year-old Richard Ramirez and his photograph was soon on television screens and newspaper front pages.

On 31 August, Ramirez was spotted by a member of the public in a liquor store in a Los Angeles suburb. He was chased through the streets and eventually cornered and overpowered by local residents. He told the police officer who arrested him, 'Shoot me, man. Kill me. I don't deserve to live.'

For procedural reasons, it took four years before Ramirez finally appeared on trial. He smirked and sneered his way through testimony given by some of his victims, at one point shouting out 'Heil Satan'. On 20 September 1989, he was found guilty of thirteen counts of murder and thirty other felonies including rape, sodomy and burglary.

Before being sentenced to death, he told the judge, 'I am beyond your experience. I am beyond good and evil, legions of the night –

night breed – repeat not the errors of the Night Prowler and show no mercy.' Ramirez joined the other 265 men waiting at that time on California's Death Row where no death sentence has been carried out for nearly twenty-five years.
[*161, 579*]

RATTEN, LEITH

Possible miscarriage of justice in Australia in which conviction for murder was obtained on dubious firearms evidence.

Police were called to a house in Echuca, a small town in Victoria, Australia on 7 May 1970 to investigate a fatal shooting. Leith Ratten explained that while he was cleaning his shotgun in the kitchen of his home the weapon accidentally discharged a shot which killed his wife. She took the blast in the chest and Beverly Ratten, who was over eight months pregnant, died instantly.

When investigators found that Ratten had been promiscuous, suspicions hardened that he might have killed his wife intentionally. Despite conflicting firearms evidence, he was charged with murder and sent for trial. The circumstantial nature of the prosecution case did not trouble the jury which found him guilty. He was sentenced to death, although in September 1971 this was commuted to life imprisonment.

Ratten's case was sent for appeal when the controversial nature of the prosecution case was exposed. According to the pathologist, the shot which killed Beverly Ratten had entered her body at an angle of 45 degrees on a downwards trajectory while she was standing. Defence experts pointed out that for this to be possible, the butt of the weapon which killed her would have been at a height of over 9 feet from the floor. This ruled out Leith Ratten as the firer, as he stood at a little over 5 feet 6 inches tall.

It was far more likely that the pathologist was in error and that the fatal shot had entered the victim's body horizontally. This was consistent with Ratten's explanation that the weapon was fired accidentally. The convicted man's appeals have been consistently turned down.
[*663*]

RATTENBURY-STONER CASE

One of the sensational murder trials of the 1930s in which a young wife took a lover who became jealous of her husband and killed him.

Francis and Alma Rattenbury lived at a house called The Villa Madeira in Bournemouth. The retired architect married the twice-wedded Alma, who was half his age, in 1928. The marriage did not work as Francis wanted a quiet life and Alma desired the opposite.

In 1934, a third party entered the Rattenburys' lives in the form of young George Stoner whom Alma had hired as a chauffeur. The driver and his mistress soon became lovers and Alma acquainted the illiterate young man with London's hotel life. Stoner believed he had made a conquest which entitled him to certain rights. He was jealous when Alma retired to her husband's bed and grew sullen to the point of refusing to carry out her instructions.

Police were called to The Villa Madeira late on the night of 24 March 1935 where they found Francis Rattenbury on the point of death. He had a severe head wound and died later. Alma, the worse for drink, told police officers that she 'did it with a mallet'. A wooden mallet, heavily bloodstained, was found in the house. While Alma was incoherent, Stoner was busily admitting that he had killed Rattenbury. Both parties had confessed to the killing but they pleaded Not Guilty when they were tried for murder at the Old Bailey in May 1935. Alma said she had no recollection of events after finding her husband and Stoner claimed that his actions were influenced by drug-taking. While Alma was acquitted, the jury found Stoner guilty and he was sentenced to death. In a tragic denouement, she committed suicide while he was reprieved. After serving a life sentence, Stoner was given a probationary sentence in 1990 for committing a sexual assault in Bournemouth.

[*405, 470, 483, 690, 773*]

RAVEN, DANIEL

Unusual case of double murder in which the motive remains obscure.

During the evening of 10 October 1949 Daniel Raven visited his wife Marie at the nursing home in Muswell Hill where she had recently given birth to their first child. Also among the young mother's visitors were her parents, Leopold and Esther Goodman.

Later the same evening, when his business partner visited Leopold Goodman at his home in Edgware, he was disturbed to gain no response. He and his wife were found lying in a pool of blood with their heads battered in. Daniel Raven, who lived in the same street, was questioned by the police and immediately aroused suspicion.

A search of his house produced a man's bloodstained suit which had been partially burned in the kitchen stove. The blood was the same group as that of the murder victims. Raven was charged with murdering his parents-in-law. He told the police that he took the Goodmans home after they had all visited his wife and new baby. He then went to see his cousins near by but returned to the Goodman's house on the way home. He found them dead and left the house in terror, soiling his clothes with blood in the process.

Raven admitted that he did not get on very well with his wife's parents but denied murdering them. He was tried at the Old Bailey and his wife testified on his behalf. He was found guilty and sentenced to death. His appeal on the grounds of insanity was based on a report that while serving in the Royal Air Force, he had suffered severe anxiety neurosis following a crash. The appeal was dismissed and Daniel Raven was hanged on 6 July 1950 at Pentonville Prison. His widow, with her infant son, remarried a year later.

[*74, 964*]

RAYNER, HORACE GEORGE

Young man, confused about his parentage, shot dead the man he believed to be his father and who refused to accept him.

On 24 January 1907, Horace Rayner walked into Whiteley's department store in Westbourne Grove, Bayswater, London and asked to see William Whiteley. He gained access to the office of the store's founder by pretending that he was on an errand from a solicitor. After meeting for half an hour in private, the two men emerged from the office. Rayner asked, 'Is that your final word?' William Whiteley replied, 'Yes', to which Rayner retorted, 'Then you are a dead man, Mr Whiteley'. He drew a revolver and fired two shots at the sixty-seven-year-old store owner, killing him instantly. Rayner then put the gun to his own head and pulled the trigger but survived.

A note in Rayner's pocket alleged that Whiteley was his father. The store owner's refusal to accept this was the apparent motive for the murder and attempted suicide. Rayner was tried for murder at the Old Bailey and pleaded not guilty on the grounds of temporary insanity. The trial proceedings were more taken up with Rayner's parentage than with his state of mind.

His supposed father, George Rayner, had refused to accept him as

his son on the grounds that his birth had been incorrectly registered, although he assumed the role of foster parent. It was alleged that George Rayner and his lady-friend often spent weekends with William Whiteley and his mistress. The fruits of these liaisons were three illegitimate children, one of whom was Horace Rayner. He believed that Whiteley was his real father. Rayner was convicted of murder and sentenced to death. He was reprieved because of the unusual circumstances of the case and sentenced to life imprisonment. He was a troublesome prisoner, and twice tried to commit suicide. He was released in 1919 but died soon afterwards.
[*269, 282, 542, 894*]

REES, MELVIN DAVID

Sex murderer who killed five times and may have been responsible for four other killings in 1957 and 1959.

An army sergeant and his girl-friend were driving in Annapolis, Maryland on 26 June 1957 when they were forced off the road by another vehicle. The driver, who was armed with a revolver, attempted to fondle the girl and, when she resisted, shot her. Her companion fled to the nearest farmhouse and called the police. By the time officers arrived at the scene, the gunman had made good his escape but a search of the vicinity led detectives to a nearby building which they believed was some kind of hideaway. The walls of the cinderblock building were festooned with pornographic pictures.

The police made little headway until January 1959 when Carroll Jackson with his wife and two children were forced off the road near Fredericksburg, Virginia. A man threatened them with a gun and ordered them to climb into the trunk of their car. The vehicle was found the next day, but there was no sign of the family. Two months later, Carroll Jackson's body was found together with that of his eighteen-month-old daughter. The bodies of Mrs Jackson and her four-year-old daughter were found near the 1957 murder scene. The girl had been bludgeoned to death and her mother had been raped and strangled. The slaughter of the Jackson family stimulated a massive manhunt which led to Melvin Rees who had drawn suspicion to himself by talking about the murders. He denied the killings but was identified by the army sergeant whose girl-friend had been shot.

A search of Rees's home turned up the murder weapon and his written account of the murder of Mrs Jackson. He was tried first in Baltimore for the Maryland killings and sentenced to life, and then in Virginia for the Jackson killings and sentenced to death. 'The Sex Beast', as he had become known, was reprieved and died in 1995. [*882*]

RIDGWAY, GARY L

One of America's greatest murder mysteries was solved in 2003 after an investigation lasting twenty-one years when Ridgway admitted to killing forty-eight women in what became known as the Green River Killings.

A spate of murders in the north west between August 1982 and March 1984 claimed the lives of dozens of young women runaways and prostitutes. The victims earned their living on the Sea-Tac strip, a three-mile stretch of the Pacific Highway near Seattle-Tacoma airport.

The first victim was sixteen year old Wendy Corfield whose body was found in the Green River on 12 August 1982. Two weeks later, Deborah Lynn Bonner was found dead in the river and three other women were found in similar circumstances. After these discoveries, bodies appeared at a rate of two or three a month in and around Washington State.

Local police forces spent millions of dollars in their efforts to capture the Green River Killer. Theories abounded and there were recriminations about the lack of progress in police investigations. The police were reticent about describing the methods used by the killer, referring to his 'homicidal violence of undetermined strength'. Psychological profiles defined the killer as male, someone who fitted in with the community, probably middle-aged, physically strong, familiar with the locality and a sexual psychopath with an urge to control others. The murders stopped in 1984 which led to speculation that the murderer might have changed his territory.

Gary Ridgway, a middle-aged truck painter, had come under suspicion in 1983 when a witness reported seeing him with one of the murder victims in his pick-up truck. There was no physical evidence at that time to link him to any crime but the police took a saliva sample from him. It was this which provided investigators with a breakthrough when in 2001, thanks to advances in DNA technology, scientists matched the sample to three of the murder victims.

Ridgway cooperated with the police, leading them to the remains of four further victims. In 2003, in a deal to avoid the death penalty, he confessed to forty-eight murders. He said he hated prostitutes and picked them up because they were easy targets. He had sex with them in his home or pick-up truck before strangling them and dumping their bodies. 'I killed so many women', he said, 'I have a hard time keeping them straight'. This was a reference to remembering where he had disposed of them.

The Green River Killer, America's most prolific serial murderer, was sentenced to forty-eight consecutive life terms without release. [*519, 772, 800, 867*]

ROBERTS, HARRY MAURICE

Leader of a gang of three car thieves who panicked when questioned by a plain-clothes police patrol. They shot dead three officers in what became known as the 'Braybrook Street Massacre'. A public outcry ensued with demands for the reintroduction of capital punishment.

The driver of a police patrol Q car designated Foxtrot-Eleven stopped his vehicle in Braybrook Street, Hammersmith on 12 August 1966. In addition to the driver, the patrol consisted of Detective Sergeant Christopher Head and Detective Constable David Wombwell – all in plain clothes. They were intent on questioning three men in a blue estate car. Head and Wombwell walked over to the car and were immediately gunned down. One of the men rushed over to the patrol car and finished off the driver by firing through the window. With three policemen dead in their wake, the gunmen made their escape.

A man driving in Braybrook Street was forced to take avoiding action when he saw a blue car reversing towards him at speed. Thinking there might have been a breakout from Wormwood Scrubs Prison, he noted the licence number, PGT 726. Ownership of the car was quickly traced to John Edward Witney who said he had sold the car to a stranger on the previous day. Publicity about the car resulted in a report that it had been seen in a railway arch garage at Lambeth rented by Witney. He was arrested and his two companions identified as John Duddy and Harry Roberts.

Duddy was quickly picked up in Glasgow, but Roberts successfully eluded the police for three months. He had served in the army in Malaya and was skilled at living outdoors. As a result of a wide-scale manhunt, Roberts's camouflaged lair was found in woods near Bishop's Stortford and he was caught in a nearby barn.

Roberts joined Witney and Duddy, who had already been sent for trial. Only Witney gave evidence and that was to the effect that he had been terrorised by Roberts. In December 1966 all three men were found guilty at the Old Bailey. In passing life sentences, the judge said, 'My recommendation is that you should not be released on licence, any of the three of you, for a period of thirty years . . .'

Following his notoriety as Britain's most wanted man, Roberts's name has been used by football crowds when they choose to taunt the police at big matches:

> Harry Roberts, he's our man;
> he shoots policemen, bang, bang, bang.

Roberts's thirty year tariff expired in 1996. A parole review began in 2001 when he was told that the police were investigating allegations against him relating to periods when he was out of prison on licence. The evidence for this was not made public but in 2005 was used to stall parole hearings.
[657, 931]

ROBERTSON, JAMES ROLAND

Policeman who contrived to make a murder look like a road accident.

Early on the morning of 28 July 1950, a taxi-driver in Prospecthill Road, Glasgow stopped to examine a bundle he saw lying in the street. He discovered the severely damaged body of a woman who appeared to have been the victim of a hit-and-run.

This conclusion changed after careful examination of the woman's injuries and the scene of the incident. The woman, who was identified as Catherine McCluskey, had sustained a blow to the head before being run over. Marks in the road indicated that she had been repeatedly run over by a car driven in figure-of-eight fashion. The car involved was found abandoned in a side street. Its owner was James Robertson, a policeman serving with the Glasgow force.

Robertson made a number of admissions including possession of the car which he knew to be stolen, absenting himself from duty without permission and making a false entry in his log about a hit-and-run report. This was designed to cover his tracks, for he later admitted knowing Catherine McCluskey, who had borne his child.

He said he saw her in the street on 28 July and declined to give her a lift. Having driven past, he then changed his mind and reversed the car to where she was standing. He discovered that he had knocked her over and her body had become tangled up under the car. He drove forwards and backwards in an attempt to free her.

Robertson was tried for murder. He was thought to have killed Catherine McCluskey because he wanted to terminate their relationship against her wishes. He denied this but the Scottish jury brought in a majority verdict and he was sentenced to death. Robertson was hanged at Barlinnie Prison, Glasgow on 16 December 1950.

[*245, 344, 862*]

ROBINSON, JOHN

Confronted with disposing of his victim's body, the murderer decided to dismember it and put the pieces into a trunk which was then deposited as left luggage.

Investigation of the 'Charing Cross Trunk Murder' began with an offensive smell pervading the atmosphere of the left-luggage office at Charing Cross railway station. The smell was traced to a large trunk which was opened on 6 May 1927 and found to contain several stinking paper-wrapped parcels. These enclosed the dismembered remains of a woman's body.

Sir Bernard Spilsbury determined that the woman had been dead for a week and reported cause of death as due to asphyxia. The left-luggage office attendant gave a description of the man who had deposited the trunk five days earlier. A laundry-mark stitched to an undergarment found in the trunk was traced to a family living in Chelsea who employed a maid called Minnie Bonati. She was the estranged wife of an Italian waiter who confirmed that the body in the trunk was that of his wife.

A taxi-driver came forward to tell the police that he had driven a man carrying a heavy trunk from 86 Rochester Row to Charing Cross station on 6 May. Attention focused on John Robinson who had opened an estate agent's office in Rochester Row. He denied knowing Mrs Bonati and none of the witnesses identified him but when confronted with new evidence, Robinson made a confession. He said that Mrs Bonati had asked him for money and went to his office where she attacked him. He fought her off and she fell back, striking her head. When he realised she was dead, he decided to dismember her body and dispose of it in the trunk.

His explanation carried little weight at his trial when an Old Bailey jury found him guilty of murder. He was sentenced to death and executed on 12 August 1927 at Pentonville Prison.
[*123, 206, 281*]

ROBINSON HILL CASE

The controversial death of a doctor's wife in Texas led to an accusation of 'murder by omission' against her husband.

Dr John Hill, a plastic surgeon in Houston, married Joan Robinson, the daughter of Ash Robinson, a wealthy Texas oilman, in 1957. Hill had a busy career as a surgeon and she was a keen horsewoman, so they tended to go their separate ways. Arguments followed when Joan realised that her husband was seeing other women and, in March 1969, she fell ill. Dr Hill treated her and after a few days had her admitted to the local hospital. Her condition grew steadily worse and she died of heart failure on 19 March.

After an inadequate post-mortem on a body which had already been drained of its fluids prior to embalming, the funeral was arranged without cause of death having been established. In highly unorthodox circumstances, death was thought to have been caused by a liver infection. Robinson was dissatisfied with this account and openly accused Dr Hill of allowing his wife to die. When Hill remarried within three months, Robinson hired detectives to follow him and pressed the district attorney to bring a murder charge. Dr Hill responded by filing a lawsuit for slander and libel.

Two Grand Juries failed to indict Dr Hill for murder, but finally, in April 1970, a third Grand Jury indicted him with causing his wife's death through 'murder by omission', which was allowable under Texas law. In the meantime, the doctor had left his second wife and she let it be known that he had admitted killing Joan Robinson. It also came out that he kept bacteriological cultures in his bathroom. A mistrial was declared in April 1971 and, as a result, Hill walked free.

Before this extraordinary case could be pursued any further, Hill was shot dead in his home by a masked gunman. Bobby Vandiver, who was paid $5000 for the hit, implicated Ash Robinson in an execution plot. Before this allegation could be investigated, Vandiver was shot dead by a police officer while trying to escape from custody.

Ash Robinson denied any involvement in a plot to kill his son-in-law, although he still held him responsible for his daughter's death. Robinson was cleared of a civil suit brought by Hill's family alleging that he had hired a gunman to kill his son-in-law. The story of Joan Robinson Hill's death and its aftermath are told by Thomas Thompson in his book *Blood and Money* which, in turn, was the basis for a television film screened in 1981. Ash Robinson died in 1985. [*416, 537, 910*]

ROBLES, RICHARD

Landmark double murder case which led to a wrongful conviction before the real murderer was caught and sentenced. The case also had important legal repercussions affecting suspects' rights.

On 28 August 1963, an intruder entered an East Manhattan apartment occupied by three young women. Pat Toller, a magazine researcher, worked that day, but her two friends, Janice Wylie and Emily Hoffert, were at home. When Pat Toller returned she found her flatmates dead. Both had been stabbed with knives taken from the kitchen and Janice Wylie's body had been mutilated. There was evidence neither of rape nor burglary although it was known that Janice had been receiving obscene telephone calls.

The 'Career Girl Murders', as they became known, received a great deal of media coverage and the police were under pressure to get results. In April 1964, George Whitmore Jr, a nineteen-year-old semi-illiterate black, was arrested on a rape charge in Brooklyn and in the course of questioning confessed to the Wylie-Hoffert murders. He later claimed the admissions were beaten out of him. Whitmore was convicted of murder and given a life sentence.

In January 1965, two young men reported that a friend, Richard Robles, had confessed to them that he was the Wylie-Hoffert murderer. The trio were involved in drugs and Robles had a reputation for his violent way of talking about women. When he was arrested, he admitted killing the two women. He said the incident began as a burglary but there was sexual activity and then 'I just went bananas.' He clubbed the women unconscious and slashed and stabbed them.

Robles was convicted of murder in December 1965 and sentenced to life imprisonment. Whitmore, who had been wrongfully convicted, was released after spending four years in prison. The manner in which Whitmore was treated by the police and his narrow escape from the electric chair led to the abolition of the death penalty in New York. In addition, the Miranda ruling was enacted in 1966 whereby the right to remain silent and to have access to a lawyer were accorded a suspect.

In 1993, Richard Robles applied for parole after serving thirty years of his life sentence. He is one of the longest-serving prisoners in the USA penal system. His application was denied despite his claim to have atoned for his crimes.

[*126, 562, 761, 839*]

ROMAND, JEAN-CLAUDE

Fantasist who constructed a bogus persona, claiming he was a doctor working for the World Health Organisation, and ended up murdering his family. On 11 January 1993 there was a fire at the home of the Romand family in the French village of Prèvissin near the Swiss border. The bodies of Florence Romand and her two children were pulled from the ruined house and declared dead. The only survivor was Jean-Claude Romand who was in a coma.

It soon became apparent that the deaths had not been caused by the fire. Mme Romand had been bludgeoned and the two children shot. The family tragedy was compounded when a relative intending to inform Romand's parents of the deaths found the elderly couple dead at their home in Clairvaux-les-lacs, some fifty miles away. They had both been shot.

Enquiries into Jean-Claude Romand's background revealed that he was thought to be a doctor who worked for the World Health Organisation in Geneva. It was soon established that the WHO did not know a 'Dr' Romand and he was not listed in the medical directories. He had studied medicine at Lyon in 1975 but did not qualify, although he maintained the fiction that he had.

Piece-by-piece the secret life of the bogus doctor was put together. Romand embezzled money from friends and family members in order to provide his income. He maintained a daily pretence of driving his children to school before going on to work at the WHO. In reality he spent his days idling away time in cafes and service stations and returning home as if from a day's work at the office. When he told his wife he was attending medical conferences in foreign cities he fabricated elaborate details, even feigning jet-lag, when he had spent the time watching TV in a hotel room.

This elaborate charade began to unravel in 1992 when a woman who had allowed him to invest some of her money asked for it back. Romand was already in financial difficulty. Around New Year 1993, he visited a gun shop where be bought cartridges and a silencer for a .22 rifle which he had borrowed from his father. After killing his wife and children and then his parents, he met the woman to whom he owed money and attacked her with tear gas and a stun-gun. She survived the ordeal and he explained that he was suffering from a terminal illness. Romand returned to his home where his family lay dead and set it it on fire. He swallowed some barbiturates and lost consciousness.

At first, he denied the crimes but eventually confessed. Psychiatrists had the feeling that they were dealing with a robotic personality incapable of feeling emotion. He was thought to be a narcissistic personality not distinguishing between reality and fantasy. Rather than confess to the secret life he had lived, he chose to murder his family. At his trial for murder he asked for forgiveness before being sentenced to life imprisonment.

[*165*]

ROSS, COLIN

Murder of a young girl in which hair evidence linked the suspect to her death.

On the last day of December 1921, a beat policeman found the body of a thirteen-year-old girl lying in a Melbourne street. The girl had been strangled and her naked body left in a cul-de-sac near Gun Alley in one of the city's markets. It seemed apparent that she had been murdered elsewhere and dumped where she was found.

Police inquiries led detectives to take an interest in Colin Ross, a wine-bar owner who had been seen in Gun Alley carrying a heavy bundle. He was known to have a predilection for girls as opposed to mature women, and admitted knowing the youngster. But he volunteered information to the police which had not at that time been made public. A search of Ross's home produced several long red hairs which matched the hair of the victim.

Ross denied the charge of murder and claimed the police were intent on framing him. At his trial much of the evidence concerned the scientific examination of hair, and the celebrated Australian forensic scientist, Dr Charles Taylor, was an expert witness. It was proved to the court's satisfaction that the girl had been in Ross's home where he had assaulted and strangled her. He was astute enough to wash the body to remove any forensic traces but was incriminated by the distinctive red hair left on a blanket.

He was convicted of the Gun Alley murder and sentenced to death. Ross was executed at Melbourne Gaol on 24 April 1922.
[*110, 333, 672*]

ROSSOUW, MARTHINUS

An unusual shooting incident in South Africa in which a man was allegedly murdered at his own request; known as the von Schauroth case.

The body of Baron Dieter von Schauroth was found dead near Cape Town on 25 March 1961. The thirty-six-year-old farmer had been shot twice in the head and robbed. There were diamonds lying on the soil by the corpse. Von Schauroth and his wife were well known in Cape Town social circles. They were regular theatre-goers and frequented the fashionable night-clubs and race meetings. He had inherited his father's farm and seemed to be prosperous. There were rumours that he was involved in illegal diamond dealings and he had recently taken out a large life insurance policy.

During his business dealings, the baron met Marthinus Rossouw who acted as his erstwhile bodyguard and go-between. Twenty-three-year-old Rossouw was a flamboyant character known to his friends as 'Killer', who was addicted to films, especially Westerns, and liked to dress as a cowboy.

In the course of investigating von Schauroth's death, the police questioned Rossouw. When his attempts to establish his alibi failed, he readily admitted killing the baron. His story was that von Schauroth, who was depressed at the unhappy state of his marriage, gave him 2300 rand and a revolver with the request that he kill him.

Rossouw carried out the request and ended up on trial for murder. He was convicted and sentenced to death at Cape Town in September 1961. Despite the outcome of the trial, one of the insurance companies declined to pay out on the dead baron's policy. Rossouw was hanged on 20 June 1962.
[*62, 649*]

ROTH, RANDOLPH G.

Married four times, he lost two wives through accidents and claimed the insurance. He was convicted of murder in 1992 in a trial which invoked references to **George Joseph Smith**.

On 23 July 1991, Randy Roth beached his rubber raft at Lake Sammamich in Washington State as his two young sons came running to meet him. They saw their mother lying blue-faced in the bottom of the raft. Their father told them to fetch a lifeguard, 'but don't make a commotion'.

Paramedics were unable to revive Cynthia (Cindy) Roth who died from drowning. Randy explained that they had been swimming in the lake and Cindy had cramp. When he tried to manoeuvre her back into the raft, the boat was overturned by a passing power boat. Randy's remarkable calm in face of tragedy was commented on by numerous people. Interest in the incident heightened when it was learned he stood to gain $365,000 from his wife's death.

Thirty-seven-year-old Roth had been married four times. Two of his wives left him and two died in accidents. His first wife, Janis, fell to her death in 1981 while they were hiking on Beacon Rock in Skamania County. They had been married only a few months and he claimed $100,000 on her insurance.

No charges were made against Roth in respect of his wife's death, but the incident was recalled after Cindy drowned. Investigators learned that he was a man who liked to control his family to the point of belittling them in public and exerting cruel discipline on his children. He claimed to have survived horrific experiences in Vietnam but, although he served in the US Marines, he did nothing more active than duty as a company clerk on Okinawa.

A former wife admitted, 'I'm scared of the guy', and Cindy left behind a disturbing letter, clearly indicating that she felt intimidated. 'Randy does not love Cindy,' she wrote. 'Randy hates Cindy.' She went on to list the things about her that he hated, including everything from her lipstick to the way she filled the bathtub.

Randy Roth was charged with Cindy's murder and the judge allowed evidence on his first wife's death to be introduced. Reference was made to the trial of George Joseph Smith, the 'Brides in the Bath' murderer, where evidence of his previous wives' deaths was allowed to demonstrate a system of murder.

Roth's explanation of the drowning proved unconvincing and the prosecution painted a picture of a cold, calculating man who killed for gain. The evidence was strongly circumstantial but it told against Roth who was found guilty of first-degree murder. He was sentenced to fifty years' imprisonment.

[*799, 866*]

ROTTMAN, ARTHUR

A plea of insane behaviour resulting from a disagreement and a state of drunkenness did not explain three axe murders.

Arthur Rottman was a German seaman unlucky enough to be on board a vessel berthed in New Zealand at the outbreak of the First World War. He was interned and sent to work on the McCann's farm at Ruahine on North Island. He seemed to get on well with Joseph and Mary McCann and their neighbours. On 27 December 1914, he made his regular run to the nearby dairy with the McCann's milk. He told the dairy workers that Joe would be away for a while shearing sheep.

On the following day there was no milk delivery to the dairy from the McCanns so the manager decided to go up to the farm. There, in a cowshed, he found Joe McCann lying dead with his head split open from an axe wound. Mary McCann's body was in the farmhouse with her dead baby close by – both had been felled by axe blows. Bloodstained axes were found on the farm premises.

Rottman had disappeared but he was traced to a construction camp at Cape Terawhiti after he reacted suspiciously at news of the 'Ruahine Axe Murders'. The murders were front page headlines everywhere and when someone asked his opinion, he pleaded with him not to tell the police. He acknowledged his guilt immediately detectives turned up to arrest him.

Rottman pleaded insanity at his trial for murder held at Wanganni. He admitted having an argument with Joe McCann over his duties and then claimed to remember nothing after he picked up an axe. His heavy drinking prior to the incident caused a great deal of discussion among the experts in court but the jury could find no mitigating circumstances. The German seaman was convicted of murder and sentenced to death. He was executed on 8 March 1915 at Terrace Gaol in Wellington.

[*260, 923*]

ROUSE, ALFRED ARTHUR

The celebrated 'Blazing Car Murder' in which the victim, chosen by accident, was never identified.

Two youths returning from a Bonfire Night dance on 5 November 1930 saw a car burning furiously on the road near Hardingstone near Northampton. They passed a man walking away who commented, 'It looks as if someone has had a bonfire.' After the fierce blaze subsided, the charred remains of a corpse were found in the car. The owner of the vehicle was traced through its registration number which had survived the fire. He was Alfred Rouse, a commercial traveller who lived in North London. He was the man seen by the two youths walking away from the fire.

Rouse told the police that while driving to Leicester he stopped on the Great North Road to pick up a man who wanted a lift. When he ran out of petrol, he took a spare can of fuel from the boot and asked his travelling companion to refill the tank while he walked down the road to answer a call of nature. Suddenly, he was aware that the car was ablaze. He rushed back but the flames were so fierce that he was unable to free the man trapped inside.

Rouse was charged with murdering an unknown man. He was a womaniser whose job gave him the freedom to drive around the country visiting his harem of girl-friends. He was tried at Northampton Assizes when the court heard expert evidence confirming that the carburettor on Rouse's car had been tampered with and a joint on the fuel supply loosened. He was convicted of murder and sentenced to death. His appeal failed and he was hanged at Bedford on 10 March 1931. The following day, his confession was published in the *Daily Sketch*. Why Rouse committed murder is unclear but it was speculated that he planned to drop into obscurity by placing his identity on the dead man.

[*152, 705, 734, 925*]

ROWLAND, WALTER GRAHAM

Unusual case in which a man convicted of murdering his baby daughter went on to face another controversial murder conviction twelve years later for which he was hanged.

The bludgeoned body of a forty-year-old prostitute, Olive Balchin, was found lying on the site of a bombed building in Manchester on 20 October 1946. The murder weapon, a brand-new bloodstained hammer, lay near by. Police inquiries led to Walter Rowland, a man who had a previous conviction for child murder, who had been seen in the dead woman's company. He admitted knowing Olive Balchin but denied harming her.

At his trial for murder in Manchester in December 1946, Rowland was convicted and before being sentenced to death lectured the judge about his innocence and claimed he was a victim of mistaken identity. Four weeks later, David John Ware, a prisoner serving a sentence for theft, told the governor of Walton Prison, Liverpool that he had killed 'Olive Balshaw' (sic).

When Rowland's appeal came up, Ware's confession was offered as fresh evidence of his innocence. The new evidence was not called and the appeal was dismissed. Following an inquiry ordered by the Home Secretary, Ware admitted that he had made false statements. Maintaining that 'I know I die for another's crime', Rowland was hanged on 27 February 1947.

Ware, who had a history of mental disturbance, was convicted at Bristol in 1951 of attempted murder. He told the police, 'I keep having an urge to hit women on the head.' He was found to be guilty but insane and was sent to Broadmoor. Rowland's conviction remains controversial, not least because he was living in a hostel and had no money. In the circumstances, it seems unlikely that he would have bought an expensive hammer to use as a murder weapon.

[*42, 169, 488, 729, 1004*]

RUSSELL, GEORGE

A thwarted attempt at robbery led to an assault on an elderly woman and to her murder, which was possibly unintended.

Eighty-five-year-old Mrs Freeman Lee lived alone in a many-roomed mansion at Maidenhead in Berkshire. She was eccentric and rumoured to be wealthy. On 1 June 1948, the milkman noticed that previous deliveries had not been taken in. He alerted the police and officers found the old lady's body in a trunk standing in the hallway. She had been bound and gagged and subjected to a beating. The house was untidy and a thick layer of dust testified to Mrs Lee's lack of attention to housework. Detectives believed her death had resulted from robbery and a search was made to determine if anything was missing. The sharp eyes of Chief Superintendent Fred Cherrill noticed that the dust on a cardboard jewellery box had been disturbed by prying fingers.

A search of the criminal records determined that the fingerprints belonged to George Russell, a convicted house-breaker working at St Albans. His possession of a head scarf belonging to Mrs Lee linked him to the crime. He said he had asked Mrs Lee about undertaking some gardening work for her because he had been told she had a lot of money. In a devastating remark to detectives he asked, 'Did I murder this poor aged woman for something she was supposed to have, and had not?' Clearly, he had searched the house for items of value and been disappointed.

The pathologist, Dr Keith Simpson, determined that Mrs Lee had died not from the beating she received but from the suffocating effect of being gagged. Murder, therefore, may not have been her assailant's intention but it was the consequence of his actions. Russell was tried for murder at Berkshire Assizes and found guilty. Sentence of death was carried out at Oxford on 2 December 1948.

[*176, 398, 855*]

RUXTON, Dr BUCK

Doctor who killed his wife out of jealousy and murdered his housemaid who witnessed the crime. His dismemberment of their bodies provided the opportunity for a celebrated piece of forensic identification.

A young woman walking along the Carlisle to Edinburgh road on 29 September 1935 made a gruesome discovery when she crossed a bridge over the River Annan. She saw a human leg in the stream which turned out to be one of many fragments of two human corpses disposed of in the area. Some of the pieces were wrapped in an edition of the *Sunday Graphic* newspaper distributed in Lancaster. This focused police inquiries who learned that two women had gone missing from the town.

Mary Rogerson, who worked in the household of Dr Buck Ruxton, had disappeared and the doctor's wife was reported to have left him. Ruxton had moved to Lancaster with Isabella van Ess, his common-law wife, in 1930. Ruxton said he did not believe that the human remains were those of his wife and Mary Rogerson. Experts from Glasgow and Edinburgh Universities proved otherwise. Using photo-imposition techniques, they identified the two sets of remains as Isabella Ruxton and Mary Rogerson despite the murderer's care in removing features, such as the teeth, which would aid identification.

It emerged that Ruxton had asked one of his patients to burn a bloodstained suit and remove soiled carpets from his house. Ruxton was tried at Manchester Assizes in March 1936 for the murder of his wife. His answer to the charge was, 'That is absolute bunkum, with a capital B.' He was nevertheless convicted and sentenced to

death. On the weekend following his hanging on 12 May 1936, the *News of the World* published his confession in which he admitted killing his wife in a jealous rage and eliminating Mary Rogerson because she was a witness.
[*90, 346, 410, 674, 757*]

S

SACCO AND VANZETTI

The execution of two Italian anarchists for murder, in what has been described as one of the most unfair trials in American history, created an international controversy.

Five men robbed the payroll during a daring raid on a shoe factory in South Braintree, Massachusetts on 15 April 1920. Over $15,000 were stolen and the paymaster and a security guard were killed by two of the robbers who escaped in a car. On 5 May, two Italians said to resemble the men seen fleeing from the hold-up were arrested and charged with murder.

Nicola Sacco, a shoemaker, and Bartolomeo Vanzetti, a fishseller, were Italian immigrants and acknowledged anarchists. That they were foreigners and possessed firearms created extreme prejudice against them. They were tried in May 1921 and found guilty on highly questionable firearms evidence. Judge Webster Thayer who condemned them to death referred to them variously as 'dagos', 'sons of bitches' and 'anarchist bastards'.

There followed protracted appeal proceedings against a background of allegations that the prosecution evidence had been falsified and in the knowledge that one of the experts had been discredited. The controversy had spread beyond the boundaries of America and was headline news around the world. After numerous stays of execution, a special commission was set up in 1927 to review the case. Despite the fact that several prosecution witnesses retracted their original evidence, and acknowledging criticism of Judge Thayer for his prejudice, the commission decided there was no miscarriage of justice. In the face of unprecedented protests in many of the world's

capitals, Sacco and Vanzetti went to the electric chair on 23 August 1927. Fifty years later, their innocence was confirmed and their names cleared in a proclamation signed by the Governor of Massachusetts.
[*266, 267, 298, 604, 665, 688*]

SAMS, MICHAEL BENNIMAN

Fifty-one-year-old tool-repairer whose plan to kidnap a wealthy victim for ransom ended in murder.

On 22 January 1992, Stephanie Slater, a twenty-six-year-old estate agent, disappeared in Birmingham. Her abductor demanded £175,000 ransom from her employer. The money was handed over but a plan to trap the kidnapper failed although he honoured his pledge to set his hostage free.

Stephanie Slater described being held for eight days, blindfolded in a metal box and completely cut off from the outside world. She determined to establish a relationship with her captor, thinking that would make it more difficult for him to kill her. Her astute reasoning probably saved her life.

Using information provided by the released hostage, the police located the place where she had been held. On 21 February 1992, they walked into a workshop at Newark in Lincolnshire and arrested Michael Sams.

The police suspected that Sams had abducted and murdered eighteen-year-old Julie Dart from Leeds in July 1991. Her body was found wrapped in a sheet in a field at Easton after an attempt had been made to obtain a ransom.

While Sams admitted kidnapping Stephanie Slater, he denied any knowledge of the earlier crime. He was nevertheless convicted of abduction and murder at his trial in Nottingham in 1993. A few days after being sentenced to life imprisonment, he finally admitted killing Julie Dart.

It was believed that Sams wanted to carry out the perfect crime in order to shame the police. He was possibly influenced by **Donald Neilson**, the 'Black Panther', whom he met in prison while serving a sentence for theft in the 1980s.
[*174, 714, 845, 863*]

SANGRET, AUGUST

A French-Canadian soldier with Cree Indian ancestry who killed a girl in wartime Britain in what became known as the 'Wigwam Murder'.

The body of nineteen-year-old Pearl Wolfe was found on 7 October 1942 partially buried in loose soil on Hankley Common in Surrey. Dr Keith Simpson ascertained that the girl had been clubbed to death, probably with a piece of wood. He also noted a number of knife wounds on the body inflicted with a weapon having a hooked blade.

Pearl Wolfe was a 'camp follower' who had been living rough in woods near Jasper Camp. Her home was a crude affair fashioned from saplings and tree branches in the style of a wigwam. She had been living with a Canadian soldier, August Sangret, serving with the Regina Rifles stationed at Jasper Camp. A letter written by Pearl Wolfe to inform him that she was pregnant was found close by. Sangret acknowledged his relationship and made a lengthy statement, concluding 'I guess I shall get the blame.' The murder weapon, in the shape of a birchwood stake with the dead girl's hair and blood on it, was found on the common but there was no sign of a knife. Sangret claimed that his clasp-knife was lost. The missing weapon was found by chance blocking a drain at the army camp. The black-handled knife with a hooked blade was identified as Sangret's by regimental police.

The soldier was tried for murder at Kingston Assizes. The prosecution case was that the initial attack on the girl was made with the knife at the wigwam. When she attempted to run away, Sangret bludgeoned her to death with the wooden stake. The victim's skull was brought into court to demonstrate how the knife blade fitted the distinctive holes in it. Sangret was found guilty but the jury added a recommendation to mercy. He was hanged on 29 April 1943 at Wandsworth Prison.

[*28, 213, 561, 929*]

SCHMID, CHARLES HOWARD

Known as 'The Pied Piper of Tucson', he exerted an influence over his young contemporaries and showed his power by killing three teenagers.

Although only a short individual – he stood at 5 feet 3 inches – Schmid had a powerful personality which won admirers. He was also an accomplished gymnast and always had girls in his entourage at the local speedway track where he was a star attraction.

Schmid had his fantasies which included wearing make-up to alter his appearance, and dyeing his red hair black. He created a weird impression in his build-up cowboy boots and painted face. Some of his fantasies were more dangerous and on 31 May 1964, while drinking with some friends, he announced that he felt like killing a girl. With help from his friends, he enticed a fifteen-year-old girl to join him and they drove out into the desert. While his friends watched, he raped the girl and then smashed her head in with a rock. They buried her in a shallow desert grave.

In August 1965, Schmid's current girl-friend, seventeen-year-old Gretchen Fritz, went missing with her younger sister. When Richard Bruns, one of his friends, remarked on their absence, Schmid said he had strangled them. When he showed him the evidence, Bruns was shocked into silence but later reported what he knew to the police. 'The Pied Piper' was arrested on 11 November 1965, together with two of his friends who subsequently turned State's Evidence. Schmid received a prison sentence of fifty-five years for the rape murder and was sentenced to death for killing Gretchen and Wendy Fritz. Implementation of the death sentence was delayed because of appeals and was cancelled when the US Supreme Court suspended capital punishment. Schmid escaped from Arizona State Prison in 1972 but was recaptured within a few days after taking hostages.

[*337, 679*]

SCHMITZ, Dr HERMAN

Austrian doctor who murdered his mistress and taunted the police over her disappearance.

On 1 April 1926, Vienna's Chief of Police received a small package through the mail. He was shocked to find that he had been sent a human finger. The well-manicured digit was from a woman's right hand and had been surgically removed. A few days later, another package arrived containing a second finger complete with 22-carat gold ring.

The surface of the ring was etched with what detectives thought might be acid of the kind used to remove tattooes. Microscopic examination of the surface of the finger revealed faint outlines of a snake tattoo. While detectives visited the city's tattoo parlours to find the source of the snake design, their inquiries took a dramatic turn when a woman's headless body, minus two fingers from the right hand, was found in a swamp.

Footprints found in the mud around the body suggested they had been made by a tall, heavily built individual. This knowledge, combined with confirmation that the fingers had been removed surgically, led detectives to search for a surgeon. By a process of elimination, their inquiries began to focus on Dr Schmitz whose once-wealthy practice had taken a knock after he had been charged with malpractice. They found both the doctor's wife and his mistress alive and well, which ruled out immediate suspicions. Inquiries revealed that his mistress frequented a particular dress shop where her purchases were charged to the doctor's account. More significantly, it became clear that his previous mistress, Anna Stein, had been in the same habit, but she was now missing.

As a result of searching Dr Schmitz's surgery, police found the missing lady's head pickled in a jar of preservative. She had been poisoned with cyanide after being replaced in the doctor's affections by another woman. The doctor's purpose in cutting off two of her fingers was to taunt the police whom he believed had earlier maliciously charged him with malpractice. His mistake was to believe that he had effectively removed the snake tattoo.

Dr Schmitz was tried for murder in Vienna but fell to his death from the top of a building during an escape attempt. He made a dying confession to murder.

[*388*]

SCHREUDER, FRANCES BRADSHAW

A mother who requested her teenage son to murder his grandfather because of a disagreement over inheritance. Franklin J. Bradshaw built up an auto-parts business which made him a millionaire and earned him the title of Utah's Howard Hughes. He lived an austere life, granting himself few luxuries and taking the view that people should work to achieve their ambitions.

This philosophy was not shared by his youngest daughter Frances, who had been married twice and faced the prospect of bringing up a young family. She was receiving psychiatric treatment and was not helped by her two sons, Marc and Lawrence, who were juvenile delinquents. Frances received limited help from her mother but without old Mr Bradshaw's knowledge. On the occasions when he became involved, his contribution was to extol the virtues of self-help.

The situation in which Frances found herself became steadily worse and her resentment at her father's refusal to assist her grew stronger. By the mid-1970s she talked openly that the only way things would improve would be if 'somebody kills my father'.

On 23 July 1978, Franklin Bradshaw, who had increasingly sought refuge in his business, was shot dead in his Salt Lake City warehouse by Marc Schreuder. The previous year his two grandsons had stolen money from him at their mother's behest and his response was to cut Frances out of his will. She and her boys joked about murdering granddad and Marc was sent out to buy a gun.

In November, Frances was reported to the police as a thief and a forger and her son was charged with murder. Marc had confessed to killing his grandfather at his mother's request. She had threatened to commit suicide because of the disinheritance. Frances did not attend her son's trial when he was found guilty of second-degree murder and sentenced to five years to life in prison.

After initially refusing, Marc agreed to testify against his mother when she came up for trial in 1983. It was clear that she had orchestrated her father's death, employing her son as an assassin. She was convicted of first-degree murder and given a sentence of life imprisonment. Schreuder died at a hospice in San Diego in March 2004.

[*9, 192*]

SCHWARTZ, CHARLES HENRY

Shrewd forensic work uncovered a murder made to look like an accident in order to claim the insurance.

Charles Schwartz ran the Pacific Cellulose Plant at Walnut Creek near San Francisco, California where he carried out research on processes to manufacture artificial silk. On 30 July 1925, the laboratory was devastated by a tremendous explosion which rocked the whole neighbourhood. When firemen entered the wrecked premises, they found in the smouldering ruins a charred corpse assumed to be that of Charles Schwartz. His wife, believing herself to be a widow with three children, collapsed on hearing the news of the accident.

Suspicions began to form when it was learned that Schwartz had insured his life against accident for $185,000 the day before the explosion. Then there was concern that the corpse might not be that of Schwartz on account of a discrepancy in height. In order to resolve the problem, the police called in Dr Edward Heinrich, the celebrated Californian criminologist. Part of the victim's right ear had survived the explosion and Heinrich saw that it bore a mole which was absent from the ear in a photograph of Schwartz. It was apparent that the victim had two teeth missing from the upper jaw, which matched Schwartz's dental records, but it was also clear that they had been removed recently.

The man who had died in the explosion was Gilbert Warren Barbe, a friend of Schwartz who had been reported missing. Schwartz was eventually traced to an apartment building in Oakland but before he could be arrested, he shot himself. He was found lying dead on his bed with an automatic pistol in his hand. He had left a note to his wife with the unlikely explanation of how a man had called at the plant asking him for work. When he declined, the man became violent and in the struggle which followed Schwartz killed him unintentionally.

[*87, 371*]

SCOTT-CROSSLEY, MARK AND MATHEBULE, SIMON

Human remains found in a lion compound at Mokwalo White Lion Project at Hoedspruit near Kruger Park in South Africa in February 2004 led to murder charges.

The remains had obviously been eaten by the lions and all that was left were a skull, rib-cage and spine and a solitary finger. Earlier, the family of Nelson Chisale, a farm worker, had reported him missing after he failed to return home from his workplace. He had visited a farm owned by Mark Scott-Crossley to collect some personal possessions after being sacked.

A fingerprint impression taken from the digit recovered from the lion compound confirmed Chisale's identity. Police enquiries at the farm produced contradictory statements from the owner, Scott-Crossley, and three of his workers. As a result, Scott-Crossley, Richard and Simon Mathebule and Robert Mnesi were arrested and charged with murder.

When the case came up for trial in January 1995 at Phalaborwa District Court, the charge against Mnesi was dropped and it was announced that he would be a witness for the prosecution. During the hearing, Richard Mathebule was taken ill with tuberculosis and proceedings against him were suspended until he was fit to stand trial. That left Scott-Crossley and Simon Mathebule to answer the murder charges.

Mnesi testified that when Chisale returned to the farm he had been attacked by the two Mathebules and tied to a tree. He further stated that Scott-Crossley had beaten his former employee and later in the day had Chisale put into a truck which was driven to the lion compound where his body was thrown over the fence. Whether he was alive or dead at the time was not clear. Scott-Crossley claimed he had distanced himself from the assault and only became involved when Mnesi made threats against his twelve year old son.

On 25 April 2005, the trial judge, sitting with two assessors, found Scott-Crossley and Simon Mathebule guilty of murder. Following the verdict, Scott-Crossley expressed his regret to the Chisale family and offered to work in order to provide them with compensation for their loss if the court approved and sanctioned a sentence of correctional supervision. Judge George Maluleke rejected this plea and on 30 September 2005, sentenced Scott-Crossley to life imprisonment and his accomplice, Simon Mathebule, to fifteen years' imprisonment with three years suspended.

SCOTT, LEONARD EWING

A murder conviction was obtained without the evidence of a victim's body and it took twenty-nine years for the truth to emerge.

Leonard and Evelyn Ewing Scott married in 1949. He was a salesman and she was a wealthy widow who had been married four times. Scott set about detaching his wife from her regular circle of friends and gradually took over the management of her financial affairs.

Evelyn Scott completely disappeared in May 1955. The sixty-three-year-old woman was last seen at her home in Bel Air, California on 16 May. Her husband explained to inquirers that she was ill and had gone away for medical treatment. This account seemed at odds with his disposal of some of her personal possessions. When Evelyn's friends learned that Leonard proposed to marry another woman, their fears about her well-being prompted them to go to the police. He told officers that his wife had left him.

The discovery of Evelyn's spectacles and dentures in the garden of their house led to further questioning as to her whereabouts.

There were also charges to be answered about financial irregularities. At this point. Leonard Scott disappeared. He was posted as a fugitive from the law and did not surface for a year. He was arrested at the Canadian border in April 1957 and charged with murdering his wife. Despite the shortage of firm evidence against him, not least the lack of his victim's body, Scott was convicted of first-degree murder and sentenced to life imprisonment. As the years rolled on, he declined to accept parole on the grounds that it would be an admission of guilt. In 1978, at the age of eighty-one, he was discharged from prison. In 1984, after nearly thirty years protesting his innocence, he admitted killing his wife and burying her body in the desert.
[*1070*]

SCRIPPS, JOHN MARTIN

An international criminal who graduated from theft, robbery and drug-smuggling to serial murder. He was jailed for drug offences in the UK in 1987 and again in 1991. On both occasions, he contrived to abscond from custody. While in Albany Prison on the Isle of Wight, he learned butchery, a trade which he later employed in his grisly career of murder and dismemberment.

In March 1995, Scripps was in Singapore where he befriended Gerard Lowe, a tourist from South Africa. The two men agreed to share a hotel room. Scripps killed his companion with a hammer and dismembered his body, later throwing the parts into Singapore Harbour. He then embarked on a spending spree using Lowe's credit card before flying off to Thailand.

A week later, Scripps approached two Canadians who he encountered at Phuket airport. He recommended a local hotel to Sheila Damude and her son Darin who were visiting Thailand for a holiday. He escorted them to Nilly's Marina Inn where he was evidently known to the hotel staff. The Damudes disappeared and parts of their dismembered bodies were later found scattered about the surrounding countryside.

He returned to Singapore on 19 March, by which time the remains of Gerard Lowe had been recovered from their watery grave and identified. Scripps was arrested by alert detectives at the airport on arrival and found to be carrying a stun-gun, hand-cuffs, a hammer and various knives. He was also in possession of the Damudes' passports and credit cards.

Scripps was tried in Singapore for the murder of Gerard Lowe, found guilty and sentenced to death. He declined to appeal against the sentence and was said to be 'impatient' for the execution to proceed. He was duly hanged at Changi Prison on 19 April 1996, earning the dubious distinction of being the first Briton to be executed for murder in Singapore. In addition to the murders in Thailand and Singapore, Scripps was believed to have killed a British backpacker in Mexico in 1994. Dubbed 'The Tourist From Hell', his criminal career spanned three continents. His speciality was to offer friendship to people he met on his travels and then to carry out brutal murders in order to plunder their bank accounts. [*1040*]

SEDDON, FREDERICK HENRY

Consumed by greed, he contrived to fleece his lodger of her investments and then poisoned her.

Seddon was a District Superintendent employed by the London and Manchester Industrial Assurance Company. His agents, bearing their collection money, called at his house in Islington, North London, where he lived with his wife and family. Seddon's favourite occupation was said to be counting his employer's money. He took no less interest in his own finances.

In July 1910, he and his wife took in a lodger. Eliza May Barrow was a middle-aged spinster of irascible temperament. Although not exactly wealthy, she had some useful financial assets. Seddon persuaded her to let him manage her investments in return for which he would give her an annuity. During the next few months, all her assets were spirited away under Seddon's control.

On 1 September 1911, Miss Barrow was taken ill with stomach pains accompanied by sickness and diarrhoea. Her doctor was in regular attendance but could do nothing to halt her decline. She died on 14 September. Seddon arranged her burial and he and his family were the only mourners at her funeral. When Miss Barrow's relatives learned of her death, they were distressed to learn that Seddon was now claiming title to her property. Dissatisfied with Seddon's explanations, Miss Barrow's, cousin, Frank Vonderhahe, wrote to the Director of Public Prosecutions.

On 20 November, Miss Barrow's body was exhumed and traces of arsenic were found. Seddon was arrested and charged with murder; his wife later joined him in custody. Frederick and Margaret Seddon were tried at the Old Bailey in March 1912 before Mr Justice Bucknill. Seddon had bought arsenical flypapers and it was alleged had leached the poison out of them which he administered to Miss Barrow in order to eliminate her once he had acquired control of her property.

The jury exonerated Margaret Seddon but found her husband guilty. Asked if he had anything to say before the judge passed sentence of death, Seddon launched into a long speech. His declaration of innocence before 'the Great Architect of the Universe' reduced Mr Justice Bucknill, a Mason like Seddon, to tears. Frederick Seddon was hanged on 18 April 1912 at Pentonville Prison.

[*261, 444, 448, 1025*]

SEYMOUR, HENRY DANIEL

Door-to-door salesman down on his luck who committed a brutal murder to acquire some ready cash.

Mrs Annie Louisa Kempson was a middle-aged widow who lived just outside Oxford and let one of her rooms to augment her pension. During August Bank Holiday 1931, she was found dead. She had been battered about the head and her throat was cut. The house had been ransacked. The murder weapon was thought to be a hammer but it could not be found.

Scotland Yard was called in to help the local police. The first clue came from a search of Mrs Kempson's desk in the form of a receipt for a vacuum cleaner. This fell into place when a woman who lived at nearby Headington Hill told the police about a salesman of electrical appliances who had called on her. Henry Seymour had visited her house on the day Mrs Kempson died. He told her a story about having his wallet stolen and she lent him some money. The same man had called on other houses in the area selling vacuum cleaners and one of his customers was Mrs Kempson.

Armed with a description of Seymour, the police caught up with him on 15 August in Brighton. Prior to that, he had stayed at a hotel in Aylesbury where he left behind a suitcase in lieu of payment. When the manager opened it, he found a recently cleaned hammer.

Seymour was tried for murder at Oxford when his defence counsel tried to show that Mrs Kempson had been seen alive after the time she was supposed to have been murdered. Although the

evidence was mainly circumstantial, there were incriminating details which weighed against him. These included the labels removed from the cleaned-up hammer which were found in his bag. He was found guilty and sentenced to death. Seymour was hanged on 10 December 1931 at Oxford Prison.
[*290, 436, 807*]

SHARK ARM CASE

Celebrated Australian case which put the spotlight on Sydney's underworld but ended inconclusively.

The main attraction at Coogee Beach Aquarium in Sydney on 25 April 1935 was a 14-foot long tiger shark caught by two local fishermen. The creature which had been put on show to entertain the public surprised spectators when it threw up the contents of his stomach which included a human arm.

The dismembered limb bore a distinctive tattoo showing a pair of boxers squaring up to each other which, with the verification of fingerprints, enabled the arm to be identified as belonging to James Smith, a former boxer who had been missing for two weeks. He had been employed by Reginald Holmes, a boat-builder, and was implicated in an incident involving drug dealing. It was learned that Smith had spent some time at Cronulla with Patrick Brady, a man with a record as a forger.

The police had stumbled on an intricate web of underworld dealings. Brady was taken in for questioning and, while he was in custody, there was an incident in Sydney harbour involving Holmes. One of his boats was boarded after it appeared to be out of control and Holmes was found with a bullet wound in the head. He claimed that he was fleeing from a gunman who had attempted to kill him. He alleged that Brady had killed Smith and disposed of his body at sea.

While Brady was awaiting trial, Holmes, the chief prosecution witness, was shot dead in his car on 13 June 1935. After a debate about whether or not the arm constituted sufficient evidence to bring a murder charge, Brady faced trial. He put the blame on the now dead Holmes and the case collapsed through lack of evidence. Brady was acquitted and, after two further abortive attempts, the 'Shark Arm Case' was considered closed.
[*168, 509*]

SHAWCROSS, ARTHUR JOHN

Released from a prison sentence for killing two children in 1987, he went on to become a serial killer, claiming the lives of eleven women in twenty months.

Shawcross was a troublesome teenager with convictions for theft and assault. In 1967 he was drafted into the army and claimed to have served in Vietnam. He later gave accounts of horrific experiences in the military in which he engaged in numerous atrocities including cannibalism. He was discharged in 1969 and immediately resumed a career of robbery and arson.

In 1972, Shawcross strangled a ten-year-old boy and an eight-year-old girl at Watertown in New York State. He threw the girl's body into the Genesee River – a favoured means of disposing of his later victims. He pleaded manslaughter to these crimes and was sentenced to twenty-five years' imprisonment. He was released in 1987 and quickly resumed the murder trail.

Between March 1988 and December 1989, he killed eleven times. Most of his victims were prostitutes working in the red-light district of Rochester in New York State. They were either strangled or beaten to death and their bodies, too, turned up in the Genesee River. He was arrested in July 1990 and confessed to a string of killings. Shawcross was tried and found guilty of all eleven counts of murder. He was sentenced to 250 years' imprisonment.

Shawcross claimed to have been abused by his mother when he was a child. Because of his childhood experiences he grew up obsessed with ideas of sex accompanied by pain. He said he became a full-blown serial killer while serving in Vietnam. He indulged in a catalogue of violent atrocities and realised he had become a monster. He was quoted as saying, 'God does not want me, Satan does.'

[*708, 722*]

SHEPPARD CASE

Celebrated American murder case in which a conviction was secured largely by one-sided press-reporting of factors detrimental to the chief suspect.

On the evening of 3 July 1954, Sam and Marilyn Sheppard entertained friends to dinner at their home near Cleveland overlooking Lake Erie. Their visitors left some time after midnight and Marilyn went straight up to bed while her husband stayed downstairs. Sheppard dozed off to sleep but was awakened by screams. He dashed upstairs but was knocked flying by an intruder. He saw his wife lying dead on the bed and chased a bushy-haired stranger out of the house. They grappled on the lake-side and Sheppard was knocked out. When he recovered he found Marilyn had been bludgeoned to death.

Sheppard worked as a neurosurgeon at Bay View Hospital where he was having an affair with a medical technician. Rumours that he had killed his wife began to take root in press coverage of the incident. His answers to questions were judged to be evasive and he was charged with murder. It appeared that morphine had been taken from the supplies in his medical bag and there was speculation that the murder weapon was a surgical instrument.

He was tried for murder at Cuyhoga in October 1954 and convicted of second-degree murder on evidence which related more to his extra-marital affairs than to the circumstances of his wife's death. Sheppard began a life sentence in Ohio State Penitentiary but was released in 1964 after gaining a retrial. At his second trial in 1966, his defence counsel, F. Lee Bailey, had the previous verdict set aside.

Sam Sheppard found it difficult to resume his former life. He married again but found no happiness and when his medical practice failed, took up wrestling. His health deteriorated and he died in 1970.

In November 2001, a new book on the case, *The Wrong Man*, concluded that Sheppard was innocent. Author James Neff spent ten years researching the case and he put the guilt on Richard Eberling as the 'bushy haired stranger' Sheppard claimed to have seen in his house at the time of the murder. Eberling died in 1998 after being imprisoned for another murder.

[*201, 234, 430, 694, 752, 846, 847*]

SHIPMAN, Dr HAROLD

Britain's worst serial killer who murdered 215 of his patients over a period of twenty-three years. Until his conviction in 2000, **Mary Ann Cotton** held the record for the greatest number of killings with her fifteen victims in the 1870s.

Shipman's first victim was seventy-one year old Eva Lyons in March 1975 and the last was Kathleen Grundy, aged eighty-one, in June 1998. In between, while he worked as a medical practitioner at two surgeries in Hyde, Greater Manchester, he murdered 171 women and 44 men.

His undoing came in 1998 when he murdered Kathleen Grundy and crudely forged her will. The victim's daughter voiced suspicions about the circumstances of death and Mrs Grundy's body was exhumed. The autopsy revealed the presence of morphine. A local doctor had already voiced concerns about the high proportion of Shipman's patients who died at home. Exhumations followed of other patients who had died while under his care and again morphine traces were found.

Shipman's distinguishing feature was his ordinariness. Many of his patients regarded him as a caring doctor with a sympathetic bedside manner, particularly with the elderly. He was though, recognised as a loner and was subject to violent mood swings. He killed his patients, faced their bereaved relatives and carried on without suspicion or remorse. He killed the terminally ill as well as those who had annoyed him or were a nuisance.

Sentencing him to life imprisonment at his trial for fifteen murders at Preston Crown Court in January 2000, Mr Justice Forbes told fifty-seven year old Shipman, 'I have little doubt that each of your victims smiled and thanked you as she submitted to your deadly administrations'. The doctor proved to be a rude and arrogant prisoner and committed suicide at Wakefield Prison in January 2004.

An inquiry into Shipman's record called for reforms in the system of issuing death certificates in the UK. In another report, Professor Richard Baker of Leicester University analysed the pattern of Shipman's murders and showed that over half of his killings were committed in the afternoon. According to this report, the likely death toll was put at 236 victims.

[*861, 1043, 1063, 1067, 1072*]

SHOWERY, ALLAN

Extraordinary murder case in which the victim named her killer in a psychic manifestation.

A Filipino woman who worked in Chicago as a hospital medical auxiliary was found dead in her apartment on 21 February 1977. Forty-eight-year-old Teresita Basa had been stabbed and burned and her body wrapped in sheets.

Teresita was well liked at the Edgewater Hospital where she

worked and the only motive police could suggest for her death was robbery. The murder inquiry was running out of impetus when police received information that a doctor from the Philippines might be able to help them. It seemed that several months after the murder, the doctor's wife had a psychic experience in which she learned the name of Teresita's killer.

The victim was said to have spoken to the doctor's wife on several occasions and to have named Allan Showery, a medical orderly at Chicago's Edgewater Hospital, as her murderer. The police overcame their natural scepticism and interviewed Showery. Their surprise at finding jewellery from the crime scene at his apartment can only be imagined.

The *Chicago Tribune* reported news of Showery's indictment for murder in March 1978 with the question, 'Did Voice from the Grave Name Killer?' The newspaper's questioning attitude reflected public opinion but his trial for murder went ahead in January 1979. The judge declared a mistrial after the jury failed to agree and, several weeks later, Showery made a confession. He was subsequently convicted of murder and sentenced to fourteen years' imprisonment. [*653*]

SLATER, OSCAR

A miscarriage of justice was compounded by an official cover-up which came to light eighty years later.

Miss Marion Gilchrist was an elderly spinster with a passion for jewellery who lived in Queen's Terrace, Glasgow. On 21 December 1908, she sent her servant, Helen Lambie, to fetch an evening newspaper. When the girl returned twenty minutes later, a man walked out of Miss Gilchrist's flat and brushed past her. On entering the flat, she found her employer lying dead in the dining-room with her head smashed in.

A diamond-shaped brooch was missing from the flat and, five days later, a man identified as Oscar Slater was reported to have offered such a brooch for sale. Detectives discovered that Slater had left England on a ship bound for the USA, on 26 December. His extradition was secured after Helen Lambie and two other witnesses identified him as the man seen at Queen's Terrace.

Oscar Slater was tried for murder at Edinburgh in May 1909. Grave doubts were shed on the identification evidence and it was known that the brooch he had offered for sale was not Miss

Gilchrist's, and that the incident occurred before she was murdered. The jury brought in a majority verdict of Guilty and Slater was sentenced to death. Twenty-four hours before he was due to be hanged he was reprieved and sent to Peterhead Prison to serve a life sentence.

In 1912, Sir Arthur Conan Doyle took up Slater's case, arguing that a miscarriage of justice had occurred and hinting that the police knew the identity of the real murderer. As a result of mounting public pressure, Slater was released in 1927 and the original verdict set aside. There the matter rested for more than sixty years before the truth of Miss Gilchrist's death was revealed.

Papers on the case released by the Scottish Record Office in 1989 contained two anonymous letters sent to the Secretary of State in May 1909, one of which named Wingate Birrell, Miss Gilchrist's nephew, as the murderer. Further papers released in 1994 showed the extent of the cover-up which had taken place to protect the murderer's name.

Following a family dispute, Miss Gilchrist excluded her relatives as beneficiaries under her will and left her estate of more than £60,000 to her former servant. This angered the Charteris branch of the family and Dr Francis Charteris gained entry to her flat, accompanied by Birrell, possibly with the intention of seizing her will. An argument ensued in which Birrell, a young man of unreliable temperament, battered the old lady to death with a chair. Because of the high standing of the Charteris family, the establishment perpetuated a cover-up and used Oscar Slater as a scapegoat.
[*249, 450, 602, 730, 788, 919, 979*]

SMART, PAMELA

Twenty-three-year-old New England educational worker who coaxed her teenage lover into killing her husband.

Gregg Smart, an insurance salesman, married Pam in 1989 and they moved into a condominium in Misty Morning Drive, at Derry in New Hampshire. Just over a year later, on 1 May 1990, Gregg was murdered with a single shot to the head; Pam found his body when she returned home from school. The young man's family was shocked and saddened by the news but Pam appeared to be totally calm. She did not shed a tear and seemed to be more worried about her dog than her dead husband. She surmised that he had disturbed intruders in their home who shot him and fled.

The widow's behaviour caused further comment when, two days after Gregg's death, she returned his belongings to his parents in a plastic garbage sack and later gave a coldly analytical interview to the press. Pam was media services director at a local school and was seen as an ambitious person who shared few of her husband's interests. Gregg liked the outdoor life and enjoyed the company of his former schoolfriends while Pam became deeply immersed in a drug awareness programme. When Gregg admitted an infidelity, their relationship became strained and she went her own way, which included her seduction of a young student, sixteen-year-old William Flynn.

Pam's cool reaction to the execution-like killing of her husband created suspicion and she admitted her involvement to a police informer. On 1 August 1990, she was arrested and charged as an accomplice to murder.

It became apparent that Flynn's infatuation with Pam turned into an obsession and the prosecution maintained that she used sex to manipulate him into murdering Gregg. They discussed the method to be used and Pam insisted on a gun as a knife was too messy and she did not want to spoil her white leather furniture. Flynn described how he pointed the gun at Gregg's head: 'I pulled the trigger . . . I didn't want to kill Gregg . . . this is what I had to do to be with Pam.'

Pam, who was dubbed 'The Ice Princess' by the press, maintained her composure during two days of cross-examination at the trial. She said she did not know why her husband was killed but supposed Flynn did it so that they could be together. Her ill-advised admissions, which were relayed to the police, she passed off as a ruse on her part to elicit information.

Pam Smart was convicted of conspiracy to commit murder and of tampering with a witness. She was sentenced to life imprisonment without parole. Flynn pleaded guilty to lesser charges in exchange for his testimony.

[*272*, *817*]

SMETHURST CASE

Convicted and sentenced to death for poisoning his bigamous wife, Dr Smethurst was pardoned on account of a technical error in evidence which shook the medical world.

Thomas Smethurst qualified in Germany and in 1828 married a young woman whose money he used to establish a hydropathic therapy clinic at Farnham, Surrey. In 1858, while he and his wife were living at Bayswater, Smethurst met forty-two-year-old Isabella Bankes, a spinster of some means. Their liaison led to a bigamous wedding and the couple moved to a house in Richmond. Mrs Smethurst, a semi-invalid, was left to her own devices.

Isabella normally enjoyed good health but, in March 1859, was taken ill and received treatment from Smethurst. When she did not improve, he called in another doctor who was uncertain as to the cause of her illness. On 3 May, after making a will leaving all her money to Smethurst, Isabella died. A third doctor had been called in and he insisted on having an analysis made of the patient's vomit which revealed traces of arsenic.

Smethurst was arrested and charged with murder. The government analyst, Dr Alfred Swaine Taylor, confirmed the presence of arsenic in the body and also in a bottle of medicine which Isabella had been taking. Smethurst's trial proved to be a sensation when Dr Taylor admitted that impurities in his chemical reagents rendered his tests for arsenic invalid. Evidence that Isabella had died of irritant poisoning still remained and Smethurst was convicted of murder.

The controversy which ensued over Dr Taylor's tests led to a Home Office inquiry, as a result of which Smethurst was first reprieved and then pardoned. He was tried for bigamy in December 1859 and sentenced to a year's imprisonment. In 1862 he brought legal proceedings which confirmed him as the beneficiary of Isabella's will.

[*32, 104, 736*]

SMITH, EDGAR HERBERT

Convicted of murdering a fifteen-year-old girl, he protested his innocence in two books written while in prison and won a sympathetic audience before admitting nineteen years later that he had indeed been a murderer.

Victoria Zielinski went missing from her home in Mahwah, New Jersey on 4 March 1957. Her partially buried body was found on the following day – she had been bludgeoned to death. The evidence trail led to Edgar Smith, a former US Marine, who had borrowed a friend's car and returned it with bloodstains on the interior. Under questioning, Smith made several conflicting statements and was charged with murder.

Despite his repeated denials, Smith was convicted of murder in May 1957 and sentenced to death. He established a record of fourteen years as a condemned man on Death Row at Trenton State Prison. He won numerous stays of execution and spent his time, encouraged by columnist William F. Buckley Jr, explaining in two books that he was an innocent man. *Brief Against Death* and *A Reasonable Doubt* won him many sympathisers and in 1971 he was granted a new trial. In a plea bargain admitting his guilt, he was convicted of second-degree murder and sentenced to twenty-five to thirty years in prison. On account of the time he had already served, he was released on probation.

In October 1976, police in San Diego, California picked up Smith after a woman had been stabbed by a kidnapper and managed to escape. He admitted the assault and, for good measure, said that he had, after all, killed Victoria Zielinski in 1957. He explained that he had finally realised that the devil lurked within him and was prepared to admit it. He was tried once more and returned to prison to serve a life sentence.

[*145, 869, 870*]

SMITH, GEORGE JOSEPH

The infamous 'Brides in the Bath' murderer drowned three 'wives' in killings made to look like accidents.

Smith was an inveterate criminal who had twice been imprisoned for theft by the time he married in 1898. Caroline Beatrice Thornhill was his only legal wife but he made a practice of contracting bigamous marriages as an easier means of acquiring money than working for a living.

By the time he met Beatrice Constance Annie Mundy in 1910, he already had two bigamous wives. He 'married' Bessie Mundy at Weymouth and they later went to live in Kent. It was at Herne Hill that Smith took Bessie to a doctor explaining that she had been experiencing fits. Bessie had already made a will leaving everything she had to her husband and he added to their domestic comforts by buying a bath.

On 13 July 1910, Smith called the doctor because Bessie had died in the bath. An inquest verdict of death by misadventure was recorded and Smith became better off to the tune of £2500. In November 1913, he 'married' Alice Burnham and went to live in Blackpool. After his 'wife' was insured, he took her to a doctor on account of her headaches. On 12 December, she was found dead in the bath. Death by misadventure was the inquest verdict and Smith recouped the insurance money.

In December 1914, Smith 'married' Margaret Elizabeth Lofty in Bath. The couple moved to Highgate, London after Mrs Smith's life was insured for a substantial sum. The bride's tragic death in the bath on 18 December was reported in the newspapers and read by Alice Burnham's father. The police were alerted to suspicions concerning Smith who was also known as Williams. He was arrested on 1 February 1915 and charged with murder.

He was tried at the Old Bailey for the murder of Bessie Mundy, and his counsel, Sir Edward Marshall Hall, failed in his efforts to have evidence of the other two drownings made inadmissible. The three deaths, taken together, clearly showed Smith's cynical premeditation. Sir Bernard Spilsbury graphically described Smith's bathtub technique for making murder look like accidental drowning.

The jury took less than half an hour to find Smith guilty and he was sentenced to death. George Joseph Smith was taken to the scaffold, allegedly in a state of complete collapse, at Maidstone Prison and hanged on Friday 13 August 1915.

[*30, 94, 244, 539, 605, 962*]

SMITH, MADELEINE HAMILTON

Tried for poisoning her lover with arsenic after an illicit love affair, she regained her freedom with a Not Proven verdict.

Madeleine was the eldest daughter of an eminent Glasgow architect. She was an intelligent and passionate nineteen-year-old girl for whom a dull life of quiet obedience did not appeal. In 1855, she met Pierre Emile L'Angelier, a shipping clerk nearly twice her age, who was smitten by her. She responded favourably to his intentions.

With the assistance of Madeleine's maid, they exchanged letters expressing passionate sentiments. The difference in their social positions made meetings virtually impossible. However, in June 1856, at Mr Smith's country home on the River Clyde, they became lovers and Madeleine referred to L'Angelier in her letters as her 'beloved husband'.

Maintaining any kind of contact proved difficult and was only possible with L'Angelier standing in the street and talking to his lover through the window of a basement room at her home. Mr Smith became aware that his high-spirited daughter was trying to pursue some kind of liaison and he forbade her to continue. Moreover, he told her that he had marriage plans for her.

This news precipitated a jealous reaction in L'Angelier and then Madeleine told him their affair was finished and demanded the return of her letters. L'Angelier's reaction was to threaten to send the letters to her father. In desperation Madeleine begged him not to carry out his threat.

L'Angelier became ill in February 1857 and died at his lodgings on 23 March. An autopsy showed the cause was arsenical poisoning. A reason for his death was seen in the discovery of Madeleine's letters and she was arrested. While she admitted buying arsenic for cosmetic reasons, she denied poisoning L'Angelier.

Madeleine's trial at Edinburgh in June 1857 was the sensation of its day, not least because of the sexual revelations that emerged. She was accused of poisoning L'Angelier when he became a nuisance by means of a chocolate drink laced with arsenic. In her defence it was pointed out that L'Angelier was an arsenic eater and he was painted as a seducing blackmailer.

On 9 July 1957, the jury returned a uniquely Scottish verdict of Not Proven and Madeleine Smith was released. She died in America at the grand old age of ninety-three in 1928, having married twice and taken the name Lena Sheehy.

[*91, 137, 256, 451, 484, 621, 676*]

SNIDER, PAUL

When his protégée developed an independent and successful career, he killed her out of jealousy and then shot himself.

Snider had the instincts of an entrepreneur and when he encountered Dorothy Ruth Hoogstratten, a beautiful young waitress in Vancouver, he had visions of making a fortune. He said as much to a friend, commenting that Dorothy, still a teenager, would make him a lot of money. With his smooth charm, he introduced her to the glamour of show business and talked her into posing for *Playboy* magazine.

Dorothy Stratten, as she became, was a great success on account of her unspoiled personality and outstanding beauty. She married Snider in 1979 and, as her career prospered, so he became jealous and resentful. She developed from a shy, unworldly teenager into a woman who knew what she wanted from life and it was clear that her talents far exceeded Snider's ability to manoeuvre her. They grew apart and arguments developed. She wanted to go her own way and he obstructed her.

Dorothy asked for a divorce which Snider refused, and he hired a detective to follow her. After a filming session in New York, Dorothy returned to their home in Los Angeles on 14 August 1980. Later that day, their bodies were found in the bedroom. It appeared that Dorothy had been killed with a shotgun blast in the face by Snider who had then taken his own life. A 12-bore shotgun lay near by.

The tragic nature of Dorothy Stratten's death at the age of twenty-one when she was on the verge of a substantial career was made into a television film, *The Death of a Centrefold*, and a movie called *Star 80*.

[93]

THE SNOWTOWN MURDERS

A missing persons enquiry in May 1999, led South Australian police to Snowtown, a small town north of Adelaide, the state capital. What they found was a murder factory in the vault of a disused bank and a bizzare trail of serial killings. Press reports quickly labelled the crimes, 'The bodies in the barrels'.

A search of the bank premises uncovered a virtual charnel house and the remains of eight people dissolving in six vats of hydrochloric acid. Various body parts were recovered including hands and feet. An assortment of knives and implements of torture was also found. At different stages, a further four bodies were discovered, making twelve in all; ten men and two women.

Exceptional forensic and detective work eventually led to the identification of the victims and also to the arrest of four murder suspects; John Justin Bunting, Robert Joseph Wagner, Mark Ray Haydon and, at a later stage, James Spyridon Vlassakis.

Bunting and Wagner were known for their virulent hatred of homosexuals and paedophiles, remarking that 'They need to be killed'. Recordings of unspeakable tortures inflicted on the victims were recovered from the crime scene. Vlassakis, aged nineteen at the time, admitted partial guilt and agreed to give evidence against his former associates. On 21 June 2001, he pleaded guilty to four murders and was sentenced to life imprisonment without parole for twenty-six years.

The trial of Bunting and Wagner began on 1 October 2002 and lasted for eleven months. Bunting pleaded not guilty to twelve murders and Wagner not guilty to seven but guilty to three. On 8 September 2003, Bunting was convicted of eleven counts and Wagner of seven counts of murder. They were both sentenced to life imprisonment. The judge said he could not envisage they would ever be found eligible for parole. In May 2005, appeals by Bunting and Wagner were dismissed by the Supreme Court.

Mark Haydon appeared on trial in August 2004, charged with two counts of murder and six of 'assisting offenders'. On 19 December 2004, he was convicted of five counts of assisting in the commission of the crimes but the jury failed to agree on the two counts of murder. In September 2005, it was announced that the two outstanding charges would be dropped and that Haydon would plead guilty to the lesser charges.

On 19 September 2005, the final horror of the Snowtown Murders case was made public in Australia. Allegations of cannibalism had been suppressed by the state Supreme Court in 2002. It appeared that Bunting and Vlassakis had been present when Wagner cooked and ate the flesh of one of the victims. In addition to torture and sadism, the Snowtown murderers added robbery to their crimes by looting their victims' credit cards and state benefits to the tune of A$100,000.
[*620, 662*]

SNYDER AND GRAY

Woman with a powerful personality who enrolled her malleable lover into a plot to kill her husband.

Ruth May Snyder was unhappily married to Albert Edward Snyder but her life brightened up when she met Henry Judd Gray in New York in 1925. Gray was a weak personality who was overawed by the woman he called 'Momsie'. They carried on an affair, meeting secretly in hotel rooms and she resolved that her husband would have to be killed.

In 1926, she took out a $48,000 double indemnity life insurance on Albert and tried to draw Gray into her web of murderous intrigue. Albert Snyder had several remarkable escapes. On two occasions he woke up to find the bedroom full of escaping gas and on another he narrowly escaped asphyxiation from car exhaust fumes in the garage. Albert proved to have a resilient constitution for he also survived several attempts at poisoning.

In February 1927, Ruth finally won over Gray on the grounds that Albert had tried to kill her. She persuaded him to assist her in murdering her husband. On 20 March 1927, while Albert was asleep, the conspirators crept into his bedroom and Gray hit him with a heavy sash-weight. The stricken man called out to his wife to help him and she hit him again with the sash-weight. They had to use chloroform to calm his struggles and resorted to strangulation with picture-wire to finish him off. Ruth was bound and gagged to make good her story of being attacked by an intruder.

When Gray's name was found in Ruth's address book, she was told that he had confessed to murder. Tricked by wily detectives, she admitted plotting to kill her husband but blamed Gray for the murder. Gray admitted his involvement and pathetically blamed Ruth for telling him what to do.

Synder and Gray were tried for murder in New York in a high-profile case which attracted great media attention. Ruth was seen as the mastermind behind the murder and was publicly reviled for her callous plotting and sustained murder attempts. Her lack of feeling earned her the title of 'Granite Woman'.

They were found guilty and sentenced to death. While awaiting for their appeals to be heard, each wrote a biography and continued to enjoy notoriety in the newspapers. They were executed at Sing Sing Prison on 12 January 1928 and, the following day, the *New York Daily News* published a photograph of Ruth Snyder in the electric chair taken secretly by a journalist with a camera strapped to his ankle.

[*47, 199, 363, 530, 635, 829*]

SOBHRAJ, CHARLES

Compulsive thief who operated in several Asian countries, robbing and murdering unsuspecting tourists after befriending them.

Hotchand Bhawanni Gurmukh Sobhraj was born in Vietnam. He acquired French citizenship in 1969 and slid into a life of gambling and crime on an international scale. In the early 1970s, he operated a car-dealing business in India interspersed with periods on the run to escape his creditors and theft when he needed to supplement his income. For several years, he made a living in

Greece and Turkey by stealing from tourists and, by 1975, was buying and selling jewellery in Bangkok. He also operated a racket by offering accommodation to young people travelling the world whom be befriended and robbed.

Robbery turned to murder and, in October 1975, he killed a twenty-three-year-old American girl whose body was found on the Thailand coast. Many visitors to Sobhraj's apartment in Bangkok fell ill and he administered his own patent cure for what he called 'Bangkok Belly'. In November 1975, a Turkish gem dealer was found dead after visiting him. This was followed by the deaths of an American couple he had met in Hong Kong. Keeping on the move, Sobhraj next turned up in Nepal where he killed an American couple and followed this with a visit to India where he left another corpse behind him. His trail of murders seemed to extend throughout Asia and he was always one step ahead of the authorities. By the end of 1976, he was wanted for questioning about eight murders. Thai officials raided his Bangkok apartment and found documents belonging to twenty people. He was finally arrested in Delhi after a plan to drug and rob a party of French tourists backfired.

In 1982, Sobhraj was convicted of murdering a student in Calcutta and was sentenced to life imprisonment. He bribed his way out of prison but was quickly recaptured. Fearing extradition to Thailand where he faced the death penalty, Sobhraj managed another prison escape. In 1997, he was extradited to France and in September 2003 was arrested in Kathmandu in connection with two unsolved murders which occurred in Nepal thirty years previously.

[*699, 911*]

SODEMAN, ARNOLD CARL

An Australian child murderer who avoided capture for five years until his workmates grew suspicious.

Twelve-year-old Mena Griffiths disappeared from her home at South Yarra in Melbourne on 9 November 1930. Her body was found two days later in a nearby derelict house. She had been strangled. Her friends reported that a tall man had given them sweets. On 10 January, a sixteen-year-old girl was murdered in the same neighbourhood. She too had been strangled. After the second murder, the investigative trail went cold for four years. Then, in

January 1935, public anxiety was reawakened when a twelve-year-old girl in Inverloch was found dead. The details of this murder were reminiscent of the previous unsolved killings. Among the thousands of men on holiday in the resort town who were questioned was Arnold Sodeman, a building worker.

In December 1936, there was another child murder, this time a six-year-old girl who had been strangled at Leongatha. On this occasion, a witness had seen a tall man with a bicycle talking to the child. After news of the murder was reported in the press, a building worker reported to the police that one of his colleagues had been behaving strangely. Arnold Sodeman had been subjected to some leg-pulling by his mates. Sodeman, normally a very even-tempered man, became violently angry when his mates jokingly suggested he was the wanted man with the bicycle.

Sodeman was questioned by the police and, after denying any involvement with the dead girls, confessed to four murders. Although happily married with a daughter, he had a history of mental illness and was prone to violence after he had been drinking. He pleaded guilty at his trial and was convicted of murder. Sentence of death was carried out at Pentridge Prison on 1 June 1936. It was shown at the autopsy that Sodeman was subject to chronic meningitis which flared up after bouts of drinking.

[*102, 246*]

SPECK, RICHARD FRANKLIN

Chicago mass murderer who was given life sentences totalling 1200 years for killing eight nurses in 1966. He had the motto 'Born to Raise Hell' tattooed on his forearm.

Speck was a drifter addicted to drugs, alcohol and comic-book culture. On 14 July 1966, he forced his way into a dormitory of the South Chicago Community Hospital where he held nine nurses captive. Armed with a gun and a knife, he promised that he would not harm them. He ordered the women to lie on the floor while he tied them up with strips of bed-sheets.

After robbing the nurses, Speck took them one at a time into another room where he either stabbed or strangled them. He also raped one of his victims. One nurse escaped. Twenty-three-year-old Corazon Amurao avoided the fate meted out to her colleagues by hiding under the bed. It was four hours later before she felt it was safe to emerge. The killer had left but eight of her friends lay dead.

Speck was identified by means of fingerprints at the crime scene. In the days following the killings he spent his time drinking heavily in a Chicago bar. When he read in a newspaper that there had been a survivor who could identify the killer, he cut his wrists. He survived the suicide attempt and told hospital staff who he was. Speck was identified by Corazon Amurao and found guilty of first-degree murder at his trial in April 1967. Sentence of death was passed but not carried out owing to the US Supreme Court's suspension of capital punishment. He was resentenced and given eight consecutive terms of between 50 and 150 years. The semi-literate former garbage collector thus faced a potential sentence of 1200 years – probably the longest sentence ever. After repeatedly denying the crimes, he confessed to a newspaper in 1978 that he had choked and stabbed the nurses.

In May 1996 embarrassment arose for the penal authorities when a videotape was discovered, apparently made by Speck in prison. He acknowledged killing the eight nurses in Chicago and bragged about the good time he was having in Stateville Prison involving sex and drug-taking.

[*14, 111, 164*]

SPENCE, DAVID WAYNE

Killed three teenagers in 1982 at Lake Waco, Texas in a murder-for-hire contract that went wrong.

Kenneth Franks, aged eighteen, and two seventeen-year-old girls, Jill Montgomery and Raylene Rice, failed to return to their homes on 13 July 1982. The trio had been to Koehne Park at Lake Waco to watch the sunset.

Their bodies were found on the following day. Franks had been stabbed several times and indications were that the two girls had been tortured before having their throats cut and suffering multiple stab wounds. The police thought the victims had been killed elsewhere and their bodies dumped in a wooded area bordering Lake Waco.

After intensive inquiries produced no result, the police decided in September to suspend their investigation. In an extraordinary act of determination, Sergeant Truman Simons persuaded the Police Department to let him carry out a lone investigation. He discovered that Kenneth Franks had been involved in an argument over a girl with Muneer Deeb, a local store-owner. Deeb had apparently taken a fancy to Franks's girl-friend and it was known that he had offered money to local girls to marry him. It was also rumoured that when the girl in question spurned Deeb's interest, he decided to kill her but, in a case of mistaken identity, Jill Montgomery was targeted instead.

Deeb was arrested and then released, but not before he implicated David Wayne Spence who was already serving a prison sentence for assault. After dogged persistence, Sergeant Simons secured a confession from Spence and demonstrated that his teeth impressions matched bite marks on the dead girls' bodies.

Spence was known to be a man of violent temper who ill-treated his female companions. He undertook to carry out Deeb's wish to kill the young woman who had rejected him. Aided by two friends, Gilbert and Tony Melendez, Spence followed the girl he had mistaken for his victim and killed her, along with Kenneth Franks and Raylene Rice, at Lake Waco.

After protracted trial proceedings, Spence was convicted and sentenced to death in June 1984 for murdering the two girls. In October 1985, he received another sentence of death following his conviction of the murder of Kenneth Franks. The Melendez brothers were sentenced to life imprisonment and Muneer Deeb was sentenced to death for hiring Spence to commit murder on his behalf.

[893]

SPENCER, HENRY

Murderer who killed for gain and embraced religion in the hope of avoiding the death sentence.

Henry Spencer turned up out of the blue at Wheaton, Illinois in June 1914. He was a complete stranger to the townsfolk but the young man, who claimed he was a salesman, had winning ways. He met Allison Rexroat, an unmarried woman, ten years older than himself, and seduced her with promises of marriage. Miss Rexroat had an attractive bank balance which Spencer persuaded her to transfer to his control.

The couple went for a picnic in the nearby countryside when Spencer battered Allison to death with a hammer and buried her body in a shallow grave. He returned to Wheaton, drew out all her savings and went to the railway station, intending to take the first train out of town. He was apprehended in the nick of time by Wheaton's sheriff who had been alerted by the local bank manager.

Spencer loudly protested his innocence and ranted at officials. He was subdued by means of a beating-up and subsequently confessed. Despite his protestations that his confession had been obtained under duress, Spencer was convicted of murder and sentenced to death.

The day before he was due to be executed, Spencer entertained members of the press corps in his cell. He told them that he was a reformed man, having taken up religion. 'I've joined the ranks of God's children,' he declared. Aided by two evangelists who sang hymns and prayed, Spencer admitted he had been a sinner but repented. Spencer's execution in August 1914 proved to be a major public event in Wheaton. Thousands of people poured into the town from outlying areas. He entertained the crowd with an extraordinary evangelical diatribe in which he said his execution was 'the happiest moment of my life'.

[*660*]

STARKWEATHER, CHARLES

Known as 'Little Red' on account of his red hair and bow-legged, unprepossessing appearance, Starkweather modelled himself on film star James Dean. At the age of nineteen, Starkweather had already killed while committing a robbery before he started on the week-long killing spree which made him a mass murderer.

On 21 January 1958, he visited the home of his girl-friend, fourteen-year-old Caril Ann Fugate, in Lincoln, Nebraska. While he waited for her to return he toyed with a .22 hunting rifle which annoyed the girl's mother who told him to stop. His answer was to shoot her on the spot and he followed this up by killing her husband. Caril Ann returned to find both her mother and stepfather dead and she watched while Starkweather choked her two-year-old sister to death.

The couple put a notice on the door telling the world, 'Every Body is Sick with the Flu'. A relative called and was fobbed off by Caril Ann but remained suspicious enough to call the police. Officers went to the house and were also deflected by the fourteen-year-old. They returned later to find the house empty save for three corpses.

An alert went out for Starkweather and his companion and, in the week of terror which followed, 'Little Red' shot and stabbed seven people. Twelve hundred police and National Guardsmen were deployed in the hunt for the pair who were eventually traced to Douglas, Wyoming.

When arrested, Starkweather attempted to absolve the girl by saying she was his hostage, but when she called him a killer, he changed his mind. In his confession he said, 'The more I looked at people, the more I hated them because I knowed there wasn't any place for me with the kind of people I knowed . . . A bunch of God-damned sons of bitches looking for somebody to make fun of . . .'

Caril Ann maintained her innocence at the couple's trial, but she was found guilty and sentenced to life imprisonment. Starkweather was condemned to death and died in the electric chair at Nebraska State Prison on 25 June 1959.

Caril Ann Fugate was released on parole in 1977 after serving eighteen years in prison. She was reported as saying that she felt sorry for the people who hated her 'because it has destroyed their lives'. One of the victims' relatives took a different view, namely that Fugate should have served fifty or sixty years, 'That's a lifetime to me,' she said.

[*11, 45, 719, 1064*]

STEPHENSON, DAVID CURTIS

Unusual case in which a successful prosecution for murder was brought after the victim of an assault committed suicide.

Thirty-four-year-old Stephenson was an ambitious member of the Ku Klux Klan in Indiana. He was reputed to have enrolled over 300,000 members and to have taken a cut of the enrolment fees for his own use. He became Grand Dragon of the Realm of Indiana and set himself up in opposition to the Klan's Imperial Wizard, Hiram W. Evans. He seceded from the national organisation in 1922 and embarked on the political trail.

Stephenson had a crush on twenty-eight-year-old Madge Oberholtzer, the daughter of an Indianapolis family, who was not similarly smitten. On 15 March 1924, he had the young woman abducted from her home and taken to his mansion. He told her that he loved her more than any women he had ever known. When she resisted his drunken blandishments, two of his aides drove her to the railway station where she and Stephenson boarded a train.

Once in their berth, Stephenson inflicted a savage assault on the girl, rendering her unconscious. They left the train at Hamilton and booked into a hotel. In severe pain from her injuries, Madge Oberholtzer persuaded one of Stephenson's cronies to take her to a drugstore. There she bought some bichloride of mercury and swallowed six tablets in a suicide attempt.

Stephenson had her driven back to Indianapolis where she was returned to her home on 17 March in an exhausted and seriously ill state. The explanation given was that she had been involved in an automobile accident. Her bruises and other injuries began to heal but she died from the effects of the poison on 14 April 1925, having told her family the full story.

Stephenson and his henchmen, Gentry and Klinck, were charged with murder and put on trial in Hamilton. There was no doubt about Stephenson's violent assault on the girl but the defence argued that homicide was not valid as the girl had plainly committed suicide. The prosecutor argued that by their acts, Stephenson and his cohorts became murderers as surely as if 'they plunged a dagger into her throbbing heart'.

Gentry and Klinck were acquitted but Stephenson was found guilty of second-degree murder and sentenced to life imprisonment. He served thirty-one years and died in 1966.

[*135, 139, 603*]

STRAFFEN, JOHN THOMAS

Mental defective who killed twice and was committed to a secure hospital from which he escaped to kill again.

After a childhood of thieving and truancy, Straffen was judged mentally subnormal and sent to a special school. When he was aged seventeen he assaulted a child and was put in an institution for the feeble-minded. Within six months of being released in 1951, he killed two girls at Bath. A five-year-old was found strangled on 15 July in woods close to the city and, on 8 August, a nine-year-old was found dead, also from strangulation.

Straffen was arrested on the basis of a witness's description of a man seen with one of the dead children. His motive for committing the murders seemed to lie in his desire to upset the police. Neither victim had been subjected to a sexual attack. Straffen was tried for murder at Taunton in October 1951 and judged to be insane. He was committed to Broadmoor.

On 29 April 1952, Straffen escaped from Broadmoor while working near the boundary wall. During a spell of several hours' freedom he killed a five-year-old girl. He was recaptured after a violent struggle but his latest crime was not discovered until the next day.

He appeared on trial for murder at Winchester in July 1952 but denied the killing, claiming he had been framed by the police. A great deal of the evidence concerned Straffen's mental status. The jury rejected the defence plea of insanity and found him guilty. He was sentenced to death, although later reprieved and sent to prison for life. The case raised important questions about criminal responsibility and insanity. For the public, however, concerns focused on how a murderer escaped to kill again.

Having spent fifty years behind bars, Straffen is Britain's longest serving prisoner. In May 2001, records came to light showing inconsistencies in the judicial process at the time he was tried and moves were made to have the case reopened. Where he was found unfit to plead concerning the two murders in 1951, he was judged to be sane eight months later when he killed after escaping from Broadmoor, a crime that he always denied. There is a suggestion that the third murder was unjustly attributed to him.

[*276, 504, 777*]

STRATTON BROTHERS

The murder of an elderly couple by the brothers Alfred and Albert Stratton marked a watershed in British criminal investigation with the use of fingerprint evidence.

The Strattons lived in Deptford, London where they made a living by theft and burglary. On 27 March 1905, acting on the rumour that a local tradesman kept large sums of money at his shop, they raided his premises. Elderly Mr and Mrs Farrow, who lived above their shop in Deptford High Street, were found the next morning. Farrow was dead and his wife died later of her injuries. They had been robbed and severely beaten.

A small cash-box had been prised open and its contents stolen. On its metal tray was a thumbprint impression. Fingerprints were taken from all those who might have handled the cash-box, including the two murder victims. None of the prints matched, leaving the police with the conclusion that the thumbprint had been made by the murderer.

The Stratton brothers, with their known criminal record, came under suspicion. They had no alibi for the night of the murders and a girl-friend reported that the pair had acted strangely when they returned home. The brothers were arrested and had their fingerprints taken. Alfred's right thumbprint proved to match perfectly the impression found at the murder scene.

They were tried for murder at the Old Bailey in May 1905 in a case that made history. Despite defence attempts to discredit the use of fingerprint evidence, the new identification method convinced the jury of the brother's guilt. The prosecution had been carefully prepared and the judge gave a balanced summing-up. The jury brought in a guilty verdict and sentence of death was passed. Alfred and Albert Stratton were hanged together on 23 May 1905.
[*44, 122, 611*]

STROUD, ROBERT FRANKLIN

One of America's most famous long-term prisoners who earned fame as the 'Birdman of Alcatraz'.

When he was aged nineteen and working as a prostitute's pimp in Alabama, Stroud shot dead a bartender following an argument. He was convicted of manslaughter and sentenced to twelve years' imprisonment. On 26 March 1916, while in Leavenworth Penitentiary prior to his release, Stroud became involved in an argument with a prison warder in the mess hall. Before a large audience, he drew a knife and killed the guard.

Stroud was convicted of murder and sentenced to death. His mother petitioned President Woodrow Wilson for clemency and succeeded in having the death sentence commuted. His punishment was to spend the whole period of his imprisonment in solitary confinement.

The prisoner used his confinement at Leavenworth to pursue his interest in birds. He wrote two books on bird diseases and became an authority on the subject. A progressively lenient attitude to his imprisonment allowed him to have a large cell, part of which was equipped as a laboratory. In 1942, he was moved to Alcatraz where the tough regime allowed him fewer privileges. He continued to study and write about birds and had a large and sympathetic following.

Stroud also compiled a history of the US Bureau of Prisons which was refused publication. Campaigns for his release failed and, in 1959, he was transferred to the Federal Medical

Centre at Springfield, Missouri. He died there in 1963, aged seventy-six. He had spent fifty-six years of his life in prison, mostly in solitary confinement.
[*27, 322*]

STUART, RUPERT MAX
The conviction of an aborigine for child murder tested the Australian legal system to its fullest and enabled the condemned man to escape the death penalty.

Nine-year-old Mary Olive Hattam disappeared on 20 December 1958. She was last seen playing with friends on a beach near her home at Ceduna, South Australia. Her friends reported that Olive stayed behind when they returned home. An intensive search was mounted and the missing child's body was found in a cave near the beach where she had been playing. She had been killed with blows directed at her head with a stone which lay near the body. She had also been sexually assaulted.

Footprints in the sandy soil, judged to have been made by an aborigine, guided the police investigation. Itinerant workers living near Ceduna were questioned by detectives. Attention focused on Rupert Max Stuart, an aborigine recently arrived in the town. He had already created an unfavourable impression by being charged with drunkenness. This was a serious crime for aborigines who were prohibited from drinking.

Stuart made a confession in which he admitted raping the girl while drunk and then bludgeoned her head with a stone. He was tried for murder at Adelaide where he was convicted and sentenced to death. Appeals followed which resulted in stays of execution. It was argued that Stuart's lack of command of the English language made it impossible for him to defend himself.

His appeal went to the Privy Council in London which rejected it, and referred the matter to a Royal Commission. Eventually, in December 1959, the Commission announced its judgement which was to uphold the original verdict. While the final appeal had failed, sentence of death was commuted to life imprisonment.

In 2004, it emerged that Rupert Murdoch as a young newspaperman in Australia, supported Stuart's lawyers in challenging the guilty verdict. Public pressure eventually led to commutation of the death sentence after execution had been

postponed several times. Stuart was released on parole in 1973 and gained his freedom in 1984. He died in 1991.
[*170, 455*]

SURADJI, AHMAD

Indonesian mystic who traded on his powers as a healer to murder his female clients. He admitted killing forty-two women in bizzare rituals.

Suradji lived in Medan, the capital of Northern Sumatra, where he enjoyed a reputation akin to a witch doctor. Using a combination of rituals and various potions, he claimed to be able to cure the sick and grant prosperity. But his most prized gift was being able to improve the physical attractiveness and sexual allure of his female clients. It was not immediately noticed that many of his clients disappeared after visiting him, possibly because many of them were prostitutes and were not missed by their families.

His world of magic and murder was uncovered in May 1997 when the father of one of the missing women reported his suspicions to the police. A search of the field next to Suradji's house revealed the remains of forty-two female bodies. He and his three wives were arrested and after admitting sixteen murders, eventually owned up to all the serial killings. He said that the ghost of his dead father had come to him in a dream to tell him that if he wanted to increase his powers, he should kill seventy women and lick the saliva from their mouths. He told investigators that he took his victims out into the field where he buried them up to the waist and strangled them while they were immobilised.

Suradji and his first wife, Tumini, went on trial for murder in December 1997. They denied the charges, claiming they had been tortured in order to extract their confessions. In April 1998, the pair were found guilty and sentenced to death. The other two wives were released.
[442]

SUTCLIFFE, PETER

Known as 'The Yorkshire Ripper', Sutcliffe terrorised a number of Yorkshire towns between 1975 and 1980, during which period he killed thirteen women. The fact that his victims were mostly prostitutes drew a powerful association with **Jack the Ripper** and earned him his nickname.

He prowled the streets of Leeds and Bradford in his car, stopping to pick up women whom he killed with blows from a hammer. He left their mutilated bodies in alleyways just footsteps away from busy thoroughfares.

His first and last murders were committed in Leeds. He killed Wilma McCann in October 1975 and Jacqueline Hill in November 1980. The killings in between were in Bradford, Manchester, Huddersfield and Halifax. A huge police investigation was mounted during which 250,000 persons were interviewed, 32,000 statements taken and 5.2 million car registrations checked at a cost of £4 million.

A great deal of police time was wasted pursuing hoaxes and the inquiry was plagued by misleading letters and tape recordings. In particular, a tape purporting to have been recorded by the murderer, beginning, 'I'm Jack . . .', was sent to the police in June 1979. The voice on the tape, which was thought to be a Wearside accent, was played in pubs and clubs in the hope that a member of the public would recognise it. The voice was not Sutcliffe's and was not identified.

On 2 January 1981, the manhunt came to an end in Sheffield. Officers in a police patrol car spotted a parked car and decided to question the driver and his companion. The man gave his name as Peter Williams but he was unable to name the woman with him. The officers were dissatisfied with the man's response and radioed police HQ to check the car registration number. Within minutes they learned that the vehicle was suspect; its licence number belonged to a car of a different make. The man, who proved to be Peter Sutcliffe, was arrested. To the embarrassment of the police, it later turned out that Sutcliffe had been questioned by them several times before during their inquiries.

Sutcliffe lived in Bradford with the girl he had married in 1967 after a courtship lasting seven years. She was a teacher and he worked as a lorry driver. Neither she nor his workmates had any idea that Sutcliffe lived a secret life of violence. He demonstrated a sense of power within by placing a notice in the window of his truck. It read, 'In this truck is a man whose latent genius if unleashed would rock the nation, whose dynamic energy would overpower those around him. Better let him sleep?'

He professed a hatred for prostitutes and said in his defence that God had given him a mission to rid the world of them. He claimed to have received instructions from the Almighty while looking out across the moors from a cemetery in Bingley.

At Sutcliffe's trial in May 1981, the jury believed him sane and responsible for his actions. He was found guilty on thirteen charges of murder and sentenced to life imprisonment.

His name has emerged in the news from time to time. In 1984 he was said to be suffering from paranoid schizophrenia and was moved from Parkhurst Prison to Broadmoor Hospital. In 1986 a press report announced that he thought he was Jesus Christ and had painted a self-portrait as a Christlike figure. In 1992 Sutcliffe confessed to previously unsolved attacks on two teenagers, both of whom survived. In 1993 a woman from North Shields believed she knew the identity of the 'I'm Jack . . .' tape. She claimed to have met Sutcliffe with this individual at the North Shields Fishermen's Mission. In 2005 a Sunderland man was charged with perpetrating the tape and letter hoax.

[*75, 132, 498, 553, 721, 1019*]

SWANGO, Dr MICHAEL J.

Doctor who made a practice of poisoning his patients over a medical career spanning twelve years and working in three US states. Despite the trail of death that followed him, his record was not seriously questioned and he always seemed to find new employment. His eventual conviction for murder raised questions about the vigilance of the hospital authorities.

In 1984 Ohio State University Hospital terminated Dr Swango's contract following the mysterious deaths of several patients. Later, while working as a paramedic in Illinois he poisoned five of his colleagues with arsenic but with non-fatal results. He was sentenced to five years' imprisonment for these crimes yet, on release, readily secured a physician's post at the Veteran Affairs Medical Center in Iowa by concealing his criminal record. When his past caught up with him, Swango was dismissed and, again, readily found employment in 1993 at the Veterans Affairs Medical Centre at Northport, New York state. After four patients in his care died, he was dismissed from his post. It was later determined that he had administered toxic injections to the victims.

Swango next travelled to Zimbabwe where he worked in Bulawayo at the Mnene Mission Hospital where he was suspected of poisoning seven patients, five of whom died.

In 1997, the murderous medic was arrested in Chicago en route to Saudi Arabia where he planned to pursue his medical career. He was charged with making false statements and later with three counts of murder relating to the deaths at Northport. At his trial in September 2000, he admitted intentionally killing a patient and administering a toxic substance which he knew was likely to be lethal. He was found guilty of murder and given three life sentences to run consecutively.

Dr Swango was believed to have committed thirty-five murders using lethal injections. During his professional career as a physician, sixty of his patients died. He was obsessed with poison and detectives found a virtual laboratory when they searched his apartment. Like **Graham Young**, he doctored his fellow workers' food and drink. He kept press cuttings about the death of Georgi Markov in London in 1978 and was fascinated by **Ted Bundy**.

When he was arrested, Swango was carrying a notebook in which he had copied extracts about death from various writers. One of these read, 'I love it. Sweet, husky, close smell of an indoor homicide'.

[*887*]

T

TANNER, JOHN

Twenty-two-year-old student convicted of the murder of Rachel McLean, an undergraduate at Oxford University who went missing on 19 April 1991.

Rachel was an attractive nineteen-year-old in her second year at St Hilda's College. She was last seen when she returned to her lodgings in Cowley after spending Easter with her parents in Blackpool. She was known to be a sensible and dutiful girl who telephoned home once a week.

Friends said she had a steady boyfriend, John Tanner, a classics student at Nottingham University. They spent a great deal of time together, including weekends at Rachel's lodgings. Tanner said he had last seen Rachel on 15 April when she saw him off at Oxford railway station. While they were waiting for his train to Nottingham, he said she was approached by a man with long, dark hair who seemed to know her.

On 29 April, Tanner attended a police conference with the missing girl's parents. He said he thought she was still alive. Later on the same day, a reconstruction was staged at Oxford railway station in the hope that a traveller might recall having seen the mysterious man described by Tanner.

Dissatisfied with Tanner's story, the police carried out a thorough search of Rachel's lodgings and on 2 May found her body beneath the floorboards under the stairs on the ground floor. She had been strangled. Tanner was arrested and committed for trial.

At Birmingham Crown Court, he pleaded not guilty to murder but admitted manslaughter. He said he could not accept that 'I had killed my love' and described himself as being encapsulated in a 'world of pseudo-reality'. It was clear from Rachel's diary that she was tired of his obsessiveness and wanted to break free. He had told the police that he flew into a blind rage when she declined his proposal to become engaged. In court, he claimed that she had been unfaithful and wanted to end their relationship. 'Something snapped in my mind,' he said, and he strangled her.

After hiding her body, he maintained a cruel charade by writing to her, expressing his love, and then attended the police reconstruction of their farewell at Oxford railway station. The prosecution accused him of an extraordinary degree of callous deliberation. The jury found him guilty of murder on a majority verdict and he was sentenced to life imprisonment.

The only encouraging aspect of the tragedy was the dignity and forgiving nature of Rachel McLean's parents who hoped that Tanner would come to terms with what he had done.
[547]

TAYLOR CASE

A famous Hollywood murder case which remained unsolved for over sixty years until a theory appeared in 1986.

William Desmond Taylor was a successful maker of silent films and chief director at Hollywood's Paramount Studios. He had led a colourful life which ranged from fighting in the First World War as a pilot in the Royal Flying Corps and working as a gold prospector. He was a cultured, charismatic person who directed some of the leading film talent in America, such as Mabel Normand, and newcomers like Mary Miles Minter.

On 1 February 1922, Taylor was found dead in his home on Wilshire Boulevard. The trickle of blood from his mouth led the doctor called to the scene to believe he suffered a fatal haemorrhage. The news of Taylor's death sent shock waves around Hollywood. Friends and acquaintances rushed to the house, not out of sympathy, but to remove articles from the house before the police arrived. It was only later, after the crime scene had been trampled underfoot, that it was realised Taylor had been shot twice in the back.

Love letters written to Taylor by Mabel Normand and the young starlet, Mary Miles Minter, were found in their hundreds. The press had a field day in which several reputations were destroyed and no progress was made in solving the crime. In 1967, King Vidor, the

Hollywood director, began an investigation into the murder which he intended to turn into a film. After his death, the inquiry was resumed by his biographer, Sidney D. Kirkpatrick. In his book, *A Cast of Killers*, published in 1986, the writer named Charlotte Shelby, mother of Mary Miles Minter, as the likely murderer. It was suggested that she was jealous of her daughter's success and particularly of the place she enjoyed in Taylor's affections. She forbade her daughter to see him and, when Mary defied her, she confronted the couple in Taylor's home and killed him with two shots.
[*343, 522*]

TESSNOW, LUDWIG

Sex murderer whose conviction rested on a new discovery which allowed scientists to differentiate between human and animal blood.

On 1 July 1901, two children from the same family disappeared from their home on the island of Rügen in northern Germany. A huge search was mounted for the six- and eight-year-old boys. Their dismembered bodies were discovered the next day in a wooded area. They had been sexually assaulted, battered to death and savagely mutilated.

The shocking news resulted in reports of a journeyman carpenter from another island who had been seen talking to the two boys. He was identified as Ludwig Tessnow and quickly taken in for questioning by the police. Some of his clothes bore evidence of recently washed stains. Tessnow said they were probably spots of cattle blood or wood stains.

The authorities learned that Tessnow had been questioned three years earlier about the murders of two girls in Osnabruck. He had been released and the crimes remained unsolved. Moreover, the carpenter had been identified by a shepherd who saw him running away from a field in which several sheep had been killed and mutilated a week after the Rügen murders. Tessnow's clothing was sent to Paul Uhlenhuth, a pioneering serologist, to examine the stains.

The forensic scientist, using newly developed tests, established that there were both sheep and human bloodstains on the garments. Tessnow was charged with murdering the two boys at Rügen and the scientific evidence of his guilt was convincing. The jury convicted him and he was sentenced to death. He was executed at Griefswald Prison in 1904.
[*914*]

TETZNER, ERICH

A blazing car murder solved by forensic scientists who proved that the victim was not who he was thought to be.

A road accident occurred on 27 November 1929 on Highway 8, near Regensburg in eastern Germany. A green Opel had crashed and caught fire, trapping the driver in the blaze. The driver was believed to be Erich Tetzner, a Leipzig businessman. Having decided he was the victim of a fatal accident, the police released the body for burial.

The dead man's widow immediately applied for the insurance, which was substantial, and premiums had been taken out with three companies. The funeral was halted at the eleventh hour and an autopsy carried out on the burned corpse. Whereas Tetzner was a broad-shouldered man, 5 feet 7 inches in height, the corpse was that of a small individual. The key finding was the absence of soot particles in the lungs and lack of carbon monoxide in the blood.

Detectives carried out surveillance on Frau Emma Tetzner. On 4 December 1929, she received a telephone call from Strasbourg in France. The caller turned out to be her husband who was quickly arrested. Tetzner made a confession in which he admitted setting out to defraud the insurance companies. He had picked up a hitch-hiker whom he strangled and then immolated in the fake car crash.

He was tried for murder at Regensburg in March 1931 and found guilty. His appeal was rejected and he was subsequently executed. The case was almost a trial run for a similar crime committed by **Alfred Arthur Rouse** in England a year later.
[*915*]

THATCHER, COLIN

Millionaire Canadian businessman who sacrificed his career in politics when he murdered his former wife out of hatred.

Forty-three-year-old Jo Ann Wilson was killed in the garage of her home in Regina, Canada on 21 January 1983. A passer-by heard her cries followed by the sound of a gunshot and a glimpse of a man fleeing from the scene.

In the snow-covered street lay a piece of paper which had dropped from the assailant's pockets as he fled. It was a credit-card receipt signed by Colin Thatcher and dated 18 January 1983. Thatcher was the dead woman's former husband whom she had divorced after bitterly fought proceedings. A previous attempt had been made on Jo Ann Wilson's life in 1981 when an unknown assailant shot at her through a window of her home.

Further acrimony ensued over custody of the three children. Thatcher was antagonistic and spoke about his ex-wife in hateful terms. Meanwhile, he had become a successful rancher and entered politics, becoming a minister in the provincial government of Saskatchewan. On several occasions, Thatcher told his American girl-friend that he wanted to kill his wife and might hire a contract gunman. He met a potential assassin while under police surveillance and their conversation was monitored.

Colin Thatcher was put on trial for murder in October 1984. His American girl-friend, from whom he had since parted, gave evidence to the court. He was hostile and confrontational in the witness-box, claiming that the incriminating credit-card slip had been planted as part of a frame-up. The jury found him guilty of first-degree murder and he was sentenced to life imprisonment. An appeal against conviction was rejected in 1985.

[*79, 853, 995*]

THAW-WHITE CASE

High-profile murder case involving a wealthy victim and assailant, and sensational sexual revelations.

On 25 June 1906, Harry Kendall Thaw shot dead the distinguished architect, Stanford White, on the roof garden of Madison Square Garden. The fact that the participants were well-known public figures guaranteed the shooting made headline news.

White had a reputation as a seducer, while Thaw, heir to a railroad fortune, was something of a playboy. Among the girls the amorous architect had seduced was sixteen-year-old, Evelyn Nesbit, who became a model and chorus girl. Still only nineteen, Evelyn met Thaw and they quickly became married. While White amused himself with his girls on a red velvet swing in his apartment, Thaw preferred to hand out whippings to girls to whom he had promised careers as showgirls.

Thaw had won Evelyn from White but took exception to the way the older man had treated her. While on a sea-cruise, Thaw beat admissions out of Evelyn which inflamed his anger against White. It is probable that he was losing his sanity anyway but he was consumed with a jealous vendetta against White. When the three participants in the drama met by chance at Madison Square

Garden, Thaw shot White dead, saying, 'You deserved this. You ruined my wife.'

Thaw was tried for murder in January 1907. The jury failed to reach a verdict and a second trial was called. He was found not guilty by reason of insanity and was to be detained for life in a mental institution. He managed to escape in 1913 and, two years later, he was declared sane. Eighteen months later, he was again declared insane, after being convicted for kidnapping a teenager. He was freed in 1922, spending his millions until the time he died in February 1947 at the age of seventy-six.

[*549, 568, 666, 697, 812, 905*]

THOMAS, DONALD GEORGE

The undoubted murderer of a police officer was fortunate to escape execution at a time when capital punishment was in abeyance.

Nathaniel Edgar, a plain-clothes policeman, stopped a man in a London street on 13 November 1948 to question him in connection with a spate of burglaries. During the questioning, the man drew a revolver and shot the officer three times. While he lay dying, the police officer told colleagues that he had written the man's name in his notebook. He was Donald Thomas and had given an address in Enfield.

A former army deserter, Thomas was well known to the military police. He had left his lodgings at Enfield but was traced to an address in Clapham where he had rented a room. As police officers burst into his room, Thomas tried to reach a Luger which he had hidden under his pillow. He was easily disarmed and quipped that he might as well 'be hung for a sheep as a lamb'. A quantity of ammunition and a firearms manual, *Shooting to Live with the One-Hand Gun*, were found in the room.

Forensic tests matched the Luger to the bullets which had killed PC Edgar, and Thomas was sent for trial. In April 1949, he was convicted of murder and sentenced to death. Owing to the suspension of the death penalty at the time, his sentence was commuted to life imprisonment.

[*74, 830*]

THOMPSON AND BYWATERS

Murder following a jealous affair was confirmed by incriminating love letters suggesting incitement.

Edith Jessie Thompson, a book-keeper for a London millinery

firm, was married to Percy Thompson, a shipping clerk. Although there were only four years' difference in their ages, Edith was restrained by the rather dull life which they led at Ilford in Essex. In June 1921, the Thompsons went on holiday to the Isle of Wight with Edith's unmarried sister and her young man, Frederick Edward Francis Bywaters. Nineteen-year-old Bywaters worked for the P&O line as a shipboard writer. He and Edith were immediately attracted to each other and became lovers.

Their affair was interrupted when Bywaters returned to sea but during his absence they wrote to each other. Edith penned long, loving letters full of frank admissions about her dreary life. She hinted at poisoning her husband and sent her lover cuttings referring to press coverage of poison trials. Bywaters returned to England in September 1922 and straight away resumed his liaison with Edith. On 3 October, as Edith and her husband were returning home late in the evening, Bywaters confronted Percy Thompson and fatally stabbed him in the neck. Edith Thompson and Frederick Bywaters were charged with murder.

Many of the letters which Edith had written to Bywaters were used in evidence at their trial at the Old Bailey in December 1922. Her suggestion that he might become jealous and 'do something desperate' was offered as incitement to murder. The judge, Mr Justice Shearman, delivered a hostile summing-up, dismissing any romantic notions about Edith's relationship with Bywaters. He said they were trying a 'vulgar and common crime'. The couple were found guilty and sentenced to death. On 9 January 1923, Edith was hanged at Holloway Prison and her lover at Pentonville.

In 2001, a film about Edith Thompson called *Another Life* pointed to uncertainties about her role in inciting Bywaters to murder her husband. It was suggested that she might have been easily drawn into her lover's scheming by notions of romance and that she was condemned as much for her loose morals as for her real guilt.
[*117, 212, 251, 264, 390, 737, 965, 1023*]

THOMPSON AND VENABLES

In the James Bulger case two eleven-year-old boys were the youngest convicted murderers in Britain for nearly 250 years.

On 12 February 1993, two-year-old James Bulger became separated from his mother at the New Strand Shopping Centre in

Bootle, Lancashire and went missing. The small boy's body was found forty-eight hours later lying across a railway line some two miles away. He had been battered to death.

News of the discovery brought forward a number of witnesses who had seen the youngster in the company of two other boys. Security video cameras at the shopping centre had also captured views of the three youngsters heading for the exit. These pictures were shown on television and led to the identification of one of the boys which, in turn, resulted in the arrest of two ten-year-olds.

They were tried for murder at Preston Crown Court in November 1993. Their real names only emerged after the judge lifted reporting restrictions. Robert Thompson and Jon Venables, who admitted killing James Bulger, were described by the judge as 'cunning and very wicked'. Both children had troubled backgrounds with a history of truancy and bad behaviour. The jury, consisting of nine men and three women, returned a Guilty verdict and the two boys were sentenced to be detained during Her Majesty's Pleasure.

There was much discussion in the press about children who kill and analysis of the possible reasons. Suggestions that the boys might serve only short sentences before being released gave rise to protests that they should be detained for life.

It was announced in June 2001 that Thompson and Venables, aged eighteen, were to be released after spending eight years in detention. The news provoked a hostile reaction in the tabloid press with fears for the safety of the two youths. Because of threats to their lives, they were given new identities. Both youths were reported to have made exceptional progress in their education and to have expressed remorse for their actions.

[*462, 678, 868, 907*]

THORNE, JOHN NORMAN HOLMES

An attempt to pass off murder as suicide failed in the face of contrary scientific evidence.

Thorne kept a chicken farm at Crowborough, Sussex where he eked out a poor living in squalid surroundings. He lived in a ramshackle hut but engaged in uplifting pursuits such as churchgoing, Sunday School teaching and preaching the virtues of temperance. Despite his unbecoming circumstances, he attracted the attentions of a twenty-three-year-old typist, Elsie Cameron, who decided she wanted to marry him. They became engaged in 1922 and the girl pressed him to name the wedding day. Thorne dillied and dallied and, in November 1924, Elsie untruthfully told him she was pregnant.

On 5 December, Elsie decided to move in with Thorne and left her parents' home in London with a few belongings. She was not seen again and when her parents enquired after her, Thorne said she had not turned up at the farm. The police were informed of the girl's disappearance and paid Thorne a visit. They appeared satisfied with his response but returned with forks and shovels. On 15 January 1925, some of Elsie's belongings were unearthed on the chicken farm. Thorne now admitted that she had visited him and said that he had found her hanging from a beam in his hut. He cut up her body and buried it in his smallholding. Her head was disinterred and its injuries provided valuable evidence.

Thorne was charged with murder and tried at Lewes Assizes. Sir Bernard Spilsbury gave evidence that the bruises found on Elsie's face and head had been caused before death. He believed that she had been clubbed to death and had not committed suicide by hanging. Lack of any rope marks on the beam in Thorne's hut tended to undermine the suicide theory of her death. Thorne was convicted of murder and was hanged on 22 April 1925 at Wandsworth Prison.

[*153, 377, 385, 487, 706*]

TINNING, MARYBETH

Describing herself in 1986, forty-four-year-old Mrs Tinning said, 'I'm not a good mother.' This followed publicity over the death of her four-month-old daughter and the knowledge that eight of her children had died before reaching their fifth birthday.

Joe and Marybeth Tinning lived in Schenectady in New York State and appeared to be an ordinary couple visited by an unusual number of personal tragedies. Their first child, aged eight days, died in 1972. This loss was followed by two more deaths in the same year, all due to natural causes.

In 1973, when the Tinnings lost fourteen-day-old Timothy due to SIDS (Sudden Infant Death Syndrome), rumours began to emerge that something suspicious was happening. No action was taken and nothing untoward occurred until September 1975 when five-month-old Nathan died of pulmonary oedema. Once again, the cause was death from natural causes with no evidence of foul-play.

Another quiet period followed but in 1979 the rate of child deaths speeded up again. Mary Frances died in February 1979, Jonathan in March 1980 and Michael (an adopted child) in March 1981. With seven child deaths in the Tinning family, suspicion rapidly hardened and exhumations were ordered of the bodies of Timothy and Nathan. Nothing indicative of foul-play was found.

Three years later, Marybeth was pregnant once more and Tami Lynne was born on 20 December 1985. Four months later her daughter was dead. Doctors felt that one child death in a family due to SIDS was unusal, two would be rare but eight was hardly conceivable. In February 1986 the police decided it was time to question Marybeth.

She admitted killing three of her children, Timothy, Nathan and Tami Lynne. 'I'm not a good mother,' she told the police when admitting that she smothered Tami Lynne with a pillow to stop her crying. Mrs Tinning was charged with intentionally causing the child's death by smothering and with showing depraved indifference to human life.

She was released on bail and immediately began legal proceedings to have her confession ruled inadmissible at trial on the grounds that her constitutional rights had been violated. Her application was rejected. On 19 July 1987 Marybeth Tinning was found guilty of second-degree murder and sentenced to life imprisonment. Her appeal was rejected in 1988.

Theories abounded regarding Marybeth's personality, including the suggestion that she had a psychological need to be pregnant but not for its consequences. A friend recalled that after losing one of her children, Marybeth had said, 'God told me to kill this one too.' [265]

TOAL, GERARD

The murderer's failure to dispose of his victim's bicycle as well as he had disposed of her body became a focus for suspicion.

Father James McKeown was the priest at a village near Dundalk in Ireland. His household was run by thirty-six-year-old Mary Callan and he employed eighteen-year-old Gerard Toal as chauffeur and handyman. When Father McKeown returned home on 16 May 1927, he expected to be greeted by his housekeeper but she was not in the house and her bicycle was gone. He questioned Gerard Toal who said simply that Mary had given him his midday meal and then left.

It was out of character for the housekeeper to behave like this and, when she failed to turn up the next day, Father McKeown began making inquiries. All his questions to local people drew negative replies. The first hint of suspicion came when the new housekeeper, Peggy Galagher, found parts of her predecessor's bicycle in Gerard Toal's room when she was cleaning. The young man's explanation was that he had stolen the cycle parts. Father McKeown decided to dispense with Toal's services and he left in April 1928, saying that he was emigrating to Canada.

As a result of the first thorough search they had made since Mary Callan disappeared, the police found more bicycle parts hidden in the priest's garden along with items of female clothing. Toal meanwhile had been arrested for stealing in Dundalk. Under pressure to explain these fresh discoveries, he admitted his dislike for the housekeeper and said they had quarrelled. Extensive searches in the neighbourhood led to the discovery of her body in a quarry near Father McKeown's house.

Toal was charged with murder and tried at Dublin in July 1928 where he was found guilty and sentenced to death. He was hanged on 29 August 1928.
[224]

TOKYO SUBWAY GAS KILLINGS

Cults have become a frightening feature of the modern world. The havoc created by the Reverend Jim Jones and the Branch Davidians at Waco, Texas were eclipsed in Japan in 1995 by the Aum Supreme Truth Cult.

Headed by a charismatic, partially blind guru calling himself Shoko Asahara, the cult rapidly attracted a wide membership, particularly among the younger intelligentsia in Japan. Propagating a mixture of ancient Eastern beliefs with a prophecy that the end of the world was imminent, disciples were manipulated with a heady cocktail of mind control and designer drugs. Those who rebelled were eliminated.

When 1995 dawned and the prophecy of Armageddon showed no signs of happening, Asahara and his cohorts decided to give it a helping hand. They obtained supplies of the nerve gas, sarin, and on the morning of 20 March despatched agents to the Tokyo subway armed with balloons containing the deadly gas which they released by piercing the containers with umbrellas. A major disaster resulted in which twelve people died and five and a half thousand required treatment in hospital. The city of Tokyo was brought to a standstill.

It did not take the police long to follow a trail to the Aum Supreme Truth Cult which had been under surveillance for some time. Hundreds of cult members were arrested and more murders were uncovered of individuals who had opposed the leadership. Those responsible for releasing the gas in the subway and the chemist who made up the deadly gas concoction were convicted of multiple murder and sentenced to death. Life sentences were handed down to the cult members who drove the carriers to the subway.

The trial of cult leader, Shoko Asahara, began in April 1996 and, following the inordinately slow standards of Japanese justice, lasted until February 2004. Finally, Asahara was found guilty of twenty-seven murders and multiple attempted murders. He was sentenced to death. The cult remains active and continues to attract surveillance. It has changed its name to Aleph, the first letter of the Hebrew alphabet and insists it is just a benign religious group.
[*501, 1041*]

TREVOR, HAROLD DORIEN

Thief turned murderer who left his name and fingerprints at the murder scene.

Trevor was an inveterate gaolbird who posed as a member of the gentry in order to carry off his numerous frauds and thefts. Although he had spent most of his adult life in prison, he was not a violent man.

After being released from prison in October 1941, he called on an elderly widow, Theodora Jessie Greenhill, at her home in Kensington, London. Posing as a likely tenant for the flat which Mrs Greenhill had to rent, he secured her confidence. The next morning, Mrs Greenhill was found dead by her daughter who had come to visit. She had been beaten over the head with a beer bottle and then strangled.

The house had been ransacked and money taken from a cash-box kept in the bedroom. The murderer had obligingly left his fingerprints on the cash-box and, better still, his name, in the form of a note written by his victim. On Mrs Greenhill's bureau was an incomplete handwritten receipt made out to Dr H.D. Trevor.

Trevor, known to the police as 'The Monocle Man' on account of his affinity for military and aristocratic titles, was arrested in Wales. He was tried for murder at the Old Bailey in January 1942. The judge, Mr Justice Asquith, asked him if he had anything to say before sentence was passed on him. In a remarkable speech, Trevor said that no fear touched his heart which had been dead since his mother died, adding, 'My life to the age of sixty-two has been all winter . . .' He was hanged at Wandsworth Prison on 11 March 1942.

[*176*]

TROPPMANN, JEAN-BAPTISTE

A nineteenth-century murderer who saw a chance of enriching himself by eliminating an entire family.

Troppmann travelled in France and Belgium selling weaving machinery. In 1868, while in Roubaix on the French-Belgian border, he met Jean Kinck, a successful local businessman. The two men had both been born in Alsace and Troppman used this bond to inveigle Kinck into accepting his plan to mine precious metals.

They arranged to meet on 26 August 1869 at Herrenfluch in Alsace. Troppmann poisoned Kinck with prussic acid and buried his body. Next, he contacted Hortense Kinck asking her for money on behalf of her husband who was incapacitated. Mme Kinck was wary of his request and agreed that her son, Gustave, should meet him in Paris. The boy did not have the money so Troppmann asked Mme Kinck to come to Paris herself with the rest of her family. Gustave, meanwhile, was murdered.

On 19 September, a cab-driver took a man and a woman, accompanied by five children, to a spot beyond the Flanders Gate. He was instructed to stop and was left to mind three of the children while the man and woman, with the other two children, went off. The man then returned alone shortly afterwards, took the remaining three children and paid off the cab-driver.

The next day, a labourer in fields on the outskirts of Paris discovered a shallow grave containing the bodies of a woman and five children. They had been hacked to death with a spade. Troppmann was traced to Le Havre and was arrested amid scenes of great public fury. He tried to place blame for the murders on Jean and Gustave Kinck but it was plain he had been systematically acquiring the businessman's assets and was determined to wipe out the family. Troppmann was convicted of all eight murders and went to the guillotine on 9 January 1870.

[*94, 244, 457*]

TRUE, RONALD

The reprieve of a man on the verge of insanity was used to draw a social distinction between two murder cases in England in 1922.

On 6 March 1922, the naked body of Olive Young was found by her cleaning lady in her basement apartment in Fulham, London. Prior to this unwelcome discovery, the cleaning lady had encountered a man she knew as 'The Major' leaving the house. Indeed, he had told her not to disturb Olive because she was sleeping. Olive Young, a twenty-five-year-old prostitute, had been battered to death and strangled. 'The Major' had left his visiting card on the sitting-room sideboard. He was arrested in a box at the Hammersmith Palace of Varieties that same evening and proved to be Ronald True, a former officer in the Royal Flying Corps.

True had led a quixotic life, having worked in many parts of the world including service with the Northwest Mounted Police in Canada. He had been severely injured in an air crash in 1916 and had been mentally unstable since then. He complained that he was being impersonated and carried a loaded firearm at all times. He was addicted to pain-killing drugs and had forged prescriptions for morphine.

There was little doubt that True had killed Olive Young and the proceedings of his trial at the Old Bailey in May 1922 revolved around his sanity. The prosecution made much of his theft of jewellery from Olive Young while the defence emphasised his undoubted history of strange behaviour. True was found guilty and sentenced to death although he was later reprieved and judged to be certifiably insane. A few weeks later, **Henry Jacoby**, the pantry-boy convicted of murdering Lady White, was hanged. Much was made of the pantry-boy's execution for murdering a titled victim while the ex-officer who killed a prostitute escaped the hangman. True died at Broadmoor in 1951 at the age of sixty.

[*166, 263, 797*]

TRUSCOTT, STEVEN MURRAY

A controversial Canadian case in which a teenaged boy was convicted of rape and murder on evidence which many thought to be weak.

Twelve-year-old Lynne Harper failed to return to her home in Goderich, Ontario on 9 June 1959. Her parents made inquiries of her friends, including fourteen-year-old Steven Truscott. Steven had been seen talking to the girl and he gave her a ride on the crossbar of his bicycle. He confirmed that he and Lynne had been out together and said that when he left her she went off with a man driving a Chevrolet.

Following an extensive local search, the missing girl's body was found at a place called Lawson's Wood near a Royal Canadian Air Force base. She had been raped and strangled. When Steven Truscott was examined by a doctor he was found to have recent scratches on his body and genital soreness. Analysis of the victim's stomach contents put time of death somewhere between 7.00 and 7.45 pm.

Steven Truscott was charged with murder and went on trial in September 1959. The prosecution contended that the marks on his body were consistent with having committed rape and he was known to be the last person seen with the victim. His defence argued that there was no evidence directly linking Truscott with the dead girl. He was found guilty and sentenced to death. After four months on Death Row, his sentence was commuted to life imprisonment.

Doubts were expressed about his conviction but the verdict was upheld after an appeal in 1960. In January 1963, he was transferred to the federal penitentiary at Kingston, Ontario. In 1966, a panel of eleven judges reviewed the evidence in the case and decided there had been no miscarriage of justice. Steven Truscott was released from prison in 1969.

[*557, 848, 926*]

TUCKER, KARLA FAYE

A savage axe murder committed in Houston in 1983 made Karla Tucker one of Death Row's most publicised inmates. She embraced religion and won over many supporters before her eventual execution in 1998.

On 13 June 1983, heavily influenced by a deadly cocktail of drugs and alcohol, Karla Faye Tucker and her boy-friend, Daniel Ryan

Garrett, broke into the ground floor apartment of Jerry Lynn Dean, seemingly intent on robbery. A friend calling on Dean found a scene of carnage. Dean lay dead on the bed, his head a bloody mess, and there was a dead girl on the floor with a pickaxe embedded in her chest, pinning her to the floor. She was identified as Deborah Thornton.

The murderers were arrested about a month later, largely due to their bragging about what they had done. Apparently Tucker disliked Dean who was the estranged husband of her best friend. In her account of what had happened she said that Dean recognised her immediately and that Garrett attacked him with a hammer. When Tucker heard Dean make gurgling noises, she finished him off with a pickaxe. Then she realised that he was not alone. Doing her best to hide behind some sheets was his girl-friend, Deborah Thornton, who was also despatched with the pickaxe.

Tucker and Garrett were tried separately. She admitted killing Dean and was tried for his murder. Garrett was charged with murdering Thornton but pleaded not guilty. The most dramatic moment in Tucker's trial came when the prosecution played a tape on which she said she had an orgasm every time the axe was driven into the victims' bodies. She denied this in court, explaining that she had said it to impress friends. She and Garrett were convicted of double murder and on 25 April 1984 the jury voted for the death penalty.

At some point during the fifteen years she spent on Death Row, Tucker adopted religion, saying 'I accepted Jesus into my heart'. The prison authorities described her as a model prisoner. Daniel Garrett died from liver disease on Death Row in 1993 and, two years later, Tucker married Dana Lane Brown, a prison minister.

In 1998, the Texas Board of Pardons and Parole denied her clemency by a unanimous vote and the State Governor, George W Bush, signed her death warrant. Under Texas law, the Governor could not overrule the Board, only grant limited stays of execution.

On 3 February 1998, Tucker was executed by lethal injection. Her last words included thoughts about her victims and their families; 'I would like to say to all of you, the Thornton family and Gerry Dean's family that I am so sorry. I hope God will give you peace with this'. A crowd gathered outside Gatesville Prison cheered when news came that the death penalty had been carried out.

[*476, 591*]

U

UDDERZOOK, WILLIAM E

A faked accident to defraud an insurance company ended in murder.

Winfield Scott Goss, a thirty-seven-year-old inventor, apparently died in a blaze which consumed his rented home near Baltimore in February 1873. He was an active man and it was thought odd that he had not escaped from the house when the fire took hold.

Goss had been visited by his brother-in-law, William Udderzook, who wanted to see one of his inventions. The kerosene lamp by which they were working failed and Udderzook went to a neighbouring house to borrow another one. The fire occurred while he was away and Goss, trapped in the blaze, was burned beyond recognition.

The insurance company was wary about paying out and suspicion grew that the dead man might not be Goss. An examination of his teeth threw further doubt on the issue. Several months after the fire, Udderzook was seen in the company of another man in a hotel in Jennerville, Pennsylvania. When blood was found in a carriage used by Udderzook, suspicion mounted rapidly. Shortly afterwards, a farmer in the locale discovered a shallow grave containing a body which was identified as Goss.

Udderzook was charged with murder and the full extent of his plotting became clear. Goss took out a large life insurance policy with the intention of faking his death so that he and Udderzook could share the pay-out. A cadaver was obtained in order to feign Goss's incineration in the fire. When Goss expressed reservations about the outcome, Udderzook killed him in order to take all the profits.

Found guilty at his trial for murder in West Chester, Udderzook was hanged in November 1874.

[*740*]

UNTERWEGER, JOHANN (JACK)

Murderer freed on parole after serving fifteen years of a life sentence in Austria who killed nine more times.

He strangled an eighteen-year-old prostitute in Graz, Austria in 1974, for which he was sentenced to life imprisonment. Unterweger had a remarkable childhood similar in many ways to that of **Henry Lee Lucas**, the serial killer. His father was an American GI and his mother a prostitute. They deserted him when he was still a baby and he was brought up by an alcoholic grandfather and an aunt who was a prostitute. The background to his childhood was one of drunkenness, pimping, violence and crime.

While in prison, the stereotype badman became a model inmate. Unterweger educated himself and became a writer and poet. His talents brought him to the attention of the literary and artistic world of Vienna whose patrons lionised him and campaigned for his freedom. He was released in May 1990, the prison governor proclaiming, 'We will never find a prisoner so well prepared for freedom.'

In September 1990, a prostitute was found strangled in Prague while Unterweger was in the city writing a story about the red-light district. The following month, two prostitutes went missing in Graz; their bodies were found in January 1991. The Austrian police believed that the killings bore all Unterweger's hallmarks and they took him in for questioning. He denied any involvement but was publicly linked to eight murders committed in Graz and Vienna.

In February 1991, the Austrian police issued a warrant for his arrest but he had flown first to Switzerland and then to the USA. He was arrested in Miami on suspicion of having murdered three prostitutes in Los Angeles while he was in the city researching a story on his favourite subject – the red-light district.

Unterweger was extradited to Austria where he stood trial for murder in Vienna. In one of the country's most notorious criminal cases, he was found guilty of nine murders in all; five in Austria, three in the USA and one in the Czech Republic. For the second time in his career, Unterweger was sentenced to life imprisonment. But he cheated the system by hanging himself in his cell six hours after the jury found him guilty on 28 June 1994. He was forty-three years of age.

The career of this criminally flawed but talented man was compared to that of **Jack Henry Abbott** whose rehabilitation also failed.

[*548, 702*]

UNRUH, HOWARD

In a few minutes of madness a mentally unbalanced gunman with a grudge against his neighbours shot and killed thirteen people.

On 5 September 1949, Howard Unruh, whose hobbies were Bible reading and a fascination with guns, left his home in Camden, New Jersey armed with two pistols. Walking along the street in the neighbourhood in which he lived, he systematically went from shop to shop, killing on the way. First the shoe-repair shop, then the barber shop, followed by the tailor's and the drugstore.

In the space of twelve minutes, Unruh shot dead thirteen people. By the time the police arrived, he had returned home. Dozens of armed police surrounded the house and tear gas was fired into the interior. Unruh emerged, declaring that he was not a psycho and adding, 'I'd have killed a thousand if I'd had bullets enough.'

Unruh had served with a tank division in Europe during the Second World War and developed his fascination for guns. After being discharged from the army he led a reclusive life and built a high fence around his house. He believed that his neighbours were talking about him and kept notes of his complaints against them. He used the basement of the house for shooting at targets to keep up his marksmanship. On 5 September, the gate which was part of his security fence was stolen. This triggered off his killing spree.

He was not brought to trial but judged to be incurably insane and committed to an institution.

[*917*]

V

VACHER, JOSEPH

An insane misfit who killed out of resentment for the misfortunes which life had imposed on him.

Born the fifteenth child in a peasant family living at Beaufort in France, Vacher grew from a dull-witted boy to a dangerous adult. He was one of nature's ugly creations, added to which he was facially disfigured by a self-inflicted gunshot wound which had never properly healed.

He was alleged to have been bitten by a rabid dog which caused his mental instability. He abandoned his work as a farm labourer and by 1894 was roaming the countryside living on his wits. Details of how he had been spending his life came to light in March 1896 after an eleven-year-old girl was attacked on her way to church. A gamekeeper came to her assistance and was attacked by her assailant who was identified as Vacher. He was arrested the following year when he attacked a woman near Tournon and was overpowered in a fierce fight by passers-by.

At first Vacher denied the charges of assault but then made a confession. In just over three years, he had murdered eleven times, killing seven women and three young men. He said that he experienced a sense of relief after each act of murder which was accompanied by rape and mutilation. He was examined extensively by several doctors who decided that he was sane and fit to stand trial.

In October 1898, he appeared at the Assizes in Ain charged with the murder of a shepherd in 1896. Vacher played the role of the madman in court but failed to convince the jury. He was convicted and condemned to death. He would not accept his fate willingly and was dragged semi-conscious to the guillotine on 31 December 1898. [*515, 577*]

VAN BUUREN, CLARENCE GORDON

A rape attack ended in murder and the time-honoured excuse of panicking on finding the dead body.

Eighteen-year-old Myrna Joy Aken went missing from her home in Durban, South Africa on 2 October 1956. A man had been calling on her at the office where she worked and it was believed they had gone off together.

Wide-scale searches failed to locate the girl and her anxious parents called on a clairvoyant to help. The medium said she would be found some distance from home lying in a culvert. Ever-widening police searches discovered her body in a culvert some sixty miles from Durban. She had been raped and mutilated. Death was caused by .22 calibre gunshot wounds.

Police inquiries in the dead girl's home community focused on a neighbour. Clarence Van Buuren, who lived across the street from the Aken family, had been convicted of theft and forgery and was questioned about her disappearance. His own married life was unhappy and he met Joy when she too was miserable. They met a couple of times and he had taken her out for a drive in his car. He said that on 2 October they went out together and she remained in the car when he stopped off at a bar.

On his return to the car, he found that it had been moved and, when he relocated it, found Joy's bloodstained body. In a state of panic, he drove away from the city and dumped her body into a road culvert. A quantity of .22 calibre ammunition in Van Buuren's possession circumstantially linked him to the girl's death. His trial jury convicted him of murdering her and he was sentenced to death. Van Buuren was hanged on 10 June 1957 at Pretoria Central Prison.

[*510*]

VAN WYK, STEPHANUS LOUIS

Acquitted of murder on a judge's concept of reasonable doubt, he went on to kill a second time.

Van Wyk was a farmer's son who decided to make a living by his wits and a glib tongue. In 1929 he served a prison sentence for committing fraud, which left him in a bitter mood. He came to believe that his nephew, Johan Moller, a legal clerk at the Bloemfontein Supreme Court, had informed on him. He made threats against Moller and determined to take his revenge.

Within days of being discharged from prison in July 1930, he visited his nephew. The two went off in Moller's car and promptly disappeared. Moller was reported missing and appeals were made in the press for Van Wyk to come forward. He responded but Moller's body had already been found in a jackal pit, dead from head injuries.

Van Wyk confirmed that he and Moller had been together and his story was that they planned to retrieve the proceeds of a robbery which he had committed in 1929. Equipped with a pick and shovel, they began digging in the dark. In the course of this activity, Van Wyk accidentally struck his companion on the head with the pick. He panicked and buried the body in the nearby jackal pit. Van Wyk was tried for murder in Bloemfontein in October 1930 and the judge's summing-up favoured acquittal. The jury pronounced Van Wyk not guilty.

In May 1931, Van Wyk once again found himself facing a murder charge. Earlier in the year he had posed as a buyer for the farm of Cyril Tucker, who was selling up to return to England. The two men agreed on the sale and while Tucker was asleep, Van Wyk killed him with a hammer. This time Van Wyk pleaded insanity but his evident premeditation persuaded the jury to convict him. He was executed on 12 June 1931, having finally confessed to killing Johan Moller.

[64]

VAQUIER, JEAN-PIERRE

An Anglo-French love affair ended in tragedy when the woman's husband was eliminated with poison.

Vaquier was a French inventor with a passion for radio who encountered an English lady in the Victoria Hotel at Biarritz where she was on holiday. Vaquier, who had been hired by the hotel to operate its radio for the guests, was attracted by Mabel Theresa Jones. Neither spoke the other's language but they developed a friendship and when Mable left to return to her husband in England, he followed. Mabel Jones was the wife of the landlord of the Blue Anchor at West Byfleet in Surrey. When Vaquier turned up in London in February 1924, he invited Mabel to visit him at his hotel. Within days of her returning once more to West Byfleet, Vaquier arrived at the Blue Anchor and settled in as a resident. He met Mabel's husband Alfred, and privately begged her to leave him.

On 1 March, Vaquier bought some chemicals, including strychnine, from a shop in London. He said they were for radio experiments and he duly signed the Poisons Register, using a false name. On 29 March, Alfred Jones came down to the bar parlour after a heavy drinking session the previous evening. He made himself a 'pick-me-up' from a jar of Bromo Salts and, protesting at its bitter taste, collapsed and died. A post-mortem on the dead landlord showed that he had been poisoned with strychnine. Traces of the poison were found in the Bromo Salts bottle. Vaquier denied any knowledge of the incident but was foolish enough to talk to the newspapers who published his photograph. Thus the chemist who had sold the strychnine identified him.

Vaquier was tried at Guildford in July 1924. His evidence was full of excuses and inconsistencies, his sole aim being to blame other people. He was convicted of murder and sentenced to death. On 12 August 1924 he was hanged at Wandsworth Prison.
[*89, 403, 469*]

VATICAN MURDERS

On the evening of 4 May 1998 five shots were fired inside Vatican City although no one heard them except the victims. The result, according to official accounts, was three deaths, two of which were murders and one suicide.

The shootings occurred in the apartment of the newly appointed commander of the Swiss Guard in the Vatican, Alois Esterman. His body and that of his Venezuelan born wife, Gladys, and a young Guardsman, Cedric Tornay, were found dead. First indications were that the Estermans had been murdered by Tornay who then took his own life.

The suggested motive was that Tornay was aggrieved because he had been overlooked for awards that he thought were due to him. The official explanation was that he had acted in a fit of madness caused by a cyst growing in his brain. Other explanations emerged later and Tornay's mother questioned the Vatican's explanation which implied her son was a murderer. She commissioned a second post mortem which arrived at different conclusions to the first autopsy. It was reported that the young NCO had been tied up before being hit about the head and then subjected to a fake suicide. No evidence was found of a cerebral cyst and the bullet which ended Tornay's life was of 7 mm calibre, whereas the weapons supplied to the Swiss Guard fired 9.4 mm ammunition.

Allegations came thick and fast in various accounts of the shootings. Conspiracy theories were thick on the ground and it was suggested that Tornay had been set up by a hit squad in a power struggle aimed at killing Esterman. There was a story that Esterman had worked for the Stasi, the secret intelligence organisation of the former East German Republic. Also thrown into the arena of speculation were stories of bullying in the Swiss Guard, homosexuality and of a love affair between Tornay and Gladys Esterman.

Cedric Tornay was a Swiss citizen and in a development in 2005, lawyers acting for his mother sought to open a murder enquiry in Switzerland. Accounts of what happened within the confines of Vatican City on 4 May 1998 vary widely. All that is certain is that three people died and that two of them were murdered.

[*380*]

VOIRBO, PIERRE

An inspired piece of detection solved the puzzle of a body found in a well.

On 26 January 1869, police were called to a restaurant in the rue Princesse in Paris following the owner's discovery of part of a human leg in his well. He noticed that the well water had become foul and his investigation was rewarded by retrieving an offensive bundle containing the limb. Police officers made their own search of the well and found a second leg.

The limbs had been wrapped in cloth which was then neatly stitched, and one of the legs was clad in a woollen sock identified with the mark + B +. A tailoress who lived above the restaurant was questioned and mentioned one of her customers, Pierre Voirbo, also a tailor, who called on her regularly with work. Inquiries established that one of Voirbo's contacts was Désiré Bodasse, an elderly upholsterer who had been missing since 14 December 1868. One of his family identified the sock with the + B + mark as Bodasse's.

When questioned by the police, Voirbo expressed concern over his friend's disappearance but this did not fool Gustave Macé, the officer in charge, who ordered a thorough search of Voirbo's room. Hidden in a cask of wines were securities belonging to Bodasse. Macé believed that Voirbo had probably killed and dismembered

Bodasse in his room, but how to prove it? The room had a tiled floor which dipped in the centre. He emptied a jug of water on to the floor and watched the fluid gravitate towards the hollow area. Lifting a few of the tiles, he saw evidence of dried blood underneath.

Voirbo confessed to murdering Bodasse because the old man had refused to make him a loan. Macé enjoyed a great triumph but his villain escaped justice by committing suicide in March 1869 before coming to trial.

[*624, 973*]

VOISIN, LOUIS

Murder committed in London during a First World War Zeppelin raid led to an ill-conceived attempt to divert the police, which merely served to incriminate.

A bundle wrapped in sacking was found by a roadsweeper in the gardens at Regent Square, London on 2 November 1917. His curiosity was rewarded by the discovery of a woman's body minus the head, legs and hands. A second bundle containing the legs was found near by. A bloodstained sheet with the body carried the laundry mark IIH, and there was also a scrap of paper bearing the words 'Blodie Belgium'. The doctor who examined the remains thought the dissection had been skilfully carried out, possibly by a butcher.

The laundry mark enabled the body to be identified as that of Emilienne Gerard, a thirty-two-year-old Frenchwoman missing from her rooms in Regent's Park. There were bloodstains in the kitchen and a signed IOU for £50. The signatory was Louis Voisin, a French butcher working in London. When Voisin was questioned, he was entertaining one of his lady friends, Berthe Roche. Asked to write the words 'Bloody Belgium', Voisin obliged and committed the same spelling error as in the note found with Emilienne Gerard's body.

In the cellar at Voisin's accommodation, police found a cask containing a head and a pair of hands. Gerard had apparently visited him on the night of 31 October 1917 during a German air raid on London. She found him with Berthe Roche and there was a quarrel which resulted in her murder. Voisin concocted the 'Blodie Belgium' note in a misguided attempt to throw the police off his trail. He was convicted and sentenced to death at

the Old Bailey, while Roche was tried later as an accessory after the fact and sentenced to seven years' imprisonment. Voisin was hanged at Pentonville Prison on 2 March 1918. Roche died in prison on 22 May 1919.
[*717, 920*]

VOLLMAN, JOHN

Murder committed on the Canadian-US border which was solved by means of matching paint fragments at the crime scene to the murderer's car.

Sixteen-year-old Gaetane Bouchard failed to return home on 13 May 1958 after finishing school. She lived at Edmundston East in New Brunswick close to the Canadian-US border. Her father discovered that she had an American boy-friend, John Vollman, from Madawaska in the bordering state of Maine. Vollman was contacted by the missing girl's father and was told that they had broken off their relationship. Despite a widespread police search for Gaetane, it was her father who discovered her body. Searching a favourite lovers' spot on the site of a gravel quarry near Edmunston, he found his teenage daughter dead from stab wounds.

A detailed examination of the area for forensic traces turned up two chips of green paint. The police had an eye-witness report from a farmer who had seen Gaetane accept a lift from the driver of a Maine-registered green Pontiac. Corroboration came from two other witnesses and inquiries showed that Vollman owned a 1952 green Pontiac. Inspection of the car's bodywork showed that it had lost paint in two spots for which the chips found at the gravel quarry were an exact match for shape, type and colour. Furthermore, strands of hair found in one of the dead girl's hands matched Vollman's head hair.

Vollman was tried for murder at Edmundston in November 1958. He admitted that Gaetane had been in his car and said they struggled after she refused his advances. He could not remember what happened after that and claimed loss of memory due to psychic shock. The jury convicted him of murder and he was sentenced to death. Sentence was later commuted to life imprisonment.
[*913*]

VONTSTEEN, FRANCISCUS WYNAND

Ménage à trois which ended in the carefully premeditated murder of one of the participants.

Following her divorce in 1960, twenty-three-year-old Sonjia Raffanti married François Swanepoel, a police officer. They lived in Pretoria, South Africa where, in 1967, she met Franciscus Vontsteen, an estate agent. She forged a love triangle by taking him as her lover. Vontsteen proved to be an obsessive, jealous man and Sonjia began to regret their liaison. She tried unsuccessfully to break off their relationship which only made Vontsteen more possessive. When Swanepoel's police duties took him to a posting in the northern part of the country, Sonjia stayed behind and lived with Vontsteen. She became pregnant and her husband accepted the child as his own, leaving Vontsteen consumed with jealousy.

Swanepoel returned to his wife in 1971 and, on 3 July, their house was burgled. A service pistol was reported stolen and, four days later, Sonjia claimed she was menaced by a man in the street armed with the missing pistol and threatening to kill her husband. On 2 August, Swanepoel was shot dead in his home, apparently by an intruder.

Vontsteen was questioned after it was learned he had sought help to kill Swanepoel. He admitted killing his rival because he believed that the policeman would inevitably track them down if he and Sonjia had gone off together. He had stolen the pistol and entered the house with Sonjia's connivance. He shot Swanepoel while he lay in bed beside his wife, all in the name of love. The couple were tried for murder at Pretoria and found guilty. Sonjia was given a fifteen-year sentence while Vontsteen was condemned to death. He was hanged in October 1971.
[259]

W

WADDINGHAM, DOROTHEA NANCY

Murder for gain at a nursing home was committed by administering a fatal dose of morphine.

After her husband died in the early 1930s, Dorothea Waddingham decided to establish a nursing home of her own at Nottingham. Apart from a period spent as a wardmaid at Burton upon Trent Workhouse Infirmary, she had no training to equip her for this task, although she began to use the title 'nurse'. Her partner was thirty-nine-year-old Ronald Joseph Sullivan who was also her lover.

In January 1935, she undertook to look after an elderly woman and her bed-ridden daughter. Mrs Baguley was eighty-nine years old and very frail. Her fifty-year-old daughter, Ada, weighed over 230 pounds and suffered from creeping paralysis. Neither patient could do much for themselves and so required a great deal of attention. After Waddingham complained that the fees were too low, Ada Baguley arranged to leave a property she owned to Waddingham in exchange for guaranteed care for her and her mother for the rest of their lives. Ada Baguley's new will in favour of Waddingham and Sullivan was completed on 6 May 1935.

Six days later, old Mrs Baguley died, to be followed on 11 September 1935 by her daughter. Suspicion was aroused when a letter, apparently written by Ada to the nursing home doctor, requested that her remains be cremated and that her relatives should not be informed of her death. Autopsies on both women revealed traces of unprescribed morphine in their bodies. Waddingham and Sullivan were charged with murdering Ada Baguley and appeared on trial at Nottingham. Waddingham's

defence was that she had administered morphine as instructed by the doctor; he denied giving any such instructions. Sullivan was released for lack of evidence against him while Waddingham was found guilty. Despite a recommendation to mercy, she was hanged at Winson Green Prison on 16 April 1936.
[*112, 716, 934*]

WAGNER, LOUIS

A man desperate for money went to extraordinary lengths of endurance to reach a lonely island where he murdered twice for a mere $20.

Wagner was a German immigrant to the USA who earned a meagre living as a fisherman in New Hampshire. On the night of 5 March 1873, he embarked on a robbery which required remarkable stamina. He stole a boat in Portsmouth harbour and rowed ten miles out to a rocky island called Smutty Nose. Three Norwegian families lived there who had taken him under their wing during previous hard times.

On this particular night, the women of the three families were alone as their menfolk were away fishing. Wagner entered the Hontvets' house where they were staying and attacked Karen Christenson. Her sister Maren came to her aid and struggled with the intruder. She shouted to Anethe to run for help but the young woman was immobilised by fear. Wagner killed Anethe and Karen with an axe and then ransacked the house, stealing $20. Meanwhile the survivor, Maren, ran off and hid until she was able to call assistance.

By the time help arrived and the three husbands returned, Wagner had rowed back to the mainland. He was arrested at his lodgings in Portsmouth and his life was threatened by roving mobs incensed by what had happened at Smutty Nose. Wagner was tried for murder at Alfred in New England. Several witnesses testified that Wagner was so hard up he had declared he was prepared to commit murder for money. Maren Hontvet identified him as the intruder who had killed her two friends. If further evidence was needed it could be seen on the palms of Wagner's hands which were a mass of blisters as a result of his feat of rowing twenty miles in a single night. Wagner was found guilty and sentenced to death. After several postponements of execution, he was finally hanged on 25 June 1875 at Thomaston Penitentiary.
[*740*]

WAGNER, WALTRAUD

Nurse who confessed to killing thirty-nine elderly patients at Lainz General Hospital in Vienna to relieve their pain.

Wagner was an auxiliary nurse who worked the night-shift at the hospital where most of the patients were geriatric. Her charges proved fractious, demanding and frequently ungrateful. Aided by three co-conspirators, she terminated the lives of many of them over a period of seven years.

Suspicion was aroused in February 1989 when Wagner and her colleagues were overheard in a beer-cellar openly discussing their methods of disposing of patients. The conversation was reported to the police who planted a detective masquerading as a patient in Wagner's ward. The fact that the man was in his fifties put her on her guard and after six weeks in which nothing suspicious occurred, the surveillance was called off.

When a doctor accused Wagner of having given a patient an unprescribed dose of insulin, she strongly denied it. But an autopsy proved beyond doubt that an overdose of insulin had been administered. Wagner was arrested in April 1989 and she confessed to killing thirty-nine patients in the hospital. Doctors feared that as many as one hundred might have been murdered. She later retracted her first statement, admitting only to ten killings.

It emerged during the trial of Wagner and her three accomplices in Vienna in March 1991 that they had perfected a technique of administering a fatal mouthwash. The patient was held down while one of the nurses pinched his nose and another poured water into his mouth and throat. The result was suffocation and the post-mortem discovery of water in the lungs of an elderly patient was not unusual. The nurses' code for dispatching the patients to the mortuary was to send him to the cellar. There appeared to be no gain in the killings apart from ridding their ward of old people who were a burden.

Thirty-year-old Wagner was found guilty of fifteen murders and seventeen attempted murders; she was sentenced to life imprisonment. Irene Leidolf was given life imprisonment. Stephenie Mayen received twenty years and Maria Gruber fifteen years.

[*184*]

WAINEWRIGHT, THOMAS GRIFFITHS

Although accused of being a prisoner, he was never convicted as such. Because of his artistic accomplishments, he has been compared with Lacenaire.

Wainewright was brought up by his grandfather, a London publisher, in an atmosphere of learning. Despite his potential as an artist, the eighteen-year-old youth joined the army but, having tasted the military life, decided to rejoin London's intellectual set. He mixed in the highest literary circles of the day and took up painting and writing. He also effected a flamboyant style and began living well beyond his means.

In 1821, he married Eliza Frances Ward but his new responsibilities did not curb his behaviour. He entertained his friends on a lavish scale and fell deeper into debt. By resorting to forgery, he sold £2000 worth of stock but, by 1828, was again in debt. In 1829, he and his wife moved in to his uncle's house in order to reduce his living expenses. When George Edward Griffiths died mysteriously, Wainewright benefited by inheriting his property. True to form, he quickly went through his inheritance.

In 1830, his mother-in-law, Mrs Abercromby, and her two daughters came to live with the Wainewrights. Mrs Abercromby died suddenly and her daughter, twenty-year-old Helen, whose life had been insured for a considerable sum, died soon afterwards. The insurance company declined to pay out and Wainewright sued them. When the case was finally settled, it went against Wainewright who escaped to France. He was arrested when he returned to England in 1837 and charged with forgery. He was tried at the Old Bailey in July 1837 and found guilty. His punishment was to be transported to Van Diemen's Land (modern Tasmania) for life. He spent his imprisonment painting and died a convict at the age of fifty-eight.

[*219, 578, 680, 704*]

WAINWRIGHT, HENRY

A perfect murder was betrayed by the need to exhume the body and transport it to a new hiding place.

Henry Wainwright manufactured brushes and had a shop in Whitechapel Road in London's East End. He was married but his roving eye lighted on a young milliner, Harriet Lane, for whom he provided a house in Mile End Road. She bore him two children and

Henry had a busy time commuting between his business, his wife and his mistress. When the business began to suffer, Wainwright cut the allowance he made to Harriet and then decided she was an encumbrance. In 1874, due to hard times, Harriet was moved to less expensive accommodation and, when last seen alive, was carrying her clothes to a house in Stepney.

In reply to inquiries about Harriet's disappearance, Wainwright said she had gone to Brighton. A year later, when his business collapsed, he asked a former employee, Alfred Stokes, to help him move some parcels. Stokes set out to carry two parcels to an address in the borough but found them too heavy to manage. He also complained of the smell. While Wainwright went off to fetch a cab, Stokes peeped into one of the parcels and was appalled to find himself looking at dismembered human remains. He kept his composure and, when Wainwright proceeded in the cab with the parcels, followed on foot, having enlisted the help of the police. Wainwright's destination was the home of his brother Thomas.

The parcels contained the remains of Harriet Lane which Wainwright had buried a year previously at his warehouse. He and his brother then exhumed the corpse and cut it into pieces to transport it to another hiding place. Harriet had been shot and her throat cut. The two brothers were tried at the Old Bailey in November 1875, Thomas receiving a prison sentence and Henry being condemned to death. He was publicly hanged at Newgate on 21 December 1875.

[*105, 133, 460*]

WAITE, ARTHUR WARREN

Ambitious dentist who murdered for greed, using poison and germs cultured in his laboratory.

Dr Waite had a fashionable dental practice in New York City and was an accomplished sportsman. After qualifying at Glasgow University, he worked in South Africa for a while and, in 1915, married into a wealthy American family. His wife's father, John E. Peck, was a millionaire drug manufacturer whose daughter Jane stood to inherit.

The Waites lived in New York's Upper West Side and were a popular couple. In addition to his dentistry work, Waite also carried out bacteriological research at Cornell Medical School. Mrs Peck, a lady in her seventies, visited her daughter-in-law at their Riverside

Drive home at Christmas 1915. She was taken ill during her stay and died suddenly of pneumonia on 30 January 1916. Grief-stricken by losing his wife, John Peck also visited Jane and Arthur Waite. The old man fell ill and lingered with various maladies until 12 March when he too died.

Arrangements to cremate John Peck did not go as planned, because the authorities demanded an autopsy. The true cause of the old man's death was found to be arsenic poisoning. By the time the police caught up with Waite, he had attempted to take his own life with a drug overdose. He recovered and was sent for trial. Waite admitted poisoning his mother-in-law by seeding her food with germs which he had cultured at his laboratory. He used a nasal spray loaded with tuberculosis bacteria on John Peck. He was quite open about his reasons for wanting to kill his parents-in-law – he wanted their money.

Convicted of murder, Waite's appeals on the grounds of insanity fell on stony ground and he went off to the electric chair at Sing Sing Prison on 24 May 1917.

[*641, 888*]

WALKER, G. DANIEL

Man on the run from prison who lived in a dangerous fantasy world but was sufficiently plausible to gain work as a photographer – with fatal consequences.

Hope Masters, recently separated from her husband, met Bill Ashlock, an advertising executive in Beverly Hills. The couple planned to marry and, in February 1973, spent a weekend at a ranch-house in Springfield, Ohio. Ashlock had arranged for Taylor Wright, a photographer, to call on them to take some pictures.

Wright arrived at the ranch on 24 February and stayed the night. At some point, Hope Masters was awoken by an intruder who tied her up. She called out for Bill Ashlock but was told he was dead. She recognised the intruder as Taylor Wright who threatened to kill her. He took her from the ranch-house to her parents' home in Beverly Hills and explained how he had found her tied up and Ashlock dead. When he was out of the house, the police were called and they promptly arrested Hope Masters. Taylor Wright kept up a barrage of communications with Hope by telephone and by sending her tape-recorded messages. Wright, whose real name was G. Daniel Walker, was arrested at a motel in Hollywood. He used the name Taylor Wright from credit cards which he had stolen from a salesman whom he had robbed and beaten up.

Charges against Hope Masters were dropped and Walker was sent for trial. He evidently lived in a fantasy world which he talked about in his numerous tape-recordings. In one, he spoke furtively of his intents and purposes in the USA which 'are definitely not to be known'. He had several convictions for armed robbery and, when arrested, was on the run as a prison escapee. In his car was the weapon used to kill Bill Ashlock. Walker was convicted of murder and sentenced to life imprisonment.

[*38*]

WALLACE CASE

Murder case which made legal history in 1931 and remained unsolved for fifty years.

William Herbert Wallace was an inoffensive man who worked for the Prudential Assurance Company in Liverpool. He played chess regularly at the Central Chess Club which received a telephone message for him on 19 January 1931. A caller naming himself as 'R.M. Qualtrough' said he wanted to see Wallace and asked him to call on the following evening at 7.30 at an address in Menlove Gardens East in Mossley Hill.

Thinking this concerned a prospective piece of business, Wallace duly set out to find the address. His first discovery was that no such place existed and his second, on returning home, was to find his wife dead. Julia Wallace had been beaten to death in the living-room of their home at Anfield. The poker was missing from its usual place and £4 appeared to have been stolen from a cash-box. There was no evidence of a break-in and detectives tended to believe that the Qualtrough message had been a ploy to keep Wallace away from home. An alternative possibility was that Wallace had concocted the whole thing to create an alibi. He was arrested and tried for murder.

Despite weaknesses in the prosecution case and a favourable summing-up by the judge, Wallace was found guilty at his trial at Liverpool and sentenced to death. He appealed against sentence and won a verdict which created legal history. But he continued to be dogged by vicious gossip and suffered ill-health. He died on 26 February 1933. In 1981, the murderer of Julia Wallace was named, in a Liverpool Radio City programme on the case, as

Richard Gordon Parry. Parry, an insurance agent, took his car with a bloodstained interior to a garage on the night of the murder to have it cleaned. This was reported to the police at the time but they believed Parry's alibi. After retiring, he went to live in Wales where he died in 1980.

[*355, 452, 687, 796, 940, 961, 984, 1017*]

WALTON CASE

Unsolved murder case with overtones of witchcraft and a strong suspect.

On St Valentine's Day 1945, seventy-four-year-old Charles Walton was reported missing from home by his niece. The old man was well known around the village of Lower Quinton in Warwickshire where he had spent his entire life. He did labouring jobs for local farmers such as picking crops and maintaining hedges. He had slightly odd ideas such as talking to birds and plants but was generally regarded as harmless.

A search was made of the farms and fields where he normally worked and his body was found after nightfall in one of Albert Potter's fields. The old man's throat had been cut with a sickle and his body was pinned to the ground with a hay-fork. Cuts on his arms testified to the struggle he had put up and the final indignity was to have the sign of the cross cut into his chest. News of the murder soon attracted rumours of witchcraft and the Evil Eye.

The local police called for assistance from Scotland Yard and Detective Inspector Robert Fabian was sent to investigate. He interviewed prisoners-of-war at Long Marston with no particular success and then set about questioning the population of Lower Quinton. He met a wall of silence – no one was willing to give more than a minimal response. Detectives picked up stories of a phantom black dog in the neighbourhood in 1885 which changed into a headless woman prior to a local woman's death. There was talk of ancient rituals still practised in the area and a suggestion that Walton's death had been a blood sacrifice. Fabian was unable to solve the mystery of the murder at Lower Quinton although it was believed he knew the murderer's identity. Albert Potter, the farmer for whom Walton worked, was a likely suspect. He owed money to the old man who had been pressing him for repayment.

[*613, 904*]

JULIE WARD CASE

The brutal murder of a twenty-eight-year-old British woman in one of Kenya's game parks in 1988 remains unsolved.

Julie Ward, a keen amateur photographer, had been in Africa for three months when she left Nairobi on 2 September 1988, heading for the Masai Mara game park. She was driving a Suzuki jeep and was accompanied by a marine biologist friend. When the vehicle broke down, her companion returned to Nairobi to fetch a spare part. In the meantime, Julie managed to fix the jeep and decided to drive the 200 miles back to Nairobi on her own.

When she did not appear as expected and when her father failed to contact her by telephone on 10 September, she was reported missing. Her father flew out to Kenya from England and organised a search for his daughter. On 13 September, her abandoned jeep was found bogged down in the Sand River. The letters, SOS had been marked out with mud on the vehicle's roof.

Some seven miles away at Keekorok, searchers found her hacked and burned remains. John Ward believed his daughter had been kidnapped and murdered but the Kenyan authorities disagreed, suggesting that she had been attacked by wild animals.

Julie's remains were returned to England for forensic examination and it was concluded that she had been killed with a machete knife. At the inquest on Julie Ward's death in Nairobi in August 1989, the Kenyan pathologist said his report confirming a machete attack had been altered by his superiors. It was clear there had been mistakes and interference in the investigation. In October, the Kenyan government accepted that Julie had died as the result of foul-play.

Following pressure from John Ward and with support from President Moi of Kenya, Scotland Yard detectives were asked in February 1990 to carry out an inquiry. Witnesses were re-interviewed and the evidence re-examined. At the Rangers' Camp at Makari, police found traces of hair which matched that of the murdered woman in one of the huts.

The two Rangers who had used the hut were Peter Metui Kipeen and Jonah Tajeu Magiroi, both in their late twenties. They were questioned and it was established that they had found Julie after she took a short cut in her jeep and became bogged down. It was believed they took her to the Rangers' Camp where she was probably raped and held hostage. When the men realised that a big hunt was on for the missing girl, they killed her and hacked her body to pieces to simulate an attack by wild animals.

Kipeen and Magiroi were tried for murder at Nairobi in February 1992. Kenya felt that its reputation as a responsible nation was under scrutiny. The judge criticised the local police for attempting a cover-up but accused the Scotland Yard officers for applying undue pressure to the suspects. The result was that the two Rangers were acquitted.

John Ward persisted in his quest for justice and in March 1993 the Kenya government agreed to reopen the case. In April 2004, an inquest at Ipswich re-examined the case after an inquest in Kenya and two criminal trials had failed to establish who murdered Julie Ward. The pathologist acting for the Kenyan government admitted signing false post mortem reports in response to the government's desire to portray the death as an accident and not a murder.

The Kenyan government admitted obstructing enquiries and there were rumours that a highly placed Kenyan citizen was involved in the murder and that a cover-up ensued to protect him. In February 2005, Kenya re-opened the investigation into Julie Ward's death.
[*329, 422, 1071*]

WEBER, SIMONE

Sixty-year-old widow convicted at Nancy in France of murdering her lover and cutting up his body with an electric saw.

Mme Weber was widowed in 1980 after her elderly husband of just three weeks died suddenly. She inherited his house and property amid much local rumour-mongering. In December 1983, she met forty-eight-year-old Bernard Hettier, foreman at a local factory and a well-known ladies' man. They became lovers but as she became increasingly obsessive, he tried to break off the relationship. In June 1985, Hettier disappeared together with his car and personal documents.

Simone Weber was among those questioned by the police about Hettier's disappearance. Although there was plenty of gossip, there was no evidence against her; nevertheless, the police decided to call in an examining magistrate. Judge Gilbert Thiel ordered a tap put on Weber's telephone. Investigators were intrigued by the calls she made to her sister in Cannes and references to 'Bernardette'. When detectives followed this up, 'Bernardette' proved to be a reference to Hettier's car. Weber was arrested on 8 November 1985.

Circumstantial evidence mounted steadily. In 1983, the elderly couple who lived in the ground-floor apartment of a house in Nancy used by Weber recalled seeing her taking a male companion upstairs. The man appeared to be drunk. That evening they heard a noise which they thought was a vacuum cleaner. The next day, they were amazed to see Weber bring down seventeen plastic sacks of refuse which she took away in her car.

It was known that Weber had hired an electric saw but failed to return it to the shop, explaining that it had been stolen. At this point, an earlier discovery came into sharp focus. In September 1985, a fisherman on the River Marne pulled a suitcase out of the water. The suitcase belonged to Bernard Hettier, and the torso, minus head and limbs, which it contained were probably his as well. Pathologists confirmed that the dismemberment had been done with an electric saw.

Weber was charged with murdering both Hettier and her former husband, Marcel Fixart. She spent five years in custody before finally coming to trial in 1991. At the age of sixty, 'La Sorciere', as she was called, was found guilty of murdering Hettier and sentenced to twenty years' imprisonment. She was acquitted of the other charge.

[*184*]

WEBSTER, JOHN WHITE

Regarded as one of America's classic murders, this killing on the campus attracted a great deal of public attention at the time.

Dr Webster was Professor of Chemistry and Mineralogy at Massachusetts Medical College where he was regarded as a man living beyond his means. He borrowed from all and sundry, including Dr George Parkman, a medical man who had made a great deal of money by trading in real estate. Parkman became irritated when Webster failed to repay his loan and gave him several reminders accompanied by threats to his reputation.

On 23 November 1849, Dr Parkman disappeared, an event which caused great consternation at the college. He was presumed to have been abducted and a reward was offered for information. Webster volunteered the information that he had met Parkman to repay him his some money. A college janitor had seen Parkman enter Webster's laboratory and noticed that the wall behind the assay oven was very hot. The curious janitor waited until the oven cooled down and then inspected its contents. He found part of a human leg and pelvis. Police investigators found other remains, including the late Dr Parkman's teeth.

Webster's trial at Boston was a sensational event which drew 60,000 people to the city. The discovery of his teeth in the oven confirmed the victim's identity despite Webster's contention that the remains were those of a medical school cadaver. He was found guilty and subsequently made a full confession. Parkman had gone to his room to demand repayment of the loan and an argument ensued. Webster killed him with a piece of wood and cut up his body for disposal in the assay oven. He was hanged on 30 August 1850.
[*240, 456, 892, 897, 912*]

WEBSTER, KATE

An example of a murderess who killed with unrivalled brutality.

Kate Webster was an Irish woman of low reputation who had been a prostitute and worked as a thief preying on lodging houses. From time to time, she took employment as a house servant and it was in that capacity that she came to work for an elderly widow at Richmond in Surrey in 1879. On 5 March of that year, a man walking along the river bank at Hammersmith noticed a wooden box lying on the shore. His curiosity was rewarded when he opened it to discover it packed with human remains. The grim relics were identified as Mrs Thomas, a widow who lived alone at 2 Mayfield Cottages, Richmond. When police learned that she had recently employed a servant who had been selling off the contents of her home and pretending to be Mrs Thomas, the hunt was on to find her.

A search of Mrs Thomas's cottage, in addition to turning up further human remains, produced a letter written to the old woman by Kate Webster from an address in County Wexford, Ireland. Webster was arrested there and returned to England to stand trial for murder at the Old Bailey.

Mrs Thomas had sacked Webster after she found her drunk and lost her life when she was attacked with an axe. Webster cut up her victim's body in the kitchen of the house and systematically destroyed it. Parts were burned and others were cooked in a steam boiler. It was later alleged that she sold some jars of dripping locally. The victim's head was never found and rumour had it that Webster carried it around with her in a black bag.

After being found guilty and sentenced to death, Kate Webster made a confession. She was hanged at Wandsworth Prison on 29 July 1879.
[*673, 718*]

WEIDMANN, EUGEN

The last murderer to be publicly guillotined in France.

Weidmann was born in Germany and at the age of fourteen led a gang of teenage thieves. He was sent to Canada in an attempt to guide him into better ways. He profited by learning fluent English and French but was quickly in trouble when he returned home. He served a five-year prison sentence for currency offences and, on his release in 1935, went to Paris. There he teamed up with two of his former prison inmates, Jean Blanc and Roger Million, and a girl called Colette Tricot. Their plan was to prey on strangers, rob them and, if necessary, kill them.

Joseph Couffy, driver to a visiting American, was found dead in September 1937. He had been robbed and shot in the neck. Roger Le Blond, a theatrical impresario, went missing on 17 October 1937. He was found later in an abandoned car, having been robbed and killed with a characteristic shot through the nape of the neck. On 20 November, Raymond Lesobre, an estate agent, disappeared after going to view a property with a prospective buyer. Like the others, he had been robbed and shot.

The police ran Weidmann to ground on 8 December 1937 when he was arrested after a gunfight with them at his home in St Cloud. Cars belonging to several of his victims were parked at the house. Weidmann confessed to committing several murders including Jean de Koven, an American dancer, and another woman, Jeannine Keller, whose body was found in caves at Fontainbleau. Weidmann and his accomplices were tried for murder. Two were acquitted but Weidmann and Million were convicted and sentenced to death. Only Weidmann went to the guillotine. He was executed on 18 May 1939.

[55, 376, 477]

WEST, ROSEMARY PAULINE

What the newspapers billed as the 'Crime of the Century' followed the discovery of the bodies of twelve women in Gloucester, some of whom had been buried for twenty years.

In February 1994, following a tip-off, police began digging in the garden of 25 Cromwell Street, Gloucester. The house belonged to fifty-two-year-old builder, Frederick West, who lived there with his second wife, Rosemary. Several bodies were discovered and West was charged with murdering his sixteen-year-old daughter Heather, who disappeared in 1987.

Digging was also carried out at two places where West had lived previously: 25 Midland Road, Gloucester and at Kempley near the village of Much Marcle. By the time digging was stopped several weeks later, nine bodies had been unearthed from the house and garden at Cromwell Street, two from the field at Kempley and one from the house at Midland Road. The bodies were all of young women who had disappeared during the early 1970s and included two of West's daughters.

The discoveries created a sensation in the media and comparisons were made with Rillington Place (see **Christie**) and Cranley Gardens (see **Nilsen**). Frederick West was charged with twelve murders and Rosemary West with ten, committed jointly with her husband.

In a further sensational development on 1 January 1995, Frederick West hanged himself in his cell at Winson Green Prison. Forty-one-year-old Rosemary West was accused of murdering ten young women and girls, including her own daughter and step-daughter, between April 1971 and February 1994. In November 1995, following a trial lasting thirty days at Winchester, she was found guilty on all ten counts of murder and sentenced to life imprisonment.
[*131, 645, 875, 959, 967, 968, 993*]

WHITEWAY, ALFRED CHARLES

Rapist who attacked and killed two girls with an axe.

Sixteen-year-old Barbara Songhurst and her friend, eighteen-year-old Christine Reed, went out on their bicycles on 31 May 1953. They were seen together late that evening on the towpath running alongside the River Thames. They were cycling in the direction of Teddington where they lived. When they failed to return, the police were alerted.

The next day, Barbara was found floating in the river near Richmond. She had been beaten, stabbed and raped. Detectives searching the river bank found the spot where the two girls had been attacked and, five days later, the second girl was found. She too had been stabbed and raped.

The police were already investigating a rape attack at Oxshott Heath in Surrey in which the victim had given a description of her attacker. A month after the double murder, another woman in the Oxshott area was accosted and threatened. She too provided a description. Police inquiries led them to Alfred Whiteway, a building labourer with a record of sexual offences. He admitted raping the girl at Oxshott Heath.

When he was arrested, Whiteway had hidden an axe under the seat of the patrol car in which he was taken to the police station. This was only found when the vehicle was undergoing routine cleaning. The axe was bloodstained and fitted the wounds inflicted on the two murder victims. Whiteway confessed to the killings. When he was brought to trial, he pleaded not guilty and repudiated his confession. An Old Bailey jury convicted him of murder and he was sentenced to death. Whiteway was executed at Wandsworth Prison on 22 December 1953.

[*311, 597, 921*]

WHITMAN, CHARLES

Former US Marine marksman who became a mass murderer when he indiscriminately shot dead sixteen people.

Whitman knew that he was mentally unstable. On 31 July 1966, he typed out a note in which he said, 'I am prepared to die. After my death, I wish an autopsy on me to be performed to see if there is any mental disorder.' He then shot and stabbed his mother and later that night killed his wife.

The next day, armed with a rifle, a shotgun, a revolver, two pistols and 700 rounds of ammunition, he climbed to the top of the observation tower at the Austin campus of the University of Texas. Preparing for a siege, he had also taken a supply of food and blocked off the stairs leading to the observation tower. As lunch-time approached and students began to emerge from the lecture halls and classrooms, he opened fire.

Whitman was a skilled marksman who, from a range of 300 yards, wounded forty-six people, killing sixteen of them. The campus looked like a battlefield with bodies strewn around. Initial efforts to stop the indiscriminate shooting failed, including an attempt to immobilise the gunman from a low-flying aircraft. Finally, the police mounted an assault from the stairway to the observation tower. Using overwhelming fire-power, they shot the marksman to pieces.

An autopsy was carried out on Charles Whitman and a tumour was found in the hypothalamus region of his brain. This may have borne out his own fears although doctors doubted that it accounted for his violent behaviour. Whitman was brought up in a domestic

atmosphere in which his father ill-treated his mother. After his parents separated in 1966, he began to behave strangely and sometimes violently. He complained of severe headaches which were attributed to his preoccupation with studying.
[*544, 882*]

WILDER, CHRISTOPHER BERNARD

Probable killer of at least eight women in Florida in 1984 who was shot dead while resisting arrest.

Rosario Gonzalez and Elizabeth Kenyon, two attractive young women who aspired to be models, disappeared within a week of each other in February 1984. The second girl's diary listed the names of a number of friends and acquaintances, including Christopher Wilder, a thirty-nine-year-old photographer.

In the course of a routine follow-up on contacts of the missing girls, the police discovered some startling facts about Wilder. Born in Australia, he went to live in the USA in 1969 following allegations about sex offences. He set up a successful building business in Boynton Beach, Florida and lived the life of an elegant bachelor. He owned an expensive house and a speedboat and liked to drive racing cars. It was not surprising with this lifestyle that he had little difficulty attracting the company of beautiful women.

But there was a sinister side to this extrovert personality. He was a voyeur, addicted to pornography and prone to committing sexual offences. In 1977 he was acquitted of sex charges and, in June 1980, was put on five years' probation when he pleaded guilty to raping a teenager. During a visit to Australia in 1982 he was accused of kidnapping two young girls but the authorities allowed him to return to the USA.

Detectives investigating the missing girls in Florida began to suspect Wilder when a filling-station attendant identified him from photographs as the man seen with one of them. When an article appeared in a local newspaper saying the police were looking for a racing driver, Wilder told his business partner that the police were trying to frame him.

Wilder left Boynton Beach and began a twenty-six day killing spree, moving from state to state and leaving a trail of either dead or distraught victims. A few lived to tell the tale, such as the young woman he kidnapped in Tallahassee, Florida and drove 200 miles to Bainbridge, Georgia. There he held her captive in a motel room where he repeatedly raped and abused her. She managed to escape and identify her attacker to the police.

By the time Wilder was traced to Colebrook, New Hampshire, he had kidnapped, tortured and murdered three women. He was spotted by an alert police patrol and during a struggle in which a police officer was wounded, he was shot dead. The date was Friday 13 April 1984. A revolver, handcuffs, rope and wire were found in Wilder's car.

The number of Wilder's victims is uncertain. Between 26 February and 12 April 1984, he attacked eleven women, eight of whom were either missing or murdered. The bodies of Elizabeth Kenyon and Rosario Gonzalez have never been discovered.

[*334, 581*]

WILKINS, WALTER KEANE

Elderly doctor who murdered his wife in order to acquire her assets through a poorly forged will.

Dr Wilkins and his third wife were in their late sixties and lived at Long Beach, Long Island. They returned home from a visit to New York City by train on 27 February 1919. The doctor called the police and said that they had surprised intruders in their home who had robbed them and beaten them up. Mrs Julia Wilkins, who had been severely injured by several blows to the head, died the following day. A broken hammer and length of lead pipe stained with blood were found by detectives. Dr Wilkins, although shaken up, was not injured.

After the murder, Wilkins went into hiding after paying a visit to his lawyer. He claimed to have found his wife's will, dated 1915, which left all her assets to him. This apparently superseded an earlier will, made before her marriage, in which all her assets were left to others. The difficulty was that the new will, being unwitnessed, was invalid.

Suspicions aroused by the appearance of the new will hardened when a detailed examination was made of the murder scene. Mrs Wilkins's gloves and hat, together with her false teeth, were found inside the house, and the hammer and lead pipe both carried her husband's fingerprints. Moreover, there were splashes of blood on the underside of Dr Wilkins's hat brim. When the missing doctor turned up in Baltimore on 18 March, he was arrested and charged with murder.

Dr Wilkins was convicted of murder in June 1919 but evaded execution at Sing Sing by taking his own life.

[*194*]

WILLIAMS, JOHN

Betrayed by a friend who named him as the murderer of a police officer.

On 9 October 1912, an intruder was seen in the act of entering the home of Countess Sztaray in Southcliffe Avenue, Eastbourne. The police were called and Inspector Arthur Walls arrived within minutes and saw a man attempting to break into the house from the portico above the front door. The inspector called out to him to come down. The reply came in the form of two shots which killed the policeman instantly and the intruder made off.

A few days later, a man walked into the police station at Eastbourne and told them the name of the murderer. Edgar Power named an acquaintance, John Williams, who he said had confessed the crime to him and sought help to avoid arrest. Williams had left his pregnant girl-friend, Florence Seymour, on the beach while he went off to commit the crime. On his return, they buried the gun in the shingle on the beach.

Williams was arrested in London, and Power and Seymour were detained after they had been found searching the beach for the murder weapon. Power, who had acted as an agent of the police, was released, leaving Florence to face the music. The young woman made a full statement implicating Williams who was tried for murder at Lewes Assizes in December 1912. In court, Florence repudiated her statement, saying she had done so at the behest of Power, who told her she would otherwise be charged with murder. Williams, an acknowledged cat-burglar, was found guilty although it did not prove possible to link the revolver found on the beach with the fatal shots. Williams was sentenced to death and Florence, who gave birth soon after the trial, was refused permission to marry him. On the eve of his execution, in a pathetic footnote to the story, Williams placed a piece of prison bread into his infant's hands with the words, 'Now nobody can ever say that your father has never given you anything.'

[*486, 1008, 1049*]

WILLIAMS, WAYNE B.

His conviction of the Atlanta murders caused a mixture of satisfaction and disquiet. Although the long-running series of killings stopped, there were allegations about suppressed evidence and an official cover-up.

Between July 1979 and May 1981, a series of murders in Atlanta, Georgia claimed twenty-eight lives. The victims were all young black males from poor backgrounds between the ages of seven and twenty-eight years. Their bodies were found either naked or partly clothed and cause of death was asphyxiation. Some of the victims had been thrown into the Chattahoochee River.

A climate of fear gripped Atlanta as the murder toll mounted and the police seemed powerless to halt it. The Federal Government voted extra funds to the city which was spending $250,000 a month on the investigation. Show business personalities gave their services to fund-raising events to boost the inquiries. There was a suggestion that the murders were the work of a white racist and many black Americans wore green ribbons denoting their frustration at the state authorities' failure to capture the killer.

In May 1981, a man was arrested after he had been seen near the Chattahoochee River behaving in a suspicious manner. Two days after Wayne Williams was arrested, the body of the latest murder victim was retrieved from the river. To the relief of everyone, the series of murders stopped. Williams was charged with two murders and sent for trial. He pleaded not guilty but was convicted by forensic evidence which linked him to one of the victims. Weighing heavily against him was the fact that since his arrest, the murders, which had been running at one a month, had ceased. In February 1982, he was convicted of murder and sentenced to life imprisonment.

[*31, 235, 411*]

WILSON, HOWARD

A former police officer convicted of murdering two policemen in the follow-up to a robbery in Glasgow.

Three armed men entered the premises of the Clydesdale Bank in Bridge Street, Linwood, Glasgow on 30 December 1969. They made off with over £14,000, part of which was in the form of bagged-up coins. One of the robbers was Howard Wilson who had a flat in the city. While the three men were in the process of transferring the canvas moneybags from their car to Wilson's flat, they were spotted by Inspector Andrew Hyslop who recognised Wilson.

Hyslop called for reinforcements and went up to the flat. There he saw a suitcase filled with money and demanded that his men make a search of the premises. Wilson's reply was to draw a gun and fire at Hyslop, wounding him. He fired at two other officers, killing one immediately, the second dying later from his wounds. While the other robbers fled, the remaining uninjured policeman disarmed Wilson.

As the three robbers had acted together in the knowledge that one of them had a gun, the law in Scotland regarded them as equally responsible for the killings even though only one of them had fired the shots. But the circumstances were such that the shooting occurred after the common purpose of the robbery had been fulfilled and in another place. Hence, Wilson alone was judged to be responsible.

In February 1970, Wilson was convicted of murder and sentenced to life imprisonment. His two companions were convicted of robbery. In 1972, Wilson took part in a prison riot at Peterhead and was given a further six months. He subsequently became a model prisoner and wrote a novel which won a literary award. In September 1994, the Scottish Police Federation protested at news that Wilson was to be released.

[*59, 295, 585*]

WOODFIELD, RANDALL BRENT

He cruised the 800-mile long I-5 highway in north-east America during 1980–1 looking for victims to rape and murder. He attacked fifty women, killing at least three and raping many more.

His reign of terror began in December 1980 with armed robbery accompanied by sexual assault. His first killing occurred in Salem, Oregon on 18 January 1981 at the Trans America office building. He held up two young women cleaners at gunpoint and shot them after forcing them to perform fellatio. One of the victims died but the other survived gunshot wounds in the head.

During the next few weeks, the I-5 killer struck again and again, usually late at night and targeting fast-food outlets where women might be working. The attacker frequently wore a false beard and a hooded jacket. Occasionally he had a band-aid across his nose. His fetish was oral and anal sodomy.

The police began to build up a profile of the attacker from victims' descriptions. He was a tall, athletic man in his late twenties who drove a gold-coloured Volkswagen 'Beetle'. The name, Randy Woodfield, also came up several times in accounts given to the police by girls who had been propositioned in bars.

On 3 March 1981, Woodfield was traced to Eugene, Oregon and

questioned by the police. He was held for a parole violation while further inquiries were made about him. He protested his innocence but frequently made contradictory statements. Five survivors of the I-5 killer's attacks identified Woodfield as their assailant.

Randy Woodfield had been a star football player at school but a promising career was blighted by sexual offences. He was sentenced to ten years' imprisonment in 1975 and put in a unit for sexually dangerous offenders. After his release on parole in 1979, he drifted from job to job, working mostly as a bartender in towns close to the I-5 highway. In his normal relationships, he tended to gravitate to young girls whom he could impress with his good looks and powerful physique, whereas more mature women saw him as shallow.

He was tried at Salem for murder, attempted murder and sodomy in June 1981. The survivor left for dead in the attack in the Trans America building in January identified him in court. He was found guilty on all three counts and given a sentence of life imprisonment plus ninety years.

Woodfield spends his time in Oregon State Penitentiary answering letters from his female admirers who send money, photographs and offers of marriage.

[*877*]

WREN CASE

Unsolved murder in which the victim, who lingered for several days after being attacked, plainly knew the identity of her attacker.

Eighty-two-year-old Miss Margery Wren kept a sweetshop at Ramsgate in Kent. On the evening of 20 September 1930, a young girl intent on buying some confectionery was surprised to find the door to the shop locked. After several loud knocks, Miss Wren opened the door. She was bleeding from injuries to her face. When the child told her parents what had happened, they went to the shop to offer help.

The elderly shopkeeper said she had tripped over a pair of fire-tongs which were seen lying in a pool of blood on the floor. When she was examined by a doctor, she was found to have several lacerations and bruises on the head and face and there were signs of an attempt at strangulation. Miss Wren made a number of statements which were confused and rambling. She repeated her story about falling over the fire-tongs but then said she had been attacked by a man in her shop.

The second story seemed the more likely and from further statements it seemed clear that she knew the identity of her assailant. In her last hours she spoke about a man whom she did not wish to suffer, saying 'He must bear his sins.' She also mentioned a number of names which featured in the police investigation of her murder but no charges were made.

The old lady's murder remains a mystery, the solution to which died with her.

[5, 485]

WRIGHT, KENNETH RAY

Convicted of a murder which involved mutilating the victim's body with razor-blades.

Eight-year-old Camellia Jo Hand failed to return home after school on 10 April 1969. Her parents, who lived in Ocoee in Florida, reported her missing and the police mounted an immediate search for the child. The family dog was also missing.

Several witnesses had seen a blue car in the neighbourhood and noticed it contained a girl and a dog. Apart from the colour of the car, the only other identifying feature were the figures 1 and 9 on the licence plate. Two days later, the body of the dog was found in woods outside the town and, close by, searchers discovered the remains of the girl in a shallow grave. The child had been sexually attacked and her body badly mutilated. Some razor-blades were found near the crime scene.

All police officers in the district were on the look-out for a blue car with the figures 1 and 9 on its licence plate. On 16 April, an alert deputy sheriff spotted a Pontiac in a car-park in the centre of Ocoee. Its licence plate included the figures which formed part of the description of the wanted vehicle and the driver was questioned. He was Kenneth Ray Wright, a painter, who admitted driving out to a refuse dump which happened to be near the crime scene. When his fingerprints were matched to impressions found on the razor-blades, the police knew they had their man.

Wright was tried for murder and found guilty on the strength of the fingerprint evidence. He maintained his innocence of the crime but the jury found him guilty and he was sentenced to life imprisonment.

[779]

WUORNOS, AILEEN CAROL (LEE)

Holds the rare distinction of being a convicted female serial killer after admitting six murders in Florida in 1990.

Florida police suspected they were searching for a woman hitch-hiker after a string of killings in which the naked bodies of men known to have been driving alone were found dead at locations close to main highways. The first such victim was fifty-one-year-old Richard Mallory, an electronics retailer from Clearwater, who went missing in November 1989. His body was found two weeks later and his abandoned car was also retrieved.

In spring 1990, there were two killings in May followed by others in June, July, September and November. In each case, the victim was a middle-aged white male travelling alone. The police formed the impression that they had stopped to pick up a female hitch-hiker who murdered them cold-bloodedly with a .22 weapon. The killer's practice of using her victim's car for short periods and of retaining stolen articles eventually helped to identify Lee Wuornos as a suspect.

She was put under surveillance on 8 January 1991 and arrested the following day. She confessed to six murders which she said had been committed in self-defence against men intent on raping her. Some of her victims' property was discovered in a rented locker at a warehouse in Daytona.

Lee Wuornos had experienced a traumatic childhood, being abandoned by her mother and brought up by her grandfather, an alcoholic who ill-treated her. She resorted to prostitution before reaching her teenage years, was pregnant at fourteen and homeless at fifteen. At the age of twenty, she married a man three times her age – the relationship lasted a month.

She had a woman lover and told friends that their relationship was like Bonnie and Clyde, 'making money and doing society a favour'. At the age of thirty-three, frequently drunk, Wuornos roamed Florida's highways selling sex and stealing as a way of living. At some point, she became a huntress and used sex to lure her victims to remote locations where she shot them dead.

When she was medically examined in prison, she was found incompetent although not insane. Doctors described her as having a borderline personality. At her trial in May 1992, she was convicted of murder and sentenced to death. Wuornos, aged forty-six, was executed by lethal injection at Florida State Prison on 9

October 2002, having served twelve years on Death Row. She became the tenth woman to be executed in the USA since capital punishment was resumed in 1977.
[*511, 774, 808, 1013*]

WYNEKOOP, Dr ALICE

When her daughter-in-law was found dead in her surgery, the doctor confessed to killing her accidentally and feigning her death at the hands of an intruder.

Sixty-two-year-old Alice Wynekoop was a respected Chicago physician with consulting rooms at 3406 W Monroe Street. On 21 November 1933, she telephoned her daughter, Catherine, also a doctor, at Cook County Hospital and told her that her brother's wife, Rheta, had been shot. The police were called and, when they entered Dr Wynekoop's basement surgery, saw a young woman lying on the operating table. Eighteen-year-old Rheta had been shot in the chest with a .32 Smith & Wesson revolver which was on a nearby table. The girl also had staining around her mouth. Dr Wynekoop said, 'It must have been a burglar.'

Rheta was married to Earle Wynekoop and, because he was out of work, the couple lodged with his mother. Dr Wynekoop was suspected of murder and was subjected to intense questioning. The angle at which the bullet had entered Rheta's body ruled out suicide and was later explained by Dr Wynekoop in her confession. She said she was examining the girl who complained of a pain in her side and administered a chloroform anaesthetic to relieve the discomfort. At this point, the girl stopped breathing and could not be revived. This was when Dr Wynekoop decided to shoot her.

Dr Wynekoop was tried for murder at Chicago in 1934 in one of that city's most celebrated homicide cases. It was widely believed that she had killed the girl to relieve her son of a burdensome wife. Others suggested she killed for the insurance money, while the defence maintained that Rheta had been murdered by an intruder. Despite her advanced years and undoubted reputation, Dr Wynekoop was convicted and sentenced to twenty-five years' imprisonment. She was paroled in 1949 and died in 1951.
[*1012*]

Y

YANG ZINHAI

Police in eastern China had been searching for three years for the perpetrator of a wave of rapes and murders in four provinces. The killings were characterised by a high level of brutality, usually involving a blunt instrument and often wiping out entire families.

Investigators in Cangzhou City made a breakthrough in November 2003 when they arrested Yang Zinhai, a migrant worker recognised by an alert police officer from descriptions of a man seen at several of the crime scenes. Yang, who had a previous conviction for rape and theft, admitted the crimes. His confession was validated by matching his DNA with that found at several of the crime scenes.

There were reports that Yang was angry at being rejected by his girl-friend but a contrary view was that he simply enjoyed violence and killing. He went on trial at Luche in Henan province on 2 February 2004 charged with sixty-seven murders and twenty-three rapes. Justice was swiftly dispensed and, amazingly, the hearing which was held behind closed doors, lasted only one hour. No details were released about the victims or their identities. It was made known that Yang used a bicycle to go about his murderous business and, curiously, that he usually wore shoes two sizes too large for his feet in order not to leave any accurate footprint evidence. He was convicted and sentenced to death.

After the trial, Yang was interviewed on Chinese television. He offered no real explanation of his motive for his killing spree only saying, 'When I killed people, I had a desire to kill more. This inspired me to kill more. I don't care whether they deserve to live or not. It is none of my concern. I have no desire to be part of society.

Society is not my concern'. He waived his right to appeal against sentence and met his end at the hands of the public executioner two weeks after his trial on 14 February 2004.
[442]

YOUNG, GRAHAM

Self-confessed poisoner who was released after nine years in Broadmoor Hospital and went on to kill twice, using thallium.

After his release, Young went to work for Hadland's, a photographic instruments firm in Hertfordshire where his duties included making the tea. In June 1971, one of his colleagues, Bob Egle, aged sixty, was suddenly taken ill at work. He was treated for peripheral neuritis but his condition deteriorated and he died in hospital.

Egle's death came after a strange illness had stricken many of Hadland's employees. No one seemed to be able to pinpoint the cause and the affliction was simply attributed to 'The Bug'. In October 1971, another employee succumbed when Fred Biggs died after three weeks of extreme suffering. Graham Young took a pathological interest in Biggs's illness and impressed his fellow workers with his medical knowledge.

When two other workers experienced stomach pains, numbness in their limbs and loss of hair, suspicion was directed at their tea which they said tasted bitter. Chemicals used in photographic processing were suspected and the factory decided to call in a medical team to carry out checks. The doctor leading the team called the staff together to answer questions. Twenty-three-year-old Graham Young, the tea-boy, was the most persistent questioner. He asked if the doctor thought the symptoms were consistent with thallium poisoning. Young was regarded as a know-all but the medical team ascertained that thallium was not used in the factory.

Young had succeeded in attracting considerable attention to himself and his firm told the police of their suspicions. When his background was investigated, his past history of poisoning his stepmother and attempting to poison two other members of his family was revealed. When he was arrested, he was found to be carrying a lethal dose of thallium. His diary contained the names of the victims he had claimed and those he intended to poison. Eventually he admitted that he had poisoned six persons and boasted that he could have killed others if he wished, 'but I allowed them to live,' he said.

Young was tried at St Albans in July 1972. Despite denying that he had killed anyone and claiming that the notes in his diary were for a novel, the jury found him guilty and he was sentenced to life imprisonment. On 2 August 1990, he was found unconscious in his cell at Parkhurst Prison and failed to respond to attempts to revive him. Newspapers reported that the multiple poisoner who had at one time experimented by poisoning pet animals had died of a heart attack.
[*427, 1028*]

YUKL, CHARLES

Sexually motivated killer who killed once and served a short term in prison before being released to kill again.

Yukl advertised his services as a music teacher in the New York City newspapers. He taught his pupils in his apartment while his wife was out at work. In August 1966, he gave voice training to a twenty-six-year-old secretary, Suzanne Reynolds, who had ambitions to be a performer. During a lesson in October, Yukl strangled his pupil and used a razor-blade to mutilate her body. After dumping her corpse, he reported her missing to the police but neglected to remove incriminating bloodstains from his clothing.

As a result of a plea bargain, Yukl made a confession and accepted a charge of manslaughter. He was given a prison sentence of which he served only five years before being paroled in 1973. He took up life where he had left off and after failing at various jobs, began posing as a film producer. In 1974 he placed newspaper advertisements inviting aspiring actresses for interview. He wined and dined several girls and enjoyed the publicity this created.

What began as a flight of fancy took a more sinister turn when, on 19 August 1974, he killed one of his would-be actresses. He strangled Karen Schlegel and mutilated her with a razor-blade. Her body was found the following day on the roof of the apartment building in which Yukl lived with his wife. The police were not slow to compare this killing with the death of the young woman in 1966. On this occasion, Yukl was reluctant to confess but, in due course, he did so. Charles Yukl, the son of an immigrant Czechoslovakian musician, was convicted of murder and sentenced to fifteen years' imprisonment. On 21 August 1982, he hanged himself in prison.
[*902*]

Z

ZEBRA KILLINGS

The citizens of San Francisco were terrorised by a series of killings in 1973–4 in which white victims were targeted on the streets by a black gang. During a reign of terror lasting six months, fifteen victims of both sexes were shot dead and eight others were wounded. On 28 January 1974, the roaming assassins attacked five people, killing four and wounding another.

A special police task-force was set up to hunt down the 'Zebra Killers', as they had been branded by the newspapers. The police suspected that the killers might be militant Black Muslims but the breakthrough came when one of the gang, Anthony Cornelius Harris, decided to accept immunity from prosecution in return for information. On 1 May 1974, acting on information received, police officers stormed an apartment block in the city and arrested seven men. Among them were Larry Green, Jesse Cook, Manuel Moore and J.C. Simon.

These four men were part of a group dedicated to eliminating the 'White Devils', as they termed the white population. They were recruited as assassins and directed to kill white victims. They professed to believe that killing whites could be excused because they were evil individuals. Once a Black Muslim had killed fourteen adults or four children, he qualified as a 'Death Angel' and was guaranteed free passage to the Holy City of Mohammed.

The trial of the four men lasted over a year and was the longest in California's history. They were all found guilty and sentenced to life imprisonment. The murders committed on 28 January had been inspired by watching the boxing match between Joe Frazier

and Mohammed Ali. This fuelled the public debate about the part played by violence shown in films and television inspiring violence in the streets.
[*387, 443*]

ZIEGLER, WILLIAM THOMAS Jr.

Forensic evidence showed that the killing of three members of the Ziegler family had been carried out by one of their own who turned his gun on himself to divert suspicion.

William Ziegler and his son Tommy ran a furniture store at Winter Garden in Orange County, Florida. On the evening of 24 December 1975, Tommy Ziegler telephoned the police saying, 'I think there's trouble . . . I'm at the store. I've been shot.'

Officers who rushed to the store found Ziegler with gunshot wounds in the abdomen surrounded by a scene of carnage. Four people lay dead in the furniture showroom, including his mother and father, his wife Eunice and a man named Charlie Mays who was a customer. Tommy Ziegler said he left the store with one of his staff, Ed Williams, to buy some Christmas drinks. When they returned, he claimed he was knocked unconscious and knew nothing about the shooting.

Williams had disappeared but when he eventually turned up, gave a different account of what had happened. He said that Tommy Ziegler had threatened him with a gun and he fled. Ziegler was charged with murder when it was learned that his unhappy wife planned to leave him and go away with her parents. He had also recently insured her life for over half a million dollars.

Forensic scientists showed that all the shots fired in the furniture showroom had come from guns belonging to him and that, in all probability, he had then inflicted a wound on himself. A trial jury convicted Ziegler on two counts of murder in the first degree and two in the second degree. While the jury recommended life imprisonment, the judge imposed the death sentence.
[*288, 573*]

ZODIAC MURDERS

Unsolved series of murders in California in 1969 in which five people were killed and two others wounded. The murders earned their name as the result of letters sent to San Francisco newspapers from 'The Zodiac' and signed with a cross and circle motif.

Zodiac Murders

Two young people were shot dead in their cars parked in a lovers' lane on 20 December 1968. On 5 July 1969, a man called the police to report an as yet undiscovered double murder. The police found the victims exactly as the caller had described. A girl was dead but her escort survived. On 27 September 1969, the police in Napa Valley received a call advising them of a double murder. A young couple had been stabbed but again one of them survived to tell the police they had been attacked by a man wearing a hood with the sign of the zodiac on it.

On 11 October a taxi-driver was shot dead and, the next day, part of the victim's shirt was sent to a San Francisco newspaper. Ten days later, a man claiming to be the Zodiac Killer called the Oakland police and offered to surrender himself provided he was represented by a famous lawyer. Melvin Belli, a well-known defence attorney, took up the challenge and received numerous telephone calls from a man calling himself the Zodiac Killer. The caller was disturbed and complained of headaches, saying, 'I've got to kill.'

This promising contact was broken off, but in 1971 the Zodiac Killer began writing to the newspapers again and this continued until 1974 when he issued threats and claimed to have killed thirty-seven times. A computer analysis of homicide patterns in the USA in 1975 confirmed that the killer might have killed forty times in locations which formed a huge letter 'Z' when plotted on a map covering several states. Contact with the killer faded and the police concluded that he had either died or been confined in some way, perhaps in a mental hospital.

[*364, 505, 746*]

SELECT BIBLIOGRAPHY

1. Abbott, Jack Henry, *In the Belly of the Beast*, London (1982)
2. ——, and Zack, Naomi, *My Return*, Buffalo, USA (1987)
3. Abinger, Edward, *Forty Years at the Bar*, London (1930)
4. Abrahamsen, David, *Confessions of Son of Sam*, New York (1985)
5. Adam, Hargrave Lee, *Murder Most Mysterious*, London (1932)
6. ——, (ed.), *Trial of George Chapman*, NBT, Edinburgh (1930)
7. ——, (ed.), *Trial of Dr Lamson*, NBT, Edinburgh (1912)
8. Alcorn, Robert Haydn, *The Count of Gramercy Park*, London (1955)
9. Alexander, Shana, *Nutcracker*, New York (1985)
10. ——, *Very Much a Lady*, Boston (1983)
11. Allen, William, *Starkweather*, Boston (1976)
12. Alpert, Michael, *London 1849*, London (2004)
13. Altick, Richard T., *Victorian Studies in Scarlet*, London (1970)
14. Altman, Jack and Ziporyn, Marvin, *Born to Raise Hell*, New York (1967)
15. Anderson, Christopher P., *The Serpent's Tooth*, New York (1988)
16. Andrews, Allen, *Intensive Inquiries*, London (1973)
17. Angelella, Michael, *Trail of Blood*, New York (1979)
18. Anspacher, Carolyn, *The Acid Test*, London (1965)
19. Anthony-Woods, Paul, *Ed Gein – Psycho*, London (1992)
20. Appleton, Arthur, *Mary Ann Cotton*, London (1973)
21. Archer, Fred, *Killers in the Clear*, London (1971)
22. Archibald, Bill, *The Bradley Case*, Sydney (1961)
23. Armbrister, Trevor, *Act of Vengeance*, London (1976)
24. Askill, John and Sharpe, Martyn, *Angel of Death*, London (1993)
25. Atkins, Susan, *Child of Satan – Child of God*, New York (1978)
26. Atlay, J.B., *Famous Trials*, London (1899)
27. Babyak, Jolene, *Bird Man*, California, USA (1994)
28. Bailey, Guy, *The Fatal Chance*, London (1969)
29. Bakos, Susan Crain, *Appointment for Murder*, New York (1989)
30. Balchin, Nigel, *The Anatomy of Villainy*, London (1950)
31. Baldwin, James, *The Evidence of Things Not Seen*, New York (1985)
32. Ballantine, Serjeant, *Some Experiences of a Barrister's Life*, London (1883)
33. Banks, Harold K., *The Strangler!*, New York (1967)
34. Bardens, D., *The Ladykiller*, London (1972)
35. Barfield, Velma, *Woman on Death Row*, Minneapolis, USA (1985)
36. Barker, Dudley, *Lord Darling's Famous Cases*, London (1936)
37. ——, *Palmer, The Rugeley Poisoner*, London (1935)
38. Barthel, Joan, *A Death in California*, New York (1981)

39. Barzun, J., *Burke and Hare: The Resurrection Men*, New Jersey USA (1974)
40. Baumann, Ed, *Step into my Parlor*, Chicago USA,(1991)
41. Beadle, William, *The Killing of Leon Beron*, Dagenham (1995)
42. ——, *Wrongly Hanged!*, Dagenham (1995)
43. Beales, Martin, *Dead Not Buried*, London (1995)
44. Beavan, Colin, *Fingerprints*, New York (2001)
45. Beaver, Ninette, Ripley, B.K. and Trese, Patrick, *Caril*, Philadelphia USA (1974)
46. Bechhofer Roberts, C.E. (ed.), *Trial of Reginald Sidney Buckfield*, London (1944)
47. ——, *The New World of Crime*, London (1933)
48. ——, *The Trial of Harry Dobkin*, London (1944)
49. ——, *Sir Travers Humphreys, His Career and Cases*, London (1936)
50. ——, *The Trial of Jones and Hulten*, London (1945)
51. ——, *Trial of Ley and Smith*, London (1947)
52. Bedford, Sybille, *The Best We Can Do*, London (1958)
53. Begg, Paul, *Jack the Ripper: The Facts*, London (2004)
54. Begg, Paul, Fido, Martin and Skinner, Keith, *The Jack the Ripper A to Z*, London (1991)
55. Belin, Jean, *My Work at the Sûreté*, London (1950)
56. Bell, Arthur, *Kings Don't Mean a Thing*, New York (1978)
57. Bell, David, *Nottinghamshire Murder Casebook*, Newbury (1997)
58. Belliveau, *John Edward: The Coffin Murder Case*, Toronto (1956)
59. Beltrami, Joseph, *The Defender*, Edinburgh (1980)
60. Benford, Timothy B. and Johnson, James R., *Righteous Carnage*, New York (1991)
61. Bennett, Benjamin, *Famous South African Murders*, London (1938)
62. ——, *The Amazing Case of the Baron von Schauroth*, Cape Town (1966)
63. ——, *The Cohen Case*, Cape Town (1971)
64. ——, *The Evil That Men Do*, Cape Town (1950)
65. ——, *The Noose Tightens*, Cape Town (1974)
66. ——, *Up for Murder*, London (1974)
67. ——, *Was Justice Done?*, Cape Town (1975)
68. Berenson, Edward, *The Trial of Madame Caillaux*, Los Angeles (1992)
69. Berg, Karl, *The Sadist*, London (1945)
70. Berrett, James, *When I Was at Scotland Yard*, London (1932)
71. Berry-Dee, Christopher and Odell, Robin, *A Question of Evidence*, London (1991)
72. ——, *Ladykiller*, London (1992)
73. ——, *The Long Drop*, London (1993)
74. Beveridge, Peter, *Inside the CID*, London (1957)
75. Bilton, Michael, *Wicked Beyond Belief*, London (2003)
76. Bingham, John, *The Hunting Down of Peter Manuel*, London (1973)
77. Bingham, Mike, *Suddenly One Sunday*, Sydney (1996)
78. Biondi, Ray and Hecox, Walt, *The Dracula Killer*, New York (1992)
79. Bird, Heather, *Not Above the Law*, Toronto (1985)
80. Birmingham, George A., *Murder Most Foul*, London (1929)
81. Bishop, Jim, *The Murder Trial of Judge Peel*, New York (1963)
82. Black, David, *Murder at the Met*, New York (1986)

83. Blackburn, Estelle, *Broken Lives*, Western Australia (1998)
84. Blashfield, Jean F., *Why They Killed*, New York (1990)
85. Bledsoe, Jerry, *Bitter Blood*, New York (1988)
86. ——, *Death Sentence*, New York (1998)
87. Block, Eugene, *The Chemist of Crime*, London (1959)
88. Blom-Cooper, Louis, *The A6 Murder*, Middlesex (1963)
89. Blundell, R.H. and Seaton, R.E., *Trial of Jean Pierre Vaquier*, Edinburgh (1929)
90. Blundell, R.H. and Wilson, G.H. (eds), *Trial of Buck Ruxton*, Edinburgh (1937)
91. Blythe, H., *Madeleine Smith*, London (1975)
92. Bocca, Geoffrey, *The Life and Death of Sir Harry Oakes*, London (1959)
93. Bogdanovitch, Peter, *The Killing of the Unicorn*, New York (1984)
94. Bolitho, William, *Murder for Profit*, London (1926)
95. Bommersbach, Jana, *The Trunk Murderess, Winnie Ruth Judd*, New York (1992)
96. Borowitz, Albert, *The Woman Who Murdered Black Satin*, Ohio, USA (1981)
97. Boswell, Charles and Thompson, Lewis, *The Carlyle Harris Case*, New York (1961)
98. ——, *The Girl in Lovers' Lane*, London (1953)
99. ——, *The Girls in Nightmare House*, New York (1955)
100. ——, *The Girl in the Stateroom*, New York (1951)
101. Boucher, Anthony, *The Quality of Murder*, New York (1962)
102. Bourke, J.P. and Sonenberg, D.S., *Insanity and Injustice*, Queensland (1969)
103. Boutet, Frederic, *International Criminals Past and Present*, London (n.d.)
104. Bowen-Rowlands, Ernest, *In the Light of the Law*, London (1931)
105. ——, *Seventy-Two Years at the Bar*, London (1924)
106. Bowker, A.E., *Behind the Bar*, London (1947)
107. Brady, Ian, *The Gates of Janus*, Los Angeles (2001)
108. Brand, Christianna, *Heaven Knows Who*, London (1960)
109. Brandon, Craig, *Murder in the Adirondacks*, New York (1986)
110. Brennan, T.C., *The Gun Alley Tragedy*, Melbourne (1922)
111. Breo, Ferris L. and Martin, William J., *The Crime of the Century*, New York (1993)
112. Bresler, Fenton, *Lord Goddard*, London (1977)
113. ——, *Scales of Justice*, London (1973)
114. ——, *The Murder of John Lennon*, London (1989)
115. Brice, A.H.M., *Look Upon The Prisoner*, London (1933)
116. Briffett, David, *The Acid Bath Murders*, West Sussex (1988)
117. Broad, Lewis, *The Innocence of Edith Thompson*, London (1952)
118. Brock, Sydney, *The Life and Death of Neville George Heath*, London (1947)
119. Brown, Stuart, *A Man Named Tony*, New York (1976)
120. Brown, Tim and Cheston, Paul, *Brothers in Blood*, London (1994)
121. Brown, Wenzell, *Introduction to Murder*, London (1953)
122. Browne, Douglas G. and Brock, Alan A., *Fingerprints: Fifty Years of Scientific Crime Detection*, London (1953)
123. Browne, Douglas G. and Tullett, E.V., *Sir Bernard Spilsbury: His Life and Cases*, London (1951)

124. Browne, G. Lathom and Stewart, C.G., *Trials for Murder by Poisoning*, London (1883)
125. Brownell, Joseph W. and Enos, Patricia W., *Adirondack Tragedy*, New York (2003)
126. Brussel, James A., *Casebook of a Crime Psychologist*, New York (1968)
127. Buchanan, A.J. (ed.), *The Trial of Ronald Geeves Griggs*, Sydney (1930)
128. Buck, Paul, *The Honeymoon Killers*, London (1970)
129. Bugliosi, Vincent and Gentry, Kurt, *The Manson Murders*, London (1974)
130. Bugliosi, Vincent and Hurwitz, Ken, *Till Death Us Do Part*, New York (1978)
131. Burn, Gordon, *Happy Like Murderers*, London (1998)
132. ——, *Somebody's Husband, Somebody's Son*, London (1984)
133. Burnaby, Evelyn, *Memories of Famous Trials*, London (1947)
134. Burt, Leonard, *Commander Burt of Scotland Yard*, London (1959)
135. Busch, Francis X., *Guilty or Not Guilty?*, London (1957)
136. ——, *They Escaped the Hangman*, London (1957)
137. Butler, Geoffrey L., *Madeleine Smith*, London (1935)
138. Butler, Ivan (ed.), *Trial of Brian Donald Hume*, Newton Abbott (1976)
139. Butler, Robert A., *'So They Framed Stephenson'*, Indiana, USA (1940)
140. Byrne, Gerald, *Borstal Boy: The Uncensored Story of Neville Heath*, London (n.d)
141. ——, *John George Haigh: Acid Bath Killer*, London (n.d.)
142. Cacopardo, J. Jerry with Weldon, Don, *Show me a Miracle*, London (1962)
143. Caffell, Colin, *In Search of the Rainbow's End*, London (1994)
144. Cahill, Tim, *Buried Dreams*, New York (1986)
145. Calissi, Ronald E., *Counterpoint*, New Jersey (1972)
146. Call, Max, *Hand of Death*, Louisiana, USA (1985)
147. Calohan, George H., *My Search for the 'Son of Sam'*, California, USA (2001)
148. Camp, John, *One Hundred Years of Medical Murder*, London (1982)
149. Campbell, Marjorie Freeman, *A Century of Crime*, Toronto (1970)
150. ——, *Torso*, Toronto (1974)
151. Camps, Frances E., *Medical and Scientific Investigation in the Christie Case*, London (1953)
152. Cannell, J.C., *New Light on the Rouse Case*, London (1932)
153. ——, *When Fleet Street Calls*, London (1932)
154. Canter, David, *Criminal Shadows*, London (1994)
155. Cantillon, Richard H., *In Defence of the Fox*, Atlanta, USA (1972)
156. Capon, P., *The Great Yarmouth Mystery*, London (1965)
157. Capote, Truman, *In Cold Blood*, London (1966)
158. Capstick, John, *Given in Evidence*, London (1960)
159. Carey, Arthur, *On the Track of Murder*, London (1930)
160. Carlin, Francis, *Reminiscences of an ex-detective*, London (n.d.)
161. Carlo, Philip, *The Night Stalker*, New York (1996)
162. Carpozi, George, *Ordeal by Trial*, New York (1972)
163. ——, *Son of Sam*, New York (1977)
164. ——, *The Chicago Nurse Murders*, New York (1967)
165. Carrere, Emmanuel, *The Adversary*, London (2000)
166. Carswell, Donald (ed.), *Trial of Ronald True*, NBT Edinburgh (1925)

167. Casswell, J.D., *A Lance for Liberty*, London (1961)
168. Castles, Alex, *The Shark Arm Case*, South Australia (1995)
169. Cecil, Henry (ed.), *Trial of Walter Graham Rowland*, Newton Abbott (1975)
170. Chamberlain, Sir Roderic, *Stuart Affair*, London (1973)
171. Chandler, Geoffrey, *So You Think I Did It?*, Melbourne (1969)
172. Chapman, Ivan, *Leonski – The Brownout Strangler*, Sydney (1982)
173. Chapman, Eunice, *Presumed Dead*, London (1992)
174. Chaytor, Rod, *Murder With Menaces*, London (1993)
175. Cheney, Margaret, *The Co-ed Killer*, New York (1976)
176. Cherrill, Fred, *Cherrill of the Yard*, London (1954)
177. Christie, Trevor L., *Etched in Arsenic*, London (1948)
178. Church, Robert, *More Murder in East Anglia*, London (1990)
179. ——, *'Well Done Boys'*, London (1996)
180. Clark, Geoffrey (ed.), *Trial of James Camb*, NBT, Edinburgh (1948)
181. Clark, Hector with Johnstone, David, *Fear the Stranger*, Edinburgh (1994)
182. Clark, Tim and Penycate, John, *Psychopath*, London (1976)
183. Clarkson, Wensley, *Doctors Who Kill*, London (2000)
184. ——, *Like a Woman Scorned*, London (1992)
185. Clegg, Eric, *Return Your Verdict*, Sydney (1965)
186. Clune, Frank, *The Demon Killer*, Sydney (n.d.)
187. ——, *The Blue Mountains Murderer*, London (1973)
188. Cobb, Christopher and Avery, Bob, *Rape of a Normal Mind*, Ontario (1977)
189. Cobb, Belton, *Murdered on Duty*, London (1961)
190. Coe, S.J., *Down Murder Lane*, London (1945)
191. Cohen, Sam D., *One Hundred True Crime Stories*, Cleveland, USA (1946)
192. Coleman, Jonathan, *At Mother's Request*, New York (1985)
193. Coleman, Robert, *The Pyjama Girl*, Melbourne (1978)
194. Collins, Ted (ed.), *New York Murders*, New York (1944)
195. Condon, John F., *Jafsie Tells All!*, New York (1936)
196. Conrad, Barnaby, *A Revolting Transaction*, New York (1983)
197. Conradi, Peter, *The Red Ripper*, London (1992)
198. Constantine-Quinn, M., *Doctor Crippen*, London (1935)
199. Cook, Fred J., *The Girl in the Death Cell*, New York (n.d.)
200. Cook, Judith, *Who Killed Hilda Murrell?*, London (1985)
201. Cooper, Cynthia L. and Sheppard, Sam Reese, *Mockery of Justice*, Boston (1995)
202. Cooper, George, *Poison Widows*, New York (1999)
203. Cooper, William, *Shall We Ever Know?*, London (1971)
204. Copeland, James, *The Butler*, London (1981)
205. Coppolino, Carl A., *The Crime That Never Was*, Tampa (1980)
206. Cornish, G.W., *Cornish of the Yard*, London (1935)
207. Costopoulos, William C., *Principal Suspect*, Philadelphia (1996)
208. Cottrell, Richard, *Blood on Their Hands*, London (1987)
209. Coulter, Jack, *With Malice Aforethought*, Perth (1982)
210. Cox, Mike, *The Confessions of Henry Lee Lucas*, New York (1991)
211. Cray, Ed, *Burden of Proof*, New York (1973)

212. Criminological Studies, *The Case of Thompson and Bywaters*, London (n.d.)
213. Critchley, Macdonald (ed.), *Trial of August Sangret*, NBT, Edinburgh (1959)
214. ——, *Trial of Neville George Cleveley Heath*, NBT, Edinburgh (1951)
215. Crocker, Art (ed.), *Celebrity Murders*, New York (1990)
216. Crow, Alan and Samson, Peter, *Bible John*, Glasgow (n.d.)
217. Cullen, Robert, *The Killer Department*, London (1993)
218. Cullen, Tom, *Crippen: The Mild Murderer*, Boston (1977)
219. Curling, Jonathan, *Janus Weathercock*, London (1938)
220. Curtin, Philip, *Noted Murder Mysteries*, London (1914)
221. Damio, Ward, *Urge to Kill*, New York (1974)
222. David, Jay, *The Scarsdale Murder*, New York (1980)
223. Davies, Nick, *Murder on Ward Four*, London (1993)
224. Deale, Kenneth E.L., *Beyond Any Reasonable Doubt*, Dublin (1971)
225. ——, *Memorable Irish Trials*, London (1960)
226. Dearden, Harold, *Aspects of Murder*, London (1951)
227. ——, *Death Under the Microscope*, London (1934)
228. Deeley, Peter, *The Manhunters*, London (1970)
229. Deeley, Peter and Walker, C., *Murder in the Fourth Estate*, London (1971)
230. Deford, Miriam Allen, *The Real Bonnie and Clyde*, London (1968)
231. De Marigny, Alfred, *More Devil Than Saint*, New York (1946)
232. De Marigny, Alfred with Herksowitz, Mickey, *A Conspiracy of Crowns*, London (1990)
233. D'enno, Douglas, *Foul Deeds and Suspicious Deaths Around Brighton*, Barnsley (2004)
234. Desario, Jack P. and Mason, William D., *Dr Sam Sheppard on Trial*, Ohio (2003)
235. Dettlinger, Chet with Prugh, Jeff, *The List*, Atlanta (1983)
236. Deverell, William, *Fatal Cruise*, Toronto (1991)
237. Devlin, Patrick, *Easing the Passing*, London (1985)
238. Dickson, Grierson, *Murder by Numbers*, London (1958)
239. Dilnot, George, *Celebrated Crimes* (1925)
240. ——, *Trial of Professor John W. Webster*, London (1928)
241. Dinnerstein, Leonard, *The Leo Frank Case*, New York (1968)
242. Dobkins, Dwight J. and Hendricks, J., *Winnie Ruth Judd: The Trunk Murders*, New York (1973)
243. Donoghue, Albert and Short, Martin, *The Krays' Lieutenant*, London (1995)
244. Douthwaite, L.C., *Mass Murder*, London (1928)
245. Dowdall, Lawrence, *Get Me Dowdall!*, London (1979)
246. Dower, Alan, *Crime Chemist*, London (1965)
247. Downs, Thomas, *Murder Man*, New York (1984)
248. ——, *The Door-to-Door Killer*, New York (1984)
249. Doyle, Sir Arthur Conan, *The Case of Oscar Slater*, London (1912)
250. Duclos, Bernard, *Fair Game*, New York (1993)
251. Dudley, Ernest, *Bywaters and Mrs Thompson*, London (n.d.)
252. Duke, Winifred, *Six Trials*, London (1934)
253. ——, *Trial of Field and Gray*, NBT, Edinburgh (1939)

254. ——, *Trials of Frederick Nodder*, NBT, Edinburgh (1950)
255. ——, *The Stroke of Murder*, London (1937)
256. Dunbar, Dorothy, *Blood in the Parlor*, New York (1964)
257. Dunboyne, Lord, *Trial of John George Haigh*, NBT, Edinburgh (1953)
258. Duncan, Ronald (ed.), *Facets of Crime*, Cornwall (1975)
259. Du Preez, Peter, *The Vonsteen Case*, Cape Town (1972)
260. Dyne, D.G., *Famous New Zealand Murders*, Auckland NZ (1969)
261. Eaton, Harold, *Famous Poison Trials*, London (1923)
262. Eddowes, John, *The Two Killers of Rillington Place*, London (1994)
263. Eddy, J.P., *Scarlet and Ermine*, London (1960)
264. Eden, Mark and Hill, Bill, *Letters from a Suburban Housewife*, London (2001)
265. Egginton, Joyce, *From Cradle to Grave*, New York (1989)
266. Ehrmann, Herbert R., *The Case That Will Not Die*, London (1970)
267. ——, *The Untried Case*, New York (1960)
268. Elkind, Peter, *The Death Shift*, New York (1990)
269. Ellis, Anthony, *Prisoner at the Bar*, London (1934)
270. Ellis, Georgie, *Ruth Ellis: My Mother*, London (1995)
271. Englade, Ken, *Cellar of Horror*, New York (1989)
272. ——, *Deadly Lessons*, New York (1991)
273. Evans, Colin, *Killer Doctors*, London (1994)
274. Evans, Richard, *The Pyjama Girl Mystery*, Melbourne (2004)
275. Fabian, Robert, *Fabian of the Yard*, London (1950)
276. Fairfield, Letitia and Fullbrook, Eric P., *Trial of John Thomas Straffen*, NBT, Edinburgh (1954)
277. Farr, Louise, *The Sunset Murders*, New York (1992)
278. Farrell, Harry, *Shallow Grave in Trinity County*, New York (1999)
279. Farrell, Michael, *Poisons and Poisoners*, London (1992)
280. Fawkes, Sandy, *Killing Time*, London (1977)
281. Fay, E.S., *The Life of Mr Justice Swift*, London (1939)
282. Felstead. S.T., *Sir Richard Muir*, London (1927)
283. Ferry, Jon and Inwood, Damian, *The Olson Murders*, British Colombia (1982)
284. Fido, Martin and Skinner, Keith, *The Peasenhall Murder*, Stroud (1990)
285. Fielder, Mike, *Killer on the Loose*, London (1994)
286. Fielding, Steve, *Lancashire Tales of Mystery and Murder*, Newbury (2005)
287. ——, *Yorkshire Murder Casebook*, Newbury (1997)
288. Finch, Peter, *Fatal Flaw*, New York (1992)
289. Firmin, Stanley, *Crime Man*, London (1950)
290. ——, *Murderers in our Midst*, London (1955)
291. Firth, J.B., *A Scientist Turns to Crime*, London (1960)
292. Fisher, Jim, *The Ghosts of Hopewell*, Wisconsin (1999)
293. Fletcher, G., *The Life and Career of Dr William Palmer of Rugeley*, London (1925)
294. Foot, Paul, *Who Killed Hanratty?*, London (1971)
295. Forbes, George and Meehan, Paddy, *Such Bad Company*, Edinburgh (1982)
296. Forbes, Ian, *Squad Man*, London (1973)
297. Fox, James, *White Mischief*, London (1982)

298. Fraenkel, Osmand, *Sacco-Vanzetti Case*, London (1931)
299. Frank, Gerold, *The Boston Strangler*, London (1967)
300. Franke, David, *Torture Doctor*, New York (1975)
301. Franklin, Charles, *The Woman in the Case*, London (1967)
302. ——, *The World's Worst Murderers*, London (1965)
303. Franklin, Eileen and Wright, William, *Sins of the Father*, New York (1991)
304. French, Thomas, *Unanswered Calls*, New York (1991)
305. Freeman, Lucy, *Before I Kill More*, New York (1955)
306. Frey, Robert Seitz and Thompson-Frey, Nancy, *The Silent and the Damned*, New York (1988)
307. Friedland, Martin L., *The Death of Old Man Rice*, New York (1994)
308. ——, *The Trials of Israel Lipski*, London (1984)
309. Frost, George, *Flying Squad*, London (1948)
310. Forster, Joseph, *Studies in Black and Red*, London (1896)
311. Furneaux, Rupert, *Famous Criminal Cases – 1*, London (1954)
312. ——, *Famous Criminal Cases – 2*, London (1955)
313. ——, *Famous Criminal Cases – 3*, London (1956)
314. ——, *Famous Criminal Cases – 4*, London (1957)
315. ——, *Famous Criminal Cases – 5*, London (1958)
316. ——, *Famous Criminal Cases – 6*, London (1960)
317. ——, *Famous Criminal Cases – 7*, London (1962)
318. ——, *Guenther Podola*, London (1960)
319. ——, *Michael John Davies*, London (1962)
320. ——, *The Medical Murderer*, London (1957)
321. ——, *The Murder of Lord Erroll*, London (1961)
322. Gaddis, Thomas E., *Birdman of Alcatraz*, New York (1955)
323. Gaddis, Thomas E. and Long, James O., *Killer: A Journal of Murder*, New York (1970)
324. Gardner, James, *The Trail of the Serpent*, Lewes (2004)
325. Garvie, Sheila, *Marriage to Murder*, Aberdeen (1969)
326. Gates, William, *The Hanging of Floss Forsyth – Book 1: Violence*, New York (1992)
327. ——, *The Hanging of Floss Forsyth – Book 2: The Trial*, London (1997)
328. Gaute, J.H.H. and Odell, Robin, *Lady Killers*, London (1980)
329. Gavron, Jeremy, *Darkness in Eden*, London (1991)
330. Gekoski, Anna, *Murder by Numbers*, London (1998)
331. Gerring, David and Brimmell, Robert, *Lucan Lives*, London (1995)
332. Geyer, Frank P., *The Holmes – Pitezel Case*, Philadelphia (1896)
333. Ghurka, Madam, *The Murder of Alma Tirtschke*, Melbourne (1923)
334. Gibney, Bruce, *The Beauty Queen Killer*, New York (1984)
335. Gilbert, Michael, *Doctor Crippen*, London (1953)
336. Gilmore, John, *Severed*, Los Angeles (1994)
337. ——, *The Tucson Murders*, New York (1970)
338. Gilmore, John and Kenner, Ron, *The Garbage People*, New York (1978)
339. Gilmore, Mikal, *Shot in the Heart*, New York (1994)
340. Gilmour, Walter and Hale, Leland E., *Butcher, Baker*, New York (1991)
341. Ginsberg, Philip, *Poisoned Blood*, New York (1989)
342. Giono, Jean, *The Dominici Affair*, London (1956)

343. Giroux, Robert, *A Deed of Death*, New York (1990)
344. Glaister, John, *Final Diagnosis*, London (1964)
345. ——, *The Power of Poison*, London (1954)
346. Glaister, John and Brash, James Couper, *Medico-Legal Aspects of the Ruxton Case*, London (1937)
347. Glamuzina, Julie G. and Laurie, Alison J., *Parker and Hulme*, Auckland NZ (1991)
348. Godwin, George, *Peter Kurten – A Study in Sadism*, London (1938)
349. ——, (ed.), *Trial of Peter Griffiths*, NBT, Edinburgh (1948)
350. Godwin, John, *Killers in Paradise*, London (1962)
351. Goodman, Derrick, *Crime of Passion*, London (1958)
352. Goodman, Jonathan (ed.), *Trial of Ian Brady and Myra Hindley*, Newton Abbott (1973)
353. ——, *The Crippen File*, London (1985)
354. ——, *The Burning of Evelyn Foster*, London (1983)
355. ——, *The Killing of Julia Wallace*, London (1969)
356. ——, *The Stabbing of George Harry Storrs*, London (1983)
357. Goodman, Jonathan and Pringle, Pat, *The Trial of Ruth Ellis*, Newton Abbott (1974)
358. Golden, Harry, *The Lynching of Leo Frank*, London (1966)
359. Gollmar, Robert H., *Edward Gein*, Wisconsin (1982)
360. Gollomb, Joseph, *Crimes of the Year*, London (1932)
361. Graham, Evelyn, *Lord Darling and his Famous Trials*, London (1929)
362. Graves, Robert, *They Hanged My Saintly Billy*, London (1957)
363. Gray, Judd, *Doomed Ship*, New York (1928)
364. Graysmith, Robert, *Zodiac*, New York (1986)
365. Green, Ben, *The Soldier of Fortune Murders*, New York (1992)
366. Greeno, Edward, *War on the Underworld*, London (1960)
367. Greenwall, Harry J., *They Were Murdered in France*, London (1957)
368. Greenya, John, *Blood Relations*, San Diego (1987)
369. Gregson, Jonathan, *Blood Against the Snows*, London (2002)
370. Greig, Charlotte, *Evil Serial Killers*, London (2005)
371. Gribble, Leonard, *Famous Feats of Detection and Deduction*, London (1933)
372. ——, *Famous Judges and Their Trials*, London (1957)
373. ——, *Famous Detective Exploits*, London (1958)
374. ——, *Great Manhunters of the Yard*, London (1966)
375. ——, *Murders Most Strange*, London (1959)
376. Grierson, Francis, *Famous French Crimes*, London (1959)
377. Grice, Edward, *Great Cases of Sir Henry Curtis Bennett*, London (1937)
378. Grombach, John V., *The Great Liquidator*, New York (1980)
379. Gross, Kenneth, *The Alice Crimmins Case*, New York (1975)
380. Guitard, Victor, *Secret Agent of the Vatican*, Paris (2004)
381. Gurr, Tom and Cox H.H., *Obsession*, London (1958)
382. Gurwell, John K., *Mass Murder in Houston*, London (1974)
383. Habe, Hans, *Gentlemen of the Jury*, London (1967)
384. Haden-Guest, Anthony, *Bad Dreams*, New York (1981)
385. Haestier, Richard, *Dead Men Tell Tales*, LOndon (1934)
386. Haines, Max, *Bothersome Bodies*, Toronto (1977)

387. ——, *True Crime Stories – 2*, Toronto (1988)
388. ——, *True Crime Stories – 3*, Toronto (1989)
389. Hall, Jean Graham and Smith, Gordon D., *The Croydon Arsenic Mystery*, Chichester (1999)
390. ——, *R. v Bywaters and Thompson*, Chichester (1997)
391. Hall, Roy Archibald, *A Perfect Gentleman*, London (1999)
392. Hallworth, Rodney and Williams, Mark, *Where There's a Will. . .* , London (1983)
393. Hambrook, Walter, *Hambrook of the Yard*, London (1937)
394. Hammer, Richard, *The CBS Murders*, New York (1988)
395. Hancock, R., *Ruth Ellis*, London (1963)
396. Harris, Jean, *Stranger in Two Worlds*, London (1987)
397. Harris, Paul, *The Garvie Trial*, Aberdeen (1969)
398. Harrison, Richard, *Criminal Calendar*, London (1951)
399. Harry, Gerard, *The Peltzer Case*, London (1928)
400. Hartman, Mary S., *Victorian Murderesses*, New York (1976)
401. Harvey, John R., *Journey to the Gallows*, Sydney (n.d.)
402. Hastings, Macdonald, *The Other Mr Churchill*, London (1963)
403. Hastings, Sir Patrick, *Autobiography*, London (1948)
404. Hatherill, George, *A Detective's Story*, London (1971)
405. Havers, Sir Michael, Shankland, P. and Barrett, A., *A Tragedy in Three Voices*, London (1980)
406. Hawkes, George H., *Hand in Glove*, Syndney (n.d.)
407. Hawkes, Harry, *Murder on the A34*, London (1970)
408. ——, *The Capture of the Black Panther*, London (1978)
409. Hawser, C. Lewis, *The Case of James Hanratty*, London (1975)
410. Hayhurst, Alan, *Lancashire Murders*, Stroud (2004)
411. Headley, Bernard, *The Atlanta Youth Murders and the Politics of Race*, Illinois (1998)
412. Hebert, Jacques, *The Coffin Affair*, Quebec (1982)
413. Heimer, Mel, *The Cannibal*, New York (1971)
414. ——, *The Girl in Murder Flat*, London (1958)
415. Helper, Albert (ed.), *The Chicago Crime Book*, London (1968)
416. Helpern, Milton with Knight, Bernard, *Autopsy*, New York (1977)
417. Henderson, William (ed.), *Trial of William Gardiner*, NBT, Edinburgh (1934)
418. Heppenstall, Rayner, *French Crime in the Romantic Age*, London (1970)
419. Herbstein, Denis, *The Porthole Murder Case*, London (1991)
420. Higdon, Hal, *The Crime of the Century*, New York (1975)
421. Hill, Paull, *Portrait of a Sadist*, London (1960)
422. Hiltzik, Michael L., *A Death in Kenya*, London (1991)
423. Hirschfield, Burt, *Bonnie and Clyde*, New York (1967)
424. Hodel, Steve, *Black Dahlia Avenger*, New York (2003)
425. Hoffman, Richard H. and Bishop, Jim, *The Girl in Poison Cottage*, London (1958)
426. Hogarth, Basil (ed.), *Trial of Robert Wood*, NBT, Edinburgh (1907)
427. Holden, Anthony, *The St Albans Poisoner*, London (1974)
428. Holgate, Mike, *The Secret of the Babbacombe Murder*, Newton Abbott (1995)

429. Holgate, Mike and Waugh, Ian David, *The Man They Could Not Hang*, Stroud (2005)
430. Holmes, Paul, *The Sheppard Murder Case*, New York (1961)
431. ——, *The Trials of Dr Coppolino*, New York (1968)
432. Holmes, W. Leslie with Northrop, Bruce, *Where Shadows Linger*, British Columbia (2000)
433. Holzer, Hans, *Murder in Amityville*, London (1980)
434. Honeycombe, Gordon, *The Murders of the Black Museum*, London (1982)
435. Hood, Lynley, *Minnie Dean – Her Life and Crimes*, Auckland NZ (1994)
436. Horwell, John E., *Horwell of the Yard*, London (n.d.)
437. Hoskins, Percy, *They Almost Escaped*, London (1937)
438. ——, *Two Men Were Acquitted*, London (1984)
439. House, Jack, *Murder Not Proven*, Glasgow (1984)
440. ——, *Square Mile of Murder*, Edinburgh (1961)
441. Houts, Marshall, *Kings X*, New York (1972)
442. Howard, Amanda and Smith, Martin, *Rivers of Blood*, Boca Raton (2004)
443. Howard, Clark, *The Zebra Killings*, New York (1979)
444. Howse, Geoffrey, *North London Murders*, Stroud (2005)
445. Huggett, R. and Berry, P., *Daughters of Cain*, London (1956)
446. Huish, Robert, *The Progress of Crime or the Authentic Memoirs of Maria Manning*, London (1849)
447. Humphreys, Christmas, *Seven Murders*, London (1931)
448. Humphreys, Sir Travers, *A Book of Trials*, London (1953)
449. Humphry, Derek and Tindall, David, *False Messiah*, London (1977)
450. Hunt, Peter, *Oscar Slater: The Great Suspect*, London (1951)
451. ——, *The Madeleine Smith Affair*, London (1950)
452. Hussey, R.F., *Murderer Scot Free*, Newton Abbott (1973)
453. Hutter, Ernie, *The Chillingworth Murder Case*, Connecticut (1963)
454. Hyde, H. Montgomery and Kisch, John H., *An International Casebook of Crime*, London (1962)
455. Inglis, K.S., *The Stuart Case*, Melbourne (1961)
456. Irving, H.B., *A Book of Remarkable Criminals*, London (1918)
457. ——, *Studies of French Criminals of the Nineteenth Century*, London (1901)
458. ——, (ed.) *Trial of Franz Muller*, NBT, Edinburgh (1911)
459. ——, (ed.) *Trial of Mrs Maybrick*, NBT, Edinburgh (1912)
460. ——, (ed.) *Trial of the Wainwrights*, NBT, Edinburgh (1920)
461. Jackson, Christopher, *Manuel*, London (1965)
462. Jackson, David, *Destroying the Baby in Themselves*, Nottingham (1995)
463. Jackson, Joseph Henry and Offord, Lenore Glen, *The Girl in the Belfry*, London (1957)
464. Jackson, Sir Richard, *Occupied With Crime*, London (1967)
465. Jackson, Robert, *Francis Camps*, London (1975)
466. ——, *The Chief*, London (1959)
467. ——, *The Crime Doctors*, London (1966)
468. Jackson, Stanley, *John George Haigh*, London (1953)
469. ——, *Mr Justice Avory*, London (1935)
470. ——, *The Life and Cases of Mr Justice Humphreys*, London (1955)

471. Jacobs, T.C.H., *Cavalcade of Murder*, London (1955)
472. Jaeger, Richard W. and Balousek, M. William, *Massacre in Milwaukee*, Oregon (1991)
473. Jakubait, Muriel with Weller, Monica, *Ruth Ellis: My Sister's Secret Life*, London (2005)
474. Japan Gazette, *Death of Mr W.R.H. Carew*, (1896)
475. Jeffers, H. Paul, *Gentleman Gerald*, New York (1995)
476. ——, *With an Axe*, New York (2000)
477. Jesse, F. Tennyson, *Comments on Cain*, London (1948)
478. ——, *Murder and its Motives*, London (1924)
479. ——, *The Trial of Samuel Herbert Dougal*, NBT, Edinburgh (1928)
480. ——, *Trials of Evans and Christie*, NBT, Edinburgh (1957)
481. ——, *Trial of Sidney Fox*, NBT, Edinburgh (1934)
482. ——, *Trial of Thomas John Ley and Lawrence J. Smith*, NBT, Edinburgh (1947)
483. ——, *Trial of Rattenbury and Stoner*, NBT, Edinburgh (1935)
484. ——, *Trial of Madeleine Smith*, NBT, Edinburgh (1949)
485. Johnson, W.H., *Kent Tales of Mystery and Murder*, Newbury (2003)
486. ——, *Sussex Tales of Mystery and Murder*, Newbury (2002)
487. ——, *Sussex Villains*, Newbury (2003)
488. Jolly, John Catherall, *Enquiry into the Confession of David John Ware*, London (1947)
489. Jonas, George and Amiel, Barbara, *By Persons Unknown*, Toronto (1977)
490. Jones, Elwyn, *The Last Two to Hang*, London (1966)
491. Jones, Frank, *Murderous Women*, Toronto (2002)
492. Jones, Jack, *Let Me Take You Down*, London (1989)
493. Jones, James L., *A Murder in West Covina*, California (1992)
494. Jones, Reginald B., *Burke and Hare*, Manchester (n.d.)
495. ——, *Palmer the Rugely Poisoner*, Manchester (n.d.)
496. Jones, Walter, *My Own Case*, Maidstone (1966)
497. Josephs, Jeremy, *Murder in the Family*, London (1994)
498. Jouve, Nicole Ward, *The Street Cleaner*, London (1986)
499. Justice, Jean, *Murder v Murder*, Paris (1964)
500. Kallio, Lauri E., *Confess or Die*, London (1999)
501. Kaplan, David E. and Marshall, Andrew, *The Cult at the End of the World*, New York (1996)
502. Karam, Joe, *David and Goliath*, Auckland NZ (1997)
503. ——, *Bain and Beyond*, Auckland NZ (2000)
504. Keeton, G.W., *Guilty but Insane*, London (1961)
505. Kelleher, Michael D. and Van Nuys, David, *'This is the Zodiac Speaking'*, Connecticut (2002)
506. Kelly, Dolores, *William Heirens: His Day in Court*, Chicago (1991)
507. Kelly, Susan, *The Boston Stranglers*, New York (1995)
508. Kelly, Vince, *The Charge is Murder*, London (1965)
509. ——, *The Shark Arm Case*, Sydney (1963)
510. Kennaugh, Robert Charles, *Contemporary Murder*, Johannesburg (1968)
511. Kennedy, Dolores with Nolin, Orlando, *On a Killing Day*, Chicago (1992)
512. Kennedy, Les and Whittaker, Mark, *Granny Killer*, Sydney (1992)
513. Kennedy, Ludovic, *The Airman and the Carpenter*, London (1985)

514. Keppel, Robert D. with Birnes, William J., *The Riverman*, New York (1995)
515. Kershaw, Alister, *Murder in France*, London (1955)
516. Keyes, Edward, *The Michigan Murders*, London (1978)
517. Kidd, Paul B., *The Knick-Knack Man*, Sydney (2002)
518. Kidder, Tracey, *The Road to Yuba City*, New York (1974)
519. King County Journal, *Gary Ridgway: the Green River Killer*, Washington (2003)
520. King, Gary C., *Driven to Kill*, New York (1993)
521. Kinder, Gary, *Victim*, New York (1982)
522. Kirkpatrrick, Sidney D., *A Cast of Killers*, New York (1986)
523. Klaus, Samuel, *The Molineux Case*, London (1929)
524. Klausner, L.D., *Son of Sam*, New York (1981)
525. Klein, Henry H., *Sacrificed*, New York (1927)
526. Knott, George H., *Trial of William Palmer*, NBT, Edinburgh (1912)
527. Knowles, Leonard, *Court of Drama*, London (1966)
528. Knowlton, Janice with Newton, Michael, *Daddy was the Black Dahlia Killer*, New York (1995)
529. Knox, Bill, *Court of Murder*, London (1968)
530. Kobler, John, *The Trial of Ruth Snyder and Judd Gray*, New York (1938)
531. Kolarik, Gera-Lind with Klatt, Wayne, *Freed to Kill*, Chicago (1990)
532. Kozenczak, Joseph and Henrickson, Karen, *A Passing Acquaintance*, New York (1992)
533. Kray, Charles, *Me and My Brothers*, London (1977)
534. Kray, Ronald and Reginald with Dineage, Fred, *Our Story*, London (1988)
535. Krivich Mikhail and Olgert, Olgin, *Comrade Chikatilo*, New Jersey (1993)
536. Kunstler, William A., *The Minister and the Choir Singer*, London (1964)
537. Kurth, Ann, *Prescription: Murder*, New York (1976)
538. La Bern, A., Haigh, *The Mind of a Murderer*, London (1973)
539, ——, *The Life and Death of a Lady Killer*, London (1967)
540. Laborde, Jean, *The Dominici Affair*, London (1974)
541. Lalor, Peter, *Blood Stain*, New South Wales (2002)
542. Lambert, Richard S., *The Universal Provider*, London (1938)
543. Lambourne, Gerald, *The Fingerprint Story*, London (1984)
544. Lambrianou, Tony with Clerk, Carol, *Inside the Firm*, London (1991)
545. Lambton, Arthur, *Echoes of Causes Célèbres*, London (n.d.)
546. ——, *Thou Shalt Do No Murder*, London (n.d.)
547. Lane, Brian, *The Murder Yearbook*, London (1992)
548. Lane, Brian and Gregg, Wilf, *The New Encyclopaedia of Serial Killers*, London (1996)
549. Langford, Gerald, *The Murder of Stanford White*, London (1962)
550. Larsen, Richard W., *Bundy: The Deliberate Stranger*, New York (1980)
551. Larson, Erik, *The Devil in the White City*, London (2003)
552. Laurence J., *Extraordinary Crimes*, London (1931)
553. Lavelle, Patrick, *Shadow of the Ripper*, London (2003)
554. Lavergne, Gary M., *A Sniper in the Tower*, Texas (1997)
555. Leasor, James, *Who Killed Sir Harry Oakes?*, London (1983)
556. Le Blanc, Jerry and Davies, Ivor, *5 to Die*, Los Angeles (1970)
557. Lebourdais, Isabel, *The Trial of Stephen Truscott*, London (1966)
558. Lebrun, George P. and Radin, Edward D., *It's Time to Tell*, New York (1962)

559. Lee, John, *The Man They Could Not Hang*, London (n.d.)
560. Lee, Sandra, *Beyond Bad*, New South Wales (2002)
561. Lefebure, Molly, *Evidence for the Crown*, London (1975)
562. Lefkowitz, Bernard and Gross, Kenneth G., *The Sting of Justice*, London (1970)
563. Leith, Rod, *The Prostitute Murders*, New Jersey (1985)
564. Le Neve, Ethel, *Her Life Story*, London (n.d.)
565. Leopold, Nathan F. Jr, *Life Plus 99 Years*, London (1958)
566. Le Queux, William, *Landru, His Secret Love Affairs*, London (1922)
567. Leslie, Jack, *Decathlon of Death*, California (1979)
568. Lessard, Suzannah, *The Architect of Desire*, London (1997)
569. Lessing, Theodore, *Monsters of Weimar*, London (1993)
570. Levitt, L., *The Healer*, New York (1980)
571. Levy, J.H. (ed.), *The Necessity for Criminal Appeal*, London (1899)
572. Levy, Steven, *The Unicorn's Secret*, New York (1988)
573. Lewis, Alfred Allen and MacDonell, Herbert Leon, *The Evidence Never Lies*, New York (1984)
574. Lewis, Arthur H., *Murder by Contract*, New York (1975)
575. Lewis, Leonard, *Trunk Crimes, Past and Present*, London (n.d.)
576. Lieck, Albert, *Trial of Dr Knowles*, NBT, Edinburgh (1933)
577. Lindsay, Philip, *The Mainspring of Murder*, London (1958)
578. Lindsey, J., *Suburban Gentleman*, London (1942)
579. Linedecker, Clifford L., *Night Stalker*, New York (1991)
580. ——, *The Man Who KIlled Boys*, New York (1980)
581. ——, *Thrill Seekers*, New York (1988)
582. Linedecker, Clifford L. and Burt, William A., *Nurses Who Kill*, New York (1990)
583. Linklater, Eric, *The Corpse on Clapham Common*, London (1971)
584. Lisners, John, *House of Horrors*, London (1983)
585. Lock, Joan, *Blue Murder?*, London (1986)
586. Loerzel, Robert, *Alchemy of Bones*, Chicago (2003)
587. Logan, Andy, *Against the Evidence*, London (1970)
588. Logan, Guy B.H., *Masters of Crime*, London (1928)
589. ——, *Verdict and Sentence*, London (1935)
590. Lourie, Richard, *Hunting the Devil*, London (1993)
591. Lowry, Beverly, *Crossed Over*, New York (2000)
592. Lucas, Norman, *The Child Killers*, London (1970)
593. ——, *The Laboratory Detectives*, London (1971)
594. ——, *The Lucan Mystery*, London (1975)
595. ——, *The Monster Butler*, London (1979)
596. ——, *The Murder of Muriel McKay*, London (1971)
597. ——, *The Sex Killers*, London (1974)
598. Lunde, Donald T. and Morgan, Jefferson, *The Die Song*, New York (1980)
599. Lustgarten, Edgar, *The Business of Murder*, London (1968)
600. ——, *The Chalkpit Murder*, London (1974)
601. ——, *The Illustrated Story of Crime*, London (1976)
602. ——, *The Woman in the Case*, London (1955)
603. Lutholtz, M. William, *Grand Dragon*, Indiana (1991)
604. Lyons, Eugene, *The Life and Death of Sacco and Vanzetti*, New York (1927)

605. Lyons, Frederick J., *George Joseph Smith*, London (1935)
606. MacCartney, Lowden, *Life and Trial of Harold Jones*, Glasgow (n.d.)
607. McClean, Fred, *Will to Kill*, Wellington NZ (1998)
608. MaClean, Harry N., *In Broad Daylight*, New York (1988)
609. McConnell, Brian, *Found Naked and Dead*, London (1974)
610. McConnell, Brian and Bence, Douglas, *The Nilsen File*, London (1983)
611. McConnell, Jean, *The Detectives*, Newton Abbott (1976)
612. McConnell, Virginia, *Sympathy for the Devil*, Connecticut (2001)
613. McCormick, Donald, *Murder by Witchcraft*, London (1948)
614. McCurtin, Peter, *Murder in the Penthouse*, New York (1980)
615. McDonald, R. Robin, *Black Widow*, New York (1986)
616. MacDonald, John, *The Murderer and his Victim*, Ohio (1961)
617. MacDonald, John D., *No Deadly Drug*, New York (1968)
618. MacDougall, A.W., *The Maybrick Case*, London (1891)
619. MacDougall, Philip, *Murder and Mystery in Kent*, London (1995)
620. McGarry, Andrew, *The Snowtown Murders*, Sydney (2005)
621. MacGowan, Douglas, *Murder in Victorian Scotland*, Connecticut (1999)
622. MacKenzie, F.A., *Landru*, London (1928)
623. McLaren, Angus, *A Prescription for Murder*, Chicago (1995)
624. Mace, Gustave, *My First Case*, London (1886)
625. Maeder, Thomas, *The Unspeakable Crimes of Dr Petiot*, Boston (1980)
626. McGinnis, Joe, *Fatal Vision*, New York (1983)
627. McKernan, M. (ed.), *The Crime and Trial of Leopold and Loeb*, New York (1957)
628. McLeave, Hugh, Chesney, *The Fabulous Murder*, London (n.d.)
629. McKnight, Gerald, *The Murder Squad*, London (1967)
630. McNeish, James, *The Mask of Sanity*, Auckland NZ (1997)
631. Mailer, Norman, *The Executioner's Song*, London (1979)
632. Malcolm, David, *Murder and Mayhem in Birkenhead*, Wirral (n.d.)
633. Mallon, Andrew, *Leonski – The Brownout Murders*, Victoria (1979)
634. Marchbanks, D., *The Moor Murders*, London (1966)
635. Margolin, Leslie, *Murderess*, New York (1999)
636. Marjoribanks, Edward, *The Life of Sir Edward Marshall-Hall*, London (1929)
637. Markman, Ronald and Bosco, Dominick, *Alone with the Devil*, New York (1989)
638. Marks, L. and Van Den Bergh, T., *Ruth Ellis: A Case of Diminshed Responsibility*, London (1977)
639. Marnham, Patrick, *Trail of Havoc*, London (1987)
640. Marriner, Brian, *A Century of Sex Killers*, London (1992)
641. ——, *Murder With Venom*, London (1993)
642. Martin, Beth, *Albany's Brush with a Mass Murderer*, Western Australia (1995)
643. Masters, Anthony and Falle, Philip, *The Newall Murders*, London (1994)
644. Masters, Brian, *Killing for Company*, London (1985)
645. ——, *'She Must Have Known'*, London (1996)
646. ——, *The Shrine of Jeffrey Dahmer*, London (1993)
647. Matthews, David A., *Crime Doctor*, London (1959)
648. Maxwell, Robert, *The Christie Case*, London (n.d.)

649. May, H.J., *Murder by Consent*, London (1968)
650. Maybrick, F.E., *Mrs Maybrick's Own Story*, London (1904)
651. Maycock, Sir Willoughby, *Celebrated Crimes and Criminals*, London (1890)
652. Melinkoff, David, *The Conscience of a Lawyer*, Minnesota (1973)
653. Mercado, Carol, *A Voice from the Grave*, New York (1994)
654. Mewshaw, Michael, *Money to Burn*, New York (1987)
655. Meyer, Gerald, *The Memphis Murders*, New York (1974)
656. Michaud, Stephen G. and Aynesworth, Hugh, *The Only Living Witness*, New York (1983)
657. Millen, Ernest, *Specialist in Crime*, London (1936)
658. Miller, James William, *Don't Call Me Killer!*, Victoria (1984)
659. Miller, Leonard, *Shadow of Deadman's Hill*, London (2001)
660. Miller, Webb, *I Found No Peace*, London (1936)
661. Milton, Joyce and Bardach, Ann Louise, *Vicki*, New York (1986)
662. Mitchell, Susan, *All Things Bright and Beautiful*, Sydney (2004)
663. Molomby, Tom, *Ratten, The Web of Circumstance*, Victoria (1978)
664. Molloy, Pat, *Not the Moors Murders*, Dyfed (1988)
665. Montgomery, Robert H., *Sacco-Vanzetti: The Murder and the Myth*, New York (1960)
666. Mooney, M.M., *Evelyn Nesbit and Stanford White*, New York (1976)
667. Moore, Kelly and Reed, Don, *Deadly Medicine*, New York (1988)
668. Moore, Sally, *Lucan: Not Guilty*, London (1987)
669. Morain, Alfred, *The Underworld of Paris*, London (1928)
670. More, John W. (ed.), *Trial of A.J. Monson*, NBT, Edinburgh (1908)
671. Morgan, Dan, *The Minister for Murder*, Victoria (1979)
672. Morgan, Kevin, *Gun Alley*, New South Wales (2005)
673. Morland, Nigel, *Background to Murder*, London (1955)
674. ——, *Hangman's Clutch*, London (1954)
675. ——, *Pattern to Murder*, London (1966)
676. ——, *That Nice Miss Smith*, London (1957)
677. ——, *This Friendless Lady*, London (1957)
678. Morrison, Blake, *As If*, London (1997)
679. Moser, Don and Cohen, Jerry, *The Pied Piper of Tucson*, New York (1968)
680. Motion, Andrew, *Wainewright The Poisoner*, London (2000)
681. Moulton, H. Fletcher, *Trial of Alexander Campbell Mason*, London (1930)
682. ——, *Trial of Stinie Morrison*, NBT, Edinburgh (1922)
683. ——, *Trial of William Henry Palmer*, London (1931)
684. Mulgrew, Ian, *Final Payoff*, Toronto (1990)
685. Muncie, William, *Crime Pond*, Edinburgh (1979)
686. Murakawi, Haruki, *Underground*, New York (2001)
687. Murphy, James, *The Murder of Julia Wallace*, Liverpool (2001)
688. Musmanno, Michael A., *Verdict!* (1958)
689. Mykyta, Anne-Marie, *It's a Long Way to Truro*, Melbourne (1981)
690. Napley, Sir David, *Murder at the Villa Madeira*, London (1988)
691. ——, *The Camden Town Murder*, London (1987)
692. Nash, Jay Robert, *Bloodletters and Badmen*, New York (1973)
693. Nassau Daily Tribune, *The Murder of Sir Harry Oakes Bt*, Nassau (1959)
694. Neff, James, *The Wrong Man*, New York (2001)

695. Neil, Arthur Fowler, *Forty Years of Manhunting*, London (1932)
696. Nelson, Polly, *Defending the Devil*, New York (1994)
697. Nesbit, Evelyn, *The Untold Story*, London (1934)
698. Neustatter, Lindesay W., *The Mind of the Murderer*, London (1957)
699. Neville, Richard and Clarke, Julie, *The Life and Crimes of Charles Sobhraj*, London (1979)
700. Newsom, Robert W. and Trotter, William, *Deadly Kin*, New York (1989)
701. Newton, Michael, *Rope*, New York (1998)
702. ——, *The Encyclopaedia of Serial Killers*, New York (2000)
703. Nicholls, Ernest, *Crime Within the Square Mile*, London (1935)
704. Norman, C., *The Genteel Murderer*, New York (1956)
705. Normanton, Helena (ed.), *Trial of Alfred Arthur Rouse*, NBT, Edinburgh (1931)
706. ——, *The Trial of Norman Thorne*, London (n.d.)
707. Norris, Joel, *Henry Lee Lucas*, New York (1991)
708. ——, *Arthur Shawcross: The Genesee River Killer*, New York (1992)
709. O'Brien, Darcy, *Murder in Little Egypt*, New York (1989)
710. ——, *Two of a Kind, The Hillside Stranglers*, New York (1985)
711. Oddie, Ingleby, *Inquest*, London (1941)
712. Odell, Robin, *Exhumation of a Murder*, London (1975)
713. ——, *Jack the Ripper in Fact and Fiction*, London (1965)
714. ——, *Landmarks of 20th Century Murder*, London (1995)
715. O'Donnell, Bernard, *Cavalcade of Justice*, London (1951)
716. ——, *Should Women Hang?*, London (1956)
717. ——, *The Trials of Mr Justice Avory*, London (1935)
718. O'Donnell, Elliot (ed.), *Trial of Kate Webster*, NBT, Edinburgh (1925)
719. O'Donnell, Jeff, *Starkweather*, Nebraska (1993)
720. O'Flaherty, M., *Have You Seen This Woman?*, London (1971)
721. O'Gara, Noel, *The Real Yorkshire Ripper Revealed*, Athlone (1989)
722. Olsen, Jack, *The Misbegotten Son*, London (1993)
723. Omoike, Isaac I., *The Columbine High School Massacre*, Baton Rouge (2000)
724. Oney, Steve, *And The Dead Shall Rise*, New York (2003)
725. O'Sullivan, J.S.O., *A Most Unique Ruffian*, Melbourne (1968)
726. Oswald, H.R., *Memoirs of a London County Coroner*, London (1936)
727. Owens, Andy and Ellis, Chris, *Killer Catchers*, London (2004)
728. Packer, Edwin, *The Peasenhall Mystery*, Yoxford (1980)
729. Paget, R.T. and Silverman, Sydney, *Hanged – And Innocent*, London (1953)
730. Park, William, *The Truth About Oscar Slater*, London (n.d.)
731. Parker, Emma and Cowan, Nell Barrow, *Fugitives – The Story of Clyde Barrow and Bonnie Parker*, Dallas (1934)
732. Parker, Tony, *The Plough Boy*, London (1965)
733. Parkin, A.M., *The Seal Chart Murder*, Kemsing (n.d.)
734. Parmiter, Geoffrey de C., *Reasonable Doubt*, London (1928)
735. Parry, Leonard A., *Some Famous Medical Trials*, London (1927)
736. ——, (ed.), *Trial of Dr Smethurst*, NBT, Edinburgh (1931)
737. Patrick, Q., *The Girl on the Gallows*, New York (1954)
738. Paul, Philip, *Murder Under the Microscope*, London (1994)
739. Payne, Leslie, *The Brotherhood*, London (1973)

740. Pearson, Edmund, *Murder at Smutty Nose and Other Murders*, London (1927)
741. ——, *Trial of Lizzie Borden*, London (1939)
742. Pearson, John, *The Profession of Violence*, London (1972)
743. Pedder, Keith, *The Rachel Files*, London (2001)
744. Peixotto, Edgar, *Trial of William Henry Theodore Durrant*, New York (1996)
745. Pejsa, Jane, *The Molineux Affair*, New York (1983)
746. Penn, Gareth, *Times 17*, (1987)
747. Penwarden, Charles, *Little Gregory*, London (1990)
748. Perry, Hamilton Darby, *A Chair for Wayne Lonergan*, London (1972)
749. Peskett, S. John, *Grim, Gruesome and Grisly*, London (1974)
750. Phagan, Mary, *The Murder of Little Mary Phagan*, New Jersey (1987)
751. Pienciak, Richard T., *Deadly Masquerade*, New York (1990)
752. Pollack, Jack Harrison, *Dr Sam*, New York (1975)
753. Pollock, George, *Mr Justice McCardie*, London (1934)
754. Porter, Edwin H., *The Fall River Tragedy*, Portland (1985)
755. Potter, J.D., *The Monsters of the Moors*, London (1966)
756. Potter, Jerry Allen and Bost, Fred, *Fatal Justice*, New York (1997)
757. Potter, T.F., *The Deadly Dr Ruxton*, Preston (1984)
758. Powell, Claire, *Murder at White House Farm*, London (1994)
759. Price, Alton, *To Build a Noose*, Ottawa (1996)
760. Pron, Nick, *Lethal Marriage*, Toronto (1995)
761. Raab, Selwyn, *Justice in the Back Room*, Cleveland (1967)
762. Radin, Edward D., *Crimes of Passion*, New York (1953)
763. ——, *Headline Crimes of the Year*, Boston (1952)
764. ——, *Lizzie Borden: The Untold Story*, New York (1961)
765. Rae, George W., *Confessions of the Boston Strangler*, London (1967)
766. Rae, Isobel, *Knox the Anatomist*, Edinburgh (1964)
767. Randall, Leslie, *The Famous Cases of Sir Bernard Spilsbury*, London (1936)
768. Ranson, Roy, *Looking for Lucan*, London (1994)
769. Raphael, John N., *The Caillaux Drama*, London (1914)
770. Rawle, John, *Minnie Dean*, Christchurch NZ (1997)
771. Raymond, R. Alwyn, *The Cleft Chin Murder*, London (1945)
772. Reichert, David, *Chasing the Devil*, New York (2004)
773. Reksten, Terry, *Rattenbury*, Victoria (1978)
774. Reynolds, Michael, *Dead Ends*, New York (1992)
775. Riddick, James, *Lord Lucan*, London (1994)
776. Rignall, Jeff and Wilder, Ron, *29 Below*, Chicago (1979)
777. Roberts, G.D., *Law and Life*, London (1964)
778. Rodell, Marie (ed.), *San Francisco Murders*, New York (1947)
779. Roen, Samuel, *Murder of a Little Girl*, New York (1973)
780. Root, Jonathan, *The Life and Bad Times of Charlie Becker*, London (1962)
781. Rose, Andrew, *Scandal at the Savoy*, London (1991)
782. ——, *Stinie*, London (1985)
783. Roughead, William (ed.), *Trials of Burke and Hare*, NBT, Edinburgh (1921)
784. ——, (ed.), *Trial of John Watson Laurie*, NBT, Edinburgh (1932)

785. ——, (ed.), *Trial of Jessie M'Lachlan*, NBT, Edinburgh (1911)
786. ——, (ed.), *Trial of John Donald Merrett*, NBT, Edinburgh (1929)
787. ——, (ed.), *Trial of Dr Pritchard*, NBT, Edinburgh (1906)
788 ——, (ed.), *Trial of Oscar Slater*, NBT, Edinburgh (1910)
789. ——, *Rogues Walk Here*, London (1934)
790. ——, *Tales of the Criminous*, London (1956)
791. Rowan-Hamilton, R.O., *The Trial of J.A. Dickman*, NBT, Edinburgh (1914)
792. Rowland, John, *Criminal Files*, London (1957)
793. ——, *Murder Revisited*, London (1961)
794. ——, *Poisoner in the Dock*, London (1960)
795. ——, *The Peasenhall Mystery*, London (1962)
796. ——, *The Wallace Case*, London (1949)
797. ——, *Unfit to Plead?*, London (1965)
798. Ruddick, James, *Death at the Priory*, London (2001)
799. Rule, Ann, *A Rose For Her Grave and Other Cases*, New York (1993)
800. ——, *Green River, Running Red*, New York (2004)
801. ——, *If You Really Loved Me*, New York (1991)
802. ——, *The Stranger Beside Me*, New York (1980)
803. Rumbelow, Donald, *The Complete Jack the Ripper*, London (2004)
804. Russell, Guy, *Guilty or Not Guilty?*, London (1931)
805. Russell, J.D., *A Chronicle of Death*, Connecticut (1971)
806. Russell, Lord, *Deadman's Hill: Was Hanratty Guilty?*, London 1965)
807. ——, *Though The Heaven's Fall*, London (1956)
808. Russell, Sue, *Damsel of Death*, London (1992)
809. Ryan, B. with Havers, Sir Michael, *The Poisoned Life of Mrs Maybrick*, London (1977)
810. Ryzuk, Mary S., *Thou Shalt Not Kill*, New York (1991)
811. Samuels, Charles, *Death Was The Bridegroom*, New York (1958)
812. ——, *The Girl in the Red Velvet Swing*, New York (1953)
813. Sanders, Bruce, *Murder Behind The Bright Lights*, London (1958)
814. ——, *They Couldn't Lose The Body*, London (1966)
815. Sanders, Ed, *The Family*, New York (1970)
816. Saunders, Edith, *The Mystery of Marie Lafarge*, London (1951)
817. Sawicki, Stephen, *Teach Me To Kill*, New York (1991)
818. Scaduto, Anthony, *Scapegoat*, London (1976)
819. Schecter, Harold, *Depraved*, New York (1994)
820. ——, *Deranged*, New York (1990)
821. ——, *Deviant*, New York (1989)
822. ——, *The Serial Killer Files*, New York (2003)
823. Schmalzbach, Oscar R., *Profiles of Murder*, Sydney (1971)
824. Schofield, Carey, *Mesrine*, London (1980)
825. Schreck, Nicholas (ed.), *The Manson File*, New York (1980)
826. Schreiber, Flora Rheta, *The Shoemaker*, New York (1983)
827. Schwartz, Ted, *The Hillside Strangler*, New York (1981)
828. Schwartz-Nobel, Loretta, *Engaged to Murder*, New York (1987)
829. Schweizer, Karl W., *Seeds of Evil*, USA (2001)
830. Scott, Sir Harold, *Scotland Yard*, London (1954)
831. Scott, Robert, *Rex v Karl Hulten and Elizabeth Jones*, Slough (n.d.)
832. Sellers, Alvin V., *The Loeb-Leopold Case*, Georgia (1926)

833. Sellwood, Arthur and Mary, *Victorian Railway Murders*, London (1979)
834. Selwyn, Francis, *Rotten to the Core*, London (1988)
835. Sereny, Gitta, *Cries Unheard*, London (1998)
836. ——, *The Case of Mary Bell*, London (1972)
837. Seth, Ronald L., *Petiot*, London (1962)
838. Shankland, Peter, *Death of an Editor*, London (1981)
839. Shapiro, Fred C., *Whitmore*, London (1969)
840. Sharkey, Joe, *Death Sentence*, New York (1990)
841. Sharp, James, *The Life and Death of Michael X*, Trinidad (1981)
842. Sharpe, F.D., *Sharpe of the Flying Squad*, London (1938)
843. Shearing, Joseph, *The Lady and the Arsenic*, London (1937)
844. Shears, Richard, *Highway to Nowhere*, Sydney (1996)
845. Sheldon, Andrew and Kiddey, Chris, *Deadly Game*, London (2003)
846. Sheppard, Sam, *Endure and Conquer*, Cleveland (1966)
847. Sheppard, Stephen, *My Brother's Keeper*, New York (1964)
848. Sher, Julian, *Until You Are Dead*, Toronto (2001)
849. Sherman, Casey, *A Rose for Mary*, Boston (2003)
850. Shore, W. Teignmouth, *Crime and its Detection*, London (1931)
851. ——, (ed.), *The Trial of Brown and Kennedy*, NBT, Edinburgh (1930)
852. ——, (ed.), *Trial of Neill Cream*, NBT, Edinburgh (1923)
853. Siggins, Maggie, *A Canadian Tragedy*, Toronto (1985)
854. Silk, Stafford, *The Bogle Mystery*, Sydney (1963)
855. Simpson, Keith, *Forty Years of Murder*, London (1978)
856. Simpson, Lesley and Harvey, Sandra, *The Killer Next Door*, New South Wales (1994)
857. Singer, Kurt (ed.), *Crime Omnibus*, London (1961)
858. ——, *My Greatest Crime Story*, London (1956)
859. Singular, Stephen, *A Killing in the Family*, London (1991)
860. ——, *Talked to Death*, New York (1987)
861. Sitford, Mikaela, *Addicted to Murder*, London (2001)
862. Skelton, Douglas, *A Time to Kill*, Edinburgh (1995)
863. Slater, Stephanie with Lancaster, Pat, *Beyond Fear*, London (1995)
864. Smith, A.D. (ed.), *Trial of Eugene Marie Chantrelle*, NBT, Edinburgh (1906)
865. Smith, Carlton, *Blood Money*, New York (1996)
866. ——, *Fatal Charm*, New York (1993)
867. Smith, Carlton and Guillen, Thomas, *The Search for the Green River Killer*, New York (1991)
868. Smith, David James, *The Sleep of Reason*, London (1994)
869. Smith, Edgar, *Brief Against Death*, New York (1968)
870. ——, *Getting Out*, New York (1972)
871. Smith, Edward H., *Famous American Poison Mysteries*, London (1926)
872. Smith, Graham, *Death of a Rose Grower*, London (1985)
873. Smith, Sir Sydney, *Mostly Murder*, London (1959)
874. Somerfield, Stafford, *The Authentic and Revealing Story of John George Haigh*, Manchester (1950)
875. Sounes, Howard, *Fred and Rose*, London (1995)
876. Speer, W.H., *The Secret History of Great Crimes*, London (1929)
877. Stack, Andy, *The I-5 Killer*, New York (1984)

878. ——, *The Want-ad Killer*, New York (1983)
879. Stagg, Colin and Kessler, David, *Who Really Killed Rachel?*, London (1999)
880. St Aubin, Giles, *Infamous Victorians*, London (1971)
881. St Clair, David, *Say You Love Satan*, New York (1983)
882. Steiger, Brad, *Mass Murderer*, New York (1967)
883. Steinhorst, Lori and Rose, John R., *When The Monster Comes out of the Closet*, Oregon (1994)
884. Stephens, Melinda, *I Accuse*, USA (1987)
885. Stevens, C.H. McCluer, *Famous Crimes and Criminals*, London (1924)
886. ——, *From Clue to Dock*, London (1927)
887. Stewart, James B., *Blind Eye*, New York (1999)
888. Still, Charles E., *Styles in Crime*, Philadelphia (1938)
889. Still, Larry, *The Limits of Sanity*, Toronto (1972)
890. Stoddart, Charles, *Bible John*, Edinburgh (1980)
891. Stone, Irving, *Clarence Darrow for the Defence*, London (1949)
892. Stone, James W., *Trial of Professor John W. Webster*, Boston (1850)
893. Stowers, Carlton, *Careless Whispers*, Dallas (1986)
894. Stratmann, Linda, *Whiteley's Folly*, Stroud (2004)
895. Sugden, Philip, *The Complete History of Jack the Ripper*, London (1994)
896. Sullivan, Gerald and Aronson, Harvey, *High Hopes: the Amityville Murders*, New York (1981)
897. Sullivan, Robert, *The Disappearance of Dr Parkman*, New York (1971)
898. ——, *Goodbye Lizzie Borden*, London (1975)
899. Sullivan, Terry and Maiken, Peter T., *Killer Clown*, New York (1983)
900. Surtees, John, *The Strange Case of Dr Bodkin Adams*, Eastbourne (2000)
901. Tallant, Robert, *Murder in New Orleans*, London (1953)
902. Tanebaum, Robert K. and Greenberg, Peter S., *The Piano Teacher*, New York (1987)
903. Taylor, Bernard and Clarke, Kate, *Murder at the Priory*, London (1988)
904. Taylor, Bernard and Knight, Stephen, *Perfect Murder*, London (1987)
905. Thaw, Harry K., *The Traitor*, New York (1926)
906. Thomas, David with Grant, Roderick, *Seek Out The Guilty*, London (1969)
907. Thomas, Mark, *Every Mother's Nightmare*, London (1993)
908. Thompson, C.J.S., *Poisons and Poisoners*, London (1931)
909. ——, *Poison Mysteries in History, Romance and Crime*, London (1925)
910. Thompson, Thomas, *Blood and Money*, New York (1976)
911. ——, *Serpentine*, New York (1981)
912. Thomson, Helen, *Murder at Harvard*, Boston (1971)
913. Thorwald, Jürgen, *Crime and Science*, New York (1967)
914. ——, *Dead Men Tell Tales*, London (1966)
915. ——, *The Century of the Detective*, New York (1965)
916. Thurlow, David, *The Norfolk Nightmare*, London (1991)
917. Tobias, Ronald, *They Shoot to Kill*, Colorado (1981)
918. Tomlinson, Gerald, *Fatal Tryst*, New Jersey (1999)
919. Toughill, Thomas, *Oscar Slater: The Mystery Solved*, Edinburgh (1993)
920. Townsend, W. and L., *Murder Will Out*, London (n.d.)
921. Traini, Robert, *Murder for Sex*, London (1960)

922. Travers, Robert, *Murder in the Blue Mountains*, London (1972)
923. Treadwell, C.A.L., *Notable New Zealand Trials*, New Plymouth NZ (1936)
924. Treherne, John, *The Strange History of Bonnie and Clyde*, London (1984)
925. Tremayne, Sydney (ed.), *Trial of Alfred Arthur Rouse*, London (1931)
926. Trent, Bill with Truscott, Stephen, *Who Killed Lynn Harper?*, Montreal (1979)
927. Trilling, Diana, *Mrs Harris*, New York (1981)
928. Triplett, William, *Flowering of the Bamboo*, Maryland (1985)
929. Trow, M.J., *The Wigwam Murder*, London (1994)
930. Trzebinski, Erroll, *The Life and Death of Lord Erroll*, London (2000)
931. Tullett, Tom, *No Answer from Foxtrot Eleven*, London (1967)
932. ——, *Portrait of a Bad Man*, London (1956)
933. ——, *Strictly Murder*, London (1979)
934. Turton, Kevin, *Foul Deeds and Suspicious Deaths in Nottingham*, Barnsley (2003)
935. Twyman, H.W., *The Best Laid Schemes . . .*, London (1931
936. Tyler, Froom, *Gallows Parade*, London (1933)
937. Valentine, Steven, *The Black Panther Story*, London (1976)
938. Vallee, Brian, *The Torso Murder*, Toronto (2001)
939. Veale, F.J.P., *The Bravo Case*, Brighton (1950)
940. ——, *The Wallace Case*, Brighton (1950)
941. Vialls, Joe, *Deadly Deception at Port Arthur*, Western Australia (1997)
942. Villasenor, Victor, *Jury*, Boston (1977)
943. Villiers, Elizabeth, *Riddles of Crime*, London (1928)
944. Wagner, Margaret Seaton, *The Monster of Dusseldorf*, London (1932)
945. Wake, Sandra and Hayden, Nicola, *The Bonnie and Clyde Book*, London (1972)
946. Wakefield, H. Russell, *Landru*, London (1936)
947. Walker, Bill, *The Case of Barbara Graham*, New York (1961)
948. Walker, Keith, *A Trail of Corn*, California (1995)
949. Walker, Kent with Stone, Mark, *Son of a Grifter*, New York (2001)
950. Wall, J.O.P., *The Trial of Minnie Dean*, Invercargill NZ (1973)
951. Wallace, Edgar (ed.), *Trial of Herbert John Bennett*, London (1929)
952. ——, (ed.), *The Trial of Patrick Mahon*, London (n.d.)
953. Wallbrook, H.M., *Murders and Murder Trials, 1812–1912*, London (1932)
954. Waller, George, *Kidnap*, London (1961)
955. Walls, H.J., *Expert Witness*, London (1972)
956. Walsh, Sir Cecil, *The Agra Double Murder*, London (1929)
957. Wambaugh, Joseph, *Echoes in the Darkness*, New York (1987)
958. ——, *The Blooding*, London (1989)
959. Wansell, Geoffrey, *An Evil Love*, London (1995)
960. Warden, Rob and Groves, Martha, *Murder Most Foul*, Ohio (1980)
961. Waterhouse, Richard, *The Insurance Man*, Croydon (1994)
962. Watson, Eric R. (ed.), *Trial of George Joseph Smith*, NBT, Edinburgh (1922)
963. Watson, Tex and Ray, Chaplain, *Will You Die For Me?*, New Jersey (1978)
964. Webb, Duncan, *Crime is my Business*, London (1953)

965. Weiss, Rene, *Criminal Justice*, London (1988)
966. Wensley, Frederick Porter, *Detective Days*, London (1931)
967. West, Anne Marie with Hill, Virginia, *Out of the Shadows*, London (1995)
968. West, Stephen and Mae, *Inside 25 Cromwell Street*, Monmouth (1995)
969. Whipple, Sidney, *The Lindberg Crime*, London (1935)
970. ——, *The Trial of Bruno Richard Hauptmann*, London (n.d.)
971. Whitbread, J.R., *The Railway Policemen*, London (1961)
972. Whitehead, Tony, *Mary Ann Cotton Dead, But Not Forgotten*, London (2000)
973. Whitelaw, David, *Corpus Delicti*, London (1936)
974. Whittaker, Mark and Kennedy, Les, *Sins of the Brother*, Sydney (1998)
975. Whittington-Egan, Molly, *Khaki Mischief*, London (1990)
976. ——, *Murder on the Bluff*, Glasgow (1996)
977. Whittington-Egan, Richard, *A Casebook on Jack the Ripper*, London (1975)
978. ——, *The Ordeal of Philip Yale Drew*, London (1972)
979. ——, *The Oscar Slater Murder Story*, Glasgow (2001)
980. ——, *The Riddle of Birdhurst Rise*, London (1975)
981. Wild, Roland, *Crimes and Cases of 1934*, London (1935)
982. ——, *The Jury Retires*, London (1937)
983. Wilkes, Roger, *Blood Relations*, London (1994)
984. ——, *Wallace – The Final Verdict*, London (1984)
985. Willcox, Philip A., *The Detective Physician*, London (1970)
986. Willesee, Amy and Whittaker, Rider, *Love and Death in Kathmandu*, London (2004)
987. Williams, Emlyn, *Beyond Belief*, London (1967)
988. Williams, John, *Hume*, London (1960)
989. Williams, John, *Suddenly at the Priory*, London (1957)
990. Williamson, W.H., *Annals of Crime*, London (1930)
991. Willis, H.A., *Manhunt*, Christchurch NZ (1979)
992. Wilson, Colin, *Murder in the West Country*, Bodmin (1975)
993. ——, *The Corpse Garden*, London (1998)
994. Wilson, Colin and Seaman, Donald, *Encyclopaedia of Modern Murder*, London (1983)
995. Wilson, Garrett and Wilson, Lesley, *Deny, Deny, Deny*, Nova Scotia (1985)
996. Wilson, H.J. (ed.), *The Bayly Case*, Wellington NZ (1934)
997. Wilson, J.G. (ed.), *The Trial of Jeannie Donald*, NBT, Edinburgh (1953)
998. Wilson, John Gray, *The Trial of Peter Manuel*, London (1959)
999. Wilson, Patrick, *Children Who Kill*, London (1973)
1000. ——, *Murderess*, London (1971)
1001. Wilson, Paul, Treble, Don and Lincoln, Robyn, *Jean Lee – The Last Woman Hanged in Australia*, Sydney (1997)
1002. Winter, Larry with Barrett, Steve and Bouda, Simon, *Garden of Evil*, New South Wales (1992)
1003. Woffinden, Bob, *Hanratty – The Final Verdict*, London (1997)
1004. ——, *Miscarriages of Justice*, London (1987)
1005. Wolf, Marvin and Mader, Katharine, *Fallen Angels*, New York (1988)
1006. Wood, Barry, *A Blood Betrayal*, London (1994)

1007. Wood, Walter, *Survivors' Tales of Famous Crimes*, London (1916)
1008. Woodhall, Edwin, *Detective and Secret Service Days*, London (n.d.)
1009. Woodland, W. Lloyd, *Trial of Thomas Henry Allaway*, London (1929)
1010. ——, *Assize Pageant*, London (1952)
1011. Wraxall, Sir Lascelles, *Criminal Celebrities*, London (1863)
1012. Wright, Sewell Peaslee, *Chicago Murders*, New York (1945)
1013. Wuornos, Aileen with Berry-Dee, Christopher, *Monster*, London (2004)
1014. Wyden, Peter, *The Hired Killers*, London (1964)
1015. Wyndham, Horace, *Consider Your Verdict*, London (1946)
1016. ——, *Crime on the Continent*, London (1928)
1017. Wyndham Brown, W.F. (ed.), *The Trial of William Herbert Wallace*, London (1933)
1018. Wyre, Ray and Tate, Jim, *The Murder of Childhood*, London (1995)
1019. Yallop, David, *Deliver us from Evil*, London (1981)
1020. Yarwood, Derek, *Outrages – Fatal and Other*, Manchester (1930)
1021. Yates, Nathan, *Beyond Evil*, London (2004)
1022. Young, Filson (ed.), *Trial of Herbert Rowse Armstrong*, NBT, Edinburgh (1927)
1023. ——, *Trial of Frederick Bywaters and Edith Thompson*, NBT, Edinburgh (1923)
1024. ——, *Trial of H.H. Crippen*, NBT, Edinburgh (1920)
1025. ——, *Trial of the Seddons*, NBT, Edinburgh (1913)
1026. Young, Gordon, *Valley of Silence*, London (1955)
1027. Young, Hugo, *My Forty Years at the Yard*, London (1955)
1028. Young, Winifred, *Obsessive Poisoner*, London (1973)

ADDITIONS TO THE BIBLIOGRAPHY

1029. Ablow, Keith Russell, *Without Mercy*, New York (1994)
1030. Anastasia, George, *The Summer Wind*, New York (1999)
1031. Annamunthodo, W. (ed.), *Malik Accused – Murder*, Trinidad (1972)
1032. ——, *Malik Guilty – Murder*, Trinidad (1972)
1033. Beattie, Robert, *Nightmare in Wichita*, New York (2005)
1034. Benns, Matthew, *When the Bow Breaks*, Sydney (2003)
1035. Bentley, Iris with Dening, Penelope, *Let Him Have Justice*, London (1995)
1036. Bentley, William George, *My Son's Execution*, London (1957)
1037. Berry-Dee, Christopher, *Shared Madness*, London (2005)
1038. Berry-Dee, Christopher and Odell, Robin, *Dad Help Me Please*, London (1990)
1039. Bird, Anne, *Blood Brother*, New York (2005)
1040. Boon Tan Ooi, *Body Parts*, Singapore (1996)
1041. Bracken, D.W., *Holy Terror – Armageddon in Tokyo*, New York (1996)
1042. Burnside, Scott and Cairns, Alan, *Deadly Innocence*, New York (1995)
1043. Clarkson, Wensley, *The Good Doctor*, London (2001)
1044. Crowley, Kieran, *The Surgeon's Wife*, New York (2001)
1045. Cullen, Lord, *The Public Enquiry into the Shootings at Dunblane Primary School on 13 March 1996*, Edinburgh (1996)
1046. Dardenne, Sabine with Cuny, Marie Therese, *I Choose to Live*, London (2005)

1047. Davey, Frank, *Karla's Web*, Toronto (1994)
1048. Duke, Winifred, *Trial of Harold Greenwood*, NBT, Edinburgh (1920)
1049. Fleeman, Michael, *Laci*, New York (2003)
1050. Forster, Joseph, *Studies in Black and Red*, London (1896)
1051. Gerrard, Nicci, *Soham – A Story of Our Time*, London (2004)
1052. Hastings, Patricia, *The Life of Sir Patrick Hastings*, London (1959)
1053. Hyde, H. Montgomery, *Trial of Bentley and Craig*, NBT Edinburgh (1954)
1054. Kennedy, Ludovic, *Ten Rillington Place*, London (1961)
1055. Lindsey, Robert A., *Gathering of Saints*, New York (1988)
1056. Lomax, S.C., *The Case of Barry George*, Hertford (2004)
1057. McDougall, Dennis, *Angel of Darkness*, New York (1991)
1058. McLagan, Graeme and Lowndes, Nick, *Mr Evil*, London (2000)
1059. McVicar, John, *Dead on Time*, London (2002)
1060. Naifeh, Steven and Smith, Gregory White, *The Mormon Murders*, New York (1989)
1061. Olsen, Jack, *The Man With the Candy*, London (1975)
1062. Paris, John, *Scapegoat*, London (1991)
1063. Peters, Carole, *Harold Shipman: Mind Set on Murder*, London (2005)
1064. Reinhardt, James M., *The Murderous Trail of Charles Starkweather*, Springfield (1960)
1065. Rule, Ann, *'. . . And Never Let Go'*, New York (1999)
1066. Selwyn, Francis, *Gangland*, London (1988)
1067. Smith, Dame Janet, *The Shipman Inquiry*, London & Manchester (2002/5)
1068. Thompson, C.J.S., *Poison Mysteries Unsolved*, London (1937)
1069. Trow, M.J. *'Let Him Have It Chris'*, London (1990)
1070. Wagner, Diane, *Corpus Delicti*, New York (1986)
1071. Ward, John, *The Animals are Innocent*, London (1991)
1072. Whittle, Brian and Ritchie, Jean, *Prescription for Murder*, London (2000)
1073. Williams, Stephen, *Invisible Darkness*, Toronto (1996)
1074. ——, *Karla – A Pact with the Devil*, Toronto (2003)
1075. Worrall, Simon, *The Poet and the Murderer*, London (2002)
1076. Yallop, David A., *To Encourage the Others*, London (1971)
1077. Berry-Dee, Christopher and Morris, Steven, *Killers on the Web*, London (2006)
1078. Bowles, Robin, *Dead Centre*, Sydney (2005)
1079. Williams, Sue, *And Then The Darkness*, Sydney (2005)

Geographical Index

Lipski, Israel
Lock Ah Tam
Loughans, Harold
Luard Case
Lord Lucan
Mackay, Patrick
Mahon, Patrick Herbert
Major, Ethel Lillie
Maltby, Cecil
Manning, Maria and Frederick
Manton, Horace William
Manuel, Peter Thomas Anthony
Marwood, Ronald Henry
Marymont, Marcus
Mason, Alexander Campbell
Maybrick, Florence Elizabeth
Merrett, John Donald
Merrifield, Louisa May
Mills, Herbert Leonard
Milsom and Fowler
M`Lachlan, Jessie
Monson, Alfred John
Moore, Alfred
Morgan, Samuel
Morris, Raymond Leslie
Morrison, Stinie
Neilson, Donald
Newall, Roderick
Newall, Susan
Rachel Nickell Case
Nilsen, Dennis
Nodder, Frederick
Onufrejczyk, Michael
Orrock, Thomas Henry
Palmer, Dr William
Pearcey, Mary Eleanor
Pitchfork, Colin
Podmore, William Henry
Podola, Guenther Fritz Erwin
Pritchard, Dr Edward William
Queen, Peter
Queripel, Michael
Rattenbury-Stoner Case
Raven, Daniel
Rayner, Horace George
Roberts, Harry Maurice
Robertson, James Roland
Robinson, John
Rouse, Alfred Arthur
Rowland, Walter Graham
Russell, George
Ruxton, Dr Buck
Sams, Michael Benniman
Seddon, Frederick Henry
Seymour, Henry Daniel
Shipman, Dr Harold
Slater, Oscar
Smethurst Case
Smith, George Joseph
Smith, Madeleine Hamilton
Spencer, Henry
Straffen, John Thomas
Stratton Brothers
Sutcliffe, Peter
Tanner, John
Thomas, Donald George
Thompson and Bywaters
Thompson and Venables
Thorne, John Norman Holmes
Trevor, Harold Dorien
True, Ronald
Voisin, Louis
Waddingham, Dorothea
Wainewright, Thomas Griffiths
Wainwright, Henry
Wallace Case
Walton Case
Julie Ward Case
Webster, Kate
West, Rosemary Pauline

Hilley, Marie Audrey
Hoch, Johann
Hofmann, Mark
Holmes, Herman Webster Mudgett
Hyde, Dr Bennett Clark
Ingenito, Ernest
Jacobson, Howard
Jones, Genene
Judd, Winnie Ruth
Kallinger, Joseph
Kappler, Dr John Frederick
Kasso, Ricky
Kemper, Edmund Emil
Kimes, Sante and Kenneth
King, Dr William Henry
Klenner, Fred
Kraft, Randy Stephen
Leopold and Loeb
List, John Emil
Lonergan, Wayne
Lucas, Henry Lee
Luetgert, Adolph Louis
Macdonald, Dr Jeffrey
McElroy Case
Main Line Murder
Maleno and Soli
Manson, Charles Miller
Molineux, Ronald Burnham
Mullin, Herbert William
Nash and Margolies
Nelson, Earle Leonard
Neu, Kenneth
Palliko, Alan
Pancoast, Marvin
Panzram, Carl
Parker and Barrow
Patrick, Albert T
Peel Case
Perry, Arthur
Peterson, Scott Lee
Pikul, Joe
Pierre, Dale Selby
Putt, George Howard
Rablen, Eva
Rader, Dennis
Ramirez, Richard
Rees, Melvin David
Ridgway, Gary L
Robinson Hill Case
Robles, Richard
Roth, Randolph G
Sacco and Vanzetti
Schmid, Charles Henry
Schreuder, Frances Bradshaw
Schwartz, Charles Henry
Scott, Leonard Ewing
Shawcross, Arthur John
Sheppard, Dr Samuel H
Showery, Alan
Smart, Pamela
Smith, Edgar Herbert
Snider, Paul
Snyder and Gray
Speck, Richard Franklin
Spence, David Wayne
Starkweather, Charles
Stroud, Robert Franklin
Swango, Dr Michael
Taylor Case
Thaw-White Case
Tinning, Marybeth
Tucker, Karla Faye
Udderzook, William E
Unruh, Howard
Wagner, Louis
Waite, Arthur Warren
Walker, Daniel G
Webster, Dr John White
Whitman, Charles